Lowe's Transport Manager's & Operator's Handbook 2012

42ND EDITION

Lowe's Transport Manager's & Operator's Handbook 2012

David Lowe

KoganPage

LONDON PHILADELPHIA NEW DELHI

The masculine pronoun has been used in this book. This stems from a desire to avoid ugly and cumbersome language, and no discrimination, prejudice or bias is intended.

First published as *The Transport Manager's Handbook* in 1970 by Kogan Page Limited
Nineteenth edition published as *The Transport Manager's and Operator's Handbook* in 1989
This forty-second edition published in Great Britain in 2012

Kogan Page Limited
120 Pentonville Road
London N1 9JN
United Kingdom
www.koganpage.com

© David Lowe, 2012

The right of David Lowe to be identified as the author of this work has been asserted by him in accordance with the Copyright, Designs and Patents Act 1988.

British Library Cataloguing in Publication Data

A CIP record for this book is available from the British Library.

ISBN   978 0 7494 6403 5
E-ISBN   978 0 7494 6410 3

Typeset by Saxon Graphics Ltd, Derby
Production managed by Jellyfish
Printed and bound in Great Britain by CPI Antony Rowe

BRIEF CONTENTS

A clear environmental policy

e preferred route for cross-Channel hauliers

of our customers agree that Eurotunnel offers a fast and easy
ce so you can make your delivery commitments with confidence*

0870 850 0721 or email freight@eurotunnel.com
t our website www.eurotunnelfreight.com

pendent Customer satisfaction study conducted by TNS Sofres in 2010.

EURO TUNNEL

Folkestone to Calais
Just 35 minutes

Eurotunnel provides unbeatable

Green advantage for customers

Eurotunnel holds the concession to operate the fixed link between the UK and France until 2086. The company was responsible for building and now operates the Channel Tunnel and its Shuttle services for passenger and freight vehicles. It also provides passage for other operators' freight and passenger trains.

Eurotunnel carries 1.1 million trucks on its Shuttles each year and over a million tonnes of goods on freight trains passing through the Channel Tunnel. Customers are increasingly aware that transporting their goods on a low carbon route is a benefit that they can sell to their end users. Showing them that Eurotunnel continues to make progress to reduce its impact on the environment is an advantage that they can use wherever sustainable development is part of the tendering process

Eurotunnel has been committed to protecting the environment since the conception and design of the electrically powered Channel Tunnel in the 1980s. Since then a continuous process of improvement has been in place to ensure that, year on year, the company makes further progress in reducing its carbon footprint from energy consumption, increases the amount of waste it recycles and improves the environment in which it sits, both in terms of the flora and fauna in situ and the access for local communities.

Eurotunnel leads the way in sustainable development in the transport sector.

In 2011, Eurotunnel became one of the first companies in the sector to be re-certified by the Carbon Trust Standard. Following on from the 44% reduction from the Channel Tunnel catenary supply project using low carbon electricity from France, in 2008, Eurotunnel reduced its transport system's carbon footprint by a further 20.5% in 2009/2010,.

The carrying capacity of the Freight Shuttles has been increased from 30 to 32 wagons, thus increasing capacity for a negligible increase in energy consumption. The delivery of two new train driving simulators, which have been developed specifically to include an "Eco-drive" function, means that Eurotunnel Shuttle Drivers are now being trained to drive more economically, consuming less energy per crossing. Since January 2011 Drivers have been introduced to this new technology which not only prepares them for the most difficult driving conditions imaginable, but also trains them how to be efficient in the use of traction power and braking at all times.

Eurotunnel is the most environmentally-friendly way to take a truck across the Channel. A truck journey on a Shuttle emits **20 times less CO$_2$** than on a ferry! In addition, not having to drive the 25 km from Folkestone to Dover saves a further 20 kg of carbon emissions each way! The position of the Eurotunnel terminal in Folkestone means that trucks crossing the Channel arrive in the UK 25 km closer to London than trucks arriving at Dover. This constitutes a real saving in terms of fuel consumption, wear and tear on vehicles and driver time.

Eurotunnel is not affected by fluctuations in oil prices, as the Shuttles run on electricity generated from clean, low carbon sources in France, so customers are protected from unexpected fuel surcharges. This enables Eurotunnel to operate a completely transparent pricing policy, enabling hauliers to understand the pricing model at a glance and guaranteeing that the prices are not impacted by outside factors.

Offering customers not only sector beating speed and reliability of service, and the greenest route across the Channel with a truck, the low carbon footprint of a journey via the Channel Tunnel means that Eurotunnel is now the operator of choice for those who put a value on the preservation of the environment and the creation of a sustainable model for transport in the future.

For further information, please contact the Freight Commercial team on 0870 850 0721 or visit www.eurotunnelfreight.com.

Drive down your costs

By taking an overall business view rather than just selling trucks, Mercedes-Benz adds value for customers.

How can transport operators maximise their profits in challenging times? The key, argues Sam Whittaker, Mercedes-Benz UK's Truck Sales & Marketing Director, is to commit to the three Ts – Training, Telematics, and Teamwork.

"At Mercedes-Benz we produce some of the finest, most fuel-efficient vehicles on the market, but it is still essential to ensure they are being driven as efficiently as possible," he says. "To do that you need to employ the best drivers, then engage with and invest in them."

Sam Whittaker, Truck Sales & Marketing Director

On training, Whittaker says the key to achieving increased productivity and efficiency is to treat drivers as valued professionals. So for the new DriverCPC rules, under which all truck drivers must have completed 35 hours of approved training by 10 September 2014, he urges operators to resist going down the 'tick box' route that merely requires attendance on a course.

Instead, they should seek to achieve genuine, tangible benefits from the training which all drivers must undergo and gain a business benefit from their investment. "Mercedes-Benz now leads the market as a provider of DriverCPC courses," he says. "This is practical training that represents excellent value for money and makes a positive contribution to the operator's bottom line.

"We've already helped more than 12,000 drivers to operate their vehicles more safely and economically. So turn to the truck experts for your training, no matter what truck you drive."

Mercedes-Benz also works closely with telematics specialist Daimler FleetBoard – they do, after all, share the same parent company, although FleetBoard's hardware is also compatible with virtually every other make and model of truck. Daimler FleetBoard offers a range of Internet-based services covering vehicle and driver management. Its system analyses driver performance against a range of criteria and pinpoints areas such as over-revving, harsh braking, idling, speeding and 'green band' driving, in which improvements can be made.

"FleetBoard allows operators to improve driving techniques, which has a direct impact on the profitability of the business," continues Whittaker. "This technology is delivering some spectacular results. Improvements in fuel performance of between seven and 10 per cent are typical. Even more impressive is the reduction in accident damage costs, which are in the range of 40 to 70 per cent, and result from the vehicle being driven more carefully."

One in four new trucks bearing a three-pointed star is now fitted with FleetBoard, and every tractor unit sold on a Mercedes-Benz Financial Services contract hire package comes with telematics hardware and three months' vehicle management services at no cost. This has proved a spectacular success.

Whittaker adds: "Mercedes-Benz is not interested in the 'quick deal' but in developing long-term partnerships with our customers. We are passionate about delivering great service, so we work hand in hand with operators to maximise the efficiency and profitability of their businesses. It's about teamwork, and together with telematics and training, it can make all the difference to a customer's bottom line."

CONTENTS

17   Safety – Vehicle, Loads and at Work 426

18   Loads – General, Livestock, Food, etc 463

BIOGRAPHICAL NOTE

David Lowe FCILT

David Lowe is a freelance writer and lecturer who has been actively involved with the road transport industry for many years.

He is the sole author of *Lowe's Transport Manager's and Operator's Handbook*, now in its 42nd year of annual publication. His many other works include two best-selling titles for CPC students: *A Study Manual of Professional Competence in Road Haulage* (12 editions) and *1001 Typical CPC Questions and Answers* (three editions), *Goods Vehicle Costing and Pricing Handbook* (four editions), *The Tachograph Manual* (two editions), and *The European Road Freighting Handbook* (1994), all published by Kogan Page. Two other works, *The Dictionary of Transport and Logistics* and *The Pocket Guide to LGV Drivers' Hours and Tachograph Law*, were published by Kogan Page in 2002 and 2006 (3rd edition) respectively.

He has written extensively for the transport press, including *Commercial Motor*, and also wrote a number of successful operator and driver handbooks for *Headlight* magazine. He was the author of the Chartered Institute of Purchasing and Supply (CIPS) graduate diploma study guides *Distribution* and *Storage and Distribution in Supply Chains* published in 2000 and 2003 respectively. Another of his works, *Intermodal Freight Transport*, was published by Elsevier in 2005.

With his detailed practical knowledge of UK and European transport law, David Lowe is well qualified to explain complex legal issues in layman's terms. He understands what the transport manager and small fleet operator need to know, and he tells them in no uncertain terms what they must and must not do to stay on the right side of the law.

He is a Chartered Fellow of the Chartered Institute of Logistics and Transport, a Freeman of the City of London and a Freeman of the Worshipful Company of Carmen. He is also a past winner of the Carmen's prestigious Herbert Crow silver medal award for 'consistent achievement for over thirty years as an outstanding freelance writer specializing in transport and logistics'.

ACKNOWLEDGEMENTS

I am grateful to all the many individuals and organizations that have provided helpful information for inclusion in this *Handbook*. During over 40 years of writing the *Handbook* I have approached so many individuals, firms and industry-related organizations for information, guidance and assistance that it really is impossible to thank them all individually. Some are consulted regularly year after year; some have been newly sought out for guidance. There is no doubt that without such help the *Handbook* would not have achieved its prominence as the so-called 'bible' for transport managers and others. To all concerned, once again, I express my sincere thanks for their help.

Reference for information has been made to many sources – the legislation itself, both British and EU; published guides and notes; to the Department for Transport (DfT) and its forebears, the Traffic Commissioners and their Traffic Area Office staff, and to the enforcement authorities. Many other relevant bodies have been consulted and both the national press and the transport trade press have provided a continuous reminder of changing legislation and developments in the industry. Similarly, a constant flow of comments and questions from consultancy clients and seminar delegates has provided the source of many leads for inclusion of information and the inspiration to continue revising the contents of the *Handbook* to include more and more legislative detail. To all these publications, organizations and nameless individuals I am greatly indebted.

My good friend John Dickson-Simpson, publisher of the monthly *Transport News Digest* and ace technical guru when it comes to vehicle engineering, very kindly provided many useful comments throughout the text and put me on the right road where necessary – for which I am extremely indebted.

I would like to thank especially my wife Patricia and the many friends in the industry who are a constant source of encouragement and, as always, too, the editorial staff of Kogan Page whose help ensures yet another edition of the *Handbook*.

PREFACE TO THE 42ND EDITION

Never before, in the 41-year history of this *Handbook*, have I been able to tell readers that they can look forward to *less* legislation in future rather than *more*, as has always been the case in the past. But this was the promise of the current coalition government in May 2011 when it launched its 'Red Tape Challenge' aimed at reducing bureaucracy. The extent to which this challenge will be successful has yet to be seen and I, like so many other people in our industry will wait with baited breath to see the extent, if at all, this filters through to road transport legislation.

In the meantime, however, significant new legislative measures are waiting on the horizon as this 42nd edition of the *Handbook* is being prepared. For a start, and most importantly, under EU Regulation 1071/2009/EC, which is currently the subject of a consultation document in the UK, our present system of national and international professional competence qualifications for transport managers are to be merged to form a single qualification. There is no doubt that this measure will have a big impact on many Handbook readers, especially those with a national CPC qualification who were intending to advance to the international qualification.

The regulation also proposes the establishment of Euro-wide national registers of transport operators and transport managers and a Euro-wide database of offences committed by operators and transport managers alike.

These provisions, like the merged 'O' licence and transport manager CPCs mentioned above are to be the subject of new UK regulations, expected to be published towards the end of 2011 and effective from 4 December 2011. These important issues will be described in detail in the next (2013) edition of the *Handbook* when they have been implemented in UK law.

Other key items of new legislation included in this edition are the law requiring conspicuity markings for trucks (this eventually became law in 2011 after a previous delay) and the requirement for all vehicles to be Continuously Insured to overcome the problems caused by large numbers of uninsured vehicles on our roads. The ADR provisions for the carriage of dangerous goods by road have been updated to refer to the 2011 version as indeed many other legislative items have been updated.

Economically, the situation for the industry in the year ahead is likely to be little better than the prospect that faced it at the beginning of 2011.

Many haulage firms are still bordering on economic collapse, others have already gone under, and even the survivors must be wondering how much longer this crisis can go on before they too have to pull the plug. The whole road haulage scenario at the present time is difficult in the extreme. The lifeblood is being squeezed out of one of the country's most vital industries at a time when it most needs help. Other industries are suffering too, that is acknowledged, but without a thriving and efficient road haulage industry to move goods around, both in the United Kingdom and internationally, for the home market, for export and import, the prospects for economic recovery look dismal.

Very few goods move without a lorry having carried them – and these goods are not fripperies; they are vital supplies needed by people and by the commercial life of this country: food, manufacturing materials, medical supplies, goods en route to the ports for export, essential imports coming in via our container ports. OK, some of the goods may be no more important than container loads of expensive electronic toys from the Far East – but why should our children not have them? And what about when the supermarket shelves, and those of garden centres and DIY stores, are nearly empty simply because the cost of transporting the goods into them is too high for economic reason?

This new 42nd edition of the *Handbook* has been updated with many snippets of new information – too numerous to specify here, but nevertheless indicating just what a constantly moving picture the whole business of transport law compliance really is.

Regrettably, the past year has been no easier for the hard-pressed haulier than preceding years and the unfortunate prospect at this time is that things may well get worse before there is any hope of an upturn in the economy.

Keeping up to date with the latest legislation is reputed to be the biggest challenge facing the road haulage industry and, in fact, there is so much legislation coming through these days that your eyes glaze over, according to Bob Durward, director of the British Aggregates Association.

On a positive note, however, readers of this *Handbook* should have no such problems comprehending the law or recognizing their statutory responsibilities since, as always, its purpose is to help goods vehicle operators, transport managers and the many other individuals responsible for road transport operations to know and understand their legal obligations. More particularly, it should help them avoid the risks of prosecution, along with the heavy financial penalties imposed these days on conviction and, even more worrying, the imposition of punitive action against their operator's licence – these being the almost certain consequences of illegal activities that the transport trade press continues to report week by week with unfailing regularity. I hope this *Handbook* will, as ever, help to steer readers clear of such problems and provide both interesting and intelligible reading as well as a useful and ready source of reference to the many and complex legal requirements relating to goods vehicle ownership and use.

Previous Editions of The Transport Manager's and Operator's Handbook

Readers may be interested to note that a full set of all previous editions of the *Handbook* (ie 41 editions to date from the first in 1970) are held by the Chartered Institute of Logistics and Transport in its Corby Library, where they may be accessed by anybody researching the progress of transport legislation over this period.

David Lowe

Wherever you are going in logistics and transport...
...our specialist knowledge will help you connect.

The Chartered Institute of Logistics and Transport in the UK is an independent professional body for individuals associated with logistics, supply chains and all transport. It aims to be the focus for professional excellence and the development of the most modern techniques in logistics and transport and encourage the adoption of policies, which are both efficient and sustainable.

Membership of CILT is represented in more than 30 countries across the world.Its 33,000 members benefit from career enhancing benefits that save them time and money, keep them informed and ensure their career development.

Logistics and transport professionals work across a wide variety of disciplines and modes and we are the Chartered Institute for everyone, wherever you are in the profession. We operate through our structure of Professional Sectors which provides a clear window into the work of each particular area of interest, whilst continuing to offer opportunities and involvement across the Forums, National/Regional Groups and Events, and all of the other Institute activities.

With over 30 special interest Forums, you have a unique opportunity to engage with the wealth of knowledge and information available within the Institute, which will help you to connect with expertise on both a national and international level. We are able to develop your career and knowledge through education and training, newsletters, articles and research as well as by networking with fellow professionals at meetings, seminars and events.

CILT members are part of the only multi modal, multi discipline professional organisation in logistics and transport. This provides members with all of the benefits of specialist learning and activities whilst offering full access to the many opportunities available across the entire profession.

The Institute also operates geographically across the nations and regions of the UK with local group meetings enabling you to take advantage of events and networking opportunities in your area. You can join/attend any group meeting near to your home or workplace.

For more information please call 01536 740104 or
e-mail: membership@ciltuk.org.uk
www.ciltuk.org.uk

**The Chartered Institute of
Logistics and Transport (UK)**™

Introduction

Historically, the road transport industry in Great Britain has had to contend with a mass of legislation which has imposed considerable restriction on operations, to say nothing of the burdens of high cost and considerable worry for the owners, operators and managers of goods vehicle fleets; but it has to be said that this is all in the interests of public safety.

The past 40 or so years in particular have seen more than their fair share of such legislation. Looking back to the days when the Road Safety Act 1967 (long defunct) and the Transport Act 1968 were about to be introduced, it would have been difficult then to foresee the mass of legal requirements which would have to be faced over the years ahead. Who could have anticipated the construction of a tunnel under the Channel and the subsequent development of combined road and rail transport networks all over Europe, or at that time that we would even be part of what is now the European Union?

In 1970 we had changes in drivers' hours and records which were eventually understood and accepted; and in place of carriers' licensing, a new system of operators' licensing was also introduced in 1970 bringing own-account operators and professional hauliers under one common scheme for the control of goods vehicle operations. This, too, was accepted and largely appreciated by the industry which recognized the need for increased road safety measures.

By 1978, however, many changes in these items alone, as respective chapters in the book show, had taken place and in 1984 further significant changes were made, and yet again in 1996. The hours regulations have become those of Europe; the records requirements changed to meet European law late in 1976 and subsequently have been largely replaced by tachographs on a mandatory basis from 1981; and the one-for-all system of 'O' licensing was torn apart to satisfy the demands for establishing standards of professional competence. In 1986 major changes were made to both the European and the British drivers' hours rules and the European tachograph rules, with the object of making the law simpler to understand and more flexible for operators to apply.

Besides these particular items of legislation there have been many more changes which earlier editions of this book have charted year by year. In fact, each year has seen something new in legal responsibilities for the vehicle operator and transport manager to digest. If it has not always been significant in transport terms it has been significant in other terms, significant Acts being the ill-fated Industrial Relations Act, the Equal Pay Act, the Health and Safety at Work etc Act, the Employment Protection Act and the Employment Protection (Consolidation) Act 1978; then the Employment Act 1980 and the Employment Act 1982.

In more recent years we have seen a much greater concentration on such issues as employment protection, health and safety, working time limits, animal welfare during transit, dangerous goods carriage and environmental controls, and indeed the introduction of digital tachographs, most of which has been brought about by the implementation of relevant EU legislation. Directives and Regulations abound, and the fear is that we are becoming an ever more regulated industry – and society. As this occurs, so too do the problems of keeping up to date with it all – and putting it into practice – become increasingly complex, time-consuming and costly.

The purpose of this *Handbook*, therefore, is to gather as much of this legislative material together as can be reasonably squeezed between the covers, to explain what it is all about in lay terms which are both easy to read and to understand and apply, and thereby to provide the hard-pressed vehicle operator or transport manager with one accessible, intelligible source of information on the responsibilities laid on him by law emanating from both the British Government and the EU.

The *Handbook* is intended for the fleet operator (whatever the size of his fleet – large or very small), the transport manager, the owner-driver haulier or anybody else, whatever his title, whose responsibilities include the day-to-day control, administration or operation of goods vehicles, and the small operator who has found that there is a lot more to running a goods vehicle besides just taxing and insuring it. In addition to its function as a ready source of reference for the main legal requirements affecting goods vehicle operation and other useful information, the book may also be found, by those studying for transport examinations, to be an additional means of acquiring a detailed knowledge of the relevant legislation currently applicable to the UK road freight industry.

The major items of legislation affecting the operator and driver of goods vehicles have been covered, together with some of the other legal requirements which are not necessarily new but which it is important for him to know about. Besides transport legislation the owner or manager has been increasingly confronted with social and environmental legislation which affects him both as an employer of staff and as the occupier of premises.

However, while this *Handbook* essentially concentrates on transport legislation rather than transport policy, it is important just to mention here two key policy documents that are helping to shape the way that governments determine their strategies for legislating the operation of goods vehicles, among other things. First of these was the UK Government's 1998 White Paper, *A New Deal for Transport: Better for Everyone,* which has been followed by a number of further documents reporting progress. Then in September 2001 the EU published its White Paper, *European Transport Policy for 2010: Time to Decide.*

Apart from this there is still a great deal more information that the operator and manager should have at his fingertips. Some of it concerns particular branches of the transport industry; the carriage of dangerous goods, abnormal loads, food or livestock, for example. The person responsible for these specialized traffics should have acquired, through experience, some knowledge of the regulations concerning his particular field. The newcomer to such operations will need to obtain the appropriate regulations direct from The Stationery Office (TSO) – see list of addresses at the end of this Introduction – or from a bookseller who stocks TSO publications, and study them carefully.

The principal Acts of Parliament which form the basis of much of the legislation explained in this book are supported by, and their provisions brought into effect by, a much larger number of regulations, orders and amendments. These are the means by which the Secretary of State for Transport (DfT) puts into effect the legal requirements laid down in principle in an Act of Parliament. Legislation contained in an Act is not of itself effective until brought into force by regulations or orders made by the Secretary of State, for which purpose he is given the necessary powers in the Act. Many provisions contained in such Acts may, in fact, never be brought into use, but they do not automatically become extinct by lack of use. They remain dormant on the statute book unless repealed by a further Act.

European legislation, of which we now have a great deal, arises as the result of draft proposals, similar to British Government White Papers, which are circulated among interested parties (the trade unions, trade associations, and so on) for comment prior to legislative action being taken, and are then enforced by means of directives and regulations of the Council of the European Union.

It is most important for transport people to be aware of the regulations affecting both their own special type of operations and transport in general. To keep up with all the individual Acts, regulations, amendments and modifications which The Stationery Office publishes on behalf of the Government in connection with transport, and the statutory publications of the European Communities, is no mean task (see accompanying list of TSO bookshops where these publications can be bought – or they can be ordered through other, TSO stockist, booksellers). A more convenient method of keeping up to date on all the new measures affecting the industry is to read the trade press regularly.

The principal journals covering the road goods transport field are *Motor Transport* and *Commercial Motor*, published weekly, and *Trucking*, published monthly. Contents include the latest industry news, new regulations with simple explanations and articles on subjects of special interest such as insurance, vehicle maintenance, road tests of new vehicles, costing, education and training, and management topics. In particular, these journals are of special interest because of their extensive reporting of court and tribunal cases, which give the reader a good indication of how the law is applied, how the enforcement agencies, and subsequently the courts, interpret legal provisions and the levels of penalties imposed on offenders and those who lose out in tribunal cases.

It must be emphasized that the fleet operator and transport manager should keep abreast of what is happening in the industry if they want to be efficient, progressive and stay on the right side of the law. To concentrate on the job in hand to the exclusion of all that is happening in the industry at large is an attitude adopted by many operators and many of them have already suffered the consequences of not being prepared to meet some of the drastic changes that have taken place in recent years.

A valuable aid to the operator is membership of one or other of the trade associations. The Freight Transport Association, which represents the own-account operator, and the Road Haulage Association, looking after the interests of the hire and reward professional haulier, provide a number of services to their members as well as keeping them informed about what is happening in the industry through their respective journals, *Freight Transport* and *Roadway*. Both organizations hold open meetings and training sessions, addressed by specialists on various topics of importance, at which members can hear first-hand details of current and new legislation, ask questions and air their views.

Additionally, for the operator or manager who wants to keep abreast of current legislation and practices in the industry there are commercial seminars and training sessions ranging from one day to over a week in duration. These provide an excellent means of keeping up to date with what is going on, and of meeting and talking to other people in the industry with similar interests and problems.

The road transport industry plays an important part in the life of Great Britain. Its safe operation is essential for the well-being of the people and its efficient operation is vital to the economy. Higher standards of management and control within the industry with a far greater awareness and understanding of the legal requirements, the operational demands and the economic considerations are necessary if these essential criteria of safety and efficient operation are to be achieved and upheld.

Special Note

It should be noted that this *Handbook* is intended purely as a practical interpretation of legal matters for the lay reader and is only a *guide* to matters current at the time of writing. It is not a definitive legal work of reference and should not be used as such. Readers are advised to check the legislation itself before committing time or expenditure to any particular course of action and any operator needing detailed legal advice is recommended to acquire it through normal legal channels. The author and publishers accept no responsibility whatsoever for decisions taken or other irrevocable actions based on the contents herein.

TSO Bookshops

Belfast   16 Arthur Street, Belfast BT1 4GD.
               Tel: 02890 238451 Fax: 02890 235401
Edinburgh   71 Lothian Road, Edinburgh EH3 9AZ.
               Tel: 0870 606 5566 Fax: 0870 606 5588

Official publications, including Statutory Instruments, may be obtained from the above TSO bookshops and at a number of TSO agency bookshops in major UK cities. Details of these agency shops can be found on the TSO website: **http://www.tso.co.uk/contact/bookshops/agents**.

The Stationery Office

PO Box 29
Norwich NR3 1GN
Tel: 0870 600 5522 (telephone orders, general enquiries, subscriptions and standing orders)
E-mail: **book.orders@tso.co.uk**
Website: **www.tso.co.uk**

Parliamentary publications may be obtained from:

The Parliamentary Bookshop
12 Bridge Street
Parliament Square
London SW1A 2JX
Telephone orders: 020 7219 3890
General enquiries: 020 7219 3890
Fax orders: 020 7219 3866
E-mail orders: **bookshop@parliament.uk**

Transport Ministers 1970 to date

The author has been asked many times about the names and dates in office of successive Transport Ministers. The following list of such Ministers in post during the life of this *Handbook* from 1970 shows what a potentially vulnerable position this is, with some incumbents lasting only a matter of months. The very first Minister of Transport was Sir Eric Geddes, who served from 19 May 1919 to 7 November 1921.

Minister for Transport Industries

- John Peyton (15 October 1970 to 4 March 1974)

Minister for Transport

- Fred Mulley (7 March 1974 to 12 June 1975)
- John Gilbert (12 June 1975 to 10 September 1976)

Secretary of State for Transport

- William (Bill) Rodgers (10 September 1976 to 4 May 1979)

Minister of Transport

- Norman Fowler (11 May 1979 to 5 January 1981)

Secretary of State for Transport

- Norman Fowler (5 January 1981 to 14 September 1981)
- David Howell (14 September 1981 to 11 June 1983)
- Tom King (11 June 1983 to 16 October 1983)

- Nicholas Ridley (16 October 1983 to 21 May 1986)
- John Moore (21 May 1986 to 13 June 1987)
- Paul Channon (13 June 1987 to 24 July 1989)
- Cecil Parkinson (24 July 1989 to 28 November 1990)
- Malcolm Rifkind (28 November 1990 to 10 April 1992)
- John MacGregor (10 April 1992 to 5 July 1995)
- Sir George Young, Bt. (5 July 1995 to 2 May 1997)

Secretary of State for Environment, Transport and the Regions

- John Prescott (2 May 1997 to 8 June 2001)

From 1997 to 2001, the Ministers of State with responsibility for Transport were:

- Gavin Strang (3 May 1997 to 27 July 1998)
- John Reid (27 July 1998 to 17 May 1999)
- Helen Liddell (17 May 1999 to 29 July 1999)
- Lord Macdonald of Tradeston (29 July 1999 to 8 June 2001)

NB: Gavin Strang and John Reid attended Cabinet meetings, but were not formally members of the Cabinet.

Secretary of State for Transport, Local Government and the Regions

- Stephen Byers (8 June 2001 to 29 May 2002) (Resigned)

Secretary of State for Transport

- Alistair Darling (29 May 2002 to 5 May 2006)
- Douglas Alexander (5 May 2006 to 28 June 2007)
- Ruth Kelly (28 June 2007 to 3 October 2008)
- Geoff Hoon (3 October 2008 to 6 October 2008)
- Lord Andrew Adonis (6 October 2008 to 11 May 2010)
- Philip Hammond (12 May 2010 to 17 October 2011)
- Justine Greening (17 October 2011 to date)

Modernizing of Government

In the course of so-called modernizing of government, a number of new departments of state were created in the prime minister's June 2007 'Machinery of Government' statement. In case readers are confused by these changes, they are as follows:

- Department for Children, Schools and Families (DCSF) – formerly the Department of Education;
- Department for Business Innovation and Skills (BIS), formerly Department for Business, Enterprise and Regulatory Reform (BERR);
- Ministry of Justice (formerly Constitutional Affairs).

A new 'Business Council for Britain' has also been created, comprising senior representatives of UK-based businesses, to advise the Prime Minister on issues that affect enterprise, business and the long-term productivity and competitiveness of the economy.

Fortunately, the good old Department for Transport retains its well-known name.

Further details of these changes can be found on the Government website at: **http://www.number10.gov.uk/output/Page30.asp.**

Goods Vehicle Operator Licensing

Operator ('O') licensing is the regulatory 'quality' control system imposed by government to ensure the safe and legal operation of most goods vehicles in Great Britain. While other individual aspects of legislation also apply to such vehicles, the 'O' licensing system provides the overriding control of road freight transport operations. Failure to observe the requirements and conditions under which 'O' licences are granted will lead to severe penalty; likewise, breach of other legislation can result in appropriate penalties as set out in respective statutes and, subsequently, will involve penalties against the operators' licence itself. Similar licensing controls apply to goods vehicle operations in Northern Ireland under the separate Road Freight Vehicle Operator's Licence scheme currently operated in the Province but soon to be replaced by the new NI operator licensing scheme (see pp 56–61).

Under the current British licensing scheme, trade or business users of most goods vehicles over 3.5 tonnes maximum permissible weight must hold an 'O' licence for such vehicles, whether they are used for carrying goods in connection with the operator's main trade or business as an own-account operator (ie a trade or business other than that of carrying goods for hire or reward) or are used for hire or reward road haulage operations. Certain goods vehicles, including those used exclusively for private purposes, are exempt from the licensing requirements. Details of the exempt vehicles to which 'O' licensing does not apply are given on pp 11–14.

The original system of operators' licensing was established by the Transport Act 1968, the relevant provisions of which are now consolidated into the Goods Vehicle (Licensing of Operators) Act 1995. This Act states that no person may use a goods vehicle on a road for hire or reward or in connection with any trade or business carried on by him except under an operator's licence.

Relevant regulations are:

- The Goods Vehicles (Licensing of Operators) Act 1995
- The Goods Vehicles (Licensing of Operators) Regulations 1995 SI 2869/1995
- The Tribunal Procedure (First-tier Tribunal) (General Regulatory Chamber) Rules 2009 SI 1976/2009
- The Goods Vehicles (Licensing of Operators) (Temporary Use in Great Britain) Regulations 1996 SI 2186/1996
- The Goods Vehicles (Licensing of Operators) (Temporary Use in Great Britain) (Amendment) Regulations 2004 SI 462/2004
- The Goods Vehicle Operators (Qualifications) Regulations 1999 SI 2430/1999
- The Goods Vehicles (Licensing of Operators (Qualifications)) Regulations 2004 SI 3222/2004
- The Transport Tribunal Rules 2000 SI 3226/2000
- The Goods Vehicles (Enforcement Powers) Regulations 2001 SI 3981/2001
- The Transport Tribunal (Amendment) Rules 2001 SI 4041/2001
- The Transport Tribunal (Amendment) Rules 2002 SI 643/2002
- The Goods Vehicle Operators (Qualifications) (Amendment) Regulations 2004 SI 3222/2004

NB: Regulations amending licence fees have not been included in this list.

Administration of Licensing System

The 'O' licensing system, which is based on the concept of ensuring legal and safe operation and thus is a system of 'quality' as opposed to 'quantity' licensing, is administered on a regional (ie Traffic Area) basis throughout Great Britain. (Northern Ireland's Road Freight Vehicle Operator Licensing system is dealt with separately by the Driver and Vehicle Agency – part of the Department of the Environment in Belfast.)

The Traffic Areas each have their own Traffic Commissioner (TC) and Traffic Area Offices (TAOs), to form the network (see Appendix I for a list). Operator licence application administration is now centralized at the following address:

VOSA Licensing Application Services
Hillcrest House
386 Harehills Lane
Leeds LS9 6NF

Post for the public inquiry and regional intelligence units, and personal post for the Traffic Commissioners, should continue to be sent to local offices.

The central licensing unit supports the existing Traffic Commissioners, and their roles as independent licensing authorities is not affected. Traffic area boundaries remain unchanged and public inquiries will continue to be held in the area of each Traffic Commissioner.

These TCs are appointed by the Secretary of State for Transport and are 'independent quasi-judicial authorities', who have the statutory power to grant or refuse operators' licences, to place road safety and environmental conditions or restrictions on such licences where necessary, and subsequently to impose penalties against licences in the event of the holder being convicted for goods vehicle-related offences.

NB: The male gender is used throughout this Handbook when referring to Traffic Commissioners although at the time of writing there are a number of female TCs. No discrimination, prejudice or bias is intended by such use.

As of 31 March 2009, 362,706 goods vehicles were specified in 91,200 'O' licences in Great Britain, of which 45,341 were restricted licences, 35,385 were standard national licences and 10,474 were standard international licences. These numbers show a small decrease overall on the previous figures, and are well below the 1989/90 figure of 132,236 valid 'O' licences in issue, covering 441,656 goods vehicles.

Source: Annual reports of the Traffic Commissioners (covering Goods Vehicle Operator Licensing) for the period 1 April 2009 to 31 March 2010.

The Operator Licensing Self-Service System

The Traffic Area Network (TAN) computer system came into operation in mid-2002. It was merged with the VOSA system and went live in October 2005 and is to be found on the VOSA website at **www.vosa.gov.uk**. Principally, this system significantly reduces the time taken to process 'O' licence changes and particularly results in the 28-day period of grace for advising the TC of vehicle changes being abolished. Operators will be expected to transact such business online. They must use a pre-registered user ID and a case-sensitive password. 'Applications and Decisions' (see pp 41–42) will subsequently be produced weekly instead of fortnightly. Additionally, the system will provide enforcement agencies with 'real-time' data to help them catch illegal operators.

This online Government service enables goods vehicle operators to add and remove vehicles from their operator's licence at any time of the day or night without the need to complete an application form and without any intervention by VOSA staff. It reduces the time taken to add a vehicle to a licence from 14 days to within a couple of minutes. Operators can register online to join the self-service system; check their own licence details held on VOSA's operator licence computer system; transfer vehicles between licences they hold in different areas; and track the progress of licence applications and set up access for other members of their staff, allowing greater access to records and transactions for larger companies. In due course the system will allow operators to pay their licence invoices and renew licences online. The site also contains a template for use by operators advertising changes to their licences in local newspapers.

'O' Licences Not for Sale

Operator's licences are issued only to applicants who meet strict criteria as set out in the regulations and as described in this chapter. As such, 'O' licences are *not* transferable between operators and may *not* be borrowed, used on loan or sold, with or without the vehicles to which they relate, by any person other than the authorized holder. Advertisements in the transport press purporting to be for the sale of such licences are misleading because they encourage respondents to act illegally and should be treated with great caution.

Exemptions from 'O' Licensing

There are a number of categories of vehicle which are exempt from 'O' licensing requirements as described below.

Small Vehicles

The principal exemption applies to 'small' vehicles identified as follows.

Rigid vehicles are 'small' if:

- they are plated and the gross plated (ie maximum permissible) weight is not more than 3.5 tonnes;
- they are unplated and have an unladen weight of not more than 1,525 kg.

A *combination of a rigid vehicle and a drawbar trailer* is 'small' if:

- both the vehicle and the trailer are plated, and the total of the gross *plated* weights is not more than 3.5 tonnes;
- either the vehicle or the trailer is not plated, and the total of the *unladen* weights is not more than 1,525 kg.

The exemption from 'O' licensing for rigid vehicles not weighing more than 3.5 tonnes gross plated weight, used in combination with trailers with an unladen weight of not more than 1,020 kilograms, has been withdrawn for operators engaged in hire and reward work. Combination of vehicles and trailers exceeding the 3.5 tonne gross plated weight, or the 1,525 kilogram unladen weight threshold, are likely to be subject to the 'O' licensing regulation unless exempt for some other reason.

However, operators engaged in 'own amount' work with vehicles that do not exceed 3.5 tonnes gross plated weight used in combination with trailers that have an unladen weight that does not exceed 1,020 kilograms remain out of scope of the 'O' licence regualations.

Articulated vehicles are 'small' if:

- the semi-trailer is plated, and the total of the *unladen* weight of the tractive unit and the plated weight of the semi-trailer is not more than 3.5 tonnes;
- the semi-trailer is not plated, and the total of the *unladen* weights of the tractive unit and the semi-trailer is not more than 1,525 kg.

Older Vehicles

Also included in the exemptions are pre-1 January 1977 vehicles which have an unladen weight not exceeding 1,525 kg and a gross weight greater than 3.5 tonnes.

Other Exemptions

Regulations list the following further specific exemptions from 'O' licensing requirements.

1 Vehicles licensed as agricultural machines used solely for handling specified goods, and any trailer drawn by them.

2 Dual-purpose vehicles and any trailer drawn by them.

3 Vehicles used on roads only for the purpose of passing between private premises in the immediate neighbourhood and belonging to the same person (except in the case of a vehicle used only in connection with excavation or demolition) provided that the distance travelled on the road in any one week does not exceed in aggregate 9.654 km (ie 6 miles).

4 Motor vehicles constructed or adapted primarily for the carriage of passengers and their effects and any trailer drawn by them while being so used.

5 Vehicles being used for funerals.

6 Vehicles being used for police, fire brigade and ambulance service purposes.

7 Vehicles being used for fire fighting or rescue work at mines.

8 Vehicles on which a permanent body has not yet been built carrying goods for trial or for use in building the body.

9 Vehicles being used under a trade licence.

10 Vehicles used in the service of a visiting force or headquarters.

11 Vehicles used by or under the control of HM United Kingdom forces.

12 Trailers not constructed for the carriage of goods but which are used incidentally for that purpose in connection with the construction, maintenance or repair of roads.

13 Road rollers or any trailer drawn by them.

14 Vehicles used by HM Coastguards or the Royal National Lifeboat Institution for the carriage of lifeboats, life-saving appliances or crew.

15 Vehicles fitted with permanent equipment (ie machines or appliances) so that the only goods carried are:

(a) for use in connection with the equipment;

(b) for threshing, grading, cleaning or chemically treating grain or for mixing by the equipment with other goods not carried on the vehicle to make animal fodder; or

(c) mud or other matter swept up from the road by the equipment.

16 Vehicles while being used by a local authority for the purpose of enactments relating to weights and measures or the sale of food or drugs.

17 Vehicles used by a local authority under the Civil Defence Act 1948.

18 Steam-propelled vehicles.

19 Tower wagons or any trailer drawn by them provided that any goods carried on the trailer are required for use in connection with the work on which the tower wagon is used.

20 Vehicles used on airports under the Civil Aviation Act 1982.

21 Electrically propelled vehicles.

22 Showmen's goods vehicles and any trailer drawn by such vehicles.

23 Vehicle of non-resident operator carrying out cabotage operations in the UK under EU regulation 3118/93/EEC.

24 Vehicles first registered prior to 1 January 1977 which are not over 1,525 kg unladen weight and are plated for more than 3,500 kg but not more than 3,556.21 kg (3.5 tonnes).

25 Vehicles used by a highway authority in connection with weighbridges.

26 Vehicles used for emergency operations by the water, electricity, gas and telephone services.

27 Recovery vehicles.

28 Vehicles used for snow clearing or the distribution of grit, salt or other materials on frosted, ice-bound or snow-covered roads and for any other purpose connected with such activities.

    NB: This exemption is not restricted solely to local authority-owned vehicles.

29 Vehicles going to or coming from a test station and carrying a load which is required for the test at the request of the Secretary of State for Transport (ie by the test station).

Exemption for Private Vehicles

Exemptions also apply to vehicles used privately (ie for carrying goods for solely private purposes and not in any way connected with a business activity) and by voluntary organizations.

Northern Ireland Vehicles

Northern Ireland-based operators do not need 'O' licences for vehicles running, laden or unladen, in or through the UK while on international journeys. Similarly, there is no requirement for 'O' licences to be held by hauliers established in other EU member states (and not established in the UK) for vehicles operating within the UK on international journeys.

Non-exempt Vehicles

All other goods-carrying vehicles over 3.5 tonnes gross weight not specifically shown as exempt in the list above must be covered by an 'O' licence. This includes such vehicles that are only temporarily in the operator's possession, or are hired or borrowed on a short-term basis, if they are used in connection with a business (even a part-time business).

No Exemption for Fast Agricultural Tractors

Fastrac-type agricultural tractors capable of pulling substantial loads at speeds of up to 40 mph on public roads must be specified on an 'O' licence if used for hire or reward haulage work. The agricultural exemption mentioned above applies only when such machines are used by farmers in connection with their own agricultural business.

These vehicles provide unfair competition to licensed road hauliers by using red diesel and under-age drivers, by paying a reduced rate vehicle excise duty and by not having any requirements to observe the law on goods vehicle plating and testing, drivers' hours, breaks and rest periods, and tachographs.

The Vehicle User

An 'O' licence must be obtained by the 'user' of the vehicle for all the vehicles he operates to which the regulations apply. The 'user' may be the owner of the vehicle or he may have hired it. If the vehicle was hired without a driver, the hirer is the 'user'. There is considerable importance attached to the word 'user', and its exact meaning, both for the purposes of 'O' licensing and in other regulations. It may be explained simply as follows:

- An owner-driver who uses his vehicle in connection with his own business is the 'user' of his own vehicle.
- If the owner of a vehicle employs a driver to drive it for him and he pays the driver's wages then the owner is the 'user' because he is the employer of the driver.
- If a vehicle is borrowed, leased or hired without a driver and the borrower or hirer drives it himself or pays the wages of a driver he employs to drive it then the borrower or hirer is the 'user'.

From this it can be seen that, in general, the person who pays the driver's wages is the 'user' of a vehicle, and it is this person (or company) who is responsible for holding an 'O' licence and for the safe condition of the vehicle on the road and for ensuring that it is operated in accordance with the law. However, it must be remembered that the driver himself, although an employee, is still also the user of the vehicle in the context of certain legislation (eg the Road Vehicles (Construction and Use) Regulations 1986, as amended) and he, too, is responsible for its safe condition on the road and is liable to prosecution if it is not in safe and legal condition.

A situation has arisen in recent times where owner-drivers of goods vehicles who cannot themselves obtain the professional competence qualification have had their vehicles specified on the 'O' licence of another operator but have nevertheless been paid as self-employed contractors to the other operator. This practice is illegal because if the driver owns the vehicle and uses it in connection with his business then by virtue of the regulations he is the 'user' and is therefore responsible for holding the 'O' licence for it.

Agency Drivers

Dependence on agencies for the supply of temporary drivers to provide relief manpower when regular drivers are not available has caused difficulty in interpretation of the term 'user' and in deciding who should hold the 'O' licence: the vehicle owner or the agency which employs the driver. It can be seen from the second bullet point item above that the person who pays the driver's wages is the 'user', and is therefore the person who should hold the 'O' licence.

However, the status of the vehicle 'user' in these circumstances has been determined by the agencies getting operators to sign agreements whereby the vehicle operator technically becomes the employer of the driver rather than the agency being the employer and consequently the operator remains the legal 'user' of the vehicle. Usually the agency asks the hirer to sign an agreement whereby the agency becomes the 'agent' of the operator for these purposes in paying the driver's wages. This practice has been proved in court to be legally acceptable on the grounds that the Transport Act 1968 section 92(2) states that 'the person whose servant or agent the driver is, shall be deemed to be the person using the vehicle'. The driver is considered to be the servant of the hirer because the hirer gives instructions and directs the activities of the driver who is temporarily in his employ. The key issue here is who controls how the drivers do their job. This must be the 'user' of the vehicle and the holder of the 'O' licence.

The great danger with agency drivers is that the operator has no sound means of establishing whether the driver is legally qualified to drive or whether he has already exceeded his permitted driving hours on previous days and whether he has had adequate rest periods. Reputable agencies usually go to considerable lengths to ensure that drivers provided by them for their clients are properly licensed and have complied with the driving hours rules in all respects. It is worth also remembering that the use of casually hired or temporary drivers (whose backgrounds and previous experiences may not be fully known) can result in jeopardy of the contract of insurance covering the use of vehicles and there could also be serious security risks as well as possible 'O' licence penalties for infringements of the law. For this reason the operator should confine himself to obtaining drivers from reputable agencies who are known to have vetted drivers satisfactorily.

Operators who use agency drivers should be aware that they may be held liable for negligence or driving offences committed by such drivers. They are also liable for ensuring the health and safety of hired drivers, and must inform them of the legal requirements of vehicle operations, such as the 'hours' law, tachographs, safe loading and vehicle checks.

A Code of Practice for the employment of agency drivers is available from offices of the Freight Transport Association (FTA), the Road Haulage Association (RHA) and the Recruitment and Employment Confederation (REC). The Code sets out the respective duties and responsibilities of the haulier on the one hand and the supplying agency on the other, with a checklist for each to ensure that full and correct information is exchanged as to the requirement for the driver (eg the skills and personal attributes required) and the particular job to be done. It also contains a model set of instructions and procedures which should be given to drivers.

Copies of the Code can be obtained from local FTA and RHA offices or from the REC at 15 Welbeck Street, London W1G 9XT (tel: 020 7462 3260).

Rental of Vehicles

Rental of vehicles on a short-term basis of a few days or a few weeks, which is the usual arrangement, does not impose onerous contractual obligations on the hirer.

'O' Licensing Provisions

However, it does involve other legal obligations in respect of the vehicle itself and its use. For a start, much depends on the gross weight of the vehicle. If it is over 3.5 tonnes permissible maximum weight and has been rented for use in connection with a trade or business, then the person or firm renting it must hold an 'O' licence and there must be a margin on that licence to cover the renting of one or more additional vehicles.

There is no need to advise the Licensing Authority (LA) of details of the vehicle unless it is to be retained on hire for more than one month, after which time the LA must be notified so an 'O' licence windscreen disc can be issued for the vehicle. If the vehicle is rented for a shorter period and then returned to the rental company to be replaced by another vehicle, the LA does not have to be notified if the combined total of the two rental periods exceeds one month unless both are part of the same rental agreement.

If the over-3.5 tonnes vehicle is rented by a firm for use in another traffic area different from the one in which the 'O' licence is held, then an 'O' licence must be obtained in that other traffic area before a vehicle is permitted to operate from a base there.

Whether or not the rented vehicle comes within the scope of 'O' licensing, the person or firm renting it carries the user responsibility for its safe mechanical condition when it is on the road. Consequently, if vehicle faults result in prosecution the user will have to pay any fines imposed (not the rental company) and the user's 'O' licence will be put in jeopardy (even if the vehicle is not specified on his 'O' licence). Therefore, careful selection of a reputable rental company with high maintenance standards is essential.

Hire and Contract Hire

Hiring of vehicles (or more specifically contract hire), as opposed to rental, implies a longer-term arrangement with a more rigid agreement as to the obligations of the parties involved. Hiring arrangements vary considerably since the vehicle provider and the customer draw up a contract to incorporate the services required. There are two principal forms of contract hire: vehicles supplied with drivers and vehicles supplied without drivers.

The important difference is that in the former case the contract hire company, as the employer of the driver, is the 'user' of the vehicles in law and therefore holds the 'O' licence and shoulders the legal responsibilities previously described, while the hirer merely operates the vehicles exclusively to suit his requirements. However, in the latter case the hirer is the 'user' and 'O' licence holder and, as with vehicles purchased and leased with his own employee drivers at the wheel, he carries the full legal responsibilities.

Advantages of Contract Hire

This method of vehicle acquisition offers a number of advantages. Principally, there is no investment of capital (generally not even an initial deposit to be found) and cash flow for transport services is predictable throughout the year, thus allowing easy budgeting. One regular monthly invoice covers all capital and operating costs. The hire charges are fully allowable against tax.

Overall, full contract hire with driver is advantageous to the operator, because it relieves him of the burdens of capital expenditure on an ancillary activity and of a welter of legal responsibilities and yet provides him with the right vehicles for his exclusive use to fulfil his delivery requirements as he wishes. He thus has the best of both worlds – all his transport needs met without the major burdens usually encountered by own-fleet operators.

A further financial advantage can arise for a firm operating its own fleet but wishing to switch to contract hire to gain the benefits outlined. Contract hire companies will usually purchase a whole existing fleet and then contract-hire it back to the operator, thus still giving him resources to meet his transport needs and yet providing him with an immediate refund of the capital tied up in vehicles. This proposition can be used to advantage in relieving cash-flow pressure.

Leasing

Leasing is a totally different concept from outright purchase or hire purchase in that the operator (ie the lessee) never actually owns the vehicle but he has the full use of it as though it were his own. It is also a different concept from rental and hiring arrangements in that it is purely a financial means of acquiring vehicles. In other words, those putting up the money are not transport or vehicle operators, they are finance houses.

Several different forms of leasing are available (basically divided by the assumption of risk, with the lessee taking the risk with a pure finance lease and the lessor retaining the risk with an operating lease) and legislation governing leasing arrangements is subject to change. Also, the way in which the accountancy profession treats leasing is subject to variation, so it is important to discuss any proposed leasing arrangement with a professional accountant before commitment to an agreement.

The general concept of leasing is that a finance house (ie the lessor) purchases a vehicle, for which the operator has specified his requirements and negotiated the price and any available discount from the supplier, and then it spreads the capital cost, interest charges, overhead costs and its profit margin over a period of time to determine the amount of the periodic repayments.

Where leasing is purely a financial arrangement, the advantages and disadvantages from an operational viewpoint are the same as for outright purchase. Because in principle the lessee operates the vehicle as though he owns it and he employs the driver, the full weight of legal responsibility, as already outlined, applies to him so he needs to have a full transport back-up of administration and operational staff, maintenance facilities and policies for selection of the correct vehicles and for replacement at the most economic intervals.

Restricted and Standard 'O' Licences

There are three main types of 'O' licence as described below and, in certain circumstances, a temporary licence known as an interim direction may be granted in exceptional circumstances (see p 33).

1 **Restricted licences:** available only to own-account operators who carry nothing other than goods in connection with their own trade or business, which is a business other than that of carrying goods for hire or reward. These licences cover both national and international transport operations with own-account goods. Restricted 'O' licence holders must not use their vehicles to carry goods for hire or reward or on behalf of customers' businesses – even if it is done only as a favour or is seen as being part of the service provided to a customer and even if no charges are raised (see below). Such activities are illegal and could result in penalties.

2 **Standard licences (national transport operations):** for hire or reward (ie professional) hauliers, or own-account operators who also engage in hire or reward operations, but restricted solely to national transport operations (ie operations exclusively within the UK). Own-account holders of such licences may also carry their own goods (but not goods for hire or reward) on international journeys.

3 **Standard licences (national and international transport operations):** for hire or reward (ie professional) hauliers, or own-account operators who also engage in hire or reward carrying, on both national and international transport operations.

National transport operations in this context include journeys to and from ports with loaded trailers which were previously considered to be international journeys.

Standard Licences for Own-Account Operators

Own-account operators may voluntarily choose to hold a standard 'O' licence for national or both national and international transport operations instead of a restricted licence provided they are prepared to meet the necessary additional qualifying requirements (principally the professional competence qualification – see Chapter 2). Among the reasons which may influence them to take this step is the desire to carry goods for hire or reward to utilize spare capacity on their vehicles, especially on return trips. Such a requirement may also arise because a firm is involved in carrying goods for associate companies on a reciprocal or integrated working basis which does not come within the scope of activities which are permitted under 'O' licensing between subsidiary companies and holding companies (see p 48) or firms may find themselves in the position where they carry goods in connection with their customers', as opposed to their own, businesses.

Firms holding restricted 'O' licences may not carry on their vehicles goods on behalf of customers (ie in connection with the trade or business of the customer rather than in connection with their own business) or other firms even if such operations are described as being a 'favour' or 'part of the service' to the customer and involve no payment whatsoever. This may occur, for example, when a vehicle delivers goods to a customer and the customer then asks the driver to drop off items on his return journey because he is 'going past the door' and their own vehicle is not available. Such activities would be illegal under the terms of a restricted 'O' licence and if two convictions for such an offence are made within five years, the licence must be revoked by the Traffic Commissioner.

Requirements for 'O' Licensing

In order to obtain an 'O' licence, applicants must satisfy certain conditions specified in regulations.

Restricted Licences

Applicants must be:

- fit and proper persons;
- of appropriate financial standing.

Standard Licences (national transport operations)

Applicants must be:

- of good repute;
- of appropriate financial standing;
- professionally competent, or must employ a person who is professionally competent, in national transport operations.

Standard Licences (national and international transport operations)

Applicants must be:

- of good repute;
- of appropriate financial standing;
- professionally competent, or must employ a person who is professionally competent, in both national and international transport operations.

Other Legal Requirements

Besides the specific requirements mentioned above, licence applicants and holders have to satisfy further legal requirements relating to the suitability and environmental acceptability of their vehicle operating centres, the suitability of their vehicle maintenance facilities or arrangements and, overall, their ability and willingness to comply with the law in regard to vehicle operating as demonstrated by signing the undertakings on the 'O' licence application form. These matters are dealt with in detail in this chapter.

Road hauliers should note that increasingly Traffic Commissioners are urging licensed operators to check carefully that any sub-contract road hauliers to whom they pass on work are fully licensed to carry out the work. See p 52.

Good Repute

For a TC to be able to grant an 'O' licence, he must determine that the applicant is of 'good repute'. Without this particular requirement being well established, the fact that the applicant may meet all other relevant criteria is of no account; no licence will be granted.

With the introduction of new provisions from EU Council Directive 98/76/EC in UK regulations (the Goods Vehicle Operators (Qualifications) Regulations 1999), much tougher good repute standards are imposed on both new and existing operators.

The term 'good repute' is defined on the basis that an individual is not of good repute if he has been convicted of more than one serious offence or of road transport offences concerning:

- pay and employment conditions in the profession (ie of road haulier);
- drivers' hours and rest periods;
- weights and dimensions of goods vehicles;
- road and vehicle safety;
- protection of the environment; and
- rules concerning professional liability.

For the purposes of the standard 'O' licensing scheme this means that the applicant for a licence (ie an individual) must not have a past record which includes more than one conviction for serious offences or conviction for road transport offences during the previous five years (excluding convictions that are 'spent' – see below) relating to the above issues. Similarly, to be a fit and proper person in order to obtain a restricted 'O' licence means that there should not be a past record of such offences. If it is a limited liability company applying for a licence and the company has relevant convictions on its record (ie for serious offences) then the TC may use his discretion in deciding whether the firm is of good repute, a facility he does not have in the case of individuals or partnership businesses.

It should be noted that the TC will not necessarily refuse to grant a licence to an applicant who has had convictions – but he must if they are for more than one serious offence, which affects the applicant's good repute – but he will consider the number and seriousness of the convictions before making a grant. He may, for example, issue a licence for a shorter period to see if the applicant has 'mended his ways', or grant a licence for fewer vehicles than the number requested. If, during the currency of a licence, an 'O' licence holder is convicted of offences related to goods vehicle operations, the TC may call the operator to a public inquiry and determine whether he is still a fit and proper person or of good repute and whether he should be allowed to continue holding an 'O' licence (see also pp 53–54).

In the case of partnership applications for licences, if one of the partners is considered not to be of good repute, then the TC will be bound to conclude that the partnership firm is not of good repute and, on that basis, he will refuse to grant a licence.

The relevant offences for which conviction damages a person's good repute are those specified in the Goods Vehicles (Licensing of Operators) Act 1995, schedules 2(4) and (5) and include matters relating to:

- unlawful use of vehicles;
- unroadworthiness of vehicles, maintenance and maintenance records;
- plating and testing;
- speed limits;
- weight limits, safe loading and overloading of vehicles;
- licensing of drivers;
- drivers' hours and record keeping (including tachographs);
- certain traffic offences (eg parking);
- certain waste-related offences;
- illegal use of rebated fuel oil;
- forgery;
- international road haulage permits.

NB: *Offences concerning protection of the environment and commercial matters such as professional liability now included in the EU Directive mentioned above will be included in UK regulations in due course.*

Increasingly, convictions for vehicle excise licensing offences are featuring in consideration of 'O' licence applicants' good repute by the TCs and a number of licences have been either refused or penalized on these grounds.

Additionally, in the case of applications for standard international 'O' licences, the TC must be told of convictions for any other offence besides those concerning the matters listed above.

Serious Offences

A serious offence, by an individual or by a company or its management, as referred to above is defined as one where, if committed in the UK, a sentence of more than three months' imprisonment, or a community service order of more than 60 hours was ordered, or a fine exceeding level four on the standard scale (currently £2,500) was imposed. If committed abroad the seriousness of the offence would be determined by assessing the punishment relative to UK standards.

Criminal Offences

Since 1 April 1998 convictions for offences such as falsifying records (eg tachograph charts), forgery (eg of insurance documents or a driving licence) and fraudulent use or display of an official document (eg an 'O' licence disc or vehicle excise licence), including aiding and abetting these offences, have branded the offender a criminal. These convictions will be recorded on the Police National Computer and can be accessed at will by the police, other organizations and possibly, in due course, the Traffic Commissioners, in determining a person's good repute for 'O' licensing purposes.

Spent Convictions

Spent convictions, which are referred to above in the context of good repute, are those which *do not* have to be declared on the licence application form, because they were incurred sufficiently long ago to be considered legally invalid for determining a person's past record. Under the Rehabilitation of Offenders Act 1974 a person who was convicted of an offence for which he was fined by a court need not disclose that conviction after five years (or 2½ years if aged under 17 at the time), or if a prison sentence of six months or less was imposed it need not be disclosed after seven years (or 3½ years if aged under 17 at the time). In the case of a prison sentence of between six months and 2½ years the rehabilitation period (after which no disclosure is necessary) is 10 years, or 5 years if aged under 17 at the time. A table showing the full range of rehabilitation periods is given below.

In Scotland, supervision requirements made by children's hearings attract similar rehabilitation periods to those for care or supervision orders.

(i) Fixed rehabilitation periods:

Sentence	Rehabilitation period
• For a prison sentence between 6 months and 2½ years	10 years (5 years if aged under 17 years at the time)
• For a prison sentence of 6 months or less	7 years (3½ years if aged under 17 years at the time)
• For a fine or a community service order	5 years (2½ years if aged under 17 years at the time)
• For an absolute discharge	6 months
• For Borstal*	7 years
• For a detention centre	3 years

(ii) Variable rehabilitation periods:

Sentence	Rehabilitation period
• A probation order, conditional discharge or bind over	1 year or until the order expires (whichever is longer)
• A care order or supervision order	1 year or until the order expires (whichever is longer)
• An order for custody in a remand home, an approved school* or an attendance centre order	A period ending 1 year after the order expires
• A hospital order (with or without a restriction order)	A period ending 1 year after the order expires 5 years or a period ending 2 years after the order expires (whichever is longer)

* NB: *These are more commonly known as 'young offenders institutions'.*

Financial Standing

The requirement for financial standing means the applicant being able to prove to, or assure, the TC that sufficient funds (ie money) are readily available to maintain the vehicles to be covered by the licence to the standards of fitness and safety required by law.

Road haulage operators must have available capital and reserves of at least £8,100 for their first vehicle and at least £4,500 for each additional vehicle; thus for a five-vehicle fleet the operator will have to prove available finances of at least £26,100 and for a 10-vehicle fleet the figure would be £48,600. These financial resources will need to be reviewed on a five-yearly basis.

These values are converted from euros, which vary daily in line with exchange rate fluctuations (in mid-2011 the euro was worth about 88 pence sterling). For the purposes of the Directive its value against national currencies is to be fixed annually based on its value on the first working day of October each year to take effect from 1 January of the following calendar year (the rate is published in the *Official Journal of the European Communities*).

The former lower figures applicable to both national operators and restricted licence holders have been abolished. All operators must now meet the standards described above.

It is important to realize that the requirement for minimum levels of capital and reserves applies to the total number of vehicles authorized on an 'O' licence, not just to the vehicles currently specified. In the case where an operator has a significant margin between the number of authorized vehicles and those actually specified, he may wish to consider decreasing this margin to reduce the amount of financial resources he has to prove to the Traffic Commissioner. The number of authorized vehicles on an 'O' licence can be reduced by application to the TC using form GV81 (see pp 46–47).

The EU Directive allows for the financial standards described above to be established by means of confirmation or assurance from a bank or from other properly qualified institutions that such funds are available, in the form of a bank guarantee, pledge or security, or by similar means.

A key point that has been reiterated recently is that proof of sufficient finances to meet the legal requirement should not relate to a single day when a bank balance may have been artificially boosted by a temporary injection of funds that are, in effect, moved away again the next day, but rather should relate to an average balance over the life of the licence. The TC has to be certain that the licence applicant or operator has sufficient funds 'available'* to establish and properly administer the business on a daily basis, not just to meet a target balance on a particular day.

*NB: 'Available' in this context means, according to the Transport Tribunal: 'capable of being used'; 'at one's disposal'; 'within one's reach'; 'easy to get at'.

Failure to pay fines, other penalties and business debts as well as non-payment of vehicle excise duties will suggest to the TC that an operator has cash-flow problems and is therefore unlikely to meet the legal requirement for financial standing. This could lead to loss of the 'O' licence.

Assessment of Financial Standing

On the fifth anniversary of the grant of a licence, the TC will carry out a 'wealth' check to determine whether the required reserves have been available during the previous five years. If they have *not*, the licence holder will be deemed to be no longer of the required financial standing and the licence will be revoked.

The TC has considerable powers to inquire into the finances of applicants, including the right to ask for the production of proof of financial standing by means of audited accounts and bank statements or bank references, savings or deposit account books or other evidence of funds stated to be available for the maintenance of vehicles. He will particularly look at the firm's balance sheet within the audited accounts and determine its liquidity (ie its capability of paying its debts as they fall due). He will examine the relevant financial ratios such as current assets to current liabilities, which ideally should not be less than 2:1, and the so-called quick ratio of quickly realizable assets (ie items which can quickly be turned into cash) to current liabilities which, in this case, should not be less than 1:1. It is believed that where a firm's accounts show a current ratio of less than 0.5:1 the TC should consult with the financial assessors he is empowered to call on.

NB: Road hauliers who make a practice of factoring their debts (ie selling their unpaid invoices at less than face value to secure a quick cash return) may find the TC questioning their financial standing on the grounds that such practices are an indicator that all is not well within a firm and that it might not meet the required financial standards for holding an 'O' licence. However, new invoice factoring arrangements established by the Royal Bank of Scotland Commercial Services (RBSCS) may satisfy the Traffic Commissioners on the financial standing of an operator.

In complex cases, usually involving companies where, perhaps, funds are moved between one subsidiary and another, and there is cross-accounting and suchlike, the TCs can call on financial experts (assessors) to help determine the true position of an applicant.

Professional Competence

Details of the professional competence requirements for standard 'O' licence holders are given in Chapter 2.

Wrong Licences

It is illegal to operate on the wrong type of 'O' licence. Applicants are required to specify which type of licence they require and those who specify restricted licences will be subject to severe penalties if they subsequently carry goods for hire or reward. Operators who specify standard licences covering only national operations and who engage in international operations will be similarly penalized.

Operating Centres

The vehicle operating centre is defined as the place where the vehicle is 'normally kept'. This is commonly taken to mean the place where the vehicle is regularly parked when it is not in use. However, places where vehicles are parked occasionally, even if on a regular basis, in circumstances that are exceptional to the normal conduct of the business, are not considered to be operating centres.

Where operators regularly permit drivers to take vehicles home with them at night and at weekends in circumstances that are not 'exceptional' to the normal conduct of the business, then the place where the drivers park vehicles near to their home becomes the vehicle operating centre. This place then must be declared on the 'O' licence application form.

In these circumstances an operator could have to declare a number of separate operating centres in addition to his normal depot or base and he could face environmental representation against each of these places and have restrictive environmental conditions placed on his licence in respect of their use. Alternatively, he could lose his licence if he fails to declare such places as operating centres. Failure to notify the TC of new or additional operating centres is an offence. Similarly, the practice of allowing drivers to take vehicles home regularly or, for other reasons, park away from the operating centre regularly (except when on genuine journeys away from base) puts the 'O' licence in jeopardy, as well as risking prosecution.

What is abundantly clear is that Traffic Commissioners expect licence applicants to be able to show that their proposed operating centre is both suitable in environmental terms and sufficiently large to accommodate all the vehicles authorized to be based there. Should this not be the case a licence may be refused or a grant made authorizing fewer vehicles (ie only as many, possibly, as can be parked at the centre).

It is useful to stress again that the use of an unauthorized operating centre or failure to notify the TC of a change of operating centre is an offence which can result in a fine of up to £2,500 on conviction and penalty against the 'O' licence.

Operating centres are subject to review as to their continued suitability at five-yearly intervals – at the TC's discretion. In other words, the TC may call an operator for review once every five years, but should he decide not to do so the centre remains 'suitable' for another five years.

Licence Application

Applications for 'O' licences are based on where the operator keeps his vehicles. In the first instance the completed application form (GV79) must be sent to the VOSA Central Licensing Office in Leeds (see Appendix I). After initial processing the application will be forwarded to the TC for each Traffic Area in which the operator has vehicles based. These bases will be the operating centres (see above for definition) for the vehicles. One 'O' licence will be sufficient to cover any number of vehicles operating at one centre and any number of operating centres in any one Traffic Area. If operating centres are in different Traffic Areas then separate 'O' licences will be required for each Traffic Area. (A list of Traffic Area Office addresses is to be found in Appendix I.)

Form GV79

Application for a licence has to be made on the appropriate form – form GV79 obtainable from the Traffic Area Office – which is straightforward and simple to answer. This form incorporates questions relating to vehicle operating centres, the previous history of licence applicants during the past five years and the type of licence required.

There are questions to be answered on the form relating to the name and address of the business, its partners or directors; information regarding vehicles currently owned and those which it is planned to acquire is also required and the address of their respective operating centres. Questions ask if the applicant company or individual or any partners of the business have convictions which are not 'spent' (under the Rehabilitation of Offenders Act 1974 a person is relieved of the obligation to disclose information about a conviction which is 'spent' – see p 22). Details are required of any such convictions including the date of the conviction, the nature of the offence, the name of the court and the penalty imposed.

Further questions require information about vehicle maintenance – who is to do it, when and where is it to be done, and what facilities there are at that place. Questions are asked about the financial status of the business proprietor, his partners or the directors of the business, in particular asking whether during the past three years any of them have been made bankrupt, been involved with a company which has gone into insolvent liquidation, or been disqualified from acting as a director or taking part in the management of a company. Details about the professionally competent person supporting the application are required, where that person lives, his actual place of work and the address of the operating centre for which he is responsible.

Undertakings

When the applicant signs the form he is not only declaring that the statements of fact made on the form are true but also, in effect, he is making legally binding promises – undertakings – that statements of what he intends to do will be fulfilled. The undertakings relate to the observation of certain aspects of the law concerned with goods vehicle operation and the maintenance of vehicles included in the licence application. If at some time during the currency of the licence the TC finds that these undertakings have not been fulfilled, as evidenced by any convictions for relevant offences, he may use his powers to revoke, suspend or curtail the licence. The basis on which the applicant makes the undertakings is that he promises the following:

I, or the licensed operator, undertake to make proper arrangements so that:

- the laws relating to the driving and operation of vehicles used under this licence are observed;
- the rules on drivers' hours and tachographs are observed, proper records are kept and that these are made available on request;
- vehicles and trailers are not overloaded;
- vehicles operate within speed limits;
- vehicles and trailers, including hired vehicles and trailers, are kept in a fit and serviceable condition;

- drivers report promptly any defects or symptoms of defects that could prevent the safe operation of vehicles and/or trailers, and that any defects are recorded in writing;

- records are kept (for 15 months) of all driver reports which record defects, all safety inspections, routine maintenance and repairs to vehicles, and that these are made available on request;

- in respect of each operating centre specified, that the number of vehicles and the number of trailers kept there will not exceed the maximum numbers authorized at each operating centre (which will be noted on the licence);

- an unauthorized operating centre is not used in any traffic area;

- furthermore, I will notify the Traffic Commissioner of any convictions against myself, or the company, business partner(s), the company directors, nominated transport manager/s named in this application, or employees or agents of the applicant for this licence and, if the licence is issued, convictions against the licence holder or employees or agents of the licence holder;

- I will ensure that the Traffic Commissioner is notified within 28 days of any other changes, for example a change to the proposed maintenance arrangements; a change in the financial status of the licence holder [eg if placed in liquidation or receivership], or a change to Limited Company status or partnership, that might affect the licence, if issued.

As already stated, the application form is straightforward and simple to answer and extensive explanatory notes are provided for guidance. The Traffic Area Office also sends applicants a free booklet, *Goods Vehicle Operator Licensing – Guide for Operators* (GV74–7/96), to provide further help. Further information is also available at the VOSA website: **www.vosa.gov.uk**. This does not, however, mean that the form should not be carefully studied or that any answer will do in an attempt to gain a licence. While it is obvious that to get an 'O' licence the undertakings must be signed, it should be remembered that the consequences of not fulfilling the stated undertakings can lead to penalties so severe as to put a small operator out of business and even to cause hardship to a large one. A warning about this in the following terms is included in the explanatory notes on the form so that applicants are left in no doubt as to the consequences of making false statements or not fulfilling statements:

'I declare that the statements made in this application are true. I understand that the licence may be revoked if the licensed operator does not comply with the undertakings made and that it is an offence to make a false declaration.'

Form GV79A

Another form is involved in making an application for an 'O' licence. This is form GV79A, which is a supplementary sheet used for supplying details of vehicles, for example, registration number, maximum gross weight, body type – flat or sided including skeletals, box body or van, tanker or other type such as cement mixer or livestock carrier – and whether the vehicle is articulated, a tipper or refrigerated. Certain designation letters and numbers are used to indicate body and vehicle type as follows:

- flat or sided including skeletals;
- box body or van;
- tanker;
- other type (such as cement mixer, livestock carrier):
    T Tipper;
    R Refrigerated;
    A Articulated.

Form TM1 (G)

When completing the GV79 application form the operator must list all of the nominated transport managers they propose to name on the licence. In addition, using form TM1 (G), each named manager must provide their personal details, and give information of other employments and particulars of previous convictions. The manager is also required to sign a 'Declaration' contained within the TM1 (G), in which he undertakes to ensure vehicles are operated in a safe and legal manner. The manager's original certificate which provides proof of their professional competence must accompany the application.

Additional Application Forms

Two supplementary application forms are used in connection with certain licence applications. These forms are GV79E (pale green in colour), dealing with environmental information, and GV79F (beige in colour), dealing with financial information. The forms are used only when the TC requires further information following the initial application on form GV79 on either or both of the relevant matters (ie environmental issues or finance).

Environmental Information

Form GV79E is sent to a licence applicant if the TC receives representations from local residents following publication of details of the applicant's proposals regarding his vehicle operating centre in the local newspaper. The form must be completed and returned to the TC, who will then consider the application in the light of this further information, the information given by those making the environmental representations and as a result of making his own enquiries.

The form requires details of the applicant's name and address, and the address of his proposed operating centre (see p 25 for definition). It then requires information about the vehicles to be normally kept at the centre and the number and types of trailer to be kept there. Information must be given about any other parking place in the vicinity of the operating centre which is to be used for parking authorized vehicles (ie those authorized on the licence). If the applicant is not the owner of the premises he must send evidence to show that he has permission or authority to use the place for parking vehicles.

A number of further questions must be answered on the form about the operating times of authorized vehicles – in particular, what time lorries will arrive at and leave the centre, whether they will use the centre on Saturdays or Sundays, what times they will arrive and leave on these days, whether maintenance work will be carried out there and between what hours, and whether any of this work will take place on Saturdays or Sundays and, if so, between what hours. The TC also wants to know whether there are any covered buildings at the centre in which this work is carried out.

A plan showing the parking positions for authorized vehicles must be sent when returning the completed form. This should show entry and exit points, main buildings, surrounding roads with names and the normal parking area for the vehicles. The scale of the plan must be indicated and this is suggested as being 1:500, which is 1 centimetre to 5 metres or, roughly, 1 inch to 40 feet. A larger scale of 1 inch to 100 feet can be used if this is more convenient when the operating centre is large. If the proposed operating centre has not previously been used as such the TC must be given information about any application for or planning permission granted for the proposed use of the site as a goods vehicle operating centre.

Financial Information

Form GV79F is sometimes sent to new standard licence applicants when the TC requires additional information to enable him to consider whether the applicant meets the financial requirements for this type of licence. An application will be refused unless the TC is satisfied that the applicant has sufficient financial resources to set up and run his business both legally and safely. This fact is pointed out clearly on the form. Answers have to be given to questions about the vehicles, their average annual mileage and the estimated running cost for each individual type of vehicle.

Details must be given about the funds available to start up the business and where these are held (eg in the bank, in savings or as agreed bank overdraft or loan facilities, or in the form of share capital), and about the start-up costs for the business including the purchase price or amount of down payments on vehicles and on premises and the sum to be held in reserve as working capital. The applicant is required to give a forecast of the annual expenditure and income for his road haulage operations for a financial year. The TC expects this information to give a clear indication of the business finances for the year ahead. In certain cases the TC may ask for monthly information.

NB: Not all TCs currently use this form; some prefer to rely on supporting financial information in other forms – bank references for example.

Date for Applications

Application for an 'O' licence should be made at least nine weeks before the day on which it is desired to take effect. In some Traffic Areas the time taken to process applications is much longer than nine weeks so new operators should be aware of the fact that it is illegal to start operating vehicles until their licence has actually been granted. Where there is an urgent need to start operations before a licence is granted through the normal processes, application can be made to the TC for an interim licence (see p 33).

Offences while Applications Are Pending

Applicants for licences have a duty to advise the TC if, in the period of time between the application being submitted and it being dealt with by the TC, they are convicted of a relevant offence which they would have had to include on the application form had the conviction been made before the application was made. Failure to notify the TC is an offence and it could jeopardize any licence subsequently granted.

Advertising of Applications

Applicants for 'O' licences who are seeking a new licence, or variation of an existing licence, are required to arrange for publication of an advertisement (following a specified format to contain the necessary information for potential environmental representors – see Figure 1.1) in a local newspaper (or newspapers) circulating in the area where the operating centre is located. If more than one operating centre is specified in the application separate advertisements must be placed for each such centre in the respective local newspapers serving those locations. The sole purpose of the advertisement is to give local residents an opportunity (given to them under the regulations) to make representations against proposals to use a particular place as a goods vehicle operating centre.

The advertisement need appear only once but it must be published during a period extending from not more than 21 days before and not more than 21 days after the licence application is made. There is no specified minimum or maximum size requirement for the advertisement but the TCs advise that it 'should not be too small and should be easy to read'. Most adverts appear in single-column format extending to a few inches of text and at an average cost estimated to be in the region of £100–150. Normally the advertisement will appear in the public or official notices section of the newspaper.

Proof that the advertisement has appeared – and is published correctly (which many are not) – must be given to the TC before he considers the application and failure to produce this proof (usually achieved by sending in the appropriate page torn from the newspaper showing the advertisement itself and the name and date of the paper) will mean that the TC, by law, must refuse to consider the application. Normally this would mean making a fresh application, which, of course, delays the whole matter, adds to the costs by requiring another advertisement and could mean vehicles having to stand until the licence or variation is granted.

Schedule 4 Application Procedure

This procedure can be used by a traffic commissioner to allow an operating centre to be accepted without the need to put an advert in a local paper, as is normally required. This would apply, for example, when transferring an operating centre, currently on one operator's licence to another operator.

However, there are particular circumstances that must be taken into consideration. These include:

- The operating centre is being given up by the original operator.

FIGURE 1.1 Format which must be used for 'O' licence newspaper advertisements

Goods Vehicle Operator's Licence

trading as _____

of _____

is applying for a licence to use _____

_____

_____

as an operating centre for _____ goods vehicles and

_____ trailers

and to use

_____

_____

_____

as an operating centre for _____ goods vehicles and

_____ trailers

Owners or occupiers of land (including buildings) near the operating centre(s) who believe that their enjoyment of that land would be affected should make written representations to the Traffic Commissioner at

_____

_____

_____

stating their reasons within 21 days of this notice. Representors must at the same time send a copy of their representations to the applicant at the address given at the top of this notice. A Guide to making representations is available from the Traffic Commissioner's Office.

Advertisement form for use with new application on GV79

FIGURE 1.1 continued

Goods Vehicle Operator's Licence

trading as _____

of _____

is applying to change an existing licence as follows

* To keep an extra _____ goods vehicles and _____ trailers at the operating centre at

_____

* To add an operating centre for _____ goods vehicles and _____ trailers at the
operating centre at _____

_____

*To change existing conditions or undertakings applying at the operating centre at

_____

from _____

_____

to _____

_____

*To remove the following conditions or undertakings which reads _____

_____ and which applies to the operating centre

at _____

Owners or occupiers of land (including buildings) near the operating centre(s) who
believe that their enjoyment of that land would be affected should make written
representations to the Traffic Commissioner at

_____

_____

stating their reasons within 21 days of this notice. Representors must at the same
time send a copy of their representations to the applicant at the address given at
the top of this notice. A Guide to making representations is available from the Traffic
Commissioner's Office.

Advertisement form for use with major variation application on form GV81

- The new operator must to use it on the same terms as the original licence holder.
- The applicant may specify only up to the total number of vehicles already specified at the operating centre of the original operator.
- Any conditions that apply to the operating centre concerned are transferred with it.

Such approval of the Schedule 4 Procedure is allowed at the discretion of the traffic commissioner.

Interim Licences

In certain circumstances the TC may grant an interim licence pending his decision on the full licence application. The circumstances under which such a licence may be granted are not precisely specified but they may be connected with some urgent need to move goods quickly because they are perishable or for some other urgent reason. A grant of an interim licence should not be taken as a guarantee that a full-term licence will be granted by the TC. An interim licence will not be granted in any case where the main requirements for 'O' licensing appear not to be met. For example, such a licence would not be granted to an applicant for a standard 'O' licence if he has not yet passed the CPC examination nor, indeed, while examination results are being awaited, nor on the assumption that the candidate will have passed. Neither will a grant of an interim licence normally be considered before the statutory 21-day waiting period for environmental representations and objections has expired.

Interim licences are not granted for any fixed period. Normally they remain in force until the TC has made his decision on the grant of a full licence or, alternatively, until they are revoked.

Duration of Licences

Operators' licences, since 1 January 1996, are valid indefinitely and will remain so unless the operator contravenes the terms under which his licence was granted or fails to pay the necessary fees by the due dates. Under normal circumstances the only reason for making a new application, and thus being subject to the risk of objection or environmental representation, is when a major variation of a licence is necessary in order to add to the number of authorized vehicles or to change an existing, or to add a new, operating centre to the licence. Despite being valid indefinitely, licences are still liable to penalty or total revocation should the operator be found to have contravened the law or breached the conditions placed on his licence. Additionally, operating centres are subject to 'review' (normally at five-yearly intervals, but not exclusively so) to determine whether they remain environmentally suitable – see p 41.

Licence Fees, Refunds and Discs

Operator licensing fees have been simplified and revised in order to part-fund enforcement and compliance activities.

Application Fees and Administrative Charges

- Application fee for a licence (GV79) or for a major (publishable) variation (GV81)   £250
- Fee payable for the issue of a licence   £391
- Charge for the continuation of an existing licence   £391
- Fee payable for the issue of an interim licence or direction   £66

Vehicle Fees were abolished from 31 March 2010.

It should be noted that all fees paid are *non-refundable*.

Termination of Licences for Unpaid Fees

It is important to note that failure to pay any of the fees described above by the due date will result in a licence being automatically terminated from the date on which the fee was due. In this event, the vehicle operation will have to cease and a new licence will have to be applied for before recommencing is permitted, if indeed it is permitted at all.

Licence Discs

'O' licence discs, issued on the grant (or variation) of a licence, must be displayed on the vehicle (normally in the windscreen) in a clearly visible position near to the excise duty disc and in a waterproof container. Licence discs are coloured as follows to differentiate between restricted and standard licences and between standard national and standard international licences:

- restricted licence – orange;
- standard licence, National – blue;
- standard licence, International – green;
- interim licence – issued in the colour appropriate to the type of licence applied for;
- copy discs – word 'COPY' in red across face of disc.

Licence discs are not interchangeable between vehicles or between operators. They are valid only when displayed on the vehicle whose registration number is shown on the disc (even if it is faded almost beyond recognition) and when that vehicle is being 'used' by the named operator to whom it was issued. Heavy fines are imposed on offenders who loan and borrow discs (this is fraudulent use and is a serious offence); their own 'O' licence may be jeopardized and the vehicle insurance could be invalidated.

Licence Surrender/Termination

The 'O' licence itself and all vehicle windscreen discs must be returned to the TC on surrender or termination of an 'O' licence.

Issue of Community Authorizations

All UK holders of standard 'O' licences covering international operations are issued (automatically) with a Community Authorization document to be kept at their main place of business together with certified copies equalling the total number of vehicles authorized on their operator's licence (which must be carried on vehicles when undertaking cross-border journeys within the EU) – more information on Community Authorizations is to be found in Chapter 26.

The TC's Considerations

When an application for an 'O' licence is made, the TC will have certain points to take into consideration before deciding whether or not to grant any licence. Mainly he has to ensure that the basic legal requirements as described previously have been met and particularly that those relating to vehicle operation and maintenance will be complied with. These points are dealt with here.

Fit Persons and Good Repute

The first point, and one of the fundamental requirements for 'O' licensing (as already described on pp 20–22, but a repeat here is useful), is whether the applicant is a fit person or is of good repute and is therefore fit to hold a licence. Basically, being a fit person and being of good repute are the same but the former relates to restricted 'O' licences over which the EU has no influence while the latter is the term used by the EU in setting its requirements for the holding of a licence to carry goods for hire or reward (ie the UK system of standard 'O' licences).

The TC, when deciding this, will take into account any previous record which the applicant (or the partners or directors of the applicant's business) might have had as an operator in terms of his ability or willingness to comply with the law in respect of vehicle operations and particularly maintenance, drivers' hours and records, overloading and the like, also any previous convictions they may have for offences relating to the roadworthiness of vehicles and for other relevant offences. The regulations require that a TC take account of 'serious offences' besides just road transport offences when determining the good repute of an individual, or of company management for a corporate 'O' licence application.

Maintenance Facilities/Arrangements

The next point that the TC will consider, and one of the most important since it is at the very foundation of the 'O' licensing system, is whether the applicant has suitable facilities or has made satisfactory arrangements for the maintenance of vehicles which are to be specified on the licence in a safe and legal condition and for keeping suitable maintenance records (this is dealt with in more detail in Chapter 16). In particular the TC will be concerned to know that vehicles are being subjected to safety inspections at regular intervals of time or mileage.

The TC for the West Midland and South Wales Traffic Areas, for example, currently suggests that for operators in his area inspections should be based on a time interval only with no mileage alternative and that a period of six weeks between inspections is the maximum that he would find acceptable. He also seeks assurances that operators are using a *written* driver defect reporting system and wall charts for planning inspection and maintenance schedules. Other TCs seek similar assurances.

Drivers' Hours and Records

The TC will consider whether there are satisfactory arrangements for ensuring that the law relating to drivers' hours and records (including tachographs) will be complied with.

Overloading

Similarly, the TC will want to be sure that arrangements are made to prevent the overloading of vehicles and that vehicle weight limits in general will be observed.

Professional Competence Requirements

The TC will want to know details of the nominated professionally competent person, who may be the applicant himself or an employee who holds a certificate of professional competence covering national or both national and international transport operations (or a person who qualifies by exemption or by having passed the appropriate OCR examination) as appropriate to the type of standard 'O' licence applied for (see Chapter 2). The First-tier Tribunal (Transport) has ruled that the named professionally competent person in respect of a standard 'O' licence must be an active employee carrying out the functions of a transport manager in an adequate manner.

In making decisions on 'O' licence applications that involve the need to nominate a qualified transport manager, the Traffic Commissioners are concerned to ensure that the individual proposed is suitable in accordance with the Guidance Notes from the Senior Traffic Commissioner set out in September 2003 in regard to such matters as:

- the number of operator licences for which that transport manager will be responsible – maximum 4 from 4 December 2011;
- the amount of time that the transport manager will spend in carrying out his duties for the operator;

- the number of operating centres and authorized vehicles for which the transport manager is responsible both on that licence and any other operator's licences – maximum 4 and 50 from 4 December 2011;
- the geographical location of the transport manager in relation to the operator's licence and the operating centres on that licence;
- any other employment or activities in which the proposed transport manager is engaged which may restrict his ability to devote sufficient time to the duties of a transport manager on that operator's licence;
- the terms upon which the proposed transport manager is to be employed.

In order to further ensure that nominated transport managers carry out their duties effectively and in accordance with the law, a proposed form of Transport Manager – Contract of Employment has been devised (see illustration on p 38), which must be completed by the 'O' licence holder and the appointed transport manager.

Number of Qualified Persons

There is no restriction under the regulations (see Chapter 2) on the number of people in a transport department or organization who may be professionally competent and consequently hold certificates of competence. Further, although restricted 'O' licence holders have no need to specify the name of a professionally competent person in order to obtain a licence, there is no restriction on such licence holders or their employees being professionally competent if they qualify personally.

In determining how many qualified persons must be named on a standard 'O' licence the TC will take account of the management structure of applicant firms, but generally there will need to be a minimum of one qualified person per 'O' licence. The TC may require the names of more qualified persons to be specified if he considers it appropriate in view of a division of responsibilities for the operation of vehicles under the licence or if vehicles specified on the licence are located at different operating centres within the Traffic Area.

Part-Time Managers

Increasingly, TCs are questioning the role of part-time and agency-provided professionally competent transport managers. There is concern that such managers are not in a position to meet the statutory requirement for managers whereby they should have 'continuous and effective responsibility' for the fleet for which they are named. In particular, the question arises of the number of clients for whom many such agency managers are acting and the remoteness from the operating bases for which they are supposedly responsible, with some such named managers being in contact only by telephone or via a fleeting visit and thus having, as one TC put it, 'little physical contact with the drivers, the vehicles and the documentation'. This TC has stated that he intends to scrutinize closely any future applications involving agency-provided transport managers.

NB: New rules affecting part-time transport managers are introduced from 4 December 2011 under EU Regulation 1071/2009/EC – see Chapter 2.

TRANSPORT MANAGER – CONTRACT OF EMPLOYMENT

Surname	First name(s)	Date of birth

Home address

(Postcode)

Address of place of work (if not the same as operating centre)

(Postcode)

Which operating centres will the nominated TM be responsible for?

All?   Yes ☐   No ☐

If no, please list individual operating centres (by first address line only)

How many hours a week is the TM contracted to work?

Will the TM be responsible for vehicles on any other licences (in *any* Traffic Area)?

Yes ☐   No ☐

If yes, please list details below

Licence number	Vehicles/trailers authorized	Hours worked per week

Declaration: In accordance with the requirements of the Goods Vehicles (Licensing of Operators) Act 1995, we declare that .... will carry out all necessary checks on the operation of the licence holder's business. We also confirm that we understand the requirements placed on both of us by the above Act.

We understand that these responsibilities include:

- the method of control of drivers' hours;
- the maintenance of the licence holder's vehicles, including the inspection of vehicles at the appropriate time, the action taken to remedy defects found and the recording of these events;
- the reporting and recording of vehicle defects by drivers;
- the method of compilation and the accuracy of all records kept;
- the making of arrangements to ensure that the licence holder's vehicle/s are not overloaded.

Signature (licence holder)   **date**

Signature (Transport Manager)   **date**

Financial Standing

In addition to these points, the TC is required under the regulations (as already stated) to establish details of the applicant's financial standing (a bank statement, a bank manager's letter of reference or an accountant's certificate of solvency may be requested, for example, or other evidence of the availability of funds) because this has a bearing on the applicant's ability to operate and maintain vehicles in a safe condition and in compliance with the law (see also pp 23–24). While considering an applicant's financial status for this purpose, the TC also has the authority to call for the services of an assessor from a panel of persons appointed by the Secretary of State for Transport, if appropriate, due to the complexity of the financial structure of the applicant's business or affairs. The TCs watch out for 'O' licence holders who are prosecuted for vehicle excise offences and those who ask for time to pay fines or request the opportunity to make payment in instalments, following conviction for offences by the courts, and they take this as good cause for investigating an applicant's financial position.

Representations by Local Residents

Opportunities are given to local residents individually to make representations against 'O' licence applications and variations on environmental grounds. Local residents are more precisely defined in the regulations as 'owners or occupiers of land within the vicinity' (ie of the operating centre). Those residents who wish to make representation must do so individually because group action is not permitted (although a group of individual representors may appoint a joint spokesperson to put forward their case), nor is representation by any environmental pressure group, political or other campaigning body. Similarly, parish councils, which regularly feature in such matters, have no right of objection *per se* unless they *own/occupy* land in the vicinity of an operating centre featuring in an 'O' licence application, in which case they may make representation as the owner/occupier of the land.

The grounds on which such owners or occupiers can make their representations are confined purely to environmental matters such as noise, vibration, fumes and visual intrusion but could include obstruction. They do not include road safety matters, which are not an environmental issue. The grounds must be stated precisely in the written representation; to state that the representation is made for 'environmental reasons' is not sufficient. The exact wording which forms the basis of representations is specified in the legislation in the following terms: 'that place (ie the operating centre) is unsuitable on environmental grounds for (such use and) any adverse effects on environmental conditions arising from that use would be capable of prejudicially affecting the use or enjoyment of the land' (ie the land owned or occupied by the person making the representation).

One of the facts that has been difficult to establish in connection with this is a definition of the term 'within the vicinity'. It has been shown that residents living along an access road to a vehicle operating centre can be considered to be in the vicinity and adverse environmental effects of vehicles travelling along the road could be taken account of by the TC in his consideration of any environmental representations against a licence application. Each TC is left to make his own determination of whether a representor lives 'within the vicinity', but as a general rule if a representor can see, hear or smell a vehicle operating centre from his property then he will be considered to be 'in the vicinity' for the purposes of making an environmental representation.

There is no opportunity for people living near an operating centre to make representations on grounds other than environmental matters or to use the opportunity to vent long-standing grudges against the vehicle operator. The TCs will not consider any representation which falls outside the terms described above or which is considered to be vexatious, frivolous or irrelevant.

Local residents will normally become aware of their opportunity to make representations against the grant of a licence or licence variation through the local newspaper advertisement placed by the applicant. Those people wishing to make a representation must do so in writing (or have their solicitor do so on their behalf), within a period of 21 days from the date of publication of the advertisement, to the TC at the Traffic Area Office address given in the advertisement. They must also send an exact copy of their representation (ie their letter to the TC) to the licence applicant at his address, which is also given in the advertisement. Their letter must clearly state the 'particulars' of the matters forming the basis of their representation so that both the TC and the licence applicant may be fully aware of the specific grounds on which the representation is made. Failure to be specific as to the facts in this letter, failure to send a copy to the licence applicant, or failure to submit the representation within the specified timescale will render the representation invalid.

Representors have no right of appeal should their case against use of the operating centre fail. These rights of representation are not to be confused with the rights of objection described later.

Suitability of Premises

TCs must inquire into and be satisfied that the place or places to be used as vehicle operating centres are suitable, cause no danger to the public, are environmentally acceptable and sufficiently large to accommodate all the vehicles authorized on the licence (or requested in the application). Local residents have rights (as described above) to make representations about the environmental consequences of the use of places for transport depots or vehicle operating centres and the TCs are bound to listen to these representations and make appropriate decisions about the application depending on the weight of the argument on either side – residents or operator (see pp 41–42). In particular, the TC, when considering the suitability of premises, will take account of the following:

- whether danger to the public may be caused where vehicles first join (or last leave) a public road;
- whether danger to the public may be caused on roads (other than public roads) along which vehicles are driven between the operating centre and a public road;
- the nature or use of any other land in the vicinity of the operating centre and the effect which the granting of the licence would be likely to have on the environment of that land;

- how much granting a licence which is to materially change the use of an existing (or previously used) operating centre, would harm the environment of the land in the vicinity of the operating centre;
- for a new operating centre, any planning permission (or planning application) relating to the operating centre or the land in its vicinity;
- the number, type and size of the authorized vehicles (including trailers) which will use the operating centre;
- the parking arrangements for authorized vehicles within and near to the operating centre;
- nature and times of use of the operating centre;
- nature and times of use of equipment at the operating centre;
- how many vehicles would be entering or leaving the operating centre, and how often.

Reviews of Operating Centres

TCs are given powers to review all operating centres, normally at five-yearly intervals counting from the date when the licence was first issued – in certain circumstances more frequent reviews may be carried out. Where the TC decides to review an operating centre he must give two months' notice in writing. Once the period has passed for the TC making a decision to review an operating centre, the licence holder can rest assured that he is safe for another five years, unless he operates outside the terms of his licence, fails to pay fees or applies for a major variation of the licence.

When carrying out the review of a centre, which will most likely be as a result of written complaints by local residents (who may now write in at any time rather than just when a licence application/variation advertisement appears), the TC will be concerned to ensure that it remains environmentally suitable, meets road safety considerations and can accommodate all the vehicles authorized on the licence, or that their parking causes no adverse effect on the local environment.

When carrying out the review the TC may decide that no action is required, but he has powers to act if necessary. For example, if an operating centre is found to be unsuitable he may attach conditions or vary any existing conditions for road safety or environmental reasons. However, the licence holder is given the opportunity to make representations about the effect that such conditions would have on his business before they are attached. The TC also has the power to remove an operating centre from a licence for non-environmental reasons (eg on the basis of road safety considerations), or because the operating centre is environmentally unsuitable by reason (only) of the parking of vehicles used under the licence at or near the centre.

Applications and Decisions

When an application for a new 'O' licence or a variation of an existing licence is received by the TC, details of the application (ie the name of the applicant and the number of vehicles and trailers included in the application) will be published in a Traffic Area notice called *Applications and Decisions (As and Ds)*. As its name implies, this notice will also contain details of licences granted by the TC and details of public inquiries to be held. The notice is published fortnightly by all Traffic Areas and may be inspected at Traffic Area Offices or purchased as an individual copy or on a regular basis. It is by means of this notice that statutory objectors (see below) are able to know when applications have been made, against which they may wish to object. They can do this within 21 days of publication of the relevant As and Ds notice. As and Ds are now available for download from the VOSA website: **www.vosa.gov.uk**.

Objections to the Application

Applications for 'O' licences are open to statutory objection by certain bodies listed below (and only by the listed bodies – no other individual or organization has this statutory right). Potential objectors to 'O' licences become aware of pending applications for new licences or variations to existing licences through the publication *Applications and Decisions* mentioned above.

Objections to applications can only be made by the bodies mentioned on the grounds that the applicant does not meet the essential qualifying criteria for the grant of a licence: namely that the applicant is not a fit person or is not of good repute; is not of adequate financial standing or does not meet the professional competence requirements (where appropriate); that the law in respect of those matters which the TC will be considering when he is deciding whether or not to grant a licence is not likely to be complied with, namely that the drivers' hours and records regulations will not be observed; that vehicles will be overloaded and that there are not satisfactory arrangements or facilities for maintaining the vehicles. The bodies may also object on environmental grounds (for example that the operating centre is environmentally unsuitable).

The bodies who may make statutory objection to an 'O' licence application are as follows:

- a chief officer of police;
- a local authority (but not a parish council – unless it owns or occupies land);
- a planning authority;
- the British Association of Removers (BAR);
- the Freight Transport Association (FTA);
- the Road Haulage Association (RHA);
- the General and Municipal Workers' Union (GMWU);
- the Rail, Maritime and Transport Union (RMTU) (formerly the National Union of Railwaymen and the National Union of Seamen);
- the Transport and General Workers' Union (TGWU);
- the Union of Shop, Distributive and Allied Workers (USDAW);
- the United Road Transport Union (URTU).

These are the only sources of objection (not to be confused with an environmental representation) to an application for an 'O' licence. If any of these bodies do make a statutory objection they are required to send a copy of their objection to the applicant at his published address at the same time as sending one to the TC and this must be within 21 days of the publication of details of the application in *Applications and Decisions*. Failure to send a copy to the applicant renders the objection invalid.

Grant or Refusal of a Licence

The TC has power to grant an 'O' licence to an applicant if he considers that all the necessary requirements are met. Alternatively, he may refuse to grant a licence or he may grant a licence for fewer vehicles than the number applied for if he doubts the ability of the applicant to be able to comply with the law with more vehicles, to be able to properly maintain more vehicles or to be able to adequately finance the operation of more vehicles. He can impose environmental conditions on any licence granted and can also refuse to accept the name put forward for the professionally competent person (in the case of standard licence applications) if he believes that the person is not of good repute. The TC may be influenced in his decision by the points made by any statutory objectors or environmental representors.

Licence Grant with Conditions

The case made by those raising valid environmental representations may influence the TC either to refuse the application altogether on the grounds that the operating centre is not environmentally suitable or alternatively to grant the licence but with environmental conditions attached. Thus to prevent or minimize any adverse effects on the environment he may place conditions or restrictions on the licence granted under the following headings:

- the number, type and size of authorized vehicles (including trailers) at the operating centre for maintenance or parking;
- parking arrangements for authorized vehicles (including trailers) at or in the vicinity of the centre;
- the times when the centre may be used for maintenance or movement of any authorized vehicle; and
- how authorized vehicles enter and leave the operating centre.

As an alternative to imposing environmental conditions on the licence, the TC may seek undertakings from the operator that he will or will not follow certain practices in order to reduce environmental disturbance of local residents (eg control the number of vehicle movements into and out of the centre). The licence holder should be aware that any such undertakings he may voluntarily give to the TC become legally binding upon him and could result in penalty against his licence if he subsequently fails to observe them.

Licence holders who find they have breached environmental conditions on their licence through unforeseen circumstances must notify the TC. Failure to comply with any of these conditions during the currency of a licence may result in the TC imposing penalties on the licence such as suspension or curtailment. In serious cases the licence may be totally revoked.

Where operators find that environmental conditions placed on their licence prove too onerous to allow them to run their businesses effectively they should apply to the TC to vary the conditions rather than ignore the conditions and become liable to a licence penalty.

Additional Vehicles

Seeking a Margin

At the time of making an application for an 'O' licence the applicant is given the opportunity to request authorization for any additional vehicles which he may need to acquire or hire during the currency of the licence. By taking this opportunity the operator saves the problems of making a fresh application when wanting to add or hire-in vehicles on a temporary basis to meet trading peaks. It also saves facing any further environmental representations or statutory objections because once the original application is granted with additional vehicles specified, extra vehicles can be added within the number authorized by completing and submitting form GV80 to the TC when they are acquired. There will be no need for the details to be advertised in a local newspaper or published in *Applications and Decisions*.

If additional vehicles were requested and the request was granted at the time of making the original application, the operator will have a 'margin' for extra vehicles on the licence. As described above, the TC will need to be notified (by submitting form GV80) from the date of actually *acquiring* the additional vehicles – *not* the date of putting them into service – so that a windscreen disc can be issued for the vehicle. From the effective date of the TAN 21 computer system (see p 10) no goods vehicle subject to operator's licensing should be on the road without a current 'O' licence windscreen disc. Vehicles found without a current disc may be subject to impounding (see p 63).

It is useful here to clarify the terms used in connection with the numbers of vehicles for 'O' licensing purposes:

Authorized vehicles	–	the maximum number of vehicles/trailers that the licence is actually granted to cover (it is illegal to operate* more than this number of vehicles at any time).
Specified vehicles	–	the actual vehicles which the operator has in possession and which are specified on the licence by registration number.
Margin	–	the difference between the numbers of authorized and specified vehicles on the licence, in other words the vehicles still to be acquired by the operator whether on a permanent or a temporary basis.

NB: 'Operate' in this context means 'use' and this applies to vehicles hired without drivers. Conversely, if they are hired with drivers, then they are operated under the hire firm's 'O' licence and not within the margin of the operator's 'O' licence (see below).

Hired Vehicles

If an operator plans to hire extra vehicles without drivers (ie where he intends to have his own or hired agency drivers to drive the vehicle/s) during the currency of his licence, whether for a short period (a day, a few days or even one or two weeks) or on a long-term contract, they must be covered by his 'O' licence and he will need to have applied for a sufficient margin of additional vehicles on his licence to cover these. If vehicles are hired within the margin the TC must be notified, and an 'O' licence disc obtained for display on the vehicle.

It is illegal to operate (ie to have employed drivers to drive) more vehicles (ie of over 3.5 tonnes gross weight) than are authorized on the 'O' licence even for a temporary period or reason (eg when an authorized vehicle is off the road for service or repairs or to cover additional delivery requirements).

Number of Extra Vehicles

When making the request for additional vehicles on the initial application for an 'O' licence, the number which may be requested is not limited in any way but it is recommended that it should be in reasonable proportion to the number of vehicles already operated (or initially required) and, most important, it should only be of a number which the applicant can maintain, and prove he can maintain (both physically and financially), on the same basis as the remainder of his fleet. If the request for additional vehicles relates to vehicles that are to be hired rather than owned it must be remembered that the person who hires a self-drive vehicle is fully responsible for the mechanical condition of the vehicle in so far as safety and legal requirements are concerned.

An applicant specifying additional vehicles on the original application should give some careful thought to the exact number of vehicles which may be needed and the reasons for needing them because the TC will ask questions about this if he calls the applicant to a public inquiry. Evidence in the form of business forecasts and trends in trade would be most useful as would figures to indicate past growth of the business; evidence also to show the financial prospects of the applicant during the currency of the licence period will help towards convincing the TC that he would be justified in granting a licence for the additional vehicles requested.

Replacement Vehicles

If for some reason an authorized vehicle ceases to be used the TC must be advised of the fact, but if at that time or later another vehicle is acquired to replace it the operator must advise the TC on form GV80 within one month of *acquiring* the replacement vehicle. This means within one month from the date of the vehicle coming into the operator's possession, not one month from the date he starts to use it. Vehicles which are not removed from the licence (even when standing in a yard or workshop smashed or cannibalized) are still counted as specified vehicles and cannot be replaced by others within the authorized number on the licence until they are removed by notifying the TC and the windscreen discs are returned to the Traffic Area Office.

Surrender of Licence

As mentioned above, form GV80 is also used when an operator wishes to surrender the whole of his licence. Question 4 on the form asks whether this is the case and requires a tick in either box 'yes' or 'no'. In Section 9 of the form (ie the Declaration) it is necessary to tick boxes showing:

- enclosure of the windscreen discs for the vehicles (Box 9a) or an indication that these have been stolen, lost or destroyed (Box 9b);
- enclosure of the licence itself and all Community Authorizations held (Box 9c) or an indication that these have been stolen, lost or destroyed (Box 9d).

Licence Variation

If the holder of an 'O' licence wishes to change the type of licence he holds – for example from restricted to standard national or from standard national to standard international – or to notify a change of transport manager, an application must be made on form GV80. It is, of course, necessary to satisfy the legal requirements for standard licences, national or international, where the application is to upgrade from a restricted 'O' licence, particularly in regard to the professional competence requirement. Similarly, a standard national licence holder who wishes to change to a licence covering international operations must satisfy the TC that he or an employee is professionally competent in international transport operations.

Where, during the currency of a licence, the licence holder needs to add extra vehicles to the fleet that were not specified on the original application then an application must be made to the TC by completing an application for major changes on form GV81 and submitting this well in advance (minimum nine weeks). This will necessitate placing an advertisement in a local newspaper as with the original application.

Unless the variation is only of a trivial nature the TC will publish details of it in *Applications and Decisions* and it may attract objectors in the same way as a new application, and the public inquiry procedure will be the same as that already described.

The licence holder must never operate more vehicles or trailers than the total number specified on his licence. When extra vehicles are required he must wait until the application for an increase in the licence is granted before actually putting the vehicles on the road – for which he should allow at least nine weeks, being the minimum application period required.

Form GV81

Form GV81 is a nine-page document called *Application for Major Changes* and must be used by applicants who wish to:

- change the total number of vehicles/trailers authorized;

- change operating centres (ie by adding another centre or stopping the use of a centre);
- change or remove a condition or undertaking recorded on the licence (including conditions on the use of operating centres).

These changes all involve the need to advertise the application in local newspapers as previously described (see p 10) and a copy of the published advertisement must be sent with the form. The usual information regarding name and address, addresses of operating centres and the number of vehicles to be based there which are in possession now or to be acquired has to be given. Also required is similar information about vehicle maintenance arrangements to that supplied on the original GV79 application (see p 26), but in relation to any additional vehicles applied for and any changed operating centres along with any request to change any of the environmental conditions or undertakings attached to the use of the operating centres. Reasons must be given as to why this change or removal is wanted.

The form has to be signed and the applicant is warned that failure to comply with conditions or undertakings recorded on a licence can result in disciplinary action being taken against the licence holder and that failure to comply with conditions is a criminal offence.

Transfer of Vehicles

If a vehicle is transferred from the Traffic Area in which it is licensed to a base in another Traffic Area for a period of more than three months, it must be removed from the original licence and specified on a licence in the new Traffic Area. Transfers for periods of less than three months are permitted with no need for notification to the TC provided an 'O' licence with a sufficient margin to cover the transferred vehicles is already held for that Traffic Area.

If the operator does not hold an 'O' licence in the other Traffic Area, or holds a licence in the area but it does not have a sufficient margin to accommodate the transferred vehicles, then an application for a new licence or a variation of the existing licence must be made to the TC for that Traffic Area. It is illegal to operate vehicles (ie over 3.5 tonnes gvw) from a base in a Traffic Area unless a licence is held in that area.

Notification of Changes

Licence holders should notify the TC in writing, within *one month,* of any changes in the legal entity of their business such as a change of name, address, ownership, if a new partnership has been formed, a limited company formed or the constitution of the partnership has been changed, as this makes a material difference to the information given in answer to questions on the original GV79 licence application. The TC must also be informed if the proprietor or persons concerned in the business die or if the business becomes bankrupt or goes into liquidation.

A change of business address as given in the original licence application must be notified to the TC within *three weeks*. A change of operating centre (or the use of an additional operating centre) also requires a variation application using form GV81 and the need to follow the newspaper advertisement procedure before any change actually takes place – it is illegal to change or add an operating centre without first seeking the TC's approval by the GV81 application procedure (ie to be submitted at least nine weeks prior to any change being required).

Other changes which must be notified in writing are those in maintenance facilities or arrangements and any breach of environmental conditions which the TC placed on the licence. Failure to notify the TC of such changes can have the same result as making false statements or failing to fulfil intentions stated in the original application, namely the risk of licence suspension, curtailment or revocation. The offender could also be prosecuted with the consequent penalties which can be imposed by the courts.

Subsidiary Companies

A holding company can include in its application for an 'O' licence vehicles belonging to any subsidiary company in which it owns more than a 50 per cent shareholding. But associate companies (ie where the shareholding arrangement is less than 50 per cent), owned by the same holding company, cannot have vehicles specified on each other's licences and separate divisions of a company are not permitted to hold separate licences unless they are separate entities in law.

The vehicles of any subsidiary company acquired during the currency of the holding company's 'O' licence can, if desired, be included in the holding company's licence either within its existing licence margin or by making application to the TC, on form GV81, to vary the licence. It is not generally likely that an application to include a subsidiary company's vehicles on the holding company's licence would be published in *Applications and Decisions* or that it would attract any objections.

Under the regulations, for the purposes of determining whether goods are carried for hire or reward in order to choose between a restricted or a standard 'O' licence, goods belonging to, or in the possession of, a subsidiary company are considered to belong to, or be in the possession of, the holding company and vice versa, so that in such cases a restricted 'O' licence would be adequate even if charges for the movement of the goods were made between the holding company and its subsidiary.

Temporary Derogation

There are provisions in the regulations to enable a standard 'O' licence to remain in force for up to one year initially and a further six months (maximum derogation is 18 months), if the TC feels it is appropriate, should the specified professionally competent person named on the licence die or become legally incapacitated (ie unable to carry out his duties due to reasons of mental disorder), in order to allow a replacement person to be found and specified.

The regulations enable the TC to defer revocation of, or refusal to grant, a standard 'O' licence in the event of the death or incapacity of the holder of the licence, a transport manager, or a partner whose professional competence is relied upon. Further, in the event of the death or incapacity of the licence holder the TC is empowered to authorize another person to carry on the business during the changeover period as though that person was the licence holder. Also, the TC may allow time for a transport business to be transferred to another person licensed to carry it on or for a transport manager or new partner to be appointed.

Where a person who was carrying on a business as a licence holder dies, becomes mentally incapacitated, becomes bankrupt or goes into liquidation, or where a partnership is dissolved, the TC must be notified within two months. The person carrying on the business will be considered by the TC to be the holder of the licence if a new licence application is made within one month in the case of restricted 'O' licences and within four months in the case of standard 'O' licences.

Production of 'O' Licences

Operator's licence holders must produce their 'O' licence (form OL 1 plus forms OL 1(R) or OL 1(S) where appropriate) for examination when required to do so by the police, DoT examiners (ie certifying officers) or by the TC or a person with his authority. The holder has 14 days in which to present the licence either at one of the operating centres authorized on the licence or at his principal place of business in the Traffic Area. In the case of production to the police this can be at a police station of the holder's choice also within 14 days.

TCs' Powers of Review

TCs have statutory powers (under the Goods Vehicles (Licensing of Operators) Act 1995, section 36) to review and, if they see fit, to vary or revoke any decision they have previously made to grant or refuse:

- an application for an operator's licence; or
- an application for the variation of an operator's licence requiring publication.

These powers to review a previous decision apply only in the following circumstances:

- if, within two months, the TC has given notice to the applicant or the licence holder that he intends to review the decision;
- if, within two months, a person who appears to the TC to have an interest in the decision has requested him to review it;
- where neither of the above situations apply, if the TC considers that there are exceptional circumstances to justify a review.

Variation or revocation of any previous decision by the TC does not make unlawful any actions relying on that decision before the variation or revocation imposed at the review comes into force.

Normally the TC will only decide to review his previous decisions where he is satisfied that a procedural requirement was not complied with in making the decision; for example, where an environmental representation or statutory objection was overlooked, or a decision was made under the wrong section of the Act.

This facility for the TCs to review their own decisions eliminates many of the situations which, hitherto, would have required appeal to the Transport Tribunal.

Licence Review Boards

Licence Review Boards (LRBs) were set up in 1990 to provide a system whereby the TCs could keep under review the 'O' licences of operators whose maintenance standards are in doubt, who have sustained relevant convictions, or who otherwise give the TCs cause for concern. The Boards are chaired by the Clerk to the TC in each of the Traffic Areas and comprise senior officials from the Vehicle Inspectorate (who deal with vehicle maintenance issues and traffic enforcement) and from the Traffic Area Office (ie managers who deal with 'O' licensing and LGV licensing matters). They meet regularly (eg fortnightly) and, where appropriate, make recommendations to the TC who may call recalcitrant operators to public inquiry.

Penalties against 'O' Licences

Warning

The TCs have warned that they are taking a harder line than ever before against 'O' licence offenders – this after being described for years as being no more than 'paper tigers'. In particular, operators are warned to pay more attention to their licence applications and what they are undertaking to do as operators. When dealing with licences the TCs are primarily concerned with road safety, fair competition and the environment.

Penalties

The maximum fine which may currently be imposed by a court for running vehicles without an 'O' licence where one is required by law is £5,000 (ie level 5). Failure to notify the TC of certain information about relevant convictions incurred by the licence holder or by his professionally competent transport manager can result in fines of up to £2,500 on summary conviction.

The TCs, as the issuing authorities for goods vehicles licences, are also given considerable legal powers to revoke, suspend or curtail an 'O' licence for a large number of reasons, of which the following are a few of the important examples:

- contravention by the licence holder of the provision, in the case of standard 'O' licences, regarding professional competence requirements;
- failure to notify the TC of changes in the business;
- convictions for failure to maintain vehicles in a fit and serviceable condition;
- contravention of speed limits, overloading or offences in connection with loading or unloading vehicles in restricted parking or waiting areas;
- failure to ensure that drivers are correctly licensed;
- convictions relating to the use of rebated (duty-free) fuel oil in vehicles (see Chapter 8);
- failure to keep records relating to vehicle inspections and repairs and driver defect reports;
- falsely stating facts on applications for 'O' licences and not fulfilling statements of intent or environmental conditions placed on the licence;
- if the licence holder becomes bankrupt or, in the case of a company, goes into liquidation;
- if a place not listed on the licence is used as a vehicle operating centre.

Offences are committed, for which prosecution and a court appearance may follow, if a:

- windscreen licence disc is not displayed;
- change of address is not notified;
- licence is not produced for examination on request;
- duplicate windscreen disc is not returned if the original is found;
- disc is not returned when a vehicle is disposed of;
- subsidiary company featured on a holding company licence is disposed of and the TC is not advised.

Furthermore, the TCs are active in preventing speeding by LGV drivers, first by imposing a penalty of suspension on the LGV driving licences of offending drivers and then by penalizing the 'O' licences of firms whose drivers persistently and wilfully exceed speed limits. Evidence of such matters is mainly obtained during routine enforcement checking of tachograph charts, where recordings showing frequent instances of driving above 100 kph are clear evidence of breach of the 60 mph maximum speed limit for vehicles exceeding 7.5 tonnes maximum laden weight.

Usually, the offending licence holder will be called to public inquiry by the TC and be required to explain why the offences occurred and what action is being taken to put matters right or to ensure they will not happen again. Depending on his reaction to such explanations, the TC may initially give a warning about future conduct and the likely consequences if there is any repetition of the contraventions of the law or he will decide that an appropriate penalty should be imposed. This will be suspension, curtailment or premature termination of the licence, or revocation. If the licence holder is found to no longer comply with the basic requirements for 'O' licensing, namely good repute, financial standing or professional competence, then the TC must revoke the licence (except where a period of temporary derogation is permitted – see below). If a restricted 'O' licence holder is convicted twice in a period of five years of operating outside the terms of the licence his licence must be revoked.

Curtailment (vehicles removed from a licence) is the most commonly imposed penalty and this implies removal of one or more authorized vehicles from the licence for any period up to the expiry of the licence. Suspension involves suspension of the whole licence and this may be combined with premature termination so the TC can review the whole operation under the provisions for consideration of a new licence application. As with premature termination of an existing licence, the need to apply for a new licence places the operator at risk of objection and environmental representation. The TC can direct that a vehicle on a licence which has been suspended or limited may not be used by another operator for a maximum of six months during the period of suspension. The increasing trend by TCs to impose short, sharp two-week 'O' licence suspensions is showing itself to be effective against errant operators, and is generally approved by the Transport Tribunal.

When the TC revokes an 'O' licence – which is not done lightly – he may order the holder to be disqualified, for a certain period or indefinitely, from holding or obtaining an 'O' licence and the order may be limited to one or may apply to more Traffic Areas. When intending to disqualify a person from holding an 'O' licence the TC should warn him of the likelihood, explain the circumstances leading to this decision and allow the person the opportunity of making submissions against disqualification. Following an order to revoke a licence, the TC may allow the licence holder to request a 'stay' to enable the operation to continue until an appeal to the Transport Tribunal is heard.

Revocation of Licences for Smuggling

Licence holders who are convicted of smuggling and related offences – mainly resulting from the illegal importation of excessive quantities of tobacco and alcohol products – risk losing their 'O' licences in addition to facing the standard penalties such as substantial fines, imprisonment in more serious cases and confiscation of vehicles. Where 'O'-licensed vehicles are involved in cross-Channel smuggling activities, HM Revenue & Customs pass details of the operators involved to the TCs for action which could include revocation of licences.

Tough new measures to combat smuggling include £1,000 penalties to recover confiscated vehicles, and permanent confiscation in the case of repeated smuggling offences. Drivers caught smuggling may also lose their driving licences and in serious cases individuals risk a prison sentence on conviction for evading alcohol and cigarette duty.

NB: An HM Revenue & Customs hotline is available for reporting excise duty smuggling – Freephone 0800 595000.

Revocation of Licences for Using Unlicensed Sub-contractors

One TC may have started a trend when he revoked an operator's 'O' licence for using unlicensed sub-contractors. This ruling may be challenged in due course but in the meantime it provides a warning to other licence holders about their conduct in this respect.

It is essential for 'O'-licensed hauliers to check carefully that any sub-contractor used is correctly licensed (as well as determining that he is using roadworthy vehicles and complies with the law on such matters as drivers' hours and tachographs). The use of an unlicensed operator may result in prosecution for aiding, abetting, counselling or procuring that operator to use a vehicle for hire or reward without an 'O' licence. This is a criminal offence carrying a maximum fine of £5,000 on conviction and could result in loss of the principal contractor's 'O' licence.

Loss of Licence for Unpaid Fees

It is worth repeating here that failure to pay 'O' licence fees when due will result in automatic termination of the licence.

Licensing Courts/First-tier Tribunal (Transport)

Inquiries and Appeals

TCs regularly hold public inquiries (PIs) to which 'O' licence applicants are called to explain the basis of their operations. A PI enables a TC to seek more information prior to determining whether he should grant a licence or not. In the event of a representation on environmental grounds or an objection being made to a licence application the TC will hold a public inquiry at which the parties (applicant, objectors or those making representations) will have an opportunity to state their case further. If the application is refused in whole or in part or if environmental conditions are attached to a licence the applicant has rights of appeal against the TC's decision to the First-tier Tribunal (Transport) which has now replaced the Transport Tribunal. Normally an existing licence will remain in force while an appeal is being heard and the TC may allow a revoked or suspended licence to continue during this time. If the TC refuses this the Tribunal can be asked to allow it to do so.

Statutory objectors also have a right of appeal to the First-tier Tribunal if an application for a licence is granted and they still feel that their objection is valid. Those individuals making representations on environmental grounds have *no* similar right of appeal if their case fails.

It should be noted that the First-tier Tribunal is the *only* source of appeal in regard to 'O' licensing matters.

Besides public inquiries conducted for the purposes of determining 'O' licence applications, such inquiries are also held at the TC's behest where it is necessary for him to examine the conduct of a licence holder for disciplinary purposes under the powers given him by the Goods Vehicles (Licensing of Operators) Act 1995. Section 26(1) of this Act empowers him to conduct such inquiries and impose penalties of suspension, curtailment or revocation of a licence (further details of this matter are given on pp 49–52).

Appeals are heard only in London whereas public inquiries are usually held in the town or city in which the TC's office (ie the Traffic Area Office – see Appendix I for addresses) is situated.

Public Inquiries

It is useful here to mention the way in which a public inquiry (PI) is conducted. It is presided over by the TC or his deputy and is open to members of the general public, other operators and interested persons, who may sit in and listen, and to the press, who may report all that is said.

TCs may restrict general attendance at a public inquiry to protect an operator's business, particularly in regard to personal matters, commercially sensitive information and other information obtained in confidence. Hitherto the TC could only close a PI to hear financial information. Further, TCs must disclose at a PI any information or evidence received in writing prior to the inquiry if it is intended that such information is to be taken into account in reaching a decision.

Verbal evidence is given to the TC by the applicant or by his legal representative if he has one – and this is strongly advised in most cases due to the complexities of making legal presentations and arguing points of law in a courtroom situation and possibly the need to cross-examine witnesses such as a vehicle examiner or an environmental representor, even though it is an inquiry, not a court. In fact, the 'call-up' letter to operators facing public inquiries, in which the TC states his reasons for calling the PI and states his powers to curtail, suspend or revoke 'O' licences, as well as giving details of the time and location for the inquiry, advises this. Such advice, if it is required, should be sought from an experienced transport lawyer who fully understands the legal basis of the whole licensing system as well as the intricacies of the PI system.

Most evidence at PIs will be given in response to the TC's questions – the TC effectively playing the role of 'prosecutor' – by the licence holder/applicant, the objectors and those making representations. The evidence, unlike in criminal or civil courts, is not given under oath and statements made at a public inquiry that are defamatory or libellous of other people do not have protection by privilege. The offended person can take civil action if such statements or comments come to his notice. Similarly, if an applicant or witness lies, he will not be prosecuted for perjury, but, where this is an applicant, anything he says in support of his application may be taken by the TC to be a statement of intent to which he will be bound for the duration of any licence granted.

Evidence in some instances may be provided in writing and the TC may ask for certain supporting documents, in which case the applicant should have these to hand with extra copies for the objectors to examine. When he has heard all the evidence the TC will normally make a decision without conferring with anybody else. He may announce this at the time or defer his decision to be given later in writing. The entire proceedings of the inquiry will be recorded and transcripts can be obtained by interested parties.

TCs must now give at least 21 days' written notice of public inquiries both to operators and other parties entitled to attend, and similar notice if they intend to vary the time or place of the inquiry. However, given the consent of all parties, this requirement can be varied.

Appeals to the First-tier Tribunal (Transport)

The Tribunal, which is under the control of the Lord Chancellor, is a completely independent judicial body supported administratively by the Ministry of Justice. The Tribunal is made up of legally qualified legal members and non-legal members, who have experience in transport operations and its law and procedure. Its offices are in London. Hearings are normally arranged in London, or (for Scottish cases) in Glasgow.

An appeal on form DSA1 may be made against a TC's decision to refuse to grant an 'O' licence; if he attaches environmental conditions to an 'O' licence; if a licence is granted authorizing fewer vehicles than the number applied for; if a licence is granted for a shorter period than that applied for; or if an existing licence is withdrawn, suspended or prematurely terminated by the TC.

A time limit of 28 days is allowed in which to make an appeal to the First-tier Tribunal following a TC's decision, counting from the date of publication of the issue of *Applications and Decisions* in which the decision is published. Where the TC's decision is not published within 21 days an appeal can be made within 49 days of notification of the decision by the TC.

Where a TC makes a disciplinary decision against an 'O' licence (ie suspension, curtailment or revocation) and the licence holder wishes to appeal, he can apply for a 'stay' of the decision until the appeal is heard, in order to keep his vehicles operating. Otherwise he would have to observe the decision irrespective of the consequences (financial and operational) on his business. An initial request for a 'stay' of the decision is made direct to the TC, but failing this an application must be made immediately to the Tribunal giving details of the decision and the reason for requesting the 'stay'. Application for a 'stay' of the decision cannot be made if there is no intention to appeal.

Appeals to the First-tier Tribunal must be in writing and six copies should be sent to the Tribunal stating the decision against which the appeal is made, the grounds for the appeal, and the names and addresses of every person to whom a copy of the appeal has been sent.

Copies of the appeal must be sent to the TC and to all objectors if the appeal is being made by a licence applicant, or to the applicant if the appeal is being made by an objector to the decision.

Although the Tribunal has the powers and status of the High Court, its proceedings are conducted informally and appellants may represent themselves or be represented by any person they choose (there are no wigs and gowns even for barristers present). However, in the best interests of the applicant, he should be legally represented at an appeal by a solicitor or barrister experienced in transport law to ensure that his case is fully and correctly made.

When an appeal is heard, the Tribunal examines the transcript of the public inquiry or the TC's statement of his reasons for the decision against which the appeal is lodged and then may ask further questions of the applicant or his advocate. No oath has to be taken and there is no protection by privilege. The proceedings are open to the public and the press. Tribunal appeal decisions may be announced at the hearing or later. All parties will be sent a full statement of the decision usually within three weeks of the hearing.

Generally, Tribunal decisions will fall into one of three categories: either to uphold the TC's decision, to change the decision or to refer the matter back to the TC with a direction that he should reconsider his decision but taking account of legal guidance from the Tribunal. In exceptional circumstances the Tribunal may review its decision subject to a request to do so made within 14 days of the appeal hearing. Decisions of the Tribunal are binding from the date they are given; in other words they have immediate effect.

Further appeals against decisions of the Tribunal may be made to the Court of Appeal or the Court of Sessions in Scotland but only on points of law, not on the original decision of the TC or the subsequent ruling of the Tribunal.

No fees are payable in respect of appeals but costs may be awarded against frivolous, vexatious, improper or unreasonable appeals.

Further details of the appeals procedure can be found in a free publication giving guidance on appeals to the Tribunal, and can be downloaded from its website at **http://www.transporttribunal.gov.uk**.

It is a requirement of new EU Regulation 1071/2009/EC, effective from 4 December 2011, that all EU Member States must have in place an electronic database of operators (ie 'O' licence holders'). The regulation specifies the minimum data required – eg the operator's name and address etc, plus a record of relevant convictions and serious infringements recorded against both the operator and the named transport manager – either in his home State or any other Member State. Similarly, findings by a Traffic Commissioner that neither the operator nor the transport manager is any longer 'fit' will be recorded. This record (ie the register) will be available throughout all the Member States so that on making an application to operate the applicant's record of convictions and transgressions will be seen by all.

Northern Ireland Licensing

Northern Ireland plans to commence its own UK-style 'O' licensing system early in 2012 under provisions contained in the Goods Vehicle (Licensing of Operators) Act (Northern Ireland) 2010. In the meantime, the existing Road Freight Operator's Licensing Scheme as described here remains in force.

Currently, goods vehicle operators in the Province do not need to obtain a short-term 'O' licence prior to entry into Great Britain. Similarly, there is no need for GB operators to obtain a short-term licence prior to entry into Northern Ireland. A goods vehicle operating on a current 'O' licence issued in Great Britain or a Road Freight 'O' licence issued in Northern Ireland is permitted to carry goods throughout the UK.

Goods vehicles from Northern Ireland engaging in own-account operations for which a Road Freight Operator's licence is not required in the Province must, while operating in Great Britain, carry a document showing details of their load and route in Great Britain.

Vehicles based and registered in England, Wales and Scotland must comply with all the normal legal requirements (eg vehicle condition, excise duty, insurance and observance of traffic rules) set out in this *Handbook* when operating in Northern Ireland, but particularly so in regard to 'O' licensing (Chapter 1), professional competence (Chapter 2), drivers' hours and record-keeping regulations (Chapters 3 and 4), tachographs (Chapter 5), driver licensing and testing (Chapters 6 and 7) and plating and testing (Chapter 14). It should be noted that in regard to road traffic and road traffic offences there are differences between the Northern Ireland requirements and those on the British mainland. A separate edition of the *Highway Code* is published for Northern Ireland.

Vehicles based and operated in Northern Ireland must comply with the law as it applies in the Province, which, although substantially similar to that applicable in the rest of the United Kingdom, does vary in some respects as shown in this section.

Road Freight Operator Licensing

In order to carry goods by road for reward (but not for purely own-account operations) with vehicles over 3.5 tonnes permissible maximum weight in Northern Ireland, it is necessary to hold a road freight operator's licence (RFOL) issued under the provisions of the Transport Act (Northern Ireland) 1967.

Since 1 January 1978 regulations have been in effect to ensure that road freight operators are better qualified. These regulations, the Road Transport (Qualification of Operators) Regulations (Northern Ireland) 1977, implement EC Directive 561/74, as amended, *On admission to the occupation of road haulage operator*. Thus the requirements for obtaining a road freight operator's licence in Northern Ireland take account of this requirement and depending on the qualifications of the operator the licence may or may not be restricted to operations within the United Kingdom. The type and scope of the licence will be indicated clearly in the licence – covering either national operations or both national and international operations.

Conditions for Grant of 'O' Licence

Under the statutory requirements for the grant of a road freight operator's licence, an operator has to satisfy the issuing authority that he is:

- of good repute;
- of appropriate financial standing;
- professionally competent or that he employs a full-time manager who is professionally competent and of good repute.

The requirements of good repute and appropriate financial standing are as stated in detail in Chapter 1 of the *Handbook*. While the professional competence requirement in Northern Ireland is largely as explained in Chapter 2, there are some differences as shown below.

Professional Competence by Examination

A separate syllabus for the Royal Society of Arts examination is applicable to Northern Ireland. It differs mainly in section C, *Access to the Northern Ireland*

Market, which covers vehicle and operators' licences and professional competence requirements. Copies of the syllabus *Examinations for the Certificates of Professional Competence in Road Transport (Northern Ireland)* may be obtained from: OCR, Westwood Way, Westwood Business Park, Coventry CV4 8HS. The current examination syllabus applicable to Northern Ireland national goods and national passenger operations was published in 1988 and both NI national examinations have taken the modular form, with a core examination common to both passenger and goods sectors.

Issuing Authority

For operations in Northern Ireland, the issuing authority for operators' and vehicle licences is: Department of the Environment (DoE) for Northern Ireland, Road Transport Licensing Branch, Upper Galwally, Belfast BT8 4FY. The new NI 'O' Licensing scheme will be administered by a new department called the Department of the Environment Transport Regulation Unit (TRU): e-mail contact tru@doeni.gov.uk.

Objections to Road Freight 'O' Licences

Objections to the grant of a road freight 'O' licence may be made to the DoE by the Road Haulage Association (RHA) and the Freight Transport Association (FTA) on the grounds that the statutory conditions for the grant of such a licence are not or will not be met.

Appeals

Appeals against refusal by the DoE to grant a road freight operator's licence or where such a licence has been suspended or revoked may be made within 28 days to the County Court.

Application for a Road Freight Operator's Licence

Application for a road freight operator's licence, which is usually valid for three years, must be made to: Department of the Environment (NI), Road Transport Licensing Branch, Upper Galwally, Belfast BT8 4FY.

Form RFL 1 is used for the application. This requires details to be supplied as follows:

1 Name and place of business.

2 Type of licence required (ie national or national and international operations).

3 Address of operating centre (ie where vehicles are to be parked when not in use). Where premises are not owned, the 'original' rental agreement must be sent with a first application.

4 Number of vehicles to be operated (original receipts or hire purchase agreements for vehicles and trailers to be operated must be sent with the application).

5 Whether professional competence requirements are met.

6 If applicant is not professionally competent, the name and address of the full-time transport manager who is qualified must be given.

7 Evidence of professional competence (the original certificate must be sent).

8 Whether the applicant or his named transport manager has any convictions for offences in the past five years which are not 'spent'.

9 Details of convictions.

10 Names and addresses (and past addresses) of the applicant, the named transport manager, and all directors and/or partners.

11 Name and address of bank from which a reference can be obtained.

12 Declaration (signature, status and date).

Further information may be required in support of a road freight operator's licence regarding the applicant's financial status and a statement of estimated operating costs for vehicles specified in the application. The former requires the applicant to send the following items:

1 Bank status report.

2 Details of any credit facilities from bank or any other financial resources available (eg deposit accounts).

3 Copy of latest bank statement.

4 Rental agreement for operating premises.

5 Receipts or hire purchase agreements in respect of vehicles.

6 Original certificate of competence.

7 A statement showing a breakdown of estimated annual costs and receipts of running the proposed road transport business.

The requirement to supply statements of estimated operating costs for vehicles involves the need to complete a form designed for this purpose. The following information must be provided:

1 Details of vehicles
   (a) type and model
   (b) registration number and date of first registration
   (c) type of trailer
   (d) gross weight
   (e) unladen weight
   (f) carrying capacity
   (g) number of tyres fitted and size (including trailer)
   (h) estimated fuel consumption (miles per gallon)
   (i) estimated annual mileage
   (j) vehicle length (in feet).

2 Estimated running costs and standing costs for one year (one vehicle only)
   (a) wages (including National Insurance)
   (b) motor tax
   (c) insurance for vehicle

(d) insurance for goods in transit

(e) fuel

(f) maintenance

(g) tyres

(h) shipping charges if applicable

(i) hire purchase payments on vehicle and trailer (if applicable)

(j) rent and rates for business premises

(k) depreciation on vehicle

(l) miscellaneous expenses (eg telephone, stationery, etc).

3 Total costs

Estimated income from one year's operation (one vehicle only).

It is generally believed (although never officially stated) that the DoE is looking for 'O' licence applicants to have at least 25 per cent of first-year operating costs in the bank at the start of the operation or assets equivalent to £7,500 for each rigid vehicle and £15,000 for each articulated vehicle either in the form of bank credits or agreed overdraft facilities.

Penalties for Improper Use

Anyone operating internationally on a road freight 'O' licence that is restricted to national operations only will be liable, on conviction, to a fine and his 'O' licence and vehicle licences may be revoked or suspended. There are also penalties laid down for using unlicensed vehicles on national operations.

Changing Licences

The holder of a road freight 'O' licence which is restricted to national transport operations may have the restriction removed to enable him to engage in both national and international operations if he can meet the additional requirements (namely professional competence in both national and international transport operations) for engaging in international operations.

Vehicle Licences

Northern Ireland motor vehicles over 3.5 tonnes gross weight may not be used to carry goods for hire or reward except under a Road Freight Vehicle Licence granted under section 17 of the Transport Act (NI) 1967 (as amended). Vehicle licences may only be granted to a person who holds a road freight operator's licence and will cover either:

1 national transport operations only (ie covering Northern Ireland and the remainder of the UK) – Blue disc;

2 national and international transport operations – Green disc.

Vehicle licences are valid for one year and are issued in the form of a disc for display in the vehicle windscreen. They are serial numbered and show the vehicle registration number, the name of the owner and the date of expiry. Application is made on form

RFL 3 to the DoE Northern Ireland enclosing both the vehicle excise licence disc and the goods vehicle certificate as evidence that the vehicle is taxed and tested, if applicable, on the date of issue of the vehicle licence.

Application for Road Freight Vehicle Licences

Applications for road freight vehicle licences have to be made on form RFL 3 to the DoE. Details which must be provided by the person or firm using the vehicles are as follows:

1 Name, address and telephone number of applicant.

2 Road freight 'O' licence number.

3 Whether the RFOL is valid for international operations.

4 **(a)** Registration numbers of vehicles which are owned or in possession under an agreement for hire, hire purchase, credit sale or loan for which road freight licences are required

   (b) Type of vehicle

   (c) Type of body

   (d) Gross weight of vehicle.

5 Address where vehicles will be parked overnight.

6 Declaration that statements given are true.

Northern Ireland Penalties for Illegal Use

Making a false statement to obtain the grant of a road freight operator's licence or a road freight vehicle licence is an offence punishable on conviction by a fine or imprisonment for up to six months, or both. The 'O' licence could also be suspended or revoked. Use of a motor vehicle on a road for the carriage of goods for reward without a road freight vehicle licence can result in a fine which increases for subsequent convictions. Since February 2011 enforcement officers of the Northern Ireland Driver and Vehicle Agency (DVA) have been empowered to issue fixed penalty notices, some of which attract penalty points on driver licences, for certain driver and vehicle offences see **www.dvani.gov.uk**.

NI Powers to Stop

Under new regulations applicable both in Northern Ireland and Great Britain (i.e. The Road Vehicles (Powers to Stop) Regulations 2011 – SI 2011 No. 996) from 30 March 2011 appointed 'stopping' officers (e.g. enforcement officers of the NIDVA and VOSA and certain police officers) are given the power to require the driver of a commercial vehicle to stop for the purposes of examining the vehicle and/or the drivers' documents and records.

Use of Light Goods Vehicles

Many existing transport operators and new entrants to the industry have sought to avoid the problems and pitfalls of 'O' licensing by using vehicles defined as 'small' vehicles – those vehicles not exceeding 3.5 tonnes maximum permissible weight. With such vehicles there is no need to obtain an 'O' licence and consequently no need to face the TC and satisfy all the conditions previously explained. The operator is also free from the legal requirements under other legislation for his drivers to operate tachographs or to keep other written records of their hours of work, and to hold LGV driving licences.

Despite this apparent freedom the operator of such vehicles does have certain obligations and responsibilities. First, if he tows a trailer with such a vehicle the combined weight of both vehicle and trailer (if over 1,020 kilograms unladen) could exceed the 3.5 tonne weight threshold above which an 'O' licence would be needed and the provisions of the EU or British driver's hours law and the relevant record-keeping or tachograph requirements may apply (see Chapters 3, 4 and 5). Second, if he also operates, or plans to operate in the future, larger vehicles which are within the scope of 'O' licensing, his conduct as an operator of small vehicles will be taken into account by the TC when deciding whether to grant or renew his 'O' licence.

The TCs have made the point that when an operator applies to renew an 'O' licence they (the TCs) would take notice of any relevant convictions in respect of smaller vehicles belonging to the operator and could call the operator to public inquiry to show cause why the 'O' licence should not be revoked or curtailed. The operator of small vehicles still has to ensure that vehicles are not overloaded and that they are kept in a safe mechanical order under other regulations; they must be tested annually after they become three years old. Drivers of these vehicles are required to observe the drivers' hours regulations with certain exceptions. All these individual legal exemptions and requirements are discussed in later chapters.

Foreign Vehicles in the UK

Vehicles entering Great Britain from other EU member states under valid Community Authorizations do not need an 'O' licence and no longer require cabotage authorization to operate in this country. Vehicles from certain non-EU countries where a bilateral agreement exists are exempt from the requirement to hold an 'O' licence under the Goods Vehicles (Licensing of Operators) (Temporary Use in Great Britain) Regulations 1996.

Foreign vehicles entering Great Britain under an ECMT permit do not need an 'O' licence provided the permit is being carried on the vehicle.

Impounding of Trucks

Impounding of the vehicles of cowboy and illegal operators – estimated to number some 8,000 vehicles – came into force on 4 January 2002. Originally envisaged in the Government's White Paper on the future of transport, *A New Deal for Transport,* published in July 1998, the provision became law under the Goods Vehicles (Enforcement Powers) Regulations 2001. Principally, impounding applies to vehicles used for hire or reward carriage without an 'O' licence in force. Such vehicles are fitted with an immobilization device (ie a clamp) either on the spot or after removal to a more suitable site, and will be marked by an immobilization notice warning against any attempt to remove the device or move the vehicle except under proper authorization. Impounded vehicles may be returned to their owner in due course provided specified conditions are met, and loads returned to their owner where title is established. Ultimately, however, without satisfactory compliance with requirements for the release of a vehicle and its load, they will be disposed of by sale or by destruction. Obstruction of authorized examiners in the course of vehicle impounding will lead to a fine at level 3 (maximum £1,000) on conviction.

An appeals procedure via the TCs initially and the Transport Tribunal subsequently allows operators to apply for the return of an impounded vehicle, although this may be unsuccessful depending on the circumstances.

Impounding of Rental/Hired Vehicles

The new impounding legislation described above has caused concern for vehicle rental, hiring and leasing companies. However, the law is clear in that the regulations permit the seizing of vehicles hired out by such firms to unlicensed operators. The TCs too have made it clear that such firms have a duty to ensure that any hiring arrangement they enter into in relation to relevant (ie over 3.5 tonne) vehicles is with an 'O' licensed operator. The situation becomes more complex where a vehicle leased to an unlicensed operator by a vehicle leasing company is subject to a finance arrangement with a third party (such as a bank or loan company), which is therefore the statutory owner of the vehicle. In such cases, it becomes necessary for the legal owner to make application to the TC for the return of the vehicle on the basis that it, the legal owner, did not know that the vehicle had been, or was being, used without an 'O' licence in accordance with the Goods Vehicles (Licensing of Operators) Act 1995 (section 2). An application for the return of a vehicle in these circumstances has to be made within 21 days of the notification of the impounding being published in the *London Gazette* or *Edinburgh Gazette* (in which all vehicle impoundings are published).

Professional Competence

Professional Competence qualifications now apply to both Transport Managers (the CPC) and to LGV and PCV Drivers (the DCPC). However, these are two totally different schemes administered by different authorities and with very different qualifying requirements for each of them, as described in this chapter – they should not be confused.

Professional Competence for Transport Managers

The legal requirement for certain people employed in hire or reward road transport operations (ie in both road freight and road passenger sectors) to be professionally competent came into effect in Britain on 1 January 1978.

Previously, the requirement to meet professional competence standards applied solely to those who held supervisory or management positions where they effectively had day-to-day control of the activities of drivers and operation of vehicles. Under a new Directive from the European Commission effective from 2008–09 goods (and passenger) vehicle drivers also have to undergo compulsory professional training in addition to meeting the existing requirements for driving, namely passing the relevant theory and practical driving tests. This subject is dealt with in the second part of this chapter.

On the road goods side of the industry, the original CPC scheme was the final outcome of many years' work on the development of a plan to make individuals more responsible for the safe operation of vehicle fleets in their charge and better qualified to understand the legal, economic and operational requirements for safe and efficient goods vehicle operation. As a result of EU influence via EC Directive 74/561 (as amended by Directives 89/438/EC, 96/26/EC and most recently by 98/76/EC of 1 October 1998 – see below), 'On Admission to the Occupation of Road Haulage Operator in National and International Operations', the current scheme, provides all those people who qualify, not just those fulfilling the role of transport manager, with either a certificate of professional competence or a professional competence qualification by exemption or by examination.

This scheme changed further from 4 December 2011 when Regulation 1071/2099/EC came into effect. One of the principal outcomes of this Regulation will be the merging of the hitherto separate national and international CPC qualifications and the consequent merging of the two examinations. Thus, in future, candidates seeking to qualify purely for managing domestic (i.e. solely within the UK) road haulage operations, will nevertheless, still have to study the whole EU syllabus and answer examination questions on matters relating to both national and international road haulage.

Under the Goods Vehicles (Licensing of Operators) Act 1995 (section 13 and schedule 3), road haulage operators (including own-account operators who wish to carry goods for hire or reward or in connection with a business which is not their own) are required to meet the professional competence requirement in order to obtain a standard operator's licence.

Own-account transport operators who have no desire to or intention of carrying goods for hire or reward or for any purpose which is not in connection with their own trade or business (including not doing favours for customers by carrying their goods also) can apply for a restricted 'O' licence, for which there is no need to meet the professional competence requirement. The important point for road hauliers and others who carry goods for hire or reward is that in order to obtain an operator's licence they must request a standard 'O' licence covering either national or both national and international operations and specify in their application the name of a person who is professionally competent and who is responsible for the operation of the vehicles authorized on the licence – the law requires the person to have 'continuous and effective responsibility' for the management of the transport operation. This person may be the applicant, if suitably qualified, or it may be a person holding the title of transport manager (or some other person – the law is not concerned as to the person's actual job-title, only that he should be the person who is responsible for the vehicle operations on a day-to-day basis) who is professionally competent and who is employed by the applicant.

Employment in this context does not necessarily mean full-time employment with the licence holder. Part-time or casual employment of a professionally competent person is permitted as a result of a regulation change in November 1991 under which a part-time qualified employee may be nominated in support of a licence application. Also, with this change in the law, a professionally competent person in one firm may be specified in support of the licence held by another, non-related, firm.

There has been a TCs' decision which indicates that a self-employed (ie freelance) transport manager may be acceptable as the professionally competent person specified on an 'O' licence. The employment requirement does not necessarily mean that the person concerned must devote all of his working time to the transport management function; he may have other duties and responsibilities in the firm (such as administration manager, works manager, company secretary, etc).

However, concern over the matter of part-time (ie so-called 'proxy') transport managers has led the EU to bring into force Article 4(c) of EU Regulation 1071/2009 (i.e. on new rules on access to the profession – professional competence) which stipulates that from 4 December 2011 a nominated transport manager may not manage more than four operations with a total number of 50 vehicles. Additionally, that person must have a 'genuine link to the undertaking' (ie as an employee, director, owner or shareholder or is administering it) and must 'effectively and continuously' manage the transport activities of the undertaking' (as now). The person must also hold a CPC in their own member state.

The new rules also set out the conditions which an operator must meet to be admitted to the profession and the criteria on which good repute will be withdrawn including drug and human trafficking.

Who May Become Professionally Competent?

Professional competence is available and applicable only to individuals. Under the regulations, a firm or a corporate body cannot be classed as being professionally competent. Any individual, whether employed with the title of 'transport manager' or not, may become professionally competent if he or she meets the necessary qualifying conditions or otherwise passes the official examination. There is no pre-qualifying standard and no requirement that the person should have any previous experience of or is working, has been working, or plans to work in the transport industry in any capacity whatsoever. It is open to absolutely anybody to become professionally competent if they so wish.

However, only those who are actually responsible for the operation of goods vehicles on a day-to-day basis will need to be 'nominated' as the professionally competent 'transport manager' in support of an application for a standard 'O' licence. Such individuals must themselves be of good repute and of appropriate financial standing .... (as well as the 'O' licence applicant - see Chapter 1) and be engaged in 'effectively and continuously' managing the transport activities of the undertaking otherwise their name may not be acceptable to the TC despite the fact that they are qualified as being professionally competent (see below).

Proof of Professional Competence

Proof that a person is professionally competent and is therefore able to satisfy the requirements of the 'O' licence system is dependent on holding one (or more) of the following:

- a 'grandfather rights' certificate of professional competence (CPC) issued by a TC (form GV203);
- an official OCR CPC examination pass certificate;
- a membership (or exemption) certificate from one of the recognized professional institutes, which confers exemption (see pp 69–70);
- a certificate issued by another EU member state which fulfils the 'mutual recognition' requirements of EC Directive 77/796 as amended by EC Directive 89/438.

No other document provides evidence of professional competence for these purposes.

Classes of Competence

Professional competence in road freight operations falls into two classes, covering national operations only or both national and international operations. As of 4th December 2011 there is only one combined qualification. A parallel scheme covers road passenger operations.

All certificates of professional competence (CPCs – form GV203) granted under the original 'grandfather rights' scheme (see below) cover both national and international operations (although it does not specifically say so on them).

In cases where people qualify for professional competence under the exemption arrangements, the level at which they qualify determines whether they are entitled to be classed as professionally competent in national transport operations only or in both national and international transport operations (see pp 69–70).

Candidates who achieve professional competence by examination will obtain appropriate documentary evidence (ie an OCR examination pass certificate) indicating that they have passed the modular examinations covering national operations only (freight or passenger) or the additional examination covering international operations (freight or passenger).

Those qualified for professional competence in national operations only will be permitted to engage in or be responsible for operations conducted on standard 'O' licences solely within the UK (ie covering national transport operations).

Holders of certificates of professional competence (form GV203) or those qualifying for professional competence in both national and international operations, by exemption or examination, will be permitted to engage in or be responsible for the operation of goods vehicles on standard 'O' licences covering national operations within the UK and international operations outside the UK.

National and International Transport Operations

Following legal decisions made in the EU the definition of what constitutes an international journey has been changed in Britain. So, for example, where loaded trailers are taken to a port for onward movement outside the UK, and the tractive unit and driver do not leave the UK, such journeys constitute national operations (previously, these were international operations), and a standard 'O' licence covering national transport operations only is needed for such operations (and the employed manager will need to be professionally competent only in national operations).

Qualifications for Professional Competence

The qualifications needed to obtain professional competence fall into four categories as follows:

1 by experience in the industry prior to 1 January 1975 (known as 'grandfather rights');

2 by exemption;

3 by examination;

4 by holding a mutual recognition certificate issued in another EU member state (see p 79).

Grandfather Rights

NB: The issue of certificates of professional competence (form GV203 – known as CPCs) under this scheme ended on 31 December 1979, since which date the only means of qualifying for professional competence is by exemption or examination. However, since many people continue to ask about the scheme it was felt useful to continue to include an explanation in the current edition of the Handbook.

Transport managers and other people employed in 'responsible road transport employment' prior to 1 January 1975 were able to obtain the grant of a so-called 'grandfather rights' certificate of professional competence (CPC), without examination, as of right. Once granted, the certificate continues to remain valid for as long as the professional competence requirement is in force.

For the purposes of the (now extinct) grandfather rights scheme, responsible road transport employment was defined as employment in the service of a person or a firm carrying on a road transport undertaking and was employment in a position where the individual had responsibility for the operation of goods vehicles used under an operator's licence.

Similar conditions applied to any person who was the holder of an 'O' licence prior to 1 January 1975. In other words, any owner-driver or small fleet operator who held an 'O' licence in his own name or under a business name qualified, having been a licence holder. In the case of an 'O' licence held by a partnership prior to this date, all the partners qualified under the grandfather rights arrangements. Where a licence was held by a limited company, the person responsible for the day-to-day operation of the vehicles under the licence (eg the transport manager) qualified for the grandfather rights grant of a CPC.

To obtain a certificate under this arrangement, application had to be made to the TCs no later than 30 November 1979. Since that date, the opportunity to obtain a CPC other than by examination or exemption has ceased.

Issue of CPC Certificates

Certificates of professional competence (form GV203) issued under the grandfather rights scheme were obtainable from the Traffic Area Offices on application provided that the necessary form and certification of appropriate qualifying experience by an employer were supplied. Although certificates carry the name of the issuing Traffic Area, they are valid for operations in all Traffic Areas and individuals had no need to obtain separate certificates for each area in which they were responsible for the operation of vehicles.

There was no fee for the issue of a CPC, and certificates thus granted remain valid for the life of the scheme. There is no system for revocation or disqualification of CPC holders but where the holder is also the 'O' licence holder, or is the nominated professionally competent transport manager employed by an 'O' licence holder, then there is a requirement that they must be of good repute (see pp 20–22) and of adequate financial standing; otherwise the 'O' licence will be subject to penalty (see pp 50–52). Grandfather rights CPCs issued on the basis of information provided which is subsequently found to be false may be withdrawn by the TC.

Qualification by Exemption

People who did not qualify for a CPC based on previous experience in road transport operations as described above and new entrants to the industry may obtain the professional competence qualification if they satisfy certain exemption criteria.

The exemption qualifications are based on holding current and valid membership of one or more of a number of professional bodies at certain levels. Additionally, the 'Certificate in Transport' qualification offered by the Chartered Institute of Logistics and Transport is recognized by the DfT and accepted as giving exemption.

There are two levels of exemption qualification: one covering both international and national operations and the other covering national operations only; these are as follows:

For both National and International Operations

- Fellow or Member of the Chartered Institute of Logistics and Transport (CILT) by examination and/or formal accreditation in Road Freight Transport.
- Fellow, Member or Associate Member of the Society of Operations Engineers.
- Fellow or Associate of the Institute of the Furniture Warehousing and Removing Industry (IFWRI), or, from 13 May 1995, Fellow or Associate of the Movers Institute.
- Certificate in Transport, awarded by the CILT.
- Associate of the Institute of Transport Administration by examination.

For National Operations Only

- Member of the CILT by examination and/or formal accreditation in Road Freight Transport.
- Certificate in Transport, awarded by the CILT.
- Associate of the Society of Operations Engineers (by examination).
- General and Ordinary Certificate in Removals Management issued by the IFWRI prior to 13 May 1995, or after that date the National Certificate in Removals Management issued by the Movers Institute.
- Royal Society of Arts (RSA) Certificate in Road Freight Transport granted on or after 1 May 1984 which specifically contains a footnote granting exemption.

There are no grounds for obtaining professional competence by exemption other than those detailed above. Valid membership of the relevant body (ie subscription paid, etc) is sufficient to confirm professional competence but, if required, the institutes will issue a confirmatory certificate or statement (ie not a certificate of competence of the type issued under grandfather rights).

Examinations

A system of examinations enables new entrants to the transport (ie road freight and road passenger) industry and those people who do not qualify under the previously mentioned grandfather rights or exemption arrangements to study for and obtain professional competence by examination. The examination scheme is organized and conducted on behalf of the DfT by the OCR (Oxford and Cambridge Royal Society of Arts) and examinations for both goods and passenger vehicle operations are held at main centres throughout the country four times each year.

Note: From 4 December 2011 the former separate road haulage national and international examinations are to be merged into a single examination providing (on successful completion) a single road haulage CPC qualification covering both national and international operations.

Examination Dates

Dates for the year 2012 examinations are as follows: Friday 2 March 2012, Friday 1 June 2012, Friday 7 September 2012 and Friday 7 December 2012. Potential candidates are advised to check dates and locations for forthcoming examinations with the OCR.

Modular Examination System

For the national examination a modular system has been adopted with a common 'core' for both road haulage and passenger subjects and then the individual modal (freight or passenger) modules. The new modular structure was introduced from the October 1999 examination as follows:

National Road Haulage CPC

- Module 1 – Core (30 multiple-choice questions), plus
- Module 2 – National Road Haulage (40 multiple-choice questions), plus
- Module 4 – National Road Haulage (case-study examination requiring eight extended response answers).

International Road Haulage CPC

- National Road Haulage CPC, plus
- Module 6 – International Road Haulage (questions requiring short written answers).

Examination Timetable

Candidates may enter for any combination of modules on any of the published examination dates. Owing to the new examination requirements, however, passenger transport modules will be timetabled to take place at the same time as the equivalent road haulage modules. Candidates cannot therefore sit a road haulage and equivalent passenger transport module on the same day.

Examinations taking place at the same time:

- Module 2 (road haulage) and module 3 (passenger transport)
- Module 4 (road haulage) and module 5 (passenger transport)
- Module 6 (road haulage) and module 7 (passenger transport).

Certification

When an examination candidate achieves the required combination of module examination successes at one sitting (ie on the same examination date), a full national or international certificate of professional competence will be issued.

Candidates who pass any individual module examination will be issued with a module certificate. When they have acquired the requisite number of individual certificates these can be exchanged for a full certificate of professional competence on application to OCR.

Examination Fees

Fees for the examinations are as follows:

- Unit 1 (core) – £15.20
- Unit 2 (road haulage national) – £25.50
- Unit 4 (road haulage national) – £44.20
- Unit 6 (international road haulage) – £36.20.

These fees are payable to the OCR. Late-entry bookings are charged extra. Additional charges may be made by examining centres for the facilities they provide. Candidates who fail examinations may apply to OCR for details of their performance. They should state where and when they sat the examination and should enclose the relevant fee.

The contact point for OCR is as follows: 01223 553998; e-mail: **vocationalqualifications@ocr.org.uk**; website: **www.ocr.org.uk**.

Examination Method

Examinations conducted for the purpose of providing the qualification for professional competence are based on the 'objective testing' or multiple-choice method. In the multiple-choice examinations the candidate is faced with either a number of questions, each of which is provided with a choice of possible answers (usually four), only one of which is correct, or alternatively statements to which a 'True' or 'False' answer must be indicated. The candidate must select and mark the correct answer to each question or statement. For the case study, examination candidates will be presented with a scenario (storyboard) followed by a number of questions. They will be required to write a short-response answer applying their knowledge to the situation in the scenario and accompanying questions.

The examinations are designed to be within the grasp of candidates whose educational standard corresponds to the level normally reached in compulsory schooling supplemented either by vocational training and supplementary technical training or by secondary-level school technical training.

Examination Syllabus

A new set of syllabuses for the CPC examinations was published by OCR early in 2006 in time for the March 2006 series of examinations. While the new documents, available from OCR or downloadable from the OCR website (**www.ocr.org.uk**), are laid out differently from the previous syllabus style, the basic content remains broadly the same. The new version of the syllabus shows, for each of the units:

- assessment objectives; and
- the knowledge, understanding and skills required.

Study Facilities

Study may be undertaken at courses organized by group training associations, trade associations or commercial organizations. Some local technical colleges and other teaching establishments also offer part-time, usually evening, classes on the subject.

The study may involve full-time or part-time attendance at such courses or it may be by correspondence course or by training or home learning package (ie notes and video) or with the aid of teaching manuals.

The Council Directive Syllabus

The syllabus for road haulage operations published in Regulation 1071/2009/EC and effective from 4 December 2011 is detailed below. It shows the assessment objectives and (in brackets) the depth of knowledge required for the examination.

A. Civil Law

Candidates must:

1 be familiar with the main types of contract used in road transport and with the rights and obligations arising therefrom (*Contracts: legal obligations; sub-contracting; legal duties of agents, employers and employees*);

2 be capable of negotiating a legally valid transport contract, notably with regard to conditions of carriage (*Legal obligations: capacity to contract; specific performance; liability; lien; laws of agency*);

3 be able to consider a claim by his principal regarding compensation for loss of or damage to goods during transportation or for their late delivery, and to understand how such claims affect his contractual responsibility (*Performance: general and specific liabilities of principal, sub-contractors and agents for the*

performance of a contract. Compensation: for losses relating to damage. Settlements: interim and full payments);

4 be familiar with the rules and obligations arising from the CMR convention on the contract for the international carriage of goods by road (*CMR liability and unwitting CMR: CMR notes to CMR convention. Successive carriers. Limits of liability. Relevance of insurance*).

B. Commercial Law

Candidates must:

1 be familiar with the conditions and formalities laid down for plying the trade, the general obligations incumbent upon transport operators (registration, keeping records) and the consequences of bankruptcy (*Trading law relating to: sole traders and partnerships; partnership agreements; rights and duties of partners; powers of partners; partners as agents; dissolution of partnerships. Company law: registered companies (private and public); AGMs; liquidation. Documentation: prospectus, memorandum of association; articles of association; certificate of incorporation*);

2 have appropriate knowledge of the various forms of commercial company and the rules governing their constitution and operation (*Types of business organization: sole traders; partnerships; private and public limited companies; co-operatives*).

C. Social Law

Candidates must be familiar with:

1 the role and function of the various social institutions that are concerned with road transport (trade unions, works councils, shop stewards, labour inspectors) (*Role of: employment tribunals; trade unions; ACAS; arbitrators; DTI. Employees' rights: trade union membership and activities*);

2 the employers' social security obligations (*Relevant parts of current legislation relating to: health and safety; discrimination; employment protection; employment rights*);

3 the rules governing work contracts for the various categories of worker employed by road transport undertakings (form of the contracts, obligations of the parties, working conditions and working hours, paid leave, remuneration, breach of contract) (*Contracts of employment: content of written statement; time limits for the issue of contracts. Employment rights: of full- and part-time employees; of self-employed; of agency staff; transfer of undertakings; remuneration and itemized pay statements; holiday entitlement; dismissal and unfair dismissal; notice to terminate employment; working time regulations*);

4 the rules applicable to driving time, rest periods and working rime, and in particular the provisions of Regulation (EEC) No 3821/85, Regulation (EC) No 561/2006, Directive 2002/15/EC and Directive 2006/22/EC, and the practical measures for applying those provisions; practical arrangements for

implementing these regulations (*Community regulations: the working week; driving time; breaks; daily and weekly rest periods; emergencies. Domestic hours' law: the working week; driving time; rest periods; emergencies. Tachograph legislation and operation: points of law; the records; driver and employer responsibilities; enforcement and inspection; calibration and sealing; malfunctions*).

5 the rules applicable to the initial qualification and continuous training of drivers [ie the Driver CPC], and in particular those deriving from Directive 2003/59/EC.

D. Fiscal Law

Candidates must be familiar with the rules governing:

1 VAT on transport services (*VAT – national operations: income threshold and registration; zero-rated goods and services; VAT returns; reclaiming VAT. Turnover tax – international operations: registration for VAT; applying VAT; submitting returns; reclaiming VAT*);

2 motor vehicle tax (*Calculation of VED: basis for calculating motor vehicle taxation on general vehicles and vehicles used in special operations and conditions applied to them*);

3 taxes on certain road haulage vehicles and tolls and infrastructure user charges (*Domestic operation: toll roads and bridges and the basis on which calculation is made. International operation: rules governing tolls and taxation of vehicles on international journeys*);

4 income tax (*Corporate taxation. Double taxation. Status: rules governing the status of employees and the self-employed and the imposition of income tax regulations. Employers' responsibilities: deduction and collection of income tax and National Insurance from employees; payment of income tax and National Insurance to the HM Revenue & Customs*).

E. Business and Financial Management of the Undertaking

Candidates must:

1 be familiar with the laws and practices regarding the use of cheques, bills of exchange, promissory notes, credit cards and other means or methods of payment (*National operation – payment methods: cash; cheques; credit cards; promissory notes; bills of exchange; debit systems and credit transfer. International operation: banking and payment systems, including the electronic transfer of funds, eg Swift*);

2 be familiar with the various forms of credit (bank credit, documentary credit, guarantee deposits, mortgages, leasing, renting, factoring) and with the charges and obligations arising from them (*Different forms of credit: overdrafts; loans; documentary credit; guarantee deposits; mortgages; leases; rents; factoring*);

3 know what a balance sheet is, how it is set out and how to interpret it (*Determine: fixed assets; net current assets; current assets; long-term liabilities; current liabilities. Interpretation: calculate and interpret*);

4 be able to read and interpret a profit and loss account (*Determine: direct and indirect costs; gross (or operating or trading) profit; net profit*);

5 be able to assess the company's profitability and financial position, in particular on the basis of financial ratios (*Determine: capital employed and return on capital employed; return on sales and assets turnover; working capital; cash flow. Use of ratios: current ratio (working capital ratio); quick ratio (liquidity ratio or acid test ratio)*);

6 be able to prepare a budget (*Construct budgets from data supplied. Use of budgets: to monitor and control performance, budgetary control, variance analysis*);

7 be familiar with their company's cost elements (fixed costs, variable costs, working capital, depreciation, etc), and be able to calculate costs per vehicle, per kilometre, per journey or per tonne (*From data supplied: identify and/or calculate fixed costs, variable costs, overhead costs, depreciation. Determine: time and distance costs*);

8 be able to draw up an organization chart relating to the undertaking's personnel as a whole and to organize work plans (*Prepare an organization chart for an: organization, department, function, unit or depot. Organizing, planning and measuring work*);

9 be familiar with the principles of marketing, publicity and public relations, including transport services, sales promotion and the preparation of customer files (*Market research (primary and secondary); segmentation; product promotion, sales and publicity. Customer: relations; research files*);

10 be familiar with the different types of insurance relating to road transport (liability, accidental injury/life insurance) and with the guarantees and obligations arising therefrom (*Insurance: risk assessment; cover; claims, risk management and improvement of risk. Types of insurance: fidelity; goods in transit; employers' liability; public liability; professional negligence; motor; plant; travel; health; property; consequential loss; cash in transit. Risks: guarantees; obligations; liability and role of trustees*);

11 be familiar with the applications of electronic data transmission in road transport (*Legislation: Data Protection Act. Hardware and software: electronic vehicle status monitoring; electronic data transmission; real-time information systems; customer information systems; depot readers; GPS; route and load planning systems; vehicle and staff scheduling; data analysis; data information systems*);

12 be able to apply the rules governing the invoicing of road haulage services and know the meaning of incoterms (agreed trading terms with legal definitions, eg FOB – the International Chamber of Commerce produces a book called *Incoterms*, ref: ISBN 92–842–0087–3) (*Transactions: the purpose of quotations, orders, consignment notes. Incoterms: principal provisions of incoterms applying to any mode of road transport, including multimodal*);

13 be familiar with the different categories of transport auxiliaries, their role, their functions and, where appropriate, their status (*Agents: various agents who assist in ensuring freight is properly and correctly transferred, eg freight forwarders, shippers, clearing houses, groupage operators*).

F. Access to the Market

Candidates must be familiar with:

1 the occupational regulations governing road transport for hire or reward, industrial vehicle rental and sub-contracting, and in particular the rules governing the official organization of the occupation, admission to the occupation, authorizations for intra- and extra-Community road transport operations, inspections and sanctions (*National operation: role of Traffic Commissioners and enforcement agencies; statutory procedures concerning operator licensing; requirements for vehicle maintenance; regulations governing domestic operation. International operation: statutory procedures concerning operator licensing; regulations governing international operations*);

2 the rules for setting up a road transport undertaking (*Rules for setting up a road transport undertaking: statutory procedures and rules concerning operator licensing*);

3 the various documents required for operating road transport services and be able to introduce checking procedures for ensuring that the approved documents relating to each transport operation, and in particular those relating to the vehicle, the driver and the goods or luggage, are kept both in the vehicle and on the premises of the undertaking (*Documents and their administration: operator licences and vehicle discs; vehicle authorizations; tachograph records; waybills/consignment notes; driving entitlement; maintenance documents; insurance documents; systems for document checking and control procedures*);

4 the rules on the organization of the market in road haulage services, on freight handling and logistics (*Market organization: 1985 Transport Act, regulatory powers of the Secretary of State, the Office of Fair Trading; the Monopolies and Mergers Commission. Role of local government regarding the movement of abnormal loads. Main provisions of third country traffic and cabotage*);

5 frontier (i.e. border) formalities, the role and scope of 'T' documents and TIR carnets, and the obligations and responsibilities arising from their use (*'T' documents, their status and rules of use. Carnets, rules governing their use. Exemptions: most practical use of various exemptions obtained by the use of various documents and the implications for operators and their customers*).

G. Technical Standards and Aspects of Operation

Candidates must:

1 be familiar with the rules concerning the weights and dimensions of vehicles in the member states of the European Union and the procedures to be followed in the case of abnormal loads that constitute an exception to these rules (*Terms used to identify the differing weight conditions. Statutory limits: weights and dimensions. Formulas used for various calculations concerned in weights and dimensions of vehicles. Main rules and most common weights and dimensions used internationally*);

2 be able to choose vehicles and their components (chassis, engine, transmission system, braking system, etc) in accordance with the needs of the undertaking (*Vehicle specifications that will improve road safety and economy, and reduce impact on the environment. Vehicle specifications to be taken into account for international operations*);

3 be familiar with the formalities relating to the type approval, registration and technical inspection of these vehicles (*Main provisions within current legislation relating to C&U and safety. Powers of enforcement agencies*);

4 understand what measures must be taken to reduce noise and to combat air pollution by motor vehicle exhaust emissions (*Main provisions of the C&U regulations; EU directives and environmental legislation. Training: awareness training*);

5 be able to draw up periodic maintenance plans for the vehicles and their equipment (*Maintenance programmes: planned preventative; methods of maintenance; operator's obligations and liabilities to maintain vehicles and equipment in a safe, roadworthy condition; responsibility for vehicles whose maintenance is contracted out*);

6 be familiar with the different types of cargo-handling and cargo-loading devices (tailboards, containers, pallets, etc) and be able to introduce procedures and issue instructions for loading and unloading goods (load distribution, stacking, stowing, blocking and chocking) (*Risk analysis and safe operations: requirements for various loads and procedures to ensure safe operations*);

7 be familiar with the various techniques of 'piggy-back' and roll-on/roll-off combined transport (*Safety requirements; vehicle specifications charging methods*);

8 be able to implement procedures for complying with the rules on the carriage of dangerous goods and waste, notably those arising from:
  - Directive 2008/68/EC with regard to the transport of dangerous goods by road;
  - Regulation (EC) 2006/1013/EC on the supervision and control of shipments of waste within, into and out of the European Community;

9 be able to implement procedures for complying with the rules on the carriage of perishable foodstuffs, notably those arising from the agreement on the international carriage of perishable foodstuffs and on the special equipment to be used for such carriage (ATP) (*Procedures to ensure correct compliance with legislation and best practice*);

10 be able to implement procedures for complying with the rules on the transport of live animals (*National and International: procedures to ensure correct compliance with legislation and best practice*).

H. Road Safety

Candidates must:

1 know what qualifications are required for drivers – driving licences, medical certificates, certificates of fitness (*Vocational entitlements: different categories, types and qualifications for driving licences and entitlements. Procedures: relating to the issue, renewal, revocation and production of licences and removal of entitlements. Disciplinary matters: procedures and appeals. Driving tests: scope and conduct and sequence of theory and driving tests. International driving permits: issue and validation*);

2 be able to take the necessary steps to ensure that drivers comply with the traffic rules, prohibitions and restrictions in force in the different member states of the European Union – speed limits, priorities, waiting and parking restrictions, use of lights, road signs (*Traffic regulations: signs and signals; variation in weights, dimensions and speed of road haulage vehicles in EU member states and non-member countries. Restrictions: imposed on the movement and speeds of road haulage vehicles*);

3 be able to draw up drivers' instructions for checking their compliance with the safety requirements concerning the condition of the vehicles, their equipment and cargo, and concerning preventive measures to be taken (*Write instructions for inspection, defect reporting and the safe use of vehicles and equipment, including cargo*);

4 be able to lay down procedures to be followed in the event of an accident and to implement appropriate procedures for preventing the recurrence of accidents or serious traffic offences (*Accident procedures: introduce measures to inform appropriate authorities and personnel of accidents; take appropriate action to minimize further dangers and to relieve suffering. The use of European Accident Statements*).

5 be able to implement procedures to properly secure goods;

6 have elementary knowledge of the layout of the road network in the Member States.

The OCR states that new legislative measures will not be included in the examination for at least three months from the date of implementation.

Those wishing to study for the examination should ensure that they have an up-to-date syllabus, covering either road haulage or passenger transport operations, from the OCR (see above for address).

Transfer of Qualifications

Provisions are made to allow an interchange of professional competence qualifications and recognition of professional competence qualification certificates between the United Kingdom, Northern Ireland and other EU member states. Thus the UK Traffic Commissioners are required, under the 'mutual recognition' requirements of EU

Directive 796/77/EEC, to take into account any certificate of professional competence or any alternative to such a certificate showing relevant experience in the road haulage industry issued either in the UK, Northern Ireland or in any other member states when considering an application for an 'O' licence. Normally, an OCR full professional competence certificate issued to UK nationals since March 1992 will be sufficient evidence of professional competence.

However, the Traffic Commissioners in the UK will issue a Certificate of Qualification form GOL55 (fee £20 – payable to the Traffic Area Office) confirming the good repute, professional competence and, where relevant, the financial standing of persons or companies from the UK who wish to be admitted to the occupation of road haulage operator, or to be employed to manage the transport operations of a goods haulage undertaking in Northern Ireland or in any other EU member state.

Where a person seeking a Certificate of Qualification is not, or has not been, an 'O' licence holder in the UK, the TCs will, of course, have no knowledge of their experience, good repute or financial standing and thus will be unable to issue a certificate. In these cases application can be made to the Secretary of State (ie for the D*f*T), who is empowered to issue a certificate to such a person on payment of the requisite fee.

Good Repute

The subject of good repute has been dealt with in detail in Chapter 1 (see pp 20–22) where it is more properly located since it is an issue which arises only when an application for an 'O' licence is made by an individual, by a partnership business or by a company. However, a great deal of attention has been focused on the 'good repute' aspect of professionally competent persons. For this reason, and to catch the attention of those who may read only this chapter rather than the 'O' licensing chapter (Chapter 1), some of the salient facts are repeated here.

As stated above, the good repute of such persons is only called into question when their names are put forward in support of a standard 'O' licence application. At that time the TC will want to know if the person has previous convictions for offences relating to the operation of goods vehicles (see below).

Following on from the previous explanation of the interchange of qualifications between the UK and other EU member states, the TCs, in considering an application for an 'O' licence and the good repute of the nominated professionally competent person, are required to take into account any convictions incurred by the person in Northern Ireland or in a country or territory outside the UK.

The relevant convictions are those which correspond to the relevant convictions under the British regulations, namely offences relating to vehicle roadworthiness, speeding, overloading, safe loading, drivers' hours and record keeping, drivers' licensing, maintenance, illegal use of rebated fuel, certain traffic offences and to the International Road Haulage Permits Act 1975.

Further, the Transport Tribunal has ruled that the TC can consider other convictions when considering a professionally competent person's good repute. The Tribunal ruled that the TC does not have to regard only those convictions mentioned above (as identified in the 1968 Transport Act) in deciding good repute.

In another instance a TC has said that a nominated professionally competent person must be clear of past financial difficulties. This followed a case where a nominated person was shown to be an adjudged bankrupt and the TC refused to accept the person's name on this account.

Rights of Transport Managers

In order to protect the rights of individuals, TCs are not permitted to examine and rule upon a transport manager's good repute or professional competence unless the individual has been notified at least 28 days in advance that this is to happen (and for what reason) and has had an opportunity to make personal representation to the TC (at a public inquiry if necessary and represented by a solicitor if he so wishes) concerning any allegations made about him.

Duties of Transport Managers

Traffic Commissioners have been increasingly tightening up on the role and duties of transport managers nominated in support of 'O' licence applications. New Guidance Notes have been issued to the TCs and a newly devised, purpose-designed Contract of Employment form has been brought into use in an effort to eliminate the practice whereby TMs are put forward in name only, with no concept of their statutory duties or any intention that they should perform this role as required by law (see also p 38).

Proposed New Rules for Transport Managers

A new, stricter and more complex set of rules for UK transport managers was proposed in a consultation paper issued by the Department for Transport based on EU Regulation 1071/2009/EC which this country is bound to comply with. Responses to the consultation were required by 20 May 2011 and regulations setting the new rules in stone were expected during the summer with an effective commencement date of 4 December 2011. This was too late for anything more than cursory details to be included in this edition of the *Handbook*.

THE DRIVER CPC

The EU is intent upon raising the standards of professionalism for LGV (and PCV) drivers by means of extended study/training periods and tough theory and practical testing, leading to a certificate of professional competence for such drivers.

An EU Directive on the qualification and training requirements for most LGV drivers (Directive 2003/59/EC of July 2003) became effective in regard to LGV drivers from 10 September 2009 (passenger vehicle drivers had to comply from one year earlier – ie 10 September 2008). The objectives are namely to improve road safety and the safety of the driver, and additionally to 'arouse young people's interest in the profession, contributing to the recruitment of new drivers at a time of shortage'.

The EC's view was that, with no more than 5–10 per cent of professional lorry drivers in Europe having undertaken any training other than what was needed to pass the relevant driving test, better-trained drivers would lead to fewer road accidents and a better quality of service being offered to customers, and harmonized training standards (which the Directive aims to achieve) would help promote growth and competition in the European transport market. Road accidents involving lorries in Great Britain in 2009 resulted in 1,439 people being killed and seriously injured (KSI) and 8,256 people being slightly injured. (Source: *DfT Transport Statistics Bulletin 2009 – Table 5.3.*)

The Directive's aim is for a system of certification of professional competence for drivers who satisfy the training requirements for 'initial' or 'accelerated initial' training and 'periodic' training. However, it is not the intention that the need to obtain an initial qualification should apply to existing drivers who have held a category C1, C1+E, C or C+E licence (or a licence recognized as being equivalent) that was issued no later than three years after the final date for this Directive coming into force (10 September 2009). They will, nevertheless, have to undergo the periodic training amounting to 35 hours every five years (which may be spread over the period by taking one 7-hour training session each year).

Exemptions will also apply to drivers of the following vehicles:

- vehicles with a maximum authorized speed not exceeding 45 kph;
- vehicles used by, or under the control of, the armed forces, civil defence, the fire service and forces responsible for maintaining public order;
- vehicles undergoing road tests for technical development, repair or maintenance purposes, or of new or rebuilt vehicles which have not yet been put into service;
- vehicles used in states of emergency or assigned to rescue missions;
- vehicles used in the course of driving lessons for any person wishing to obtain a driving licence or a certificate of professional competence (CPC);
- vehicles used for non-commercial carriage of passengers or goods for personal use;
- vehicles carrying material or equipment to be used by the driver in the course of his work, provided that driving the vehicle is not the driver's principal activity.

Initial Training

The Driving Standards Agency (DSA) is responsible, on behalf of the UK Government, for implementing the EU Driver Training Directive (2003/59/EC) and, in conjunction with Skills for Logistics (and GoSkills representing the passenger transport industry), has established the regime for CPC training to comply with the Directive. Two levels of training requirement must be met by professional LGV drivers, namely:

- initial training (set at the level of NVQ 2) for newcomers to LGV driving from 10 September 2009;
- periodic training, which will need to be undertaken by pre-existing LGV drivers who held their vocational entitlement prior to 10 September 2009.

Initial training applies to new drivers who acquire their entitlement to drive vehicles in categories C1, C1+E, C or C+E from 10 September 2009. These drivers will need to complete the initial training *in addition to* obtaining their vocational licence before they will be allowed to drive LGVs on the public highway.

This initial training will involve additional theory and practical testing beyond that required to obtain the LGV vocational licence as follows:

- basic licence theory test of 1½ hours plus 2½ hours of extra theory testing for CPC – making four hours in total;
- basic driving test of 1½ hours plus half an hour of extra practical testing for CPC – making two hours total.

The basic theory test mentioned above will be in two parts comprising:

- 100 multiple choice questions (85 per cent pass mark required) and a 20-video-clip hazard perception test;
- a number of case studies using diagrams, pictures and graphics as well as text, in which the candidate is presented with a defined scenario on which questions will be based.

Where appropriate, the test presentation will be screen-based and will be undertaken at existing DSA driving theory test centres (see Further Information on p 664).

Fees for Theory and Practical Tests

Module 1a Theory Test MPC* = £35
Module 1b Theory Test HPT** = £15
Module 2 Theory Test Case Studies = £30
Module 3 Practical Test = £115
Module 4 Practical Demonstration Test = £55

* Multiple choice test
** Hazard perception test

Initial Training for Young Drivers

The pre-existing Young LGV Driver scheme operated on behalf of the DfT by Skills for Logistics and the transport associations (RHA, FTA, etc) is superseded by the new Driver CPC scheme. In consequence of this the standard minimum age for professional LGV drivers is reduced to 18 years and, on gaining an 'accelerated initial qualification', such drivers will be allowed to drive goods vehicles in licence categories C1 and C1+E.

This 'accelerated' qualification must include the teaching of all subjects in the syllabus over a minimum study period, including a specified number of hours driving in a relevant approved test vehicle, followed by tests as described above.

Periodic Training

All existing LGV driving licence holders as at the date of commencement of the new scheme (10 September 2009) are required to undergo approved periodic training sessions amounting to 35 hours in total within the five years to September 2014 and in each subsequent five-year period. The training periods must be organized by an approved training centre, and each individual period must be of at least seven hours duration – this means seven hours of actual direct contact with the trainer within a 24-hour period. Thus, to achieve this training requirement, drivers could undertake one day of training each year or a week's training once every fifth year, either way amounting to 35 hours in total within the five years. The training objective could be to provide 'up-skilling' in general to improve overall driver performance and safety awareness, or specific training, to account for new technological developments in vehicle design for example, or operating 'best practices' as and when they occur.

Training, Testing and Certification

The whole of the new Driver CPC scheme is based on a system of approved methods of training and certification provided by approved trainers and working within approved training centres. Approval for trainers, training centres and training courses is given only by the Joint Approvals Unit for Periodic Training (JAUPT) – see Appendix II for contact details.

For these purposes, the JAUPT falls within the auspices of the Driving Standards Agency (DSA) and the Driver Vehicles Testing Agency and the schemes are managed by the Sector Skills Councils: namely, Skills for Logistics for the goods vehicle operating sector and GoSkills for the passenger vehicle operating sector.

What should be made clear here is that the Driver CPC qualification cannot be acquired by any means other than via these approved training methods. There are no facilities within the scheme for distance learning, study by correspondence course or other types of home study.

However, readers of this *Handbook* should understand that a great deal of knowledge of transport law and operating methods is needed to meet the CPC qualifying standard. Much of this can, of course, be obtained through 'hands-on' experience and practical tuition such as that provided by the approved trainers. Nevertheless, it is also clearly necessary to spend some time studying subjects that cannot necessarily be demonstrated adequately in a practical manner. This is where, in opportune moments, quiet reading of a suitable text, such as this *Handbook*, will help.

Minimum Age for Driving LGVs

Under the new Driver CPC scheme, from 10 September 2009 the minimum age for driving LGVs is reduced to 18 years, but this applies only to drivers holding a Driver Qualification Card who have completed the requisite period of initial training.

Driving Tests

The established system of driver testing continues, with the exception that from April 2008 the number of theory test questions have increased to 100 (85 pass mark) and the hazard perception test to 20 video clips. The practical driving test remains at 1½ hours duration but this will be supplemented by a series of questions that require the candidate to demonstrate knowledge of vehicle safety matters.

Availability of Training

At the time of writing this *Handbook*, quite a number of training centres have received the necessary approval to offer Driver CPC training; a current list of these can be found on the JAUPT website at: **http://www.drivercpc.org**.

Testing and Certification

Pre-existing LGV driving licence holders as at the date when the new scheme came into operation (10 September 2009 for LGV licence holders) are not required to undertake any tests to acquire a Driver CPC; they have what is known as 'acquired rights' and therefore are deemed to be 'professionally competent' drivers, albeit without an actual CPC document (to be known as a 'Driver Qualification Card' – DQC) to prove the fact. Their CPC qualification will be evidenced, if such proof is required, by the date on their driving licence that shows when their entitlement to drive LGVs came into effect.

NB: This is a further reason why drivers should carry their vocational licences with them at all times when driving – they may be asked for such evidence (see also below).

Such pre-existing LGV licence holders will eventually obtain the Driver CPC on completion of their first (35-hour) spell of periodic training. This will then be renewed on completion of each subsequent five-yearly session of periodic training.

New drivers who have not held an LGV driving entitlement prior to 10 September 2009 will need to complete the Driver CPC initial training, as described above, at the time of undertaking their LGV driving test. Without this extra qualification it will be illegal for them to drive goods vehicles professionally (ie for payment) unless the vehicle is one that falls into an exempt category (see pp 11–14).

Certification of the fact that a new driver holds the CPC qualification will be by holding a Driver Qualification Card. These cards will be issued by the Driver and Vehicle Licensing Agency (DVLA) on meeting the necessary qualification by passing the various tests outlined above.

A record of all driver training undertaken at approved centres will be held on a central database by the DSA, and it is on the basis of this record of training hours achieved that the DSA will notify the DVLA when to send the candidate his or her Driver Qualification Card. Drivers themselves may also check up on their own personal accumulated training hours by enquiry to the DSA, and employers will have the same facility provided they have the individual's permission to make such enquiries.

Enforcement, Offences and Penalties

Strict enforcement of the new Driver CPC scheme is promised by the authorities, with offenders being in line to receive tough penalties for failure to comply with the legal requirements.

Enforcing Authorities

In this case the enforcing authorities are the police and VOSA, both of which will have direct access to the centrally held data at the DVLA, enabling them to instantly check any dubious claims or records.

Offences and Penalties

From 10 September 2009 all such LGV drivers must carry evidence of their Driver CPC qualification and may be asked to produce this at the time of a roadside check.

- For pre-September 2009 LGV licence holders the evidence will be the date on their vocational licence – so the message here is clear: LGV drivers must carry their driving licence at all times when actually driving or when undertaking work that may involve LGV driving.

- For new LGV drivers from 10 September 2009 the evidence will be their Driver Qualification Card issued to them on satisfactory completion of the initial CPC training achieved in conjunction with their driving qualification – this card must also be carried at all times when driving as described above.

Failure by drivers to produce their DVQ or their driving licence with date evidence on request by a VOSA enforcement officer or police officer carries a fixed penalty fine of £30.

The more serious offence that drivers are at risk of committing is failure to have undergone the mandatory 35 hours of periodic training within the preceding five years. Whether this occurs through forgetfulness or deliberate avoidance of the training regime matters not; an offending driver could be fined up to £1,000 on conviction.

Since the Driver CPC scheme applies throughout the whole EU community, British drivers must, when driving abroad, carry with them their driving licence (showing evidence of their pre-September 2009 driving qualification) or their DVQ. They risk an on-the-spot penalty if caught out in breach of this requirement. Similarly, foreign LGV drivers operating within the UK face the prospect of the £30 fixed penalty fine if found not to have the requisite documentation with them, but there is an anomaly in the case of the more serious offence mentioned above. Due to the current inadequacy of the DVLA database, which does not carry training records for non-UK drivers, such drivers will avoid the £1,000 fine for having either failed to complete, or totally avoided, the periodic training requirement.

Minimum Training and Qualification Requirements

List of Subjects

The knowledge to be taken into account when establishing the driver's qualification and training must include at least the subjects in this syllabus.

Trainee drivers must reach the level of knowledge and practical competence necessary to drive the relevant categories of vehicle with safety.

The minimum level of a driver's knowledge must not be less than the level reached during compulsory education, supplemented by professional training.

Syllabus

1 Advanced training in rational driving based on safety regulations

1.1 Objective: to learn the characteristics of the vehicle transmission system in order to use it to the best possible effect:
- curves relating to engine torque and power;
- specific consumption of an engine;
- area of optimum use of revolution counter;
- gearbox-ratio cover diagrams.

1.2 Objective: to learn the technical characteristics and operation of the safety controls in order to control the vehicle, minimize wear and tear and prevent dysfunctioning:
- specific features of hydraulic, vacuum and servobrake circuits;
- limits to the use of brakes and retarder;
- combined use of brakes and retarder;
- making better use of speed and gear ratios;
- making use of vehicle inertia;
- using ways of slowing down and braking on downhill stretches;
- action in the event of failure.

1.3 Objective: to learn how to optimize fuel consumption:
- optimization of fuel consumption by applying know-how as regards the above-mentioned points in 1.1 and 1.2.

1.4 Objective: to acquire the ability to load a vehicle with due regard for safety rules and proper vehicle use:
- forces affecting vehicles in motion;
- use of gearbox ratios according to vehicle load and road profile;
- calculation of payload of vehicle or assembly;
- calculation of total volume and load distribution;
- consequences of overloading the axle;
- vehicle stability and centre of gravity;
- types of packaging and pallets;
- main categories of goods needing securing;
- damping and securing techniques;
- use of securing straps;
- checking of securing devices;
- use of handling equipment;
- placing and removal of tarpaulins.

2 Application of regulations

2.1 Objective: to understand the social environment of road transport and the rules governing it:

- maximum working periods specific to the transport industry;
- principles, application and consequences of Regulations (EEC) Nos. 3820/85 and 3821/85;
- penalties for failure to use, improper use of and tampering with the tachograph;
- knowledge of the social environment of road transport;
- rights and duties of drivers as regards initial qualification and periodic training.

2.2 Objective: to learn the regulations governing the carriage of goods:

- transport operating licences;
- obligations under standard contracts for the carriage of goods;
- drafting of documents which form the transport contract;
- international transport permits;
- obligations under the Convention on the Contract for the International Carriage of Goods by Road (ie CMR);
- drafting of the international consignment note;
- crossing borders;
- freight forwarders;
- special documents accompanying goods.

3 Health, road safety and environmental safety, service, logistics

3.1 Objective: to make drivers aware of the risks of the road and of accidents at work:

- types of accidents at work in the transport sector;
- road accident statistics;
- involvement of lorries;
- human, material and financial consequences.

3.2 Objective: to learn how to prevent trafficking in illegal immigrants:

- trafficking in illegal immigrants and illegal immigration;
- general information;
- implications for drivers;
- preventive measures: checklist;
- legislation on transport operator liability.

3.3 Objective: to learn how to prevent physical risks:

- ergonomic principles;
- movements and postures that pose a risk;

- physical fitness;
- handling exercises;
- personal protection.

3.4 Objective: to understand the importance of physical and mental ability:
   - principles of healthy, balanced eating;
   - effects of alcohol, drugs or any other substance likely to affect behaviour;
   - symptoms, causes and effects of fatigue and stress;
   - fundamental role of the basic work/rest cycle.

3.5 Objective: to learn how to assess emergency situations:
   - behaviour in an emergency situation;
   - assessment of the situation;
   - avoiding complications of an accident;
   - summoning assistance;
   - assisting casualties and giving first aid;
   - reaction in the event of fire;
   - evacuation of occupants of a lorry;
   - ensuring the safety of all passengers;
   - reaction in the event of aggression;
   - basic principles for the drafting of an accident report.

3.6 Objective: to learn how to adopt behaviour to help enhance the image of a service undertaking:
   - behaviour of the driver and company image;
   - importance for the company of the standard of service provided by the driver;
   - the roles of the driver and people with whom the driver will be dealing;
   - vehicle maintenance;
   - work organization;
   - commercial and financial effects of a dispute.

3.7 Objective: to understand the economic environment of road haulage and the organization of the market:
   - road transport in relation to other modes of transport (competition, shippers);
   - different road transport activities (transport for hire or reward, own account, auxiliary transport activities);
   - organization of the main types of transport company and auxiliary transport activities;
   - different transport specializations (road tanker, controlled temperature, etc);
   - changes in the industry (diversification of services provided, rail–road, sub-contracting, etc).

Goods Vehicle Drivers' Hours and Working Time

This chapter has been expanded to incorporate both the EU driving hours rules and the legal provisions relating to working time for LGV drivers. With the EU's Directive on Working Time extended to include mobile workers (most predominantly LGV drivers), it was thought to be more appropriate to deal with the subject here along with the long-established driving hours rules.

EU Driving and Rest Time Rules

Any person who uses a vehicle for the carriage of goods for commercial or business purposes (ie not including those used for purely private purposes and other vehicles specifically exempted – see pp 11–14) irrespective of the vehicle weight must conform to strict rules on the amount of time he may spend driving. For most goods vehicle drivers the rules also include requirements relating to minimum breaks to be taken during the driving day and to both daily and weekly rest periods.

Enforcement and Penalties

The driving hours rules are applied solely to protect public safety, especially to protect road users from the dangers of overworked and tired drivers of heavy vehicles. Enforcement is vigorously undertaken by both the police and VOSA enforcement officers, and convicted offenders are dealt with severely by the courts to emphasize the importance of these road safety measures.

Drivers who are convicted for contravening the rules risk heavy fines, while the most serious of offences can result in imprisonment. LGV driving entitlements may be revoked in consequence, losing a driver his job.

Besides prosecution for infringements and its consequent penalties, provisions brought in by the Transport Act 2000 (ie section 266, which amends section 99 of the Transport Act 1968) and effective since 1 February 2001 authorize enforcement officers of VOSA to detain drivers found to be in breach of the drivers' hours rules.

Where it is determined during a roadside check that a UK driver has not taken sufficient break or rest periods prior to that time, he will be prohibited from continuing his journey. In the case of break period infringements the delay at the roadside will be until a full 45-minute break period has been taken. Where breaches of the daily or weekly rest period requirements are detected, the driver and his vehicle will be escorted by the police to a suitable parking area (eg service area or truck stop) where he will have to remain until he has taken a full 11-hour daily rest or 24-hour weekly rest.

The vehicle operator may send a relief driver to take over the vehicle and continue its journey, but this driver will be subject to scrutiny by VOSA to ensure that he has sufficient time available within legal limits to drive the vehicle.

Employers of convicted drivers also risk prosecution and heavy fines for similar offences. Additionally, they may have penalties imposed against their 'O' licences by the Traffic Commissioners (TCs) since they promised in the declaration of intent at the time of their 'O' licence application that they would make arrangements to ensure the drivers' hours law would be observed.

It is also a specific requirement of the EU rules that employers must make periodic checks to ensure the rules are observed and must take appropriate action if they discover breaches of the law to ensure there is no repetition of offences.

In mainland Europe, breaches of the rules detected in roadside checks may result in drivers incurring heavy on-the-spot fines which must be paid immediately, otherwise the vehicle may be impounded and the driver held until the fine is paid.

Reporting of Illegal Operations

Under the Public Interest Disclosure Act 1998 employees are protected if they report corruption, wrongdoing or danger at work, or if they are unduly pressured by an unscrupulous employer to break the law.

For example, in the context of the drivers' hours law, where drivers are encouraged or pressured to breach the driving hours or tachograph rules, they would have protection under the Act if they reported such matters either to VOSA or to the TC.

The Act came into force in July 1999. This new so-called 'whistle-blowing' charter entitles workers to unlimited compensation if their employer penalizes them for exposing breaches of the law or unsafe practices. Besides this legal protection, the United Road Transport Union (URTU) provides a confidential hotline service for drivers on freephone 0800 526639.

Which Rules Apply?

Goods vehicle driver employers and drivers themselves need to understand the hours rules clearly, and especially which particular set of rules applies to them depending on the vehicle being driven or the nature of the transport operation on which they are engaged. Three main sets of rules apply, the EU rules, the British domestic rules and what are known as the AETR rules for international journeys outside the EU (fully aligned with the EU rules). The specific requirements under each of these sets of rules are explained in the following pages.

European Union Rules

The drivers' hours EU rules, formerly contained in Regulation 3820/85/EEC, which came into effect in the UK on 29 September 1986, are repealed and replaced by similar provisions contained in EU Regulation 561/2006/EC which took effect from 11 April 2007 apart from the digital tachograph provisions (ie in Articles 10(5), 26(3) and (4), and 27) described in Chapter 5, which became effective from 1 May 2006.

Vehicles Covered

EU rules always take precedence over national rules. Therefore, since all goods vehicles and other vehicles used for the carriage of goods in connection with business activities as stated above are covered by one or other of the sets of drivers' hours rules (ie EU, British or AETR), the requirements of specific EU legislation must be considered first. Mainly, this involves examination of the list of EU rules exemptions to determine whether the vehicle or the transport operation falls within scope of the rules or outside.

Where a vehicle has a maximum permissible weight not exceeding 3.5 tonnes it is exempt from the EU rules or if it is one identified on the EU exemption list or is used for a purpose which is shown in the list as exempt as mentioned previously (eg vehicles used by the public utilities and local authorities, etc) it automatically comes within the scope of the British domestic rules set out in the 1968 Transport Act as described in detail on pp 100–102.

Where vehicles are over 3.5 tonnes permissible maximum weight, including the weight of any trailer drawn, and are not exempt as shown by the list or are not used for an exempt purpose, the EU hours law applies.

Where vehicles are over 3.5 tonnes permissible maximum weight, including the weight of any trailer drawn, and are not exempt as shown by the list or are not used for an exempt purpose, the EU hours law applies. Similarly, the law applies to vehicles 'used for the carriage of goods', such as 'off-road' vehicles and so-called 4 × 4s towing trailers, and where the combined weight of the towing vehicle and the trailer exceeds 3.5 tonnes.

Exemptions from EU Rules

EU Regulation 561/2006/EC (in Article 3) lists a number of exemptions and national governments (eg the British Government) are permitted to make certain other exemptions (derogations) if they so wish, as shown below.

International Exemptions (under EU regulations)

1 Vehicles used for the carriage of passengers on regular services where the route covered by the service in question does not exceed 50 km.

2 Vehicles with a maximum authorized speed not exceeding 40 km per hour.

3 Vehicles owned or hired without a driver by the armed services, civil defence services, fire services, and forces responsible for maintaining public order when the carriage is undertaken as a consequence of the tasks assigned to these services and is under their control.

4 Vehicles, including vehicles used in the non-commercial transport of humanitarian aid, used in emergencies or by road rescue operations.

5 Specialized vehicles used for medical purposes.

6 Specialized breakdown vehicles operating within a 100 km radius of their base.

7 Vehicles undergoing road tests for technical development, repair or maintenance purposes, and new or rebuilt vehicles which have not yet been put into service.

8 Vehicles or combinations of vehicles with a maximum permissible mass not exceeding 7.5 tonnes used for the non-commercial carriage of goods.

9 Commercial vehicles which have an historic status according to the legislation of the member state in the countries in which they are being driven, and which are used for the non-commercial carriage of passengers or goods.

National Exemptions (under UK derogations)

1 Passenger vehicles constructed to carry not more than 17 persons including the driver.

2 Vehicles used by public authorities to provide public services which are not in competition with professional road hauliers.

3 Vehicles used by agricultural, horticultural, forestry or fishery* undertakings, for carrying goods within a 100 km radius of the place where the vehicle is normally based, including local administrative areas the centres of which are situated within that radius.

To gain this exemption the vehicle must be used to carry live fish or to carry a catch of fish which has not been subjected to any process or treatment (other than freezing) from the place of landing to a place where it is to be processed or treated.

4 Vehicles used for carrying animal waste or carcasses not intended for human consumption.

5 Vehicles used for carrying live animals from farms to local markets and vice versa, or from markets to local slaughterhouses.

6 Vehicles specially fitted for and used:
   – as shops at local markets and for door-to-door selling;
   – for mobile banking, exchange or savings transactions;
   – for worship;
   – for the lending of books, records or CDs;
   – for cultural events or exhibitions.

7 Vehicles (not exceeding 7.5 tonnes gvw) carrying materials or equipment for the driver's use in the course of his work within a 50 km radius of base provided the driving does not constitute the driver's main activity and does not prejudice the objectives of the regulations.

8 Vehicles operating exclusively on islands not exceeding 2,300 sq km not linked to the mainland by bridge, ford or tunnel for use by motor vehicles (this includes the Isle of Wight, Arran and Bute).

9 Vehicles (not exceeding 7.5 tonnes gvw) used for the carriage of goods propelled by gas produced on the vehicle or by electricity.

10 Vehicles used for driving instruction (but not if carrying goods for hire or reward).

11 Tractors used after 1 January 1990 exclusively for agricultural and forestry work.

12 Vehicles used by the RNLI for hauling lifeboats.

13 Vehicles manufactured before 1 January 1947.

14 Steam-propelled vehicles.

15 Vintage vehicles (ie over 25 years old) not carrying more than nine persons including the driver, not being used for profit, and being driven to or from a vintage rally, museum, public display or a place where it has been or is to be repaired, maintained or tested.

Note: In exemption 2 above relating to vehicles used by public authorities, the exemption applies only if the vehicle is being used by:

a a health authority in England and Wales, a health board in Scotland or a National Health Service (NHS) Trust
   – to provide ambulance services in pursuance of its duty under the NHS Act 1977 or NHS (Scotland) Act 1978; or
   – to carry staff, patients, medical supplies or equipment in pursuance of its general duties under the Act;

b a local authority to fulfil social services functions, such as services for old persons or for physically and mentally handicapped persons;

c HM Coastguard or lighthouse authorities;

d harbour authorities within harbour limits;

e airports authority within airport perimeters;

f British Rail, London Regional Transport, a Passenger Transport Executive or local authority for maintaining railways;

g British Waterways Board for maintaining navigable waterways.

Exemption for Military Reservists

An exemption from EU drivers' hours rules is now available to military reservists who drive trucks or buses for a living which enables them to take part in weekend military training without breaching the rules on weekly rest requirements. It allows a driver who finishes his normal driving duties on a Friday to complete a 34-hour period of military training, and then resume his normal driving duties again on a Monday morning – providing specified safeguards are met. The exemption applies to volunteer reservists in the Territorial Army, the Royal Naval Reserve, the Royal Marine Reserve, and the Royal Auxiliary Air Force, as well as cadet instructors.

The following safeguards are imposed to ensure that road safety is not jeopardized: the exemption will apply to 15 days' annual camp and 10 weekend training sessions per annum – a total of 35 days; and weekend training will not be allowed to take place on consecutive weeks (other than during the 15-day annual camp). Also:

- A regular daily rest period of 11 hours must be taken between the end of weekend training and start of work for the primary employer.
- A 45-hour weekly rest period must be taken no later than at the end of the sixth day following a period of weekend training.

The Ministry of Defence plans to issue guidelines as to how drivers can manage their volunteer reserve service in accordance with the exemption.

Regulation 561/2006/EC

To apply the rules as required and appreciate their implications it is necessary to understand the definitions of certain words and phrases used as follows:

- 'Vehicle' means a motor vehicle, tractor, trailer or semi-trailer or a combination of these vehicles, defined as:
  - a 'motor vehicle' is any self-propelled vehicle travelling on the road, other than a vehicle permanently on rails, and normally used for carrying passengers or goods;
  - a 'tractor' is any self-propelled vehicle travelling on the road, other than a vehicle permanently running on rails and specially designed to pull, push or move trailers, semi-trailers, implements or machines;
  - a 'trailer' is any vehicle designed to be coupled to a motor vehicle or tractor;
  - a 'semi-trailer' is a trailer without a front axle coupled in such a way that a substantial part of its weight and the weight of its load is borne by the tractor or motor vehicle.

- 'Driver' means any person who drives the vehicle, even for a short period, or someone who is carried in a vehicle as part of his duties to be available for driving if necessary.
- 'Break' means any period during which a driver may not carry out any driving or any other work and which is used exclusively for recuperation.
- 'Other work' means all activities which are defined as working time in Article 3(a) of Directive 2002/15/EC except 'driving', including any work for the same or another employer, within or outside of the transport sector.
- 'Rest' means any uninterrupted period during which a driver may freely dispose of his time.
- 'Daily rest' means the daily period during which a driver may freely dispose of his time and covers a 'regular daily rest period' and a 'reduced daily rest period':
  - 'regular daily rest period' means any period of rest of at least 11 hours. Alternatively, this regular daily rest period may be taken in two periods, the first of which must be an uninterrupted period of at least 3 hours and the second an uninterrupted period of at least 9 hours;
  - 'reduced daily rest period' means any period of rest of at least 9 hours but less than 11 hours.

- 'Weekly rest period' means the weekly period during which a driver may freely dispose of his time and covers a 'regular weekly rest period' and a 'reduced weekly rest period':
  - 'regular weekly rest period' means any period of rest of at least 45 hours;
  - 'reduced weekly rest period' means any period of rest of less than 45 hours, which may, subject to the conditions laid down in Article 8(6) [ie relating to compensated rest], be shortened to a minimum of 24 consecutive hours.

- 'A week' means the period of time between 00.00 hrs on Monday and 24.00 hrs on Sunday.
- 'Driving time' means the duration of driving activity recorded:
  - automatically or semi-automatically by the recording equipment as defined in Annex 1 and Annex IB of Regulation 3821/85/EEC; or
  - manually as required by Article 16(2) of Regulation 3821/85/EEC.

- 'Daily driving time' means the total accumulated driving time between the end of one daily rest period and the beginning of the following daily rest period or between a daily rest period and a weekly rest period.
- 'Weekly driving time' means the total accumulated driving time during a week.
- 'Maximum permissible mass' means the maximum authorized operating mass [ie weight] of a vehicle when fully laden.
- 'Multi-manning' means the situation where, during each period of driving between any two consecutive daily rest periods, or between a daily rest period and a weekly rest period, there are at least two drivers in the vehicle to do the

driving. For the first hour of multi-manning the presence of another driver or drivers is optional but for the remainder of the period it is compulsory.

- 'Driving period' means the accumulated driving time from when a driver commences driving following a rest period or a break. The driving period may be continuous or broken.

Employers' Responsibilities

Under the EU rules employers have specific responsibilities as follows:

- They must organize drivers' work in such a way that the requirements of the regulations are not broken (ie on driving times, breaks and rest periods, etc).
- They must make regular checks (ie of tachograph charts – see Chapter 5) to ensure the regulations are complied with.
- Where they find any breaches of the law by drivers, they must take appropriate steps to prevent any repetition.

Additionally, of course, it goes without saying that employers should ensure their drivers do understand how the law in this respect applies to them and how to comply with its detailed provisions. Although it is no excuse in court for a driver to say he did not know the law, the court would expect the employer to have instructed the driver in its requirements and might well convict the employer for 'failing to cause' the driver to conform to the law (or for permitting offences) if it felt that insufficient attention had been given to this matter.

Driving Limits

Goods vehicle drivers are restricted in the amount of time they can spend driving before taking a break and the amount of driving they can do between any two daily rest periods (or a daily and a weekly rest period), in a week and in a fortnight. The maximum limits are as follows:

- Maximum driving before a break: 4½ hours
- Maximum daily driving normally: 9 hours
- Extended driving on 2 days in week only: 10 hours
- Maximum weekly driving: 6 daily driving shifts*
- Maximum fortnightly driving: 90 hours

*NB: The High Court ruled in 1988 that drivers can exceed the maximum of six daily driving shifts within six days as specified in the EU rules provided they do not exceed the maximum number of hours permitted in six consecutive driving periods. It should be noted that where a driver spends the maximum amount of driving time behind the wheel in one week (ie 4 × 9 hours plus 2 × 10 hours = 56 hours), during the following fixed week he may drive for a maximum of only 34 hours.

NNB: It should be noted here that the so-called '12-day rule' reintroduced for coach drivers on international journeys from June 2010 (under article 29 of regulation 1073/2009/EC) which allows such drivers to postpone their weekly rest period for up to 12 consecutive 24-hour periods does not apply to goods vehicle drivers.

Break Periods

Drivers are required by law to take a break or breaks if in a day the aggregate of their driving time amounts to 4½ hours or more. If the driver does not drive for periods amounting in aggregate to 4½ hours in the day there is no legal requirement for him to take a break during that day.

Break periods must not be regarded as parts of a daily rest period and during breaks the driver must not carry out any 'other work'. However, waiting time, time spent riding as passenger in a vehicle or time spent on a ferry or train are not counted as 'other work' for these purposes.

The requirement for taking a break is that immediately the 4½-hour driving limit is reached a break of 45 minutes must be taken, unless the driver commences a rest period at that time (see below). This break may be replaced by a break of *at least* 15 minutes followed by a break of at least 30 minutes each distributed over the driving period or taken during and immediately after this period, so as to equal at least 45 minutes and taken in such a way that the 4½-hour limit is not exceeded. To re-emphasize the point, once the 45 minutes' break requirement has been met, the slate is effectively wiped clean and the next 4½-hour period can begin.

A break period which was otherwise due in accordance with this requirement does not have to be taken if immediately following the driving period the driver commences a daily or weekly rest period, so long as the 4½ hours' aggregated driving is not exceeded.

NB: It is important to note that break periods (ie especially the 45-minute period as well as the alternative minimum 15-minute periods) should not be curtailed even by a minute or two. Prosecutions have been brought for offences relating to break periods which are alleged not to conform to the law even though they have been only a matter of minutes below the minimum specified in the regulations. Such matters are, of course, shown clearly on tachograph recordings, which provide ample evidence for the prosecution case.

Rest Periods

Rest periods are defined as uninterrupted during which the driver 'may freely dispose of his time'. Daily rest periods, and particularly rest periods which are compensating for previously reduced rest periods, should not be confused with, or combined with, statutory break periods required to be taken during the driving day as described above.

It has been held that time spent by drivers on weekend training courses (eg Hazchem courses and suchlike), even where there is no direct payment of wages by the employer, breaches the requirements under EU rules for drivers to have a period of weekly rest during which they may freely dispose of their time.

Daily Rest Periods

Once each day drivers are required to observe either a regular, a reduced or a split daily rest period during which time they must be free to dispose of their time. These daily rests are to be taken once in each 24 hours commencing at the time when the driver activates the tachograph following a weekly or daily rest period. Where the daily rest is taken in two separate periods (see below), the calculation must commence at the end of a rest period of not less than 9 hours. Thus in each 24-hour period as defined here one or other of the following daily rest periods must be taken:

- Regular daily rest: 11 hours
  or alternatively,

- Reduced rest: 9 hours – may be taken no more than three times between any two weekly rest periods

- Split rest: Where the daily rest period is not reduced (as above), the rest may be split and taken in two separate periods during the 24 hours, provided:
  - the first period must be at least 3 hours;
  - the last period must be at least 9 hours.

Split Daily Rest

When a regular daily rest period is split into two or three separate periods (shown above to be permitted under the rules) it should be noted, as a result of a European Court of Justice ruling, that the 9-hour period must be in the last portion of the rest. Previously it was thought that the separate components of a split rest period could be taken in any order.

Multi-manned Vehicles

Where a vehicle is operated by a two-man crew, the daily rest period requirement is that each man must have had a minimum of 9 hours' rest in each period of 30 hours counting from the end of a daily or weekly rest period.

NB: In the case of multi-manning, it should be noted that the hours law applies to the crew members from the commencement of the journey (or their day's work if that commenced earlier) but for the first hour the presence of another driver is optional.

Daily Rest on Vehicles

Daily rest periods may be taken on a vehicle provided:

- the vehicle has a bunk so the driver (but not necessarily a mate or attendant) can lie down; and
- the vehicle is stationary for the whole of the rest period.

It follows from this that a driver on a multi-manned vehicle cannot be taking part of his *daily rest period* on the bunk while a co-driver continues to drive the vehicle. He could, however, be taking a *break* at this time while the vehicle is moving or he could merely spend his time lying on the bunk, with his tachograph chart recording other work. It is permissable for the co-driver to book a period of availability when not driving, instead of a break or other work. This can only be applied when all the qualifying conditions exist for him to do so.

Daily Rest on Ferries/Trains

Normal 11-hour daily rest periods which are taken when a vehicle is carried for part of its journey on a ferry crossing or by rail may be interrupted, not more than twice, by other activities (such as embarkation or disembarkation) provided:

- the interruption must be 'as short as possible' and in any event must not be more than 1 hour;
- during both parts of the rest (ie in the terminal and on board the ferry/train) the driver must have access to a bunk or couchette.

Weekly Rest Period

After six successive 24-hour periods a regular weekly rest period totalling 45 hours must be taken. A weekly rest period which begins in one fixed week and continues into the following week may be attached to either of these weeks but not to both.

While the normal weekly rest period is 45 hours as described above, this may be reduced to a rest period of at least 24 hours whether at base or away from base.

Reduced weekly rest periods must be compensated (ie made up) by an equivalent amount of rest period time taken *en bloc* and added to another rest period of at least 9 hours' duration before the end of the third week following the week in which the reduced weekly rest period is taken.

Compensated Rest Periods

When reduced weekly rest periods are taken, the compensated time must be attached to another rest period of at least 9 hours' duration and must be granted, at the request of the driver, at the vehicle parking place or at the driver's base. Compensation in this respect *does not* mean compensation by means of payment; it means the provision of an equivalent amount of rest time taken on a later occasion but by the end of the third following week in the case of compensated weekly rest periods.

Summary of EU Rules

The following table summarizes the EU rules applicable to both national and international goods vehicle operations:

- Maximum daily driving: 9 hours
  10 hours on 2 days in week
- Maximum weekly driving: 56 hours
- Maximum fortnightly driving: 90 hours
- Maximum driving before a break: 4½ hours
- Minimum breaks after driving: 45 minutes or one break of at least 15 minutes and one of at least 30 minutes each to equal 45 minutes
- Minimum daily rest (normally):   11 hours
- Reduced daily rest: 9 hours on up to 3 days per week between any two weekly rest periods

- Split daily rest:

  A regular daily rest period may be split into two periods – the first at least 3 hours, the other at least 9 hours. This gives a minimum total rest of 12 hours

- Minimum weekly rest (normally): 45 hours once each fixed week

- Reduced weekly rest:

  24 hours (any reduction must be made up *en bloc* by the end of the third following week)

- Rest on ferries/trains:

  Normal daily rest (11 hours) may be interrupted not more than twice:
  – no more than 1 hour between parts
  – drivers must have access to a bunk or couchette for both parts of rest

Emergencies

It is permitted for the driver to depart from the EU rules as specified above to the extent necessary to enable him to reach a suitable stopping place when emergencies arise where he needs to ensure the safety of persons, the vehicle or its load, providing road safety is not jeopardized. The nature of and reasons for departing from the rules in these circumstances must be shown on the tachograph chart or on a printout from a digital tachograph. The driver should note the reasons when he reaches a suitable stopping place.

Prohibition on Certain Payments

The EU rules prohibit any payment to wage-earning drivers in the form of bonuses or wage supplements related to distances travelled and/or the amount of goods carried unless such payments do not endanger road safety.

British Domestic Rules

The current British drivers' hours rules contained in the 1968 Transport Act (as amended) came into effect on 29 September 1986. They apply to goods vehicle drivers whose activities are outside the scope of the EU requirements as described above (ie which are specified as exempt from the EU rules) and comprise only limits on daily driving and daily duty.

NB: Detailed provisions which previously applied in regard to daily and weekly duty, daily spreadover and daily and weekly rest period limits were completely abolished when these rules changes were introduced.

It is important to emphasize that drivers who are exempt from the EU rules, either because their vehicle does not exceed 3.5 tonnes permissible maximum weight or because the activity in which they are engaged falls within the scope of the EU exemptions list (see pp 92–94), must observe the British domestic rules.

NB: It should be noted that:

- *Although no records of driving or working times are required to be kept, drivers of light goods vehicles (ie not exceeding 3.5 tonnes permissible maximum weight) must still conform to the legal limits on maximum daily driving and maximum daily duty.*

- *If a trailer is attached to a vehicle not exceeding 3.5 tonnes permissible maximum weight (which itself is exempt from the EU rules on account of its weight) thereby taking the combined weight to over 3.5 tonnes then the EU rules must be followed as described in the foregoing text (unless it is exempt for other reasons, namely the nature of the operations on which it is engaged) and a tachograph must be fitted to the vehicle and used by the driver for record-keeping purposes (see Chapter 5).*

Exemptions and Concessions

The British domestic rules apply to drivers of all goods vehicles which are exempt from the EU regulations as described earlier but with the following further exceptions which are totally exempt from all hours rules control:

- the armed forces;
- police and fire brigade services;
- driving off the public road system;
- driving for purely private purposes (ie not in connection with any trade or business).

The British domestic rules do not apply:

- to a driver who on any day does not drive a relevant vehicle; or
- to a driver who on each day of the week does not drive a vehicle within the rules for more than 4 hours (note: this exemption *does not* apply to a driver whose activities fall within scope of the EU rules).

Driving and Duty Definitions

For the purposes of the British domestic rules:

- Driving means time spent behind the wheel actually driving a goods vehicle and the specified maximum limit applies to such time spent driving on public roads. Driving on off-road sites and premises such as quarries, civil engineering and building sites and on agricultural and forestry land is counted as duty time, not driving time.

- Duty time is the time a driver spends working for his employer and includes any work undertaken including the driving of private motor cars, for example, and non-driving work which is not driving time for the purposes of the regulations. The daily duty limit does not apply on any day when a driver does not drive a goods vehicle.

Summary of British Domestic Rules

- Maximum daily driving: 10 hours
- Maximum daily duty: 11 hours
- Continuous duty: no specified limit
- Daily spreadover: no specified limit
- Weekly duty: no specified limit
- Breaks during day: no requirement specified
- Daily rest: no specified requirement (but obviously a minimum of 13 hours so as not to exceed the daily 11-hour duty limit)
- Weekly rest: no specified requirement

Emergencies

The daily driving and duty limits specified above may be suspended when an emergency situation arises. This is defined as an event requiring immediate action to avoid danger to life or health of one or more individuals or animals, serious interruption in the maintenance of essential public services for the supply of gas, water, electricity, drainage, or of telecommunications and postal services, or in the use of roads, railways, ports or airports, or damage to property. Details of the emergency should be entered by the driver on his record sheet when the limits are exceeded.

Light Vehicle Driving

As explained above, drivers of light goods vehicles not exceeding 3.5 tonnes permissible maximum weight – as with drivers of other goods vehicles which fall within scope of these rules – must observe the daily limits on driving (10 hours) and duty (11 hours). However, only the 10-hour daily driving limit applies when such vehicles are used:

- by doctors, dentists, nurses, midwives or vets;
- for any service of inspection, cleaning, maintenance, repair, installation or fitting;
- by a commercial traveller, and carrying only goods used for soliciting orders;
- by an employee of the AA, the RAC or the RSAC;
- for the business of cinematography or of radio or television broadcasting.

Mixed EU and British Driving

It is possible that a goods vehicle driver may be engaged in transport operations which come within scope of both the EU drivers' hours rules and the British domestic hours rules on the same day or within the same week. When such a situation arises he may conform strictly to the EU rules throughout the whole of the driving/working period or he may take advantage of the more liberal British domestic rules where appropriate. If he decides on this course of action and thereby combines both British and EU rules he must beware of the following points:

- time spent driving under the EU rules cannot count as an off-duty period for the British rules;
- time spent driving or on duty under the British rules cannot count as a break or rest period under the EU rules;
- driving under the EU rules counts towards the driving and duty limits for the British rules;
- if any EU rules driving is done in a week the driver must observe the EU daily and weekly rest period requirements for the whole of that week.

AETR Rules

Drivers on journeys to certain non-EU countries that have signed up to the European Agreement Concerning the Work of Crews of Vehicles Engaged in International Road Transport 1971 – better known as AETR (see following list), are required to observe the hours rules laid down in the AETR Regulations.

AETR Countries
Albania
Andorra
Armenia
Azerbaijan
Belarus
Bosnia and Herzegovina
Croatia
Kazakhstan
Liechtenstein
Macedonia
Moldova
Monaco
Montenegro
Russia
San Marino
Serbia
Switzerland
Turkey
Turkmenistan
Ukraine
Uzbekistan

When undertaking journeys to AETR signatory countries EU drivers must follow the AETR rules for the whole journey, including any EU countries passed through. Importantly, since September 2010, the AETR rules have been amended to align with the (EC) Drivers' Hours Regulations 561/2006 and also recognize the digital tachograph.

Working Time

Among all the strict regulation that the road transport industry has had to contend with in recent years, there is no doubt that the imposition of the EU's Road Transport Directive (Directive 2002/15/EC – the RTD), which took effect from 4 April 2005, has had a significant impact on transport operators and LGV drivers alike.

The first step in this particular legislative process started with the European Council Directive 93/104/EC of November 1993 commonly referred to as the working time directive (WTD). This Directive introduced a number of provisions to control working time for most employees in the interest of improving work environments and ensuring better protection for workers by limiting maximum weekly working hours, setting minimum daily and weekly rest periods and minimum in-work breaks, setting minimum annual holidays and requiring regular health checks for night workers. In particular, the Directive specified a maximum 48-hour working week and limited night working in any 24-hour period. These requirements are enforced in the UK by our own domestic working time regulations (see below).

However, while this Directive originally excluded the transport sector, further proposals originally published in 1997 were intended to bring road haulage (and other previously excepted worker categories) into the scope of the working time principles. From 1 August 2003 came the Horizontal Amending Directive (Directive 2000/34/EC – abbreviated to HAD), which amended the original WTD by setting rules for those employment sectors that were expressly excluded from the WTD, such as non-mobile transport workers and mobile workers not covered by the EU drivers' hours rules (for example, light vehicle drivers).

These two EU Directives are given the force of law in Great Britain by a number of regulations as follows:

- the Working Time Regulations 1998 (SI 1998 No. 1833);
- the Working Time Regulations 1999 (SI 1999 No. 3372) (amending regulations);
- the Working Time (Amendment) Regulations 2001 (SI 2001 No. 3256) (dealing mainly with annual leave);
- the Working Time (Amendment) Regulations 2002 (SI 2002 No. 3128) (dealing mainly with provisions regarding young people at work);
- the Working Time (Amendment) Regulation 2003 (SI 2003 No. 1684) (implementing the provisions of the HAD).

In the following section, the working times rules are explained in order of their relevance to the road transport industry; namely, first the RTD that applies to LGV drivers, second the HAD that applies to LGV drivers and finally the WTD itself, which is applicable to most other workers.

The Road Transport Directive (RTD)

LGV drivers who fall within scope of the drivers' hours law contained in EU Regulation 561/2006/EC, namely most drivers of goods vehicles exceeding 3.5 tonnes gross weight, are covered by the RTD (Directive 2002/15/EC), which deals specifically with working time for those persons performing mobile transport activities within the scope of the EU drivers' hours rules (mainly LGV drivers), but with the exception of self-employed mobile workers.

This Directive was implemented in the UK from 4 April 2005, following publication of Statutory Instrument SI 2005 No 639.

NB: It is important to note that the RTD does not replace the present EU drivers' hours rules. Instead, it supplements both the current Regulation and the AETR Agreement, so drivers who fall within the scope of these regulations when driving a goods vehicle must also take note of and comply with the provisions of the RTD.

Definitions

It is useful to consider the definitions for certain terms used and the specific provisions set out in the RTD as follows.

Mobile Transport Activities

Any activity carried out by workers in the course of their employment within a road transport operation.

Mobile Worker

Any worker who forms part of the travelling staff of an undertaking that operates goods or passenger transport for hire or reward or on its own account – obviously this means drivers, but also includes other crew members, trainees and apprentices.

Self-Employed Drivers

These are similarly categorized as mobile workers (ie driving in a road transport operation) except that such workers are not tied to an employer by an employment contract (see below).

Working Time

This is time spent at work and at the employer's disposal carrying out his activities or duties. This includes travelling as part of job- and work-related training, but not commuting between home and work, or rest breaks where no work is done, or 'on-call' time when at home.

Periods of Availability

These periods are not working time and do not count as such, nor are they breaks or daily or weekly rest periods. They could include waiting time (for example, to load or unload or while waiting for a ferry) if the driver is free to dispose of his time during that period of waiting, but not, for example, if he has to remain with his vehicle in a queue – this would be working time. The key to this is whether the waiting period could have been foreseen in advance: if it could, it counts as non-working time; if it could not be foreseen, it is working time.

Working Week

The working week is 48 hours work (with a maximum of 60 hours in a week) averaged over a 4-month (ie 17-week) reference period, which may be extended by agreement to 6 months. The total working time is calculated excluding breaks during the working day and any periods of availability (see above). It should be noted that there is NO opt-out from the working time limits under this Directive as there is with the other Directives (ie the WTD and the HAD).

Breaks

Breaks taken during the working period must amount to a minimum of 30 minutes if working between 6 and 9 hours; or 45 minutes if working over 9 hours. Breaks should be of at least 15 minutes duration.

Night Work

This is defined as a 4-hour period between midnight and 4.00 am. Night working will be limited to 10 hours in any 24-hour period although a collective or workforce agreement will allow this to be extended.

NB: This night work definition should not be confused with the night work definition contained in either the HAD or the WTD.

Holidays

Holidays are to comprise a minimum of 5.6 weeks (ie 28 days). It is to be an important provision of new regulations that mobile workers must tell their employer, in writing, of any time they spend working for other employers if they are engaged in road transport activities. Driving and other activities must be declared when working for employers involved in road transport.

Record Keeping

Irrespective of which of the three Directives (the WTD, HAD or RTD) applies in any particular work situation, employers must keep detailed records of employee working time and provide copies of such records to their employees when asked for them. There is no officially prescribed system for record keeping or special format for individual records, but whatever system is used the records must be kept for two years and be made available to VOSA enforcement officers on request.

Health Assessments

Employers will be required to provide free health assessments for night workers. Employers have a duty to determine exactly who is a night worker for this purpose and provide the health assessment accordingly. The assessment should include a questionnaire devised and monitored by a qualified health professional and, where necessary, backed up by a medical examination.

Enforcement

The RTD regulations will be enforced mainly by VOSA, most likely when they are checking compliance with the EU drivers' hours and tachograph rules, or as a result of complaints made to them.

Self-Employed Workers

The original intention of the directive was that it should apply to self-employed drivers from 23 March 2009. However, despite discussions on implementing this aspect of the directive no changes have been made. At the time of writing, self-employed drivers remain excluded from the legislation.

The Horizontal Amending Directive (HAD)

The WTD referred to above originally excluded the transport sector, but publication of an amending Directive, 2000134/EC (the so-called Horizontal Amending Directive – HAD), which took effect from 1 August 2003, brought all employed road transport personnel, including office-based staff, referred to collectively as 'non-mobile workers', and other previously excepted employment categories, into line.

This Directive, which has applied to all employed road transport personnel (ie apart from those subject to the EU drivers' hours law) since 1 August 2003 as mentioned above, requires all relevant transport employees to comply with the provisions set out below. Drivers will also remain subject to the EU drivers' hours rules set out in Regulation 3820185/EEC.

Four particular provisions of the HAD apply to drivers who fall outside the scope of the Road Transport Directive – ie drivers of smaller vehicles and drivers of other vehicles that are exempt from the EU drivers' hours rules. These are:

- the 48-hour average working week;
- the requirement to have four weeks' paid annual leave;
- regular health checks for night workers;
- the need for 'adequate rest'.

Under these regulations, workers are allowed to opt out of the 48-hour average working week. However, mobile workers covered by the RTD are only entitled to the annual leave and health checks provisions (see above).

The Working Time Directive (WTD) for Non-mobile Workers

The Working Time Directive (Directive 93/1104/EC) of November 1993, commonly referred to as the Working Time Directive (WTD), introduced a number of provisions to control working time for employees, including the concept of a maximum 48-hour working week and shift working restrictions under which night workers may not work more than a specified average number of working hours in any 24-hour period. This Directive specifically excluded the transport sector (eg road, rail, sea, air, inland waterway, etc), which is now covered by other, subsequently published Directives, namely the RTD and HAD described above.

Under the WTD provisions:

- Employers are required to limit average weekly working time to a maximum of 48 hours, including overtime, calculated over successive periods of 17 weeks (ie 4 months), or for the period of employment where this is less than 17 weeks.

- The opt-out clause which would have allowed non-mobile workers to exceed the average 48-hour working week has now been withdrawn by the European Parliament.

- Employers are required to limit night working to no more than 8 hours in 24 hours taken as an average over a 17-week reference period (see sections above regarding the RTD and HAD on this topic). For night workers (ie those who work for at least 3 hours at night) whose work involves special hazards or heavy physical or mental strain, the limit is a straight 8 hours in 24 hours with no averaging out.

- Employers are required to provide free health assessments for night workers, and the opportunity for employees to transfer to day work if their health is affected by night working.

- Employers are required to allow workers a daily rest period of at least 11 consecutive hours in each 24-hour period and an uninterrupted rest break of at least 20 minutes when their daily work exceeds 6 hours.

- Employers are required to allow workers a weekly rest period of not less than 24 hours in each 7 days.

- Employers are required to allow workers who have been employed continuously for 13 weeks to have at least 4 weeks' paid annual leave, which may not be exchanged for payment in lieu except where it occurs on termination of the employment.

- Employers are required to keep records of workers' hours of work that are adequate to show that the legal requirements are complied with, and retain these records for at least two years from the date on which they were made.

The WTD regulations set more restrictive standards for young workers and exempt certain special classes of worker such as Crown servants, the police, trainees and agricultural workers.

Unfair Dismissal

The Employment Rights Act 1996 is amended by the addition of new provisions to make it unfair to dismiss an employee for refusing to comply with a requirement contrary to the working time regulations, or to forgo his rights.

The National Minimum Wage

The national minimum wage provisions introduced by the National Minimum Wage Regulations 1999 under the National Minimum Wage Act 1998, which came into force in the UK on 1 April 1999, have been further amended by the National Minimum Wage Regulations 1999 (Amendment) Regulations 2008. These require that workers (other than self-employed persons) aged 21 years or over must be paid at least £6.08 per hour, and workers aged from 18 to 20 years at least £4.98 per hour. The development rate for 16–17-year-olds is £3.68 per hour. The minimum wage applies to most workers in the UK, including agency workers (eg agency drivers), part-time and casual workers and those paid on a commission basis.

NB: *These rates were increased from 1 October 2010.*

Assessing Minimum Pay

For the purposes of assessing minimum pay, payments to employees comprising bonuses, incentives and performance-related awards count as part of the pay package, but other allowances not consolidated into an employee's pay are not counted. Similarly, overtime payments and shift payments do not count. Benefits in kind, such as the provision of overnight subsistence, meals, uniforms and workwear allowances, are also excluded. Gross pay, with all deductions and reductions subtracted, should be divided by the number of hours worked to determine whether the resulting hourly pay rate at least matches, if not exceeds, the national minima stated above.

Types of Work

The work hours for which an employer has to pay are calculated according to the type of work employees are engaged upon. Mainly this is as follows:

- time work, where an employee is paid for working a set number of hours or a set period of time;
- salaried work, where an employee has a contract to work a set number of basic hours annually in return for an annual salary paid in equal instalments;
- unmeasured work, where employees are paid to do specific tasks (eg driving), but are not set specific hours for the work.

NB: *In this case the employer must agree with the employee (in writing) a daily average of hours to be spent carrying out the assigned tasks. The employer must be able to show that the number of hours agreed is realistic.*

Enforcement and Penalties

Enforcement of the minimum wage provisions is by HM Revenue & Customs and by the employees themselves, who have a right to complain if they are not being paid the national minimum wage.

Employers obviously need to keep accurate records of the hours worked and hourly rates paid to employees in case such information is called into question later – for a minimum of three years. An employee (or any other qualifying worker) may make a written request for access to his own records, and this must be allowed within 14 days unless extended by agreement. Should a dispute arise, the burden of proof is on the employer to show that the national minimum wage has been paid, not on the employee to prove that it has not.

Refusal to pay the national minimum wage is a criminal offence carrying a maximum fine of up to £5,000 on conviction. Dismissal of an employee who becomes eligible for the national minimum wage or for a higher rate of pay will constitute unfair dismissal, with no qualifying period to be served by workers to secure protection against this form of unfair dismissal.

Self-Employment

The road haulage industry is renowned for the number of self-employed workers, especially owner-driver lorry operators. However, not all such so-called self-employed persons are genuinely self-employed in terms that meet legal requirements of HMRC in regard to payment of tax and National Insurance contributions.

To satisfy HMRC a self-employed person needs to meet a series of so-called 'tests' under which the self-employed person:

- decides, broadly, how and when specified work is to be carried out, the actual hours he works and when breaks and holidays are taken, and is not subject to the disciplinary provisions of an employer;
- provides his own tools and equipment and is free to send another person (or sub-contractor) in his place to carry out work where necessary;
- has no entitlement to payment for public or annual holidays or sickness; is not included in an employer's pension scheme, and has no rights to claim redundancy payments, unfair dismissal or any entitlement to unemployment benefit if his services are no longer required;
- takes financial risk with the aim of making a profit, is responsible for paying his own income tax and national insurance contributions, and charges for the services provided by submitting an invoice;
- is free to work for other employers as required if he so wishes (a self-employed person who works for only one employer is likely to be considered to be an employee of that employer).

A number of instances have arisen in transport where the self-employed status of owner-drivers has been questioned by HMRC (mainly because they work for only one firm). In such cases, where HMRC has ruled that owner-driver agreements are merely employment contracts, the employer becomes liable for back tax and NI contributions for its sub-contractors. This is especially so where the owner-driver works under the 'O' licence of the employing company – and if he is genuinely self-employed, then, in any event, this practice is illegal under 'O' licensing legislation.

Tax Relief on Driver Allowances

Sleeper Cab Allowances

The amount paid to drivers for overnight subsistence varies considerably from area to area – the national general figure is currently £32.20 (2011 figure). HM Revenue & Customs has agreed that LGV drivers can be paid night-out allowances on a tax-free basis amounting to £30.75 per night where the vehicle does not have a sleeper cab, reducing to £23.06 per night where a sleeper cab is available. Payment of such amounts is subject to the employer being satisfied that:

- the individual did necessarily spend the night away from his home and normal place of work and that he used a sleeper cab;
- the employee necessarily incurred extra expense in doing so; and
- the amounts paid are no more than reasonable reimbursement of the average allowable expenses of the driver (ie for payment of an evening meal, breakfast, washing facilities and the upkeep of bedding).

Owner-drivers are dealt with differently for tax purposes and may NOT claim such night-out allowances against their tax liability.

There have been recent reports about tax inspectors querying payment of night-out allowances where drivers have stayed only a few miles from base. Currently the agreement with HM Revenue & Customs for night-out payments is as stated above and this applies for nights-out without receipts, except where alternative figures have been agreed, in which case an annual increase of 9.3 per cent on the previously agreed figure is acceptable. These payments should only be made where the employee does actually spend the night away and incurs extra expense. If he uses the bunk in a sleeper cab the allowable amount is only that required to meet the expenses he incurs, not the full night-out allowance.

HM Revenue & Customs may refuse claims for tax-free payments of night-out allowances above the general limit. Employers who have paid in excess of this amount (or a locally agreed rate) without deduction of tax may find themselves liable to meet the tax due on the additional amounts paid, except where it can be proved that the expense was genuinely incurred (by production of a valid receipt); alternatively they should include it as part of the wages within PAYE.

Charts Retained for Tax Purposes

Where tachograph charts are used to justify payment of night-out and other subsistence expenses to drivers these become part of the tax record and as such must be retained for six years instead of the normal one year.

Meal Expenses

Where LGV drivers receive from their employers a contribution towards midday meal expenses either by the issue of meal vouchers or by means of a cash payment, these contributions may be treated as not taxable provided they:

- are of a reasonable amount only (ie not exceeding £2.00 per day); and
- are paid to long-distance drivers only whose duties oblige them to take meals away from home and their normal place of employment, but not to drivers who have fixed or local routes.

Any amount paid in excess of £2.00 per day must be subject to income tax deduction unless acceptable evidence of the expenditure is provided to the employer or where HM Revenue & Customs has given dispensation.

Personal Incidental Expenses

Employee drivers may be paid additional amounts by way of 'personal incidental expenses' in relation to genuine expenditure (eg newspapers, laundry and calls home) during a qualifying absence (ie when working away from home) up to a tax-free limit, without any tax consequences for the employee – or NI – for the employer up to the value of £5 per day if in the UK, or £10 per day outside the UK. (*Source: Road Haulage Association website:* **www.rha.net/public/adviceandinfo/subsistence.shtml**).

Tax Relief for International Drivers

International LGV drivers who spend less than 91 days in the UK during a tax year (ie from 6 April to 5 April annually) can claim 'non-resident' status and qualify for their wages to be paid tax-free. Previously, the limit was less than 60 days but this was increased to 91 days by the March 1998 Budget.

Goods Vehicle Drivers' Records

Drivers of goods vehicles and other vehicles used for the carriage of goods (eg off-road vehicles and so-called 4 × 4s) over 3.5 tonnes gross weight must keep records of the time they spend driving such vehicles and their working times. Most drivers are also required to record breaks taken during driving periods and their daily and weekly rest periods. Where vehicles fall within the scope of the EU drivers' hours law as described in Chapter 3 (ie unless they are specifically exempt as shown in the relevant exemptions list) the record-keeping requirement is based on the mandatory use of tachographs as described in Chapter 5.

Where a vehicle is outside the scope of the EU rules then the British domestic (ie 1968 Transport Act – as amended) driving hours rules apply (see Chapter 3) and the driver of such a vehicle is required to keep written records by means of a 'log-book' system.

To summarize the main record-keeping alternatives, these are as follows:

- Goods vehicles not exceeding 3.5 tonnes permissible maximum weight – NO RECORDS.
- Goods vehicles over 3.5 tonnes permissible maximum weight (including the weight of any trailer drawn) operating within EU rules – TACHOGRAPH RECORDS.
- Goods vehicles over 3.5 tonnes permissible maximum weight exempt from EU rules – WRITTEN 'LOG-BOOK' RECORDS (but subject to further exemption in certain cases).
- Goods vehicles over 3.5 tonnes permissible maximum weight exempt from both EU and British domestic rules (eg military vehicles) – NO RECORDS.

This chapter describes the record-keeping requirements applying to drivers falling within the third item above, namely those operating under the British domestic rules, who must keep written 'log-book' records.

Exemptions from Record Keeping

Written records do not have to be kept in the following cases:

- by drivers of vehicles which are exempt from 'O' licensing, except that the exemption does not apply to drivers of Crown vehicles which would have needed an 'O' licence if the vehicle had not been Crown property;
- by drivers of goods vehicles on any day when they drive for four hours or less and within 50 kilometres of the vehicle's base (NB this exemption is applicable only in the case of domestic operations – it does not apply to tachograph use – see pp 100–02);
- by drivers voluntarily using an EU tachograph for record-keeping purposes which has been calibrated and sealed at a DETR-approved tachograph centre.

Record-Keeping System

Prior to 29 September 1986, when the EU rules and British domestic hours rules last changed, the written record-keeping requirement related to the use of the EC diagrammatic-type International Control Book (ICB). From this date there was a transitional arrangement for phasing out the use of this record book and the introduction of a new style of simplified British record which relates specifically to the British domestic driving hours rules. Regulations brought the 'simplified' record book into use from 2 November 1987, with the old-type diagrammatic control book ceasing to have any further legal standing from that date.

Record Books

Ready-printed record books can be purchased 'off the shelf' or firms can have their own version pre-printed with their own name and logo if desired. In the latter case it is important that the specific requirements of the regulations are observed in both the format and the printing of the book.

The book must be a standard A6 format (105 mm × 148 mm) or it may be larger if preferred. It must comprise a front sheet on which is entered relevant information, a set of instructions for the use of the book, and a number of individual weekly record sheets with facilities for completing these in duplicate (ie with carbon paper or carbonless copy paper) and for the duplicate sheet to be detached for return to the employer when completed.

There is no legal requirement for the numbering of record books or for their issue against an entry in a register of record book issues as previously required.

Weekly record sheets in the book must follow the format set out in the regulations with appropriate spaces for entries to be made under the following headings:

- driver's name;
- period covered by sheet week commencing . . . week ending . . .;
- registration number of vehicle(s);

- place where vehicle(s) based;
- time of going on duty;
- time of going off duty;
- time spent driving;
- time spent on duty;
- signature of driver;
- certification by employer (ie signature and position held).

Issue and Return of Record Books

Employers must issue their employee drivers with record books when they are required to drive vehicles to which the British domestic driving hours regulations apply and where records must be kept. Before issuing the book, the employer must complete the front cover to show the firm's name, address and telephone number, preferably with a rubber stamp if he has one.

When a record book is issued to the driver he should complete the front cover with his surname, first name(s), date of birth and home address and the date he first used the book. When the book is completed he should also enter the date of the last entry (ie date of last use). There is space to record the name and address of a second employer.

Books issued by an employer to an employee-driver must be returned to that employer when complete (subject to the requirement for the driver to retain it for two weeks after use) or when the employee leaves that employment. He must not take it with him to his new employer. Any unused weekly sheets and all duplicates must be included when the book is returned.

Two Employers

Where a driver has two employers who employ him to drive goods vehicles to which the British domestic hours rules apply, the first employer must issue the record book as described (completed weekly record sheets and completed record books must be returned to this employer), and the second employer must write or stamp his firm's name and address on the front cover of the record book with a statement that the holder is also a driver in his employment. When the driver does part-time driving work for another employer he must disclose to each employer, if requested, details of his working and driving times with the other employer. Similarly, when a driver changes to a new employer the former employer must give the new employer details of the driver's previous driving and working times if requested.

Record Book Entries

The driver must make entries on the weekly sheet for each day on which a record is required (instructions on the correct use of the book are printed inside the cover). Care must be taken to ensure that an exact duplicate of the entry is made simultaneously (ie two separately written repeat entries are *not* acceptable even if no carbon paper is available). When completing a daily sheet he must enter all the required details under each of the headings. If he changes vehicles during the day he must write in the registration number for each vehicle. He must then sign the sheet before returning it to his employer.

Completion of the record is straightforward, the driver having to enter the vehicle registration number, the time of coming on duty, and at the end of the day the time at which he went off-duty, and he must sign the sheet. He may enter any remarks concerning his entries, or point out corrections which should be made, in the appropriate box at the foot of the record. The employer may also use this space if required for making comments regarding the record. This space may also be used for recording the name of a second driver.

Corrections

Entries in the record book must be in ink or made by a ballpoint pen and there must be no erasures, corrections or additions. Mistakes may only be corrected by writing an explanation or showing the correct information in the remarks space. Sheets must not be mutilated or destroyed.

Return and Signing of Record Sheets

On completion of the weekly sheet, and after it has been signed by the driver, the duplicate copy must be detached from the book and handed to the employer within seven days of the date of the last entry on the sheet, and then within a further seven days the employer must have examined and signed the duplicate sheet. However, if in either case it is not reasonably practicable to do so within this time, these actions must be carried out as soon as it is possible to do so.

Retention and Production of Record Books

The driver should carry his record book with him at all times when working and must produce it for inspection at the request of an authorized examiner. The book should be shown to the employer at the end of every week or as soon as possible after the week so he can examine and countersign the entries. Following completion of the book the driver must continue to keep it with him for a further two weeks (available for inspection by the enforcement authorities) before returning it to his employer.

Completed record books must be retained by the employer, also available for inspection by the enforcement authorities, for not less than 12 months.

Record Sheets for Germany

It has been reported that the German authorities require, under their own domestic legislation, foreign drivers of goods vehicles of between 2.8 tonnes and 3.5 tonnes gross weight (ie which are exempt from record keeping by means of the tachograph) entering the country to carry and complete AETR-type log books. These are the old-type log books long since abolished in the UK and the rest of Europe. Failure to carry such a log book could result in delays and penalties.

FIGURE 4.1 Simplified record sheet for British domestic transport operations

WEEKLY RECORD SHEETS

WEEKLY SHEETS

DRIVER'S NAME

2. PERIOD COVERED BY SHEET
WEEK COMMENCING (DATE) ....
TO WEEK ENDING (DATE) ....

DAY ON WHICH DUTY COMMENCED	REGISTRATION NO. OF VEHICLE(S) 3.	PLACE WHERE VEHICLE(S) BASED 4.	TIME OF GOING ON DUTY 5.	TIME OF GOING OFF DUTY 6.	TIME SPENT DRIVING 7.	TIME SPENT ON DUTY 8.	SIGNATURE OF DRIVER 9.
MONDAY							
TUESDAY							
WEDNESDAY							
THURSDAY							
FRIDAY							
SATURDAY							
SUNDAY							

10. CERTIFICATION BY EMPLOYER

I HAVE EXAMINED THE ENTRIES IN THIS SHEET
SIGNATURE ....
POSITION HELD ....

Tachographs – Fitment and Use Requirements

Tachograph instruments installed in goods and passenger vehicles provide a means of recording time and the speed and distance travelled by the vehicle. This record enables drivers' working activities and driving practices to be monitored to ensure that legal requirements – especially observance of the drivers' hours rules – have been met.

There are now two very distinctly different and separate tachograph recording systems legislated for use both in the UK and across the rest of the EU. First is the analogue system which has been in existence for many years (originating as the so-called hated 'spy in the cab'), but now we have a digital system (commonly referred to as the 'digi-tach') which came into force from May 2006. These two systems run in parallel; drivers of older vehicles having to use the former system and those driving post-May 2006 registered over 3.5 tonne gross weight vehicles using the latter system. Some drivers, however, encounter both older and newer vehicles in their work and thus have to contend with both systems – sometimes changing as often as daily when swapping from one vehicle to another, and producing, as a consequence, both round, flat wax-coated charts which must be kept flat to avoid damage, and tally-roll printouts which instantly roll up and are very difficult to keep flat.

'D' Day for Digital Tachographs

Regulation 561/2006/EC, amending Regulations 3281/85/EEC and 2135/98/EC, was published on 15 March 2006, with its various provisions relating to digital tachographs and the drivers' hours law effective from 1 May 2006 and 11 April 2007 respectively. The drivers' hours law issues contained in this regulation (which replaces the repealed Regulation 3820/85/EEC) are dealt with in Chapter 3.

In this chapter we cover both the pre-existing tachograph provisions relating to analogue instruments as set out in Regulation 3821/85/EEC and digital instruments, the technical provisions for which are described fully in Annex 1B of Regulation 3821/85/EEC and the operational provisions for which are defined in Regulation 561/2006/EC.

It is important to note that despite the introduction of the digital tachograph from May 2006 in all new goods vehicles over 3.5 tonnes gross weight (apart from those specifically exempt under the legislation), existing analogue tachographs fitted to goods vehicles will remain valid and effective until such time as the vehicle reaches the end of its useful life or the analogue tachograph instrument itself ceases to function. In the latter case, where the vehicle exceeds 12 tonnes maximum weight, the replacement tachograph fitted must be of the digital type. On this basis, it is clear that analogue (or chart-type) tachographs will continue in use for many years to come, giving both fleet operators and their drivers the headache of dealing with a dual system, both of which will have to be operated correctly within the law and adequately integrated to provide a full statutory record of driver activities as required by the European legislation.

A driver who has failed to obtain a digital 'smart card' cannot legally drive a vehicle fitted with a digital tachgraph.

Legal Requirements for Existing Analogue Tachographs

The fitment of tachographs and their use in relevant vehicles (ie those operating within the scope of the EU driving hours rules – see Chapter 3) for record-keeping purposes originally became a legal requirement in the United Kingdom on 31 December 1981. EU regulations (3821/85/EEC) which came into effect on 29 September 1986 amended some of the original requirements.

The legislation requires the fitment and use of tachographs in most goods vehicles and other vehicles used for the carriage of goods over 3.5 tonnes permissible maximum weight with certain EU-approved exemptions as listed in the following section of this chapter. Since the list of exemptions is limited, many categories of goods vehicle which may be thought to be exempt are not so.

It should be stressed that unless a vehicle is used for private purposes only or is specifically exempted as shown by the exemption list, the law applies to:

- any goods vehicle over 3.5 tonnes gvw, or a combination of a goods vehicle and goods-carrying trailer which together exceed 3.5 tonnes permissible maximum weight; and

- any other vehicle (such as off-road vehicles and so-called 4 × 4s) used for the carriage of goods which when towing a trailer has a combined permissible maximum weight exceeding 3.5 tonnes.

In particular, it should be noted that there is no exemption for short-distance operations, infrequent-use vehicles or occasional driving. Once a relevant vehicle is on the highway the law applies in full.

This means that a tachograph instrument must be installed in the vehicle and that whosoever drives it must keep a tachograph record and observe the EU drivers' hours law in full both for the day on which the driving takes place and for the week in which that day falls. It should also be noted that vehicles which are exempt from the tachograph rules are not necessarily exempt from record-keeping requirements (for example, those operating under the British domestic hours rules). See Chapter 4 for details of activities where written records must be kept.

Under the EU regulations a number of specific basic requirements relating to tachograph use must be met as follows:

- The tachograph instrument must conform to the technical specification laid down in the EU regulations (561/2006/EC – see pp 136–39).

- The instrument must be calibrated and officially sealed at an approved calibration centre to ensure that accurate (ie legally acceptable) records are made (see pp 126–29).

- The instrument must be used in accordance with the regulations, with individual responsibilities being observed by both employer and driver.

- Electronic tachographs must be capable of detecting interruptions in the power supply.

- Driving time must be recorded automatically.

- Facilities must be provided for the removal and subsequent refitting, by an approved centre, of recording equipment seals to enable speed limiters to be fitted.

- Cables connecting electronic tachographs to the transmitter (ie sender unit) must be protected by a continuous steel sheath (ie a tamper-proof armoured cable).

Exemptions

There is no requirement for the fitment and use of tachographs in vehicles in the following list or in vehicles used in connection with the particular transport operations specified in the exemption list.

Changes in regulations (ie the Community Drivers' Hours and Recording Equipment (Amendment) Regulations 1998 – effective from 24 August 1998) brought within the scope of the tachograph rules vehicles which are not in themselves considered to be goods vehicles (eg four-wheel-drive off-road vehicles) and therefore were previously exempt from the rules. However, when such vehicles are drawing a trailer for the carriage of goods for commercial purposes, and the combined weight of the towing vehicle and trailer exceeds 3.5 tonnes, the fitment and use of tachographs as described in this chapter is necessary and the driver must observe the EU drivers' hours law as set out in Chapter 3.

National and International Exemptions

1 Vehicles not exceeding 3.5 tonnes gross weight including the weight of any trailer drawn.

2 Passenger vehicles constructed to carry not more than nine persons including driver.

3 Vehicles on regular passenger services on routes not exceeding 50 kilometres.

4 Vehicles with legal maximum speed not exceeding 40 kph (approx 25 mph).

5 Vehicles used by the armed services, civil defence, fire services, forces responsible for maintaining public order (ie police).

6 Vehicles used in connection with sewerage; flood protection; water, gas and electricity services; highway maintenance and control; refuse collection and disposal; telephone and telegraph services; carriage of postal articles; radio and television broadcasting; detection of radio or television transmitters or receivers.

NB: Item 4 above includes certain works trucks and industrial tractors which have a statutory 30 kph speed limit imposed upon them but this does not include forklift trucks, which may come within the scope of the rules.

NB: Under a European Court ruling, British Gas must fit tachographs to vehicles it uses for the delivery of gas appliances, gas cylinders and meters to ensure fair competition with private transport operators. The point at issue, and contended by British Gas, was that its vehicles engaged on such deliveries were being used in connection with gas services.

Also: Vehicles used for private waste collection (ie not on behalf of local authorities) on journeys exceeding a 50 km radius from the place where they are normally based must be fitted with a fully calibrated tachograph, following a European Court of Justice ruling.

7 Vehicles used in emergencies or rescue operations, including humanitarian aid.

8 Specialized vehicles used for medical purposes.

9 Vehicles transporting circus and funfair equipment.

10 Specialized breakdown vehicles operating within 100 km of their base.

11 Vehicles undergoing road tests for technical development, repair or maintenance purposes, and new or rebuilt vehicles which have not yet been put into service.

12 Vehicles used for non-commercial carriage of goods for personal use (ie private use).

13 Vehicles used for milk containers or milk products intended for animal feed.

Further Derogations in National Operations only

14 Vehicles with between 10 and 17 seats used exclusively for the non-commercial carriage of passengers.

15 Vehicles used by public authorities to provide public services which are not in competition with professional road hauliers.

16 Vehicles used by agricultural, horticultural, forestry or fishery* undertakings, for carrying goods within a 100 km radius of the place where the vehicle is normally based, including local administrative areas the centres of which are situated within that radius.

*NB: To gain this exemption the vehicle must be used to carry live fish or to carry a catch of fish which has not been subjected to any process or treatment (other than freezing) from the place of landing to a place where it is to be processed or treated.

17 Vehicles used for carrying animal waste or carcasses not intended for human consumption.

18 Vehicles used for carrying live animals from farms to local markets and vice versa, or from markets to local slaughterhouses within a radius of 50 km.

19 Vehicles specially fitted for and used:
   - as shops at local markets and for door-to-door selling;
   - for mobile banking, exchange or savings transactions;
   - for worship;
   - for the lending of books, records or CDs;
   - for cultural events or exhibitions.

20 Vehicles (not exceeding 7.5 tonnes gvw) carrying materials or equipment for the driver's use in the course of his work within a 50 km radius of base provided the driving does not constitute the driver's main activity and does not prejudice the objectives of the regulations.

21 Vehicles operating exclusively on islands not exceeding 2,300 sq km not linked to the mainland by bridge, ford or tunnel for use by motor vehicles (this includes the Isle of Wight, Arran and Bute).

22 Vehicles (not exceeding 7.5 tonnes gvw) used for the carriage of goods propelled by gas produced on the vehicle or by electricity.

23 Vehicles used for driving instruction (but not if carrying goods for hire or reward).

24 Tractors used after 1 January 1990 exclusively for agricultural and forestry work.

25 Vehicles used by the RNLI for hauling lifeboats.

26 Vehicles manufactured before 1 January 1947.

27 Steam-propelled vehicles.

28 Vintage vehicles (ie over 25 years old) not carrying more than nine persons including the driver, not being used for profit, and being driven to or from a vintage rally, museum, public display or a place where it has been or is to be repaired, maintained or tested.

NB: In the exemption above relating to vehicles used by public authorities, the exemption applies only if the vehicle is being used by:

a *a health authority in England and Wales, a health board in Scotland or a National Health Service (NHS) Trust*

  – *to provide ambulance services in pursuance of its duty under the NHS Act 1977 or NHS (Scotland) Act 1978; or*

  – *to carry staff, patients, medical supplies or equipment in pursuance of its general duties under the Act;*

b *a local authority to fulfil social services functions, such as services for old persons or for physically and mentally handicapped persons;*

c *HM Coastguard or lighthouse authorities;*

d *harbour authorities within harbour limits;*

e *airports authority within airport perimeters;*

f *British Rail, London Regional Transport, a Passenger Transport Executive or local authority for maintaining railways;*

g *British Waterways Board for maintaining navigable waterways.*

Declaration of Exemption

When presenting a vehicle for the goods vehicle annual test which the operator believes is exempt from the tachograph regulations in accordance with the list above, a 'Declaration of Exemption' form has to be completed.

Employers' Responsibilities

The employer needs to determine whether his transport operation and his vehicles fall within scope of the EU tachograph requirements – by reference to the exemption list above – and take appropriate steps regarding the fitment and calibration of instruments as described in this chapter. He must also instruct his drivers accordingly. Additionally, the regulations place specific responsibilities on the employer of a driver who drives within the EU rules as follows:

- The employer must organize the driver's work in such a way that he is able to comply with both the drivers' hours and tachograph rules.

- The employer must supply drivers with sufficient numbers of the correct type of tachograph charts (ie one chart for the day, one spare in case the first is impounded by an enforcement officer, plus any further spares which are necessary to account for any charts which become too dirty or damaged to use), and he must ensure that completed charts are collected from drivers no later than 42 days after use.

- The employer must periodically check completed charts to ensure that the law has been complied with (ie that the driver has made a chart for the day, that he has completed it fully and properly and that he has observed the driving hours rules). If breaches of the law are found, the employer must take appropriate steps to prevent their repetition.

- The employer must retain completed charts for 12 months for inspection by VOSA examiners, if required.
- The employer must give copies of the record to drivers concerned who request them.

A number of recent court cases have highlighted the extent of employer responsibilities for tachograph operation as follows:

- It has been made clear that employers who do not check tachograph records are permitting drivers' hours offences and can be prosecuted and convicted accordingly.
- Employers can be charged with failing to use the tachograph in accordance with the regulations in cases where a driver is unable to produce charts to show his driving and other work activities (eg when requested to do so in a roadside check).
- Where employers allow drivers to take their tractive units home after their day's work they must ensure that such driving is recorded on a tachograph chart and is counted as part of the driver's legally permitted driving and working time for that day – it is not part of his rest period.

Drivers' Responsibilities

Drivers of vehicles operating within the EU rules must observe the tachograph requirements. In particular this means understanding what the law requires and how to comply with it. The specific responsibilities of the driver in regard to the law are as follows:

- Drivers using tachograph charts must ensure that a proper record is made by the instrument:
    - that it is a continuous record;
    - that it is a 'time right' record (ie recordings are in the correct 12-hour section of the chart – daytime or night-time hours).

- In the event of instrument failure or in circumstances where no vehicle is available when the driver is working he must make manual recordings of his activities on the chart 'legibly and without dirtying' it.
- Drivers must produce for inspection on request by an authorized inspecting officer a current chart/record for that day plus the charts relating to the previous 28 days (see section below on Production of Charts/Records).
- Drivers must return completed charts and/or records to their employer no later than 42 days after use.
- Drivers must allow any authorized inspecting officer to inspect the charts and tachograph calibration plaque, which is usually fixed inside the body of the instrument.

In cases where drivers take their tractive units home at the end of their working shift, this time must be recorded on the tachograph chart and counted as part of the daily maximum driving time and the driver's day's work – it is not part of his rest period.

Production of Charts/Records

Under the new digital tachograph legislation (ie Regulation 561/2006/EC – Article 26, which amends provisions in Regulation 3821/85/EEC) drivers must be able to produce records (ie charts or digital printouts) to the enforcement authorities (eg VOSA and the police) as follows:

When driving vehicles with analogue tachographs

- The record sheet (ie chart/s) for the current day and those used in the previous 28 calendar days.

When driving vehicles with digital tachographs or a combination of both digital and analogue types

- Record sheets (ie charts) for the day of driving with the analogue instrument and for the previous 28 days.
- Any manual record and printout made by a digital instrument during the current week and for the previous 28 days.

Drivers who drive vehicles fitted with digital tachographs must also be able to produce on request their driver Smart Card.

NB: The 28-day timescale referred to above means the records made during the previous 28 days of working/driving. It does not mean the previous 28 sets of records. Thus, for example, if the driver has not worked at all during those previous 28 days he will have no records to produce or, if he has worked on only some of the days, he will need to produce records for those days but not the other days.

Two-Crew Operation

Reference above to a driver also includes any other driver who is carried on the vehicle to assist with the driving. In this case a two-man tachograph must be fitted and both drivers must use it to produce records as follows:

- The person who is driving must have his chart located in the uppermost (ie number 1) position in the instrument and use the number 1 activity mode switch to enable his activities and vehicle speed and distance recordings to be made on the chart as appropriate.
- The person who is riding passenger must have his chart in the rearmost (ie number 2) position and must use the number 2 activity mode switch to record his other work activities, or break or rest periods. Only time-group recordings

are made on this chart; driving, speed and distance traces are *not* produced on the second-man chart.

NB: *Following a High Court ruling it has become clear that the second man on a double-manned vehicle operation must insert his chart in the 2nd-man position of the instrument from the commencement of the journey, not from the later time when he commences his period of driving.*

Tachograph Calibration, Sealing and Inspection

To make legally acceptable records, tachograph installations in vehicles must be calibrated initially at an approved tachograph centre (a list of DfT-approved tachograph fitting and calibration centres can be found on the DfT website at: **http://www.dft.gov.uk/pgr/freight/road/workingtime/approvedtachographcalibratio3237**) and subsequently must be inspected every two years and fully recalibrated every six years or after repair at an approved centre.

NB: *Problems have arisen over the date when two-yearly checks on tachographs are due. Operators of new vehicles have missed these dates, having assumed that the two years run from when they first took delivery of the vehicle, but in fact they run from the date of original calibration, which may have been some months earlier.*

VOSA specifies and approves the premises (and the display of approved signs), equipment, staff (including their training) and procedures for the installation, repair, inspection, calibration and sealing of tachographs. Such centres must be approved to the BS 5750 Part 2 quality assurance standard before they can gain VOSA approval. No other workshops or individuals are permitted to carry out such work and any work carried out by unauthorized agents would render the installation incapable of producing legally acceptable records.

Tachograph Installation Offences

It is an offence for any unauthorized person to carry out work on tachograph installations. It is also an offence for a vehicle operator (maximum fine £5,000) to obtain and use a tachograph instrument repaired by a firm which is not BS 5750 approved.

Calibration

The calibration process requires the vehicle to be presented to an approved tachograph centre in normal road-going trim, complete with body and all fixtures, unladen, and with tyres complying with legal limits as to tread wear and inflated to manufacturer's recommended pressures. At the centre, the necessary work on the installation is carried out to within specified tolerances.

The regulations specify tolerances within which the tachograph installation must operate and are valid for temperatures between 0° and 40°C as follows:

	On bench test	On installation	In use
Speed	3kph	4kph	6kph
Distance	1%	2%	4%
Time	in all cases, ± 2 minutes per day with a maximum of 10 minutes per 7 days		

In the case of both speed and distance figures shown above, the tolerance is measured relative to the real speed and to the real distance of at least 1 kilometre.

Calibration and Periodic Inspection Fees

Official fees charged for tachograph calibration and periodic inspections are as follows:

- calibration £46.00 plus VAT (the official time for this task being 1½ hours);
- two-yearly inspection £32.00 plus VAT;
- six-yearly inspection £46.00 plus VAT.

NB: These prices are exclusive of any replacement parts used.

Sealing of Tachographs

Approved centres seal tachograph installations after calibration or two-yearly inspections with their own official seals (each of which is coded differently) and details of all seals are maintained on a register by VOSA. The seals are of the customs type whereby a piece of wire is passed through each of the connecting points between the vehicle and the tachograph itself and then a lead seal is squeezed tight on to the wire with special pliers which imprint the centre code number in the metal. Attempts to remove any of the seals or their actual removal will show and need to be accounted for.

The purpose of sealing is to ensure that there is no tampering with the equipment or any of its drive mechanism or cables which could either vary the recordings of time, speed or distance or inhibit the recording in any way. Such tampering is illegal and once seals are broken the installation no longer complies with the law and legally acceptable records cannot be made.

Besides the seals inside the body of the instrument head, the following points are sealed:

- the installation plaque;
- the two ends of the link between the recording equipment and the vehicle;
- the adaptor itself and the point of its insertion into the circuit;
- the switch mechanism for vehicles with two or more axle ratios;
- the links joining the adaptor and the switch mechanism to the rest of the equipment;
- the casings of the instrument;

- any cover giving access to the means of adapting the constant of the recording equipment to the characteristic coefficient of the vehicle.

Seal Breakage

Obviously, there are occasions when certain of the seals have to be broken of necessity to carry out repairs to the vehicle and replacement of defective parts (eg the vehicle clutch or gearbox). The only seals which may be broken in these circumstances are as follows:

- those at the two ends of the link between the tachograph equipment and the vehicle;
- those between the adaptor (ie the tachograph drive gearbox) and the point of its insertion into the circuit;
- those at the links joining the adaptor and the switch mechanism (ie where the vehicle has a two-speed rear axle) to the rest of the equipment.

With the introduction of the statutory speed-limiter fitment on many heavy vehicles, the EU now permits operators to break tachograph seals for the purpose of fitting such devices, but the seals must be replaced – at an approved tachograph centre – within seven days.

While it is permitted to break the particular seals listed above for other authorized purposes (eg in connection with vehicle maintenance), a written record must be kept of the seal breakage and the reason for it. The installation must be inspected or recalibrated and fully sealed following repair or seal breakage as soon as 'circumstances permit' and before the vehicle is used again. It is illegal to remove any of the other seals and tampering with seals by drivers is tantamount to committing fraud (ie for the purposes of making fraudulent records, which is an offence liable to lead to a prison sentence).

Under new arrangements, VOSA is planning to check that all tachograph head seals are intact when vehicles are submitted for their annual goods vehicle test. This tougher regime is intended to crack down on rogue operators who are fiddling their tachographs to avoid compliance with both statutory speed limits and the drivers' hours rules. Following trial inspections in three of its regions VOSA found that tachograph instruments in up to one in five vehicles had been illegally interfered with to produce false recordings.

Calibration Plaques

When a tachograph has been installed in a vehicle and calibrated, the approved centre must fix, either inside the tachograph head or near to it on the vehicle dashboard in a visible position, a plaque giving details of the centre, the 'turns count' and the calibration date. The plaque is sealed and must not be tampered with or the sealing tape removed. When an instrument is subjected to a two-year inspection or recalibration a new plaque must be fitted. If a vehicle is found on the road with an 'out-of-date' plaque an offence will have been committed and prosecution may follow.

The normal sequence for plaques is that one will show the initial calibration date, the next (two years later), which is fitted alongside the first plaque, will show the date of the two-year inspection and a third plaque will show the second two-year inspection. After a further two years a six-year recalibration of the installation will be due and at this time all the previous plaques will be removed, the new calibration plaque will be fitted and the procedure described above starts again. In between times, following certain repairs, a 'minor work' plaque may be fitted but this does not alter the sequence of dates for the two-year inspection and the six-year re-calibration plaques.

The two-year and six-year periods referred to above for inspections and calibrations are counted to the day/date, *not* to the end of the month in which that day/date falls.

Tachograph Breakdown

If tachograph equipment becomes defective (or the seals are broken for whatever reason, including authorized breakage, as described above, to carry out mechanical repairs to the vehicle, or unauthorized interference) it must be repaired at an approved centre as soon as 'circumstances permit', but in the meantime the driver must continue to record manually on the chart all necessary information regarding his working, driving, breaks and rest times which are no longer being recorded by the instrument. There is *no* requirement to attempt to record speed or distance.

Once a vehicle has returned to base with a defective tachograph, it should not leave again until the instrument is in working order and has been recalibrated (if necessary) and the seals replaced. If it cannot be repaired immediately, the vehicle can be used so long as the operator has taken positive steps (which he can satisfactorily prove later if challenged by the enforcement authorities – see paragraph below) to have the installation repaired as soon as reasonably practicable.

If a vehicle is unable to return to base within *one week* (ie seven days) counting from the day of the breakdown, arrangements must be made to have the defective instrument repaired and recalibrated as necessary at an approved centre *en route* within that time.

Defence

There is a defence in the regulations against conviction (ie not against prosecution) for an offence of using a vehicle with a defective tachograph. This has the effect of allowing subsequent use of a vehicle with a defective tachograph provided steps have been taken to have the installation restored to a legal condition as soon as circumstances permit and provided the driver continues to record his driving, working and break period times manually on a tachograph chart. In such circumstances it will be necessary to satisfactorily prove to the enforcement authorities – and to the court if they proceed with prosecution – that a definite booking for the repair had already been made at the time the vehicle was apprehended and that this appointment was for the repair to be carried out at the earliest possible opportunity.

It is also a defence to show that at the time it was examined by an enforcement officer the vehicle was on its way to an approved tachograph centre to have necessary repairs carried out. However, this defence will fail if the driver did not keep written records of his activities in the meantime.

Use of Tachographs

Drivers are responsible for ensuring that the tachograph instrument in their vehicle functions correctly throughout the whole of their working shift in order that a full and proper recording for a full 24 hours can be produced. They must also ensure that they have sufficient quantities of the right type of charts (see below) on which to make recordings.

Time Changes

Drivers must ensure that the time at which the instrument clock is set and consequently recordings are made on the chart agree with the official time in the country of registration of the vehicle. This is a significant point for British drivers travelling in Europe, who may be tempted to change the clock in the instrument to the correct local European time rather than, for example, having it indicate and record the time in Britain. To re-emphasize the point, this means that for British drivers in British-registered vehicles the tachograph chart recording must accord with the official time in Britain regardless of the country in which that recording was made – the tachograph clock must *not* be reset to show local time when travelling abroad.

Dirty or Damaged Charts

If a chart becomes dirty or damaged in use, it must be replaced and the old chart should be securely attached to the new chart which is used to replace it.

Completion of Centre Field

Before starting work with a vehicle in which tachograph charts are to be used, the driver must enter on the centre field of his chart for that day the following details:

- his surname and first name (not initials);
- the date and place where use of the chart begins;
- vehicle registration number;
- the distance recorder (odometer) reading at the start of the day.

At the end of a working day, the driver should then record the following information on the chart:

- the place and date where the chart is completed;

- the closing odometer reading;
- by subtraction, the total distance driven – in kilometres (It is not a legal requirement for the driver to carry out this calculation).

Making Recordings

When the centre field has been completed the chart should be inserted in the tachograph instrument, ensuring that it is the right way up (it should be impossible to fit it wrongly) and that the recording will commence on the correct part of the 24-hour chart (day or night). The instrument face should be securely closed. The activity mode switch (number 1) should be turned as necessary throughout the work period to indicate the driver's relevant activities, namely driving, other work, break or rest periods. While some drivers find difficulty in getting into the habit of turning the switch to coincide with each change of activity, nevertheless this is what the law requires and it is an offence to fail to do so (ie not keeping proper records).

New Recording Rules

New Regulation 561/2006/EC specifies in Article 26 (amending Article 15 of Regulation 3821/85/EEC) that the use to which the tachograph crossed hammers and rectangle symbols are put must, from 1 May 2006, be as follows:

 use to record 'other work' (ie any activity other than driving) done for both the driving employer and any other employer outside of transport;

 use to record 'periods of availability' as defined in EU Directive 2002/15/EC – The Road Transport Directive – and as described on page 93 of the book.

Other Work and Overtime Recordings

The High Court has ruled that drivers must record *all* periods of work on their tachograph charts. This makes it clear that work undertaken for the employer after the daily driving shift has been completed (eg in a yard, warehouse, workshop or office), and whether deemed part of the normal day or overtime working, must be recorded on the chart for that day – ie either by the instrument if this is convenient or otherwise manually. A contention that since tachographs were intended primarily to record driving time in the interests of road safety they should be used for that purpose only and not for recording other working activities was ruled to be contrary to the provisions of both the EU legislation and section 97 of the Transport Act 1968.

Overnight Recordings

At the end of his shift the driver can leave the chart in the instrument overnight to record the daily rest period or alternatively it can be removed and the rest period recorded manually on the chart. Generally, enforcement staffs prefer an automatic recording of daily rest made by the instrument but this is not always practicable where the vehicle may be used on night-shift work, may be driven for road testing or other purposes by workshop staff, or moved around the premises by others when the driver is at home having the rest period. Also, if the driver is scheduled to start work later on the following day, there will be an overlap recording on the chart which is illegal.

Vehicle Changes

If the driver changes to another vehicle during the working day he must take the existing chart with him and record details of the time of change, the registration number of the further vehicle(s) and distance recordings in the appropriate spaces on the chart. He then uses that chart in the next vehicle to record his continuing driving, working activities and break periods. This procedure is repeated no matter how many different vehicles (except those not driven on the public highway) are driven during the day so the one chart shows all of the driver's daily activity. This assumes that the tachograph chart is compatible with the tachograph instrument. If the chart and the instrument are not compatible, a new chart must be used by the driver. The charts used by the driver must be kept together to show a complete days' work.

Mixed Tachographs

It is important to note that the various makes and models of tachograph currently available in the UK have different charts and they cannot all be interchanged. So, the driver who switches from a vehicle with one make of instrument to a vehicle with a different make during the working day will have to make fresh entries on a second or even third chart. At the end of the day all the charts used should be clipped together to present a comprehensive (and legal) record for the whole day. However, there are some charts now available on the market suitable for dual use in different makes of tachograph. It is the employer's duty to issue drivers with the correct charts (ie with matching type approval numbers to those on the tachograph instrument in use) in sufficient numbers for the schedule which the driver has to operate.

NB: Where instruments are standardized in a fleet, one chart will suffice for the whole day and the driver must take this with him from one vehicle to the next, recording changes as previously described.

Manual Records

Drivers are responsible for ensuring that the instrument is kept running while they are in charge of the vehicle and should it fail or otherwise cease making proper records they should remove the chart and continue to record their activities manually on it as previously described. They must also make manual recordings on the chart of work done or time spent away from the vehicle (for example, periods during the day spent working in the yard, warehouse or workshop). Manual recordings must be made legibly and in making them the sheet must not be 'dirtied'.

Records for Part-time Drivers

The rules on the use of tachographs described in the foregoing text apply equally to part-time or occasional drivers such as yard and warehouse staff, office people and even the transport manager. The rules also apply fully even if the driving on the road is for a very short distance or period of time; a five-minute drive without a tachograph chart in use would be sufficient to break the law and risk prosecution. Vehicle fitters and other workshop staff who drive vehicles on the road for testing in connection with repair or maintenance are specifically exempt from the need to keep tachograph records when undertaking such activities (see exemption list on p 121) but this exemption *does not* apply to them when using vehicles for other purposes (eg collecting spare parts, ferrying vehicles back and forth, taking replacement vehicles out to on-road breakdowns, taking and collecting vehicles to and from goods vehicle test stations, etc).

Retention, Return and Checking of Tachograph Charts

Drivers must retain and be able to produce, on request by authorized examiners (including the police), completed tachograph charts for the current day and for the previous 28 days.

Charts must be returned by drivers to their employer no later than 21 days after use and on receiving the charts the employer must periodically check them to ensure that the drivers' hours and record-keeping regulations have been complied with. Failure by an operator to check charts for possible offences by drivers can lead to charges of 'permitting' the commission of certain tachograph and drivers' hours offences (should such offences be proven) – in one case a transport manager was held to be 'reckless' because his chart-checking system was not sufficiently thorough. Charts must then be retained, available for inspection if required, for a period of one year.

Where a driver has more than one employer in a week (eg as with agency drivers), he must return the tachograph charts to the employer who first employed him in that week. This provision clearly presents a problem for those firms which regularly employ agency drivers and which may find difficulty in securing the return of charts for driving work done with their vehicles. At the present time, there is no legal solution to this issue.

Retention of Charts for Tax Records

Where tachograph charts are used by employers to justify payment of driver night-out and other subsistence expenses for tax purposes, then the charts constitute part of the legal recording system for tax purposes and as such must be retained for six years instead of the normal one-year period as described above.

Driver records for non-driving days

Drivers must make records for work completed on any non-driving days, within a working week, when they have undertaken some driving that comes within the scope of the EU drivers' hours rules, since their last weekly rest.

For example, a driver who drives a vehicle within the scope of the EU rules on a Monday, and then works in a warehouse from Tuesday to Friday, of the same week, must complete non-driving records for the work completed from Tuesday to Friday

The driver can make the record in a number of ways by:

- making manual records on a tachograph chart;
- making manual records on a printout from a digital tachograph;
- using the manual input facility on a digital tachograph;
- making manual records in a domestic log book for days when they are working under the domestic drivers' hours rules and a record is legally required.

Records for non-driving days do not need to be complex. They may merely show the name of the driver, the date, and the start and finish of the shift. The driver should always carry these records on the vehicle (for the previous 28 days) to be able produce them to enforcement officers for the relevant period.

Official Inspection of Charts

An authorized inspecting officer (which means a traffic examiner of VOSA or a person authorized by a Traffic Commissioner (TC), in either case on production of their authority if requested, or a police officer) may require any person to produce for inspection any tachograph chart on which recordings have been made. This includes:

- any charts for the current day and for the previous 28 *calendar* days;
- any legally required manual records made in the previous 28 days;
- plus his driver smart card, if he has one.

Further, he may enter a vehicle to inspect a chart or a tachograph instrument (he should be able to read the recordings relating to the nine hours prior to the time of his inspection) and the calibration plaques and detain a vehicle for this purpose. At any reasonable time he may enter premises on which he believes vehicles or tachograph charts are kept and inspect the instruments in such vehicles and the completed charts. He can require (by serving a notice in writing) charts to be produced at a Traffic Area Office at any time on giving at least 10 days' notice in which to do so. Where a chart is suspected of showing a false entry he may 'seize' the chart (but not for reasons other than evidence of a false entry, or an entry intended to deceive, or an entry altered for such purposes) and retain it for a maximum period of six months, after which time, if no charges for offences have been made, the chart should have been returned. If not, the person from whom it was taken can apply to a magistrate's court to seek an order for its return.

In practice, TCs regularly ask operators to provide batches of tachograph charts covering one or more of their vehicles for a short period or possibly some months either on a routine basis or following investigations into, or leads about, hours law or tachograph infringements – and where it is suspected that drivers are regularly exceeding speed limits. These charts are then analysed for contraventions of the law. The courts have ruled that examiners do have powers to remove tachograph charts from operators' premises when acting on the instructions of a TC – this follows the successful prosecution of a haulage firm that refused to allow charts to be removed from its premises.

Cases have been reported where the police have demanded that operators should send in to them, by post, tachograph charts required for inspection. This has been shown to be an illegal practice: there is no provision in the law which allows random collection of charts by the police or demands for charts to be submitted by post. Only in cases where an on-the-spot examination reveals possible offences can the police then request copies of the relevant chart for that day, other charts for that week and for the last day of the previous week. VOSA enforcement officers, on the other hand, may take random selections of charts away for examination.

It is an offence to fail to produce records for inspection as required or to obstruct an enforcement officer in his request to inspect records or tachograph installations in vehicles.

Offences

Some tachograph-related offences have already been mentioned in connection with specific requirements of the law but there are other overriding, and very serious, offences to be considered. In particular, it is an offence to use, cause or permit the use of a vehicle which does not have a fully calibrated tachograph installed; for the driver to fail to keep records by means of a tachograph (or manually if the instrument is defective) and to make false recordings. Further, it is an offence for the driver to fail to return used charts to his employer within 21 days after use or to fail to notify his first employer of any other employer for whom he drives vehicles to which the regulations apply.

In many cases offences committed by the driver result in charges against the employer for 'causing' or 'permitting' offences. For example, where tachograph charts go missing and cannot be produced for examination by the enforcement authorities, the employer may be charged with any one of three (or even all three) relevant offences: namely, failing to cause the driver to keep a record, failing to preserve the record, failing to produce the record. It is in such cases that sound legal representation should be sought and a good defence put forward where possible.

Two other types of offence that have come to the forefront is recent times and have featured in extensively reported prosecutions concern:

- missing mileages when charts are compared;
- interference of tachograph systems by various means of wires and so-called 'magic buttons'.

Penalties on summary conviction for offences under these regulations can be a fine of up to level 4 on the standard scale (currently £2,500) and conviction for such offences can jeopardize both the employers' 'O' licence and the driver's LGV driving entitlement. Conviction for the more serious offences of making false entries on a tachograph chart and forgery can result in level 5 fines of up to £5,000 (per offence) or imprisonment for up to two years. Since April 1998 tachograph falsification has been a 'recordable' offence, meaning that a person convicted of such an offence carries a criminal record.

TCs have made it clear that heavy goods drivers convicted for using wires to interfere with their tachograph will be disqualified from holding an LGV driving licence for a period of one year.

Much heavier penalties are likely for those transport operators and LGV drivers found guilty in UK courts of forging tachograph charts and chart entries relating to international journeys. These penalties are contained in the provisions of the Forgery and Counterfeiting Act 1981, which the Court of Appeal now allows the police to use for bringing prosecutions for tachograph chart offences committed outside the UK. Fines may be in excess of the current level 5 standard scale maximum of £5,000, and custodial sentences longer than those available to the courts under other legislation.

The courts have ruled that in cases where a driver or transport operator claims not to have known that the tachograph instrument in a vehicle had been fitted with a device intended to interfere with its operation (ie a trip device to aid the production of false records) this was no excuse and an offence of 'strict liability' was committed, to which there is no defence.

Tachograph Charts as Evidence

In the past it has been made clear that tachograph charts, while providing evidence of 'the facts shown' for drivers' hours purposes, would not be used by the police and enforcement authorities as evidence to bring prosecutions against drivers for speeding offences – not to be confused with the TCs' actions in imposing short-term LGV driving bans on drivers found from their charts to have regularly exceeded maximum speed limits. However, the DETR is currently considering the possibility of changing the law to permit the retrospective checking of tachograph charts for speeding and prosecution of drivers where such evidence is shown. This follows publicity surrounding a number of serious coach and lorry crashes where speeding was thought to be a contributory factor.

The Tachograph Instrument

A tachograph is a cable or electronically driven speedometer incorporating an integral electric clock and a chart recording mechanism. It is fitted into the vehicle dashboard or in some other convenient visible position in the driving cab. The instrument indicates time, speed and distance and permanently records this information on the chart as well as the driver's working activities. Thus, the following factors can be determined from a chart:

- varying speeds (and the highest speed) at which the vehicle was driven;
- total distance travelled and distances between individual stops;
- times when the vehicle was being driven and the total amount of driving time;
- times when the vehicle was standing and whether the driver was indicating other work, break or rest period during this time.

Recordings

Recordings are made on special circular charts, each of which covers a period of 24 hours (Figure 5.1), by three styli. One stylus records distance, another records speed and the third records time-group activities as determined by the driver turning the activity mode switch on the head of the instrument (ie driving, other work, breaks and rest periods). The styli press through a wax recording layer on the chart, revealing the carbonated layer (usually black) between the top surface and the backing paper. The charts are accurately pre-marked with time, distance and speed reference radials and when the styli have marked the chart with the appropriate recordings these can be easily identified and interpreted against the printed reference marks.

Movement of the vehicle creates a broad running line on the time radial, indicating when the vehicle started running and when it stopped. After the vehicle has stopped, the time-group stylus continues to mark the chart but with an easily distinguishable thin line. The speed trace gives an accurate recording of the speeds attained at all

FIGURE 5.1 A typical tachograph chart showing recordings of times, distance and speed times throughout the journey, continuing to record on the speed base line when the vehicle is stationary to provide an unbroken trace except when the instrument is opened. The distance recording is made by the stylus moving up and down over a short stroke, each movement representing 5 kilometres travelled; thus, every 5 kilometres the stylus reverses direction, forming a 'V' for every 10 kilometres of distance travelled. To calculate the total distance covered the 'V's are counted and multiplied by 10 and any 'tail ends' are added in, the total being expressed in kilometres.

When a second chart is located in the rear position of a two-man tachograph, only a time recording of the second man's activities (ie other work, break or rest) is shown. Traces showing driving, vehicle speed or distance cannot be recorded on this chart.

Precautions against interference with the readings are incorporated in the instrument. It is opened with a key and a security mark is made on the chart every time the instrument is opened.* When checking the chart it can be easily established at what time the instrument was opened and thus whether this was for an authorized reason or not. Interference with the recording mechanism to give false readings, particularly of speed, can be determined quite simply by an experienced chart analyst.

NB: Changes to the EU tachograph specification to reduce the possibility of fraudulent recordings were introduced to apply to new instruments receiving Type Approval from 1991. These include a provision for the chart to be marked at every interruption of the power supply (eg when a fuse is removed).

Faults

Tachographs are generally robust instruments, but listed below are some of the faults which may occur:

- failure of the cable drive at the vehicle gearbox;
- failure of the cable drive at the tachograph head;
- failure of the adaptor/corrector/triplex gearbox;
- cable breaking or seizure;
- electrical faults affecting lights in the instrument or the clock;
- incorrect time showing on the 24-hour clock (eg day-shift work becomes shown against night hours on the charts);
- failure of the tachograph head;
- damage to the recording styli;
- failure of the distance recorder;
- damage to charts because of incorrect insertion.

Fiddles

A key feature of tachograph recordings is that careful observation will show results of the majority of faults in recordings as well as fiddles and attempts at falsification of recordings by drivers. The main faults likely to be encountered will show as follows:

- Clock stops – recordings continue in a single vertical line until the styli penetrate the chart.

- Styli jam/seize up – recordings continue around the chart with no vertical movement.
- Cable or electronic drive failure – chart continues to rotate and speed and distance styli continue to record on base line and where last positioned respectively. Time-group recordings can still be made but no driving trace will appear.

Attempts at falsification of charts will appear as follows:

- Opening the instrument face will result in a gap in recordings.
- Winding the clock backwards or forwards will leave either a gap in the recording or an overlap. In either case the distance recording will not match up if the vehicle is moved.
- Stopping the clock will stop the rotation of the chart so all speed and distance recordings will be on one vertical line (see the first item in the previous list about how faults in instruments show on charts).
- Restricting the speed stylus to give indications of lower than actual speed will result in flat-topped speed recordings while bending the stylus down to achieve the same effect will result in recordings below the speed base line when the vehicle is stationary.
- Written or marked-in recordings with pens or sharp pointed objects are readily identifiable by even a relatively unskilled chart analyst.

NB: *This is only an outline list of a large number of possible faults and attempts at falsification likely to be encountered. Some driver fiddles are one-off attempts, crudely and clumsily executed and naively obvious; others are much more sophisticated in their execution, often as part of an ongoing violation of legal requirements. These are more difficult, but not impossible, for the transport manager or fleet operator to detect and would certainly be picked up quickly by an experienced chart analyst.*

EU Instruments and Charts

Tachographs may only be used for legal record-keeping purposes if they are type-approved and comply with the detailed EU specification. Such instruments have provision for indicating to the driver, without the instrument being opened, that a chart has been inserted and that a continuous recording is being made. They also provide for the driver to select, by an activity mode switch on the instrument, the type of recording which is being made. In the UK this must be one of the following:

- driving time;
- other work time;
- break and rest periods.

Two-man instruments are also provided with a means of simultaneously recording the activities of a second crew member on a separate chart located in the rear position in the instrument.

The charts used for legal purposes must also be type-approved as indicated by the appropriate 'e' markings printed on them. It is illegal to use non-approved charts or charts which are not approved for the specific type of instrument being used. Care should be taken that charts used have accurate time registration – cheap and non-type-approved versions, which are illegal anyway, have been found in the past to be significantly inaccurate in the way they are printed, thus producing inaccurate and worthless records.

Chart Analysis

Analysis of the information recorded on tachograph charts can provide valuable data for determining whether drivers have complied with the law on driving, working, break and rest period times, and have conformed to statutory speed limits. The data can also be extremely useful as a basis for finding means of increasing the efficiency of vehicle operation and for establishing productivity monitoring and payment schemes for drivers.

Many fleet operators use and rely upon the services of tachograph analysis agencies for checking their charts for conformity with the law. However, it should be noted that should such firms fail to recognize and notify the operator of deficiencies in their records, it is the operator who is at risk and his licence, not the analysis bureau. The TCs repeatedly remind operators that responsibility for driver compliance with the hours law rests entirely with them, not outside agencies. Generally, also, the checking carried out by such firms is for standard hours law infringements only, which are mainly picked up by computerized analysis and may not include identification of other irregularities or cleverly executed false entries or fraudulent recordings. Similarly, such analysis may not identify driver abuse of vehicles or frequent and excessive speeding.

Tachograph manufacturers supply accessories to enable detailed chart analysis to be carried out. A chart analyser magnifies the used chart to the extent that detailed analysis beyond the scope of a normal visual examination can be made of the vehicle's minute-by-minute and kilometre-by-kilometre progress. Journey times, average running times and speeds, delivery times, route miles, traffic delays and many other relevant factors can be readily established. With the aid of a fixed hairline cursor on the magnifier to allow precise definition of the time and speed scales and recordings on the chart, even vehicles' rates of acceleration and deceleration can be determined.

The German company Siemens VDO (formerly Kienzle), which is the leading tachograph manufacturer, has undertaken considerable research into chart analysis and is able to offer users the service of its analysis experts both in Germany and the UK as well as in other countries to determine the activities of vehicles and particularly the progress of a vehicle immediately prior to an accident and at the point of impact. In some instances such analysis has shown that witnesses' accounts of the speed of the vehicle and its braking force just before the accident have been far from correct.

It is also claimed that by detailed analysis of the charts and by keeping drivers aware of the information obtained, driving methods can be improved, thus saving fuel and cutting down on the wear and tear on vehicle brakes, tyres, transmission and other components.

Digital Tachographs

European Council Regulation (561/2006/EC) amending the previous tachograph regulations (3821/85/EC and 2135/98/EC) by the introduction of a new generation of digital tachographs was published on 15 March 2006 and came into effect on 1 May 2006. From this date all new goods vehicles exceeding 3.5 tonnes gross weight (except those specifically exempt under the regulations) have needed to be fitted with the new-type digital instruments in which the driver inserts his own, personalized, micro-chip 'smart' card on which his driving, working and rest activities will be held, along with vehicle speeds and distances driven. The 'smart' card is capable of storing 28 days of average activity. Average activity is deemed to be 93 activity changes. Therefore, if a driver is engaged in an operation where more than 93 activity changes occur in a day, then the card may hold less than 28 days of data. Once the card's memory is full the oldest data will be overwritten.

There is no requirement for retrospective fitment of digital tachographs to existing vehicles except that where, after 1 May 2006, a pre-existing vehicle exceeding 12 tonnes gross weight suffers tachograph failure requiring replacement, that replacement will have to be a new-type digital instrument.

The Regulations

The new regulation (561/2006/EC) which is outlined here has been introduced for a number of reasons including:

- to prevent infringement and fraud in application of the driving hours rules;
- to monitor automatically driver performance and behaviour;
- to overcome problems of monitoring compliance due to the numbers of individual record sheets (charts) that have to be held in the vehicle cab;
- the need to introduce advance recording equipment with electronic storage devices and personal driver cards to provide an indisputable record of work done by the driver over the last few days and the vehicle over a period of several months; and
- to devise a system which ensures total security of the recorded data.

Definitions for Digital Tachographs and Ancillaries

The new-type equipment will feature a number of key components defined in the technical Annex IB to Regulation 3185/85/EC as follows:

- *Recording equipment* is amended to mean the total equipment intended for installation in road vehicles to show, record and store automatically or semi-automatically details of the movement of such vehicles and of certain work periods of their drivers. This equipment includes cables, sensors, an electronic driver information device, one (two) card reader(s) for the insertion of one or two driver memory card(s), an integrated or separate printer, display instruments, facilities for downloading the data memory, facilities to display or print information on demand, and facilities for the input of the places where the daily work period begins and ends.

- *Data memory* means an electronic storage system built into the recording equipment, capable of storing at least 365 calendar days from the recording equipment. The memory should be protected in such a way as to prevent unauthorized access to and manipulation of the data and detect any such attempt.

- A '*driver card with memory*' means a removable information transfer and storage device allocated by the authorities of the member states to each individual driver for the purposes of identification of the driver and storage of essential data. The format and technical specifications of the driver card must meet the requirements laid down in the technical annex to the regulations (not yet adopted).

- A '*control card*' means a removable data transfer and storage device for use in the card reader of the recording equipment, issued by the authorities of the member states to competent authorities to get access to the data stored in the data memory or in the driver cards for reading, printing and/or downloading.

- A '*company data card*' means a removable data transfer device issued by the member state's authorities to the owner of vehicles fitted with recording equipment. The company data card allows for displaying, downloading and printing of the data stored in the recording equipment fitted in the company's vehicle(s).

- *Downloading* means the copying of a part of or a complete set of data stored in the data memory of the vehicle or in the memory of the driver card, but which does not alter or delete any stored data, allows for the origin of downloaded data to be authenticable and to be kept in a format that can be used by any authorized person, and ensures that any attempts to manipulate data are detectable.

Function and Use of Digital Instruments

The regulations require digital instruments to be able to record, store, display and print out specified statutory information as follows.

Recording and Storing in the Data Memory

The instrument will be required to record and store:

- Distance travelled by the vehicle with an accuracy of 1 km.
- Speed of the vehicle:
  - momentary speed of the vehicle at a frequency of 1 s for the last 24 hours of use of the vehicle;
  - exceeding the authorized speed of the vehicle, defined as any period of more than 1 minute during which the vehicle speed exceeds 90 kph for N3 vehicles or 105 kph for M3 vehicles (with time, date, maximum speed of the over-speeding, average speed during the period concerned).

- Periods of driving time (times and dates), with an accuracy of 1 minute.
- Other periods of work or of availability (times and dates) with an accuracy of 1 minute.
- Breaks from work and daily rest periods (times and dates) with an accuracy of 1 minute.
- For electronic recording equipment which is equipment operated by signals transmitted electrically from the distance and speed sensor, any interruption exceeding 100 milliseconds in the power supply of the recording equipment (except lighting), in the power supply of the distance and speed sensor, and any interruption in the signal lead to the distance and speed sensor, with date, time, duration and driver card issue number.
- The driver card issue number with times and dates of insertion and removal.
- For each driver card that is inserted for the first time after it was used in another item of recording equipment:
  - current driving time since the last break or rest period;
  - driving time for the day after the last rest period of at least eight hours;
  - driving times for the day between two rest periods of at least eight hours for the preceding 27 calendar days with date, time and duration;
  - total of the driving times for the current week and the preceding week and the total of the driving times of the two completed preceding weeks;
  - rest periods of at least eight hours' duration for the day and the preceding 27 calendar days in each case with date, time and duration;
  - the VRN (vehicle registration number) of the vehicles driven.

- Date, time and duration of driving without an inserted or a functioning driver card.
- Data recorded on the places at which the daily work period began and ended.
- Automatically identifiable system faults of the recording equipment with date, time and driver card issue number.
- Faults in the driver card with date and time and driver card issue number.
- Workshop card number of the authorized fitter or workshop with date of at least the last installation inspection and/or periodic inspection of the recording equipment.
- Control card number with date of control card insertion and type of control (display, printing, downloading). In the case of downloading, the period downloaded should be recorded.
- Time adjustment with date, time and card issue number.
- Driving status (single/crew driving – driver/co-driver).

Storage on the Driver Card

The driver card must be capable of storing:

- the essential data for a period of at least the last 28 days combined with the VRN identification of the vehicle driven and the data as required above;
- the events and faults mentioned above with the VRN identification of the vehicle driven;
- the date and time of insertion and removal of the driver card and distance travelled during the corresponding period;
- the date and time of insertion and removal of the co-driver card with issue number.

Data must be recorded and stored on the driver card in such a way as to rule out any possibility of falsification.

Recording and Storing for Two Drivers

Where vehicles are used by two drivers the driving time must be recorded and stored on the driver card of the driver who is driving the vehicle. The equipment must record and store in the data memory and on the two driver cards simultaneously, but distinctly, details of the information listed above.

Recording Driver Walk-Round

Increasingly, VOSA examining officers are checking on recordings of the time that drivers spend doing their daily walk-round checks of the vehicle before starting out on their journey. Where no such recording is shown, their assumption is that no such check was carried out, which could lead to further enquiries by VOSA. Conversely, if the driver insists he did check his vehicle this may lead the examiner to allege that the driver has failed to keep a proper record or has falsified his record, both of which are offences for which prosecution may follow.

Recording Multi-drop Deliveries

The accuracy of digital tachograph recording within an accuracy of 'one minute' may lead to problems for the multi-drop delivery drivers, according to the Road Haulage Association, because of the way in which they 'over-record'. This may result in showing that the driver spent more time driving than was actually the case because part-minutes have been 'rounded up' to full minutes. It has been suggested that in certain circumstances this 'over-recording' could amount to as much as 20–30 minutes in a day, which would be sufficient to cause the driver to appear to be exceeding his statutory limits.

Displaying or Printing for an Authorized Examiner

The equipment must be capable of displaying or printing, on request, the following information:

- Driver card issue number, expiry date of the card.
- The surname and first name of the driver who is the cardholder.

- Current driving time since the last break or rest period.
- Driving time for the day after the last rest period of at least eight hours.
- Driving times for the day between two rest periods of at least eight hours for the preceding 27 calendar days on which the driver has driven, with date, time and duration.
- Total of the driving times for the current week and the preceding week and the total times for the two completed preceding weeks.
- The other periods of work and availability.
- Rest periods of at least eight hours' duration for the day and the preceding 27 days in each case with date, time and duration.
- VRN identification of vehicles driven for at least the last 28 calendar days with the distance travelled per vehicle and day, time of first insertion and last removal of the driver card and the time of change of vehicle.
- Time adjustment with date, time and card issue number.
- Interruption of power supply to the recording equipment with date, time, duration and driver card issue number.
- Sensor interruption with date, time, duration and driver card issue number.
- The VIN and/or VRN identification of the vehicle driven.
- Driving without driver card as defined above for the last 28 calendar days.
- Details of the information stored concerning the driver.
- Recorded data on the places where the daily work period began and ended.
- The automatically identifiable system faults of the recording equipment with date, time and driver card issue number.
- The faults in the driver card with date and time and driver card issue number.
- Control card number with date of control card insertion and type of control (display, printing, downloading). In the case of downloading, the period downloaded should be recorded.
- Exceeding the authorized speed as defined above, with date, time and driver card issue number for the current week and in any case including the last day of the previous week.
- Summary reports to permit compliance with the relevant regulations to be checked.

Figure 5.2 shows a list of the pictograms used in digital tachographs, both on-screen and on the printouts while Figure 5.3 is a sample printout with the explanation of the coding (both courtesy of Siemens VDO).

Smart Cards

Crucial to the whole system is the driver ('smart') card, which is personal to the individual and carries identification information and other essential data about him. It has a capacity to store relevant data on driving and working times, breaks and rest periods covering at least 28 days, and comprises the legal record in place of the current tachograph chart. The card itself is tamper-proof, and strict regulatory systems are established by national governments to prevent fraudulent issue, use and transfer of cards within their territories. Cards are valid for five years, after which time they should be renewed by application to the DVLA no later than 15 days before the expiry of the card.

A tachograph 'smart card' (officially called a 'tachograph card') is a plastic card similar in size to a photocard driving licence or credit card, with a microchip embedded into it. There are four such cards for use with digital tachographs as follows:

- driver cards – which the driver inserts at the commencement of his journey to record driving and working activities (see Figures 5.4 and 5.5);
- company cards – for use by vehicle operators to protect and download the data;
- workshop cards – available only to approved tachograph calibration centres;
- control cards – for use only by VOSA examiners and the police for carrying out enforcement activities.

Before **commencing a journey** the driver is required to insert his driver card into the 1st (driver) or 2nd (co-driver) slot on the front of the Vehicle Unit (VU) – where the vehicle has two drivers (ie multi-crewing) the DfT has advised that both drivers must insert their respective driver cards into the vehicle unit when they start using the vehicle. While the vehicle is moving, time spent as the second driver will be recorded as a period of availability and the mode cannot be changed to other work or to a break until the vehicle comes to rest. The time setting (and all manual entries) must be in UTC (Universal Time Co-ordinated), which is the same as Greenwich Mean Time (GMT), and must remain so both in the UK and throughout Europe. The 'centre field' details, with digital instruments, will be recorded automatically by the tachograph – ie driver name, vehicle registration number, start and finish odometer readings and name of place code.

In the same way that drivers and co-drivers currently **record their different activities** – driving, other work, breaks and rest – by changing the mode switch and by swapping the position of charts in the tachograph head, with digital tachographs the mode switch will have to be turned and digital smart cards will need to be swapped between driver and co-driver slots in the instrument when double-manning a vehicle.

Details of time spent **working away** from the vehicle that are currently written on the rear of the tachograph chart (ie record sheet) will have to be input manually into the digital tachograph. The system will also record details of any faults, interference, errors and over-speeding that occur.

All this information will be stored for at least **28 days** on the driver's personal smart card and for at least a year in the VU.

FIGURE 5.2 Pictograms used in digital tachographs

Basic pictograms

People

⌂	Company
⬡	Controller
○	Driver
⊤	Workshop/ Test station
⊟	Manufacturer

Activities

⧄	Available
○	Drive
⊢	Rest
⚡	Work
‖	Break
?	Unknown

Equipment

1	Driver slot
2	Co-driver slot
▯	Card
☉	Clock
□	Display
⊤	External storage
÷	Power supply
▼	Printer/ Print-out
⊓	Sensor
⊟	Vehicle/ Vehicle Unit

Miscellaneous

!	Event
×	Fault
•	Location
🔒	Security
>	Speed
☉	Time
Σ	Total/Summary

Qualifiers

24h	Daily
I	Weekly
II	Two weeks
→	From or To

Pictograms list

Actions

	Control
	Driving
	Inspection/ Calibration

Duration

	current availability period
	continuous driving time
	current rest period
	current work period
	cumulative break time

Functions

	Downloading
	Printing

Pictograms Combinations

⬡ •	Control pace
• →	Location begin
→ •	Location end
☉→	From time
→☉	To time
>>	Overspeed

Cards

○▯	Driver card
⌂▯	Company card
⬡▯	Control card
⊤▯	Workshop card

Driving

○○	Crew driving
○ I	Driving time for one-week
○ II	Driving time for two weeks

Print-outs

24h ▯▼	Daily driver activities from driver card print-out
24h ⊟▼	Daily driver activities from VU print-out
!×▯▼	Events and faults from driver card print-out
!×⊟▼	Events and faults from VU print-out
⊤☉▼	Technical data print-out
>>▼	Overspeed print-out

Faults

×▯1	Card fault (driver slot)
×▯2	Card fault (Co-driver slot)
×□	Display fault

FIGURE 5.3 Example of a typical printout from a digital tachograph

```
Driver Activities Card Daily Print-Out
+---------------------------------+
| ▼ 15/10/1997 15:15 (UTC) |    1   Printing - Date & Time (UTC)
|-------------▼-----------|            Delimiter Print-out general information
| # DavidFish            |    2   Controller - Name
| #◘B/4803992633         |            Controller - Card Number
|                        |
| #→ ..................   |    3   Control Place (Hand written)
|                        |
|                        |
| ◘ WALSTER              |    5   Driver - Last Name
|   Nick D.              |            Driver - First Name
| ◘◘GB/135798642         |    6   Driver Card - Number
|   14/05/2004           |            Driver Card - Expiry Date
|                        |
| ♠ XAD1117483A          |    7   Vehicle - VIN
|   B/PV1772             |            Vehicle - Nation + VRN
|                        |
| Tacho-Manufacturer     |    8   Tachograph - Manufacturer Name
| Tacho-Part-Number      |            Tachograph - Part Number
| T Workshop-Name        |            Last Inspection/Calibration - Workshop Name
| T◘GB/159482637         |            Workshop Card Number
| T 05/03/1997           |            Date
|----------◘----------|            Delimiter driver information
|◘▼14/10/1997           |    4   Type of Print-Out (Card) & Enquiry date
|                        |
|? 00:00  06:17  06h18  |    9   Card not inserted. Activity unknown
|-------------------|          10   Card insertion
|♠ B/PV1772             |            Insertion in VRN No
|  42000 km             |            Odometer at card insertion
|⊙ 14:12  16:03  01h52  |         11   Detailed activities
|✗ 16:04  18:00  01h57  |
|ト 18:01  18:01  00h01  |
|  81111 km; 111 km     |         12   Odometer, Distance travelled at Card withdrawal
|                        |
|? 18:02  23:59  05h58  |    9   Card not inserted. Activity unknown
|------------Σ---------|            Summary information
|→✗06:19 F              |         13   Start daily work time Country/Region Odometer
|✗→18:00 E    CAT       |            End daily work time Country/Region Odometer
|                        |
|  ⊙ 04h59  374 km      |         14   Activity totals
|  ✗ 03h42  ▨ 00h11     |
|  ト 01h14  ? 13h54     |
|                        |
|◘2 05h25               |         15   Duration of crew status
|----------!◘✗--------|         16   Delimiter Cards Events and Faults
|!S12/09/1997 18:24     |            Event Security breach attempt and VRN number
|B/PV1772               |            of the vehicle in which this event/fault occurred
|!✦12/09/1997 18:23     |            Event Power supply interruption and VRN
|B/PV1772               |            number of the vehicle in which this event/fault
|                        |            occurred
|----------!♠✗--------|         17   Delimiter Vehicle Unit Events and Faults
|!л05/09/1997 06:35     |            Event  Sensor interruption
|◘◘IT/836254363         |            Driver Card Number
|✗♠21/08/1997 12:45     |            Fault VU
|◘◘---                  |            No card inserted
|✗▼21/08/1997 12:46     |            Fault Printer
|◘◘---                  |            No card inserted
|------------------|
|                        |
|◘ ..................    |         18   Driver's signature if applicable
|                        |
|# ..................    |         19   Controller's signature if applicable
+---------------------------------+
```

FIGURE 5.4 Front view of driver 'smart' card

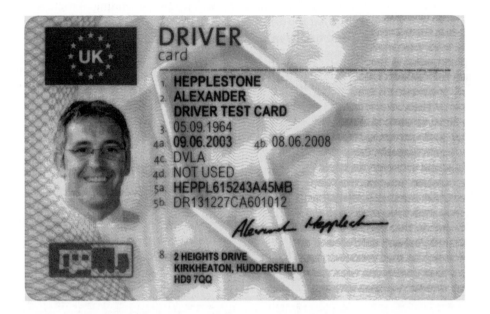

FIGURE 5.5 Rear view of driver 'smart' card

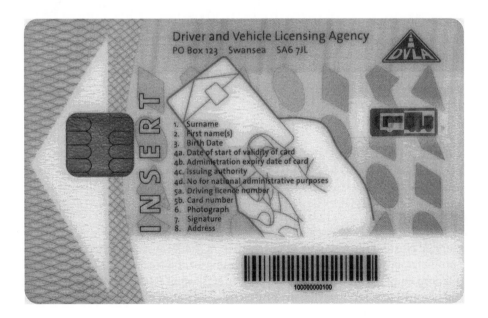

New Recording Rules

New Regulation 561/2006/EC specifies in Article 26 (amending Article 15 of Regulation 3821/85/EEC) that the use to which the tachograph crossed hammers and rectangle symbols are put must, from 1 May 2006, be as follows:

 use to record 'other work' (ie any activity other than driving) done for both the driving employer and any other employer outside of transport;

 use to record 'periods of availability' as defined in EU Directive 2002/15/EC – The Road Transport Directive – and as described on page 103 of the book.

Fees for Digital Tachograph Cards (ie Smart Cards)

The following table of fees has been set by the DVLA for digital tachograph 'smart' cards.

NB: *Further information on digital tachographs can be found on the official Government website:* **www.digitaltachograph.gov.uk**.

Transaction	Driver card	Company card	Workshop card	Control card
Card application	£38	£38	£0	£0
Renewal after 5 years	£19	£19	£0	£0
Replacement – lost/stolen	£19	£19	£0	£0
Exchange	£0	£38	£0	£0
Malfunction	£0	£0	£0	£0

Typical Digital Equipment

Typical equipment comprises a recording unit (ie the VU) incorporating a mass memory fitted into the vehicle instrument panel. This is connected to an intelligent sensor to enable transmission of 'driving' pulses to the recording unit and to the instrument cluster for displaying road speed, time and distance travelled. Connections are provided (ie data interfaces) to allow readout of the stored data via an office PC or a laptop computer, and for it to be printed out to hard copy via a suitable printer where required. Various warning functions are incorporated and a keypad connection can be made to input additional commands and relevant data.

Production of Digital Records

Operator Responsibility for Digital Records

For road safety reasons, and to ensure compliance with legal requirements regarding the monitoring and preservation of digital tachograph records, operators should ensure that they follow the guidance given by VOSA in its Safe Operator's Guide (pp 11–15), which is summarized below. In particular, it is important that the operator can show that his drivers are keeping to the hours and record keeping regulations by having a good monitoring and control system in place.

Digital tachographs require the electronic downloading of data from driver smart cards and from tachograph instruments; this will support improved methods of analysis but requires different administrative processes to those used for analogue tachograph records. The downloading and monitoring system should cover the following requirements, which are the responsibility of the transport manager or a delegated person.

Issue of Tachograph Record Sheets (Charts) and Print Rolls

- Record the quantity and type of charts/print rolls issued (ie make and Type Approval number).
- Record the driver's name and date of issue.

Return of Record Sheets and Printouts

- Record the date and time of chart returns and/or printouts.
- Record other relevant details (eg damaged or defaced charts and missing records).

Checking and Downloading of Driver Smart Cards

- Download data from driver smart cards at regular intervals – ie at a maximum of 28-day intervals and sufficiently often that no data are lost (NB: smart cards generally hold up to 28 days' data, overwriting the oldest records when the card is full).
- Routinely check and download smart cards, particularly for agency and part-time drivers to ensure that the cards are valid and that drivers have adequate time to complete their duties.

NB: *A digital download tool is needed for this purpose, such as the Dig-fob available from T+M Ingenieur Buero (***www.t-m-ingbuero.de***).*

Locking-in and -out of Digital Tachographs with a Company Card

Company cards allow operators to download data from the digital tachograph (ie the vehicle unit – VU), which should be done routinely within the legal maximum time (ie at a maximum of 56-day intervals) to ensure that data are complete and accurate and to enable operators to take timely action to remedy any problems. This download will identify all driving activities, driver cards used and driving where no card has been used, and any 'events' or 'faults' recorded by the instrument.

Analysing Digital Data

Digital data downloading from the instrument itself or from driver smart cards requires IT equipment and software to analyse the data. Alternatively, analysis can be carried out remotely by a third party. Such data must be available from the operator to anybody authorized to inspect the data.

Records of Analysis of Driver Record

Records should be kept of the analysis and the results from both analogue and digital tachographs, particularly why journeys were not completed as scheduled, breakdown, traffic delays, etc, and whether the driver has endorsed the back of the chart or the printout as appropriate.

Lists of Faults and Offences

Lists should be kept of all drivers' hours and records offences, occurrences of tachograph faults and instances of speeding found during analysis. A procedure should be in place to bring these promptly to the attention of the person running the operation (ie the CPC holder) and to drivers.

Monitoring and Training of Drivers

A system should be in place to interview drivers when offences are discovered with a view to arranging suitable training programmes and, where necessary, imposing sanctions.

Repairing Tachographs

Adequate procedures should be in place for ensuring that tachograph malfunctions are dealt with, bearing in mind that it is an offence to use a vehicle with a defective tachograph.

Storing Record Sheets and Printouts

It is a legal requirement that tachograph records (ie both charts and printouts) are kept for at least one year from the date they were made – filed in date order under either the driver's name or the vehicle registration numbers.

Storing Digital Data

Downloaded data from digital instruments and driver smart cards must be stored for at least one year. These data must be stored in their downloaded format (in accordance with the technical data in Regulation 1360/2002/EC) and operators are legally required to ensure that the downloading equipment used (by themselves or by contracted outside agencies) can fulfil this requirement. The data may be stored remotely from the operating centre (eg at the premises of an analysis bureau), provided they can be made readily available on request (eg by e-mail transfer if necessary).

Working Time Records

Records of work by employees under the provisions of the Working Time Directive must be maintained by employers and stored for at least two years following the period to which they relate. This may be done through the payroll system. Workers must, on request, be given copies of the records of hours worked.

Production of Digital Records

Drivers working with digital tachographs must be able to produce for inspection on request by an inspecting officer:

- their digital tachograph card;
- any printouts and manual records for the current day and for the previous 28 calendar days;
- any analogue tachograph charts relating to the use of such instruments during this period.

See also pp 124–26.

Drivers who fail to produce such records on request may find themselves prohibited from driving for 48 hours and fined up to £200. Such actions will be recorded against the Operator's Compliance Risk Score (OCRS) and may result in his vehicles being pinpointed more frequently during roadside enforcement checks.

Signing of Digital Records

In instances where their smart card malfunctions, drivers are required by law to produce two copies of the digital printout from the tachograph, one at the beginning of the journey and the other at the end. These copies must be annotated to show the driver's name and he must sign each copy.

Return of Records

Digital records (ie printouts and downloads) must be returned by the driver to his employer or the vehicle operator, normally within 30 days, but this may vary according to circumstances. Where this is not possible, the enforcement authorities will require evidence that the employer/operator has adequate alternative systems in place for controlling drivers' compliance with the driving hours and working time regulations.

New Anti-Fraud Measures

The EC has adopted a two-part package of measures aimed at:

- detecting and preventing abuses of the tachograph system; and
- providing the use of dedicated, type-approved adaptors for light vehicles that are required to comply with the Drivers' Hours and Tachograph rules.

First, member states are required to develop dedicated equipment and software that can be used to analyse the data from the digital tachograph. Additionally, best practice guidance is given for national control authorities when carrying out checks of vehicles and the recording equipment, whether at the roadside, at company premises, or at workshops.

Second, in the case of certain light vehicles (ie vehicles in classes M1 and N1) in which it was technically not possible to install tachograph equipment so that it could meet the necessary requirements, the use of a dedicated, type-approved adaptor for these vehicles is allowed.

Digital Tachographs – the 'One Minute Rule'

Changes under EU Regulation 1266/2009/EC will make digital tachograph readings more secure and enable drivers to more accurately comply with the regulations. This will overcome the controversy surrounding what has become known as the 'One Minute Rule'. Under existing legislation, when a vehicle is driven for any part of a minute this would be recorded on the digital tachograph and driver's card, in each case, as a full minute of driving. The new regulations will alter the way driving time is calculated and will abandon the former calculating process. In future, if a vehicle is in motion for the shortest portion of a minute and then stationary for longer during the same minute, the dominant seconds will determine how the minute is recorded. Thus, if the vehicle is moving for 29 seconds within a calendar minute, and remains stationary for the next 31 seconds, under the new system the entire minute will be recorded as rest time. If the situation is reversed and the vehicle is in motion for 31 seconds, this, conversely, would record as a full minute of driving time. Although relatively insignificant, the changes could benefit multi-drop drivers by allowing them up to as much as 30 minutes more driving time during their working day.

Driver Licensing and Licence Penalties

Driver Licensing

Any person wishing to drive a motor (ie mechanically propelled) vehicle on a public road in the UK or within Europe must hold a licence showing a driving entitlement (either full or provisional) for the relevant category of vehicle. Specifically in the case of goods vehicle driving, drivers must hold a current licence showing a relevant LGV vocational driving entitlement (either full or provisional). This is the legal responsibility of the individual concerned and heavy penalties are imposed on any person found to be driving either without a licence, without a licence covering the correct category of vehicle, or while disqualified from driving by a court.

Furthermore, it is the responsibility of the employer of any person required to drive for business purposes to ensure that such employee-drivers, irrespective of their function, status or seniority, are correctly licensed to drive company vehicles. The fact that a driver may be disqualified or has allowed his licence to lapse without the employer knowing is no defence for the employer against prosecution on a charge of allowing an unlicensed person to drive a vehicle.

Offences

The law states that it is an offence to drive, or to cause or permit another person to drive, a vehicle on the road without a current and valid driving licence. In the case of large goods vehicles (LGVs) it is an offence to drive, or to cause another person to drive, without a valid licence (ie full or provisional) giving entitlement to drive vehicles in categories C or C+E.

Checking Licences

Haulage employers are advised by the police to check their drivers' licences on a regular basis – always initially when giving a driver a job and then at least once every three to six months – otherwise they leave themselves wide open to prosecution for a range of licensing offences and for the vehicle insurance to be invalidated. When checking licences only an original licence should be accepted, never a photocopy. Check that all of a driver's given names shown on the licence match those in the company record, and that the date of birth shown also coincides with that recorded at the time of employment.

Employers can check the validity of a driving licence and verify the holder's driving entitlements by contacting the DVLA's Data Subject Enquiry Department at Swansea for a printout of the details currently held on file. It is necessary to obtain written authorization from the individual concerned before making application and this authorization together with a fee of £5.00 must be submitted. For details contact the DVLC on 01792 310075. Form P57, which lists conviction codes and what they stand for, can also be obtained free from the DVLA.

Where a driver has a new-type photocard licence, it is important to examine both the photocard and the accompanying 'counterpart'. One without the other is not valid.

Invalidation of Insurance

Driving without a current and valid driving licence covering the category of vehicle being driven can invalidate insurance cover (which is itself an offence and is usually included among the charges for an unlicensed person driving) and could result in any accident or damage claim being refused by the insurance company under the terms of its policy contract – which is invariably conditional upon the law being complied with in full.

Licensing Provisions

The licensing provisions described in this chapter are principally contained in:

- the Road Traffic Act 1988;
- the Road Traffic (Driver Licensing and Information Systems) Act 1989;
- the Road Traffic (New Drivers) Act 1995;

and the following regulations:

- The Motor Vehicles (Driving Licences) (Large Goods and Passenger Carrying Vehicles) Regulations 1990 (which deal with entitlements to drive large goods vehicles over 7.5 tonnes gross weight and passenger-carrying vehicles which are used for hire and reward operations), plus a number of subsequent amendments;
- The Motor Vehicles (Driving Licences) Regulations 1999;
- The Motor Vehicles (Driving Licences) Amendment Regulations (updating fees).

The licence-scheme changes brought about by this legislation involved significant change in vocational (ie HGV/PSV) licensing. In particular, the terminology changed so that heavy goods vehicles (HGVs) and public service vehicles (PSVs) as they were previously known, are now called large goods vehicles (LGVs) and passenger-carrying vehicles (PCVs), respectively, and goods vehicles are no longer classified by the number of axles.

For driver licensing purposes:

- a 'large goods vehicle' is 'a motor vehicle (not being a medium-sized goods vehicle) which is constructed or adapted to carry or haul goods and the permissible maximum weight of which exceeds 7.5 tonnes';

- a medium-sized goods vehicle is defined as one having a permissible maximum weight exceeding 3.5 tonnes but not exceeding 7.5 tonnes;

- a large passenger-carrying vehicle is a vehicle constructed or adapted to carry more than 16 passengers;

- a small passenger-carrying vehicle is a vehicle which carries passengers for hire or reward and which is constructed or adapted to carry more than 8 but not more than 16 passengers.

Driving Licences

Major changes to Britain's ordinary and HGV driving licence schemes were introduced in 1990–91 as the UK harmonized with EU requirements. Since 1 April 1991 the pink and green European model, 'unified' driving licence (Euro-licence), which shows all of an individual's entitlements to drive (ie for motorcycle, car, light and large goods vehicles, and passenger carrying vehicles as appropriate), has been issued from the DVLA, Swansea. Traffic Commissioners (TCs) no longer have responsibility for issuing large goods and passenger vehicle licences. The Euro-licence carries the words 'European Communities Model' and has 'Driving Licence' printed in the 11 languages of the EU (besides the language of the country of issue – eg English), including Greek and Gaelic, on the front. British-issued Euro-licences also show, where appropriate, provisional driving entitlements and any endorsements of penalty points or licence disqualification made by the courts. This part of the document is called the 'counterpart' and is coloured green.

Further driving licence rule changes are to be made following introduction of the provisions of EC Directive 2006/126/EC of 20 December 2006. This Directive is intended to ensure uniformity of licences across all Member States (currently 110 different driving licences are in use across the EU), to prevent fraud and to guarantee free movement of driving licence holders throughout the whole of the EU. Eventually, all driving licences will be of the credit card type carrying a photograph of the holder and with a microchip inserted on which other driver details will be recorded. There will be universal medical requirements for drivers and universal periods of validity for licences.

Green Licences Still Valid

National driving licences issued in EU member states are still recognized throughout the EU and existing British 'green' ordinary driving licences continue to be valid both in Britain and in other countries which recognize British licences.

Existing UK Licence Holders

For a large proportion of British ordinary driving licence holders (ie those who have no vocational – LGV or PCV – entitlements) who currently hold 'licences-for-life', the changes mentioned above will not be noticed unless or until they apply to change the details on their licence (eg to record a new address or, in the case of a woman, applying for a new licence to show her married name), when they will be issued with the Euro-licence.

The DVLA no longer issues paper driving licences. An EU directive requires all member states to issue driving licences in a card format containing the licence holder's photograph and signature.

The photocard driving licence, which is made entirely from polycarbonate (and is valid for 10 years, after which it has to be surrendered for renewal), has a number of enhanced security features that were not available on the older licences. One of the main differences between the two is that the current photocard has a black and white photo while the older version had a coloured one.

The photocard driving licence is said to offer numerous benefits as follows:

- A secure format reduces the chance for misrepresentation.
- It makes certain that the person getting a provisional licence, taking the test and getting a full driving licence is one and the same.
- It makes certain that the person obtaining the licence is the right age to do so.
- It cuts the chances of a person holding more than one licence, either by accident or design.
- It increases the accuracy of the DVLA database, which will in turn provide better information to the police and courts.

Application can be made online at **https://motoring.direct.gov.uk** to exchange a paper licence for a photocard licence, or apply by post to the DVLA, Swansea SA99 1BU.

Organ Donor Option

Since 1 March 1993 UK-issued Euro driving licences have incorporated an organ donor consent section (in the green counterpart of the licence document). Previously, only provisional driving licences had this facility and separate donor cards were enclosed by the DVLA when sending out full driving licences. Completion of the section is entirely voluntary and both the DfT and the Department of Health have jointly confirmed that a consenting donor's organs would not, in any event, be removed without the prior permission of the deceased's next of kin. The separate organ donor card remains valid for existing licence holders.

The Issuing Authority

Responsibility for the issue of vocational driving entitlements rests with the Driver and Vehicle Licensing Agency (DVLA), Swansea. However, it should be noted that the TCs still retain a disciplinary role in regard to vocational entitlements as described on p 166.

All applications in connection with driver licensing (ie for both ordinary and vocational driving entitlements) should be addressed to the DVLA, Swansea followed by the appropriate postal code, ie:

- SA99 1AD for first provisional licences;
- SA99 1AB for renewals, duplicate and exchange licences;
- SA99 1BJ for first full car and motorcycle licences; and
- SA99 1BR for all vocational entitlement applications (including minibuses).

Online licence applications can be made via the Directgov website at **www.direct.gov.uk**.

Further information on driver licensing can be obtained from the Customer Enquiries Unit, DVLA, Swansea SA6 7JL (tel: 01792 772151; fax: 01792 783071 for general enquiries about the licensing system). Ring 01792 782787 to use minicom owing to hearing difficulties.

Minimum Age for Drivers of Small, Medium and Large Vehicles

Certain minimum ages are specified by law for drivers of small, medium and large motor vehicle as follows:

Small Goods Vehicle

- Small goods vehicle not exceeding 3.5 tonnes maximum authorized mass (including the weight of a trailer not exceeding 750 kilograms maximum authorized mass)
  Category B   *17 years**
  *16 if receiving a Disability Living Allowance (ie mobility allowance)

- Small goods vehicle not exceeding 3.5 tonnes maximum authorized mass (including the weight of a trailer exceeding 750 kilograms maximum authorized mass)
  Category B + E   *17 years*

Medium Goods Vehicles

- Medium-sized goods vehicle constructed or adapted to transport goods which exceeds 3.5 tonnes maximum authorized mass but not 7.5 tonnes maximum authorized mass (including the weight of a trailer not exceeding 750 kilograms maximum authorized mass)
  Category C1   *18 years**
  *17 if member of the armed services

- Combinations of vehicles where the towing vehicle is in subcategory C1 and its trailer has a maximum authorized mass (MAM) of more than 750 kilograms maximum authorized mass, provided that the maximum authorized mass of the combination thus formed does not exceed 12,000 kilograms and the maximum authorized mass of the trailer does not exceed the unladen mass of the towing vehicle. (If driver passed category B test prior to 1 January 1997 he will be restricted to a total weight not more than 8,250 kilograms)

  Category C1+ E   *21 years* * * **

  *17 if member of the armed services

  ** 18 if:

  - after passing a driving test for this category and Driver Certificate of Professional Competence (Driver CPC) initial qualification
  - learning to drive or taking a driving test for this category or Driver CPC initial qualification
  - while undergoing a national vocational training course to obtain a Driver CPC initial qualification
  - if driving licence attained before 10 September 2009

Large Good Vehicles

- Vehicles over 3,500 kilograms maximum authorized mass with a trailer up to 750 kilograms maximum authorized mass

  Category C   *21 years* * * **

  *17 if member of the armed services

  ** 18 if:

  - after passing a driving test for this category and Driver Certificate of Professional Competence (Driver CPC) initial qualification
  - learning to drive or taking a driving test for this category or Driver CPC initial qualification
  - while undergoing a national vocational training course to obtain a Driver CPC initial qualification
  - if driving licence attained before 10 September 2009

- Vehicles over 3,500 kilograms maximum authorized mass with a trailer over 750 kilograms maximum authorized mass

  Category C + E   *21 years* * * **

  *17 if member of the armed services

  ** 18 if:

  - after passing a driving test for this category and Driver Certificate of Professional Competence (Driver CPC) initial qualification
  - learning to drive or taking a driving test for this category or Driver CPC initial qualification
  - while undergoing a national vocational training course to obtain a Driver CPC initial qualification
  - if driving licence attained before 10 September 2009

Road Rollers

A person under 21 but not less than 17 years old may drive a road roller if it:

- is propelled by means other than steam;
- has an unladen weight of not more than 11,650 kg;*
- is fitted with metal or hard rollers;
- is not constructed or adapted to carry a load other than water, fuel, accumulators and other equipment used for the purpose of propulsion, loose tools, loose equipment and any object which is specially constructed for attachment to the vehicle so as to increase, temporarily, its unladen weight.

NB: If this weight is exceeded, the minimum age for driving a roller is 21 years.

Agricultural Tractors

A person under 17 but over 16 may drive an agricultural tractor only if it is:

- of the wheeled type;
- not more than 2.45 metres wide including the width of any fitted implement;
- specially licensed for excise duty purposes as an agricultural machine;
- not drawing a trailer other than one of the two-wheeled or close-coupled four-wheeled type which is not more than 2.45 metres wide.

A 16-year-old must not drive an agricultural tractor on a road unless he has passed the appropriate test.

Vehicle Categories/Groups for Driver Licensing

For driver licensing purposes vehicles are defined according to specified groupings or categories, which are shown on licences by means of capital letters as indicated in the following lists.

EU Vehicle Categories

Under the Euro-licensing system, the old British system of vehicle groups has been replaced by EU vehicle categories as listed below. All future licences will specify driving entitlements against these vehicle categories.

Category	Vehicle type
Cars and light vans	
B	Motor vehicles not exceeding 3.5 tonnes mass and with not more than eight seats (excluding the driver's seat) including drawing a trailer not exceeding 750 kg mass. Including combinations of category B vehicles and a trailer where the combined weight does not exceed 3.5 tonnes and the weight of the trailer does not exceed the unladen weight of the towing vehicle. *Additional categories covered: F, K, P*
B1	Motor tricycles and three/four-wheeled cars and vans up to 550 kg unladen with a design speed not exceeding 50 kph and if fitted with an internal combustion engine, a cubic capacity not exceeding 50 cc. *Additional categories covered: K, P*
B+E	Motor vehicles in category B drawing a trailer over 750 kg where the combination does not come within category B.
Medium goods vehicles	
C1	Medium goods vehicles between 3.5 tonnes and 7.5 tonnes (including drawing trailer not exceeding 750 kg) – maximum weight of the combination must not exceed 8.25 tonnes.
C1+E	Medium goods vehicles between 3.5 tonnes and 7.5 tonnes and drawing a trailer over 750 kg but does not exceed the unladen weight of the towing vehicle – maximum weight of the combination must not exceed 12 tonnes. *Additional category covered: B+E*
Large goods vehicles	
C	Large goods vehicles over 3.5 tonnes (but excluding vehicles in categories D, F, G and H) including those drawing a trailer not exceeding 750 kg.
C+E	Large goods vehicles in category C drawing a trailer exceeding 750 kg. *Some C+E licences, where the holder was previously qualified to drive vehicles in old HGV class 2 or 3, show a restriction limiting driving to drawbar combinations only. Additional category covered: B+E*
Minibuses	
D1	Passenger vehicles with between 9 and 16 seats including drawing trailer not exceeding 750 kg.
D1+E	Motor vehicles in category D1 drawing a trailer over 750 kg – the weight of the trailer must not exceed the unladen weight of the towing vehicle and the maximum weight of the combination must not exceed 12 tonnes. *Additional category covered: B+E*

Category	Vehicle type
Passenger vehicles	
D	Passenger vehicles with more than 8 seats including drawing a trailer not exceeding 750 kg.
D+E	Passenger vehicles in category D drawing a trailer over 750 kg. *Additional category covered: B+E*
Other vehicles	
F	Agricultural or forestry tractors but excluding any vehicle in category H.
G	Road rollers.
H	Track-laying vehicles steered by their tracks.
K	Mowing machine or pedestrian-controlled vehicle with up to three wheels and not over 410 kg.
L	Electrically propelled vehicles.
P	Mopeds.

NB: *In the above table, vehicle/trailer weights, unless otherwise specified, are to be taken as the maximum authorized mass (mam), which is the same as the permissible maximum weight (pmw) for the vehicle/trailer – commonly referred to as the 'gross weight'.*

Restricted Category for Pre-1997 Drivers

Drivers of goods vehicles with trailers in category C1+E who passed their category B test prior to 1 January 1997 are restricted to a total combination weight of 8,250 kilograms. The restriction is marked on the driver's licence with the code 107. Driving a combination up to the 12-tonne limit requires an additional test.

NB: *A full list of licence restrictions and information codes can be found on the DVLA website at:* **http://www.dvla.gov.uk/media/pdf/leaflets/ins57p.pdf**.

Restricted Categories for Post-1997 Drivers

Since 1 January 1997, new drivers passing the car and light vehicle test (ie with vehicles not exceeding 3.5 tonnes permissible maximum weight) for the first time are not permitted to drive vehicles above this weight without securing additional driving categories on their licence. It is stressed that this restriction to 3.5 tonne driving applies *only* to those who first pass their test since this date; it will not be applied retrospectively to existing licence holders – their existing entitlements are preserved.

Drivers who pass their car test (ie category B) are not permitted to:

- drive minibuses (in category D1);
- drive medium-sized goods vehicles (in category C1); or
- tow large (ie over 750 kg) trailers (in categories B+E, C1+E and D1+E).

They must take a further test if they wish to drive such vehicles or vehicle combinations.

Any driver wishing to drive a vehicle towing a heavy trailer (ie one with a gross weight over 750 kg) must first pass a test in the associated rigid vehicle. Learner drivers in categories B, C1, C, D1 and D cannot drive a vehicle towing a trailer of any size.

NB: The Driving Standards Agency has warned that 'heavy trailers' in this context includes twin-axled caravans, horsebox trailers and boat trailers. If such trailers are towed, a full B+E driving entitlement is required.

Towed and Pushed Vehicles

It has been ruled that a person who steers a vehicle being towed (whether it has broken down or even has vital parts missing, such as the engine) is 'driving' the vehicle for licensing purposes and therefore needs to hold current and valid driving entitlement covering that category of vehicle. Conversely, it has been held that a person pushing a vehicle from the outside (ie with both feet on the ground) is not 'driving' a vehicle, nor are they 'using' the vehicle.

Incomplete Vehicles

Drivers of incomplete goods vehicles comprising a chassis and cab only (ie before bodywork is fitted) and of articulated tractive units not yet fitted with a fifth-wheel coupling need (from 1 January 1998) must hold either a category C1 driving entitlement for such vehicles weighing between 3.5 and 7.5 tonnes, or a category C entitlement for such vehicles weighing over 7.5 tonnes. Prior to this date incomplete vehicles could be driven on a category B licence covering motor cars and light vans.

Tractive Units

Drivers of heavy (ie over 3.5 tonne) articulated tractive units with no semi-trailer attached need hold only a category C driving entitlement – contrary to popular misconception, a category C+E driving entitlement is not required.

Learner Drivers

Learner drivers must hold a provisional driving entitlement to cover them while driving under tuition. This provisional driving entitlement is shown on the green 'counterpart' of the licence.

Full category C LGV entitlement holders can use this entitlement in place of a provisional entitlement for learning to drive vehicles in category C+E (ie drawbar combinations and articulated vehicles). But it should be noted that full entitlements in categories B and C1 *cannot* be used as a provisional entitlement for learning to drive vehicles in categories C or C+E. A proper provisional entitlement for these classes is required.

Learner drivers must be accompanied, when driving on public roads, by the holder of a full entitlement covering the category of vehicle being driven (see also below) and must not drive a vehicle drawing a trailer, except in the case of articulated vehicles or agricultural trailers. (*NB: Full licence holders must have held the licence for 3 years.*)

An 'L' plate of the approved dimensions must be displayed on the front and rear of a vehicle being driven by a learner driver (see Chapter 7). Learners driving in Wales may alternatively display a 'D' plate.

Learner drivers of category B vehicles are not allowed to drive on motorways. However, learner LGV drivers seeking a licence for category C1, C and C+E vehicles and who hold full entitlements in licence categories B and C1 may drive such vehicles on motorways while under tuition.

Compulsory Retests for Offending New Drivers

From 2 June 1997, newly qualified drivers who tot up six or more penalty points on their licence within two years of passing the test revert to learner status (ie with the display of 'L' plates and the need to be accompanied by a qualified driver) and have to repass both the theory test and the practical driving test before regaining a full licence.

Supervision of 'L' Drivers

Qualified drivers who supervise learner drivers in cars and in light, medium and large goods vehicles must:

- be at least 21 years old;
- have held a full driving entitlement for a continuous period of at least three years (excluding any periods of disqualification); and
- for accompanying learner LGV drivers, have held a relevant entitlement (ie for the type of vehicle on which they are supervising) for at least three years.

Contravention of these requirements could lead to prosecution of the supervising driver and, on conviction, a fine of up to £400, the imposition of two driving licence penalty points and possibly licence disqualification.

Insurance Scheme for New Drivers

A government scheme of insurance incentives was launched in 1995 to encourage newly qualified drivers to take additional lessons after passing their driving test. The 'Pass Plus' scheme is aimed particularly at young drivers who have not previously taken out motor insurance. It comprises six training sessions, normally taken within 12 months of passing the test, and includes driving in all weather conditions, at night, on motorways and dual carriageways and in town. Some 20 insurance companies offer preferential insurance premiums to 'Pass Plus' certificate holders.

Exemptions from Vocational Licensing

Exemptions from the need to hold an LGV driving entitlement (ie in categories C or C+E) apply when driving certain vehicles as follows (in most cases such vehicles may be driven by the holder of a category B licence):

1 Steam-propelled vehicles.

2 Road construction vehicles used or kept on the road solely for the conveyance of built-in construction machinery.

3 Engineering plant, but not mobile cranes*.

4 Works trucks.

5 Industrial tractors.

6 Agricultural motor vehicles which are not agricultural or forestry tractors.

7 Digging machines.

8 Vehicles used on public roads only when passing between land occupied by the vehicle's registered keeper and which does not exceed an aggregate of 9.7km in a calendar week.

9 Vehicles, other than agricultural vehicles, used only for the purposes of agriculture, horticulture or forestry, between areas of land occupied by the same person and which do travel more than 1.5km on public roads.

10 Vehicles used for no purpose other than the haulage of lifeboats and the conveyance of the necessary gear of the lifeboats which are being hauled.

11 Vehicles manufactured before 1 January 1960 used unladen and not drawing a laden trailer.

12 Articulated goods vehicles with an unladen weight not exceeding 3.05 tonnes.

13 Vehicles in the service of a visiting military force or headquarters as defined in the Visiting Forces and International Headquarters (Application of Law) Order 1965.

14 Any vehicle being driven by a police constable for the purpose of removing it to avoid obstruction to other road users or danger to other road users or members of the public, for the purpose of safeguarding life or property, including the vehicle and its load, or for other similar purposes.

15 Breakdown vehicles which weigh less than 3.05 tonnes unladen, provided they are fitted with apparatus for raising a disabled vehicle partly from the ground and for drawing a vehicle when so raised, are used solely for the purpose of dealing with disabled vehicles, and carry no load other than a disabled vehicle and articles used in connection with dealing with disabled vehicles.

16 A passenger-carrying vehicle recovery vehicle other than an articulated vehicle with an unladen weight of not more than 10.2 tonnes which belongs to the holder of a PSV 'O' licence, when such a vehicle is going to or returning from a place where it is to give assistance to a damaged or disabled passenger-carrying vehicle or giving assistance to or moving a disabled passenger-carrying vehicle or moving a damaged vehicle.

17 A mobile project vehicle, which is defined as a vehicle exceeding 3.5 tonnes pmw constructed or adapted to carry not more than eight persons in addition to the driver and which carries mainly goods or burden comprising play or educational equipment for children or articles used for display or exhibition purposes.

*NB: Drivers of mobile cranes must hold a full LGV vocational entitlement covering vehicles in category C1 for driving cranes between 3.5 and 7.5 tonnes and category C for driving cranes over 7.5 tonnes mpw (applicable since 1 January 1999).

Application for Licences and Vocational Entitlements

Applications for driving licences have to be made to Swansea on form D1 for ordinary licences and form D2 for vocational licences. Forms are obtainable from main post offices, direct from Swansea via the internet (at **www.direct.gov.uk**) or from Local Vehicle Registration Offices.

Questions on the form are concerned with personal details of the applicant, the type of licence required, any previous licence held and whether the applicant is currently disqualified. LGV/PCV entitlement applicants are asked about any convictions they may have recorded against them.

Health Declaration

Applicants are asked to declare information about their health, particularly as to whether they have:

- had an epileptic event (ie seizure or fit);
- sudden attacks of disabling giddiness, fainting or blackouts;
- severe mental handicap;
- had a pacemaker, defibrillator or anti-ventricular tachycardia device fitted;
- diabetes controlled by insulin;
- angina (heart pain) while driving;
- had a major or minor stroke;
- Parkinson's disease;
- any other chronic neurological condition;
- a serious problem with memory;
- serious episodes of confusion;
- had any type of brain surgery, brain tumour or severe head injury involving hospital in-patient treatment;
- any severe psychiatric illness or mental disorder;
- continuing or permanent difficulty in the use of arms or legs which affects the ability to control a vehicle safely;

- been dependent on or misused alcohol, illicit drugs or chemical substances in the previous three years (excluding drink/driving offences);
- any visual disability which affects both eyes (short/long sight and colour blindness do not have to be declared).

Applicants for LGV/PCV entitlements (unless submitting a medical report – form D4 – see below) are required to state whether they have:

- sight in only one eye;
- any visual problems affecting either eye;
- angina;
- any heart condition or had a heart operation.

Where licence applicants have previously declared a medical condition, they are required to state what the condition is, whether it has worsened since it was previously declared and whether any special controls have been fitted to their vehicle since the last licence was issued.

The DVLA's Considerations for Vocational Entitlements

Applicants for vocational driving entitlements must meet specified conditions as follows:

- They must be fit and proper persons.
- They must meet laid-down eyesight requirements.
- They must satisfy a medical examination and specifically must not
  - have had an epileptic attack in the previous 10 years (see below), or
  - suffer from insulin-dependent diabetes.

The decision as to whether or not an applicant will be granted an LGV driving entitlement rests entirely with the DVLA and in making this decision it will take into account any driving convictions for motoring offences, drivers' hours and record offences, and offences relating to the roadworthiness or loading of vehicles against the applicant in the 4 years prior to the application, and any offence connected with driving under the influence of drink or drugs during the 11 years prior to the application. The applicant has to declare such convictions on the licence application form (D2) but the DVLA has means of checking to ensure that applicants have declared any such convictions against them.

TCs' Powers in Respect of Vocational Entitlements

Although the issue of vocational (ie LGV/PCV) entitlements is the prerogative of the DVLA, TCs still have powers to consider the fitness of persons applying for or holding such entitlements. This disciplinary role allows a TC to call upon applicants or entitlement holders to provide information as to their conduct (and if necessary to appear before him to answer in person), to refuse the grant of an entitlement, and to suspend or disqualify a person from holding such an entitlement. The TC's decision must be communicated to the person concerned, upon whom it is binding, and to the Secretary of State for Transport (effectively the DVLA).

Date for Vocational Applications

Application for an LGV driving entitlement should be made not more than three months before the date from which the entitlement is required to run. Reminders will be sent out by the DVLA to existing licence/entitlement holders two months prior to the expiry date of their existing licence/entitlement.

Medical Requirements for Vocational Entitlements

Strict medical standards for vocational entitlement holders are legally established to ensure that those wishing to drive large goods or passenger-carrying vehicles are safe to do so and are not suffering from any disease or disability (especially cardiovascular disease, diabetes mellitus, epilepsy, neurosurgical disorders, excessive sleepiness, nervous or mental disorders, vision problems, or the excessive use of prescribed medicines or illicit drugs, for example) which would prevent them from driving safely.

Even tougher medical standards for vocational entitlement holders were brought in from 1 January 1997 when the EU's 'second' driver licensing Directive came into force. In particular these concern eyesight (see pp 175–76) and a number of other serious problems which are added to the list of medical disabilities that may result in failure of the medical examination and refusal of a driving licence (see below).

UK applicants for LGV driving entitlements must satisfy such medical standards on first application and subsequently. To do so, they must undergo a medical examination and have their doctor complete the medical certificate portion of the application form D4 not more than four months before the date when the entitlement is needed to commence.

A further examination and completed medical certificate is required for each five-yearly renewal of the entitlement after reaching age 45 years. After reaching the age of 65 years a medical examination is required for each annual renewal of the entitlement. Further medical examinations may be called for at any time if there is any doubt as to a driver's fitness to drive.

The form D4 requests applicants' consent to allow the DVLA's medical adviser to obtain reports from their own doctor and any specialist consulted if this helps to establish their medical condition.

Driving Following Medical Disqualification

Where an application for a full driving licence is made following the revocation of a licence or the refusal of its renewal on medical grounds, the applicant may be required to take a driving test (or an 'on-road assessment') to determine whether he is fit to regain his licence. A provisional licence may be granted for this purpose (ie to authorize driving on the road), but its use is restricted to driving only during the period preceding and while taking the test, and its authority ceases immediately upon conclusion of the test or assessment.

Medicals for New Category C1 Drivers

Since 1 January 1997 new drivers of vehicles over 3.5 tonnes gross weight (ie covered by driving licence category C1) require the same medical examination that previously applied only to over 7.5 tonnes vocational licence holders and must follow the same regime as described above for subsequent medical examinations (ie five-yearly after age 45 years, and annually after age 65 years).

Medical Examination Fees

Doctors charge a fee for conducting such medical examinations, which the candidate must pay himself. These examinations are not available on the National Health Service in the UK – current fees are around £100 to £120. The medical fee for licence/entitlement renewal can be claimed as an allowable expense for income tax purposes.

Diabetes

Normally, insulin-dependent diabetes sufferers are barred from holding an LGV entitlement, but if they held an HGV driving licence, and the TC was aware of their condition prior to 1 January 1991, an entitlement may be granted. From 5 April 2001, new rules have removed the blanket limitation on driving category C1 vehicles between 3.5 and 7.5 tonnes by persons who suffered from diabetes before 1998 and held a relevant licence at the end of 1996. The new rules allow individual assessment of drivers wishing to drive vehicles of this category and extend this to cover also vehicles in category C1+E. Any person who lost his C1 licence under the 1997 rules can reapply for a licence, as can new drivers and new insulin users.

Epilepsy

A person will now be prevented from holding an LGV/PCV entitlement *only* if he has a 'liability to epileptic seizures'. Applicants must satisfy the DVLA that:

- he has not suffered an epileptic seizure during the 10 years prior to the date when the entitlement is to take effect;
- no epilepsy treatment has been administered during the 10 years prior to the starting date for the entitlement; and
- a consultant nominated by the DVLA has examined the medical history and is satisfied that there is no continuing liability to seizures.

Car, light vehicle and certain other drivers (ie in licence categories A, B, B+E, F, G, H, K, L and P), but not LGV/PCV drivers, who suffer from epilepsy can obtain a licence to drive such vehicles provided they:

- have been free from an epileptic attack during the period of one year from the date the licence is granted; or,
- if not free from such an attack, had an asleep-attack more than three years before the date on which the licence is granted and have had attacks only while asleep between the date of that attack and the date when the licence is granted; and
- provided the DVLA is satisfied that driving by them will not cause danger.

Coronary Health Problems

Drivers who have suspected coronary health problems are permitted (since April 1992) to retain their LGV driving entitlements while medical enquiries are made. (Previously the rule was to revoke the licence pending enquiries into the holder's health.) Such drivers no longer have to submit to coronary angiography (ie angiogram testing). The DVLA says that ECG exercise tests will be undertaken no earlier than three months after a coronary event and providing the driver displays no signs of angina or other significant symptoms, he is allowed to keep his driving entitlement while investigations are made, but subject to the approval of his own doctor.

Drivers who have suffered, or are suffering from, the following heart-related conditions must notify the DVLA:

- heart attack (myocardial infarction, coronary thrombosis);
- coronary angioplasty;
- heart valve disease/surgery;
- coronary artery bypass surgery;
- angina (heart pain);
- heart operation (other than a heart transplant).

The DVLA's Drivers Medical Branch has the following advice for heart sufferers:

- Following a heart attack or heart operation, driving should not be recommenced for at least one month following the attack or operation. Driving may be resumed after this time if recovery has been uncomplicated and the patient's own doctor has given his approval.
- A driver suffering from angina may continue to drive (whether or not he is receiving treatment) unless attacks occur while driving, in which case he must notify the DVLA immediately (see below) and *stop driving*.
- A driver who suffers sudden attacks of disabling giddiness, fainting, falling, loss of awareness or confusion must notify the DVLA immediately (see below) and *stop driving*.

Any driver who has doubts about his ability to continue to drive safely is advised to discuss the matter with his own doctor, who has access to medical advice from the DVLA.

Alcohol Problems

Persons with repeated convictions for drink-driving offences may be required to satisfy the DVLA (with certification from their own doctor) that they do not have an 'alcohol problem' before their licence is restored to them.

Other Medical Conditions

Other disabilities which may cause failure of the driver's medical examination include:

- sudden attacks of vertigo ('dizziness');

- heart disease which causes disabling weakness or pain;
- a history of coronary thrombosis;
- the use of hypertensive drugs for blood pressure treatment;
- serious arrhythmia;
- severe mental disorder;
- severe behavioural problems;
- alcohol dependency;
- inability to refrain from drinking and driving;
- drug abuse and dependency;
- psychotrophic medicines taken in quantities likely to impair fitness to drive safely.

A licence will be refused to a driver who is liable to sudden attacks of disabling giddiness or fainting unless these can be controlled.

Those who have had a cardiac pacemaker fitted are advised to discontinue LGV driving, although driving vehicles below the 7.5 tonnes LGV threshold is permitted if a person who has disabling attacks which are controlled by a pacemaker has made arrangements for regular review from a cardiologist and will not be likely to endanger the public.

Notification of New or Worsening Medical Conditions

Once a licence has been granted (ie whether ordinary or covering vocational entitlements), the holder is required to notify the Drivers Medical Group, DVLA at Swansea SA99 1TU of the onset, *or worsening*, of any medical condition likely to cause him to be a danger when driving – *failure to do so is an offence*. Examples of what must be reported are:

- giddiness;
- fainting;
- blackouts;
- epilepsy;
- diabetes;
- strokes;
- multiple sclerosis;
- Parkinson's disease;
- heart disease;
- angina;
- 'coronaries';
- high blood pressure;
- arthritis;
- disorders of vision;
- mental illness;

- alcoholism;
- drug-taking;
- loss, or loss of use, of any limb.

In many cases the person's own doctor will either advise reporting the condition to the DVLA himself, or the doctor (or hospital) may advise the DVLA direct. In either case the driving licence will have to be surrendered until the condition clears.

There is no requirement to notify the DVLA of temporary illnesses or disabilities such as sprained or broken limbs where a full recovery is expected within three months.

Enquiries about medical conditions can be raised with the Drivers Medical Group at the DVLA. Telephone the Customer Enquiries Unit on 08702 411879.

New EU Health Standards for Drivers from 2013

The UK is to align the current driver health standards by 2013 with those contained in EU Directive 2006/126/EC. Principally, the changes concern eyesight, diabetes and epilepsy as follows:

- The eyesight requirements are to be reduced – licence applicants will only have to read a number plate from 17.5m instead of the currently distance of 20m. Bus and lorry drivers will be able to take vision tests wearing glasses or contact lenses, and the rules for drivers who have reduced sight in one eye will be relaxed.

- HGV drivers who are being treated with insulin will be able to apply to drive provided strict medical monitoring is carried out. Previously they could only drive vehicles up to 7.5 tonnes gross weight.

- The new rules set out a definition of epilepsy under which drivers will have to surrender their licence if they have two or more epileptic seizures in five years and that they will not be able to reapply for their licence for a further five years. The UK proposals are that two attacks in 10 years will mean the loss of a licence and a driver not being able to reapply for 10 years.

- Drivers will still be required to notify the DVLA of any health issues, including heart problems, that their doctor has warned could affect their ability to drive.

Medical Appeals and Information

The final decision on any medical matter concerning driving licences rests with the Drivers Medical Group of the DVLA. However, there is the opportunity of appeal, within six months, in England and Wales to a magistrate's court, and within 21 days in Scotland to a sheriff's court. In other cases the refused driver may be given the opportunity to present further medical evidence which the medical adviser will consider.

Further information on medical conditions relating to driving are to be found in a booklet, *Medical Aspects of Fitness to Drive*, price £6, available from the Medical Commission on Accident Prevention, 35–43 Lincoln's Inn Fields, London WC2A 3PN (tel: 020 7242 3176). Useful information for diabetic drivers may be obtained from the British Diabetic Association, 10 Queen Anne Street, London W1M 0BD (tel: 020 7636 6112; fax: 020 7462 2732).

Cover Against Loss of Licence/Entitlement on Medical Grounds

In view of the risk of losing their LGV entitlement in later life due to the onset or worsening of a medical condition and therefore jeopardizing their employment prospects, it is possible for drivers (or their employers) to insure against loss of driving licence/vocational entitlement. Special insurance schemes to cover such an eventuality are offered by, among others, the FTA, RHA and the drivers' union, the TGWU; the last promotes a scheme provided by Unity Trust. Various other independent schemes are offered by district offices of the TGWU.

Drugs and Driving

Official sources say that drugs are a major cause of one in five fatal road accidents. Another source says that driving after smoking cannabis could be a greater danger than drink-driving, and that as many as 3 million people could be driving under the influence of this drug. Yet another report has highlighted the fact that drivers who use tranquillizers are involved in 1,600 road accidents every year – 110 of them fatal.

Illegal Drugs

Among the drugs which may be detected and which can affect driving are:

- cannabis – produces slow reaction times;
- cocaine – may increase reaction times, but severely affects accuracy and judgement; has potential to cause hallucination;
- amphetamines – may increase reaction times in the short term, but severely affect accuracy and judgement;
- ecstasy – may increase reaction times, but severely affects accuracy and judgement;
- heroin – produces reduced reaction times and causes drowsiness and sleep.

Prescribed Drugs

Prescribed tranquillizers, sedatives and antidepressants, as well as diabetes and epilepsy drugs, may have an adverse effect on a driver's judgement and reactions, and therefore increase the risk of an accident. These include a number of anti-anxiolytic benzodiazepines (prescribed to reduce stress and anxiety), including:

- Valium;
- Librium;
- Ativan.

The sedatory effect of these drugs is substantially compounded by the addition of alcohol, even when taken in relatively small quantities, resulting in a potentially significant loss of co-ordination. Similarly, sleeping tablets (eg diazepam, temazepam and nitrazepam), including the new drug zopiclone, may also have a continuing sedatory effect on a driver the following morning. Furthermore, a whole range of other proprietary medicines such as painkillers, antihistamines, cold and flu remedies, eye drops, cough medicines and common painkillers taken in sufficient quantities may have similar effects.

If a driver feels drowsy, dizzy, confused, or suffers other side effects that could affect reaction times or judgement, *he should not drive.*

Drug Testing

Trial drug testing of drivers in random roadside spot checks was carried out by the police in spring 1998. Principally the scheme was designed to test the 'Drugwipe' testing kit, which is wiped across the driver's forehead to pick up any traces of drugs in his sweat. This is a foretaste of what may become standard practice.

Drug testing of LGV drivers by their employers is becoming an increasing practice in the UK, especially among tanker fleet operators, following the pattern in the United States which has had mandatory testing since 1992. In fact, Unilabs UK, one of the leading drug-testing laboratories, has reported a substantial increase in requests for testing by haulage companies in recent times. While there is no suggestion at this stage that the practice should become mandatory in this country, most of Britain's major oil companies now carry out random testing for both alcohol and drug problems – Shell has produced a staff booklet identifying 11 banned substances (including amphetamines) and warning of the consequences of drink or drug abuse.

In mid-2000, emergency tests were introduced for road users because of a sharp rise in drug-related road deaths. Drivers suspected of having taken drugs are asked, among other physical tests, to walk in a straight line and count their steps. Suspects are then taken to a police station for further tests. Fines of up to £5,000 may be imposed on convicted offenders, together with a mandatory driving ban and risk of a prison sentence.

Join the Fight against Drugs

If you have any information about drugs or drug smugglers, HM Revenue & Customs request that you ring the 24-hour hotline **0800 59 5000**. You don't have to tell them who you are, but for important information you may be eligible for a cash reward.

Eyesight Requirement

The statutory eyesight requirement mentioned above for ordinary (ie car and light goods vehicle) licence holders is for the driver to be able to read, in good daylight (with glasses or contact lenses if worn), a standard motor vehicle number plate from 20 metres (ie 65.6 feet). Under new EU proposals the number plate reading distance is to be reduced to 17.5m. A 120-degree-wide field of view is also required. It is an offence to drive with impaired eyesight and the police can require a driver to take an eyesight test on the roadside. If glasses or contact lenses are needed to reach these vision standards they must be worn at all times while driving. It is an offence to drive with impaired eyesight. There are proposals for drivers to undergo regular eye tests.

Eyesight Standards for Vocational Licence Holders

Tougher eyesight standards for LGV and PCV drivers were introduced from 1 January 1997. Specifically, drivers of vehicles in categories C, C1, C+E, C1+E, D, D1, D+E and D1+E (effectively trucks over 3.5 tonnes and passenger vehicles with more than nine seats) must have eyesight which is at least:

1 6/9 on the Snellen scale in the better eye,* and

2 6/12 on the Snellen scale in the other eye,* and

3 3/60 in each eye without glasses or contact lenses.

NB: these standards may be met with glasses or contact lenses if worn.

To achieve these standards means being able to read the top line of an optician's chart (ie Snellen chart) with each eye from a distance of *at least* 3 metres without the aid of glasses or contact lenses – if it can only be read from, say, 2.5 metres or less, the test is failed. Wearers of spectacles or contact lenses must have vision of at least 6/9 in the better eye and at least 6/12 in the weaker eye, which means being able to read the sixth line of an optician's chart at 6 metres. Besides these requirements, all drivers must meet existing eyesight standards, which include having a field of vision of at least 120° (horizontal) and 20° (vertical) in each eye with no double vision.

Drivers who held a licence before 1 January 1997 and who do not meet these higher standards are advised to check their licensing position with the Drivers Medical Group at the DVLA (see above for address and telephone number).

Licence Fees and Validity

Current fees for driving licences are as follows:

Licence type		
First provisional		
Car	£50.00	
Bus or lorry	FREE	
First full		
Car	£20.00	(if provisional licence has been lost,
Bus or Lorry	FREE	otherwise FREE)
Renewal		
From age 70	FREE	
For medical reasons	FREE	
Bus or lorry	FREE	
After disqualification	£65.00	
HRO* disqualification	£90.00	
After revocation	£50.00	

Duplicate	
Replace lost or stolen licence	£17.50
Paper licence for photocard licence	£17.50
Full Northern Ireland licence	FREE
Full EC/EEA or other foreign licence (inc. Channel Islands or IoM)	FREE
Exchange	
Add or remove entitlement	FREE
Remove expired endorsements	£20.00
Change photo on licence	£20.00
Replacement	
Change of name and/or address	FREE

* High-risk offender disqualified for drink/driving convictions

Licence Validity

An LGV/PCV driving entitlement is normally valid for five years or until the holder reaches the age of 45 years, whichever is the longer. After the age of 45 years, five-year entitlements are granted subject to medical fitness, but may be for lesser periods where the holder suffers from a relevant or prospective relevant disability. From the age of 65 years, vocational entitlements are granted on an annual basis only. Ordinary driving licences are valid until age 70 years after which they may be reviewed at 3-yearly intervals subject to meeting the health requirements. Photographs on photocard driving licences need to be renewed at 10-yearly intervals.

Tax Deductions

The cost of renewing LGV driving entitlements and for undergoing medical examinations in connection with licence renewals is income tax deductible against Schedule E earnings – but not the costs of first obtaining such an entitlement.

Lost or Mislaid Licences

Drivers who lose or mislay their driving licences should apply for a duplicate licence in the normal way using the standard application form, form D2, at a cost of £20.00.

UK drivers moving to live abroad who have mislaid their driving licence may obtain a temporary 'Certificate of Entitlement' (commonly referred to as a cover note), valid for one month, either from the DVLA at Swansea (free of charge) or from local Vehicle Registration Offices (VROs), subject to proof of their identity. This document is valid for proving entitlement to drive to enable such persons to apply for and obtain an equivalent driving entitlement in their new country of residence. Applicants for these certificates will be able to complete an application for a duplicate licence at the VRO and this will be sent on to the DVLA in Swansea for processing.

Production of Driving Licences

Both the police and enforcement officers of VOSA can request a driver – and a person accompanying a provisional entitlement holder – to produce his licence showing ordinary and vocational entitlements to drive. If he is unable to do so at the time, it may be produced without penalty:

- if the request was by a police officer, at a police station of his choice within 7 days; or
- if the request was by an enforcement officer, at the Traffic Area Office within 10 days.

In either case, if the licence cannot be produced within the 7 or 10 days it can be produced as soon as reasonably practicable thereafter. A TC can also require the holder of an LGV/PCV driving entitlement to produce his licence at a Traffic Area Office for examination within 10 days.

Failure to produce a licence on request is an offence.

A police officer can ask a driver to state his date of birth – British ordinary driving licences carry a coded number which indicates the holder's surname and date of birth. The name and address of the vehicle owner can also be requested.

NB: In the case of the photocard driving licence, it is necessary to produce also the paper 'counterpart' that accompanies it. One without the other is not valid.

When required by a VOSA examiner to produce his licence, an LGV entitlement holder may be required to give his date of birth and to sign the examiner's record sheet to verify the fact of the licence examination. This should not be refused.

Licence holders apprehended for endorsable fixed penalty (ie yellow ticket) offences are required to produce their driving licence to the police officer at that time or later (ie within seven days) to a police station and surrender the licence, for which they will be given a receipt. Failure to produce a licence in these circumstances means that the fixed penalty procedure will not be followed and a summons for the offence will be issued requiring a court appearance. Drivers summoned to appear in court for driving and road traffic offences must produce their driving licence to the court on, at least, the day before the hearing.

International Driving Permits

Certain foreign countries do not accept British ordinary driving licences (see the AA website for a list of such countries: **www.theaa.com/getaway/idp**), in which case an international driving permit (IDP) will be required by British licence holders wishing to drive in those countries. These permits (issued under the auspices of the 1949 Geneva Convention on Road Traffic) are obtainable from the RAC, RSAC, AA or Green Flag. The statutory fee is £5.50 and a passport-type photograph is required for attachment to the permit. Applicants must be UK residents, over 18 years of age and hold full driving entitlements for the category of vehicle which the IDP is required to cover. Permit providers may charge an extra admin fee.

The AA warns drivers to beware of bogus IDPs on sale mainly on the internet, but also in magazines and newspapers. Such documents are counterfeit and are not recognized by countries that are party to the United Nations Convention on Road Traffic.

Exchange of Driving Licences

British driving licence holders can exchange their licence if necessary in order to:

- add new categories to a full licence;
- remove out-of-date endorsements or suspension details;
- add or take off provisional motorcycle entitlement;
- exchange an old-style pink or green licence for a new-style one.

Exchanging a Foreign Licence for a GB Licence

Northern Ireland Licences

Full NI driving licences or a test pass can be exchanged for a GB licence. Alternatively, a driver can continue to use an NI licence in Britain until it expires.

EU/EEA Licences

A valid full licence issued in any EU or EEA country (ie all EC countries plus Liechtenstein, Iceland and Norway) need not be changed immediately for a GB licence. So long as such a licence remains valid, the holder can drive in Great Britain until he reaches 70 years of age or for three years after becoming resident in Great Britain, whichever is the longer period.

Foreign drivers of large vehicles can drive in Great Britain until aged 45 or for five years after becoming resident, whichever is the longer period. Drivers aged over 45 years but under 65 can drive until their 66th birthday or for 5 years after becoming a GB resident, whichever is the shorter. Drivers aged 65 years or older may drive for 12 months after becoming a resident in Great Britain.

In order to continue driving after this time, a British driving licence must be obtained by making application on form D2. Application can be made for a British licence at any time, even after expiry of the foreign national licence.

Non-EC (Designated) Countries and Gibraltar

A full valid car licence issued in any of the following countries can be exchanged for a British licence: Australia, Barbados, British Virgin Islands, Gibraltar, Hong Kong, Japan, Kenya, Malta, New Zealand, Cyprus, Singapore, Switzerland and Zimbabwe.

Holders of lorry and bus licences from any of the above countries should contact the DVLA's Customer Enquiry Unit (at Swansea SA6 7JL) for further information.

Full Jersey or Isle of Man car, lorry or bus licences, or a full Guernsey car licence, can be exchanged for a British licence if they were valid within the past 10 years.

Certain driving licences for vehicles up to 3.5 tonnes issued in South Africa and Canada may now be exchanged for an equivalent GB licence.

A foreign car, lorry or bus driving licence can be used in Great Britain for one year only provided it remains valid, but exchange of a driving licence issued in any of the above-listed countries can be made up to five years after taking up residence in Great Britain.

Visitors from other countries not mentioned above cannot exchange their national licence for a British equivalent but they can drive in Great Britain on such licences (or on an International Driving Permit) for up to one year.

All foreign licence holders who for various reasons cannot obtain an exchange licence or who wish to drive vehicles which their national licence does not cover must apply for provisional entitlement in the normal way using form D1.

Full GB driving licences can only be issued to foreign nationals who become normally resident in Great Britain.

Visitors Driving in the UK

Visitors to the UK may drive vehicles in the UK provided they hold a domestic driving licence issued in their own country (ie outside the UK and the EU) or a Convention Driving Permit (issued under the 1949 Geneva Convention on Road Traffic by a country outside the UK). Holders of such permits are entitled to drive vehicles of a class which their own national or international licence covers for a period of 12 months from the date of their entry into the UK.

Driving While Tired

Drivers must be encouraged to STOP when they feel tired, whether during the night-time hours or during daytime, and rest for a short while, no matter what the pressures of the job or the particular journey in which they are engaged. Employers have responsibilities under health and safety legislation to assess such potential risks and take proper action to eliminate them. A VOSA prosecutor dealing with a case of a haulier permitting a driver to take insufficient rest said, 'Haulage bosses should become amateur policemen and keep a close watch on their drivers to make sure they have sufficient rest.'

Think – Don't Drive Tired

Since tiredness has been established as the principal factor in around 10 per cent of all accidents the DfT has launched a campaign to combat tiredness among both car and LGV drivers, *Think – Don't Drive Tired*. The main points for drivers to observe are that they should:

- make sure they are fit to drive, particularly before undertaking any long journeys (over an hour) – avoid such journeys in the morning without a good night's sleep or in the evening after a full day's work;

- avoid undertaking long journeys between midnight and 6 am, when natural alertness is at a minimum;
- plan their journey to take sufficient breaks. A minimum break of at least 15 minutes after every two hours driving is advised;
- if they feel at all sleepy, stop in a safe place and either take a nap for not more than 15 minutes, or drink two cups of strong coffee.

Driving Licence Penalty Points and Disqualification

Driving licence holders may be penalized following conviction by a court for offences committed on the road with a motor vehicle. These penalties range from the issue of fixed penalty notices for non-endorsable offences, which do not require a court appearance unless the charge is to be contested, and incur no driving licence penalty points, although the relevant fixed penalty has to be paid; to those for endorsable offences when penalty points are added on the licence counterpart and the fixed penalty is incurred or a heavy fine imposed on conviction if a court appearance is made.

In other cases, licence disqualification for a period (extending to a number of years in serious cases – especially for drink-driving-related offences), and in very serious instances imprisonment of the offender, may follow conviction in a magistrate's court or indictment for the offence in a higher court. Holders of vocational driving entitlements may be separately penalized for relevant offences which could result in such entitlements being suspended or revoked and in serious circumstances the holder being disqualified from holding a vocational entitlement – see below.

The Penalty Points System on Conviction and Disqualification

Driving licence endorsement of penalty points following conviction for motoring offences is prescribed by the Road Traffic Offenders Act 1988 with further provisions relating to driving offences being contained in the Road Traffic Act 1991 – see list below.

The penalty points system grades road traffic offences according to their seriousness by a number or range of penalty points, between 2 and 10, imposed on the driving licence of the convicted offender. Once a maximum of 12 penalty points has been accumulated within a three-year period counting from the date of the first offence to the current offence (not from the date of conviction), disqualification of the licence for at least six months will follow automatically.

Most offences rate a fixed number of penalty points to ensure consistency and to simplify the administration; but a discretionary range applies to a few offences where the gravity may vary considerably from one case to another. For example, failing to stop after an accident which only involved minor vehicle damage is obviously less serious than a case where an accident results in injury.

Unless the court decides otherwise, when a driver is convicted of more than one offence at the same hearing, only the points relative to the most serious of the offences will normally be endorsed on the licence. Once sufficient points (ie 12) have been endorsed on the driving licence and a period of disqualification has been imposed (six months for the first totting-up of points), the driver will have his 'slate' wiped clean and those points will not be counted again. Twelve more points would have to be accumulated before a further disqualification would follow, but to discourage repeated offences the courts will impose progressively longer disqualification periods in further instances (minimum 12 months for subsequent disqualifications within three years and 24 months for a third disqualification within three years).

Licence Endorsement Codes and Penalty Points

Following conviction for an offence, the driver's licence (ie the green counterpart) will be endorsed by the convicting court with both a code (to which employers and prospective employers should refer so they can assess the offences which drivers have committed) and the number of penalty points imposed as follows:

Code		Penalty points
	Accident offences	
AC 10	Failing to stop after an accident	5–10
AC 20	Failing to report an accident within 24 hours	5–10
AC 30	Undefined accident offence	4–9
	Disqualified driver	
BA 10	Driving while disqualified	6
BA 20	Driving while disqualified on age grounds	2
BA 30	Attempting to drive while disqualified	6
	Careless driving	
CD 10	Driving without due care and attention	3–9
CD 20	Driving without reasonable consideration for other road users	3–9
CD 30	Driving without due care and attention or without reasonable consideration for other road users	3–9
CD 40	Causing death through careless driving when unfit through drink	3–11
CD 50	Causing death by careless driving when unfit through drugs	3–11
CD 60	Causing death by careless driving with alcohol level above the limit	3–11
CD 70	Causing death by careless driving then failing to supply a specimen	3–11
	Construction and use offences	
CU 10	Using a vehicle with defective brakes	3
CU 20	Causing or likely to cause danger by reason of unsuitable vehicle or using a vehicle with parts or accessories (excluding brakes, steering or tyres) in a dangerous condition	3

Code		Penalty points
CU 30	Using a vehicle with defective tyre(s)	3
CU 40	Using a vehicle with defective steering	3
CU 50	Causing or likely to cause danger by reason of load or passengers	3
CU 60	Undefined failure to comply with C&U Regulations	3
	Reckless/dangerous driving	
DD 40	Dangerous driving	3–11
DD 60	Manslaughter or culpable homicide while driving a vehicle	3–11
DD 80	Causing death by dangerous driving	3–11
	Drink or drugs	
DR 10	Driving or attempting to drive with alcohol level above limit	3–11
DR 20	Driving or attempting to drive while unfit through drink	3–11
DR 30	Driving or attempting to drive then failing to supply a specimen for analysis	3–11
DR 40	In charge of a vehicle while alcohol level above limit	10
DR 50	In charge of a vehicle while unfit through drink	10
DR 60	Failure to provide a specimen for analysis in circumstances other than driving or attempting to drive	10
DR 70	Failing to provide a specimen for breath test	4
DR 80	Driving or attempting to drive when unfit through drugs	3–11
DR 90	In charge of a vehicle when unfit through drugs	10
	Insurance offences	
IN 10	Using a vehicle uninsured against third-party risks	6–8
	Licence offences	
LC 10	Driving without a licence	2
LC 20	Driving otherwise than in accordance with a licence	3–6
LC 30	Driving after making a false declaration about fitness when applying for a licence	3–6
LC 40	Driving a vehicle having failed to notify a disability	3–6
LC 50	Driving after a licence has been revoked or refused on medical grounds	2
	Miscellaneous offences	
MS 10	Leaving a vehicle in a dangerous position	3
MS 20	Unlawful pillion riding	3
MS 30	Contravention of the Road Traffic Regulations provisions on street playgrounds	2
MS 40	Driving with uncorrected defective eyesight or refusing to submit to a test	3

Code		Penalty points
MS 50	Motor racing on the highway	3–11
MS 60	Offences not covered by other codes as appropriate	–
MS 70	Driving with uncorrected defective eyesight	3
MS 80	Refusing to submit to an eyesight test	3
MS 90	Failure to give information as to identity of driver, etc	3
	Motorway offences	
MW 10	Contravention of Special Roads Regulations (excl speed limits)	3
	Pedestrian crossings	
PC 10	Undefined contravention of Pedestrian Crossing Regulations	3
PC 20	Contravention of Pedestrian Crossing Regulations with moving vehicle	3
PC 30	Contravention of Pedestrian Crossing Regulations with stationary vehicle	3
	Provisional licence offences	
PL 10	Driving without 'L' plates	3–6
PL 20	Not accompanied by a qualified person	3–6
PL 30	Carrying a person not qualified	3–6
PL 40	Drawing an unauthorized trailer	3–6
PL 50	Undefined failure to comply with conditions of a provisional licence	3–6
	Speed limits	
SP 10	Exceeding goods vehicle speed limits	3–6
SP 20	Exceeding speed limit for type of vehicle (excluding goods or passenger vehicles)	3–6
SP 30	Exceeding statutory speed limit on a public road	3–6
SP 40	Exceeding passenger vehicle speed limit	3–6
SP 50	Exceeding speed limit on a motorway	3–6
SP 60	Undefined speed limit offence	3–6
	NB: Disqualification is obligatory where the relevant speed is in excess of 30 mph over the statutory limit.	
	Traffic directions and signs	
TS 10	Failing to comply with traffic light signals	3
TS 20	Failing to comply with double white lines	3
TS 30	Failing to comply with a 'Stop' sign	3
TS 40	Failing to comply with direction of a constable or traffic warden	3
TS 50	Failing to comply with a traffic sign (excluding 'Stop' signs, traffic lights or double white lines)	3
TS 60	Failing to comply with a school crossing patrol sign	3
TS 70	Undefined failure to comply with a traffic direction or sign	3

Code		Penalty points
	Special Code	
TT 99	To signify a disqualifaction under 'totting up' procedure. If the total of penalty points reaches 12 or more within 3 years, the driver is liable to be disqualified	
	Theft or unauthorized taking	
UT 10	Taking and driving away a vehicle without consent or an attempt thereat	8
UT 20	Stealing or attempting to steal a vehicle	8
UT 30	Going equipped for stealing or taking a vehicle	8
UT 40	Taking or attempting to take a vehicle without consent; driving or attempting to drive a vehicle knowing it to have been taken without consent; allowing oneself to be carried in or on a vehicle knowing it to have been taken without consent	8
UT 50	Aggravated taking of a vehicle	3–11

Where the offence is one of aiding or abetting, causing or permitting or inciting, the codes are modified as follows:

Aiding, Abetting, Counselling or Procuring

Offences as coded, but with zero changed to 2, eg UT 10 becomes UT 12.

Causing or Permitting

Offences as coded, but with zero changed to 4, eg LC 20 becomes LC 24.

Inciting

Offences as coded, but with zero changed to 6, eg DD 30 becomes DD 36. The length of time for periods of disqualification is shown by use of the letters D = days, M = months and Y = years. Consecutive periods of disqualification are signified by an asterisk (*) against the time period. The symbol + means that 3 to 11 points are added to a licence if for exceptional reasons disqualification is not imposed.

Disqualification

The endorsing of penalty points will also arise on conviction for offences where disqualification is discretionary and where the court has decided that immediate disqualification is not appropriate (for example if acceptable 'exceptional' reasons are put forward – see also below). In this case the offender's driving licence will be endorsed with four points. The courts are still free to disqualify immediately if the circumstances justify this.

Offences carrying obligatory disqualification are shown in the following list:

- causing death by dangerous driving and manslaughter;
- dangerous driving within three years of a similar conviction;
- driving or attempting to drive while unfit through drink or drugs;
- driving or attempting to drive with more than the permitted breath-alcohol level;
- failure to provide a breath, blood or urine specimen;
- racing on the highway.

Driving while disqualified is a serious offence which can result in a fine at level 5 on the standard scale (see below), currently £5,000 maximum, or six months' imprisonment, or both.

Special Reasons for Non-disqualification

The courts have discretion in exceptional mitigating circumstances (ie when there are 'special reasons') not to impose a disqualification. The mitigating circumstance must not be one which attempts to make the offence appear less serious and no account will be taken of hardship other than exceptional hardship. Pleading that you have a wife and children to support or that you will lose your job is not generally considered to be exceptional hardship for the purposes of determining whether or not disqualification should be imposed.

If account has previously been taken of circumstances in mitigation of a disqualification, the same circumstances cannot be considered again within three years.

Where a court decides, in exceptional circumstances as described above, not to disqualify a convicted driver, 3 to 11 penalty points will be added to the driver's licence in lieu of the disqualification.

Driving Offences

Dangerous Driving

The previous charge of reckless driving was replaced from 1 July 1992 by a charge of 'dangerous' driving. A person is to be regarded as driving dangerously if the way he drives 'falls far short of what would be expected of a competent and careful driver, and it would be obvious to a competent and careful driver that driving in that way would be dangerous'. Driving would be regarded as dangerous 'if it was obvious to a competent and careful driver that driving the vehicle in its current state would be dangerous' – this obviously applies to the vehicle's mechanical condition or the way it is loaded. Also, 'dangerous' refers to danger either of injury to any person or of serious damage to property. The principal offences to which this relates are dangerous driving and causing death by dangerous driving.

Interfering with Vehicles, etc

It is an offence for any person to cause danger to road users by way of intentionally and without lawful authority placing objects on a road, interfering with motor vehicles, or directly or indirectly interfering with traffic equipment (eg road signs, etc).

Penalties

Penalties for these offences are heavy. For example, causing death by careless driving while under the influence of drink or drugs carries a maximum penalty of up to five years in prison and/or a fine. For causing a danger to road users the maximum penalty is up to seven years' imprisonment and/or a fine.

In addition to disqualification and the endorsement of penalty points on driving licences, courts may impose fines and, for certain offences, imprisonment. The maximum fine for most offences is determined by reference to a scale set out in the Criminal Justice Act 1991 as follows:

Level 1	£200
Level 2	£500
Level 3	£1,000
Level 4	£2,500
Level 5	£5,000

Offences such as dangerous driving, failing to stop after an accident or failure to report an accident, and drink-driving offences, carry the current maximum fine of £5,000, as do certain vehicle construction and use offences (eg overloading, insecure loads, using a vehicle in a dangerous condition, etc) and using a vehicle without insurance.

Under new provisions included in the Criminal Justice Act 2003, the maximum penalty for the offence of causing death by dangerous driving has been increased from a 10-year prison sentence to 14 years. This measure has been taken, according to the then Home Secretary, to ensure that drivers who kill can be 'properly punished'.

New Driver Penalties

The Road Traffic (New Drivers) Act 1995 concerns new drivers who first passed their driving test on or after 1 June 1997. Where such drivers acquire six or more penalty points on their licence within two years of passing that test (the so-called 'probationary period') the DVLA will automatically revoke the licence on notification by a court or fixed penalty offence. Such drivers have to surrender their full licence and obtain a provisional licence to start driving again as a learner. They will have to pass both the theory and practical tests again in order to regain their full driving licence.

Penalty points counting towards the total of six include any incurred before passing the test, if this was not more than three years before the latest penalty point offence. Points imposed after the probationary period will also count if the offence was committed during that period.

Passing the retest will not remove the penalty points from the licence; these will remain and if the total reaches 12, the driver will be liable to disqualification by a court.

Short-Period Disqualification (SPD)

When drivers are disqualified for less than 56 days, the court will stamp the counterpart of their driving licence and return it to them. The stamp will show how long disqualification is to last. The licence does not have to be renewed when the short-period disqualification ends – it becomes valid again the day following expiry of the disqualification.

Removal of Penalty Points and Disqualifications

Penalty points endorsed on driving licences can be removed (by application to the DVLA Swansea on form D1 and on payment of a fee of £22.00).

The waiting period before which no such application would be accepted is four years from the date of the offence, except in the case of reckless/dangerous driving convictions when the four years is taken from the date of conviction. Endorsements for alcohol-related offences must remain on a licence for 11 years.

Licences returned after disqualification will show no penalty points but previous disqualifications (within four years) will remain and if a previous alcohol/drugs driving offence disqualification has been incurred, this will remain on the licence for 11 years.

Application may be made by disqualified drivers for reinstatement of their licence after varying periods of time depending on the duration of the disqualifying period as follows:

- less than 2 years – no prior application time;
- less than 4 years – after 2 years have elapsed;
- between 4 years and 10 years – after half the time has elapsed;
- in other cases – after 5 years have elapsed.

The courts are empowered to require a disqualified driver to retake the driving test before restoring a driving licence, and following the introduction of provisions contained in the Road Traffic Act 1991 it is now mandatory for them to impose 'extended' retests following disqualification for the most serious of driving offences, namely, dangerous driving, causing death by dangerous driving and manslaughter by the driver of a motor vehicle (in Scotland, the charge is culpable homicide).

The fee charged for replacement licences following disqualification is £60.00, but where the disqualification was for drink-driving-type offences the fee for a replacement is £85.00.

Retests for Offending Drivers

Where drivers are convicted of the offences of manslaughter, causing death by dangerous driving or dangerous driving, and mandatory disqualification is imposed, an 'extended' retest (involving at least one hour's driving) must be taken before the driving licence is restored. This also applies to drivers disqualified under the penalty points totting-up procedure. Courts may also order drivers disqualified for lesser offences to take an appropriate (ie ordinary) driving test.

Drink-Driving and Breath Tests

It is an offence to drive or attempt to drive a motor vehicle when the level of alcohol in the breath is more than 35 micrograms per 100 millilitres of breath. This is determined by means of an initial breath test, conducted on the spot when the driver is stopped, and later substantiated by a test on a breath-testing machine (eg Lion Intoximeter) at a police station. The breath/alcohol limit mentioned above equates to the blood/alcohol limit of 80 milligrams of alcohol in 100 millilitres of blood or the urine/alcohol limit of 107 milligrams of alcohol in 100 millilitres of urine.

Failure to Produce a Breath Sample and Low Breath-Test Readings

If those suspected of an alcohol-related offence cannot, due to health reasons, produce a breath sample, or if a breath test shows a reading of not more than 50 micrograms of alcohol per 100 millilitres of breath, they are given the opportunity of an alternative test, either blood or urine, for laboratory analysis. This test can only be carried out at a police station or a hospital and the decision as to which alternative is chosen rests with the police (unless a doctor present determines that for medical reasons a blood test cannot or should not be taken). Similarly, if a breath test of a driver shows the proportion of alcohol to be no more than 50 micrograms in 100 millilitres of breath, the driver can request an alternative test (ie blood or urine) as described above for those who cannot provide a breath sample for analysis.

A House of Lords ruling says that a driver recording a breath sample that does not exceed 50 micrograms in 100 millilitres of breath must be given a police statement to this effect.

Prosecution for Drink-Driving Offences

Prosecution will follow a failure to pass the test, which will result in a fine or imprisonment and automatic disqualification from driving. Failure to submit to a breath test and to a blood or urine test are serious offences, and drivers will find themselves liable to heavy penalties on conviction and potentially long-term disqualification or driving licence endorsement (endorsements for such offences remain on a driving licence for 11 years).

The police *do not* have powers to carry out breath tests at random but they *do have* powers to enter premises to require a breath test from a person suspected of driving while impaired through drink or drugs, or who has been driving, or been in charge of a vehicle which has been involved in an accident in which another person has been injured.

In a highly publicized case in 1991, charges against an LGV driver breathalysed by police having been woken from sleep on the sleeper berth of his vehicle cab (and with his tachograph set to record rest) were dismissed by the court. Although presumably over the statutory limit (otherwise no charge would have been brought), the driver was clearly making no attempt to drive his vehicle and the vehicle was parked in a proper (ie non-public) place. Since the court dismissed the case there was no opportunity to obtain a ruling from a higher court as to the precise legal position of drivers in such circumstances. It is considered that drinking and then sleeping in a vehicle cab does present risk of prosecution for drivers.

Drink-Driving Disqualification

Conviction for a first drink-driving offence will result in a minimum one-year period of disqualification and for a second or subsequent offence of driving or attempting to drive under the influence of drink or drugs longer periods of disqualification will be imposed by the court. If the previous such conviction took place within 10 years of the current offence the disqualification must be for at least 3 years.

Drivers convicted twice for drink-driving offences may have their driving licence revoked altogether. Offenders who are disqualified twice within a 10-year period for any drink-driving offences and those found to have an exceptionally high level of alcohol in the body (ie more than 2½ times over the limit) or those who twice refuse to provide a specimen will be classified as high-risk offenders (HROs) by the Driver and Vehicle Licensing Agency. They will be required to show that they no longer have an 'alcohol problem' by means of a medical examination (including blood analysis of liver enzymes) by a DVLA-approved doctor before their licence will be restored to them. A higher than normal fee (ie £75) will be charged for the renewal of such licences.

Drink-Driving Courses

The Road Traffic Act 1991 contained provisions whereby certain (but not all) drink-driving offenders may have the period of their disqualification reduced if they agree to undertake an approved rehabilitation course and satisfactorily complete it. The provision applies only where the court orders the individual (who must be over 17 years of age) to be disqualified for at least 12 months following conviction under the Road Traffic Act 1988 for:

- causing death by careless driving when under the influence of drink or drugs;
- driving or being in charge of a motor vehicle when under the influence of drink or drugs;
- driving or being in charge of a motor vehicle with excess alcohol in the body; or
- failing to provide a specimen (of breath, blood or urine) as required.

The court has a duty to ensure that a place on an approved course is available for the offender. It must explain to the offender 'in ordinary language' the effect of the order (to reduce the disqualification period), the amount of the fees and that these must be paid in advance, and it must seek the offender's agreement that the order should be made – in other words, it is a completely voluntary scheme and there is no question of force.

Given these provisos, the court can order the period of disqualification to be reduced by not less than 3 months and not more than one-quarter of the unreduced period (for example, with a 12-month disqualification, the reduction will be 3 months, leaving a 9-month disqualification period to be served).

The latest date for completion of one of these rehabilitation courses is two months prior to the last day of the reduced disqualification period (so, in the nine- month example given above, the course would have to be completed by the last day of the seventh month). On completion of the course the offender is given a certificate which must be returned to the clerk of the supervising court (named in the order) in order to secure the reduction. Failure to complete the course or to produce the certificate on time will result in the loss of this facility.

A number of approved courses have now been established around the country (with fees of between £50 and £200) and these will require attendance for between 16 and 30 hours, made up of a number of separate sessions, during which the offender will learn about the effects of alcohol on the body and on driving performance and behaviour, about drink-driving offences, and about the alternatives to drinking and driving. A range of relevant advice will also be given.

Drug-Driving Code of Practice

A Code of Practice has been established (effective from 9 December 2004) to tackle the dangers caused by drivers under the influence of drugs. This includes prescription drugs and medicines as well as illegal drugs. The Code requires suspected drivers to submit to a roadside impairment test by the police. This test will be carried out in accordance with the Code and will include the so-called pupilliary test, the walk and turn test and the one-leg stand. Refusal to participate in the test will render a driver liable to the same penalty as refusal to undertake a breath test.

Penalties against Vocational Entitlements

Where a licence holder is disqualified from driving following conviction for offences committed with cars or other light vehicles, or as a result of penalty point totting-up, any vocational entitlement which that person holds is automatically lost until the licence is reinstated. Additionally, the holder of an LGV/PCV vocational entitlement may have this revoked or suspended by the DVLA without reference to the TC – see below – and be disqualified from holding such entitlement, for a fixed or an indefinite period, at any time on the grounds of misconduct or physical disability. Furthermore, a person can be refused a new LGV/PCV driving entitlement following licence revocation, again either indefinitely or for some other period of time which the Secretary of State (ie via the DVLA) specifies. A new vocational test may be ordered before the entitlement is restored – see further below.

Disqualification from holding an LGV vocational entitlement as described above does not prevent a licence holder from continuing to drive vehicles within the category B and C1 entitlements that he holds.

The TCs continue to play a disciplinary role under the new licensing scheme in regard to driver conduct, but only at the request of the DVLA. They have powers under the new provisions to call drivers to public inquiry (PI) to give information and answer questions as to their conduct. Their duty is to report back to the DVLA if they consider that an LGV/PCV entitlement should be revoked or the holder disqualified from holding an entitlement. The DVLA must follow the TCs' recommendation in these matters.

Failure to attend a PI when requested to do so (unless a reasonable excuse is given) means that the DVLA will automatically refuse a new vocational entitlement or suspend or revoke an existing entitlement.

LGV drivers who have been off the road for a period of time after being disqualified are having to prove themselves capable of driving small goods vehicles legally and safely for a period of time before their LGV driving entitlement may be restored by the TCs. One TC has said that banned LGV drivers must prove themselves on vehicles up to 7.5 tonnes before being allowed to drive vehicles up to 38 tonnes again.

Rules on disciplining LGV entitlement holders require TCs to follow a set of recommended guidelines in imposing penalties against such entitlements. Under these rules, and where there are no aggravating circumstances, a driver being disqualified for 12 months or less should be sent a warning letter, with no further disqualification of the LGV entitlement. Where a driving disqualification is for more than one year, offenders should be called to appear before the TC and should incur an additional suspension of their LGV entitlement, amounting to between one month and three months. The intention here is to allow them to regain their driving skills and road sense in a car before driving a heavy vehicle again. Where two or more driving disqualifications of more than eight weeks have been incurred within the past five years, and the combined total of disqualification exceeds 12 months, the driver should be called to public inquiry and a further period of LGV driving disqualification imposed amounting to between 3 and 6 months.

In the case of new LGV entitlements, for applicants who already have nine or more penalty points on their ordinary licence, the guidelines recommend that the TC should issue a warning as to future conduct or suggest that the applicant tries again when the penalty points total on his licence has been reduced.

Removal of LGV Driving Licence Disqualification

Drivers disqualified from holding an LGV/PCV entitlement, as described above, may apply to have the disqualification removed after 2 years if it was for less than 4 years, or after half the period if the disqualification was for more than 4 years but less than 10 years. In any other case including disqualification for an indefinite period an application for its removal cannot be made until 5 years have elapsed. If an application for the removal of a disqualification fails another application cannot be made for three months.

The DVLA will not necessarily readily restore LGV/PCV driving entitlements on application following disqualification of a driving licence. An applicant may be called to public inquiry by a TC, who will inquire into the events which led to the disqualification and at which he may also decide that the applicant must wait a further period before applying again, must spend a period driving small (ie up to 7.5 tonnes) vehicles or must take a new LGV/PCV driving test in order to regain the vocational entitlement.

Appeals

If the DVLA refuses to grant an application for an LGV/PCV driving entitlement or revokes, suspends or limits an existing entitlement, the applicant or entitlement holder may appeal against the decision under the Road Traffic Act 1988. The first step is for them to notify the DVLA, and any TC involved in consideration of the applicant's conduct, of their intention to appeal. The appeal can then be made to a magistrate's court acting for the petty sessions in England or Wales, or in Scotland to the local sheriff.

Driver Testing and Training

This chapter deals with the legal requirements for driving tests (including the Advanced Commercial Vehicle Driving Test and the Master Driving Certificate), the New Young Driver training scheme, training for the use of lorry loaders and training for dangerous goods carrying.

Driving Tests

The main purpose of driver testing is to ensure that all drivers taking a vehicle on the road:

- are safe and competent to do so;
- know the rules of the road and the significance of traffic signs and signals; and
- appreciate the dangers arising from moving vehicles.

The purpose of the additional tests for LGV/PCV entitlements is to ensure that such drivers are competent to drive these large vehicles on the roads in safety – especially when carrying heavy loads or passengers. Vocational testing also provides a measure of professionalism among goods and passenger vehicle drivers.

New driver testing procedures, following the requirements of the EU's 'second' driver licensing Directive, were introduced for car and light vehicle drivers from 1 July 1996 and from 1 January 1997 for large goods and passenger vehicle drivers – including car and LGV theory tests. The main objective of the LGV/PCV test remains, which is to ensure that goods and passenger vehicle drivers are competent to drive large vehicles on the roads in safety. It also provides a measure of professionalism among commercial vehicle drivers. The test is more comprehensive and more complex than the ordinary (ie car and light goods) driving test and, consequently, demands greater skill and knowledge from the driver who wishes to pass.

Proof of Identity

Candidates for both ordinary and vocational (ie LGV and PCV) driving tests must produce satisfactory photographic evidence of identity when arriving for a test. Acceptable identity documents for this purpose include existing driving licences (ordinary, LGV or PCV or an overseas driving licence), a passport or an employer-issued identity card bearing the holder's name, signature and photograph. If a test candidate cannot produce satisfactory means of identification the test will not be conducted and the fee forfeited.

This measure is necessary to combat a rising incidence of persons with false identities taking multiple LGV driving tests on behalf of others who cannot themselves pass the test, but are prepared to pay large sums to acquire a test pass certificate.

Ordinary Driving Test

Before persons can be granted a licence to drive a motor vehicle on the road they must pass both a written theory test and a practical driving test on the class of vehicle for which they require the licence. An entitlement to drive will not be gained until both parts of the test are passed – the theory test having to be passed before the practical driving test can be taken.

The Theory and Hazard Perception Tests

Driving test candidates must take and pass a 'touch screen' theory test and a hazard perception test – which replaces the old, verbal, questioning to test the candidate's knowledge of the *Highway Code* – carried out on behalf of the Driving Standards Agency (DSA – an Executive Agency of the Department for Transport, D/T) at a network of practical test centres across Britain.

The test comprises 50 multiple-choice questions of which the candidate must get at least 43 correct to achieve a pass certificate. The questions concern such matters as driver attitude, traffic signs and regulations, the effects of alcohol and drugs, driver fatigue and safety, and environmental aspects of vehicles. All these topics are covered in the *Highway Code* and the DSA's *Driving Goods Vehicles: The Official DSA Syllabus*. The DSA has also published *The Official Theory Test for Drivers of Large Vehicles,* which explains the test and lists the 900-odd bank of questions from which test papers are set, together with the correct answers. All these publications are available from The Stationery Office or main booksellers.

The theory test is computerized with the questions appearing on screen, which the candidate has only to touch to indicate the correct answer. This system makes the test more accessible to the general public, and is particularly helpful for people with special needs. Candidates are advised of the result of their theory test immediately.

Online versions of sample theory test questions can be found at: **www.dsa.gov.uk/ mockpaper/theory/intro.htm**.

The hazard perception part is also computerized, and the candidate responds by clicking a button on the mouse. There are 14 separate video clips featuring everyday road scenes and in each one there will be at least one developing hazard – one of the clips features two such hazards. To achieve a high score the candidate must respond to the hazards quickly; the maximum score on each is five. The pass mark for the car hazard perception test is 44 out of 75.

Practical Driving Tests

The practical driving test (lasting approximately 38–40 minutes) is carried out by examiners from the Driving Standards Agency. Candidates must present a theory test pass certificate – practical driving tests will not be carried out without the candidate having first passed the theory test.

Test candidates have to meet the following requirements:

- They must show that they are fully conversant with the contents of the *Highway Code*.
- They must prove that they are able to read in good daylight (with the aid of spectacles, if worn) a motor vehicle's registration number in accordance with the vision requirements (see p 175).
- They must show that they are competent to drive without danger to and with due consideration of other users of the road, including being able to:
  - start the engine of the vehicle;
  - move away straight ahead or at an angle;
  - overtake, meet or cross the path of other vehicles and take an appropriate course;
  - turn right-hand and left-hand corners correctly;
  - stop the vehicle in an emergency and in a normal situation, and in the latter case bring it to rest at an appropriate part of the road;
  - drive the vehicle backwards and while doing so enter a limited opening either to the left or to the right;
  - cause the vehicle to face the opposite direction by the use of forward and reverse gears;
  - carry out a reverse parking manoeuvre which involves stopping the vehicle next to and parallel with a parked vehicle, then reversing to position and park the vehicle in front of or behind the other vehicle, level with and reasonably close to the kerb;
  - indicate their intended actions at appropriate times by giving appropriate signals in a clear and unmistakable manner (in the case of a left-hand-drive vehicle or a disabled driver for whom it is impracticable or undesirable to give hand signals there is no requirement to provide any signals other than mechanical ones);
  - act correctly and promptly on all signals given by traffic signs and traffic controllers and take appropriate action on signs given by other road users.

The driving test may be terminated in the event of a serious driving error which jeopardizes public safety.

Cars used for the ordinary (ie category B) driving test must be fitted with a seat belt and a head restraint for the front seat passenger and an additional rear view mirror for use by the examiner.

Candidates who fail the driving test are given an oral explanation of the reasons for their failure.

Extended Driving Tests

Since 6 January 1992 the courts have been vested with powers to impose an extended driving test on any person who has been convicted of dangerous driving offences, or convicted of other offences involving obligatory disqualification.

Loss of a driving licence for dangerous driving or related offences involving obligatory disqualification means that the licence holder returns to 'learner' status and has to conform to the normal rules applicable to provisional licence holders. A theory test must be taken and passed for the category of vehicle on which the extended practical driving test is to be taken. This extended driving test is longer and therefore more demanding than the normal, lasting for about 70 minutes and covering a wide variety of roads, usually including dual carriageways. Candidates for the extended retest are advised to prepare by taking suitable instruction from an Approved Driving Instructor (ADI). The higher fee (as indicated below) reflects the length of the test.

The purpose of retesting is not intended to be punitive; rather it is a road safety measure, designed to recheck the driver's competence.

Driving Test Fees

The fee for lorry and bus theory tests is £50.00 – this includes the multiple-choice questions test (£35.00) and the hazard perception test (£15.00).

The fee for an ordinary driving test (conducted on weekdays up to 4.30 pm) is £62.00, or £75.00 if conducted on a weekday evening or on a Saturday.

Driving tests for lorries and buses cost £115.00 on weekdays (up to 4.30 pm) and £141.00 if conducted in the evening or on a Saturday.

Higher test fees of £124.00 on weekdays (up to 4.30 pm) and £150.00 on Saturdays are payable where an extended retest is ordered following obligatory disqualification of a driving licence (see above).

Driver CPC tests cost £30.00 for the theory case studies and £55.00 (or £63.00 for evening and weekend testing) for the practical test – this includes the issue of a Driver Qualification Card (DQC).

Test fees are forfeited unless at least 10 clear days' notice of cancellation is given.

Driving Instruction

Only approved instructors (ADIs – approved by the Driving Standards Agency) are permitted to give driving instruction for payment on vehicles legally defined as 'motor cars', which basically means the following classes of vehicle:

- private cars;
- goods vehicles not exceeding 3,050 kg unladen weight.

Tuition given for payment on heavy goods vehicles does not come within the scope of this legislation despite a certain amount of transport industry opinion that it should do so. However, to ensure that the level of driving instruction available to learner LGV drivers is of a consistently high standard a new scheme for the voluntary registration of LGV driving instructors has been established. Entry to the register is currently via a three-part examination of both driving and instructional abilities.

LGV Driver Testing

In order to drive a large vehicle (ie goods or passenger) it is necessary to pass both the large vehicle theory test and a practical driving test on either a large goods or passenger vehicle of the appropriate category for which a licence is required.

Theory and Hazard Perception Testing

Since 1 January 1997 large vehicle (ie LGV/PCV) driving test candidates must take and pass a 'touch screen' theory test – which has replaced the old, verbal, questioning to test the candidate's knowledge of technical and safety matters and the *Highway Code*. This test has been expanded with the inclusion of a wider range of topics such as fuel economy, environmentally sensitive driving and safety issues.

Theory tests are carried out on behalf of the Driving Standards Agency (DSA) at their dedicated test centres nationwide. The test comprises 100 multiple-choice questions; a pass is achieved with 85 correct answers. Full details of the theory test are contained in *The Professional LGV Drivers' Handbook* (by David Lowe, and available from Kogan Page).

The Hazard Perception Test is as previously described on pp 194–95, with the exception that for bus and lorry drivers there will be 19 video clips, with a pass mark of 67 out of 100.

The LGV Driving Test

In order to undertake a large goods or passenger vehicle (LGV/PCV) driving test, candidates must, since 1 January 1997, produce a large vehicle theory test pass certificate. Without this the examiner will not conduct the practical driving test.

The 90-minute large goods vehicle practical driving test is conducted by DSA examiners and booking has to be made through the Driving Standards Agency. Certain test centres offer Saturday morning LGV and PCV driver testing.

The staged system of testing means that:

- Applicants for LGV tests must already hold a full category B (car and light vehicle) driving entitlement before taking a test to obtain a category C entitlement.
- Category B entitlement holders have to pass a test on a rigid goods vehicle in category C before being able to take a test to qualify for driving articulated vehicles and drawbar combinations in category C+E.
- Category C1 entitlement holders wishing to drive vehicles in category C1+E must take a further test for this type of vehicle combination.

In each case the driver must hold a provisional entitlement for the category of vehicle on which he wants to be tested.

Application and Fees

Large vehicle theory tests cost £50.00. This test must be passed before the practical driving test is taken.

Applications for the large vehicle practical driving test have to be made on form DLG26, obtainable from local DSA offices. The current test fee of £115.00 (£141.00 for Saturday and weekday evening tests) must be sent with the application (see also page 81 for driver CPC test fees). Test applications can also be made by telephone with payment by credit or debit card.

Applicants are warned to apply for a test in good time. This is important if an LGV driving entitlement is required – subject to passing the test – from a particular date; and applicants must also ensure that their driving is of a sufficiently high standard to be able to pass the test.

Test Cancellation

Should a candidate need to cancel a test appointment this should be done at least 10 clear working days in advance, otherwise the fee will be forfeited.

Identification

Test candidates must be able to produce satisfactory photographic identification on arrival at the test centre, otherwise the examiner may refuse to conduct the test and the fee will be forfeited (see p 194).

Vehicles for the LGV Driving Test

The candidate has to provide the vehicle (or arrange for the loan of a suitable vehicle) on which he wishes to be tested and it must comply with the following requirements:

- it must be unladen and of the category (ie a 'minimum test vehicle') for which an LGV driving entitlement is required – see below;
- it must display 'L' plates front and rear;
- it must be in a thoroughly roadworthy condition;
- seating accommodation in the cab must be provided for the examiner;
- it must have sufficient fuel for a test lasting up to two hours.

Minimum Test Vehicles

All vehicles used for Categories C1, C1+E, C and C+E tests must:

- have externally mounted nearside and offside mirrors;
- have seat belts fitted to seats used by the examiner or any person supervising the test;
- be fitted with a tachograph;
- have an anti-lock braking system (ABS)

NB trailers don't need ABS.

All vehicle combinations must operate the appropriate service brakes and utilize a heavy duty coupling arrangement suitable for the weight.

NB: An articulated tractor unit is not considered to be a suitable vehicle for category C or C1 test.

Category C1

- A medium-sized lorry with a MAM of at least 4 tonnes;
  - at least 5 metres in length;
  - capable of 80 kph (50 mph); and
  - with a closed box cargo compartment at least as wide and as high as the cab.

Category C1+E

- A drawbar combination comprising a Category C1 vehicle;
  - towing a trailer of at least 2 tonnes MAM;
  - with a combined length of at least 8 metres;
  - capable of 80 kph (50 mph);
  - with a closed box trailer slightly less wide than the towing vehicle, but rearview must be by external mirrors only; or
- A medium-sized articulated lorry with a MAM of at least 6 tonnes;
  - with a combined length of at least 8 metres;
  - capable of 80 kph (50 mph);
  - with a closed box trailer slightly less wide than the towing vehicle, but rear view must be by external mirrors only.

Category C

- A rigid goods vehicle with a MAM of at least 12 tonnes;
  - at least 8 metres in length;
  - at least 2.4 metres in width;
  - capable of 80 kph (50 mph);
  - with at least 8 forward gears;
  - a closed box cargo compartment at least as wide and as high as the cab; and
  - a maximum length of 12 metres (39 ft 4 in).

Category C+E

- A drawbar outfit comprising a combination of a Category C vehicle and trailer with a MAM of 20 tonnes;
  - with a combined length of at least 14 metres;
  - with a trailer at least 7.5 metres in length from coupling eye to extreme rear;
  - at least 2.4 metres in width;

- capable of 80 kph (50 mph);
- with at least 8 forward gears;
- with a closed box cargo compartment at least as wide and as high as the cab; and
- a maximum length of 18.75 metres (61 ft 5 in); or
- An articulated lorry with a MAM of at least 20 tonnes;
  - with a minimum length of 14 metres;
  - a maximum length of 16.5 metres (54 ft);
  - at least 2.4 metres in width;
  - capable of 80 kph (50 mph);
  - with at least 8 forward gears;
  - with a closed box cargo compartment at least as wide and as high as the cab.

The LGV Driving Test Syllabus

The recommended syllabus to be studied by candidates preparing for the LGV driving test is as follows. See also the DSA publication *Driving Goods Vehicles: The Official DSA Syllabus Manual* (available from The Stationery Office) and *The Professional LGV Drivers' Handbook* (by David Lowe, available from Kogan Page).

The syllabus comprises seven main sections containing advice and detailing specific requirements for the test as well as an introductory section outlining the prior 'thorough' knowledge that a candidate should acquire before attempting the test.

The syllabus contains the following main headings:

Part One: Getting Started

- Selecting an instructor.
- Applying for your licence.
- The theory test.
- Medical requirements.
- Professional standards.
- Responsibility and attitude.

Part Two: Understanding Large Goods Vehicles

- Understanding LGVs.
- Forces affecting your vehicle.
- Vehicle characteristics.
- Vehicle limits.
- Braking systems.
- Gear systems.
- Load restraint.

Part Three: Limits and Regulations

- Environmental impact.
- Drivers' hours and records.
- Other regulations.

Part Four: Driving Skills

- Professional driving.
- Driving at night.
- Motorway driving.
- All-weather driving.
- Accidents.
- First aid.
- Breakdowns.

Part Five: Preparing for the Driving Test

- About the driving test.
- The theory test.
- How to apply for your test.
- Before attending your test.
- Legal requirements.
- At the test centre.
- The official syllabus.

Part Six: The LGV Driving Test

- The reversing exercise.
- The braking exercise.
- The vehicle controls.
- Other controls.
- The gear-changing exercise.
- Moving off.
- Using the mirrors.
- Giving signals.
- Acting on signs and signals.
- Awareness and anticipation.
- Making progress.
- Controlling your speed.
- Separation distance.
- Hazards.

- Selecting a safe place to stop.
- Uncoupling and recoupling.
- If you pass.
- If you don't pass.

Part Seven: Additional Information

- Disqualified drivers.
- DSA services.
- DSA offices.
- LGV test centres.
- Traffic Commissioners and Traffic Area Offices.
- Other useful addresses.
- Categories of LGV licences.
- Minimum test vehicles.
- Hazard labels.
- Cone positions.
- Glossary.

New LGV Tests from September 2003

A number of significant changes to the vocational (LGV) driving test were made from September 2003 as follows.

For a start, drivers seeking vocational licence entitlement are expected to be experienced and technically expert. Test candidates are asked five 'show me' and 'tell me' type questions, with a driving fault being recorded for each incorrect answer up to a maximum of four driving faults. If all five answers are given incorrectly, a serious fault will be recorded.

Examples of safety check questions are as follows.

Identify where:

- you would check the engine oil level and tell me how you would check that the engine has sufficient oil.
- you would check the engine coolant level and tell me how you would check that the engine has the correct level.
- the windscreen washer reservoir is and tell me how you would check the windscreen washer level.

Tell me how you would check:

- your tyres to ensure that they are correctly inflated, have sufficient tread depth and that their general condition is safe to use on the road.
- that the brake lights are working.

- the condition of the reflectors on this vehicle.
- the condition of the windscreen and windows on this vehicle.
- the condition of the windscreen wipers on this vehicle.
- the condition of the suspension on this vehicle.
- that the condition of the body is safe on this vehicle.
- that the power-assisted steering is working.

Tell me:

- how you would operate the loading mechanism on this vehicle (vehicle specific, ie tail lift).
- the main safety factors involved in loading this vehicle.

Show me how you would check:

- that the headlamps, sidelights and tail lights are working.
- that the direction indicators are working.
- the operation (specify) of the audible warning devices on this vehicle.
- the wheel nuts are secure on this vehicle.
- the condition of the mudguards on this vehicle.
- for the correct air pressure on this vehicle.
- for air leaks on this vehicle.
- that your cargo doors are secure.
- that your cab locking mechanism is secure.

Show me how you would:

- replace the tachometer disc on this vehicle.

Show me:

- what instrument checks you would make before and after starting the engine on this vehicle.
- where the emergency exits are and how you would check that they are operating correctly.
- where the first aid equipment is on this vehicle.
- where the fire extinguishers are on this vehicle.

The Braking Exercise

From 2011 drivers undertaking the LGV driving test are no longer required to carry out off-road braking tests. These tests will be carried out on the road in normal traffic conditions. This is thought to be a more realistic test of a driver's ability to bring his vehicle to rest in a safe and timely manner taking account of prevailing road and traffic conditions.

The Safe Parking Test

Candidates will be asked to carry out the current reversing exercise, but at the end of the reversing bay there will be a simulated loading platform up to which the candidate will be required to reverse (stopping with the extreme rear of the vehicle within a stopping area marked by black and yellow hatched lines) and park safely for loading and unloading.

Stopping short of the marked stopping area will be assessed as a serious fault. Reversing through the marked stopping area and dislodging the simulated loading/unloading platform will be assessed as a serious fault. Stopping within the marked stopping area but unacceptably short of the platform will be assessed as a driving fault. A total loss of vehicle control, which causes actual danger to the driver, examiner or another road user, will be assessed as a dangerous fault.

It is recognized that some professional drivers reverse, under control, up to a loading/unloading platform until they gently touch the platform. This will be acceptable on test as long as the platform is not dislodged.

The Uncoupling and Recoupling Exercise

After uncoupling the candidate will be required to park the towing vehicle alongside the trailer and then realign the towing vehicle with the trailer before recoupling. The competencies of control, accuracy and effective observation will be assessed during the exercise. A fault involving actual danger to the driver or another road user will be assessed as a dangerous fault. A fault that would be potentially dangerous to the driver or another road user will be assessed as a serious fault. Faults that reflect that the driver does not have the required competencies to carry out the exercise following industry best practice and recognized procedures will be assessed as driving or serious faults, depending upon the severity of the fault.

EU LGV Driving Test Standards

Under European Commission Directive 2000/56/EC, which amended an earlier Directive on driving licences (91/439/EEC), the conduct of the practical driving test itself was revised and applied to tests conducted from September 2003.

The following text summarizes Annex II to the Directive in so far as it applies to LGV driving tests only.

Driving Skills and Behaviour for LGV Drivers

Driving test candidates must demonstrate the following key skills:

- Preparation and technical check of the vehicle for the purposes of ensuring road safety. Applicants must demonstrate that they are capable of preparing to drive safely by satisfying the following requirements:
  - adjusting the seat as necessary to obtain a correct seated position;
  - adjusting rear-view mirrors, seat belts and head restraints if available;
  - random checks on the condition of the tyres, steering, brakes, lights, reflectors, direction indicators and audible warning device;

- checking the power-assisted braking and steering systems; checking the condition of the wheels, wheel nuts, mudguards, windscreen, windows and wipers, fluids (eg engine oil, coolant, washer fluid); checking and using the instrument panel including the recording equipment as defined in Regulation (EEC) No 3821185 [ie the tachograph];
- checking the air pressure, air tanks and the suspension;
- checking the safety factors relating to vehicle loading: body, sheets, cargo doors, loading mechanism (if available), cabin locking (if available), way of loading, securing load;
- checking the coupling mechanism and the brake and electrical connections (categories C+E, C1+E only);
- reading a road map, route planning, including the use of electronic navigation systems (optional).
- Special manoeuvres to be tested with a bearing on road safety:
  - coupling and uncoupling, or uncoupling and recoupling a trailer from its motor vehicle; the manoeuvre must involve the towing vehicle being parked alongside the trailer (ie not in one line) (categories C+E, C1+E only);
  - reversing along a curve;
  - parking safely for loading/unloading at a loading ramp/platform or similar installation.
- Behaviour in traffic. Applicants must perform all the following actions in normal traffic situations, in complete safety and taking all necessary precautions:
  - driving away: ie after parking, after a stop in traffic, when exiting a driveway;
  - driving on straight roads; passing oncoming vehicles, including in confined spaces;
  - driving round bends;
  - crossroads: approaching and crossing of intersections and junctions;
  - changing direction: left and right turns; changing lanes;
  - approach/exit of motorways or similar (if available): joining from the acceleration lane; leaving on the deceleration lane;
  - overtaking/passing: overtaking other traffic (if possible); driving alongside obstacles, eg parked cars; being overtaken by other traffic (if appropriate);
  - special road features (if available): roundabouts; railway level crossings; tram/bus stops; pedestrian crossings; driving up/downhill on long slopes;
  - taking the necessary precautions when alighting from the vehicle.

Marking of the Skills and Behaviour Tests

In assessing driver competence, the examiner will be looking for the ease with which the applicant handles the vehicle controls and his capacity to drive in complete safety in traffic. Importantly, the examiner must be made to feel safe throughout the test.

The examiner will also pay special attention as to whether the applicant shows defensive and social driving behaviour, in particular ensuring the safety of all road users, especially those who are the weakest and most exposed, by showing due respect for others. Overall, drivers are expected to make progress in an economically and environmentally friendly manner.

During the test, the examiner will be checking to ensure that the test candidate makes proper use of safety belts, rear-view mirrors, head restraints; driving seat; lights and other equipment; clutch, gearbox, accelerator, braking systems (including third braking system, if available) and the steering. He will also be checking the driver's control of the vehicle under different circumstances and at different speeds; his steadiness on the road (this means no fast acceleration, smooth driving and no hard braking); the weight and dimensions and characteristics of the vehicle; the weight and type of load.

Additionally, drivers must show that they are capable of detecting any major technical faults in their vehicles, especially those posing a safety hazard, and know how to have them remedied in an appropriate fashion.

LGV Test Passes and Failures

A driver who passes the LGV/PCV driving test is issued with a certificate to that effect, valid for a period of two years, and the holder can apply for an LGV driving entitlement of the appropriate category to be added to his unified driving licence.

A driver who fails the LGV/PCV driving test is given a written statement of failure and an oral explanation of the reasons for his failure. He may apply for an immediate retest to be taken after an interval of at least three days.

Advanced Commercial Vehicle Driving Test

For many years the advanced driving test organized by the Institute of Advanced Motorists has been looked upon as a severe test of driving skills requiring a high degree of knowledge of the 'rules of the road' for private car drivers. Commercial vehicle drivers who wish to show that they too have attained an exceptional level of proficiency can take the advanced driving test designed specially for commercial vehicles and on passing they may display the coveted IAM badge.

The advanced commercial vehicle driving test is organized by the Institute of Advanced Motorists, IAM House, 510 Chiswick High Road, London W4 5RG (tel: 020 8996 9600; fax: 020 8996 9601; website: **www.iam.org.uk**) and is open to any heavy goods vehicle driver, subject to certain conditions as follows:

- Loads, if carried on test vehicles, must be properly secured.

- A safe seat at the front of the vehicle must be available for the examiner.

- The driver must not, by taking the test, contravene the drivers' hours and record-keeping rules.

On passing the test, the applicant becomes eligible for admission to membership of the Institute of Advanced Motorists.

Fees

The IAM has introduced a combined fee of £139 under its *Skill for Life* programme, which includes the following:

- a copy of the IAM's Advanced Driving/Motorcycling Manual;
- associate membership of one of the many local IAM Groups;
- a place on an IAM course to prepare for the Advanced Driving Test;
- the fee for the IAM Advanced Test;
- a First-Year Membership of the IAM after passing the Advanced Test.

Exemption from the Test

Certain specially qualified drivers may apply to become Members of the Institute without taking the advanced driving test:

- Royal Navy, Army and Royal Air Force LGV instructors and qualified testing officers who have passed an LGV instructor's course and whose application is supported by the recommendation of the applicant's commanding officer.
- Holders of the Road Transport Industry Training Board Instructor's Certificate.
- Fire Service LGV instructors who have completed an LGV instructor's course, and whose application is supported by the senior instructor.
- LGV driving examiners.

The Advanced Test

To pass the test the driver should show 'skill with responsibility', and any driver of reasonable experience and skill should be able to pass without difficulty. The Institute examiners are all ex-police drivers holding a Class 1 Police Driving Certificate, and they test candidates on routes located all over Britain.

The test lasts about two hours, during which the test route of some 35–40 miles is covered. The route incorporates road conditions of all kinds including congested urban areas, main roads, narrow country lanes and residential streets. Candidates are not expected to display elaborate driving techniques. Examiners prefer to see the vehicle handled in a steady, workmanlike manner without exaggeratedly slow speeds or excessive signalling. Speed limits must be observed (driving in excess of any limit results in test failure) and the driving manner must take into consideration road, traffic and weather conditions. However, the examiners expect candidates to drive briskly within the limits and to cruise at the legal limit (ie either on the road or the vehicle, whichever is lower) whenever circumstances permit.

Drivers will be asked to reverse around a corner and to make a hill start. There will be spot checks on the driver's power of observation (ie the examiner will ask questions about road signs or markings recently passed or about other significant landmarks).

Examiners ask a number of questions of candidates but these are not trick questions. The previous requirement for the driver to give a running commentary during a portion of the route no longer exists – although the test regulations do state that candidates are free to give a commentary if they wish to make extra clear their ability to 'read the road'.

Test Requirements

The examiner will consider the following aspects of driving:

- *Acceleration*: must be smooth and progressive, not excessive or insufficient, and must be used at the right time and place.
- *Braking*: must be smooth and progressive, not fierce. Brakes should be used in conjunction with the driving mirror and signals. Road, traffic and weather conditions must be taken into account.
- *Clutch control*: engine and road speeds should be properly co-ordinated when changing gear. The clutch should not be 'ridden' or slipped and the vehicle should not be coasted with the clutch disengaged.
- *Gear changing*: should be smooth and carried out without jerking.
- *Use of gears*: the gears should be correctly selected and used and the right gear engaged before reaching a hazard.
- *Steering*: the wheel should be correctly held with the hands and the 'crossed-arm' technique should not be used except when manoeuvring in confined spaces.
- *Driving position*: the driver should be alert and should not slump at the wheel. Resting an arm on the door while driving should be avoided.
- *Observation*: the driver should 'read' the road ahead and show a good sense of anticipation and the ability to judge speed and distance.
- *Concentration*: the driver should keep his attention on the road and should not be easily distracted.
- *Maintaining progress*: taking account of the road, traffic and weather conditions, the driver must keep up a reasonable pace and maintain good progress.
- *Obstruction*: the candidate must be careful not to obstruct other vehicles by driving too slowly, taking up the wrong position on the road or failing to anticipate and react correctly to the traffic situation ahead.
- *Positioning*: the driver must keep to the correct part of the road, especially when approaching and negotiating hazards.
- *Lane discipline*: the driver must keep to the appropriate lane and be careful not to straddle white lines.
- *Observations of road surfaces*: the driver must keep an eye on the road surface, especially in bad weather, and should watch out for slippery conditions.
- *Traffic signals*: signals, signs and road markings must be observed, obeyed and approached correctly and the driver should show courtesy at pedestrian crossings.

- *Speed limits and other legal requirements*: these should be observed. The examiner cannot condone breaches of the law.
- *Overtaking*: must be carried out safely and decisively, maintaining the right distance from other vehicles and using the mirror, signals and gears correctly.
- *Hazard procedure and cornering*: road and traffic hazards must be coped with properly, and bends and corners taken in the right manner.
- *Mirror*: the mirror must be used frequently, especially in conjunction with signals and before changing speed or course.
- *Signals*: direction indicator, and hand signals when needed, must be given at the right place and in good time. The horn and headlamp flasher should be used as per the *Highway Code*.
- *Restraint*: the driver should show reasonable restraint, but not indecision, at the wheel.
- *Consideration*: sufficient consideration and courtesy should be shown to other road users.
- *Vehicle sympathy*: the driver should treat the vehicle with care, without overstressing it by needless revving of the engine and by fierce braking.
- *Manoeuvring*: manoeuvres (reversing) should be performed smoothly and competently.

Driver Training

Driver Training for Lorry Loaders

No mandatory requirements exist at the present time for goods vehicle drivers to hold certificates of competence to operate lorry-mounted cranes. However, under the Health and Safety at Work etc Act 1974 employers have a statutory duty to provide adequate instruction and safety training for all employees.

A voluntary certification scheme is run by the Construction Industry Training Board (CITB) to improve safety on construction sites. This scheme is strongly supported by the construction industry, which may refuse entry to its own sites to non-certified lorry drivers. Mainly, the Board's scheme is concerned with ensuring a sound understanding of safety procedures for the use of a wide range of equipment, including lorry-mounted cranes and skip loaders. Under the scheme, the Board provided certification of existing lorry-loader and skip-loader operators who could show by means of employer confirmation that they were experienced in the use of such equipment.

Existing operatives prior to June 1993 who could produce the employer declaration could obtain the Board's safety certificate for lorry-mounted crane operation under a grandfather rights arrangement. A similar arrangement applied to skip-loader operatives until the end of 1994. Newcomers seeking first-time certification and drivers renewing grandfather rights certificates have to undergo (re-) training and site-based assessment to show that they can operate such equipment with complete safety. CITB safety certificates are renewable at five-yearly intervals.

Another scheme is run by the Contractors' Mechanical Plant Engineers (CMPE), although this requires no specific training, certification being based solely on employers' references. Training is also provided by most member firms of the Association of Lorry Loader Manufacturers and Importers (ALLMI). Additionally, the Association itself publishes a Code of Practice for safe application and use of loaders, and is currently preparing a training programme. Details are available from the Association at 14 Manor Close, Droitwich, Worcestershire WR9 8HG (tel: 01905 770892 or 01905 451040). Other organizations providing suitable lorry-loader training include the Freight Transport Association, Centrex (previously the RTITB) and a number of commercial training firms.

Driver Training for ADR

The Carriage of Dangerous Goods and Use of Transportable Pressure Equipment Regulations 2009 (regulation 5), replace previous regulations of this title. These regulations require that dangerous goods drivers are trained in accordance with section 8.2.1 of the European Agreement Concerning the International Carriage of Dangerous Goods by Road (commonly referred to as the ADR) and that they hold Vocational Training Certificates issued by the Driver and Vehicle Licensing Agency (DVLA), Swansea, and gained by attending an approved course and passing a written examination set by the Scottish Qualifications Authority.

Relevant Vehicles

The regulations apply broadly to the carriage of specified dangerous goods in:

- road tankers with a capacity exceeding 1,000 litres; or
- tank containers with a capacity greater than 3,000 litres (with certain exceptions); or
- vehicles carrying radioactive materials or explosives; or
- vehicles carrying packed dangerous goods the amount of which exceeds certain thresholds, as set down by the ADR regulations.

Driver Responsibilities

Vocational training certificates are valid for a period of five years and are renewable, subject to the holder attending an approved refresher course and taking a further examination within the 12 months prior to the expiry date of an existing certificate. Drivers must carry the certificate with them when driving relevant vehicles and must produce it on request by police or a goods vehicle examiner. It is an offence to drive a dangerous goods vehicle without being the holder of a certificate, or to fail to produce such a certificate on request.

Employer Responsibilities

It is the responsibility of the employer to ensure that dangerous goods drivers receive training so they understand the dangers arising from the products they are carrying and what to do in an emergency situation, and that they hold relevant certificates covering the vehicle being driven and the products carried. The employer has a duty to provide necessary training leading to the certificate and the official C&G examination. The employer must retain records of all instruction and training given to drivers.

Approved Training and the City and Guilds Examination

The Department for Transport has approved suitable establishments where dangerous goods driver training can be obtained and the C&G examination taken.

The syllabus for the examination involves both theoretical sessions and practical exercises. The examination itself comprises a core element designed to assess candidates' practical and legal knowledge plus a specialist element for either road tanker and tank container drivers or packaged goods drivers (or both if required). Additionally, candidates have to pass individual 'dangerous substance' examination papers, which cover each of nine classes of dangerous goods, to test their specialist knowledge of the products they carry in their work.

Candidates who pass the examination (by achieving a pass mark of at least 75 per cent in each element – ie core, tanker/package and substance) will receive their certificate direct from the DVLA, Swansea. Those who fail can apply to resit the examination without further training within a period of 16 weeks from receipt of the notification of failure.

Further information on the training and examinations may be obtained from Area Offices of the Health and Safety Executive (see local telephone directory).

Transport Training

NVQs in Transport

Occupational training standards for the road haulage industry are established by Skills for Logistics, an employer-led independent body. These standards underpin a number of National Vocational Qualifications (NVQs) which have been developed for use within the industry as follows:

- NVQ level 1
  Assisting in road haulage and distribution operations
  - covers basic operational skills which may involve helping other more skilled staff.
- NVQ level 2
  Transporting goods by road
  - aimed at the driver of a small or large goods vehicle.

  Distribution and warehousing
  - aimed at someone engaged in the storage and despatch of goods.

  Organizing road transport operations
  - aimed at the traffic planner or clerk who is concerned with traffic operations.

- NVQ level 3
  Supervisory management
  - aimed at supervisors within the road haulage and distribution industry performing road haulage and distribution operations.
- NVQ level 4
  Management
  - aimed at managers in the road haulage and distribution industry.

Continuing Professional Development

Constant changes in business, industry and technology mean that executives need to keep their skills and knowledge up to date in order to maximize professional opportunities and their market value. Continuing professional development (CPD) schemes, such as those operated by the Chartered Institute of Logistics and Transport in the UK (CILT) for its members, enables individuals to improve their knowledge and competence systematically throughout their working life – a concept supported by the Government.

Professional development is the key to career enhancement. Although it is possible to train as and when suitable courses become available, this approach can leave the individual with key needs unfulfilled. A CPD scheme offers personal development solutions structured to fit around a certain career and lifestyle. Planning career development in this systematic way brings the following developments:

- It makes the best use of training and learning opportunities.
- It encourages the individual to look for alternative ways of meeting training/ learning needs.
- It enables the individual to become aware of less obvious knowledge or skills gaps.
- By periodic evaluation of development individuals can judge whether they are meeting their personal objectives.
- Records are kept to track progress.

Learning Activities

Formal learning usually comprises:

- company training;
- study courses including open learning;
- teaching and making presentations;
- attendance at conferences, seminars and meetings related to the individual's work or professional interests.

Informal learning includes:

- reading;
- networking;

- mentoring and coaching;
- project work.

CPD places emphasis on helping individuals to plan and progress their professional future. Normally, schemes focus on outputs without prescribing a minimum number of hours or particular courses to attend; professional persons are expected to take responsibility for their own learning. The CILT, for example, helps members to identify opportunities and provides accreditation of their learning log.

Further details of the CILT and its CPD scheme can be obtained from:

Training and Personal Development
The Chartered Institute of Logistics and Transport in the UK
Earlstree Court
Earlstree Road
Corby
Northants NN17 4AX
www.cilt.org.uk

Vehicle Registration, Excise Duty and Trade Licences

Vehicle Registration

N ew vehicles must be registered with Local Offices of the DVLA or at Swansea and a registration number obtained for each. A one-off first registration charge of £55 is made to cover the DVLA's administrative costs. See Appendix VII for a list of DVLA Local Offices and new vehicle registration marks, also described on pp 362–63.

The registration number must be displayed on plates mounted on the front and rear of the vehicle. These must conform to legal requirements as specified in the Road Vehicles (Display of Registration Marks) Regulations 2001 as amended (see pp 362–63 for full details).

Annual registration prefix changes were replaced by six-monthly changes from 1 March 1999 (prefix 'T') until 1 September 2001, when an entirely new format for registration plates was introduced. This comprises two letters representing the place of registration (ie 1 of 19 areas followed by a letter for the office of registration). Two numbers denote the year of registration. The last three letters are randomly selected.

Form V55, which is used for motor vehicle registrations, consists of a single sheet used for first-licensing and registration purposes and a two-sheet section with carbon paper inserts, so that details of the vehicle and the dealer's name and town (but nothing more) will copy through on to those sheets. These are sent to an agency acting for the motor industry and the DfT for the assembly of official vehicle registration statistics.

A feature of these additional sheets is a voluntary statistical section in which applicants are invited to voluntarily supply information of value for government and motor industry statistical purposes. It includes questions about the purchaser's occupation and previous vehicle and about the main use to which he intends to put the new vehicle. The information given will help the industry to obtain a better knowledge of the market and therefore to give the best possible service to its customers. Also, if purchasers choose to give their name and address, this will enable the manufacturer to get in touch with them direct over any safety matters that may arise. Any information given in this section will be treated as confidential.

Most of the main vehicle manufacturers and importers will have entered the details of each vehicle on the form before it reaches the dealer. This has two advantages, both for motor dealers and for purchasers. First, they no longer have to fill in the details themselves, and second, the association of one form with one vehicle right from the start is intended to make it more difficult to register a stolen vehicle as new. If the manufacturer or importer has not completed the form in advance, copies are available on demand at licensing offices.

Documents

A completed form V55, a certificate of insurance, a copy of the supplier's invoice, and an appropriate Type Approval Certificate (TAC) for goods vehicles subject to the type approval regulations, are required when first registering a goods vehicle. When an excise licence is required for vehicles exempt from annual testing a completed form V112G (Declaration of Exemption) must also be produced.

Vehicle Registration Documents

A Registration Document/Certificate shows the registered keeper of a vehicle. The registered keeper is the person who keeps the vehicle on a public road, but is not necessarily the legal owner. The Certificate gives the keeper's name and address, the registration mark and other details of the vehicle, including engine, VIN and Type Approval numbers, the category into which it falls, its body type, maximum mass (ie weight) etc. A new Registration Certificate is issued each time the DVLA updates the record with any change to the existing details. The vehicle keeper should make sure that the details on this certificate are accurate and must tell the DVLA immediately if any changes are necessary. It may be difficult to sell the vehicle if any of the information is inaccurate. However, it is important to note that the Registration Document/Certificate is *not* a document of title (ownership).

Since January 2004 anyone applying for a V5 Registration Document will have been issued with the new-style Vehicle Registration Certificate (V5C). This new Registration Certificate has been developed to comply with European Directive 1999/37/EC, which required member states to introduce a common format for Registration Certificates no later than June 2004, with the aim of helping to identify vehicles in international traffic and to allow for the re-registration of vehicles throughout the EU.

Future issues of the V5C document will show the vehicle engine's Euro status (e.g. currently Euro V for new vehicles). This will enable operators to show the vehicle's compliance with emission standards for toll charging purposes.

On receipt of the Registration Certificate, vehicle keepers should check that the details are correct, put the document in a safe place (together with the guidance notes) and destroy the existing old-style Registration Document if it is still in their possession.

NB: A statutory charge of £55.00 is made by the DVLA for first registration of a new vehicle and of £25.00 for replacing a lost, stolen, destroyed or damaged vehicle registration document.

Police officers and certain officers of VOSA may request production of the registration document for inspection at any reasonable time.

Issue of Licence Disc

On payment of the relevant amount of vehicle excise duty (VED) for a vehicle, the DVLA issues a circular licence disc indicating the period of validity, the vehicle registration number, and the fee paid. This licence must be displayed in the vehicle windscreen where it can be clearly seen from the nearside.

Since October 2003 a new-style windscreen disc has been issued with enhanced anti-fraud security features, particularly a bar code, which enables licensing information to be electronically transferred to the DVLA.

Number Plates

As part of the DVLA's measures to combat vehicle crime, it has been a requirement since the beginning of 2003 that vehicle number (registration) plates may be produced only by registered manufacturers, who must keep records of the plates they sell, to whom they are sold and whether that person is authorized to require the plates. Purchasers of plates need to produce evidence as to who they are (a passport or photocard driving licence) and that they have a right to the plates for the vehicle in question (generally by producing the vehicle registration document (form V5) or a letter of authorization from the vehicle owner). Drivers of vehicles with dirty or fancy number plates caught on ANPR (Automatic Number Plate Recognition) systems may be prosecuted under rules introduced in 2006.

Registration of 'O' Licence Vehicles

The Traffic Commissioners have ruled that vehicles specified on British 'O' licences must be registered in the UK.

The DVLA has also warned that British VED must be paid on vehicles unless the operator has a genuine business abroad.

Vehicle Excise Licences

All mechanically propelled vehicles, whether used for private or business purposes, which are used or parked on public roads in Great Britain, must be covered by, and display, a vehicle excise licence indicating that the appropriate amount of vehicle excise duty (VED) has been paid – except when being driven, by previous appointment, to a place to have their annual test.

It is an offence to use or keep an unlicensed vehicle on the road for any period, however short. Conviction for such an offence will result in heavy fines, and back duty may be claimed (see also p 229). Furthermore, new vehicle licensing rules from 1 January 2004 mean that the registered keeper of a vehicle (the person named on DVLA's record) remains responsible for taxing a vehicle (or making a SORN declaration) until that liability is formally transferred to a new keeper. To avoid liability for taxing it, the keeper needs to inform DVLA when the vehicle is off the road, or has been sold, transferred, scrapped or exported. Once DVLA has been notified about a sale/transfer or that the vehicle is off-road they will issue an acknowledgement letter, which should be kept as proof that the vehicle record has been changed. Failure to re-license a vehicle or make a SORN declaration will incur an automatic penalty of £80 (reduced to £40 if paid within 28 days). Determined offenders will be faced with prosecution and could be fined a minimum of £1,000. Operators' licence holders also jeopardize their 'O' licences when committing excise duty offences.

The present system of excise licences for most goods vehicles is based on gross weights (ie the 'revenue weight') and axle configurations, while goods vehicles not exceeding 3,500 kilograms gross weight are in the same class as private vehicles, which is called private/light goods (PLG) (see p 519 for full details).

Exemptions

Exemption from vehicle excise duty (as specified in the Vehicle Excise and Registration Act 1994) applies to the following:

1 Vehicles used for police, fire brigade, ambulance or health services (including veterinary ambulances).
2 Mines rescue vehicles.
3 Vehicles used for the haulage of lifeboats and lifeboat gear.
4 Vehicles for disabled people.
5 Vehicles used solely for forestry, agriculture or horticultural purposes travelling on public roads to pass between land occupied by the same person and the distance travelled on public roads is not more than 1.5km per journey.
6 Vehicles travelling to or from a place where they are to have an annual roadworthiness test by prior appointment.
7 Vehicles for export.
8 Vehicles in the service of a visiting force or headquarters.

The special concessionary rate which formerly applied has been abolished and the following vehicles that were included in this class are now free of vehicle excise duty and are thus added to the exempt class along with the above-listed vehicles:

- An agricultural or off-road tractor which is a tractor used on public roads only for purposes relating to agriculture, horticulture, forestry or cutting verges, hedges or trees bordering public roads. An off-road tractor is one which is not an agricultural tractor but which is designed and constructed primarily for use otherwise than on roads and is incapable of exceeding 25 mph on the level.

- A light agricultural vehicle is a vehicle with a revenue weight not exceeding 1,000 kg which is designed and constructed to seat only the driver and primarily for use otherwise than on roads; and is used only for agriculture, horticulture or forestry.
- An agricultural engine.
- Mowing machines.
- Steam-powered vehicles.
- Electrically propelled vehicles.
- Vehicles when used, or going to or from a place for use, or kept for use, for clearing snow on public roads by means of a snow plough or similar device.
- Vehicles constructed or adapted and used only for the conveyance of machinery for spreading material on roads to deal with frost, ice or snow.

Special Vehicles

Special vehicles over 3.5 tonnes – current and annual rate of duty £165. This class includes mobile cranes, digging machines, works trucks, road rollers and showmen's goods and haulage vehicles. Vehicles classed as 'mobile pumping vehicles' have been added to this category.

Rates of Duty

The rate of duty payable varies depending on the way in which the vehicle is constructed, the way that it is used and, in the case of light vehicles, their unladen weight, and for heavy goods vehicles, their 'revenue' weight and the number of axles. The current rates of duty shown have been effective since 1 December 2001.

Revenue Weight

Revenue weight means either the 'confirmed maximum weight' as determined under the plating and testing regulations (ie by the issue of a plate and plating certificate), or the 'design weight' for vehicles not subject to plating and testing and currently known as restricted HGVs (this is the maximum laden weight at which non-plated vehicles can legally operate on roads in the UK).

Down-Plating

For various operational reasons heavy goods vehicles are specified to a higher standard and gross weight than payload weights demand. However, to avoid the higher rates of vehicle excise duty that would normally be payable, such vehicles may be down-plated without making any technical change to the specification – see p 384 for details of how this can be done.

Reduced Pollution Vehicles

Reduced rates of vehicle excise duty (by up to £1,000 for the heaviest vehicles) apply to certain buses, haulage vehicles and heavy goods vehicles which have been built or adapted to ensure reduced pollution exhaust emissions under the provisions of the Vehicle Excise Duty (Reduced Pollution) Regulations 1998 (as amended). These regulations:

- set out the reduced pollution requirements to be satisfied in order for a vehicle to qualify for reduced rates of excise duty;
- provide for the issue of reduced pollution certificates where the specified requirements have been met;
- set out the procedure for applying for a vehicle examination in order to obtain a reduced pollution certificate.

Reduced Pollution Certificates are available to heavy goods vehicles and buses that attain (under test) the full Euro-V exhaust emission standard, and meet both the on-board diagnostic (OBD) and torque control (de-powering) requirements. This applies up to the end of September 2009 when the mandatory introduction of Euro-V came into force (ie from 1 October 2009).

Articulated Combinations

In the case of articulated tractive units which are used with a variety of trailers, the determining factor for taxation purposes is the number of axles on the trailer likely to be used with it. This is so that the maximum amount of duty is paid to prevent a vehicle operating on the road at a rate less than that which is applicable. In general terms, the system operates so that the fewer the axles the greater the duty payable and vice versa. This is because the duty relates to the road damage caused and greater damage arises with fewer axles. In consequence of this it is illegal to operate a vehicle on a road for which the incorrect (ie insufficient) excise duty has been paid.

Trailers

Where drawbar trailers are drawn, if the gross weight of the trailer exceeds 4 tonnes and the gross weight of the towing vehicle exceeds 12 tonnes, additional duty is payable in accordance with published duty tables but not otherwise. So, if the towing vehicle or the trailer falls below these weights, no trailer duty is payable.

Goods-Carrying Vehicles

The goods vehicle rate of duty is payable if the vehicle is built or has been converted to carry goods, and is actually used to carry goods in connection with a trade or business. In general this rate of duty applies to all types of lorries, vans, trucks, estate cars, dual-purpose vehicles and also passenger vehicles if they are converted for carrying goods. If, however, dual-purpose vehicles (see below) and goods vehicles (over 3.5 tonnes) are never used for carrying goods in connection with a trade or business they may be licensed at the private heavy goods rate of duty, which is currently £165 per year.

Following a High Court ruling in March 1999, heavy vehicles carrying wide loads in excess of 4.3 metres must be taxed at the 'Special Types' rate of duty, currently £2,585 per year (£2,085 for reduced pollution vehicles), irrespective of their gross weight. This duty is based on the use of a vehicle rather than its construction, and when carrying a wide load under the Motor Vehicles (Authorization of Special Types) General Order 2003, the relevant Special Types duty rate must be applied.

In yet another interpretation case, the Crown Court has ruled that concrete-pumping vehicles must be taxed at the goods vehicle rate of duty, and not at the reduced rate applicable to mobile cranes.

Driver Training and Non-Goods-Carrying Vehicles

Heavy goods vehicles which are used exclusively for driver training purposes may be licensed at the private heavy goods rate of duty even if they carry ballast (eg concrete blocks) to simulate driving under loaded conditions – *but not other loads*. Similarly, other goods vehicles used for private purposes (ie carriage of goods but not in connection with a trade or business – for example, privately used horseboxes) may be licensed at the private heavy goods vehicle rate of duty – currently £165 for vehicles over 3.5 tonnes.

Private-Rate Taxation of Heavy Vehicles on International Work

The use of heavy vehicles for goods carrying in the UK or within other EU member states while taxed only at the private heavy goods rate of duty is illegal both in the UK and in Europe (see also section on penalties, p 229). Furthermore, running a vehicle on the Continent with an expired UK tax disc, on the assumption that the tax can be renewed on the vehicle's return to the UK, is also illegal. Under the provisions of bilateral agreements and under International Conventions on the Taxation of Road Vehicles, vehicles on which the correct rate of vehicle excise duty has been paid in their country of registration are exempt from payment of further duty on being temporarily imported into the territories of other parties to the agreements. Where the correct duty is not paid in the 'home' country, there is a liability for payment of additional duty in each other country through which the vehicle travels.

Dual-Purpose Vehicles

For the purposes of the regulations a dual-purpose vehicle (as referred to above) is defined as a vehicle, built or converted to carry both passengers and goods of any description, which has an unladen weight of not more than 2,040 kilograms and has either four-wheel drive or:

- has a permanently fitted roof;
- is permanently fitted with one row of transverse seats (fitted across the vehicle) behind the driver's seat (the seats must be cushioned or sprung and have upholstered back-rests);
- has a window on either side to the rear of the driver's seat and one at the rear.

The majority of so-called estate cars, shooting-brakes, station wagons, hatchbacks, certain Land Rovers and Range Rovers are dual-purpose vehicles under this definition. It should be noted, however, that vehicles used for *dual operations* are not dual-purpose vehicles in terms of the legal requirements.

VED Tables

These rates of duty apply to all licences taken out from 1 April 2010.

- *Private/Light Goods Vehicles registered before 1 March 2001 (ie goods vehicles not over 3,500kg revenue weight)*

	12-month rate £	6-month rate £
Not over 1,549cc	125.00	68.75
Over 1,549cc	205.00	112.75

- *Light goods vehicles (ie not over 3,500 kg revenue weight, registered on or after 1 March 2001)*

	12-month rate £	6-month rate £
Light vans	200.00	110.00

	12-month rate £	6-month rate £
Euro-IV Light Goods Vehicles (vehicles not over 3,500 kg) (registered 1 March 2003–31 December 2006)	125.00	68.75
Euro-V Light Goods Vehicles (vehicles not over 3,500 kg) (registered 1 January 2009–31 December 2010)	125.00	68.75

- *Buses*

Seating capacity (excluding driver)	12-month rate £	6-month rate £	Reduced pollution vehicle 12-month rate £	6-month rate £
10–17	165.00	90.75	165.00	90.75
18–36	220.00	121.00	165.00	90.75
37–61	330.00	181.50	165.00	90.75
62 and over	500.00	275.00	165.00	90.75

- *General haulage vehicles*

12-month rate £	6-month rate £	Reduced pollution vehicle 12-month rate £	6-month rate £
350.00	192.50	165.00	90.75

- *Trade licences*

	12-month rate £	6-month rate £
Trade licences available for all vehicles	165.00	90.75

- *Recovery vehicles*

Over	Not over	12-month rate £	6-month rate £
3,500 kg	25,000 kg	165.00	90.75
25,000 kg	–	410.00	225.50

- *Private HGV (exceeding 3,500 kg)*

	12-month rate £	6-month rate £
	165.00	90.75

Annual VED Rates from 1 December 2001

A new, simplified structure for heavy vehicle excise duty rates was introduced from 1 December 2001.

Rigid vehicles

Vehicle weight	2-axled rigid	3-axled rigid	4 or more-axled rigid
Not over 7,500 kg	A	A	A
Not over 15,000 kg	B	B	B
Not over 21,000 kg	D	B	B
Not over 23,000 kg	D	C	B
Not over 25,000 kg	D	D	C
Not over 27,000 kg	D	D	D
Not over 44,000 kg	D	D	E

Trailer duty
NB: *Where vehicles draw trailers weighing 4,000 kg or below they do not come within a trailer taxation class and no additional trailer duty is payable.*

Trailer duty Where the drawing vehicle has a weight of over 12,000 kg and draws laden trailers over 4,000 kg, additional trailer duty is payable				Reduced pollution trailer duty	
Over	Not over	12-month rate £	6-month rate £	12-month rate £	6-month rate £
4,000	12,000	165.00	90.75	165.00	90.75
12,000	–	230.00	126.50	230.00	126.50

Example: A two-axled vehicle with a weight of 16,260 kg that draws trailers with a weight of 12,130 kg would pay £650 plus £230 annual rate.

Two-axled tractive unit articulated vehicles

Vehicle weight	1 or more-axled semi-trailer	2 or more-axled semi-trailer	3 or more-axled semi-trailer
Not over 25,000 kg	A	A	A
Not over 28,000 kg	C	A	A
Not over 31,000 kg	D	D	A
Not over 34,000 kg	E	E	C
Not over 38,000 kg	F	F	E
Not over 44,000 kg	G	G	G

Three-axled tractive unit articulated vehicles

Vehicle weight	1 or more-axled semi-trailer	2 or more-axled semi-trailer	3 or more-axled semi-trailer
Not over 28,000 kg	A	A	A
Not over 31,000 kg	C	A	A
Not over 33,000 kg	E	C	A
Not over 34,000 kg	E	D	A
Not over 36,000 kg	E	D	C
Not over 38,000 kg	F	E	D
Not over 44,000 kg	G	G	E

	Key to VED bands			
Lorry VED band	**Standard**		**Reduced pollution**	
	12-month rate £	**6-month rate £**	**12-month rate £**	**6-month rate £**
A	165.00	90.75	*160.00	*88.00
B	200.00	110.00	*160.00	*88.00
C	450.00	247.50	210.00	115.50
D	650.00	357.50	280.00	154.00

Key to VED bands continued				
Lorry VED band	Standard		Reduced pollution	
	12-month rate £	6-month rate £	12-month rate £	6-month rate £
E	1,200.00	660.00	700.00	385.00
F	1,500.00	825.00	1,000.00	550.00
G	1,850.00	1,017.50	1,350.00	742.50

* Where two or more bands show the same rate of duty the renewal remainder may display one band only.
SOURCE: Reproduced from DVLA website with acknowledgement.

- *Special Types vehicles*

	12-month rate £	6-month rate £	Reduced pollution vehicle	
			12-month rate £	6-month rate £
Used to carry abnormal indivisible loads under the Special Types General Order	2,585.00	1,421.50	2,085.00	1,146.50

Payment of Duty

Excise duty is payable once annually, or every six months. Application for initial registration or renewal of duty is made on the appropriate form as follows:

- First registration
  - – form VE 55/1 for new vehicles
  - – form VE 55/5 for reimported vehicles
- Renewal of duty (12 or 6 months)
  - – form V10 for all vehicles up to 3,500 kg
  - – form V11 renewal reminder, which enables vehicles to be re-licensed at a post office
  - – form V85 for heavy goods vehicles, which may only be re-licensed at VROs.

Display of Licence Discs

A circular licence disc is issued by the Driver and Vehicle Licensing Agency (DVLA) – or a post office when renewing licences there – when the duty is paid and this must be displayed in the vehicle windscreen where it can be clearly seen from the nearside. It is an offence to fail to display a current and valid vehicle excise licence disc – those not displaying discs will be reported to the DVLA and the operator may face a fine of up to £25,000 plus back duty and costs.

Reduced, Extended Periods and Refunds

A vehicle may be licensed for only six months at a time if this is preferred but this method of licensing means that a higher amount of duty is paid annually. All licences are valid only from the first day of the month in which they come into force. Alternatively, new vehicles may be licensed part-way through a month (but only at local VROs) with the duty period commencing on the 10th, 17th or 24th day of the month and continuing through to the end of the 12-month period from the first day of the following month.

In cases where a vehicle is to be used for a shorter period than either 6 or 12 months or is taken out of service during the currency of the licence, a licence has to be taken out for one or other of these periods and then surrendered to the VRO (see local telephone directory for addresses of local VROs) when it is no longer required; the VRO will refund the duty for each complete month remaining on the licence. To gain a full month refund the licence must be surrendered at least by the last day of the previous month. Application for a refund should be made on form V14.

Statutory Off-Road Declaration Scheme

As part of its initiative to recover the estimated £175 million lost each year to road tax evasion, a new scheme requires registered vehicle keepers to notify the Driver and Vehicle Licensing Agency (DVLA) whenever a vehicle is off the road untaxed. By law, vehicle keepers must provide a Statutory Off-Road Notice (SORN) declaring to the DVLA that the vehicle is not being used and is not being kept on a public road and is therefore not liable to vehicle excise duty.

The Government introduced new vehicle tax rules from 1 January 2004 under which keepers of vehicles who have not paid their tax (VED) within the month will be identified from the DVLA computer database and will receive an *automatic* £80 penalty. This is reduced to £40 if the tax is paid within 28 days; but determined offenders could face prosecution and a minimum fine of £1,000. The changes mean that for the first time registered keepers of vehicles are now legally responsible for taxing them. If they do not tax their vehicle, or fail to inform the DVLA that the vehicle is off-road or has had a change of keeper, then they will be liable for the £80 penalty – even if the vehicle belongs to someone else.

This scheme will enable the Government to crack down further on 'vehicle cheats' who do not tax their vehicles, many of whom also drive without insurance or a valid test certificate. Currently there are estimated to be some 1.75 million untaxed vehicles on UK roads. As a test certificate (for light vehicles over three years old and LGVs over one year old) and insurance certificate are needed to purchase a vehicle tax disc, this measure, according to the Government, will not only cut the number of untaxed vehicles, but also cut the number of unsafe and illegal vehicles on our roads.

Making a false 'off-road' declaration will result in prosecution and a maximum fine of £5,000 or two years' imprisonment on conviction.

Renewal of Licences

When the licence expires after 6 months or 12 months it has to be renewed by completing renewal form V10 or form V85. Renewal reminders are sent out from the DVLA on form V11 and this may be used as an alternative to form V10 to renew the licence at certain post offices (provided the vehicle is not over 3,500 kg gross weight where form V10 is used, there is no change in ownership or address which has not been recorded and no change to the vehicle or its use), or at DVLA Local Offices. Form V85 is used for goods vehicles over 3,500 kg gross weight. The vehicle registration document, the appropriate fee, a valid certificate of insurance and, if the vehicle is subject to annual testing, a current test certificate, must accompany the application.

Where to Apply

Applications for renewal of duty may be made as follows:

- If you have the official licence renewal reminder, form V11 (provided there is no change in the details on the form)

  In person to main post offices or Local Offices, or by post to Local Offices.

- If you have form V11 but there are changes in the details

  In person or by post to Local Offices.

- If the vehicle is a heavy goods vehicle for which no form V11 has been received

  In person or by post to Local Offices.

Payment of Excise Licence duty can now be made by credit card, for which a statutory extra charge of £2.50 is made. Re-licensing of vehicles can also be carried out online via the DVLA's website at: **www.dvla.gov.uk/vehiclelicence**.

Replacement Licences and Discs

Duplicates or replacements for lost or defaced vehicle licence windscreen discs are available on application, using form V20 at VROs. They cost £7 each (except in certain exceptional cases – eg if stolen with the vehicle, if for a VED-exempt vehicle, if lost in the post). Replacements for lost, stolen or destroyed vehicle registration documents/certificates (or the new keeper supplement) can be obtained by applying to the DVLA using form V62 (Vehicle Registration Certificate V5C Application Form), which is available from DVLA Local Offices or certain post office branches, or can be downloaded from the DVLA website at: **www.dvla.gov.uk/vehicles**. An existing registered vehicle keeper on the DVLA computer may apply by telephoning 0870 240 0010 using a debit/credit card for payment, provided there are no changes in the registration details. A statutory fee of £19 is charged.

Alteration of Vehicles

If a vehicle is altered during its life by adding or removing equipment, by changing the type of body or even the colour of the vehicle, by changing the plated weight or increasing the unladen weight by fitting a heavier body or heavier components, the DVLA must be advised of the changes at once. If the changes mean that the vehicle goes into a higher weight range, then the additional licence duty becomes payable from the date of the changes.

If a van is converted to carry passengers or has side windows fitted to the body behind the driver's seat the owner becomes liable to pay car tax to HM Revenue & Customs. The amount of tax payable is based on the current wholesale value of the vehicle. Any person making such a conversion must report the fact to the HM Revenue & Customs authorities immediately.

Sale of Vehicles

When a vehicle is sold, the seller must notify the DVLA by completing the bottom tear-off portion of the registration document (form V5), which is perforated for this purpose, with the name and address of the new owner of the vehicle. It is an offence to fail to notify a change of vehicle ownership (maximum fine £1,000) and it can lead to the original owner being prosecuted for offences committed with the vehicle by the new owner and leaving the previous owner to pay any fixed penalty fines incurred. The new owner has to fill in his name and address in the changes section of the registration document and send the document to the DVLA for registration in his name. If a vehicle is sold for scrap or is broken up, the registration document has to be sent to the DVLA with a note advising them of this.

Under a new vehicle keepership scheme, the police and the DVLA will combine reporting of the offences of failing to register a vehicle (ie by the new owner) and vehicle excise duty evasion. This scheme is intended to clamp down on those who fail to notify disposal or acquisition of a vehicle.

Unrepairable Vehicles

Where a motor vehicle is unrepairable and the insurer notifies the DVLA of this fact, or the vehicle registration document has been surrendered to the DVLA, it must undergo an examination (ie a Vehicle Identity Check) to confirm it is the originally registered vehicle before a new registration document can be issued. A charge of £35 is made for the VIC.

Production of Test Certificates

A valid goods vehicle test certificate has to be produced at the time of re-licensing any goods vehicle over one year old (ie vehicles over 3,500 kilograms gross weight and articulated vehicles which are subject to the goods vehicle annual test), and a light vehicle or private car type (ie MoT) test certificate when re-licensing any vehicle not over 3,500 kilograms gross weight which is over three years old and is subject to the light vehicle annual test scheme.

Vehicles Exempt from Plating and Testing

When applying to license or re-license goods vehicles which are exempt from plating and testing, a declaration has to be made on form V112G (available from VROs) to cover the non-production of a valid test certificate.

Where a person does not intend to use a vehicle during the period of an excise licence except for a purpose which is specifically exempt from testing requirements (see list on pp 386–88), a 'Form of Declaration' must be made as specified in the Goods Vehicles (Evidence of Test Certificates) Regulations 2004 (SI 2004 No 2577).

Penalties and Payment of Back Duty

Offenders prosecuted for evasion of vehicle excise duty face fines of up to £1,000 for cars and £25,000 for heavy goods vehicles. This also applies to payment at an incorrect (ie too low) rate of duty or payment by means of a cheque which defaults, while making a false 'off-road' declaration will lead to a fine of up to £5,000 or two years' imprisonment on conviction, as previously mentioned. Additionally, an offender may be ordered to pay an amount of back duty. Previously the amount of back duty payable could be reduced if the offender could prove non-use of the vehicle during any particular month, but this provision has been rescinded. Failure by a vehicle keeper to notify the DVLA of a change of name or address could result in a £1,000 fine on conviction.

Foreign-Registered Vehicles in Great Britain

Foreign-registered cars and light vehicles brought into Great Britain temporarily by overseas residents are exempt from UK registration and licensing. See p 519 for further details.

Data Protection

In accordance with the provisions of the Data Protection Act the DVLA at Swansea is registered as a Data User and as such must make available, on request, details held on file concerning individual persons. Such information is normally shown on driving licences and vehicle registration documents but an enquiry to establish details held on file can be made (on payment of a fee) to the Vehicle Enquiry Unit (Data Protection Queries), DVLA, Swansea SA99 1AN.

Trade Licences

Trade licences (trade plates) are available for use by motor traders and vehicle testers to save them the inconvenience of having to license individually every vehicle which passes through their hands. Probationary licences are available to those setting up in business where a trade licence can be legally used.

Fees and Validity

A trade licence can be obtained from the local VRO in whose area the applicant has his business; it is valid either for one year or for six months (licences are issued on 1 January and 1 July) and the licence fee is £165 for one year and £90.75 for six months. Replacements for lost or defaced trade plates (which remain the property of the local VRO) cost £13.50 per set of two plates or £18 for a set of three plates. A replacement holder for the licence costs £2 and a replacement (ie duplicate) licence is £7. Besides the 12-month and 6-month licences, it is now possible to obtain such a licence for periods between 7 months and 11 months at pro-rata rates to the six monthly rate (ie 55 per cent of the annual rate for six months, plus one-sixth of this amount for every month in excess of six months).

Display of Trade Licences

The VRO will, when they have approved the application, issue a pair of special number plates with the registration number in red letters on a white background – an additional plate is available in certain circumstances. One of the plates has a licence holder attached to it and the licence affixed (it does not have to be displayed on the windscreen); this plate must always be carried at the front of the vehicle on which the plates are being used. The other plate is carried at the rear.

Issue of Licences

There are considerable restrictions on the issue and use of trade licences; as already mentioned they are issued only to:

- motor traders, defined as 'manufacturers or repairers of, or dealers in mechanically propelled vehicles' (this also includes dealers who are in business consisting mainly of collecting and delivering mechanically propelled vehicles), plus those who modify vehicles (eg by fitting accessories) and those who provide valet services for vehicles, who may use the licence for all vehicles which are from time to time temporarily in their possession in the course of their business as motor traders;
- vehicle testers for all vehicles which are from time to time submitted to them for testing in the course of their business as vehicle testers.

Vehicles such as service vans or general runabout vehicles owned by motor traders cannot be used under trade licences; the full rate of duty has to be paid for such vehicles.

Use of Trade Licences

The following are the purposes for which vehicles operated under a trade licence may be used by a motor trader or vehicle tester:

- for test or trial in the course of construction or repair of the vehicle or its accessories or equipment and after completing construction or repair;

- travelling to or from a weighbridge to check the unladen weight or travelling to a place for registration or inspection by the council;
- for demonstration to a prospective customer and for travelling to or from a place of demonstration;
- for test or trial of the vehicle for the benefit of a person interested in promoting publicity for the vehicle;
- for delivering the vehicle to a purchaser;
- for demonstrating the accessories or equipment to a prospective purchaser;
- for delivering a vehicle to, or collecting it from, other premises belonging to the trade licence holder or another trader's premises;
- for going to or coming from a workshop in which a body or equipment or accessories are to be, or have been fitted, or where the vehicle is to be or has been valeted, painted or repaired;
- for delivering the vehicle from the premises of a manufacturer or repairer to a place where it is to be transported by train, ship or aircraft or for returning it from a place to which it has been transported by these means;
- travelling to or returning from any garage, auction room or other place where vehicles are stored or offered for sale and where the vehicle has been stored or offered for sale;
- travelling to a place to be tested (and returned), dismantled or broken up.

It should be noted that the use of a vehicle on trade plates does not exempt the driver or operator from the need to ensure that it is in sound mechanical condition when on the road, even if being driven for the purposes of road testing or fault finding prior to repair or after repair. The police will prosecute if they find trade-licensed vehicles on the road in an unsafe or otherwise illegal condition.

Carriage of Goods on a Trade Licence

Goods may only be carried on a vehicle operating under a trade licence:

- when a load is necessary to demonstrate or test the vehicle, its accessories or its equipment – the load must be returned to the place of loading after the demonstration or test unless it comprised water, fertilizer or refuse;
- when a load consists of parts or equipment designed to be fitted to the vehicle being taken to the place where they are to be fitted;
- when a load is built in or permanently attached to the vehicle;
- when a trailer is being carried for delivery or being taken to a place for work to be done on it;
- if the goods are another fully licensed vehicle being carried for the purpose of travel from or to the place of collection or delivery (ie the driver's own transport to get him out or back home).

Carriage of Passengers on a Trade Licence

The only passengers who are permitted to travel on a trade licensed vehicle are:

- the driver of the vehicle, who must be the licence holder or his employee – other persons may drive the vehicle with the permission of the licence holder but they must be accompanied by the licence holder or his employee (this latter proviso does not apply if the vehicle is only constructed to carry one person);

- persons required to be on the vehicle by law; a statutory attendant, for example;

- any person carried for the purpose of carrying out his statutory duties of inspecting the vehicle or trailer;

- any person in a disabled vehicle being towed including persons from the disabled vehicle being carried provided this is not for hire or reward;

- a prospective purchaser or his servant or agent;

- a person interested in promoting publicity for the vehicle.

NB: *It is illegal for transport fleet operators to road-test their own vehicles on trade plates. This has been established on the grounds that the vehicles are not 'temporarily' in their possession and are therefore outside the permitted terms of trade licence use.*

Recovery Vehicles

A separate class of VED at an annual rate of duty of £165 or £410* currently applies to these vehicles. Any vehicle used for recovery work which does not conform to the definition given below must be licensed at the normal goods vehicle rate according to its class and gross weight.

The annual rates of duty for recovery vehicles based on design weights are as follows:

- *3.5 to 25 tonnes*   *£165.00 (£90.75 for 6 months)*
- *over 25 tonnes*   *£410.00 (£225.50 for 6 months)*

Definition of Recovery Vehicle

For the purpose of this taxation class, a recovery vehicle is one which is 'either constructed or permanently adapted primarily for the purpose of lifting, towing and transporting a disabled vehicle, or for any one or more of those purposes'. A vehicle will no longer be a recovery vehicle under the regulations (ie the Vehicles Excise and Registration Act 1994, Schedule 1 part V) if at any time it is used for a purpose other than:

- the recovery of a disabled vehicle (a maximum of two disabled vehicles may be recovered at any one time);

- the removal of a disabled vehicle from the place where it became disabled to premises at which it is to be repaired or scrapped;

- the removal of a disabled vehicle from premises to which it was taken for repair to other premises at which it is to be repaired or scrapped;

- carrying fuel and other liquids required for its propulsion and tools and other articles required for the operation of, or in connection with, apparatus designed to lift, tow or transport a disabled vehicle;
- travelling to a place where it will be available to recover or remove a disabled vehicle and to go from a place where it has recovered a disabled vehicle or to any place to which it has removed a disabled vehicle;
- repairing a vehicle at the place at which it became disabled or to which it had been taken for safety;
- towing or carrying one trailer which had previously been towed or carried by the vehicle immediately prior to it becoming disabled;
- removing a vehicle from the road to a nominated place on the instruction of a police constable or a local authority under their statutory powers.

The Act allows the carriage of people and/or goods on a recovery vehicle under the first two items listed above, provided they were either a driver or passenger in the vehicle immediately prior to it becoming disabled, or goods being carried on the vehicle immediately prior to it becoming disabled. The driver and/or passenger of a disabled vehicle (and his personal effects) may also be carried from the place where the disabled vehicle is to be repaired or scrapped to his original destination.

The use of a recovery vehicle, subject to VED at the recovery vehicle rate, for purposes other than those described above is illegal and may lead to prosecution and demands for payment of duty (and back duty) at the full goods vehicle rate.

Operation of Recovery Vehicles

Recovery vehicles licensed under the recovery vehicle taxation class are not exempt from goods vehicle plating and testing unless they satisfy the definition of a 'recovery vehicle' (see above). Such vehicles, however, are exempt from 'O' licensing, the EU drivers' hours rules and the tachograph requirements but those persons who drive them must comply with the British domestic driving hours rules (see pp 100–02 for details).

Rebated Heavy Oil

Commercial vehicles powered by diesel (heavy oil) engines must use diesel fuel on which the full rate of duty has been paid. A lower rate of duty is payable on fuel used for purposes other than driving road vehicles, such as driving auxiliary equipment, for contractors' plant which does not use public roads, bench-testing of engines and space heating. Fuel on which the lower rate of duty has been paid is known as rebated heavy oil but is more commonly called gas oil or red diesel. It is illegal to use this type of fuel, or kerosene, in road vehicles, as is the use of other marked diesel such as that with the Solvent Yellow 124 marker used in all EU member states.

Rebated heavy oil must be marked, when delivered from bonded oil warehouses, with a red dye so that its use can easily be detected, and the supplier must deliver to the recipient a delivery note bearing a statement that the oil is 'not to be used as road fuel'. If both rebated and unrebated oils are stored in the same place a notice bearing the same wording must be placed at the outlet of the rebated oil supply.

Supplies of so-called 'green' diesel have become available from the Irish Republic. This fuel is to be regarded in the same way as 'red' diesel. In other words, it is illegal for normal goods vehicle use on UK roads and in Europe.

Road fuel testing units staffed by officers of Revenue & Customs operate throughout the UK to test fuel in vehicles and in storage tanks. Under the Hydrocarbon Oil Regulations 1973 and the Hydrocarbon Oil (Marking) Regulations 2002, Revenue & Customs officers are empowered to examine any vehicle and any oil carried in it or on it and may also enter and inspect any premises and inspect, test or sample any oil on the premises whether the oil is in a vehicle or not. Vehicle owners and drivers must give the officers facilities for inspecting oils in vehicles or on premises.

The following vehicles may use rebated heavy oil as fuel. All other vehicles must use unrebated (full-duty paid) oil at all times:

- vehicles not used on public roads and not licensed for road use;
- road rollers;
- road construction machinery (vehicles used or kept on a road solely for carrying built-in road construction machinery);
- vehicles licensed as 'limited use vehicles' and used for agriculture, horticulture or forestry which pass only between areas of land occupied by the same person and which travel on public roads between such places for no more than 1.5 km;
- agricultural machines (ie tractors);
- trench digging and excavating machines;
- mobile cranes;
- mowing machines;
- works trucks.

Heavy penalties, including fines of up to £500, repayment of duty and even arrest and impounding of vehicles, are imposed on offenders convicted of using illegal diesel fuel.

It should be noted particularly by international hauliers that use of 'red diesel' (ie untaxed diesel fuel) carried in reserve or 'belly' tanks or fed from diesel tanks on refrigerated semi-trailers and used once outside the UK is an illegal practice (NB: red diesel can legally be used for powering refrigeration units on vehicles). It is also illegal to carry red diesel in unconnected or disconnected additional vehicle tanks. Although Customs checks abroad on vehicle fuel tanks are limited, any operator found running on or illegally carrying such fuel within the EU is likely to face heavy penalties.

Customs may question operators with unusually large diesel tanks mounted on reefer semi-trailers to determine whether such fuel is being illegally used to power the vehicle as well as the fridge unit.

The maximum legal capacity for an engine-connected diesel tank on a vehicle is 1,500 litres. Revenue & Customs policy is that vehicle manufacturer-fitted fuel tanks are acceptable, but any additional tank fitted to the vehicle, or the exchange of a standard manufacturer tank for a large-capacity tank, infringes the rules and will incur a penalty. Above 1,500 litres it is considered that the vehicle would have to operate under ADR regulations (see Chapter 20). It should also be noted that transferring fuel purchased abroad for use in another vehicle is illegal and may result in charges for evasion of duty.

With estimated losses of some £600 million annually through illegal use of duty-free red diesel, and to eliminate unfair commercial advantage gained through its use, the Government (through HM Revenue & Customs) is anxious to implement further controls over its permitted use. It has issued a consultation document in which it outlines proposals for:

- banning road construction vehicles from using red diesel unless they can be classed as 'works vehicles' operating within 1km of a site;
- banning lorry or van-mounted elevated working platforms from using red diesel but allowing mobile cranes to continue the use of this fuel;
- banning the use of red diesel in unlicensed vehicles that are not used on public roads unless a SORN (Statutory Off-Road Notification) has been made;
- continuing to allow tractors and agricultural engines to use this fuel, but subject to a definition for their legitimate use;
- deciding what legislative changes (if any) are needed in relation to the defined use of farm vehicles, subject to discussions with interested parties.

Oil Storage

Many haulage firms need to store oil in large quantities and will therefore need to be aware of the Control of Pollution (Oil Storage) (England) Regulations 2001, which came into effect in 2003, but with certain key provisions that came into force from 1 September 2005. These regulations apply to all types of oil (with the exception of waste mineral oil) stored above ground in containers of more than 200 litres at industrial or commercial premises. The regulations set minimum standards for oil storage (ie tanks to have a 110 per cent bund capacity) with the objective of preventing pollution and protecting the environment, oil being a major pollutant of watercourses and toxic to plants and animals. Fines for non-compliance are up to £5,000 but if pollution is caused they could be up to £20,000 or three months' imprisonment. Further information can be obtained from the following websites: **www.defra.gov.uk** and **www.environment-agency.gov.uk/business/ppg**.

Insurance (Vehicles and Goods in Transit) and Conditions of Carriage

O wners and operators of motor vehicles using the public highway must insure against third-party* injury and passenger claims. Further, an essential part of any investment in property (buildings, vehicles, plant, etc) is to obtain protection by insurance against loss or damage by theft, fire or other eventuality. It is also wise to be protected against claims made by third parties for compensation following injury to themselves or damage to their property as a result of some occurrence involving you, your employees, your property, or taking place on your premises.

The insurance company is the first party, the insured person(s) is the second party, and anybody else involved (particularly if they make a claim for compensation) is termed the third party.

Motor Vehicle Insurance

Third-Party Cover

The Road Traffic Act 1988 (s143) requires that all motor vehicles, except invalid carriages and vehicles owned by local authorities or the police, used on a road must be covered against third-party risks. This can be achieved by means of a conventional insurance policy or, alternatively, by a deposit of £500,000 in cash or securities to the Accountant-General of the Supreme Court but this is only applicable if authorization is granted by the Secretary of State for Transport. Normally, such authorization is only granted to public bodies and authorities and to major organizations with access to the substantial funds which may be needed to meet major accident claims.

Where the cover is obtained by conventional insurance means the Road Traffic Act 1988 stipulates that such cover is valid only if taken out with insurers who are members of the Motor Insurers' Bureau (MIB), which is a body established to meet claims for compensation (in respect of death or personal injuries only) by third parties involved in accidents with motor vehicles which subsequently prove to be uninsured against third-party risks.

Sections 145 (3a) and (3c) of the 1988 Act state that the insurance policy

> must insure such person, persons or classes of persons as may be specified in the policy in respect of any liability which may be incurred by him or them, in respect of the death or bodily injury to any person or damage to property caused by, or arising out of, the use of the vehicle on a road in Great Britain . . . [and] must also insure him or them in respect of any liability which may be incurred by him or them . . . relating to payment for emergency treatment.

NB: *Since April 2000, the term 'on a road' used above has been extended to include 'or other public place'.*

Passenger Liability

Passenger liability insurance cover for motor vehicles is compulsory. This requirement applies to all vehicles which are required by the Road Traffic Act to have third-party insurance and the cover must extend to authorized passengers (other than employees of the insured, who are covered separately by the compulsory employers' liability insurance), other non-fare-paying passengers and also to what may be termed 'unauthorized passengers' such as hitchhikers and other people who are given lifts.

Unauthorized Passengers

The display in a vehicle of a sign which says 'No passengers' or 'No liability' does not indemnify a vehicle operator or driver from claims by so-called 'unauthorized' passengers who may claim for injury or damage received when travelling in or otherwise in connection with the vehicle resulting from the driver's or vehicle operator's negligence. The law ensures that such liabilities are covered within the vehicle policy of insurance.

Property Cover

In accordance with an EU Directive (EC 5/84), from 1 January 1989 all UK motor insurance policies have been required to cover liability for damage to property (up to a maximum liability of £250,000 arising from one accident or a series of accidents from one cause). Damage to property in this context includes that caused by the weight of the vehicle (eg to road surfaces, paving slabs, etc) and by vibration which may damage services (eg gas and water mains, gullies and sewers, telephone cables, etc) below the road surface, and third parties whose property is damaged in a vehicle accident have the right to request details of the vehicle insurance.

Certificate of Insurance

A policy of insurance does not provide the cover required by the Act until the insured person or organization has in their possession a Certificate of Insurance. Possession means, in this context, exactly what it says: 'promised' or 'in the post' is not sufficient to satisfy the law. The policy itself is not *proof* of insurance cover; it only sets out the terms and conditions for the cover and the exclusion and invalidation clauses.

The Certificate (or a temporary cover note proving cover until the Certificate is issued), which is *proof* (or evidence) of cover, must show the dates between which the cover is valid, give particulars of any conditions subject to which the policy is issued (eg the permitted purposes for which the vehicle may be used and those which are not permitted) and must relate to the vehicles covered, either individually by registration number or by specification, and to the persons who are authorized to drive them.

Production of Insurance Certificate

It is necessary to produce a current Certificate of Insurance when making application for an excise licence (road tax) for a vehicle. Alternatively, a temporary cover note may be produced and this will be accepted, but the insurance policy document itself is not acceptable.

Regulations effective from 21 February 1997, and applying only where a fleet comprises 250 vehicles or more, remove the normal requirement for the production of individual Certificates of Insurance for fleet vehicles when applying for vehicle excise licences.

Further regulations, effective from 17 September 1999, exempt an applicant for a vehicle licence from producing evidence of insurance in cases where that applicant's insurer maintains a database from which the DVLA can verify that a policy of insurance is in force when the licence has effect.

The owner (ie registered keeper) of a motor vehicle must produce a Certificate of Insurance relating to the vehicle if required to do so by a police officer. If he is not able to produce the Certificate on the spot, or if an employed driver is required to produce a Certificate of Insurance for the vehicle he is driving, it may be produced for inspection, no later than seven days from the date of the request by the police officer, at any police station which the owner or driver chooses. The person to whom the request is made does not have to produce the Certificate personally, but may have somebody else take it to the nominated police station for him. A valid temporary cover note would suffice instead of the Certificate if this has not yet been issued.

Duty to Give Information

If requested to do so, the owner of a vehicle must give the police any information they request to help determine whether on any particular occasion a vehicle was driven without third-party insurance cover in force. The owner must also give information about the identity of a driver who may at any time have been driving a vehicle which is registered in his name, or information which may lead to identification of a driver if he is asked to do so by the police.

When the vehicle or vehicles concerned in such a request are the subject of a hiring agreement, the term 'owner' for the purposes of these insurance provisions includes each and every party to the hiring agreement.

The Motor Insurance Database

Under European law (the Fourth Motor Insurance Directive), vehicle fleet operators are required to register with the Motor Insurance Database (MID), which will hold details of the insurance arrangements for every vehicle on our roads. Failure to register will result in prosecution for the fleet operator, whose duty it is to provide details of the current fleet and any subsequent changes including the use of any temporary vehicles. Information about privately owned vehicles is provided to the MID directly by the insurer.

Registration of details may be made via the internet to, and further details obtained from, the Motor Insurers' Information Centre at: **www.miic.org.uk**.

Checking Uninsured Vehicles

With over 1 million uninsured people reportedly driving on UK roads, the police are anxious to identify and seize uninsured vehicles, for which they have been given powers. However, under another new DfT initiative it is suggested that vehicles must be insured at all times, whether on a road or not. If this proposal is implemented, it would become an offence to be the registered keeper of any vehicle for which there was no certificate of insurance in force, initially carrying a fixed penalty of £100. But if the vehicle remained uninsured, then prosecution would follow, resulting in a fine at level 3 (ie up to £1,000), with liability resting upon the registered keeper of the vehicle, although it would not be an endorsable offence. Exemption would be provided for vehicles genuinely 'off the road' for repairs or 'laid-up', but in that case a SORN declaration would need to have been made to the DVLA beforehand. With this system, an offender would not have to be caught driving an uninsured vehicle; simply their vehicle would not show up as a match when the DVLA's records are compared with the Motor Insurers' Database – as is now the practice when re-licensing vehicles via the internet; ie no documentary proof of insurance is required, it is simply achieved by comparing the computer databases.

Continuous Insurance Enforcement

With the introduction of new legislation in February 2011 (The Motor Vehicles (Insurance Requirements) Regulations 2011 – SI 2011 No. 20) establishing a system of Continuous Insurance Enforcement (CIE), it is now a legal requirement for registered vehicle keepers to insure their vehicle(s) at *all* times. The registered keeper does not have to be driving the vehicle to be caught. It is an offence to *keep* a vehicle without insurance unless the DVLA has been notified that the vehicle is being kept off the road and a valid Statutory Off Road Notification (SORN) has been obtained. It's one or the other – valid insurance cover or SORN – an old vehicle parked-up in a yard, for example, needs to be covered by insurance or on SORN.

Under the new system, the Motor Insurers' Bureau (MIB) and the DVLA will work in partnership to identify uninsured vehicles by comparing DVLA vehicle records against those held on the Motor Insurance Database (MID). The registered keeper will be sent an Insurance Advisory Letter (IAL) telling them that their vehicle appears to be uninsured and warning them that they will be fined unless they take action. If the keeper fails to comply with the advice set out in the letter they will face the prospect of :

- a fixed penalty notice of £100
- the vehicle being clamped, seized and disposed of
- prosecution with a potential maximum fine of £1,000.

It should be noted that these new measures are in addition to the powers the police already have to seize an uninsured vehicle and fine the driver.

Vehicle owners and keepers wishing to check that their vehicles are recorded as insured may do so by accessing the MID via its website at: **www.askMID.com**.

Invalidation of Cover

Insurance cover may be invalidated and claims for compensation refused if policy conditions are not strictly adhered to. In particular, these circumstances may arise if the vehicle is operated illegally (for example, in excess of its permissible weight, without a valid test certificate, in an unsound mechanical condition, outside the terms of an 'O' licence, with an incorrectly licensed or unlicensed driver or one who is disqualified, or if replacement components fitted to the vehicle are not to manufacturer's specification).

By way of example, a case was reported where liability was rejected by an insurance company when a fast sports saloon motor car was found to be fitted with tyres not rated for the top speed of which the car was capable (well in excess of 100 mph), although the claim arose out of an accident at less than 30 mph.

It is important to stress the need to examine carefully all the clauses contained in a motor insurance policy and to take steps to avoid any action which may invalidate the policy. The employment of unlicensed or incorrectly licensed drivers or the use of unroadworthy vehicles (ie vehicles which do not comply with legal requirements or are found to be on the road in a dangerous condition) are two examples of the most likely ways of invalidating a motor insurance policy. Similarly, the policy should cover *all persons* who may be required (or may need in an emergency) to drive vehicles, not just employees.

Use of Unfit Drivers

It is important not to use drivers who are, or who are believed to be, medically unfit to drive. Insurance companies have a duty to notify the Secretary of State for Transport of the names and addresses of people refused insurance cover on medical grounds so their driving licences can be withdrawn.

Payment to Travel

Previously, motor insurance cover could be invalidated if passengers paid towards the cost of car running expenses. As a result of provisions in the Transport Act 1980, the receipt of travel expenses contributions from passengers in private cars does not invalidate insurance policies provided no profit is made.

Cancellation of Insurance

When an insurance policy is cancelled, the Certificate of Insurance – there may be one or more depending on the number of vehicles covered by the policy – relating to that policy must be surrendered to the insurer within seven days of the cancellation date.

Cover in EU Countries

It is a requirement that every motor insurance policy issued in an EU country, including Britain, must include cover against those liabilities which are compulsorily insurable under the laws of every other EU member state (*Article 7 (2) of the EEC Directive on Insurance of Civil Liabilities arising from the use of Motor Vehicles (No 72/166/CEE)*) and some non-EU states (eg Switzerland).

Motor policies issued in the UK contain provisions for such cover but this only provides very limited legal minimum cover and, while an international motor insurance 'green card' is no longer essential to enable EU member state boundaries to be crossed by vehicles (private or commercial), it is wise to obtain a green card when travelling or sending goods vehicles abroad, in order to obtain the much wider cover provided by the policy. Possession of a green card provides adequate evidence of insurance when abroad and it also eliminates problems of language and different procedures in foreign countries.

International Accident Report Form

A special accident report form has been devised by the European Insurance Committee (CPA) for use as an agreed statement and accident report to be completed by drivers at the time of an accident when travelling in a foreign country (ie country other than that in which the vehicle is insured). The use of such a form (available from insurers), particularly when dealing with persons from other countries who cannot speak your language, can help to resolve matters later.

Fleet Insurance

Most large fleet operators obtain insurance cover on a 'blanket' basis. Under this arrangement vehicles are not specified on the Certificate of Insurance by registration number but there is a statement on the Certificate to the effect that cover is provided for any vehicle owned, hired or temporarily in the possession of the insured person or company. With blanket insurance it is normal to advise the insurance company by means of a quarterly return of the registration numbers of all vehicles added to or deleted from the fleet strength during that period.

The basic insurance premium is calculated on the total fleet at the beginning of the policy year and adjustments are made by the insurance company issuing debit or credit notes as necessary following receipt of the quarterly returns. This system saves the insurance companies having continually to issue and cancel cover notes and Certificates for vehicles in fleets where there may be many changes during a year because of staggered replacement programmes. The insured company also benefits by not having to get in touch with its insurers every time a vehicle is obtained or disposed of and, further, by being able to obtain an excise licence for a new vehicle without having to wait to receive a cover note from the insurance company.

Additional Insurance Cover

Extended Cover

The minimum cover against third-party risks mentioned above is not sufficient protection for the owner of a vehicle in the event of it being involved in an accident, damaged in any way (eg by vandals or by another vehicle when the driver was not present) or stolen. To obtain extra protection against such contingencies it is necessary to extend the insurance cover beyond the third-party legal minimum. This can be done in varying stages depending on what the vehicle owner considers necessary for his purpose. The basic policy can be extended to cover loss of the vehicle or damage to it as a result of fire or theft. The insurance can be further extended to give comprehensive cover which provides protection against third-party claims, fire and theft risks and accidental damage to the vehicle itself.

GAP Cover

This is an extra insurance policy, usually taken out when buying a vehicle by means of hire purchase. In the event of a total loss claim, it is intended to cover the difference between the current market value of the vehicle (ie the amount the insurance company pays out) and the amount still owing under the finance agreement.

Loading and Unloading Risks

Goods vehicle insurance policies should include clauses which give protection against claims arising from the loading or unloading of vehicles or the activities of employees engaged on such work.

Loss of Use

Most motor vehicle policies do not include cover for the loss of use of a vehicle or for the hire of a replacement vehicle following an accident. If the accident proves to be the fault of the third party, a claim has to be made against the third party for the loss of use or the hiring charges incurred but such claims are often difficult to substantiate (particularly the value of loss of use of the vehicle) and may result in only meagre awards. An extension to the policy covering such eventualities is the most satisfactory means of protection against this type of loss.

Mechanical Failure

Mechanical failure is another item which is not normally included in motor insurance policies and generally it is not possible to obtain this type of cover for motor vehicles (although it is for some items of heavy engineering plant). Damage to engines caused by frost is covered in the majority of commercial vehicle insurance policies although there are certain qualifications. It is necessary, for example, if a claim is to be met, for the vehicle to have been sheltered in a properly constructed garage between specified hours of the night. It is a condition of all policies that all reasonable steps should be taken to safeguard the vehicle from such loss or damage, and this clause particularly is one which the insurance company can use to escape a claim if it feels the policy conditions were not complied with.

Windscreen Breakage

Insurance companies normally provide cover for windscreen breakage within the standard motor insurance policy. Claims made for broken windscreens are generally limited to a fixed amount but are paid to the policy holder without detriment to any existing no-claims bonus and irrespective of whether or not an 'excess' clause is in force on the policy. Similar cover applies on most goods vehicle policies providing for the cost of replacement of the broken windscreen and for repairs to paintwork damaged by the broken glass.

Medical Expenses

When drivers are required to travel abroad they should be covered for medical expenses incurred in foreign countries, for compensation for taking relatives out to visit them if they are detained in hospital and for bringing the patient back to the UK for further treatment if necessary. Compensation for the loss of drivers' personal effects and baggage can usually be included in this type of policy.

For 25 years, the Transmed scheme, purpose-designed for the international road transport industry, has been rescuing drivers from abroad. The firm can be contacted on: 020 8399 6003.

Towing

Insurance cover for towing a vehicle which has broken down is normally provided under a goods vehicle policy, but the cover does not extend to damage caused to the vehicle while it is being towed, or to loss or damage of any goods being carried by the broken-down vehicle.

Damage by Weight

A goods vehicle insurance policy should provide cover against claims for damage caused to roads, bridges, manhole covers and suchlike by the weight of the vehicle passing over them. Some policies have a limit on the maximum liability acceptable for damage to property and this amount should be checked to ensure that it is adequate to meet likely claims in this respect.

Defence Costs

A motor insurance policy can be extended to cover legal costs incurred in defending a driver faced with manslaughter or causing death by reckless driving charges.

Goods in Transit Insurance

Motor vehicle insurance does not provide cover for claims made for damage or loss to goods carried on or in the vehicle. Goods in Transit (GIT) insurance cover is needed to provide protection for this eventuality.

Most GIT insurance policies provide cover in accordance with the limits included in the Road Haulage Association Conditions of Carriage, which is normally a maximum liability of £1,300 per tonne for goods carried within the UK. If goods are of relatively low value (bulk traffics, such as coal, gravel and other excavated materials, for example) a lower limit of liability and consequently a lower premium can be considered. However, in many cases the £1,300 per tonne limit can be totally inadequate. Many loads these days are valued at tens of thousands of pounds with an equivalent value per tonne way in excess of the RHA level and it is necessary to ensure that the insurance is adequate to cover the value of such loads. Owner-drivers, in particular, are advised to examine their goods-in-transit policies with great care; many such policies become automatically invalidated if high-value loads are left unattended (some loads must be accompanied *at all times*).

When goods of this level of value are carried regularly the insurance company will provide suitable annual cover but in some instances goods vehicle operators may find that a lower level of cover is suitable for most of their activities since they only occasionally carry high-value loads. It is important when this happens that the haulier makes himself aware of the load value and that the insurance company is advised of such loads and the appropriate cover obtained. Failure to do so could leave a haulier facing expensive loss or damage claims from his own pocket.

Some GIT policies specifically exclude certain high-risk loads such as cigarettes, tobacco, spirits, livestock, computers, etc, so the operator faced with a request to carry such a load should check that his policy covers the value and consult his insurers before accepting an order to move the goods.

The GIT policy can be on an 'All-Risks' basis but it is usual for the policy to meet the particular requirements of the operator to give him protection against the liabilities he assumes when he accepts goods for carriage. Such liabilities may be accepted under conditions of carriage (see later in this chapter) or under a contract or agreement or, in the absence of any specific contract or conditions, at common law. If the operator is carrying his own goods in addition to other people's he should make sure that these are also covered under the policy.

Carrier Liability for Goods

Most transport managers are aware that it is essential that they should effect a GIT insurance policy in respect of the goods carried, but it is most important to consider very carefully the liabilities which are assumed for the goods handled on behalf of customers and that there is full understanding of the GIT insurance contract which has been arranged.

If transport contractors for commercial reasons assume total responsibility for very high-value loads and do not in any way limit their liability by contract or by the application of conditions of carriage (see below), they will soon realize that the claims which are being handled by their GIT insurers become so expensive that the premium subsequently demanded will be far too high to bear.

It is for this reason that the majority of transport contractors find it sensible to limit their liability in accordance with Conditions of Carriage such as those published by the RHA (its most recent Conditions are dated 1998 – these are the copyright of the RHA and may not be used by non-members) where the liability is based on a value of £1,300 per tonne on the actual weight of the goods carried or on the computed weight if the volume of the goods exceeds 80 cubic feet per tonne. This limit can be varied on the insurance policy to suit individual demands but otherwise retaining for the operator the legal liability limitations.

New conditions have also been drawn up by the Freight Transport Association (FTA) in conjunction with the Institute of Purchasing and Supply (IPS), and these specify a liability limit of £2,000 per tonne. These are not copyright and may be used by hauliers although legal difficulties may arise where RHA conditions and the new FTA/IPS conditions are applied to the same movement contract (ie one set by the customer and one by the haulier).

High-Value Loads

There may be a temptation for haulage contractors to accept high-value loads because the freight rate being offered by the consignor is generous in comparison to normal haulage rates. Such loads, however, are notoriously attractive to thieves so it is important before accepting them to examine the GIT insurance policy to make sure that such high-value goods are not specifically excluded and that any special requirements which the insurance company may have imposed regarding overnight parking and general vehicle security and protection are complied with.

Night Risk and Immobilizer Clauses

Insurance policies frequently contain clauses requiring vehicles carrying high-value goods to be securely parked in locked or guarded premises overnight (known as the 'Night Risk' clause) or to be fitted with approved vehicle protection devices such as steering column locks, engine immobilizers and alarm systems (known as the

'Immobilizer' clause). It is a condition of the insurance that such devices must be maintained in good working order and must be put into effect when the vehicle is left unattended. Failure to comply with such conditions can render the cover invalid.

Sub-contracting

Before valuable loads are sub-contracted to other hauliers, operators should take considerable pains to satisfy themselves as to the genuineness of any driver calling at their premises for a load (telephoning the driver's employer is one suggested method of checking). Experience shows that drivers with criminal intent will state that they are employed by a certain firm and that they require a return load; documents are frequently handed to the driver in such cases; he picks up the load and disappears. A few days later, when investigations are made, it is only then discovered that the driver obtained the load by false pretences. GIT insurers may not accept responsibility for such losses, or indeed any losses involving sub-contracted loads unless they have had prior notification of the loads and the circumstances.

GIT on Hired Vehicles

The increasing use of vehicles on contract hire raises an important issue regarding liabilities for goods carried. Normally under the terms of the hire contract it is made quite clear by the hire company supplying the vehicle that it assumes no responsibility for loss or damage to the goods which are carried on the vehicle.

Vehicles Hired with Drivers

If, however, under the terms of the contract the hire company offers to provide a driver, the driver acts under its instructions. Should he act in a way which would be considered contrary to normal reasonable action (for example, leaving a fully laden vehicle overnight in the open when he had been specifically instructed to empty the vehicle or to place it in a locked garage), the hire company may find itself held liable at law for a 'fundamental breach of contract' and be faced with having to pay the full amount of any loss incurred. A method of overcoming this difficulty is for the hire company to arrange with the owner of the goods for a GIT insurance policy to be effected in their joint names and for the owners of the goods to pay the premium in the contract hire agreement.

Conditions of Carriage

An operator carrying goods for hire or reward is advised to set out conditions of carriage under which he contracts to carry goods. In these conditions the carrier can define his liabilities by stipulating limits on the value of goods for which he will normally accept responsibility, with goods of higher value being carried only on special terms, and stating circumstances and provisions under which no compensation is payable. For example, an operator could make it a condition that he accepts no liability under the following circumstances:

- act of God;
- act of war or civil war;
- seizure under legal process;
- act or omission of the trader, his employees or agents;
- inherent liability to wastage in bulk, or weight; latent defect, inherent defect, vice or natural deterioration of the merchandise;
- insufficient or improper packing;
- insufficient labelling or addressing;
- riots, civil commotions, strikes, lock-outs, stoppage or restraint of labour from whatever cause;
- consignee not taking or accepting delivery within a reasonable time;
- loss of a particular market whether held daily or at intervals;
- indirect or consequential damages;
- fraud on the part of the trader. In this context trader means either consignor or consignee;
- if non-delivery of a consignment, whether in part or whole, is not notified in writing within a specified number of days of despatch and a claim made in writing within a further specified number of days of despatch;
- if pilferage or damage is not notified in writing within a specified number of days of delivery, and a claim made in writing within a further specified number of days of delivery.

A note to the effect that goods are carried only under the Conditions of Carriage should be made on all relevant business documents, particularly consignment and delivery notes, invoices and quotations. Conditions of Carriage should always be drawn to the customer's attention and copies made available for customers to examine before they give orders for movements to commence.

RHA Conditions of Carriage

The Conditions of Carriage used by members of the Road Haulage Association are an excellent example of the sort of conditions which could be used by a haulage contractor to define his responsibilities. The Association's current Conditions are dated 2009 – these limit liability to £1,300 per tonne unless agreed otherwise. Further sets of conditions for livestock carrying and sub-contracting are also prepared for members.

NB: The RHA Conditions of Carriage are the copyright of the Association and their use by a non-member would be a breach of copyright and therefore illegal – the RHA has taken legal action in cases of unauthorized use of its Conditions.

Unfair Contract Terms

The Unfair Contract Terms Act 1977 affects such contracts as conditions of carriage. The effect of this legislation is to increase the liability of transport operators, particularly in respect of instances where liability for negligence is disclaimed by contract or by notice. Further, it prevents a business from excluding its liabilities for breach of contract when dealing with the general public. Consequently, any term in a contract purporting to exclude liability for personal injury by negligence is void. Any term excluding liability for damage to property by negligence is also void unless the term used is reasonable as between the parties to the contract.

Cover for International Haulage Journeys

The GIT cover described above is not sufficient or even legally acceptable where vehicles are engaged on international haulage work. In most cases, such operations are governed by the provisions of the Convention on the Contract for the International Carriage of Goods by Road, commonly known and referred to as the CMR Convention. This Convention automatically applies where an international haulage journey takes place between different countries at least one of which is party to the Convention (with the exception of UK–Eire and UK mainland–Channel Islands journeys, which are ruled not to be international journeys for this purpose).

Road hauliers who carry goods on any part of an international journey, whether they choose to know it or not, fall within the legal confines of the CMR Convention under which compensation levels for loss or damage to goods are much higher than the standard Conditions of Carriage GIT cover applicable in national transport operations. CMR levels of cover vary according to a set standard which is published daily in the financial press. For this reason it is important to obtain adequate cover when involved in international transport.

Additionally, where hauliers undertake cabotage operations they should discuss the levels of cover required with their insurers – indeed, they should see if extended cover is available to cover certain liabilities such as losses from unattended vehicles. Difficulties may arise where local conditions of carriage are imposed, and claims and legal wrangling arise under law other than English law; under French law, for example, minimum liability is set at a value equivalent to approximately £12,000 per tonne and as this is a domestic requirement it may not be covered by a UK haulier's CMR policy (see p 582).

Security

Insurance claims relating to vehicle thefts have increased in recent years and this is a serious problem of concern to insurance companies as well as to vehicle operators and the police. It is important that when away from base drivers should be encouraged to park their vehicles, especially if they are loaded with valuable goods, in guarded security parks. While the number of suitable security parks is limited and they are not conveniently located, it is nevertheless in everybody's interest that vehicles should not be left parked overnight on the roadside or on pieces of wasteland. Some insurers are now refusing to pay out on loss or theft claims if keys are left in or on a vehicle.

Security Warning

The RHA issues a security warning to members as follows:

- Make every effort to ensure you are employing honest staff. Take up references over at least the previous five years and be suspicious of unexplained gaps. When checking references by telephone be sure to look in the telephone directory yourself for the number. A number supplied by a dishonest applicant could connect you to his accomplices. A staff enrolment form is available on application to RHA Area Offices and this form or a similar one should be completed.

- Until you have seen his driving licence and have in your possession his P45 tax form and photograph, do not allow a newly engaged driver to take out a vehicle.

- Fit a vehicle immobilizer and/or alarm in as inaccessible a position as possible. Choose one which provides protection without the driver having to perform any operation which he normally would not have to do to stop his vehicle. Inspect the device frequently.

- Drivers of vehicles carrying valuable loads should not get out of their cab if stopped. Even if a police officer requests them to do so, they should offer to go to the nearest police station. Bolts on the inside of the cab doors give added protection against hijackers.

- A trouble-free cash bonus, from which a driver can be fined if he does not observe your security drill, is helpful.

- Vehicles should not be left unattended for long periods, especially at night. At no time should keys be left in an unattended vehicle. Remember, a stationary vehicle with its windscreen wipers or indicators operating gives a clear signal to any watching criminal that it is his for the taking.

- Discourage drivers from using the same cafés at the same time each day, particularly where their vehicles are not parked within sight.

- Starter or ignition switches, security lock keys: remove numbers and keep the keys for each vehicle on a ring which is welded so that they cannot be separated.

- If a vehicle's keys are lost, change switches and locks. It is much cheaper than losing a load.

- Invite drivers to report to the police any suspicious circumstances, such as transfer of goods from one vehicle to another without apparent reason, which they might see on their travels, or the registration number of any vehicle which is persistently following them.

- When disposing of a vehicle, remove the name of your firm so that a thief cannot use it to secure a load by false pretences.

TruckPol

With the closure of the National Stolen Lorry Load Desk in 2003, the Metropolitan Police in partnership with The Road Haulage Association established TruckPol, an intelligence unit dedicated to cutting road freight crime across the United Kingdom. TruckPol acts as a single point of contact, collating crime reports and intelligence from a variety of sources.

Contact: **www.truckpol.com**; tel: 02476 516 246.

NB: Incidents of truck crime should first be reported to the police locally.

Road Traffic Law

Road traffic regulations are very complex and are to be found in a number of Acts and statutory instruments relating to all aspects of road use by pedestrians, cyclists and motorcyclists, motorists and, of course, large goods and passenger vehicle drivers and operators. In recent years new traffic offences have been introduced along with tougher measures to deal with drink-drivers (with five years' imprisonment for drink-drivers who cause a death) and with vandals who place road users' lives at risk by placing dangerous objects on a road or interference with traffic signs or signals (with up to seven years' imprisonment for convicted offenders).

One of the most recent pieces of legislation concerning traffic law is the Traffic Management Act 2004. While the Act is predominantly concerned with traffic management matters and roads issues, one of the key provisions that relates more specifically to transport operators is the establishment of a uniformed on-road traffic officer service to manage the traffic consequences of such incidents as accidents, vehicle breakdowns, obstructions and debris on the carriageway, etc. These traffic officers operate under the auspices of the Highways Agency and have the power to stop and direct traffic in the interests of keeping traffic flowing.

Definition of Roads

For the purposes of most aspects of road traffic law a 'road' is defined in the Road Traffic Act 1988 (section 192) for England and Wales as 'any highway and any other road to which the public has access, and includes bridges over which a road passes'. In Scotland, the Roads (Scotland) Act 1984 applies and defines a public road as 'any road and any other way to which the public has access, and includes bridges over which a road passes'.

NB: *It has been held that so-called 'private' dock roads at ports from which ferry services operate are in fact 'open to the public' and therefore public roads on which drivers are subject to the normal road traffic rules applicable to all other public roads.*

The term 'highway' has its meaning in common law as a way over which all members of the public have the right to pass and repass. This might be on foot, on horseback, accompanied by a beast of burden or with cattle, or with a vehicle. For the purposes of the Highways Act 1980 a 'highway' includes the whole or part of the highway other than a ferry or waterway, and where it passes over a bridge or through a tunnel, the bridge or tunnel is part of the highway. This Act makes it an offence for a person, without lawful authority or excuse, in any way wilfully to obstruct free passage along the highway of whatever type.

The Highway Code

Many of the particular legal requirements relating to the use of vehicles on the road are identified in the *Highway Code** (the current edition of which was published in 2007), along with much useful advice on driving and road usage, although it should be remembered that the *Code* is intended for guidance and is not, in itself, a book of definitive traffic law. However, many of the rules in the *Code* are legal requirements and failure to comply with these will render a driver liable for prosecution, and if convicted he may face a fine, penalty points being imposed on his driving licence, and even disqualification from driving. In any case, even where a specific offence has not been committed, such as in the event of an accident, failure to follow advice given in the *Code* on safe driving may still result in attachment of blame.

A revised edition of the *Code* was published in June 2007. Among the changes from the previous version is the legal requirement for drivers to comply with directions (including to stop if required) given by VOSA and Highways Agency staff (rules 107 and 108). Drivers are also advised always to carry high-visibility jackets in the vehicle for use during breakdowns. There is also advice about not throwing litter from vehicles, extra information on what to do when becoming tired while driving and warnings about smoking being a distraction. The *Code* advises that parking 'against the flow of traffic' is prohibited and, in anticipation of forthcoming EU regulations, draws attention to new rules regarding exemptions from seat belt wearing by delivery drivers (ie with a 50-metre between-drops distance limit). The rules regarding over 3.5 tonne vehicles (ie those requiring a speed limiter) not using motorway third lanes are stated. Also included is a kilometres-to-miles conversion table – both imperial and metric measures are stated throughout the text.

It is intended that a future edition of the *Code* will include a section on heavy goods vehicles (HGVs). No date has yet been set for its publication.

*NB: Available from The Stationery Office and via its website **www.tsoshop.co.uk**, most booksellers and many newsagents, price £2.50.*

Speed Limits

Excessive speed is said to be a contributory factor in one in three road casualties. How fast we drive is crucially important to how safe our roads are, according to a Government statement in March 1999, when launching a 'far-reaching' review of road safety strategy. In the meantime the Government's message is to 'Kill your Speed', and a new system of speed enforcement has been introduced – see pp 255–56.

Three levels of speed limit for vehicles are imposed on road users:

- limits applying to vehicles using particular roads;
- limits applying to particular classes of vehicle (including limits imposed by the mandatory fitment of speed limiter devices);
- temporary speed limits on vehicles introduced for special reasons such as in potentially hazardous situations and in times of fuel shortages.

Speed Limits on Roads

On roads where street lights are positioned at intervals of not more than 200 yards (defined as a 'restricted' road), an overall speed limit of 30 mph applies to all classes of vehicle unless alternatively lower speeds are indicated by signs or unless the vehicle itself is subject to a lower limit by reason of its construction or its use. In some instances, speeds in excess of 30 mph are permitted on such roads and this is indicated by appropriate signs showing the higher maximum limits.

The present maximum speed limits on roads outside built-up areas are 60 mph on single-carriageway roads and 70 mph on dual-carriageway roads and motorways, except where specified temporary or permanent lower limits are in force. In certain high-accident risk areas (eg housing estates) 20 mph speed limit zones are being introduced in conjunction with road humps. The first was started in Norwich in January 1991 and others have followed. Other so-called 'traffic calming' measures being increasingly used to improve road safety include road-narrowing chicanes.

Advisory speed limits on motorways should be observed. These are shown by illuminated signs which indicate hazardous situations and roadworks ahead and by temporary speed limits signs at roadworks. The amber flashing warning lights positioned on the nearside of motorways (two lights, one above the other) indicate an advisory slowing down until the danger, and the next non-flashing light, is passed. Mandatory speed limits may also be seen at roadworks sites on motorways (indicated by white signs with black letters and a red border). Failure to comply with these mandatory motorway speed warning signs can result in prosecution.

Speed Limits on Vehicles

Vehicles are restricted to certain maximum speeds according to their construction, weight or use but when travelling on roads which themselves are subject to speed restrictions it is the lowest permitted speed (ie of the vehicle or of the section of road) which must be observed.

Table of Vehicle Speed Limits

	Motorway mph	Dual-carriageway mph	Other roads mph
Private cars			
– solo	70	70	60
– towing caravan or trailer	60	60	50
Buses and coaches			
– not over 12 metres length	70 (65)*	60	50
– over 12 metres length	60	60	50
NB: Coaches over 7.5 tonnes subject to speed limiter legislation are restricted to 65 mph.			
Goods vehicles			
Car-derived vans			
– solo	70	70	60
– towing caravan/trailer	60	60	50
Not exceeding 7.5 tonnes mlw			
– solo	70	60	50
– articulated	60	60**	50
– drawbar	60	60**	50
*** In Northern Ireland the speed limit for vehicles in these two categories is 50 mph only.*			
Over 7.5 tonnes mlw			
– solo	60	50	40
– articulated	60	50	40
– drawbar	60	50	40

NOTE: m/w means maximum laden weight (ie maximum gross weight for a vehicle as specified in construction and use regulations).

NB: See text below for speed limits for Special Types and other vehicles.

Special Types Vehicles

Vehicles operating outside the Construction and Use (C&U) regulations for the purposes of carrying abnormal indivisible loads come within scope of the Special Types General Order (STGO) as described in Chapter 19 and must conform to specified speed limits depending on their category. These speed limits are stated on p 476 but are repeated here with other speed limits for ease of reference:

Vehicle category	Motorways	Dual-carriageways	Single-carriageways
Category 1	60 mph	50 mph	40 mph
Category 2 and 3	40 mph	35 mph	30 mph

Works Trucks and Industrial Tractors

The maximum speed limit for works trucks and industrial tractors is 18 mph but the latter are not permitted on motorways.

Motor Tractors/Locomotives

Where such vehicles (including their trailers) are fitted with springs and wings their maximum permitted speeds are 40 mph on motorways and 30 mph on other roads. When they do not have springs and wings the maximum speed limit is 20 mph on all roads.

Emergency Vehicles

Fire, police and ambulance service vehicles are exempt from all speed limits if, by observing the speed limit, they would be hampered in carrying out their duties. However, drivers of such vehicles have a duty to take particular care when exceeding statutory limits and could face proceedings if an accident results while exceeding the limits.

Speed-Enforcement Cameras

The Road Traffic Act 1991 legally authorized the use of photographs as evidence by courts in cases of alleged speeding (and traffic-light jumping). Cameras have been installed at key sites since 1 July 1992 to catch speeding drivers and traffic-light offenders. The so-called Gatso cameras (named after their inventor, Dutch ex-racing driver Maurice Gatsonides) produce film showing the vehicle and its number plate (which can be enhanced by scientific means for purposes of clarity – and can even decipher the registration number of vehicles fitted with plates which have been photo-reflective sprayed), date, time and the vehicle speed.

However, digital speed-enforcement cameras are being progressively introduced to overcome the physical constraints of the present system, which requires the manual loading, unloading, removal and storage of film from the roadside units – a costly and time-consuming operation for already hard-pressed police forces.

Legislation allows for a prescribed device which 'captures and records images of motor vehicles at two positions on the road and calculates the average speed of the vehicle between those positions'. The new device, announced in August 1999, and called a Speed Violation Detection Deterrent (SVDD), was first installed on the M2 between junctions 4 and 5. Two cameras are set 1 mile apart and linked by digital signal to a computer centre where the time a vehicle takes to pass the two points is measured and the average speed instantly calculated. Where the statutory speed limit has been exceeded the vehicle and registered keeper are identified from DVLA records and a relevant penalty is imposed.

New digital SPECS speed-enforcement cameras were launched in Nottingham on 28 July 2000. The system measures average speeds between pairs of cameras mounted on distinctive SPECS columns a distance apart which create Speed Controlled Zones.

NB: *The blue poles that have sprouted with amazing rapidity on Britain's roadsides are not speed cameras – they are part of a £10 million development of the Trafficmaster network of traffic monitoring sensors (see p 287).*

Lighting-Up Time

All mechanically propelled vehicles must display front and rear position lights and headlamps (where required by regulations) between sunset and sunrise and during daytime hours when visibility is seriously reduced (see Chapter 13 for lighting details).

Night Parking

Goods vehicles not exceeding 2,500 kg gross vehicle weight do not require lights at night when standing on restricted roads (ie on which a 30 mph speed limit – or lower limit – is in force) if they are parked either in a recognized parking place (ie outlined by lamps or traffic signs) or on the nearside, close to and parallel to the kerb, facing the direction of travel and with no part of the vehicle within 10 metres of a junction (ie on the same side as the vehicle or on the other side of the road). On any road where these conditions are not met lights must be shown (ie front and rear position lights).

All goods vehicles exceeding 2,500 kg gross vehicle weight must display lights at all times when parked on roads between sunset and sunrise. Trailers and vehicles with projecting loads must not be left standing on roads at night without lights.

Vehicles should be parked on the nearside of the road when left standing overnight except when parked in a one-way street or in a recognized parking place and they must not cause obstruction.

Increasing attention is being given by the police and local authorities to drivers sleeping overnight in heavy vehicles with sleeper cabs while parked in lay-bys. Drivers should be warned against this practice, which is usually considered illegal on the grounds that the vehicle is causing an obstruction. A similar situation applies when drawbar trailers and semi-trailers are left in lay-bys.

Parking in lay-bys, separated from the main carriageway only by a broken white line, without sidelights and other obligatory lights as appropriate being lit after lighting-up time, is an offence and the driver will be prosecuted if caught. This does not apply where the lay-by is segregated from the highway.

Stopping, Loading and Unloading

Leaving Engine Running

Whenever a driver leaves his vehicle on a road, the engine must be stopped (except in the case of fire, police or ambulance service vehicles or when the engine is used to drive auxiliary equipment or to power batteries to drive such equipment). Hitherto, the requirement for stopping a vehicle engine when stationary was to prevent noise, but an amendment to the C&U regulations, effective from 2 February 1998, makes preventing exhaust emissions an additional reason for the requirement.

Obstruction

A vehicle must not be left in a position where it is likely to cause obstruction or danger to other road users, eg near an entrance to premises, near a school, a zebra crossing or a road junction (also see p 262).

Trailers (including articulated semi-trailers) must not be left on a road when detached from the towing vehicle.

Loading and Unloading Restrictions

Vehicles must not stop or park on clearways to load or unload. In some areas loading and unloading restrictions are indicated by yellow lines painted on the kerb at right angles to it as follows:

- A single yellow line at intervals indicates a ban on loading and unloading between the times shown on a nearby plate (eg Mon–Sat 8.30 am – 6.30 pm).
- Double yellow lines at intervals indicate a complete ban on loading and unloading at any time.

The precise terms of the restriction are indicated on signs mounted on nearby lamp posts, walls, etc. Delivery drivers should check these carefully to avoid any infringement of the law.

Waiting and Parking Restrictions

Single, double or broken yellow lines painted on the road parallel to the kerb apply to waiting and parking at various times, but they do not indicate a ban on loading or unloading and the same applies to 'no waiting' prohibitions indicated by 'no waiting' signs (see the *Highway Code* for full details of waiting and parking restrictions).

Parking Meter Zones

Loading and unloading in parking meter zones during the working day (the times are indicated on signs) is not allowed unless a gap between meter areas or a vacant meter space can be found. A vehicle using a meter space for loading or unloading can stop for up to 20 minutes without having to pay the meter fee (this does not apply when parking for any purpose other than loading or unloading the vehicle).

Motorway Driving

Motorway driving requires special care and observance of the motorway regulations. In particular, vehicles not capable of exceeding 25 mph on the level are prohibited from using motorways, including vehicles operating under the Special Types General Order (see also Chapter 19) if they cannot exceed this speed.

Vehicles must not stop on motorways except through mechanical defect or lack of fuel, water or oil, due to an accident, the illness of a person in the vehicle or for other emergency situations (including giving assistance to other persons in an emergency), or to permit a person from the vehicle to recover or remove objects from the carriageway. It is illegal to drive on the hard shoulder or the central reservation, to reverse or to make a 'U-turn' on a motorway. Vehicles which must use the hard shoulder for emergency reasons as described above must remain there only for so long as is necessary to deal with the situation.

Use of Lanes

Goods vehicles with maximum laden weights in excess of 7.5 tonnes and vehicles drawing trailers (and certain other heavy motor cars not included in the categories mentioned) must not use the outer or offside lane of three- and four-lane motorways.

On some steep slopes of two-lane motorway sections large goods vehicles (ie over 7.5 tonnes) are banned from using the outside lane; these bans are clearly signposted on the approaches to the appropriate section indicating the extent of the banned section and the vehicles prohibited from using the outer lane.

From 1 January 2005 the range of vehicles prohibited from using the outer (offside) lane of three-lane motorways was extended to include goods vehicles with a maximum laden weight exceeding 3.5 tonnes, which are fitted with speed limiters as required by the Road Vehicles (Construction and Use) Regulations, also with effect from 1 January 2005 (see also pp 329–31).

Temporary Speed Limits

Where carriageway repairs take place on motorways or where contraflow traffic systems are used an *advisory* 50 mph speed limit is usually imposed. This is considered by the police to be a maximum speed, and they may prosecute drivers found speeding in these sections for a 'driving without due consideration' type of offence. However, it is becoming more common for a *mandatory* temporary speed limit to be imposed in such cases and where drivers are detected speeding in these sections they will be prosecuted for this offence.

Speed Limits for Recovery Vehicles on Motorways

For the purposes of motorway speed limits, recovery vehicles may travel at up to 60 mph. This follows a High Court ruling (on an appeal by the Director of Public Prosecutions) that such vehicles are constructed to carry a load and therefore may travel at the same maximum speed as other heavy goods vehicles. Previously such vehicles were required to observe the 40 mph maximum limit applicable to vehicles classified as motor tractors, light and heavy locomotives.

Other Vehicles on Motorways

Light and heavy locomotives which do not comply with C&U regulations, dump trucks, engineering plant and vehicles for export which do not comply with the C&U regulations may be driven on motorways provided they are capable of attaining a speed of 25 mph on the flat when unladen and not drawing a trailer.

Learner Drivers on Motorways

Learner drivers are not allowed to drive on motorways, but holders of provisional LGV driving entitlements may drive heavy goods vehicles on motorways provided they hold a full ordinary driving entitlement (ie category B) and are accompanied by a qualified driver.

Lights, Markings and Signs on Motorways

Hazard Warning

Motorways are equipped with amber hazard warning lights located on the nearside verge and placed at 1 mile intervals. When these lights flash, vehicles must slow down until the danger which the lights are indicating, and a non-flashing light, has been passed.

Rural Motorways

Rural motorways have amber lights, placed at not more than 2-mile intervals and usually located in the central reservation, which flash and indicate either a maximum speed limit or, by means of red flashing lights, that one or more lanes ahead are closed. The speed limit indicated applies to *all* lanes of the motorway and should not be exceeded.

Urban Motorways

Urban motorways have overhead warning lights placed at 1,000-yard intervals. Amber lights flash in the event of danger ahead and indicate a maximum speed limit or an arrow indicating that drivers should change to another lane. If red lights flash above any or all of the lanes, vehicles in those lanes must stop at the signal. It is as much of an offence to fail to stop at these red lights as it is to ignore automatic traffic signals.

Information Signs

A new system of overhead information signs has been installed on the M1 motorway between Junctions 4 (Elstree) and 6a (Abbots Langley). The 18 overhead driver information signs operated from the National Traffic Control Centre in Birmingham and by the police from the Highways Agency regional control room at South Mimms notify drivers of incidents and conditions on the road ahead and warn of delays.

Motorway Road Markings

Experimental road markings designed to reduce the risk of nose-to-tail collisions are being tried out on some sections of motorway (eg the M1 near Leicester). The chevron-shaped markings are painted on the road surface at 10-metre intervals for 5 kilometres (ie 3 miles). Drivers are advised to keep at least two chevrons (ie two seconds) between themselves and the vehicle in front.

Local Radio Station Frequency Signs

Under new arrangements with the DfT, local radio stations can have their broadcasting frequencies indicated on motorway signs. It is a condition of such signposting that the station in question provides traffic news relevant to the location of the signs and of benefit to long-distance travellers 24 hours a day, seven days a week with at least four broadcasts per hour at peak times and two per hour during off-peak times, with programme interruptions for important announcements. The signs do not carry the station name or logo, only the broadcasting frequency, enabling drivers quickly to tune into the appropriate wavelength.

Emergency Telephones on Motorways

Emergency telephones are located at 1-mile intervals on the hard shoulders of each side of motorways – there is no need (and it is both dangerous and illegal) to cross the carriageways to reach an emergency telephone. Arrows on the back of posts on the hard shoulder indicate the direction to the nearest telephone. The use of the telephone is free, and it connects directly to the police, who should be given full details of the emergency, who is calling and the vehicle involved. A woman travelling alone is advised to tell the police of this fact. After making the call you should return immediately to your vehicle to await help – a police patrol may arrive within minutes.

Driving in Fog

To help drivers avoid the grave hazards of driving in fog, the *Highway Code* clearly advises, in Rule 210, that drivers should:

- use headlights as required by the *Code* (ie switch them on when visibility is reduced to 100 m – 328 ft);
- keep a safe distance behind the vehicle in front, remembering that the other vehicle's rear lights can give a false sense of security;
- be able to pull up within the distance they can see clearly, especially on motorways and dual-carriageways, where vehicles are travelling much faster;
- use the windscreen wipers and demisters;
- beware of other drivers not using headlights;
- not accelerate to get away from a vehicle which is being driven too close behind;
- check mirrors before slowing down and use the brakes so the brake lights warn drivers behind that their vehicle is slowing down;

- stop in the correct position at a road junction with limited visibility and listen for traffic until it is safe to cross, then do so positively without hesitating in a position directly in the path of approaching vehicles.

The *Code* also states that drivers MUST NOT use front or rear fog lights unless visibility is seriously reduced as they dazzle other road users and can obscure the brake lights. These lights must be switched off when visibility improves.

M25 Automatic Fog-Warning System

An automatic fog-warning system operates on the M25 motorway. Detectors installed alongside the motorway identify when visibility falls below 300 metres and automatically switch on the existing matrix signals to display the message 'FOG'. The signals are located at strategic points where unexpected pockets of fog may occur as identified by the Meteorological Office (30 such zones are identified and 54 danger spots within those zones). When the fog signs are on, drivers should slow down and proceed at a speed where they can safely stop within their range of vision.

Hazard Warning Flashers

Four-way direction-indicator flasher systems fitted to vehicles may be legally used to indicate that a vehicle is temporarily obstructing the road or any part of the carriageway either while loading or unloading, when broken down or for emergency reasons (previously their use was only permitted in emergencies). Further details of vehicle lighting requirements are to be found in Chapter 13.

Temporary Obstruction Signs

New regulations (ie the Traffic Signs (Temporary Obstructions) Regulations 1997) from 1 March 1998 authorize drivers to place on the road, behind a broken-down vehicle:

- a minimum of either four traffic cones, traffic delineators (a flattened cone) or traffic pyramids;
- a red warning triangle; and
- a flashing amber warning lamp with any of these warning devices.

They can also place, on the vehicle itself, a 'Road Vehicle Sign', described as a highly visible flexible yellow sheet depicting a red warning triangle.

The person in charge of, or accompanying, an emergency or breakdown vehicle that is causing an obstruction is authorized to place a 'keep right' sign to indicate a route past the vehicle.

Lights During Daytime

If visibility during the daytime is poor, because of adverse weather conditions, drivers of all moving vehicles must switch on both front position lights and headlamps or front position lights and matched fog and spotlights. This applies in the case of heavy rain, mist, spray, fog or snow or similar conditions. When vehicles are equipped with rear fog lights (see pp 356–57) these should be used when the other vehicle lights are switched on in poor daytime visibility conditions. Further details of vehicle lighting requirements are to be found in Chapter 13.

Parking

Drivers who park their vehicles in a position which causes danger or obstruction to other road users can be prosecuted and their driving licence endorsed with penalty points on conviction (usually three) or they can be disqualified from driving.

The *Highway Code* lists the many places where drivers should not or must not park, in paragraphs 213 to 226. Drivers should study these lists to avoid causing danger or committing an offence.

There are not many parking places for the goods vehicle driver who has collections or deliveries to make, particularly in town, and for this reason drivers should be instructed to take reasonable care when parking in congested areas to avoid causing obvious obstruction or danger. For example, drivers should not double-park, block entrances and exits of business or private premises, or park near dangerous junctions or near pedestrian crossings, as well as avoiding the areas mentioned in the *Highway Code*.

Parking on Verges

The Road Traffic Act 1988 (sections 19 and 20) makes it an offence to park a heavy commercial vehicle (ie a vehicle over 7.5 tonnes maximum laden weight including the weight of any trailer) on the verge of a road, on any land between two carriageways or on a footway whether the vehicle is totally parked on those areas or only partially so.

There are exemptions to this: when a vehicle is parked on such areas with the permission of a police officer in uniform, or in the event of an emergency, such as for the purposes of saving life or extinguishing fire, or for loading and unloading, provided that the loading or unloading could not have been properly performed if the vehicle had not been so parked and that the vehicle was not left unattended while it was parked.

It is an offence (under the Road Traffic Act 1988 section 34) for any person to drive a motor vehicle on to common land, moorland or other land which does not form part of a road, or on any footpath or bridleway beyond a distance of 15 yards, except where legal permission exists to do so, but then only for the purposes of parking or to meet an emergency such as saving life or extinguishing fire.

Lorry Road User Charging

LKW-Maut and GO-Box Systems

Germany, Austria and Switzerland have their own lorry road toll (Maut) systems. Germany's LKW-Maut scheme, which applies solely to heavy trucks over 12 tonnes gross weight using the country's motorways, was finally inaugurated on 1 January 2005 after two previous false starts due to technological hiccups. Austria's Maut system, colloquially known as the GO-Box system, was introduced in 2004 to replace both that country's former Eco-points and 'vignette' systems. Switzerland's system is a mileage-based truck tax that goes by the acronym LSVA. Further details of these systems can be found in Chapter 26.

Lorry Routes and Bans

Local authorities identify preferred routes for heavy vehicles passing through their areas and display on them appropriate signs that:

- mark the most suitable route between dock areas and the nearest convenient connection with the primary route/motorway network;
- mark a suitable alternative route at any place on the primary route network where drivers of goods vehicles might be advised to avoid a particular part of that route, but where it is not appropriate to direct all traffic on to the alternative route, or to the primary route itself;
- mark routes from the primary/motorway route system to local inland centres which generate a high level of goods vehicle traffic (industrial estates, for example).

Certain areas, and especially London, impose bans on the movement of goods vehicles and the parking of goods vehicles. These bans and restrictions are always marked with appropriate signs and operators are advised to ensure that their drivers observe them.

London Bans

Vehicles over 18 tonnes pmw are prohibited from travelling along many routes through Greater London at certain times unless the operator holds an exemption permit (issued under the London Lorry Control Scheme), which must be carried on the vehicle in a conspicuous position. Vehicles are also required to be fitted with air-brake silencers (hush kits).

The routes on which the ban applies are well signposted and the times at which it applies are also given on the signs. It is an offence for a driver of a goods vehicle over 18 tonnes pmw to travel on the banned routes at the relevant times unless a valid exemption permit has been issued and is carried on the vehicle. Application for exemption permits and vehicle plates should be made to the ALG Transport and

Environment Committee, Traffic Enforcement Unit, New Zealand House, 80 Haymarket, London SW1Y 4TE (tel: 020 7747 4770; fax: 020 7930 2719).

The London ban applies (to vehicles without permits) at the following times:

- Sunday   at all times
- Monday to Friday   midnight to 7 am and 9 pm to midnight
- Saturday   midnight to 7 am and 1 pm to midnight

Westminster Council, London, intends to ban from its designated low emission zones (LEZs) heavy vehicles that cannot meet either: 1) Euro-II emission levels with retro-fitted exhaust after-treatment; or 2) Euro-III emission levels. Operators with such vehicles wishing to enter the LEZs will be required to pay an £80 annual fee.

London 'Red Route' Scheme

The 'Red Route' scheme to prevent traffic congestion on certain primary routes in London has been extended. Originally about 6.5 miles of roadway between Archway Road and the Angel, Islington, was designated as a red route but other sections have been, and are being, progressively introduced until the full 315-mile red route network is complete. Each section is identified by single or dual red road markings and accompanying red route signs. Vehicles may only stop to collect or deliver at specified times (or not at all), only for limited periods (ie 20 minutes only between the hours of 10.00 am and 4.00 pm), and only in marked (ie white-painted) loading bays. Generally the red route bans will apply between 7.00 am and 7.00 pm.

Failure to comply with the restrictions can lead to severe penalties. A red parking ticket (penalty currently £100) will be issued by police or traffic wardens, but if the driver argues or refuses to move, an impoundment order may be issued and the vehicle taken away. This will cost the driver or operator £150 to get the vehicle back, plus the £100 penalty and a £25 daily storage charge.

London Congestion Charging

Congestion charges of £8 (but only £7 for fleet vehicles) per day apply in a central area of London on weekdays only (Monday to Friday) between the hours of 7.00 am and 6.00 pm excluding public holidays.

The charging zone covers any route that crosses the River Thames by Lambeth, Westminster, Waterloo, Blackfriars, Southwark or London Bridges. Not included in the charging area are Euston Road, Tower Bridge, Elephant and Castle, and Vauxhall Bridge. On 4 January 2011 the Central London Congestion Charge Zone was reduced to exclude most of the boroughs of Kensington and Chelsea, and Westminster. Cameras are located at 85 per cent of the boundary intersections and at random points within the zone. These cameras record vehicle registration numbers and cross-check via computer with records of charges paid.

Vehicles running on gas or electricity are exempt after paying a £10 registration fee. All other commercial vehicles are included, unless they are emergency service vehicles or are vehicles on municipal duty, not competing with private firms.

Drivers who regularly enter the charging zone may pre-register and pay a fee, otherwise payment of the daily fee may be made by credit card – a call centre will process credit-card numbers – or by buying carnets from newsagents and convenience stores and from ticket terminals in car parks, hospitals and other local amenities. Any driver who has not paid prior to entry into the charging zone may pay later that day – up to midnight – or pay £10 until midnight on the following charging day. Payment can be made by calling 0845 900 1234 or through the Congestion Charge website at: **www.cc.london.com**.

Failure to pay the daily charge will result in evaders incurring an £80 penalty, issued to the vehicle owner (not necessarily the driver), but this is halved to £40 if paid within two weeks. There is an appeals procedure.

London Low Emission Zone

The Low Emission Zone (LEZ) across London commenced on 4 February 2008. According to Transport for London, the aim of the LEZ is to improve air quality in London by deterring users of the most polluting vehicles from driving them in the area. The vehicles affected are older diesel-engined lorries, buses, coaches, large vans, minibuses and other heavy vehicles that are derived from lorries and vans such as motor caravans and motorized horseboxes. There has been a phased introduction of the scheme from 4 February 2008 which will continue through to January 2012.

Compliance with the emission zone requirement is by reference just to particulates in exhausts – quoting a maximum contained in the Euro-III approval limits. The particulate limits can, in fact, be attained by many engines made before Euro-III came into force.

Different vehicles will be affected over time and increasingly tougher emissions standards will apply. Cars, motorcycles and small vans are not included in the Low Emission Zone (LEZ).

Vehicle types and definitions are shown on the following chart.

Vehicle type	Compliance dates	Required emissions standards
Lorries Heavier lorries in this context are heavy diesel-engined vehicles exceeding 3.5 tonnes gvw, including goods vehicles, motor caravans, motorized horseboxes and other specialist vehicles.	Euro-IV vehicles: 3 January 2012.	*NB: From 3 January 2012 the required emissions standards are raised to Euro-IV. All Euro-IV vehicles will meet the LEZ standard.* 1. Vehicles first registered as new on or after 1 October 2006 are assumed to be Euro-IV and so will meet the emissions standards. 2. Vehicles not meeting the emissions standards could be made to do so by modifying them to meet the Euro-IV standard for particulate matter. 3. Vehicles not meeting the emissions standards will need to pay a daily charge if used within the LEZ.
Large vans Large vans are diesel-engined vehicles between 1.205 tonnes unladen and 3.5 tonnes gvw and motor caravans and ambulances between 2.5 tonnes and 3.5 tonnes gvw.	Euro-III vehicles: 3 January 2012	*All Euro III vehicles will meet the LEZ standard.* 1. Vehicles registered as new on or after 1 January 2002 are assumed to be Euro-III, so will meet the LEZ emissions standards. 2. Vehicles not meeting the emissions standards could be made to do so by modifying them to meet the Euro-III standard for particulate matter. 3. Vehicles not meeting the emissions standards will need to pay a daily charge if used within the LEZ.

NOTE: Vehicle weight is a good guide as to when a vehicle will be affected by the LEZ. If the type of vehicle operated does not appear above the weight limits used for lorries and large vans should be used as a guide. Alternatively, contact the vehicle manufacturer or Transport for London (TfL) for guidance: **www.tfl.gov.uk**

LEZ Charges

Operators of vehicles which do not meet the LEZ emissions standards must pay the daily charge if they wish to use the vehicle in the Zone. The daily charge for lorries is £200 and that for large vans £100. Different vehicles will be affected over time and increasingly tougher emissions standards will apply. Operators should check the timings for when different vehicles are affected by the LEZ.

Payments may be made up to 64 working days in advance of travel, on the day of travel or until midnight on the next working day after travelling in the LEZ. Payments must be made for a specific vehicle on a nominated day. The daily charging period runs from midnight to midnight. Once the operator has paid for a day the vehicle can be driven within the Zone as many times as the operator wishes on that day. Payment will need to be made for every day that the vehicle is used in the Zone. For example, a vehicle being driven within the Zone at 10 pm on one day but leaving at 2 am the next day would need to pay for two days. Payment can be made by cheque or using a debit or credit card, or online.

LEZ Compliance Test

Hauliers can book low-emission certificate (LEC) tests to prove their older vehicles comply with the requirements of London's low-emission zone (LEZ), which began in February 2008. These LEC tests, costing £28, were introduced after it was realized that some Euro-I and Euro-II vehicles can reach the Euro-III standard for particulate matter. Inspections are available at VOSA goods vehicle testing stations.

Exemptions

A small number of GB-registered vehicles are granted an exemption from the LEZ. These vehicles will not need to be registered with TfL and can be used within the Zone without being subject to the daily charge.

Exempt vehicles are those which are designed and built for mainly off-road use, but which may be used on the road for limited purposes. Such vehicles include agricultural and forestry tractors, mowing machines, agricultural and farm machinery and equipment, mobile cranes, and road and building construction machinery. Historic vehicles (those constructed before 1 January 1973) and military vehicles registered in Great Britain are also exempt.

Note that non-GB (including Northern Ireland) vehicles need to register with TfL to be eligible for an exemption.

Vehicles Entitled to a Discount

A 100 per cent discount will apply to showman's vehicles which have been custom built and are permanently fitted with equipment forming part of the show. Operators of these vehicles will need to register them with TfL in order to qualify for the discount.

Penalty Charges

If a vehicle that does not meet the required emissions standards, is not exempt or entitled to a 100 per cent discount is driven in the LEZ without payment of the daily charge, the operator may be liable for a penalty charge. This will be issued to the registered keeper of the vehicle.

For lorries the penalty charge is £1,000 per day. This will be reduced to £500 if paid within 14 calendar days, but increased to £1,500 if not paid within 28 calendar days. For large vans the penalty charge is £500 per day. This will be reduced to £250 if paid within 14 calendar days, but increased to £750 if not paid within 28 calendar days. A penalty charge may be issued if the charge has not been paid by midnight on the next working day after the day of travel, or if an incorrect Vehicle Registration Mark (VRM) or day of travel was supplied when the charge was paid. Where a vehicle is found to have three or more outstanding penalty charges against it then further enforcement proceedings may be taken and TfL has the power to clamp and/ or remove these vehicles.

TfL website: **http://www.tfl.gov.uk/roadusers/lez/vehicles/2535.aspx**

Bus Lanes

Traffic lanes on urban roads reserved solely for use by buses are a common feature in many towns and cities. Uniform traffic signs and road markings indicate bus lanes. A single wide solid white line is used to mark the edge of the reserved lanes. Upright signs incorporating international symbols combined with arrows show to other traffic the number of lanes available for their use. When the signs and restrictions are in operation on a road, all other vehicles, except for pedal cycles (and taxis if signed to this effect), are prohibited from using the bus lane.

Level Crossings

Most railway level crossings are now fitted with automatic half-barrier crossing gates and appropriate warning signs are given in advance. When a train is approaching such crossings, red lights flash and a bell rings to warn drivers and pedestrians. Once these warnings start the barrier comes down immediately, and drivers should not zig-zag around the barriers. When the train has passed, the barriers will rise unless another train is following, in which case the warnings will continue.

Drivers of vehicles which are large or slow (ie that with their loads are more than 2.9 metres (9 ft 6 in) wide or more than 16.8 metres (55 ft) long or weighing more than 38 tonnes gross or incapable of a speed of more than 5 mph) wishing to cross one of these crossings must, before attempting to cross, obtain permission to do so from the signalman by using the special telephone which is provided at the crossing. Failure to do this is an offence. In the event of a vehicle becoming stuck on the crossing the driver should advise the signalman immediately by using the telephone.

Weight-Restricted Roads and Bridges

Where signs indicate that a particular section of road or a bridge is restricted to vehicles not exceeding a specified weight limit or axle weight limit, unless otherwise expressly stated, the weight limit shown relates to the actual weight of the vehicle or to an individual axle of the vehicle, not the relevant plated weights.

Signs protect weak bridges by restricting vehicles according to their maximum authorized gross weight (ie their plated weight) – indicated as 'mgw'. These have replaced existing signs as described above where the weight shown relates only to the actual weight of the vehicle and load at the time. The new signs apply even if the vehicle, with a plated weight greater than the limit shown, is unladen at the time and therefore well below the maximum weight limit for the bridge (unless the sign permits 'empty vehicles'). Where doubt exists about any particular sign it is advisable to consult the local authority responsible for its erection and to determine the precise wording of the Traffic Management Order under which authority the sign would have been erected.

Owner Liability

Under the Road Traffic Offenders Act 1988 responsibility for payment of fixed penalty fines or excess parking charges rests with the registered vehicle owner (ie the keeper of the vehicle, not necessarily the legal owner), if the driver who committed the offence cannot be identified or found. The registered owner of the vehicle is sent details of the alleged offence and is obliged to pay the fine or submit a 'Statutory Statement' of ownership in which he states whether he was the vehicle owner at the time of the alleged offence (in which case he should name the driver), had ceased to be the owner at that time or had not yet become the owner at that time. Where the person was not the owner he must give the name of the previous owner or the new owner to whom he transferred the vehicle, if he knows it.

When a vehicle is hired out for less than six months, and such an incident arises, the hiring company can declare that the vehicle was on hire and send a copy of the hiring agreement together with a signed statement of liability from the hirer accepting responsibility for the fine or excess parking charge. Such a clause is normally included in the hiring agreements which the hirer signs. Failure to pay a fixed penalty or excess charge, or to give information as required by the police in such matters, can result in a fine of up to £1,000 on conviction (or even £5,000 in certain circumstances).

Fixed Penalties

In order to reduce the pressure on the courts, a system of fixed penalties exists by which both Civil Enforcement Officers (CEOs) and the police can issue fixed penalty notices requiring the vehicle driver or owner to pay the fixed penalty or to elect to have the case dealt with in court in the normal way. The fixed penalty system operates on two levels: non-endorsable offences (mainly dealt with by CEOs), and driving licence endorsable offences which only the police can deal with since CEOs have no general authority to request the production of driving licences (see p 274). Additionally, two London area parking offences are included in the fixed penalty system.

Non-endorsable Offences

For non-endorsable offences a white ticket/notice (penalty £30) is issued either to the driver if present or is fixed to the vehicle windscreen. Since no driving licence penalty points are involved for such offences there is no requirement to examine the licence. CEOs have authority to issue fixed penalty tickets for the following non-endorsable offences:

- leaving a vehicle parked at night without lights or reflectors;
- waiting, loading, unloading or parking in prohibited areas;
- unauthorized parking in controlled parking zone areas;
- contravention of the Vehicle Excise and Registration Act 1994 by not displaying a current licence disc;
- making 'U' turns in unauthorized places;
- lighting offences with moving vehicles;
- driving the wrong way in a one-way street;
- overstaying on parking meters, returning to parking places before the expiry of the statutory period, or feeding meters to obtain longer parking facilities than those permitted in a meter zone;
- parking on pavements or verges by commercial vehicles exceeding 3,050 kg unladen weight (see p 262).

Endorsable Offences

The extended fixed penalty system covers driving licence endorsable offences, which can be dealt with only by the police (ie not CEOs) – this includes some 250 driving and vehicle use offences. For endorsable offences a yellow ticket/notice with a different level of penalty applies as described below.

For driving licence endorsable offences the police issue a yellow ticket/notice for which a penalty of £60 is payable. These tickets are only issued after the police officer has seen the offender's driving licence and has established that the addition of penalty points appropriate to the current offence, when added to any points already on the licence, will not result in automatic disqualification under the 12-point totting-up procedure. If this is the case, the ticket will be issued and the driving licence will be confiscated (an official receipt, covering the holder for non-possession or production of his licence, will be given – valid for two months), being returned to the holder with the appropriate penalty points added when the penalty has been paid.

If the offender does not have his driving licence with him at the time the penalty notice will not be issued on the spot but will be issued at the police station if the driving licence is produced there within seven days – subject again to the number of penalty points already on the licence.

Where the addition of further points in respect of the current offence would take the total of penalty points on the licence to 12 or more, thus leading to automatic disqualification, the ticket will not be issued and the offence will be dealt with by the offender being summoned to appear in court in the normal manner.

London Area Parking Offences

The fixed penalty system includes two specific London area parking offences, namely parking on a 'Red Route' (see p 264), for which the penalty is currently £60, and parking in other prohibited places, for which the penalty is £40.

Payment or Election to Court

Fixed penalty notices must be paid in accordance with the instructions on the notice and within the specified time limit of 28 days. Alternatively, the offender can elect to have the charge dealt with by a court so he has the opportunity of defending himself against the charge or, even if he accepts that he is guilty of the offence, of putting forward mitigating circumstances which he feels may lessen any penalty which may be imposed.

The address of the fixed penalty office to which the penalty payment should be sent is given in the notice together with instructions for making application for a court hearing if this course of action is chosen.

Failure to Pay

With both the white and yellow ticket systems, failure to pay the statutory penalty within the requisite period of 28 days will result in the offender being automatically considered guilty and the penalties being increased by 50 per cent (ie to £45 and £90 respectively). These increased amounts become fines and continued non-payment will lead to the arrest of the offender and appearance before a court in the district where the offence was committed. This could be many miles from where the offender lives and may necessitate him being transported there under arrest and possibly held overnight.

Summary of Offences

Among the many offences covered by the fixed penalty scheme are the following:

- parking at night without lights or reflectors;
- waiting, parking, loading or unloading;
- breach of controlled parking zone regulations;
- failing to display a current excise licence disc;
- making 'U' turns in unauthorized places;
- lighting offences with a moving vehicle;

- driving the wrong way in a one-way street and making banned right turns;
- contravening traffic regulation orders;
- breach of experimental traffic orders;
- breach of experimental traffic scheme in Greater London;
- contravening motorway traffic regulations;
- using a vehicle in contravention of a temporary prohibition or restriction of traffic on a road;
- driving in contravention of an order prohibiting or restricting driving on certain classes of road;
- breach of pedestrian crossing regulations;
- contravention of a street playground order;
- breach of parking orders on roads, and of parking place designation orders and other offences committed in relation to them, except failing to pay an excess charge;
- contravening minimum speed limits;
- speeding;
- driving or keeping a vehicle not showing a registration mark;
- driving or keeping a vehicle with a registration mark or hackney carriage sign obscured;
- failing to comply with traffic directions or signs;
- leaving a vehicle in a dangerous position;
- failing to wear a seat belt;
- breach of a restriction on carrying children in the front or rear of vehicles;
- driving a vehicle elsewhere than on the road;
- parking a vehicle on a footpath or verge;
- breach of construction and use regulations;
- contravening lighting restrictions on vehicles;
- driving without a licence;
- breach of provisional driving licence conditions;
- failing to stop when required to do so by a uniformed police officer;
- obstructing the highway with a vehicle;
- overtaking on a pedestrian crossing;
- failing to display a registration mark (ie number plate) on a vehicle;
- driving on a footpath.

Table of Fixed Penalties

The following is the current list of fixed penalties for both road traffic and other offences.

- Fixed penalty under section 143 of the Road Traffic Act 1988   £200
- Fixed penalty offence under section 172 of the Road Traffic Act 1988   £120
- Any other fixed penalty offence involving obligatory disqualification   £60
- Fixed penalty parking offence committed in Greater London on a Red Route   £60
- Any other fixed penalty parking offence committed in Greater London   £40
- Fixed penalty offence under section 47 of the Road Traffic Act 1988   £60
- Fixed penalty offence under section 33 of the Vehicle Excise and Registration Act 1994   £60
- Any other fixed penalty offence   £30

The Graduated Fixed Penalty and Deposit Scheme

A new scheme of graduated fixed penalties (GFP) and deposits for both UK and foreign truck drivers who break the law was introduced from 1 April 2009 in an amendment to the Fixed Penalty Order 2000. The scheme is operated by the police and by VOSA examiners who have the power to issue such notices.

Fixed penalties, issuable by police, already exist for a range of traffic and roadworthiness offences for all categories of vehicle. Their use provides a quick and effective method of dealing with minor offending which reduces the burden on the courts and saves police time. Acceptance of a fixed penalty provides the offender with the opportunity of discharging all liability for that offence, requires no admission of guilt, results in no criminal record and saves him the need to attend court.

The new provisions create powers to introduce fixed penalties for commercial vehicles as a means of dealing effectively with cases such as multiple offences arising from the commercial operation of vehicles which currently can prove cumbersome and time-consuming to process. Certain penalties will be graduated to reflect the number and severity of the offences.

The scheme will cover offences, mainly relating to commercial vehicles, as follows:

- drivers' hours and tachograph record offences;
- overloading;
- roadworthiness;
- construction and use of vehicles;
- driver licensing;
- community authorizations;
- goods vehicle plating and testing;
- vehicle excise duty;
- vehicle exhaust emissions.

The amounts of the graduated fixed penalty payable vary according to the type and degree of the alleged offence at three levels, namely, £60, £120 and £200.

Additionally, powers are included in the legislation to:

- enable the number of penalty points endorsed on driving licences to be varied according to type, location and severity of offence;
- require operators to notify the Traffic Commissioner of fixed penalty notices issued against them under the new GFP scheme;
- allow enforcement officers to issue endorseable fixed penalties to non-GB driving licence holders through checks of their 'driving record';
- require financial deposit payment (£300 up to £900) by drivers who do not have a satisfactory UK address (intended to enforce against foreign drivers who otherwise have been able to avoid a fixed penalty or prosecution in the UK);
- immobilize vehicles subject to a prohibition (again, primarily directed at foreign drivers).

Civil Enforcement Officers

In addition to the powers of Civil Enforcement Officers (CEOs) (from 31 March 2008) to issue fixed penalty tickets as described in the previous section, they also have powers to act as parking attendants at street parking places, to carry out special traffic control duties, to inquire into the identity of drivers of vehicles, to act in connection with the custody of vehicles at car pounds and to act as school crossing patrols.

They may demand to know the names and addresses of those believed to have committed parking, obstruction, traffic sign and excise licence offences and to see the driving licence of any person who is reasonably suspected of such offences. If the licence cannot be produced at that time the warden may issue a form HO/RT 1 requiring its production at a police station within seven days. CEOs have no powers to request the production of insurance certificates or vehicle test certificates.

CEOs' powers extend (since December 2002) to include stopping vehicles for testing and other purposes and escorting abnormal loads – duties previously the prerogative of the police only.

NB: *This new name also applies to former parking attendants.*

Pedestrian Crossings

There are two main types of pedestrian crossing. Zebra crossings are bounded on either side by areas indicated by zig-zag road markings in which overtaking, parking and waiting are prohibited. The marked areas extend to about 60 ft on either side of the crossing. A 'give way' line 3 ft from the crossing is the point at which vehicles must stop to allow pedestrians to cross. Pelican crossings are controlled by traffic lights which vehicle drivers must observe and pedestrians should cross only when the green light signal indicates that they should do so (at many pelican crossings an audible bleeper is provided to assist blind people to cross with safety). With this type of crossing, if there is a central refuge for pedestrians, each side of the refuge is still considered to be part of a single crossing. Only if the two parts of the crossing are offset does it become two separate crossings.

Builders' Skips

Provisions are contained in the Highways Act 1980 to control the placing of builders' skips on the road. Before such a skip is placed on the road, permission must be obtained from the local authority. This will be given subject to conditions relating to the size of the skip, its siting, the manner in which it is made visible to oncoming traffic, the care and disposal of its contents, the manner in which it is lit or guarded and its removal when the period of permission ends.

Owners must ensure that skips carry proper reflective markers (see pp 371–72), are properly lit at night, are clearly marked with their name and telephone number or address, and that they are moved as soon as is practical after they have been filled.

The police and highway authorities have powers to reposition or remove a skip from the road and recover the cost of doing so from the owner, and a penalty may be imposed.

For the purposes of the Act the definition of a builder's skip is 'a container designed to be carried on a road vehicle and to be placed on a highway or other land for the storage of builders' materials, or for the removal and disposal of builders' rubble, waste, household and other rubbish or earth'.

Abandoned Motor Vehicles

It is an offence under the Road Traffic Regulation Act 1984 to abandon a motor vehicle or any part of, or part removed from, a motor vehicle in the open air or on any other open land forming part of a highway. Such offences, on conviction, can lead to fines of up to £200 for a first offence and up to £400 and a term of up to three months' imprisonment or both for a subsequent offence.

Vehicles which are illegally or obstructively parked can be removed and a statutory charge of £105 imposed. An additional charge for storage of a removed vehicle is £12 per day and £50 is charged for its disposal. Removed and impounded vehicles are not released until all relevant charges have been paid.

Retention and Disposal of Seized Vehicles

Where a police officer has seized and removed a vehicle as authorized under section 165A of the Road Traffic Act 1988, certain legal procedures must be followed; namely, the constable must give a seizure notice to the driver (unless it is impracticable to do so) and must also give a seizure notice to the registered keeper and the owner (where that appears to be someone different) requiring him to claim the vehicle within a specified period (but not less than seven working days). The notice must indicate the charges payable to reclaim the vehicle – amounting to £105 for the seizure and £12 for each 24 hours or part thereof that the vehicle is in custody, counting from noon on the first day after the seizure – and the person claiming the vehicle must produce a valid driving licence and certificate of insurance at a specified police station, the vehicle being retained until these conditions are met. Where the police cannot issue a seizure notice or the conditions of the notice are not met, the vehicle may be disposed of after 14 days. If disposal is by means of a sale, the net proceeds must be paid to the owner if he makes a claim within one year of the sale.

Wheel Clamps

Vehicles which are illegally parked or which cause obstruction in a wide area of Central London will be immobilized by the Metropolitan Police or by contractors on their behalf. A wheel clamp, known as the 'Denver Boot', will be fixed to one wheel of the vehicle, thereby preventing it being driven away. A notice will be stuck to the vehicle giving the driver notice of the offence committed and instructions for securing release from the clamp.

It is an offence to try to remove a wheel clamp or to attempt to drive off with one fitted. Vehicle drivers finding a clamp fixed to their vehicle must go to the Metropolitan Police pound in Hyde Park underground car park and request removal of the clamp. Both a removal charge (currently £38) and a fixed penalty (currently £30) have to be paid before the clamp is removed. If the vehicle has been removed by the police a removal charge of £105 is payable, in addition to any fixed penalty, to secure its release.

Overloaded Vehicles

It is an offence to drive an overloaded vehicle on a road. Under the Road Traffic Act 1988 (sections 70 and 71) an authorized examiner or police officer may prohibit the use of an overloaded vehicle on the road until the weight is reduced to within legal limits and may direct, in writing, the person in charge of an overloaded vehicle to remove the vehicle to a specified place. See also pp 304–305.

A driver may be instructed to drive for a distance of up to 5 miles to a weighbridge for the weight of his vehicle and load to be checked. If he is directed to drive more than 5 miles to the weighbridge and his vehicle is found to be within the maximum permitted weights then a claim may be made against the appropriate highway authority for the costs incurred.

The maximum fine for an overloading offence is £5,000 but any one instance of an overloaded vehicle could result in conviction for more than one offence, each of which carries this maximum penalty. Subsequent convictions for such offences could lead to higher fines. Convictions for overloading offences also jeopardize the operator's licence (see also Chapter 11 on vehicle weights and overloading).

NB: *It is useful to note the fact that in-motion axle weight weighers are being introduced by VOSA/Trading Standards enforcement staff on some UK roads beyond the main Dover road, where they were first employed to spot overweight outbound and inbound vehicles. Axle weights above the legal maximum trigger cameras, but it seems unlikely that the system can actually recognize the vehicle plated weights except by back-referencing data via the vehicle's number plate.*

Road Traffic Accident Procedure

Road accidents are said to have caused more than 41,000 deaths and 1.7 million reported injuries throughout the EU in 2000 at a cost of £124 billion. The relevant figures for the UK alone in 2009 were 2,222 people killed; and there were 222,146 road casualties in Great Britain in 2009.

Any driver involved in a road accident in which personal injury is caused to any person other than himself, or damage is caused to any vehicle other than his own vehicle, or damage is caused to any animal* other than animals carried on his own vehicle, or to any roadside property (see below for definition) MUST STOP. Failure to stop after an accident is an offence and fines of up to £5,000 can be imposed on conviction.

The driver of a vehicle involved in an accident must give to anybody having reasonable grounds for requiring them his own name and address, the name and address of the vehicle owner and the registration number of the vehicle.

If the accident results in injury or damage to any person other than the driver himself or to any other vehicle or to any reportable animal,* or to roadside property, then the details of the accident must be reported to the police *as soon as reasonably practicable afterwards, but in any case no later than 24 hours after the event.* This obviously does not apply if police at the scene of the accident take all the necessary details. Failure to report an accident is an offence which also carries a maximum fine of £5,000.

*NB: *For these purposes an animal means any horse, ass, mule, cattle, sheep, pig, goat, dog (in Northern Ireland only, a 'hinnie' is added to this list).*

Reportable incidents include those that occur 'in any public place' as well as on the road. Any public place would include, for example, supermarket, rail station and multi-storey car parks.

Under the Road Traffic Act 1988 the need to stop following accidents extends to cover any damage caused to any property 'constructed on, fixed to, growing on, or otherwise forming part of the land in which the road is situated or land adjacent thereto'. This means that if a vehicle runs off the road and no other vehicles or persons are involved the driver still has to report damage to fences, hedges, gateposts, street bollards, lamp posts, and so on.

Third parties injured in accidents who find when making claims for damages that the vehicle was uninsured at the time can make a claim for their personal injuries to the Motor Insurers' Bureau (MIB) (see also Chapter 9). More recently the MIB compensation scheme has been extended to cover claims for damage to property by uninsured vehicles. Such claims for property damage will only be accepted if the vehicle driver is traced – not otherwise – and provided no claim for the damage can be made elsewhere. There is a limit of £250,000 on claims and they are subject to a £175 excess clause.

Road Humps – Traffic Calming

Regulations permit the construction of road humps on sections of the highway where a 30 mph speed limit is in force. The road hump will be treated as part of the highway provided it complies with the regulations. New regulations were introduced in 1989 to enable local authorities to reduce pedestrian casualties by the introduction of more road humps (see also p 253 regarding 20 mph speed limit zones).

Increasing use is being made of a variety of so-called 'traffic-calming' measures to reduce vehicle speeds and cut accident risks. Besides road humps (often called 'sleeping policemen'), other measures include rumble strips which draw the driver's attention by extra road noise and vibration, mini-roundabouts and artificial chicanes (ie pinch points). However, these steps are seen in some quarters as being a countermeasure, driving fast traffic on to other vulnerable routes and impeding emergency vehicles.

Sale of Unroadworthy Vehicles

It is an offence to sell, supply, offer to sell or expose for sale a vehicle in such a condition that it does not comply with the construction and use regulations, and is therefore legally unroadworthy. Under the Road Traffic Act 1988 offenders are liable to a fine of up to £5,000.

This means that to display a vehicle for sale which needs attention to bring it up to the required standard is an offence, even though the intention would have been to remedy any defects before a purchaser paid for or took the vehicle away. However, it would not be an offence if the buyer was made aware of the defects and he intended to remedy them or have them remedied before using the vehicle on the road.

It is also an offence to fit any part to a vehicle which, by its fitting, makes the vehicle unsafe and causes it to contravene the regulations. For example, fitting a tyre which is below the limits regulating tread depth would be to commit such an offence.

Under the Road Traffic Act 1991 the law relating to the sale of unroadworthy vehicles has been tightened: in particular, the seller of such a vehicle now has a statutory duty to take steps to ensure that the buyer is aware that the vehicle is in an unroadworthy condition. Previously the seller could rely on the defence that he believed that the vehicle was not to be used on the road until made roadworthy.

Seat Belts

Legislation specifying the compulsory wearing of seat belts in motor vehicles came into force on:

- *31 January 1983*
  for drivers and front-seat passengers of motor cars, light vehicles not exceeding 1,525 kg unladen weight registered on or after 1 April 1967 and vehicles not exceeding 3,500 kg gross weight registered since 1 April 1980.
- *1 July 1991*
  for adults (ie persons aged 14 years or over) travelling in the rear of motor cars to wear seat belts where they are fitted – *irrespective of the age of the car.*
- *2 February 1993*
  for the driver and any person sitting in a seat which is equipped with a seat belt (even on a voluntary basis) to wear the belt provided – this includes drivers of goods vehicles over 3.5 tonnes gross weight which are fitted with seat belts on a voluntary basis since there is no legal requirement for such vehicles to be so fitted. Also, from this date:
  - It is illegal to carry any unrestrained child in the front seat of a motor vehicle.
  - Children under three years of age travelling in the front seat of a vehicle must be restrained by a suitable child restraint.
  - Children under 12 years of age and under 1.35 metres (approx 4ft 5in) tall travelling in vehicles must be restrained by an approved device adapted to their weight.
  - Children over 1.35 metres tall may use an adult seat belt.

NB: Seat belts have been fitted to all new cars and taxis since 1987.

Legislation requiring compulsory fitment of seat belts in new goods vehicles over 3.5 tonnes gross weight came into effect from 1 October 2001. Belts must be fitted to all forward-facing front seats and exposed rear seats.

Responsibility for Seat Belt Wearing

It is the individual responsibility of the vehicle driver and any adult passengers (ie persons 14 years of age and over) to wear the seat belt provided for the seat in which they are sitting (ie front or rear). The driver is *not* liable where adult passengers fail or refuse to comply with the law in this regard. However, in the case of children under 14 years of age it is the driver's responsibility to ensure that the law is complied with, irrespective of whether the child's parents, guardians or other responsible person in whose charge they are, are in the vehicle.

Bench-Type Seats

Where a light goods vehicle is fitted with a bench-type or double front passenger seat, it is illegal to occupy the centre part of the seat (ie next to the driver), where a belt may not be provided, if the outer part of the seat with the belt provided is unoccupied.

Failure to Wear Seat Belts

Failure by a person to wear a seat belt as required by law could result in a fixed penalty (currently £20) or a fine of up to £500 if convicted by a court. In a case relating to illegally carrying an unrestrained child a fine of up to £200 could be imposed.

A court has ruled that if, as a result of an accident, injuries were sustained which might have been prevented or lessened had the injured person been wearing a seat belt, then the damages awarded to that person in any claim should be reduced by an appropriate amount. Subsequently, other cases involving motor accident claims have followed the same lines.

Exemptions

Exemption from seat belt wearing applies:

- When holding a valid medical certificate giving exemption (see further details below).
- When driving a vehicle constructed or adapted for the delivery or collection of goods or mail to consumers or addresses, while engaged in making local rounds of deliveries or collections, but only where such journeys do not exceed 50 metres in length.
- When driving a vehicle at the time of carrying out a manoeuvre which includes reversing.
- When accompanying a learner driver as a qualified driver and supervising the provisional entitlement holder while that person is performing a manoeuvre which includes reversing.
- In the case of a driving test examiner (but *not* an instructor) who is conducting a test of competence to drive and who finds that wearing a seat belt would endanger himself or any other person.
- In the case of a person who is driving or riding in a vehicle being used for fire brigade or police purposes, or for carrying a person in lawful custody, including a person being so carried.
- In the case of a driver of a licensed taxi who is seeking hire, answering a call for hire, or carrying a passenger for hire; or of a driver of a private hire vehicle which is being used to carry a passenger for hire.
- When *riding* in a vehicle being used under a trade licence for the purposes of investigating or remedying a mechanical fault in the vehicle.

NB: *this particular exemption refers specifically to 'riding' in a vehicle and does not include 'driving' a vehicle for the same or similar purposes – therefore, it must be concluded that the driver of a vehicle using it for the purpose described would not be exempt from wearing a seat belt whereas a passenger riding in the vehicle for the same purpose would be exempt.*

- In the case of a disabled person, wearing a disabled person's seat belt.
- In the case of a person *riding* (see note above) in a vehicle while it is taking part in a procession organized by or on behalf of the Crown. This exemption

also applies to a person riding in a vehicle which is taking part in a procession held to mark or commemorate an event which is commonly or customarily held in the police area in which it is being held, or for which a notice has been given under the Public Order Act 1986.

The regulations also do not apply to a person who is:

- driving a vehicle if the driver's seat is not provided with an adult seat belt;
- riding in the front of a vehicle in which no adult belt is available to him;
- riding in the rear of a vehicle in which no adult belt is available to him.

It should be noted that these exemptions relate to the non-wearing of seat belts where they are not provided, but this circumstance may involve other infringements of the law relating to the non-fitment of seat belts.

Stowaways

From April 2008, a new authority has taken over responsibility for securing the UK's borders and control of migration. The UK Border Agency now manages border control and enforces immigration and customs regulations – including dealing with applications for permission to enter or stay in the UK, citizenship and asylum issues, smuggling and border tax fraud.

Concern about the number of illegal immigrants (legally termed 'clandestine entrants') entering this country stowed away in heavy goods vehicles has resulted in severe penalties being imposed on drivers and operators caught with such stowaways hidden in their vehicles. The Immigration and Asylum Act 1999 sets penalties of £2,000 for each immigrant found in a lorry trailer, with confiscation of the vehicle as the sanction should the fine not be paid. However, under existing legislation (ie the Immigration Act 1971, section 25) it is already an offence to aid illegal immigrants to enter Great Britain. On conviction, an offending driver could face a heavy fine or up to seven years' imprisonment.

Despite a Court of Appeal ruling in February 2002 that these illegal immigrant fines are contrary to human rights and therefore illegal, the Home Office has continued to impose them on drivers and operators caught with illegal stowaways in their vehicles.

Proof of 'due diligence' may be accepted in defence of any charges under the legislation, but it is important for an accused driver to clearly show that he followed the Code of Practice, which has yet to be formally established. In the meantime, the Road Haulage Association provides the following advice to its members to pass on to their drivers:

- Never leave ignition keys in the vehicle. Lock cab doors and secure the vehicle's load space whenever the vehicle is unattended.
- Avoid routine stops for papers, cigarettes, etc, particularly within 100 km of Channel ports.
- Always ensure windows are closed when away from your vehicle.

- If sleeping in the vehicle, lock all doors and try to block access to the rear doors by parking up against a wall or other secure barrier.
- Be on the lookout for bogus officials or staff.
- Never leave keys hidden for a relief driver.
- On arrival at your destination, do not leave your vehicle in someone else's care.
- Look out for and report any security defects on your vehicle, such as faulty locks or straps.
- Use pre-planned secure overnight parking wherever possible.
- Try to keep your vehicle in sight if you leave it unattended.
- Make sure your vehicle is correctly loaded.
- If you make the same journey frequently, consider whether the route or schedule can be varied.
- Report any irregularity of loading, sealing or documentation.
- Never accept unsolicited offers of assistance.
- Avoid talking about your route over the radio.
- When returning to a vehicle, check for suspicious vehicles/people nearby and if concerned note descriptions, registration numbers, etc.
- After every stop look for signs of tampering with doors, straps, curtains, etc.
- Managers should ensure that operational procedures are constantly reviewed.
- Report to base when you arrive at an unoccupied site, or when you see suspicious activity.
- If you are uncomfortable opening your vehicle for potentially bogus authorities, ask for their details so you can check up on them and offer to open your vehicle at the nearest police station.

Hauliers are advised to turn in any stowaways found in their vehicles, despite the onerous civil penalties involved. Facilitating the entry of illegal immigrants is a serious criminal offence that carries a maximum prison sentence of 10 years.

Home Office Civil Penalty Code of Practice

This Code of Practice is issued in accordance with section 33 of the Immigration and Asylum Act 1999, now amended by the Immigration, Asylum and Nationality Act 2006. This sets out the measures to be taken and the procedures to be followed by persons operating a system for preventing the carriage of clandestine entrants to the United Kingdom in respect of road vehicles.

Under section 34(3) of the 1999 Act, where it is alleged a person is liable to a penalty under section 32 of that Act for bringing a clandestine entrant to the United Kingdom, it is a defence to show that:

- he did not know and had no reasonable grounds for suspecting that a clandestine entrant was, or might be, concealed in the transporter;

- there was an effective system in operation in relation to the transporter to prevent the carriage of clandestine entrants;
- on the occasion concerned, the person or persons responsible for operating that system did so properly.

Regard will be had to this Code of Practice in determining whether such a system is effective (section 34(4) of the 1999 Act).

Part 1: Road Haulage and Other Commercial Vehicles

'Commercial vehicle' means any vehicle excluding buses, coaches, cars, taxis, mobile homes and caravans.

'Vehicle' refers to the entire vehicle, including any attached trailer(s) and any container carried. It also refers to a detached trailer, in the case of which any reference to 'driver' is to be read as 'operator'.

1.1 Measures to be taken to secure vehicles against unauthorized entry

1.1.1 Before final loading takes place, all existing cuts or tears in the outer shell or fabric of the vehicle that exceed 25 centimetres in length must be repaired and sealed so as to prevent unauthorized entry.

1.1.2 If present at the time of final loading, the owner, hirer or driver of the vehicle must check it to ensure that no persons have gained entry and are concealed within. It must then be locked, sealed, or otherwise made secure to prevent unauthorized entry. If not present at the time of final loading, the owner, hirer or driver must, where possible, ensure that such checks are conducted at that point by reputable persons. The owner, hirer or driver must then obtain written confirmation from those persons that these checks were properly conducted and that the vehicle did not contain concealed persons at the time of final loading and securing.

1.1.3 When the final loading has been completed, the load space must be secured immediately by lock, seal or other security device that will prevent unauthorized entry.

1.1.4 Tilt cords and straps, where used, must be undamaged, pass through all fastening points, made taut and be secured by lock, seal or other security device.

1.1.5 There must be no means of entry to the load space, other than via access points which have been secured by lock, tilt cord/strap and seal, or other security device.

1.1.6 Locks, tilt cords, straps and other devices used to secure the load space must be effective and of robust quality.

1.1.7 Seals, other than Customs seals, must be distinguished by a number from a series that is unique to the owner, hirer or driver. This must be recorded in the documentation accompanying the vehicle.

1.1.8 When a sealed container (except a container sealed by Customs) is loaded on to a vehicle, the owner, hirer or driver must, where possible, check to ensure that it does not contain unauthorized persons. It must then be resealed and made secure in accordance with the above requirements. These actions and the number of the new seal used must be recorded in documentation accompanying the vehicle.

1.1.9 The same checking, securing and recording procedure detailed in paragraph 1.1.8 above must be followed when the load space in the vehicle has been opened by the owner, hirer, driver, or any other person before the final checks detailed in section 1.2 below are carried out.

1.1.10 Where a new driver becomes responsible for the vehicle *en route* to the United Kingdom, he should ensure that it does not contain unauthorized persons and that the requirements detailed above have all been met.

1.1.11 Paragraphs 1.1.1–1.1.10 above will not apply in relation to any vehicle that it is not possible to secure by means of lock, seal or other security device. However, in such circumstances, it will be for the owner, hirer or driver concerned to establish alternative arrangements to prevent unauthorized entry, and to be able to demonstrate that such arrangements have been made and complied with.

1.2 Measures to be taken immediately prior to the vehicle boarding the ship, aircraft or train to the United Kingdom, or before arrival at the UK immigration control at Coquelles.

1.2.1 Where used, check tilt cords and straps for evidence of tampering, damage or repair.

1.2.2 Where used, check that seals, locks or other security devices have not been removed, damaged or replaced. In order to ensure that there has been no substitution, numbers on seals must be checked to confirm that they correspond with those recorded on the documentation accompanying the vehicle.

1.2.3 Check the outer shell/fabric of the vehicle for signs of damage or unauthorized entry, paying particular attention to the roof, which may be checked from either inside or outside the vehicle.

1.2.4 Check any external storage compartments, toolboxes, wind deflectors and underneath the vehicle.

1.2.5 Check inside the vehicle. Effective detection devices may be used for this purpose at the discretion of the owner, hirer or driver, but this will not obviate the requirement that the other checks be carried out (detailed above). Where it is not possible to secure a vehicle lock, seal or other security device, a thorough manual check of the load and load space must be conducted.

1.3 *General principles*

1.3.1 Vehicles should be checked regularly *en route* to the United Kingdom to ensure that they have not been entered, particularly after stops when left unattended.

1.3.2 A document detailing the system operated to prevent unauthorized entry must be carried with the vehicle, so that it may be produced immediately on demand to an immigration officer in the event of a possible liability to a penalty.

1.3.3 A report detailing the checks that were carried out must be carried with the vehicle. If it is possible to arrange it, the report should be endorsed by a third party, who has either witnessed or carried out the checks himself by arrangement with the owner, hirer or driver, as the report will then be of greater evidential value.

1.3.4 While owners, hirers or drivers may contract with other persons to carry out the required checks on their behalf, they will nevertheless remain liable to any penalty incurred in the event of failure to have an effective system in place or to operate it properly on the occasion in question.

1.3.5 Where the checks conducted suggest that the security of the vehicle may have been breached, or the owner, hirer or driver otherwise has grounds to suspect that unauthorized persons have gained entry to the vehicle, it must not be taken on to the ship, aircraft or train embarking for the United Kindom, or to the UK immigration control at Coquelles. Any such circumstances must be reported to the police in the country concerned at the earliest opportunity, or at the latest, to the passport control authorities at the port of embarkation. In the event of difficulties arising, owners, hirers or drivers should contact the UK Immigration Service at the proposed port of arrival for advice.

Use of Radios and Telephones in Vehicles

The *Highway Code* contains advice against using a hand-held microphone or telephone handset while the vehicle is moving except in an emergency. Drivers should not stop on the hard shoulder of a motorway to answer or make a call, no matter how urgent. The *Code* recommends that a driver should only speak into a fixed, neck-slung, or clipped-on microphone when it would not distract his attention from the road.

Penalties for Mobile Phone Use

Under provisions contained in the Road Safety Act 2006, penalties for the illegal use of mobile phones or other similar hand-held devices were increased to a £60 fixed penalty notice and a three-point penalty added to the driver's licence. Should offenders decide to take the case to court rather than accept the fixed penalty, on conviction they would face a maximum fine of £1,000 for car drivers and £2,500 for van and lorry drivers.

Traffic and Weather Reports

Drivers concerned about prevailing or likely weather conditions prior to making a journey, or even while en route, can check forecasts from local and national newspapers and get an update of the current situation by listening to radio and television bulletins. In particular, the following are useful for traffic and weather forecasts:

Radio

BBC Radios 1, 2, 4 and 5 and local BBC and commercial radio stations broadcast regular weather and traffic bulletins.

The DfT signposts show tuning frequencies for local radio stations on some motorways. These wavelengths broadcast 24 hours a day, 7 days a week, giving as many as four local traffic and weather reports an hour at peak times, and two during off-peak times, with programme interruptions for important traffic announcements.

National radio covers major traffic and weather problems, and the BBC's Radio Data System (RDS) enables drivers listening to BBC radio to be interrupted with relevant travel news. Receivers using additional data, Enhanced Other Networks (EON), can switch drivers from a BBC national radio station, or CD, to a BBC local radio station for a travel bulletin.

Television

BBC 2 Ceefax, ITV Teletext and various news channels (for digital viewers) provide up-to-date travel information.

Online

AA Roadwatch and Weatherwatch (**www.theaa.com/travelwatch**) provide national motorway and A-road information, while the RAC Traffic News (**www.rac.co.uk/web/trafficnews**) provides information on traffic in London and regionally.

On-Board Traffic Information

Sophisticated modern technology can now provide drivers with on-board (ie in-vehicle) visual information on traffic routes and conditions. Three systems are currently in use:

Autoguide

This system, operating within the M25 London orbital motorway, gives drivers recommended routes to their destination via a dashboard-mounted display screen activated by roadside mounted beacons which also update the central computer. It is self-compensating, so does not shift traffic jams from one location to another.

AA Roadwatch Pager

The AA Roadwatch Pager displays dynamic traffic news on the screen of its pocket-sized pager unit, taking account of the current location of the unit. For more information call 0800 300 300 (toll free).

Trafficmaster

Despite what many road users think, the blue poles sprouting up on Britain's roadsides are not speed cameras. They are part of the Trafficmaster live traffic- monitoring network of infrared sensors and roadside beacons on over 8,000 miles of motorway and trunk roads. The system provides information on traffic conditions and real-time information on journey times on over 95 per cent of the country's main roads and can predict when traffic is at its worst – and therefore enable drivers to determine when is the best time to travel.

The system works by using specially developed infrared sensors, installed approximately 4 miles apart, to measure the time taken for a vehicle to travel between each sensor site. Computers at each site continuously transmit this information back to Trafficmaster's National Control Centre in Milton Keynes, where it is processed and transmitted directly to vehicles fitted with Trafficmaster receivers.

Trafficmaster claims that its technology is playing a key role in helping to cut the cost and time wasted in congestion by providing accurate, high-quality, dynamic information directly to drivers, resulting in significant reductions in both journey times and stress levels.

Trafficmaster can be contacted via **www.trafficmaster.co.uk**.

Smuggling

The Customs authorities are becoming increasingly concerned about the volumes of smuggled goods, particularly tobacco products, being brought into the UK. It is estimated that tobacco smuggling alone amounts to some £3.5 billion annually.

Besides new measures to detect smuggling such as the use of sophisticated X-ray equipment, tougher new penalties have been introduced which could result in convicted offenders losing their vehicle (all goods vehicles found to be carrying contraband goods are seized: 300 HGVs were impounded in the first year of operation) and their driving licence, and facing up to seven years in prison.

The maximum legal limits for personal importation of goods into the UK are as follows:

From within the EU:

3,200 cigarettes	400 cigarillos
200 cigars	3 kg of smoking tobacco
110 litres of beer	10 litres of spirits
90 litres of wine	20 litres of fortified wine (eg port or sherry)

From outside the EU:

200 cigarettes, or	600cc/ml of perfume
100 cigarillos, or	250cc/ml of toilet water
250 grams of tobacco	£145 worth of all other goods including gifts and souvenirs

NB: For these purposes, the EU is the enlarged EU of 25 countries, but in the case of Cyprus goods from any area of Cyprus which is not under the effective control of the Government of the Republic of Cyprus are treated as non-EU imports. Similarly, Spain does not include the Canary Islands and neither the Channel Islands nor Gibraltar are counted as EU territories.

Any amounts of such goods brought in exceeding these limits may be confiscated and penalties imposed.

The High Court (in August 2002) has ruled that UK Customs & Excise policing of cross-Channel shopping expeditions by means of random searches and routine confiscations causes 'injustice and hardship'. The court established that there should be a presumption in favour of the free movement of individuals, and their goods, across internal EU borders. Instead of random checks, the court said that customs officers should act only when there are reasonable grounds for suspicion that excise goods have been acquired for commercial purposes. It also held that travellers should no longer bear the burden of proving that their excise goods fall within acceptable limits 'and the mere fact that a traveller is transporting a significant cargo does not constitute a "persuasive presumption" that he has acquired them for commercial purposes.

'Transporting large quantities of excise goods into this country may suggest a possible commercial intent. But that should be for Customs to prove, beyond reasonable doubt, in court. Why should citizens be forced to justify their appetite for wine, consumption levels of beer or fondness for cigarettes to outside authority to prevent their purchases being impounded? Citizens have a right to be presumed dissolute before any court may find them guilty of criminality.'

In a more recent ruling, the European Court of Justice has determined that truck drivers caught with smuggled goods on their vehicles are to be held responsible for the duty payable even if they are proven to be the innocent victims of deceit.

Customs has a special telephone number for reporting suspected cases of smuggling: Customs Confidential 0800 59 5000.

Road Safety Act 2006

Despite Great Britain having one of the best road safety records in the world, the Government introduced its Road Safety Act in 2006 with the objective of achieving further casualty reduction targets and further improving safety on our roads.

The Act targets the following main areas:

- introduction of graduated fixed penalties for offences and graduated penalty point endorsement for speeding (eg 2, 3 or 6 points) depending on their seriousness;

- mandatory notification of fixed penalty offences to Traffic Commissioner; also offence of failing to do so;

- introduction of a new offence of death by careless driving (which may be tried in the magistrate's court or the Crown Court, with prison sentence penalty available to both);

- introduction of a new offence of being involved in a fatal accident when unlicensed, disqualified or uninsured – carrying a prison sentence on conviction;

- introduction of a system of roadside financial deposits for drivers who cannot establish a fixed address in the UK; vehicles to be grounded pending payment of a financial deposit, which is offset against any fine imposed by a court in due course;

- unlawful use of hand-held mobile phones becomes a 3-point driving licence endorsable offence;

- increase in penalty for failure to notify driver details on request by the police from 3 to 3–6 penalty points;

- provisions to enable county councils to create French motorway-style rest areas;

- provisions concerning the phasing out of old-style (ie green and paper) driving licences and the creation of driver records in order to be able to endorse the driving records of drivers present within the UK who do not hold UK licences;

- 12-month mandatory disqualification for two separate construction and use (C&U) offences committed within a three-year period;

- provisions to combat high-risk drivers committing excess alcohol or unfit to drive offences;

- provisions to permit VOSA enforcement officers to issue fixed penalties for non-moving traffic offences (eg C&U contraventions).

Goods Vehicle Dimensions and Weights

E uropean and British law relating to the weights and dimensions of goods vehicles and trailers is extremely complex. Much of it is difficult for operators to comprehend and apply, and even worse for their drivers, who may, when loading, have to make on-the-spot decisions which could later prove to be wrong, thereby breaching the law and bringing possible prosecution for themselves and their employers. We have seen many weight and dimensional changes in recent years which have been documented in previous editions of this *Handbook*.

Interest is still being shown for increased overall lengths for vehicle and trailer combinations up to 25.25 metres. Currently vehicles at this length can operate legally in Sweden and Finland and, with certain restrictions, in Denmark and the Netherlands. Trials with articulated vehicles of the same length as truck and trailer combinations are in progress in Germany. Britain, however, has rejected the concept of these longer, heavier vehicles (LHVs), as reported in *Transport News Digest* in May 2008 – then Secretary of State Ruth Kelly confirmed to Parliament that trials of either longer or heavier vehicles would not be permitted.

The maximum permitted dimensions and weight limits for goods vehicles and trailers in Great Britain are set out in the Road Vehicles (Construction & Use) Regulations 1986 (C&U regulations), as amended, and the Road Vehicles (Authorised Weight) Regulations 1998, which introduced from 1 January 1999 the following specific weight increases:

- two-axle rigids (including buses) increase from 17 to 18 tonnes;
- three-axle articulated buses increase from 27 to 28 tonnes;
- four-axle combinations increase from 35 to 36 tonnes;
- four-axle articulated vehicles fitted with road-friendly suspension on the drive axle increase from 35 to 38 tonnes;

- five-axle combinations increase from 38 to 40 tonnes;
- five-axle (3+2) articulated vehicles at 44 tonnes permitted for the carriage of 40-foot ISO containers on international combined transport operations;
- drive axles at 11.5 tonnes for all the above except 41-tonne combinations.

These changes are detailed in this chapter, along with existing C&U regulation limitations on vehicle weights which remain in force. Information on weights and dimensions for vehicles carrying abnormal indivisible loads under other legislation is to be found in Chapter 19.

Since 1 February 2001, 44-tonne lorries have been permitted for general haulage operations within the United Kingdom. A 10.5-tonne maximum drive axle weight applies to vehicles grossing 41 tonnes or more; otherwise the limit is 11.5 tonnes. Tractive units of combinations operating at 44 tonnes gross weight must have engines that are regarded as meeting low pollution emission standards – ie either a gas-fuelled engine or a diesel engine that complies with at least the Euro-II emission standard.

European limits on vehicle weights and dimensions are to be found in EC Directive 96/53/EC of 25 July 1996, which repeals previous Directive 85/3/EEC on this subject and its various amendments.

Definitions

The following definitions apply when considering the lengths, widths and weights of goods vehicles and trailers:

Overall length – the distance between the extreme forward and rearward projecting points of the vehicle/trailer inclusive of all parts, but excluding load-securing sheets and flexible coverings, receptacles for customs seals and tailboards (provided they are not supporting the load in which case they are included in the overall length). In the case of drawbar trailers overall length *excludes* the length of the coupling.

Overall width – the distance between the extreme projecting points on each side of the vehicle/trailer inclusive of all parts but excluding driving mirrors, distortion of the tyres caused by weight, receptacles for customs seals, load-securing sheets and flexible coverings.

Weight – the maximum gross (or design) weight (gvw) for a vehicle/trailer is that at which it has been designed to operate. The permissible maximum weight (pmw) for a vehicle/trailer is the limit set by law (and is shown on the 'Ministry' plate attached to the vehicle), which must not be exceeded on the road in Great Britain.

Length

Rigid Vehicles

The maximum overall length permitted for rigid vehicles is 12 metres.

Articulated Vehicles

For certain articulated vehicles the maximum permitted length is 16.5 metres (see also below), provided the combination can turn within minimum and maximum swept inner and outer concentric circles of 5.3 metres radius and 12.5 metres radius respectively (see Figure 11.1); otherwise the maximum permitted length is 15.5 metres. The swept circle requirements do not apply to:

- low loader or step-frame low-loader combinations;
- car transporters;
- articulated vehicles constructed to carry indivisible loads of exceptional length;
- articulated vehicles with semi-trailers built or converted to increase their length prior to 1 April 1990;
- articulated vehicles not exceeding 15.5 metres overall length.

Articulated vehicles first used since 1 June 1998 which are fitted with a lift axle must meet the turning circle requirement (described above) both with and without all the wheels in contact with the ground.

For the purposes of enforcement of the turning circle requirements, VOSA has notified vehicle manufacturers that it will take a notional measurement from the kingpin to the centre-line of the semi-trailer bogie. Where such a dimension does not exceed 8.155 metres the combination will be assumed to comply in the case of 2.5-metre wide semi-trailers; 8.135 metres if 2.55 metres wide and 8.115 metres if 2.6 metres wide. Where this dimension exceeds 7.8 metres VOSA reserves the right to demand a turning circle demonstration on a steering pad.

The maximum overall length for an articulated vehicle incorporating a low-loader semi-trailer (but not a step-frame semi-trailer) is 18 metres. Such vehicles do not have to meet the turning circle requirements described above.

Where an articulated vehicle is designed to carry indivisible loads of exceptional length there is no length restriction (an indivisible load means 'a load which cannot without undue expense or risk of damage be divided into two or more loads for the purpose of conveyance on a road').

Vehicle and Trailer Drawbar Combinations (Road Trains)

When a rigid motor vehicle is drawing a trailer the maximum overall length for the combination is 18.75 metres, subject to certain other minimum dimensional requirements being met (see below).

FIGURE 11.1 The maximum and minimum outer and inner swept circles within which articulated vehicles over 15.5 metres long and certain other vehicles (see text for details and exceptions) must be able to turn

The 18.75-metre maximum length for road train combinations incorporates:

- a maximum loadspace of 15.65 metres to be shared between the two bodies;
- a minimum gap of 0.75 metres (to provide a 16.4-metre 'envelope' of load and coupling space); and
- a minimum cab length of 2.35 metres (see Figure 11.2).

When a trailer is designed for carrying indivisible loads of exceptional length the length of the drawing vehicle must not exceed 9.2 metres and the whole combination must not exceed 25.9 metres.

When two or more trailers are drawn, the overall length of the combination must not exceed 25.9 metres unless an attendant is carried and two days' notice is given to the police. When two trailers are drawn within the 25.9 metre limit mentioned here (ie only legally permissible with a vehicle classed as a motor tractor or locomotive), only one of the trailers may exceed an overall length of 7 metres. When three trailers are drawn (ie only legally possible with a vehicle classed as a locomotive), none of the trailers may exceed a length of 7 metres.

The limits do not apply when a broken-down vehicle (which is then legally classed as a trailer) is being towed.

Trailers

The maximum length for any drawbar trailer which has four or more wheels and is drawn by a vehicle which has a maximum gross weight exceeding 3,500 kg is 12 metres. The same 12-metre maximum length limit also applies to agricultural trailers.

FIGURE 11.2 The maximum dimensions for drawbar vehicle combinations

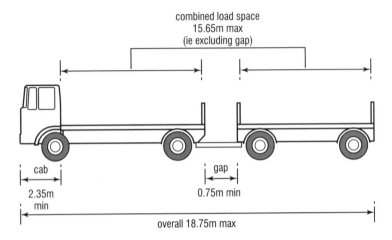

combined load space
15.65m max
(ie excluding gap)

cab
2.35m min

gap
0.75m min

overall 18.75m max

NB: The term 'loading area' includes the thickness of the bulkhead. Towing equipment is not counted in the measurement of the truck-trailer gap.

NB: *Although the maximum individual lengths for both rigid drawing vehicles and trailers are 12 metres as stated, two such maximum-length units obviously cannot be combined within the overall 18.75-metre limit for drawbar combination described above.*

The maximum permitted length for all other drawbar trailers is 7 metres.

Composite trailers (see p 310) having at least four wheels and drawn by a goods vehicle over 3,500 kilograms permissible maximum weight or by an agricultural vehicle, may be up to 14.04 metres long.

Articulated Semi-trailers

The maximum permitted length for certain articulated vehicles is 16.5 metres. This applies where such vehicles include a semi-trailer with a distance from the centre-line of the kingpin to the rear of the trailer which does not exceed 12 metres and where the distance from the kingpin (or foremost kingpin if more than one) to *any point* on the front of the trailer does not exceed 2.04 metres (4.19 metres for car transporters) – see Figure 11.3.

Articulated semi-trailers built since 1 May 1983 are limited to a maximum length of 12.2 metres. There is no specified length limit for semi-trailers built prior to this date. In measuring the 12.2-metre dimension no account need be taken of the thickness of front or rear walls or any parts in front of the front wall or behind the rear wall or closing device (ie door, shutter, etc). The thickness of any internal partitions must be included in the length measurement. This means effectively that the dimension relates only to load space between the front and rear walls.

FIGURE 11.3 The maximum dimensions for articulated vehicles and semi-trailers (see above for details and exceptions)

The 12.2-metre length limit for semi-trailers as described does not apply to a trailer which is normally used on international journeys, part of which are outside the UK. Similarly, articulated vehicles operating within the 15.5-metre limit on international journeys do not have to meet the turning circle requirements described on p 292 for 16.5-metre-long vehicles.

The 13.7 metre Container Problem

The carriage of standard 13.7 metre pallet-wide ISO-type shipping containers cannot be carried out legally on maximum-length articulated vehicles on account of the limitation on swing radius as set out in Community Directive 96/53/EC. This was particularly worrying for European intermodal road hauliers who needed to use the 13.7 metre pallet-wide container, the only size longer than 12.1 metre that would enable them to compete effectively against the traditional road hauliers using 13.6-metre-long semi-trailers. However, this problem has been overcome by use of the Geest (ie Geest North Sea Line bv)-designed 'Euro-Casting' fitted to the front end of a 13.7 metre container, which successfully meets the crucial swing radius of 2.04 metres – measured from the centre of the kingpin to any point at the front end of the container or skeletal semi-trailer – as well as the 12.0-metre length requirement measured from the centre of the kingpin to the rearmost point of the semi-trailer (see Figure 11.3).

NB: Department for Transport issued a consultation document in March 2011 seeking industry views on its proposals to amend the Road Vehicles (Construction and Use) Regulations 1986 and Road Vehicles (Approval) Regulations 2009 in order to allow an increase of 2.05 metres in the permitted length of semi-trailers for articulated lorries. This would increase the maximum loading length of a semi-trailer from 13.6 metres to 15.65 metres giving up to 13 per cent increase in capacity.

Measurement of Length

In measuring vehicle or trailer length account must be taken of any load-carrying receptacle (eg demountable body or container) used with the vehicle. Excluded from the overall length measurement are such things as rubber or resilient buffers and receptacles for customs seals. In the case of drawbar combinations the length of the drawbar is excluded from overall length calculations. With dropside-bodied vehicles the length of the tailboard in the lowered (ie horizontal) position is excluded unless it is supporting part of the load, in which case it must be included in the overall length measurement and for the purposes of establishing overhang limits (see below).

Overhang

Overhang is the distance by which the body and other parts of a vehicle extend beyond the rear axle. The maximum overhang permitted for rigid goods vehicles (ie motor cars and heavy motor cars) is 60 per cent of the distance between the centre of the front axle and the point from which the overhang is to be measured. The point from which overhang is measured is, in the case of two-axled vehicles, the centre line through the rear axle, and in the case of vehicles with three or more axles two of which are non-steering rear axles, 110 millimetres to the rear of the centre line between the two rear axles (Figure 11.4).

This regulation does not apply to vehicles used solely in connection with street cleansing; the collection or disposal of refuse; the collection or disposal of the contents of gullies or cesspools; works trucks; or tipping vehicles, provided the total overhang does not exceed 1.15 metres (3 ft 9 in approx). There is no specified overhang limit on trailers.

NB: Overhang is not always measured from the rear axle but from the turning axis of the vehicle – as the caption to Figure 11.4 points out. In other words, this is not always the middle of the rear bogie of a six or eight-wheeler: when one of the axles steers or is lifted, the turning centre becomes the driven axle. There is also an alternative to the 60 per cent of the distance from front axle to vehicle turning point. It can instead conform to European Directive 92/27/EEC, in accordance with which the swing-out of a rear corner is limited to 0.8 metre when the vehicle is following the 12.5-metre radius swept circle (see p 292).

Width

Motor Vehicles

The overall width of motor tractors, motor cars and heavy motor cars (most goods vehicles are included in these classifications) must not be more than 2.55 metres (see note below about refrigerated vehicles) and the maximum width of locomotives must not be more than 2.75 metres.

FIGURE 11.4 How to measure body overhang on vehicles with two axles, three axles and more (this measurement applies equally to two- and three-axle tractive units) (see details and exceptions in text above)

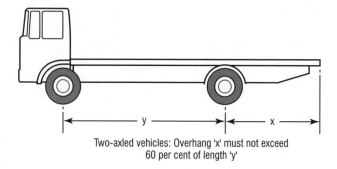

Two-axled vehicles: Overhang 'x' must not exceed
60 per cent of length 'y'

110mm behind centre line
of two axles

Vehicles with three axles or more: Overhang 'x' measured
from 110mm behind the centre-line of the two rear axles
must not exceed 60 per cent of the length of 'y', which is
the distance beween the centre-line of the front wheel to
the centre-line of the two rear axles plus 110mm

Trailers

The maximum permissible width for trailers is 2.55 metres provided the drawing vehicle has a maximum permissible weight exceeding 3,500 kilograms. If the towing vehicle is below this weight, the width of the trailer must not exceed 2.3 metres.

Refrigerated Vehicles

The maximum permitted width for refrigerated (ie reefer) vehicles, semi-trailers and drawbar trailers is 2.6 metres provided that the thickness of the side walls (inclusive of insulation) is at least 45 millimetres. For the purposes of this regulation 'refrigerated vehicle' means a vehicle (or trailer) specially designed to carry goods at low temperature.

Height

There are currently no legal maximum height limits for goods vehicles or for loads in Britain (see below) but these are, obviously, governed by the height of bridges on the routes on which the vehicles are operated. For general information, the minimum height of bridges on motorways is normally 4.8 metres to 5 metres and the maximum heights for buses is 4.57 metres (see also item regarding high loads on p 479).

NB: *The Blackwall Tunnel (on the A102(M)), the River Thames crossing to the east of London, is limited to a maximum height of 4 metres northbound and 4.72 metres southbound.*

The operator must bear in mind, however, that if he loads vehicles to a height which could cause danger he would be liable to prosecution under the construction and use regulations. Also, if a vehicle were to be loaded to a height whereby the load hit a bridge on the route being used, the operator could be accused under these regulations of using a vehicle on a road for a purpose for which it was so unsuitable as to cause, or to be likely to cause, danger.

EU regulations specify a height limit of 4 metres but this does not apply in the UK.

Height Limit on Vehicles over 35 Tonnes

The maximum height limit of 4.2 metres on both articulated vehicles and drawbar combinations operating at (ie laden to) weights in excess of 35 tonnes (previously 32.5 tonnes) was abolished from 1 June 1995.

Height Marking and Route Descriptions

Since 1 October 1997 all vehicles with an overall travelling height of more than 3 metres must have a notice prominently displayed in the driver's cab indicating the actual travelling height of the vehicle, its load or equipment in feet and inches (or in both feet and inches and metres).

The height marking, where this is shown in feet and inches only, must be in letters and figures at least 40 mm tall, But where the height is shown in both imperial and metric measure the figures shown must not differ by more than 50 mm.

As an alternative to the height marking described above, in circumstances where the driver is operating on a particular journey during which he is unlikely to be confronted with any bridge or overhead structure which does not exceed the maximum travelling height by at least 1 metre, a document may be carried on the vehicle (within easy reach of the driver) which describes the route, or a choice of routes, which the driver must follow in order to avoid any risk of the vehicle, its load or equipment colliding with any bridge or overhead structure.

Where vehicles are fitted with 'high-level equipment' (defined as power-operated equipment) with a maximum height of more than 3 metres they must have a warning device which gives visible warning to the driver if the height of the vehicle exceeds a predetermined level. This applies to vehicles first used and trailers first made from 1 April 1998.

Bridge Bashing

Bridge bashing remains a major problem despite new legislation on height marking as described above. In 1990, 800 such accidents were recorded, of which 11 resulted in train derailments, and in a recent instance an owner-driver was left facing a compensation claim for more than £100,000. Some 20 or so key railway bridges have been identified as providing risk of potential disaster, should they be struck by a large vehicle. Infrared warning systems are to be installed at these key sites, which will trigger alarms when over-height vehicles approach.

The *AA Trucker's Atlas of Britain* (scale 3 miles to 1 inch), recommended by both Railtrack and the RHA, shows 1,500 road- and rail-bridge heights. It contains useful advice on how not to be a 'bridge basher' and suggests that by not knowing their vehicle height, drivers risk the consequences of bridge bashing from causing rush-hour chaos to losing their job, or even causing loss of life. It warns that drivers should not hit and run but should report incidents – failure to do so being an offence. Most rail bridges have a sign indicating the Railtrack contact number (ie 020 7928 4616) to be telephoned following contact with a bridge structure and advising that the police should also be notified immediately by dialling 999.

Vehicles for Combined Transport

Swap-body and container-carrying goods vehicles running to and from rail terminals on intermodal operations may operate at up to 44 tonnes gross weight provided they are:

- articulated vehicles and drawbar combinations equipped with:
  - at least six axles; and
  - road-friendly suspensions (or having no axle exceeding 8.5 tonnes); and
- articulated vehicles comprising specially built bimodal semi-trailers (ie capable of running on road or rail).

For these purposes, containers and swap-bodies are defined as being receptacles at least 6.1 metres long designed for repeated carriage of goods and for transfer between road and rail vehicles.

To comply with the law, the driver must carry with him documentary evidence to show that the swap-body or container load is on its way to a rail terminal (the document must show the name of the rail terminal, the date of the contract and the parties to it), or is on its way back from a rail terminal (in which case the document must show the terminal and the date and time that the unit load was collected). There is no restriction on the distance that may be travelled to or from a rail terminal for the purposes of complying with this legislation.

Authorized Weight Regulations

UK lorry weights have been aligned with EC Directive 96/53/EC since 1 January 1999 under the Road Vehicles (Authorized Weight) Regulations 1998 (SI 1998 No 3111), which specify maximum authorized weights for vehicles (ie weights not to be exceeded in any circumstances). These regulations make new provision for the weights of vehicles and trailers of the types defined in EC Directive 70/156/EEC (see list on page 310) but they do not apply to vehicle combinations that meet the requirements for combined transport in the C&U regulations. Vehicles that comply with C&U are taken to comply with the Authorised Weight regulations.

The pre-existing vehicle and axle weight limits set out in the Call regulations (as amended) remain in force largely unchanged, apart from three particular provisions listed below which were implemented when these regulations were amended in consequence of the making of the new authorized weight regulations.

- An increase in the maximum total weight of all trailers drawn at any one time by a locomotive.

- An increase in the maximum weight permitted for uncompensated steering axle from 7,120 kg to 8,500 kg.

- Amendments to the provisions relating to vehicles used in combined transport operations.

Maximum Authorized Weights for Rigid Vehicles and Tractor Units

Description of vehicle	Number of axles	Maximum authorized weight (kg)
Rigid motor vehicle	2	18,000
Tractor unit	2	18,000
Trailer (not a semi-trailer or centre-axle trailer)	2	18,000
Trailer (not a semi-trailer or centre-axle trailer)	3 or more	24,000
Rigid motor vehicle	3	25,000
Rigid motor vehicle(1)	3	26,000
Tractor unit	3 or more	25,000
Tractor unit(1)	3 or more	26,000
Articulated bus	any number	28,000
Rigid motor vehicle	4 or more	30,000
Rigid motor vehicle(1)	4 or more	32,000

(1) Applies to vehicles with either:
    (a) the driving axle, if it is not a steering axle fitted with twin tyres and road-friendly suspension; or
    (b) each driving axle fitted with twin tyres and not exceeding 9,500 kg.

Maximum Weight determined by Axle Spacing

The authorized weight (in kilograms) for the vehicles shown below must equal the product of the distance measured in metres between the foremost and rearmost axles of the vehicle multiplied by the factor specified in the third column and rounded up to the nearest 10 kg, if that number is less than the 'maximum authorized weight' (ie in accordance with the table immediately above).

Description of vehicle	Number of axles	Factor to determine maximum authorized weight
Rigid motor vehicle	2	6,000
Tractor unit	2	6,000
Trailer which is not a semi-trailer or centre-axle trailer	2	6,000
Rigid motor vehicle	3	5,500
Tractor unit	3 or more	6,000
Trailer which is not a semi-trailer or centre-axle trailer	3 or more	5,000
Rigid motor vehicle	4 or more	5,000
Articulated bus	any number	5,000

Maximum Authorized Weights for Vehicle Combinations

Description of combination	Number of axles	Maximum authorized weight (kg)
Articulated vehicle	3	26,000
Rigid motor vehicle towing a trailer	3	22,000
Rigid motor vehicle towing a trailer(1)	3	26,000
Articulated vehicle	4	36,000
Articulated vehicle(2)	4	38,000
Rigid motor vehicle towing a trailer	4	30,000
Rigid motor vehicle towing a trailer(1)	4	36,000
Articulated vehicle	5 or more	40,000
Rigid motor vehicle towing a trailer	5 or more	34,000

Description of combination	Number of axles	Maximum authorized weight (kg)
Rigid motor vehicle towing a trailer(1)	5 or more	40,000
Articulated vehicle(3)	6 or more	41,000
Rigid motor vehicle towing a trailer(1 & 3)	6 or more	41,000
Rigid motor vehicle towing a trailer(1, 3 & 4)	6 or more	44,000

(1) Applies to vehicles that have a distance between the rear axle of the motor vehicle and the front axle of the trailer of not less than 3 m.

(2) Applies to combinations where:
  (a) the combination is a 2-axle tractor unit and 2-axle semi-trailer;
  (b) the weight of the tractor unit comprised in the combination does not exceed 18,000 kg;
  (c) the sum of the axle weights of the semi-trailer does not exceed 20,000 kg; and
  (d) the driving axle is fitted with twin tyres and road-friendly suspension.

(3) Applies to vehicles where:
  (a) the weight of each driving axle does not exceed 10,500 kg; and
  (b) either
      (i)   each driving axle is fitted with twin tyres and road-friendly suspension; or
      (ii) each driving axle that is not a steering axle is fitted with twin tyres and does not exceed 8,500 kg;
  (c) each axle of the trailer is fitted with road-friendly suspension; and
  (d) each vehicle comprised in the combination has at least 3 axles.

(4) Applies to vehicles powered by low pollution engines (ie gas or diesel complying with emission requirements).

Weight by Reference to Axle Spacing

The maximum authorized weight in kilograms for an articulated vehicles 'shall be the product of the distance measured in metres between the kingpin and the centre of the rearmost axle of the semi-trailer multiplied by the factor specified and rounded up to the nearest 10 kg, if that weight is less than the authorized weight' (ie in accordance with the table above).

Description of vehicle combination	Number of axles	Factor to determine maximum authorized weight
Articulated vehicle	3 or more	5,500

Maximum Authorized Axle Weights

Description of axle	Maximum authorized weight (kg)
Single driving axle	11,500
Single non-driving axle	10,000
Driving tandem axle	18,000
Driving tandem axle(1)	19,000
Non-driving tandem axle	20,000
Tri-axle	24,000

(1) Applies to axles where:
    (a) the driving axle is fitted with twin tyres and road-friendly suspension; or
    (b) each driving axle is fitted with twin tyres and no axle has an axle weight exceeding 9,500 kg.

Where maximum weights are less than those in the fourth table above.

Description of axle	Specified dimension	Length (metres)	Maximum authorized weight (kg)
Driving tandem axle	Distance between the 2 axles	Less than 1	11,500
Driving tandem axle	Distance between the 2 axles	Not less than 1 but less than 1.3	16,000
Non-driving tandem axle	Distance between the 2 axles	Less than 1	11,000
Non-driving tandem axle	Distance between the 2 axles	Not less than 1 but less than 1.3	16,000
Non-driving tandem axle	Distance between the 2 axles	Not less than 1.3 but less than 1.8	18,000
Tri-axle	Distance between any 1 axle and the nearer of the other 2 axles	1.3 or less	21,000

Overall Weight Limits

The total weight of the load on a vehicle, together with the weight of the vehicle itself, must not exceed the maximum permitted weight for each individual axle or for the vehicle.

Load Movements – C&U Regulations versus Special Types Order

The majority of general haulage loads moved in this country fall within scope of the weights, lengths and width limitations set out in the Road Vehicles (Construction and Use) Regulations 1986 (C&U) as described in this chapter. However, an increasing number of long, heavy and/or wide loads are being transported which, due to C&U restrictions on load lengths, widths and weights, are required to be moved under the abnormal indivisible loads (AIL) provisions of the Road Traffic Act 1988 Section 44(1) detailed in the Motor Vehicle (Authorization of Special Types) General Order 2003 (STGO) as described in Chapter 19 of this *Handbook*. In particular, it should be noted that maximum vehicle and load lengths permitted under Regulation 7 of C&U must not be confused with those authorized under the STGO.

ISO Container Dimensions and Weights

Shipping containers to ISO standards present a complexity of dimensions and weights, mainly identified by a 'Type Designation'. A table showing the relevant internal and external heights, widths and lengths plus maximum gross weights and cubic capacity in metric and imperial measures is to be found in Appendix X.

Weight Offences

It is an offence on the part of both the driver and the vehicle operator (ie the driver's employer) to operate a goods vehicle on a road laden to a weight above that at which it has been plated by VOSA (ie above the maximum permitted gross and individual axle weights) and both are liable to prosecution. Such offences are 'absolute' in that once the actual overweight has been established the fact that it was a deliberate action to gain extra revenue or purely accidental, unintentional, outside the driver's or vehicle operator's control or loading was in a place where no weighing facilities existed, is of no consequence in defending against the charge.

Currently, the policy adopted by VOSA is that if a vehicle exceeds its weight limits by more than 5 per cent (up to a maximum of 1 tonne) it will be prohibited from proceeding on its journey until the weight is reduced to within legal limits – see below. Where an overload exceeds 10 per cent of the vehicle's legal limits or a maximum of 1 tonne, a prosecution will follow with heavier penalties being imposed on conviction. Trading Standards Officers may not take such a lenient view in their dealing with overloaded vehicles.

Defence

There is no defence of 'due diligence' against charges of overloading, something for which the Road Haulage Association has been campaigning, but it is a defence under the Road Traffic Act 1988 (section 42) to prove that at the time the contravention was detected the vehicle was proceeding to the nearest available weighbridge or was returning from such weighbridge to the nearest point at which it was reasonably practicable to remove the excess load. There have also been instances reported where successful defences have been made against conviction where the operator was able to show that he had no way of knowing or controlling the weight placed on a vehicle.

It is a further defence, where the weight exceeds maximum limits by not more than 5 per cent, to prove that the weight was within legal limits at the time of loading the vehicle and that no person had since added anything to the load.

Penalties

Overloading offences are looked upon very seriously by the enforcement authorities and by the courts and very heavy penalties are imposed on offenders. In addition to punitive fines (currently a maximum of £5,000 per offence – an overloaded vehicle could result in a number of individual offences related to gross and axle weights), the operator risks losing his 'O' licence and the driver could put his LGV driving entitlement in jeopardy.

Prohibition of Overweight Vehicles

Any vehicle on a road found by a vehicle examiner to be overloaded to the extent that it could endanger public safety will be ordered off the road immediately. The necessary powers to enable this step to be taken are included in section 70 (2) and (3) of the Road Traffic Act 1988 and they empower an authorized officer to prohibit the driving of a goods vehicle on a road if after having it weighed it appears to him that the vehicle exceeds the relevant weight limits imposed by the Construction and Use Regulations, and as a result would be an immediate risk to public safety if it were used on a road. The officer may be one of VOSA's examiners or a specially authorized weights and measures inspector or a police constable.

A prohibition notice, form TE160, will be issued to the driver of a vehicle found to be overweight and it is the driver's responsibility to remove the excess weight to his own satisfaction and clear the TE160 before proceeding on his journey. The penalty for ignoring a prohibition notice is a fine of up to £5,000.

Official Weighing of Vehicles

Under the Road Traffic Act 1988 an authorized officer can request the person in charge of a vehicle to drive it to a weighbridge to be weighed. If the journey is more than 5 miles and on arrival the vehicle is found to be within the legal limit then the vehicle owner can claim for the loss involved in making the journey. It is an offence to refuse to go to a weighbridge if requested (maximum fine currently £5,000). Once a vehicle has been weighed the official in charge should give the driver a 'certificate of weight' (whether it is overloaded or not) and the vehicle will be exempt from further requests for weighing while carrying the same load on that journey.

The following Codes of Practice are currently in use by VOSA for vehicle weighing.

Code of Practice for Conventional Weighing

The procedure will be as follows:

- Normally only one authorized officer will check-weigh a vehicle.
- The driver and any passengers should remain in the vehicle during weighing as they are part of the weight transmitted to the road.
- When requested, the driver should move the vehicle smoothly on to the weighbridge plate.
- The engine should be switched off but left in gear during weighing. When a vehicle's individual axles are being check-weighed both the hand and foot brakes should be released.
- If the vehicle is too long to go on the weighing plate or is over the weight capacity of the machine it may require two or more weighings to get a total weight for the vehicle (see note below).
- The driver may be required to have the axle weights checked, and in positioning the vehicle he should carefully follow instructions given by the authorized officer.
- A certificate of weight will be issued for each vehicle weighed and will be handed to the driver. In some cases, where circumstances permit, he may be invited to see the weight recorded on the indicator. The certificate of weight exempts a vehicle from being weighed again on the same journey *with the same load* if stopped at another weight check. The driver should give the certificate of weight to his employer as soon as he reaches his base.
- The driver should also note that previous overloading offences may be detected by checks on weighbridge records.

NB: *Operation of Weighing Equipment*
Weighbridges will be operated only by or under the supervision of a duly authorized officer fully conversant with the operation of the weighing equipment and with approved methods of weighing. Weighing by the method known as 'double-weighing' will only be carried out by a Trading Standards Officer whose professional qualifications and experience will enable him to give expert evidence as to the accuracy of this weighing procedure; or by a duly authorized officer at sites which have been examined and approved as suitable for double-weighing by the local Trading Standards Officer, and who will if necessary be available to give expert evidence in court. NOTE: double-weighing occurs when the results of two or more individual weighings of a vehicle's axles are summated to produce the total gross weight of the vehicle.

Dynamic Weighing

The use of dynamic axle weighing machines is permitted under regulations (the Weighing of Motor Vehicles (Use of Dynamic Axle Weighing Machines) Regulations 1978), which specify that an enforcement officer can require a vehicle to be driven across the weighing platform of a machine for this purpose. The permitted weights for the vehicle are measured to within plus or minus 150 kg for each axle and within plus or minus 150 kg multiplied by the total number of axles to determine the tolerance on the total vehicle weights.

The Department for Transport has a 'Code of Practice for Weighing Goods Vehicles on Dynamic Axle Weighers' (see below), which must be followed by enforcement officers to secure a successful prosecution for vehicle overloading. This Code supplements the regulations and provides enforcement officers as well as vehicle operators and drivers with information on the correct setting up and operational use of weighing machines and on periodical (ie maximum six-monthly) accuracy tests which must be carried out. Among other things, the Code specifies standards for the approach and exit from the concrete apron of the equipment (ie plus or minus 3 mm for a distance of 8 metres on each side of the weigh beam, and the finished surface must not deviate from the level by more than 3 mm under a 3-metre-long straight edge).

Portable Weighers

There have been reports of Trading Standards Officers in some areas using portable axle weigh-pads as a means of checking vehicle/axle weights and have brought overloading prosecutions against operators based on such weighings. There is considerable doubt about the accuracy of such machines and the Road Haulage Association has expressed its concern about their use.

Code of Practice on Dynamic Weighing

The following procedure should be adopted for weighing vehicles:

- The vehicle to be weighed is to be stopped a minimum distance of 6 metres from the weigh beam on a level approach; avoid stopping on uneven ground, eg with one or more wheels on the kerb.
- Possible errors caused by surges in the liquid load of a single compartment unbaffled tanker should be taken into account.
- The enforcement officer operating the console is to recheck and reprint the Low and High indication, set the equipment in the dynamic mode and, where appropriate, set the direction selector switch to suit the vehicle approach. He must also press the totalizer button to ensure that any residual information in the totalizer has been cleared.
- Where vehicles under 3 tonnes unladen weight are to be checked, and the equipment has a Low Weight mode, this button should be depressed before weighing commences.
- An enforcement officer should then instruct the driver of the vehicle to drive across the weigh beam at a steady speed not exceeding 2.5 miles per hour; during this run the driver must neither accelerate nor use his brake. This can normally be achieved by engaging lowest forward gear and driving at tick-over speed across the weighbridge.
- The vehicle is to be observed at all times during the weighing procedure to ensure that a consistent speed is maintained. In the case of a foreign driver

who cannot speak English it is desirable for him to be guided by an enforcement officer walking alongside the vehicle.

- If at any time during the weighing a driver accelerates above the permitted speed, thus causing a red printout, or no printout, to be registered, or if he uses his brakes to cause a sharp deceleration, the weighing should be disregarded and the vehicle weighed again until a satisfactory weighing and an all-black printout is achieved.

- At the conclusion of a satisfactory weighing, with an all-black printout showing axle weights, the operator should press the appropriate button to give a summation of the axle weights. The registration number of the vehicle should then be written on the printout adjacent to the readout.

- Each weighing is to be followed by a zero and high indication check which will be shown on the print-roll.

- Following weighing of the vehicle, normal Road Traffic Act procedures are to be followed in the light of the Weighing of Motor Vehicles (Use of Dynamic Axle Weighing Machines) Regulations 1978. The prescribed Certificate of Weight should be issued to the driver. The recorded weights should be assessed in the light of the presumed accuracy limits, laid down in the regulations, of ±150 kg per axle, with a consequent accuracy limit on gross vehicle weight of ±150 kg, multiplied by the number of axles; compensating axles as usual should continue to be assessed as a combined weight against the combined plated weights.

- The print-roll should be left intact for the complete day's weighings, then removed, dated and retained by the enforcement staff.

Construction and Use of Vehicles

I n constructing goods vehicles and trailers, manufacturers and bodybuilders must observe requirements regarding the specification and standards of construction of components and the equipment used in the manufacture. While some of these items are covered by the Type Approval scheme (see p 347), the majority are included in the Road Vehicles (Construction and Use) Regulations 1986, Statutory Instrument (SI) 1078/1986 (available from The Stationery Office) and subsequent amendments to these regulations, which, collectively, are commonly referred to as the C&U regulations. Certain EU legislation also applies, as indicated in the text.

Once a goods vehicle or trailer has been built and put into service, it is the operator as the vehicle user (see pp 14–15) who must then ensure that it complies fully with the law regarding its construction and use when on the road. It is worth pointing out that where a vehicle on the road is found to contravene the constructional aspects of the regulations, it is the operator who will be prosecuted and if convicted he will be liable to meet the penalty and may find that it jeopardizes his 'O' licence. It is no defence or excuse to say that the fault with the vehicle rests with the manufacturer, bodybuilder or even the supplying dealer.

Only the main items from the regulations and amendments which concern the goods vehicle operator and transport manager are included in this chapter. Those aspects of the regulations dealing with the limitations on vehicle weights and dimensions are covered in Chapter 11. The provisions of the C&U regulations dealing with safe operation and safety of vehicles and loads are explained in Chapter 17. Many other points relating to a wide variety of other types of vehicle (motor bicycles and invalid carriages, for example) are not included because they are not generally thought to be relevant to the reader of this *Handbook*.

Definitions of Vehicles

For the purpose of these regulations the following definitions, as given in the Road Traffic Act 1988, apply:

- A **goods vehicle** is a vehicle or a trailer adapted or constructed to carry a load.
- A **motor car** is a vehicle which, if adapted for the carriage of goods, has an unladen weight not exceeding 3,050 kg but otherwise has an unladen weight not exceeding 2,540 kg.
- A **heavy motor car** is a vehicle constructed to carry goods or passengers with an unladen weight exceeding 2,540 kg.
- A **motor tractor** is a vehicle which is not constructed to carry a load and has an unladen weight not exceeding 7,370 kg.
- A **light locomotive** is a vehicle which is not constructed to carry a load and which has an unladen weight of more than 7,370 kg but not exceeding 11,690 kg.
- A **heavy locomotive** is a vehicle which is not constructed to carry a load and which has an unladen weight exceeding 11,690 kg.
- An **articulated vehicle** as defined in the C&U regulations is a motor car or heavy motor car with a trailer so attached that when the trailer is uniformly loaded at least 20 per cent of the weight of the load is imposed on the drawing vehicle.
- A **composite trailer** is a combination of a converter dolly and a semi-trailer, and is treated as one trailer only when considering the number of trailers which may be drawn.
- **Engineering plant** means movable plant or equipment in the form of a motor vehicle or trailer which is specially designed and constructed for the purposes of engineering operations and which cannot, for this reason, comply with the C&U regulations. Also, it is constructed to carry only materials which it had excavated from the ground and which it is specially designed to treat while being carried. It also means mobile cranes, which do not conform in all respects with the C&U regulations.
- An **agricultural motor vehicle** means a motor vehicle that is constructed or adapted for use off roads for the purposes of agriculture, horticulture or forestry and which is primarily used for one or more of those purposes.
- A **pedestrian-controlled vehicle** means a motor vehicle which is controlled by a pedestrian and which is not constructed or adapted to carry a driver or passenger.
- A **works truck** means a motor vehicle (other than a straddle carrier) designed for use in private premises and used on a road only in delivering goods from or to such premises, or from a vehicle on a road in the immediate neighbourhood, or in passing from one part of the premises to another or to other private premises in the immediate neighbourhood, or in connection with roadworks or in the immediate vicinity of the site of such works.
- A **works trailer** means a trailer used for the same purposes as a works truck.

International Vehicle Classifications

Goods vehicles are classified according to the following international categories:

- Category M: Motor vehicles having at least four wheels, or having three wheels when the maximum weight exceeds 1 metric ton, and used for the carriage of passengers:
  - *Category M1*: Vehicles used for the carriage of passengers and comprising no more than eight seats in addition to the driver's seat;
  - *Category M2*: Vehicles used for the carriage of passengers, comprising more than eight seats in addition to the driver's seat, and having a maximum weight not exceeding 5 metric tons;
  - *Category M3*: Vehicles used for the carriage of passengers, comprising more than eight seats in addition to the driver's seat, and having a maximum weight exceeding 5 metric tons.
- Category N: Motor vehicles having at least four wheels, or having three wheels when the maximum weight exceeds 1 metric ton, and used for the carriage of goods:
  - *Category N1*: Vehicles used for the carriage of goods and having a maximum weight not exceeding 3.75 metric tons;
  - *Category N2*: Vehicles used for the carriage of goods and having a maximum weight exceeding 3.75 but not exceeding 12 metric tons;
  - *Category N3*: Vehicles used for the carriage of goods and having a maximum weight exceeding 12 metric tons.
- Category O: Trailers (including semi-trailers):
  - *Category O1*: Trailers with a maximum weight not exceeding 0.775 metric ton;
  - *Category O2*: Trailers with a maximum weight exceeding 0.775 metric ton but not exceeding 3.75 metric tons;
  - *Category O3*: Trailers with a maximum weight exceeding 3.75 but not exceeding 10 metric tons;
  - *Category O4*: Trailers with a maximum weight exceeding 10 metric tons.

Constructional and Maintenance Requirements

Brakes

All goods vehicles must meet specified braking efficiencies. The regulations state minimum efficiencies for the service brake, for the secondary brake and for the parking brake or handbrake. On pre-1968 vehicles the secondary brake can be the handbrake and on post-1968 vehicles it can be a split or dual system operated by the footbrake. If it is the latter it must be capable of meeting the secondary requirement if part of the dual system fails. The parking brake must achieve the required efficiency by direct mechanical action or by the energy of a spring without the assistance of stored energy.

Every vehicle must have a parking brake system to prevent at least two wheels from turning when it is not being driven. All vehicles first used after 1 January 1968 must have an independent parking brake.

Anti-lock (ie anti-skid) braking systems are required on certain new articulated vehicles and drawbar trailer combinations under EU legislation (for which Category 1 – wheel-by-wheel systems are necessary) and under British C&U regulations. The vehicles affected are articulated tractive units and rigid goods vehicles over 16 tonnes equipped to draw trailers and first used from 1 April 1992, and trailers over 10 tonnes built on or after 1 October 1991.

From 1 March 2002* anti-lock braking systems (ABS) are required on all newly registered goods vehicles over 3.5 tonnes gross weight. In due course the requirement will be for electronic braking systems (EBS) on heavy vehicles.

*NB: This date has been further deferred.

Specified Braking Efficiencies

Vehicles used before 1 January 1968:

Two-axle rigid vehicles	Service brake	45 per cent
	Secondary brake	20 per cent
Multi-axled rigid vehicles, trailer combinations and articulated vehicles	Service brake	40 per cent
	Secondary brake	15 per cent

Vehicles First Used on or after 1 January 1968:

All vehicles	Service brake	50 per cent
	Secondary brake	25 per cent
	Parking brake must be capable of holding the vehicle on a gradient of at least 1 in 6.25 without the assistance of stored energy (1 in 8.33 with a trailer attached).	

Maintenance of Brakes

The braking system on a vehicle, including all of its components and means of operation, must be maintained in good and efficient working order and must be properly adjusted at all times.

Braking Standards

The regulations reflect the requirements for braking standards laid down in EC Directives 320/1973, 524/1975 and 489/1979 (as amended). These call for the fitment of load sensing valves or anti-lock braking on drive axles – most modern tractive units already comply with these requirements – and the overall emphasis is on stability, eliminating jackknifing and trailer swing. EU rules permit the use of two-line air braking systems instead of the traditional British three-line systems. Most older tractive units in the UK have three-line braking systems fitted with yellow, blue and red couplings.

Vehicles built to the European standard have only two lines (red and yellow or two black). Coupling three-line tractive units to three-line trailers, two-line tractive units to two-line trailers and two-line tractive units to three-line trailers presents no difficulties. Problems arise when coupling three-line tractive units to two-line trailers. Such combinations must not be used unless they are specially designed or modified by fitting a fourth coupling or internal valves and connecting pipework.

On tractive units first registered before 1 April 1983 a notice should be displayed stating that the system is suitable for coupling. If no such notice is displayed the driver should check the system to see if it is suitable for coupling.

Failsafe Handbrake Alarms

Plans are afoot to introduce mandatory handbrake-off alarms following a number of deaths from runaway vehicle incidents.

Anti-lock Brakes

The following goods vehicles must be fitted with anti-lock brakes:

- Motor vehicles first registered on or after 1 April 1992 with design gross vehicle weight greater than 16,000 kg and authorized to tow trailers with total design axle weight exceeding 10,000 kg.
- Trailers with total design axle weight exceeding 10,000 kg manufactured on or after 1 October 1991.
- New Category N vehicles from 1998 were required to have anti-lock braking fitted as part of their type approval.
- All Category N2 and N3 vehicles and Category O3 and O4 trailers registered from April 2002 were required to have anti-lock braking systems fitted.

Anti-lock systems must conform to Annex 10 of the EU braking directive (Council Directive 71/320/EEC).

A journey in a vehicle with a faulty anti-lock braking system may be completed if the fault arose *en route,* or the vehicle may be driven to a place where the fault is to be repaired. However, this does not apply if the defective braking system does not meet specified braking efficiency requirements.

Endurance Braking Systems

From 1 January 1995 UK braking requirements were harmonized with those of the EU, thereby requiring new vehicles from this date carrying dangerous goods to be fitted with endurance braking systems. Older vehicles are likely to have to be retro-fitted in due course.* EU vehicles over 16 tonnes gross weight on cross-border ADR work have required such braking systems since 1 July 1993.

NB: A 2002 planned date for implementation has been further deferred.

The purpose of endurance braking systems is to relieve excess loadings on the normal vehicle service brakes, particularly, for example, on long downhill gradients, where they tend to fade due to overheating. A variety of proprietary retarders are available to meet this requirement.

Brakes and Couplings on Trailers

Trailers constructed before 1 January 1968 must have an efficient braking system on half the number of wheels. Trailers constructed after this date must be fitted with brakes operating on all wheels which are capable of being applied by the driver of the drawing vehicle and having maximum efficiencies matching the braking requirement for the drawing vehicle, emergency brakes operating on at least two wheels and a parking brake capable of holding the trailer on a gradient of at least 1 in 6.25.

New lightweight trailers (ie weighing not more than 750 kg) made after 1 January 1997 must be fitted with a secondary safety coupling. Such trailers must also be marked with their date of manufacture.

Overrun Brakes

Overrun brakes may be fitted to trailers not exceeding 3,500 kg gross weight (or 3,560 kg if made before 27 February 1977). Overrun brake couplings must be damped and matched with the brake linkage. Normally, to ensure that these standards are met, the coupling design needs to be type approved. Trailer braking efficiency must be at least 45 per cent and the parking brake must be capable of holding the laden trailer on a gradient of 1 in 6.25 (ie 16 per cent). Modern braked trailers must also be fitted with an emergency device which automatically applies the brakes if the trailer becomes uncoupled from the towing vehicle. This does not apply to single axle trailers up to 1,500 kilograms gross weight provided they are fitted with a safety chain or cable to stop the coupling head touching the road if the trailer becomes detached.

Light Trailer Brakes

Light trailers must be fitted with brakes if:

- their maximum gross weight exceeds 750 kg and their unladen weight exceeds 102 kg;
- their maximum gross weight exceeds 750 kg and they were built on or after 1 October 1982; or
- their laden weight on the road exceeds half the towing vehicle's kerbside weight (this does not apply to agricultural trailers or to trailers whose unladen weight does not exceed 102 kg and which were built before 1 October 1982).

Unbraked trailers must have their maximum gross weight marked in kilograms in a conspicuous position on the nearside.

Parked Trailers

When trailers are detached from the towing vehicle they must be prevented from rolling by means of a brake, chain or chock applied to at least one of their wheels.

Braking Coils

Braking coils to ISO 7638 standard must be used when both drawing vehicle and trailer are fitted with connections. A prohibition notice will be issued where these coils are found unconnected in roadside checks.

Exhaust Emissions

Since 1 April 1991 newly registered diesel-engined goods vehicles exceeding 3.5 tonnes gross weight have been required to comply with EC Directive 88/77, which sets gaseous emission (ie exhaust emission) limits (see Chapter 21 for details of emission requirements for fleet cars and light vans). These limits have already been applied in Type Approval regulations to vehicles first used from 1 April 1991 (later for cars/vans with engines over 1,400 cc and those with diesel engines).

The purpose of the EU's legislative programme (under EC Directive 91/542) is to reduce the amount of nitrous oxide (NO_x), carbon monoxide (CO) and unburned hydrocarbons (HC) blown into the atmosphere from vehicle exhausts. The first stage of this programme (ie the so-called Euro-I standard) applied to all new Type Approved goods vehicles from 1 July 1992 (and to earlier Type Approved vehicles from 1 October 1993). Tougher Euro-II standards applied to new vehicles over 3.5 tonnes pmw from 1 October 1996; and progressively more stringent emission controls have applied since 1 October 2000. Euro-IV limits have been in force since 1 October 2005. The Euro-V standard came into force from 1 October 2008. Euro-VI is to apply from 1 January 2013.

The following table indicates the relevant emissions standards with the date of implementation and the emissions and smoke limits.

Emissions Standards

Tier	Date	CO	HC	NOx	PM	Smoke
Euro IV	10.2005	1.5	0.46	3.5	0.02	0.5
Euro V	10.2008	1.5	0.46	2.0	0.02	0.5
Euro VI	01.2013	1.5	0.13	0.4	0.01	–

The vehicle user is required by law to keep the engine of his vehicle and any emission control equipment (ie catalytic converter) in good working order and in tune.

Emissions Developments

The next round of pollution emissions limits for lorries and buses has been proposed by the European Commission, and this time the requirement will change from being a directive to a regulation. The proposal is to cut nitrogen oxide emissions by 80 per cent and particulate matter by 66 per cent compared with the Euro-V standard, which will require particulate filters to be fitted to all diesel vehicles. The decision to have Euro-VI as an EC regulation means the limits will become directly binding and will not need to be transposed into national law. The stricter limits are said to be likely to cause a mild rise in CO_2 from trucks and buses. Apparently, the Commission has dropped its idea of proposing Euro-VII standards at the same time as Euro-VI.

EGR v SCR

For vehicles to achieve the Euro-IV standard – from 1 October 2005 and Euro-V from 1 October 2008, necessary for all vehicles over 7.5 tonnes gross weight – operators have needed to choose between two technologies: EGR (Exhaust Gas Recirculation), which requires no additions to either engine or silencer box, or SCR (Selective Catalytic Reduction), which achieves its effect through the addition of a chemical substance called 'AdBlue'. Current opinion suggests that EGR is preferable because it is cheaper, has no additional maintenance, has an absence of moving parts and is a proven technology. AdBlue is a synthetic urea solution which, when used with SCR engine technology, converts exhaust pollutants (mainly nitrogen oxides or NO_x and particles) into water vapour and harmless nitrogen. It requires intervention from the driver, by way of regular topping up of the AdBlue tank, otherwise the engine will run at reduced power.

Towards Euro-VI

By way of an example as to how heavy vehicle manufacturers are approaching the forthcoming requirement for meeting the tough Euro-VI emission standard, Swedish manufacturer Scania has announced its plans. It says two new Euro-VI engines are available during 2011 in its G-Series and R-Series tractive unit ranges, with multi-axle rigid models following in 2012. These Euro-VI engines are based on Scania's existing Euro-V 12.7-litre, in-line-six-cylinder engine and will be available at outputs of 440 and 480hp. In addition to the engines' existing EGR system, Scania is using variable geometry turbo-charging, a diesel particulate filter, SCR and an ammonium slip catalyst to clean up exhaust emissions. The new engines are designed to give the same performance and fuel-efficiency as their existing Euro-V counterparts. These engines, Scania says, make it possible for operators to take the next step and invest in the greenest technology available. They will be able to benefit from lower motorway charges and other incentives that may be introduced by the authorities and will also command a higher second-hand value on resale.

On-Board Diagnostic Equipment

All heavy diesel-engine vehicles complying with Euro-IV and Euro-V emissions standards must be fitted with onboard diagnostics (OBD) or onboard management (OBM) equipment to monitor their emissions performance. If this diagnostic equipment fails or it records a malfunction in the emissions system the vehicle can only be operated at very much reduced power levels... and the driver has a slow journey home.

Public Service Vehicle Emissions

Many vehicles operating within the public service sector will need to comply with tougher emissions standards in the future. Under European Commission proposals, vehicles owned or used under contract by Government departments or local authorities will be required to meet the European EEV (enhanced environmental vehicle) standard, which is tougher than Euro-V on particulates, smoke and, for gas engines, tailpipe methane.

London Low Emission Zone

In an effort to improve air quality in London, which is currently among the worst in Europe, Greater London has been designated a Low Emission Zone (LEZ), the objectives of which were to move London closer to achieving national and EU air quality objectives for 2010, and to improve the health and quality of life of people who live and work in London, through improved air quality.

The LEZ aims to achieve reduced air pollution by discouraging the most polluting vehicles from driving in Greater London. These are generally older, diesel-engined goods vehicles, buses and coaches (cars and light vans are not to be included in the scheme), which contribute significantly to the pollutants most harmful to health, namely, particulate matter (PM_{10}).

The LEZ commenced on 4 February 2008 and applies to a range of vehicles as shown on pp 265–68, where details of the payment system, exemptions and penalties are also shown.

Local Authority Emissions Testing

Several local authorities, including Birmingham, Bristol, Canterbury, Glasgow, Middlesbrough, Swansea and the City of Westminster, are currently operating roadside emission testing schemes under Section 83 of the Environment Act 1995. Drivers of vehicles that fail the test will be issued with a fixed penalty notice requiring payment of £60, rising to £90 if unpaid within 28 days. The test levels are the same as those that vehicles would be expected to meet at annual test. Commercial vehicles that fail an emission test invariably have poorly maintained engines. The scheme covers all types of vehicles, including commercial vehicles, and if the tests prove successful they will be extended nationally.

Towards the Euro-VI Standard

With the Euro-V emission standard now in being, the transport industry is beginning to look towards Euro-VI under Regulation 595/2009/EC due to be implemented from 31 December 2013 for new vehicle Type Approvals and a year later, in January 2014, for all newly registered diesel-engined goods vehicles over 3.5 tonnes maximum laden (i.e. gross) weight.

Basically, the Euro-VI standard seeks to achieve a halving of particle emissions from the current Euro-V standard of 0.02 grams/kWh to a maximum of 0.01grams/kWh and a reduction in Nitrogen Oxides (NO_x) of some 77 per cent. These reductions are important because they are the component gases of the exhaust emission that do most harm both to people and to the atmosphere, plus of course, there are the emissions of unburnt hydrocarbons (reduced to 0.13 for Euro-VI from 0.46 for Euro-V) and carbon monoxide (one of the so-called greenhouse gases).

To put these reductions into context, information disseminated by Volvo Trucks via the internet, shows that, whereas the environmental footprint of exhaust emissions for a Euro-I diesel engine in 1993 equated roughly to the area of a tennis court, the exhaust emissions for a Euro-VI diesel engine will equate to the miniscule area of a postage stamp. The technology needed to achieve this reduction involves the use of existing exhaust gas recirculation (EGR) systems combined with selective catalyst reduction (SCR) technology together with variable geometry turbo-charging, a diesel particulate filter, and an ammonium slip catalyst to effect a further clean-up of NO_x emissions at the tailpipe.

Smoke

Vehicles must not emit smoke, visible vapour, grit, sparks, ashes, cinders or oily substances that might cause damage to property or injury or danger to any person.

Excess Fuel Devices

Excess fuel devices must not be used on diesel vehicles while the vehicle is in motion. Such devices are incorporated in the vehicle fuel pump to enable extra fuel to be fed to the engine to aid cold-starting. Their use when the engine is warm slightly increases the power of the engine, but in doing so black smoke is emitted from the exhaust. For this reason their use is forbidden while the vehicle is in motion.

Smoke Opacity Limits

Diesel-engined vehicles first used after 1 April 1973 (but not manufactured before 1 October 1972) must comply with smoke opacity limits specified in BS AU 141a/1971. Engines fitted to such vehicles must be of a type for which a type test certificate in accordance with the British Standard Specification for *The Performance of Diesel Engines for Road Vehicles* has been issued by the Secretary of State. The certificate will indicate that engines of that type do not exceed the emission of smoke limits set out in the BS Specification.

Offences

It is an offence to use a vehicle to which this type test applies if the fuel injection equipment, the engine speed governor or other parts of the engine have been altered or adjusted in such a way that the smoke emission of the vehicle is increased. An offence is committed if a vehicle emits black smoke or other substances even without alteration or adjustment of the parts (eg as a result of lack of maintenance). VOSA has promised tougher enforcement of goods-vehicle smoke emissions, particularly at the time of submitting vehicles for annual test.

Control of Fumes

Petrol-engined vehicles first used after 1 January 1972 must be fitted with a means of preventing crankcase gases escaping into the atmosphere except through the exhaust system.

Fuel Tanks

Vehicle fuel tanks must be constructed so as to prevent any leakage or spillage of fuel. In particular, there is concern about leakage from heavy vehicle fuel tanks on to the road, where it causes exceptional danger to cyclists and motorcyclists. Failure to maintain diesel fuel tanks in good condition (and especially filler caps) is now an offence in its own right and gives the police the opportunity to prosecute without having to actually observe spillage from the tank. Fines of up to £2,000 could be imposed on conviction for such offences.

Vehicles first used since 1 July 1973 and manufactured since 1 February 1973 that are propelled by petrol engines must have metal fuel tanks fitted in a position to avoid damage and prevent leakage. This provision does not apply where the vehicle complies with relevant EU regulations (EC 221/70) and is marked accordingly.

NB: See pp 536–37 for information on fitting long-range fuel tanks.

Ground Clearance for Trailers

Minimum ground clearances are specified for goods-carrying trailers manufactured since 1 April 1984. Such trailers must have a minimum ground clearance of 160 mm if they have an axle interspace of more than 6 metres and not more than 11.5 metres. If the interspace is more than 11.5 metres, the minimum clearance is 190 mm.

Measurement of the axle interspace is taken from the point of support on the tractive unit in the case of semi-trailers or the centre line of the front axle in other cases to the centre line of the rear axle or the centre point between rear axles if there is more than one.

In determining the minimum ground clearance no account should be taken of any part of the suspension, steering or braking system attached to any axle, any wheel and any air skirt. Measurement of the ground clearance is taken in the area formed by the width of the trailer and the middle 70 per cent of the axle interspace.

Horn

All vehicles with a maximum speed exceeding 20 mph, except works trucks and passenger-controlled vehicles, must be equipped with an audible warning instrument. The sound emitted by a horn must be continuous and uniform and not strident. Gongs, bells, sirens and two-tone horns are only permitted on emergency vehicles, though a concession allows similar instruments, except two-tone horns, to be used on vehicles from which goods are sold to announce the presence of the vehicle to the public. Any vehicle first used since 1 August 1973 must not be fitted with multi-toned or musical horns.

Regulations effective from October 2005 permit the fitting of a bell, gong, siren or two-tone horn to vehicles used by HM Revenue & Customs when used for investigating serious crime, and defence vehicles used in case of radiation accident or emergency.

Restriction on Sounding Horns

Audible warning instruments must not be sounded at any time while the vehicle is stationary or in a built-up area (ie where 30 mph speed restriction is in force) between 11.30 pm and 7.00 am (see also item about reversing alarms on p 345). The use of the horn on a stationary vehicle in an emergency situation (ie 'at times of danger due to another, moving vehicle on or near the road') is allowed.

Horns Used as Anti-theft Devices

Audible warning instruments that are gongs, bells or sirens may be used to prevent theft or attempted theft of a vehicle provided a device is fitted that will stop the warning sounding continuously for more than five minutes. Hazard lights and interior lights may be set to operate continuously for (a maximum of) five minutes if the vehicle is tampered with.

Mirrors

Goods vehicles and dual-purpose vehicles must be fitted with at least two mirrors. One of these must be fitted externally on the offside and the other must, in the case of vehicles first used since 1 June 1978, be fitted in the driver's cab or driving compartment. When an interior mirror does not provide an adequate view to the rear, a mirror must be fitted externally on the nearside. The mirrors must show traffic to the rear or on both sides rearwards. Mirrors fitted to vehicles over 3,500 kg must conform to Class II and those fitted to other vehicles with Class II or III as described in EC Directive 2003/97/EC.

Definitions for Classes of Mirrors

Classes of mirrors are defined in EC Directive 2003/97/EC as follows:

- Class I – being an interior rear-view mirror;
- Class II and III – being main exterior rear-view mirrors;
- Class IV – being a wide-angle exterior mirror;
- Class V – being a close-proximity exterior mirror;
- Class VI – being a front mirror (ie one that gives a view across the front of the vehicle).

In all these cases very specific and detailed angles of vision are prescribed and illustrated in the Directive.

Fitment of Mirrors

External mirrors with a bottom edge less than 2 metres from the ground (when the vehicle is loaded) must not project more than 20 cm beyond the overall width of the vehicle or vehicle and trailer. Mirrors fitted on the offside must be adjustable from the driving seat unless they are of the spring-back type. Internal mirrors fitted to vehicles first registered on or after 1 April 1969 must be framed with material (usually plastic beading) which will reduce the risk of cuts to any passenger who may be thrown against the mirror.

Type Approval for Mirrors

Since 1 June 1978 vehicles must be fitted with rear-view mirrors bearing the EU Type Approval 'E' mark. The relevant date for implementation of this requirement for Ford Transit vehicles was 10 July 1978, rather than 1 June 1978, which was the date for all other vehicles.

Close Proximity and Wide-Angle Mirrors

Goods vehicles over 12 tonnes maximum permissible weight first used since 1 October 1988 must be fitted with additional mirrors that provide close proximity and wide-angle vision for the driver in accordance with EC Directives 205/85 and 562/86.

Since January 2007 all new trucks have required more mirrors as a result of two EU Directives (ie Directives 2003/97/EC as amended by 2005/27/EC). Besides the existing requirements described in this section:

- Vehicles between 3.5 tonnes and 7.5 tonnes gross weight need two Class IV (wide-angle) mirrors and a Class V (close-proximity) mirror.
- Vehicles between 7.5 tonnes and 12 tonnes gross weight need two Class IV (wide-angle) mirrors, a Class V (close proximity) mirror and a Class VI (front) mirror.
- Heavy vehicles over 12 tonnes gross weight need additional Class IV (wide-angle) and Class V (close-proximity) mirrors plus a Class VI (front) mirror.

Fresnel Lenses

A great danger caused by left-hand drive (ie foreign) vehicles on British roads – and conversely by British vehicles driving on continental roads – is that of 'side-swiping' vehicles overtaking in the passenger-side blind spot.

Fresnel lenses placed on the passenger-side window are said to give the driver a wider view of overtaking vehicles that would otherwise be lost in the driver's blind spot. VOSA has been trialling the use of these lenses, hoping to help reduce the 400-odd side-swipe incidents that occur annually on British roads.

Safety Glass

Goods vehicles must be fitted with safety glass (ie toughened or laminated glass which, when fractured, does not fly into fragments likely to cause severe cuts) for windscreens and windows in front of and on either side of the driver's seat. The windscreen and all windows of dual-purpose vehicles must be fitted with safety glass. Glass bearing an approval mark under EC Directive 92/22 is regarded as meeting the requirement stated above for safety glass.

The glass must be maintained so as not to obscure the vision of the driver while the vehicle is being driven on the road. This means that a driver could be prosecuted for having a severely misted up, iced up or otherwise dirty windscreen.

Seat Belts

Seat belts for the driver and one front-seat passenger must be fitted to goods vehicles not exceeding 1,525 kg unladen registered since 1 April 1967 and goods vehicles not exceeding 3,500 kg gross weight first used since 1 April 1980. From 1 October 1988 goods vehicles over 3,500 kg must be fitted with seat belt anchorage points for each forward-facing seat to which lap-strap type seat belts can be fixed (see Chapter 10 for details of seat-belt fitment requirements in fleet cars).

Since 1 March 2001 seat belts have been required by law to be fitted in new goods vehicles over 3.5 tonnes gross weight (although many new vehicles were fitted with seat belts by manufacturers on a voluntary basis long before this date).

Vehicles to which this regulation applies, first used since 1 April 1973, must be fitted with belts that can be secured and released with one hand only and also with a device to enable the belts to be stowed in a position where they do not touch the floor. Vehicles to which this requirement applies will fail the annual test if seat belts are not fitted, are permanently obstructed or are not in good condition.

The legal requirement for drivers and passengers to wear seat belts came into effect in January 1983 with certain exemptions (see pp 279–81).

Since 1 February 1997 it has been illegal to use a minibus or coach for carrying a group of three or more children (aged between 3 and 16 years) on an organized trip unless as many forward-facing passenger seats as there are children are fitted with seat belts.

Sideguards

Most heavy vehicles and trailers must be fitted with sideguards to comply with legal requirements except certain vehicles and trailers that are exempt from the fitting requirement as listed at the end of this section.

Sideguards must be fitted to the following vehicles and trailers:

- goods vehicles exceeding 3.5 tonnes maximum gross weight manufactured since 1 October 1983 and first used since 1 April 1984;

- trailers exceeding 1,020 kg unladen weight manufactured since 1 May 1983 and which, in the case of semi-trailers, have a distance between the foremost axle and the centre line of the kingpin (or rearmost kingpin if there is more than one) exceeding 4.5 metres (Figure 12.1);

- semi-trailers made before 1 May 1983 with a gross weight exceeding 26,000 kg and used in an articulated combination with a gross train weight exceeding 32,520 kg.

FIGURE 12.1 Measurements of relevant distance between foremost axle and centre of kingpin for semi-trailers to determine if sideguards must be fitted

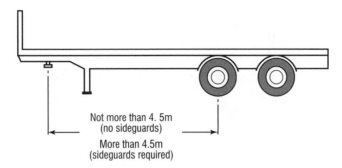

Not more than 4. 5m
(no sideguards)

More than 4.5m
(sideguards required)

Sideguards are not required on vehicles and trailers, other than semi-trailers, where the distance between any two consecutive (ie front and rear) axles is less than 3 metres (Figure 12.2).

Strength of Sideguards

Sideguards must be constructed so they are capable of withstanding a force of 200 kg (2 kilonewtons) over their length, apart from the rear 250 mm, without deflecting more than 150 mm. Over the last 250 mm the deflection must not be more than 30 mm under such force (Figure 12.3). These force resistance requirements *do not* apply where sideguards were fitted to existing semi-trailers (ie those built before 1 May 1985, and which were used at weights above 32,520 kg).

Fitment of Sideguards

The fitting position for sideguards depends on the type of vehicle or trailer as follows:

- Rigid vehicles: at front – not more than 300 mm behind the edge of the nearest tyre and the foremost edge of the sideguard; at rear – not more than 300 mm behind the rearmost edge of the sideguard and the edge of the nearest tyre (Figure 12.4).
- Trailers: at front – not more than 500 mm behind the edge of the nearest tyre and the foremost edge of the sideguard; at rear – not more than 300 mm behind the rearmost edge of the sideguard and the edge of the nearest tyre (Figure 12.5).
- Semi-trailers with landing legs: at front – not more than 250 mm behind the centre line of the landing legs and the foremost edge of the sideguard; at rear – not more than 300 mm behind the rearmost edge of the sideguard and the edge of the nearest tyre (Figure 12.6).
- Semi-trailer without landing legs: at front – not more than 3 metres behind the centre line of the rearmost kingpin and the foremost edge of the sideguard; at rear – not more than 300 mm behind the rearmost edge of the sideguard and the edge of the nearest tyre (Figure 12.7).

FIGURE 12.2 Measurements of two consecutive axles on drawbar trailers – the same dimension applies to rigid vehicles – to determine if sideguards must be fitted

Not more than 3m
(no sideguards)

More than 3m
(sideguards required)

FIGURE 12.3 How force resistance applies to sideguard on new vehicles and trailers (it does not apply to sideguard fitted to existing semi-trailers)

Maximum deflection 150mm

Force resistance 200kg (2 kilonewtons)

Last 250mm

Maximum deflection 30mm

FIGURE 12.4 Fitting position for sideguard on rigid vehicles

Maximum 300mm

Maximum 300mm

In all cases sideguards must be fitted so they are not inset more than 30 mm from the external face of the tyre, excluding any distortion due to the weight of the vehicle (Figure 12.8).

FIGURE 12.5 Fitting position for sideguard on trailers

Maximum 500mm   Maximum 300mm

FIGURE 12.6 Fitting position for sideguard on semi-trailers with landing legs

Maximum 250mm   Maximum 300mm

FIGURE 12.7 Fitting position for sideguard on semi-trailers without landing legs

Maximum 3m   Maximum 300mm

FIGURE 12.8 Inboard mounting position for sideguards – all vehicles and trailers

Inboard maximum 30mm from outer face of tyre

The upper edge of sideguards must be positioned as follows:

- In the case of vehicles or trailers with a body or structure that is wider than the tyres, no more than 350 mm from the lower edge of the body or structure (Figure 12.9).
- In the case of vehicles or trailers with a body or structure that is narrower than the tyres or that does not extend outwards immediately above the wheels, a vertical plane taken from the outer face of the tyre must be measured upwards for 1.85 metres above the ground. If this plane is dissected by the vehicle structure within 1.85 metres from the ground, the sideguard must extend up to within 350 mm of the structure where it is cut by the vertical plane (Figure 12.11); if the vertical plane is not dissected by the vehicle structure, the upper edge of the sideguard must extend to be level with the top of the vehicle structure to a minimum height of 1.5 metres from the ground (Figure 12.10).

The lower edge of sideguards must not be more than 550 mm from the ground. This dimension is to be measured on level ground and, in the case of a semi-trailer, when its load platform is horizontal.

When sideguards are to be fitted to extendible trailers and to vehicles and trailers designed to carry demountable bodies or containers, the following fitting provisions apply:

- Sideguards must be fitted to extendible trailers in compliance with the original fitting specifications in regard to spacings from the nearest wheel, kingpin or landing leg when the trailer is at its shortest length. When the trailer is extended beyond its minimum length the spacings between the front edge of the sideguard and the semi-trailer landing legs or kingpin (if it has no landing legs) and the rear edge of the sideguard and the foremost edge of the tyre nearest to it are no longer applicable.
- Sideguards must be fitted to vehicles and trailers that are designed and constructed (not merely adapted) to carry demountable bodies or containers so that when the body or container is removed the sideguards remain in place.

This means that if the vehicle runs without a body or container it must still comply with the sideguard requirements.

Vehicles that are fitted with sideguards complying with EC Directive 89/279 do not have to comply with the fitting requirements specified in the UK regulations as detailed above.

Construction of Sideguards

All parts of the sideguard that face outwards must be 'smooth, essentially rigid and either flat or horizontally corrugated'. Each face of the guard must be a minimum of 100 mm wide (including the inward face at the forward edge) and the vertical gaps between the bars must not be more than 300 mm wide.

FIGURE 12.9 Fitting position for sideguards where body or structure is wider than the tyres

FIGURE 12.10 Fitting position for sideguards where body or structure is narrower than the tyres up to a height of 1.85 metres

FIGURE 12.11 Fitting position for sideguards where body or structure is narrower than the tyres

Maintenance of Sideguards

Sideguards must be maintained free of any obvious defect that would impair their effectiveness. It is important to ensure that the fitting dimensions are observed, particularly when the sideguards are damaged (eg by forklift truck impact).

Exemption to Fitting Dimensions

The specific requirements relating to the fitting positions for sideguards as previously described only apply so far as is practicable in the case of the following vehicles and trailers:

- Those designed solely for the carriage of a fluid substance in closed tanks permanently fitted to the vehicle and provided with valves and hose or pipe connections for loading and unloading.
- Those vehicles that require additional stability during loading and unloading or while working and which are fitted with extendible stabilizers on either side (eg lorry-mounted cranes, tower wagons, inspection platforms).

Exemptions

Sideguards do not have to be fitted to vehicles and trailers in the following list:

- vehicles incapable of a speed of more than 15 mph on the level under their own power;
- agricultural trailers;
- engineering plant;
- fire engines;
- land tractors;
- side and end tipping vehicles and trailers;
- vehicles with no bodywork fitted and being driven or towed for the purposes of a quality or safety check by the manufacturer, distributor or dealer in such vehicles, or being driven by prior arrangement to have bodywork fitted;
- vehicles being driven or towed to a place by prior arrangement to have sideguards fitted;
- vehicles designed solely for use in connection with street cleansing, the collection or disposal of refuse or the collection or disposal of the contents of gullies or cesspools;
- trailers specially designed and constructed to carry round timber, beams or girders of exceptional length;
- articulated tractive units;
- naval, military or air-force vehicles;
- trailers specially designed and constructed (not merely adapted) to carry other vehicles loaded from the front or rear (eg car transporters);
- temporarily imported foreign semi-trailers;
- low-loader trailers where:
  - the upper surface of the load platform is not more than 750 mm from the ground; and
  - no part of the edge of the load platform is more than 60 mm inboard from the external face of the tyre (discounting the distortion caused by the weight of the vehicle).

Silencer

An adequate means of silencing exhaust noise and of preventing exhaust gases escaping into the atmosphere without first passing through a silencer must be fitted to all vehicles. Silencers must be maintained in good and efficient working order and must not be altered so as to increase the noise made by the escape of exhaust gases.

Speedometer

Speedometers (and/or tachographs, as appropriate – see Chapter 5) must be fitted to all vehicles registered since 1 October 1937 except those that cannot or are not permitted to travel at more than 25 mph, agricultural vehicles that are not driven at more than 20 mph and works trucks first used before 1 April 1984. In the case of vehicles first used since 1 April 1984 the speedometer must indicate speed in both miles per hour and kilometres per hour. The instrument must be maintained in good working order at all material times and kept free from any obstruction that might prevent it being easily read.

Defence

It is a defence to be able to show that a defect to a speedometer or a tachograph occurred during the journey when the offence was detected or that at that time steps had been taken to get the defect repaired with all reasonable expedition (ie as soon as reasonably practicable).

Speed Limiters

In a move to reduce the number and severity of road accidents, legislation requires certain heavy vehicles to be fitted with speed limiters. The Government says that this will also have beneficial effects for operators in terms of fuel economy – possibly saving as much as 150 million litres annually when all relevant vehicles are fitted – and benefit the environment by an annual reduction of an estimated 0.5 million tonnes of carbon monoxide (CO) pumped, by way of exhaust emission, into the atmosphere. At the same time, the EU requires certain vehicles also to be fitted with speed limiters set to a maximum of 90 kph (approx 56 mph), and this has led to no end of confusion since the two sets of requirements do not align.

The UK regulations, which came into effect on 1 August 1992, limit relevant vehicles to a maximum speed of 60 mph (ie 96.5 kph). They apply to all new goods vehicles exceeding 7.5 tonnes permissible maximum weight that are capable of a speed in excess of 60 mph on the flat and which were first registered on or after 1 August 1992.

Vehicles not capable of travelling at or above 60 mph (eg refuse collection and certain highway maintenance vehicles) are exempt from the regulations, as are the following vehicles:

- those being taken to a place to have a speed-limiter device fitted or calibrated;
- those owned and being used by the army, navy or air force;

- those being used for military purposes while driven by a person under military orders;
- those being used for fire brigade, ambulance or police purposes;
- those exempt from excise duty because they do not travel more than 6 miles per week on public roads.

Speed limiter equipment must comply with BS AU 217 (or an acceptable equivalent), be calibrated to a set speed not exceeding 60 mph and be sealed by an 'authorized sealer'. Existing speed limiters, fitted on a voluntary basis prior to 1 August 1992, were permitted and did not have to be sealed by an 'authorized sealer' as stated above.

Speed limiters must be maintained in good working order, though it is a defence to show that where a vehicle is driven with a defective limiter, the defect occurred during that journey or that at the time it is being driven to a place for the limiter to be repaired.

EU Requirements

The speed limiter requirements of EC Directive 92/6/EEC apply from 1 January 1994 and require new goods vehicles first registered from this date and which exceed 12 tonnes gross weight to be fitted with speed limiters. Speed limiters should be set at a speed of not more than 85 kph (52.8 mph), allowing a stabilized speed of not more than 90 kph (56.0 mph).

Speed Limiter Plates

Vehicles that are required to be fitted with speed limiter equipment must carry a plate (fitted in a conspicuous and readily accessible position in the vehicle cab) on which is shown the words:

- 'SPEED LIMITER FITTED' (in large letters at the top);
- the Standard with which the installation complies (eg BS AU 217 Part 1A 1987);
- the speed setting in mph/kph;
- the vehicle registration number;
- the name/trademark of the firm which carried out the calibration; and
- the place where the speed limiter was fitted and the date of fitment.

Plates that refer to a maximum speed of 56 mph must be changed (as of 1 September 1997) to show 85 kph. Normally replacement plates will be supplied (free of charge) by VOSA when relevant vehicles are presented for their annual test after this date.

Warning – Penalties in France

It is reported that the French authorities are imposing stringent penalties where vehicles are found to have defective or incorrectly set speed limiters (ie above the 85 kph legal limit). These include substantial fines and the need for the vehicle to undergo a French-style annual goods vehicle test. This is resulting in long delays for those operators affected.

Speed Limiters for Larger Vans and Light Trucks

Since 1 January 2007 all goods vehicles over 3,500 kg gvw fitted with Euro-III engines and first registered from 1 October 2001 to 31 December 2004 should have been fitted with a speed limiter calibrated to a maximum speed not exceeding 56 mph (90 kph). Euro-III vehicles already have the facility to have a top speed limiter built into the engine electronic control unit, thus ensuring that the calibration procedure does not involve the fitment of brackets, air cylinders or piping.

The same date, 1 January 2007, is also the date from which over 3.5 tonne gross weight vans have been prohibited from using the outside lane of a three- or more lane motorway.

Spray Suppression

Regulations require certain vehicles and trailers to be equipped with anti-spray devices. The following vehicles and trailers must be fitted with approved equipment from the dates shown:

- Motor vehicles over 12 tonnes gross weight made on or after 1 October 1985 and first used on or after 1 April 1986. Fitment required from date when vehicle first used on road from 1 April 1986.
- Trailers over 3.5 tonnes gross weight made on or after 1 May 1985. Fitment required from date trailer first used on road from new.
- Trailers over 16 tonnes gross weight with two or more axles.

Exemptions

Anti-spray requirements do not apply to those vehicles and trailers that are fitted with such devices in accordance with EC Directive 91/226 (and marked accordingly) and to those that are exempt under the C&U regulations from the need for wings. Further exemptions are as follows:

- four-wheel and multi-wheel drive vehicles;
- vehicles with a minimum of 400 mm (approximately 16 in) ground clearance in the middle 80 per cent of the width and the overall length of the vehicle;
- works trucks;
- works trailers;
- broken-down vehicles;
- vehicles that cannot exceed 30 mph on the level under their own power owing to their construction;
- vehicles specified in regulations as exempt from sideguards:
  - agricultural trailers and implements;
  - engineering plant;
  - fire engines;
  - side and end tippers;
  - military vehicles used for military, naval or air-force purposes;

    – vehicles with no bodywork fitted being driven on road test or being driven by prior appointment to a place where bodywork is to be fitted or for delivery;

    – vehicles used for street cleansing, or the collection or disposal of the contents of gullies or cesspools;

    – trailers designed and constructed to carry round timber, beams or girders of exceptional length;

    – temporarily imported foreign semi-trailers;

- concrete mixers;
- vehicles being driven to a place by prior arrangement to have anti-spray equipment fitted;
- land locomotives, land tractors and land implement conveyors;
- trailers forming part of an articulated vehicle or part of a combination of vehicles having, in either case, a total laden weight exceeding 46,000 kg.

British Standard

The British Standard on spray suppression was originally contained in two documents, BS AU 200 (parts 1 and 2) 1984, which applied to vehicles fitted before 1 May 1987 and has now been replaced by BS AU 200 (parts 1a and 2a) 1986, which apply to fitment since this date. The regulations require anti-spray devices to conform to the Standard set out in these documents. However, there is no requirement for existing equipment fitted to the requirements of the original BS AU Standard to be changed to equipment that meets the new BS AU Standard.

In order to comply with the law, relevant vehicles and trailers must be fitted with anti-spray systems that fall into one of two main categories:

- a straight valance across the top of the wheel and a flap hanging vertically behind the wheel, all made from approved spray-suppressant material; or
- a semicircular valance following the curvature of the wheel with either:
  - air/water separator material round the edge; or
  - a flap of spray suppressant material hanging from the rear edge.

Spray-Suppressant Material

Two types of material are referred to in the Standard. These are generally identifiable as follows:

- spray-suppressant material – designed to absorb or dissipate the energy of water thrown up from the tyre in order to reduce the degree to which water shatters into fine droplets on hitting a surface;
- air/water separator – 'a device forming part of the valance and/or wheel flap which permits air to flow through while reducing the emission of spray'.

Maintenance of Anti-spray Equipment and Devices

The regulations stipulate that all devices fitted to comply with the legal requirement (and every part of such a device) must be maintained, when the vehicle is on the road, so that they are free from 'any obvious defect which would be likely to affect adversely the effectiveness of the device'. It is also important that fitting dimensions are maintained, especially if the flaps are damaged.

Fitment – Valances and Flaps

Where the choice is for spray suppression to be achieved by the use of valances and flaps (particularly on rear vehicle wheels and trailer wheels) the specific requirements for fitment are as follows:

NB: Capital letters in brackets in the following text refer to items on the adjacent diagrams illustrating fitment details.

- Valances of spray suppressant material must extend across the top of the tyre from a line vertical with the front edge of the tyre (A) to a line beyond the rear wheel which will allow the rear flap to be suspended no more than 300 mm from the rear edge of the tyre (B). The valance must be at least 100 mm deep (C).

- The valance must extend downwards to be level with the top of the tyre (D) or it may overlap the top of the tyre (E).

- In the case of multiple-axle bogies the relevant dimensions are shown below with the additional requirement that where the gap between the rear edge of the front tyre and the front edge of the rear tyre is greater than 250 mm (F) a flap must be fitted between the two. *Note: No middle flap is required if the distance does not exceed 250 mm.*

NB: The top of the valance may be in two separate sections (see shaded part) so long as it otherwise conforms to the dimensions.

This section
can be omitted

F
More than
250mm

Maximum
300mm

- Valances must extend the full width of the tyre and beyond to a maximum of 75 mm (G) in the case of the rear wheels (non-steerable) and 100 mm (H) in the case of steered wheels.

Rear wheels

Steered wheels

G
Maximum
75mm

H
Maximum
100mm

- If the valance extends below the level of the tyre on fixed wheels, the gap between the tyre face and the valance can be extended to 100 mm (J). There must be no gaps between the valance and the vehicle body.

- Flaps used in conjunction with valances as described above must conform to the following dimensions:
  - They must extend to the full width of the tyre/tyres (K).
  - They must reach down to within 200 mm of the ground (L) when the vehicle is unladen (300 mm on rearmost axles of trailers used on roll-on/ roll-off ferries or on any axle where the radial distance of the lower edge of the valancing does not exceed the radius of the tyres fitted).

- When flaps are used in conjunction with mudguard valances the top of the flap must extend upwards at least to a point 100 mm above the centre line of the wheel irrespective of the position of the lower edge of the mudguard.

Flap used in conjunction with mudguard valance

- Where the flap extends inside the guard it must be at least the width of the tyre tread pattern.
- If the flap used is of a type with an air/water separator device (ie bristles) fitted to the bottom edge, the following dimensions apply:
  - Rear edge of tyre to flap – maximum distance 200 mm (M).
  - The edge of the device must come to within 200 mm of the ground (N).

Deflection of Flaps

Wheel flaps must not be capable of being deflected rearwards more than 100 mm when subjected to a force of 3N (ie 4 lbs) applied near the bottom of the flap.

Fitment – Mudguards and Air/Water Separator Devices

Where the choice for compliance with the regulations is by means of conventional mudguarding there are specific dimensions to be observed:

- If the mudguard is covering a steerable wheel (see later note about steerable axles on drawbar trailers), the radius of the edge of the valance must be not more than 1.5 times the radius of the tyre measured at three points (P) and in the case of non-steerable wheels, 1.25 times the same radius.
  - Vertically above the centre of the tyre.
  - A point at the front of the tyre 20 degrees above the horizontal centre line of the tyre (non-steerable wheels) or a point 30 degrees above the horizontal centre line of the tyre (steerable wheels).

– A point at the rear of the tyre 100 mm above the horizontal centre line of the tyre.

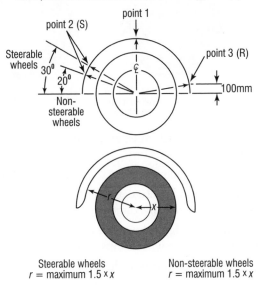

Three points of measurement of radial for mudguards (P)

Steerable wheels
r = maximum 1.5 × x

Non-steerable wheels
r = maximum 1.5 × x

- Mudguard valances must be at least 45 mm deep behind a point vertically above the wheel centre. They may reduce in depth forward of this point (Q).

Depth of mudguard valances

45mm or less

Minimum 45mm

- In the case of drawbar trailers, the 1.5 times radius dimension applies as above for the front steerable axle unless the mudguards are fitted to the turntable and thus turn with the wheels, in which case the maximum radius for the valance is 1.25 times the tyre radius.
- If the valancing on fixed-wheel mudguards is provided by means of air/water separator material (ie bristles), the edge must follow the periphery of the tyre. On steerable wheels the edge must be not more than 1.05 times the tyre radius.

Fixed wheel   Steerable wheel

Edge of bristle
level with tyre
periphery

$r \times 1.05$

Edge of bristle
1.05 times
tyre radius

The valances on mudguards must extend downwards at the front and rear to at least the following dimensions:

– at rear – to within 100 mm above the centre line of the axle (point 3) (R).

– at front – to within a line 20 degrees above the centre line of the axle. In the case of steerable wheels this dimension is raised to 30 degrees (point 2) (S).

- In the case of multi-mudguarding over tandem axles or bogies, the intersection of the guards between the wheels must conform to one of the two dimensions:

  – The gap between the guards at the valance edges must not exceed 60 mm (T); or

  – The edges must come down to within 150 mm of the horizontal centre line across the wheels (V).

- If the gap between the tyre edges is greater than 250 mm, a flap must be provided between the wheels. If the gap is more than 300 mm, the wheels should be treated as though separate for mudguarding purposes (W).

Notes

- All dimensions in the regulations are to be taken when the vehicle is unladen, when steerable wheels are straight ahead and when the load platforms of articulated semi-trailers are level.

- All suppression material or devices and air/water separator material or devices must be permanently and legibly marked with the following mark: BS AU 200/2, plus 'the name, trademark or other means of identification of the responsible manufacturer'.

Tyres

It is an offence to use, or cause or permit to be used on a road, a vehicle or a trailer with a pneumatic tyre which is unsuitable for the use to which the vehicle is being put. It is also an offence to have different types of tyres fitted to opposite wheels of the vehicle or trailer; for example, radial-ply tyres must not be fitted to a wheel on the same axle as wheels already fitted with cross-ply tyres and vice versa. Tyres must be inflated to the vehicle or tyre manufacturers' recommended pressures so as to be fit for the use to which the vehicle is being put (for example, motorway work or cross-country work). No tyre must have a break in its fabric or a cut deep enough to reach the body cords, more than 25 mm or 10 per cent of its section width in length, whichever is the greater; also there must be no lump, bulge or tear caused by separation or partial fracture of its structure; neither must there be any portion of the ply or cord structure exposed.

Approval Marks on Tyres

It is an offence to sell motor car tyres unless they carry an 'E' mark to show compliance with EU load and speed requirements. It is also an offence to sell retreaded car or lorry tyres unless they are manufactured and marked in accordance with British Standard BS AU 144b 1977.

Since 1 October 1990 it has been a requirement for tyres on heavy goods vehicles to show load and speed markings in accordance with UN ECE Regulation 30 or 54. It is a legal requirement that these limits of both loading and speed performance are strictly observed. Failure to do so can result in prosecution and could invalidate insurance claims in the event of an accident to a vehicle loaded above the weight limit of the tyres or travelling at a speed in excess of the tyre limit.

Tread Depth

All tyres on goods vehicles of over 3,500 kg gross weight must have a tread depth of at least 1 mm across three-quarters of the breadth of the tread and around the entire circumference of the tyre. This 1 mm tread depth must be in a continuous band around the entire circumference of the tyre. Further, on the remaining one-quarter of the width of the tyre where there is no requirement for the tread to be 1 mm deep, the base of the original grooves must be clearly visible.

The minimum tread depth for cars, light vans (not exceeding 3,500 kg gross weight) and light trailers was increased to 1.6 millimetres from 1 January 1992, and this applies across the central three-quarters of the width of the tyre and in a continuous band around the entire circumference. The 1 mm limit stated above remains in force for heavy goods vehicles.

Re-cut Tyres

Re-cut tyres may be fitted to goods vehicles of over 2,540 kg unladen weight which have wheels of at least 405 mm rim diameter and to trailers weighing more than 1,020 kg unladen weight and electric vehicles. They must not be used on private cars, dual-purpose vehicles, goods vehicles or trailers of less than the weight or wheel size specified.

Run-Flat and Temporary Use Spare Tyres

The regulations permit the legal use of 'run-flat' tyres in a partially inflated or flat condition and what are described as temporary-use spare tyres. This is of more consequence to motor car users because the only tyres of the former (ie run-flat) type currently available are designed for a limited range of private cars (eg Dunlop Denovo tyres). Where a temporary-use spare tyre is being used the vehicle speed must not exceed 50 mph otherwise the legal provision which permits their use ceases to apply. The temporary use spare tyre or the wheel to which it is fitted must be of a different colour to the other wheels on the vehicle and a label must be attached to the wheel giving clear information about the precautions to be observed when using the wheel.

Lightweight Trailer Tyres

Tyres fitted to lightweight trailers since 1 April 1987 must be designed and maintained to support the maximum axle weight at its maximum permitted speed (ie 60 mph).

Front Under-run Protection

Since August 2003 it is a requirement under EC Directive 2000/40/EC that all goods vehicles exceeding 3.5 tonnes gross weight should be fitted with an approved form of front under-run protection (ie bumper) system (FUPS). This bumper must extend to the full width of the vehicle, must be fitted no higher than 400 mm from the ground when the vehicle is unladen and must meet the same strength requirements specified for rear under-run bumpers (see below). Vehicles over 16 tonnes gross weight used for off-road purposes (ie principally tippers – in European category N2 and N3) and vehicles whose 'use is incompatible with the provisions of front under-run protection' are exempt from the legal requirements.

Rear Under-run Bumpers

Rear under-run bumpers (referred to in legislation as rear under-run protection) must be fitted to most rigid goods vehicles over 3.5 tonnes gross weight manufactured since 1 October 1983 and first used since 1 April 1984. Trailers, including semi-trailers, over 1,020 kg unladen weight manufactured since 1 May 1983 must also be fitted with bumpers. Certain vehicles and trailers are exempt (see below) from the fitting requirements and there were no retrospective fitting requirements for existing vehicles.

Strength of Bumpers

Rear under-run bumpers must be constructed so they are capable of withstanding a force equivalent to half the gross weight of the vehicle or trailer or a maximum of 10 tonnes, whichever is the *lesser*, without deflecting more than 400 mm measured from the rearmost point of the vehicle or trailer – not from the original vertical position of the bumper.

Fitment of Bumpers

Bumpers must be fitted as near as possible to the rear of the vehicle and the lower edge must be not more than 550 mm from the ground (see Figure 12.12). Normally, only one bumper would be fitted, but where a tail-lift is fitted or the bodywork or other parts of the vehicle make this impracticable, two or more bumpers may be fitted. When a single full-width bumper is fitted it must extend on each side of the centre to within at least 100 mm from the outermost width of the rear axle, but must not in any case extend beyond the width of the rear axle measured across the outermost face of the tyres. When two or more bumpers are fitted, for the reasons mentioned above, the space between each part of the bumper must not exceed 500 mm and the outermost edge of the bumpers must extend to within at least 300 mm from the outermost width of the rear axle (see Figure 12.13). Bumpers must not protrude beyond the width of the vehicle or trailer and the outside ends of the bumper must not be bent backwards.

Maintenance of Bumpers

Rear bumpers must be maintained free from any obvious defect that would adversely affect their performance in giving resistance to impact from the rear. It is also important to ensure that the dimensional requirements are met, particularly if the bumper is damaged (for example by forklift truck impact or reversing on to loading bays).

Exemptions

Rear under-run bumpers do not have to be fitted to vehicles and trailers in the following list:

- vehicles incapable of a speed exceeding 15 mph on the level under their own power;
- tractive units of articulated vehicles;;
- agricultural trailers, trailed appliances and agricultural motor vehicles;
- engineering plant;
- fire engines;
- road spreading vehicles (ie for salt and grit);
- rear tipping vehicles;

FIGURE 12.12 Illustration of the rear under-run bumper force resistance requirements and ground clearance dimension

FIGURE 12.13 Illustrations of the fitting dimensions for single and multiple rear under-run bumpers

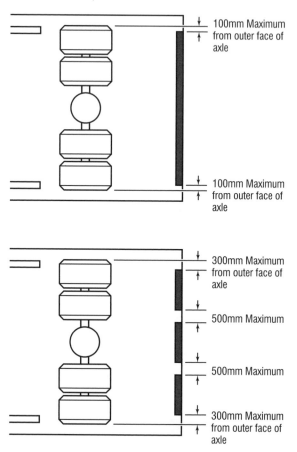

- military, naval or air-force vehicles;
- vehicles being taken to have bodywork fitted, or being taken for quality or safety checks by the manufacturer, distributor or dealer in such vehicles;
- vehicles being driven or towed to a place to have a rear under-run bumper fitted by prior arrangement;
- vehicles designed to carry other vehicles which are loaded from the rear (eg car transporters);
- trailers designed and constructed (not just adapted) to carry round timber, beams or girders of exceptional length;
- vehicles fitted with tail-lifts where the tail-lift forms part of the floor of the vehicle and extends to a length of at least 1 metre;
- temporarily imported foreign vehicles and semi-trailers;

- vehicles specially designed (not just adapted) for carrying and mixing liquid concrete;

- vehicles designed and used solely for the delivery of coal by means of a conveyor fixed to the vehicle so as to make the fitment of a rear under-run bumper impracticable.

View to the Front

Drivers must have a full view of the road and traffic ahead at all times when driving. Obstructing the windscreen with mascots, stickers, stone guards and other such things could result in prosecution and/or failure of the vehicle when it is presented for annual test.

Vehicles with closed-circuit television (CCTV) rear-view monitors mounted in the cab in such a position that the driver's view to the front is obscured, or partly obscured, will be failed in their annual test by VOSA. This particularly applies to refuse collectors and ambulances, which traditionally use such equipment (see also pp 344–45).

Windscreen Wipers and Washers

Windscreen Wipers

All vehicles must be fitted with one or more efficient automatic windscreen wipers capable of clearing the windscreen to provide the driver with an adequate view to the front and sides of the vehicle. They must be maintained in good and efficient working order and must be adjusted properly. This provision does not apply if the driver has an adequate view of the road without looking through the windscreen.

Windscreen Washers

Vehicles required to be fitted with windscreen wipers must be fitted with a windscreen washer that is capable, in conjunction with the wipers, of clearing the area of the windscreen swept by the wipers of mud or dirt. Washers are not required on land tractors, track-laying vehicles and vehicles that cannot travel at more than 20 mph.

A vehicle should not be driven on the road with defective windscreen wipers or washers. This is an offence which could result in a fine of up to £1,000 (as with many other C&U regulation offences).

Wings

Goods vehicles and trailers must be fitted with wings to catch, as far as practicable, mud and water thrown up by the wheels unless adequate protection is provided by the bodywork.

Articulated vehicles and trailers used for carrying round timber are exempt from these requirements in respect of all except the front wheels of the tractive unit. Vehicles and trailers in an unfinished condition that are proceeding to a bodybuilder for work to be completed and works trucks are also exempt from the need to have wings.

Use of Vehicles

In addition to the foregoing constructional requirements, which are mainly the responsibility of the vehicle manufacturer or the person building the bodywork, there are requirements regarding the use of vehicles which are the responsibility of the operator. However, as mentioned earlier, the vehicle user carries full legal responsibility for the mechanical condition of a vehicle on the road and its compliance with the constructional requirements even if the fault which led to an offence could be laid at the door of the chassis manufacturer, the bodybuilder, an ancillary equipment supplier or the dealer.

These requirements cover such items as vehicle weights (which were dealt with earlier), towing, fumes, the condition and maintenance of vehicles and their components, noise, smoke, and general safety in the use of vehicles. They also include the regulations regarding the number of trailers which a vehicle may draw.

Gas-Powered Vehicles

Regulations specify technical standards for fuel tanks or containers, the filling system and valves and general requirements for gas propulsion systems in motor vehicles. The regulations permit the use of LPG only in gas-propelled vehicles, though this may be combined with petrol fuel systems, and the use of methane or hydrogen is prohibited. The DfT has published a free guide *Gas Installations in Motor Vehicles and Trailers*, which is available from: Department for Transport, B3, Victoria Road, South Ruislip, Middlesex HA4 0NZ.

A new article (17A) and new schedules (5A and 5B) to the Motor Vehicles (Authorisation of Special Types) General Order 1979 – inserted by virtue of Amendment No 2 of 1 December 1998 to the Order – authorize the use on roads of vehicles propelled by compressed natural gas (CNG), notwithstanding that they do not comply with the requirements of the C&U regulations. They must, however, comply with the provisions of the new schedules as to constructional requirements and the requirements for testing gas containers used in these systems.

Noise

It is an offence to use, or cause or permit to be used, on a road a motor vehicle or trailer which causes an excessive noise because of a defect, lack of repair or faulty adjustment of components or load. Also, no motor vehicle must be used on a road in such a manner as to cause any excessive noise which could have been reasonably avoided by the driver. Noise for these purposes is the combined noise emitted by the exhaust plus that from the tyres, engine, bodywork and equipment, and the load. Noise levels for goods vehicles are measured by special meters either by the police or by VOSA examiners at goods vehicle testing stations and occasionally on roadside tests. The noise measured is that of the 'whole' vehicle, not just the exhaust and engine.

Noise Limits

It is no longer a legal requirement for goods vehicles to maintain the noise standards set when the vehicle was manufactured. The regulations covering noise emissions are adequately covered under other provisions (see above).

Reversing Alarms

It is legally permissible to fit reversing alarms to certain goods and passenger vehicles if desired – *the regulations do not make it mandatory to do so*. Such alarms may be voluntarily fitted and used on the following vehicles:

- commercial vehicles over 2 tonnes gross weight;
- passenger vehicles with nine or more seats;
- engineering plant;
- works trucks.

Time Restriction on Use of Reversing Alarms

The alarms are subject to the same night-time restrictions that apply to the sounding of horns in built-up areas (ie not after 11.30 pm and before 7.00 am – 23.30 to 07.00) and the sound emitted must not be capable of being confused with the pelican crossing 'safe to cross' signal.

Restriction on Fitment of Reversing Alarms

Such alarms *must not* be fitted to light goods vehicles below 2 tonnes gross weight or to motor cars.

Advice on Use of Alarms

A number of cases have arisen following reversing accidents resulting in death or injury where the Health and Safety Executive has prosecuted the vehicle operators concerned for not voluntarily fitting reversing alarms. In other words, the HSE line is that the offenders had not taken sufficient steps to ensure safety when their vehicles were reversing by fitting equipment which the law permits, but does not mandatorily require, them to do.

Televisions in Vehicles

It is illegal for a vehicle to be fitted with television receiving apparatus where the driver can see the screen either directly or by reflection, except where such equipment displays nothing other than information:

- about the state of the vehicle or its equipment;
- about the location of the vehicle and the road on which it is located;
- to assist the driver to see the road adjacent to the vehicle (eg to the rear when reversing); or

- to assist the driver to reach his destination.

NB: *See also p 343.*

Towing

Goods vehicles may draw (ie tow) only one trailer. An exception to this is when a rigid goods vehicle tows a broken-down vehicle on a towing ambulance or dolly, in which case although this is counted as towing two trailers it is allowed. In a case where an articulated vehicle has broken down, this may be towed by a rigid goods vehicle so long as the articulated vehicle is not loaded. In these circumstances the outfit is treated as one trailer only, but if it is loaded, an articulated outfit being towed is considered to be two trailers and it would be illegal for a normal goods vehicle (ie a heavy motor car) to tow it. Only a locomotive can tow a broken-down articulated vehicle which is laden (see below).

Motor tractors may draw one laden or two unladen trailers, and locomotives may draw three trailers (see p 310 for definitions).

Composite Trailers

The C&U regulations make it permissible for rigid goods vehicles (apart from locomotives and motor tractors) to draw two trailers instead of only one, when one of the trailers is a towing implement (ie a dolly) and the other is an articulated-type semi-trailer secured to and resting on, or suspended from, the dolly. This combination of dolly and semi-trailer is known as a composite trailer (Figure 12.14).

To comply with the regulations, the dolly needs to have two or more wheels and be specifically designed to support a superimposed semi-trailer. Dollies must display a manufacturer's plate and they are subject to the annual heavy goods vehicle test.

Towing Distance

The distance between the nearest points of two vehicles joined by a tow rope or chain must not exceed 4.5 metres. When the distance between the two vehicles exceeds 1.5 metres the rope, chain or bar must be made clearly visible from both sides of the vehicles. There is no specified maximum distance limit if a solid tow bar is used for towing.

FIGURE 12.14 A conventional six-wheeled rigid vehicle drawing a dolly mounted semi-trailer for which the maximum overall length is 18.35 metres

Maximum length 18.35m

Trailer and Semi-Trailer Coupling and Uncoupling

Over time, the procedure of coupling and uncoupling trailers and semi-trailers has proved to be a high-risk activity, prone to accident and dangerous incident, unfortunately costing far too many lives. In 2006 a new Code of Practice was launched by the Society of Operations Engineers (SOE) in conjunction with the Institute of Road Transport Engineers (IRTE) and the Health and Safety Executive (HSE) in an effort to ensure that safe practices are adopted and followed by drivers and others when carrying out this high-risk procedure. The Code is divided into five sections dealing with safe procedures for standard and close-coupled semi-trailers and both centre-axle and turntable drawbar trailers.

The Code has particular relevance due to the latest developments in corporate killing legislation, in which failure by employers to ensure that safe practices are adopted can lead to company bosses facing charges in the event of such fatal accidents in work scenarios. Copies of the Code are available from the SOE and online at: **www.soe.org.uk**.

Type Approval

Type Approval is a scheme which requires vehicle manufacturers to submit new vehicles (ie new designs, new models and changes of specifications for existing approved models) for approval before they are put on the market. The Department for Transport examines the vehicle submitted to ensure that it meets all legal requirements and also meets minimum standards of construction and performance. When a vehicle has been approved the manufacturer is then required by law to build all vehicles of a similar type to exactly those standards and certify this fact to the customer by the issue of a Certificate of Conformity.

An EU directive lays down the basic procedures for the Type Approval scheme for vehicles and components. Subsidiary directives have also been issued setting out agreed standards on some aspects of vehicle safety or pollution. They cover the same ground as existing national regulations. The directives do not yet cover all vehicle features which need to be regulated so until the programme is complete both EU directives and national regulations apply to relevant items. The UK established a non-compulsory scheme to enable exporting vehicle manufacturers to gain the necessary Type Approval in order to sell their products in EU countries.

Vehicles Covered

EC approval of most road vehicles is based around a 'Whole Vehicle' framework directive, Directive 70/156/EEC as most recently amended by Directive 2007/46/EC – implemented in all EU member states from 29 April 2009 – which specifies the range of aspects of the vehicle that must be approved under separate technical directives. In order to gain EC whole vehicle type approval, a vehicle must first be approved in regard to its brakes, emissions, noise, etc – in fact, up to 48 different standards for a typical vehicle. The issuing of the whole vehicle approval does not in itself involve testing, but a *production* sample of the complete vehicle is inspected to check that its specification matches the specifications contained in all the separate directive approvals.

Broadly, the whole vehicle framework document covers any vehicle with four or more wheels intended for use on roads, except agricultural or forestry tractors, mobile machinery, and vehicles with a design maximum speed of less than 25 kph. Separate technical directives and regulations allow (or require) the approval of individual systems as part of a type of vehicle and some allow for the approval of separate devices. System and component approval requires that a sample of the type to be approved is tested by the Technical Service to the requirements of the relevant Directive. Its technical specification is documented and that specification forms part of the approval.

Exemptions from Type Approval

Type Approval does not apply to the following vehicles:

- vehicles manufactured before 1 October 1982, whenever they are first registered;
- vehicles manufactured on or after 1 October 1982, providing they were first licensed before 1 April 1983;
- temporarily imported vehicles;
- vehicles proceeding for export from the UK;
- vehicles in the service of visiting forces or headquarters;
- certain vehicles which are, or were formerly, in use in the public service or the Crown;
- prototypes which are not intended for general use on the roads;
- motor tractors, light locomotives and heavy locomotives;
- engineering plant, pedestrian-controlled vehicles, straddle carriers, works trucks and track-laying vehicles;
- vehicles specially designed and constructed for use in private premises for moving excavated materials, vehicles fitted with movable platforms and vehicles designed and constructed for the carriage of abnormal indivisible loads;
- tower wagons;
- fire engines;
- roadrollers;
- steam-propelled vehicles;
- vehicles constructed for the purpose of preventing or reducing the effect of snow or ice on roads;
- two-wheeled motorcycles with or without sidecars;

- electrically propelled vehicles;
- breakdown vehicles;
- any vehicle not exceeding 3,500 kg maximum gross weight which is constructed or assembled by a person not ordinarily engaged in the manufacture of goods vehicles of that description;
- vehicles not exceeding 3,500 kg maximum gross weight provided that:
  - the vehicle has been purchased outside the UK for the personal use of the individual importing it or his dependants;
  - the vehicle has been so used by that individual or his dependants on roads outside the UK before it is imported;
  - the vehicle is intended solely for such personal use in the UK; and
  - the individual importing the vehicle intends, at the time when the vehicle is imported, to remain in the UK for not less than 12 months from that date.

Responsibility for Compliance

Responsibility for complying with the complex construction standards rests with the manufacturer although users are still responsible for maintaining vehicles in roadworthy condition. The construction standards applied by the scheme are limited to those which can be approved during the primary stage of manufacture. The standards are identical to those already required under the Construction and Use Regulations but under this scheme vehicles have to be approved before they can be used on the road.

Effects on Plating and Testing

The scheme requires plated weights for heavy goods vehicles to be set during the Type Approval process instead of waiting until the first annual plating and testing examination. This means that heavy vehicle operators need a Type Approval Certificate in order to get a Ministry plate for display in the vehicle cab (see Chapter 14). However, annual testing is retained so as to check the condition of vehicles and to ensure that plated weights are accurate.

Responsibility for Type Approval

All aspects of Type Approval are the responsibility of VOSA.

The Standards Checked

To obtain goods vehicle national Type Approval it is first necessary to obtain individual systems approvals for the following items:

- power-to-weight ratio (not applicable to petrol-engined vehicles or dual-purpose vehicles);
- gaseous exhaust emissions (petrol-engined vehicles only);
- particle emission (ie exhaust smoke) (diesel-engined vehicles only);
- external noise level;
- radio-interference suppression (petrol-engined vehicles only);
- brakes.

Arrangements for First Licensing of Vehicles

For vehicles over 1,525 kilograms unladen weight or which form part of an articulated vehicle, application for first licensing on form V55 must be accompanied by two copies of the Type Approval Certificate, which should have been supplied with the vehicle. On one of these the applicant must complete a declaration saying whether or not the vehicle is exempt from the plating and testing regulations (see Chapter 14 for full details) and whether it has been altered in any way that has to be notified to VOSA under the Type Approval regulations and, if so, whether any action arising from the notification has been satisfactorily completed.

Issue of Plates

When application is made for first licensing a vehicle which is subject to plating and testing, the local Vehicle Registration Office (VRO) will send a copy of the Type Approval Certificate with the applicant's declaration to the Goods Vehicle Centre (GVC) at Swansea. The second copy will be stamped and returned to the applicant to serve as a temporary Ministry plate. When the GVC receives the copy of the certificate, and if the details compare satisfactorily with those on the copy sent direct by the vehicle manufacturers, it will issue a Ministry plate and laminated plating certificate. These will be sent direct to the person or company in whose name the vehicle is registered. Thus, operators buying new vehicles receive their first plate and plating certificate for the vehicle from the GVC at the time of licensing rather than from the goods vehicle testing station when the vehicle is presented for its first annual test as under previous arrangements. When application is made for licensing a vehicle which is exempt from plating and testing, a copy of the certificate and the declaration will be sent to the GVC so that it is aware that it is exempt.

Refusal to Licence

Since 1 April 1983 no vehicle subject to the Type Approval regulations will be first licensed unless the DVLA registration form V55 has a valid Type Approval number on it or it is an exempt vehicle.

Alteration to Vehicles

If a vehicle which has been issued with an Approval Certificate and supplied to a dealer or direct to an operator is modified by them, prior to first licensing, they must notify the Vehicles and Components Approvals Division (VCA) at Bristol and send the certificate for the vehicle together with a completed VTG10 form, full technical details, drawings of the alterations and details of the weights on the certificate which need, or may need, changing.

The VCA will judge whether the alterations affect the vehicle's compliance with the regulations; if they do not affect compliance the certificate will be returned so the vehicle can be licensed. If they do contravene compliance, the certificate will be cancelled and fresh approval will need to be obtained before the vehicle can be licensed. This is a complex and costly procedure that most operators will want to avoid; they can do so by registering and licensing the vehicle before any alterations are carried out.

Vehicle Lighting and Marking

The legal requirements for vehicles to be fitted with and to display lights at night and other times, and for the fitment of reflectors and other markings on vehicles, are contained in the Road Vehicles Lighting Regulations 1989 (as amended). These regulations specify in considerable detail all the requirements for the position of lamps and reflectors and the angles from which they must be visible. This chapter can only include a summary of the relevant requirements and dimensions as they apply to goods vehicles, which, for most normal purposes, is satisfactory because vehicles and trailers are generally ready-fitted with lamps and reflectors conforming to legal requirements when supplied from new. However, for a variety of reasons, operators may find it necessary to replace and relocate lamps from time to time when carrying out repairs and conversions, and at this time they are advised to check the regulations carefully to ensure strict compliance with the law. Not only can prosecution follow for incorrectly positioned or non-functioning lights and reflectors, but vehicles could fail their annual test on this account, which adds to operating costs and wastes time. There are also the safety considerations with the lives of both vehicle drivers and other road users at risk if vehicles are not showing correct or adequate lights.

The regulations require that lights and reflectors which are fitted to vehicles must be maintained so as to enable them to be driven on a road between sunset and sunrise (times are published in most daily and local newspapers), or in seriously reduced visibility between sunrise and sunset, or to be parked on a road between sunset and sunrise without contravening the regulations. All lights must be kept clean and in good working order. It is an offence to cause undue dazzle or discomfort to other road users by the use of lights or through their faulty adjustment, or to have defective or obscured lighting on a vehicle at any time. There is no longer a defence to a charge of having defective lights on a vehicle (see below).

Obligatory Lights

Between sunset and sunrise vehicles used on a public road must display the following obligatory lights, other lights and reflectors:

- two front position lamps (ie sidelamps) showing white lights to the front;
- two rear position lamps (ie rear lamps) showing red lights to the rear;
- two head lamps showing white lights to the front (alternatively, the light may be yellow);
- illumination for the rear number (ie registration) plate when the other vehicle lights are on;
- certain goods vehicles and trailers additionally require side marker lamps plus side-facing reflectors and rear reflective markings – see below;
- one or two red rear fog lamps on post-1 April 1980 vehicles;
- two red reflex retro-reflectors at the rear;
- end-outline marker lamps;
- any other lights or lighting devices with which the vehicle is fitted (eg stop lamps, hazard warning signals, running lamps, dim-dip devices and headlamp levelling devices).

It is illegal except in certain specified cases for a goods vehicle to show a white light to the rear (showing such a light when reversing and indirect illumination of the rear registration plate are permitted, for example) or a red light to the front.

Head lamps

Motor vehicles must be fitted with two head lamps capable of showing a white or yellow light to the front – both lamps must emit the same colour light. Head lamps must be either permanently dipped or fitted with dipping equipment. Vehicles first used since 1 April 1987 must have dim-dip lighting devices unless their lighting equipment complies with EU requirements (see below).

Head lamps must be mounted so that they are not lower than 500 mm from the ground and not higher than 1,200 mm. They must be placed on either side of the vehicle with their illuminated areas not more than 400 mm from the side of the vehicle. They must be equipped with bulbs or sealed-beam units of not less than 30 watts in the case of vehicles first used before 1 April 1986. For vehicles used since this date no minimum wattage requirement is specified.

Head lamp Exemptions

Certain vehicles are exempt from the head lamp requirements. These include vehicles with less than four wheels, pedestrian-controlled vehicles, agricultural implements, land tractors, works trucks, vehicles not capable of travelling at a speed of more than 6 mph and military vehicles.

Head lamps on Electric Vehicles

Electrically propelled goods vehicles with four or more wheels registered before October 1969 and electric vehicles with two or three wheels first used before 1 January 1972 and capable of a speed of more than 15 mph are required to comply with the head lamp requirements. Those electrically propelled vehicles which are incapable of speeds of more than 15 mph are exempt from the head lamp requirements.

Use of Head lamps

Head lamps must be adjusted so that they do not cause undue dazzle or discomfort to other road users. When vehicles which require head lamps are being driven on unlit roads between sunset and sunrise and in seriously reduced daytime visibility the head lamps must be illuminated. They must be switched off when the vehicle is stationary except at traffic stops.

Incorrect aim of vehicle headlights is reported to be one of the most common reasons for annual goods vehicle test failure. Correction can be effected by simple adjustment, or by changing bulbs – inconsistent filament positioning on some low-quality bulbs being a possible cause of incorrect headlight aim.

NB: Unlit roads are roads on which there are no street lamps or on which the street lamps are more than 200 yards apart.

Head lamps in Daylight

It is a legal requirement for vehicles to use side-position lights (ie sidelights) and dipped headlights when travelling in seriously reduced daytime visibility conditions such as in fog, smoke, heavy rain, spray or snow. If matching fog or fog and spot lights are fitted in pairs these may be used instead of headlights, but sidelights must still be used and the other vehicle lights must be on (eg side marker lights).

There is no specific definition of 'seriously reduced visibility' in the regulations.

It is left to drivers to judge whether it is advisable and sensible to use their lights to enable their vehicle to be seen by others.

Dim-Dip Lighting

Since 1 April 1987 newly registered vehicles must be fitted with dim-dip lighting devices which operate automatically when the obligatory lights of the vehicle are switched on and ensure that either 10 per cent (with halogen) or 15 per cent (with grading filament lamps) of the normal dipped beam intensity shows when the vehicle ignition key is switched on or the engine is running. The European Court of Justice has ruled that it is unfair for the British Government to legislate for the fitment of dim-dip lighting devices for vehicles which already comply with the EU Lighting Directive (EC 756/1976 as amended by EC 663/1991), which has no dim-dip requirement.

Front Position Lamps (sidelamps)

Two front position lamps (ie sidelamps) emitting a white light through a diffused lens must be fitted to all motor vehicles (with three or more wheels) and trailers (except those not more than 1,600 mm wide), those no longer than 2,300 mm (excluding the drawbar) built before 1 October 1985 and those used for carrying and launching boats. If such lamps are incorporated within a head lamp showing a yellow light then the side position lamps may be yellow. No minimum wattage is specified for these lights. The lights must be equal in height from the ground and mounted not more than 1,500 mm from the ground (in exceptional circumstances this height can be increased to 2,100 mm) in the case of vehicles first used on or after 1 April 1986 and 2,300 mm in other cases, and not more than 400 mm from the outer edge of the vehicle for vehicles first used since 1 April 1986 and 510 mm in other cases. No minimum height above the ground is specified.

Rear Position Lamps (rear lamps)

Two red rear position lamps (ie rear lamps) must be fitted to all motor vehicles and trailers. There is no specified wattage for these lights. They must be mounted not less than 350 mm and not more than 1,500 mm (2,100 mm in exceptional circumstances) from the ground. They must be at least 500 mm apart (no specified distance on pre-1 April 1986 registered vehicle) and not more than 400 mm (800 mm on pre-1 April 1986 registered vehicle) from the outside edge of the vehicle.

Stop Lamps

All goods vehicles (except those not capable of more than 25 mph) must be fitted with red stop lamps which are maintained in a clean condition and in good and efficient working order. Vehicles registered before 1 January 1971 need only one such lamp, which must be fitted at the centre or to the offside of the vehicle, although a second matching lamp may be fitted on the nearside. Vehicles registered since that date need two such lamps (specified wattage 15 to 36 watts except with pre-1 January 1971 registered vehicles) mounted not less than 350 mm from the ground and not more than 1,500 mm (in exceptional circumstances this may be increased to 2,100 mm) and they must be at least 400 mm apart. Such lamps must be visible horizontally from 45 degrees on either side and normally from 15 degrees above and below vertically (from only 5 degrees below where fitted less than 750 mm from the ground and only 10 degrees below when fitted not more than 1,500 mm from the ground).

Reversing Lamps

White reversing lamps (not more than two) may be fitted to vehicles provided they are only used while the vehicle is reversing and operate automatically only when reverse gear is selected. Alternatively, they may be operated manually by a switch (which serves no other purpose) in the driver's cab provided that a warning device indicates to the driver that the lights are illuminated. The lights must be adjusted so as not to cause dazzle to other road users. Such lamps when bearing an 'e' approval mark do not have to meet minimum wattage requirements but those without approval marks must not exceed 24 watts.

Number Plate Lamp

Rear number plates (ie registration plates) on vehicles must be indirectly illuminated when the other obligatory lamps on the vehicles are lit. The light must be white and must be shielded so that it only illuminates the number plate and does not show to the rear.

Rear Fog Lamps

Rear fog lamps (at least one, but two may be fitted) must be fitted to new vehicles and trailers manufactured on or after 1 October 1979 and first used since 1 April 1980. There is no legal requirement to fit such lamps on pre-1 October 1979 registered vehicles but if they are fitted voluntarily they must comply with the regulations in regard to mounting position, method of wiring and use.

Rear Fog Lamps on Articulated and Towing Vehicles

In the case of articulated combinations, the relevant date in this connection is the date of the older of the tractive unit or semi-trailer. Thus, if a post-April 1980 registered tractive unit is coupled to a pre-October 1979-built trailer there appears to be no legal requirement for the vehicle to carry rear fog lamps. This means there is no retrospective fitting requirement for such lamps on older trailers. A broken-down vehicle being towed does not need rear fog lamps. However, it is important to remember the dangers which arise if such a combination is used when the tractive unit or towing vehicle itself has rear fog lamps which would, in some instances, be visible to following motorists who, in bad visibility, might not be aware of some 12 metres of trailer or another vehicle on tow behind the lights.

Mounting of Rear Fog Lamps

Rear fog lamps must be mounted either singly in the centre or on the offside of the vehicle or in a matched pair not less than 250 mm and not more than 1,000 mm from the ground (in the case of agricultural vehicles this height limit is increased to 1,900 mm or in cases where, because of the shape of the vehicle, 1,000 mm is not practical it may be increased to 2,100 mm). The lamps must be at least 100 mm from existing stop lamps.

Restriction on Wiring of Rear Fog Lamps

The lights must be wired so that they only operate when the other statutory lights on the vehicle are switched on; they must not be wired into the brake/stop light circuit and the driver must be provided with an indicator to show him when the lights are in use.

Use of Rear Fog Lamps

The lights should only be used in conditions affecting the visibility of the driver (ie in fog, smoke, heavy rain or spray, snow, dense cloud, etc), when the vehicle is in motion or during an enforced stoppage (a motorway hold-up, for example). They must not cause dazzle. The *Highway Code* recommends these lights should not be used unless visibility is below 100 metres.

Side Marker Lamps

Side marker lamps must be fitted on vehicles and trailers as follows:

- Vehicles first used on or after 1 April 1991 and trailers made from 1 October 1990 and being over 6 metres long:
  - one lamp on each side within 4 metres of the front of the vehicle;
  - one lamp on each side within 1 metre of the rear of the vehicle;
  - additional lamps on each side at 3 metre intervals (or if impracticable 4 metres) between front and rear side marker lamps.
- Vehicles (including a combination of vehicles) over 18.3 metres long (including the length of the load):
  - one lamp on each side within 9.15 metres of the front of the vehicle;
  - one lamp on each side within 3.05 metres of the rear of the vehicle;
  - additional lamps on each side at 3.05-metre intervals between front and rear side marker lamps.
- Vehicles in combination between 12.2 metres and 18.3 metres long (but not articulated vehicles) carrying a supported load:
  - one lamp on each side within 1,530 mm of the rear of the rearmost vehicle in the combination;
  - one lamp on each side within 1,530 mm of the centre of the load, if the load extends further than 9.15 metres to the rear of the drawing vehicle.
- Trailers more than 9.15 metres long (6 metres for post-1 October 1990 trailers):
  - one lamp on each side within 1,530 mm of the centre of the trailer length.

Side marker lamps fitted to pre-1 October 1990-built trailers may show white side marker lights to the front and red lights to the rear; in all other cases such lights must be amber. They must be positioned not more than 2,300 mm from the ground.

End-Outline Marker Lamps

Vehicles (except those less than 2,100 mm wide and those first used before 1 April 1991) and trailers (except those less than 2,100 mm wide and those built before 1

October 1990) must be fitted with two end-outline marker lamps visible from the front and two visible from the rear. They must be positioned no more than 400 mm in from the outer edges of the vehicle/trailer and mounted at the front at least level with the top of the windscreen. They must show white lights to the front and red lights to the rear.

Lighting Switches

On vehicles first used since 1 April 1991 a single lighting switch only must be used to illuminate all front and rear position lamps, side and end-outline marker lamps and rear number plate lamp although one or more front or rear position lamps may be capable of being switched on independently.

Visibility of Lights and Reflectors

A part, at least, of each front and rear position light, front and rear-mounted direction indicator lamp and rear retro-reflector required to be fitted to a vehicle/trailer must be capable of being seen from directly in front or behind the lamp or reflector when the vehicle doors, tailgate, boot lid, engine cover or other movable part of the vehicle is in a fixed open position.

Lights on Projecting Loads

Details of the requirements for the display of lights on projecting loads are given fully in Chapter 19, which covers this subject.

Direction Indicators

All goods vehicles must be fitted with amber-coloured direction indicators (on pre-September 1965 registered vehicles, indicators can be white facing to the front and red facing to the rear) at the front and rear which must be fixed to the vehicle not more than 1,500 mm (2,300 mm in exceptional cases) and not less than 350 mm above the ground, at least 500 mm apart and not more than 400 mm from the outer edges of the vehicle. Side repeater indicators are required on vehicles first used since 1 April 1986 and these must be fitted within 2,600 mm of the front of the vehicle. Normally vehicles should have one indicator on each side at the front and rear but may have two on each side at the rear. They must not have more than one on each side at the front.

Indicators bearing approval marks do not have to meet minimum wattage requirements but those without such marks must be between 15 and 36 watts. They must flash at a rate of between 60 and 120 times a minute and a visible or audible warning must indicate to the driver when they are operating. The indicators must be maintained in a clean condition and in good and efficient working order.

Semaphore Arm Indicators

Vehicles first registered before 1 September 1965 are allowed to have either semaphore arm or flashing indicators. The semaphore arm type must be amber in colour but the flashing indicators may show a white light to the front and a red light to the rear.

Hazard Warning

Direction indicators operating on both sides of the vehicle simultaneously as a hazard warning to other road users are required by law on all vehicles first used since 1 April 1986. They must be actuated by a switch solely controlling that device and a warning light must indicate to the driver that the device is being operated. The hazard indicators may be used when the vehicle is stationary on a road, or any part of the road (ie not just the carriageway), because of a breakdown of it or another vehicle, an accident or other emergency situation, or when the vehicle is causing a temporary obstruction on a road when loading or unloading.

Emergency Warning Triangles

As an additional warning of a hazard drivers *may* (ie it is not compulsory to do so) place a red warning triangle on the road to the rear of a vehicle causing a temporary obstruction (eg through breakdown). The triangle must be made and marked to British Standard Specification BS AU 47: 1965. It must be placed upright on the road, 45 metres to the rear of the obstruction and on the same side.

Other safety devices may be used to warn of vehicles broken down on the roadside. These include traffic cones, warning lamps and traffic pyramids, as well as conventional warning triangles mentioned above.

Optional Lamps

Optional main-beam head lamps (which includes spot lamps) may be fitted to a vehicle but they must be capable of being dipped, and if fitted as a matched pair they must also be capable of being switched off together – not individually. They must emit either a white or yellow light, must be adjusted so that they do not cause dazzle to other road users and must not be lit when the vehicle is parked. If optional front fog lamps are fitted and used singly, the headlamps must also be illuminated.

These optional lamps should be positioned not more than 1,200 mm from the ground and not more than 400 mm from the sides of the vehicle. They should be aligned so that the upper edge of the beam is, as near as practicable, 3 per cent below the horizontal when the vehicle is at its kerbside weight and has a weight of 75 kg on the driver's seat.

Vehicles first registered since 1 April 1991 may be fitted with only one pair of extra dipped-beam head lamps and then only on vehicles intended to be driven on the right-hand side of the road. They must be wired so that only one pair of dipped-beam head lamps can be used at any one time. Pre-April 1991 registered vehicles may have any number of additional dipped-beam head lamps.

Any number of extra main-beam head lamps (including spot/driving lamps) may be fitted and there is no restriction on their fitment or use except that they must not cause dazzle to other road users.

Blue Lights

There is an increasing trend towards the use of blue lights on the front of, or in the windscreens of, both cars and commercial vehicles, giving rise to questions about their legality. As the law stands at present it appears that it is not illegal to fit or use such lights as long as they do not flash in the same manner as those on emergency service vehicles. The police, however, are opposed to their use and are anxious to see them prohibited by law, because of the risk of confusion with emergency service vehicles and because of their potential use by criminals purporting to be police. A number of prosecutions and fixed penalty notices have been issued to drivers displaying such lights, and others can expect to be challenged, although it will take a test case to fully determine the legal position.

Drivers variously believe that the ultraviolet light emitted by such lamps reduces in-cab white-light glare from oncoming vehicle headlights and that they help to 'confuse' roadside enforcement cameras.

Warning Beacons

Amber warning beacons must be fitted to vehicles with four or more wheels and having a maximum speed no greater than 25 mph when using unrestricted dual-carriageway roads except where such use is merely 'for crossing the carriageway in the quickest manner practicable in the circumstances'.

Amber warning beacons may also be fitted to vehicles used at the scene of an emergency, when it is necessary or desirable to warn of the presence of a vehicle on the road (eg Special Types vehicles carrying abnormal loads) and to breakdown vehicles used at the scene of accidents and breakdowns and when towing broken-down vehicles.

Green warning beacons may be used on vehicles by medical practitioners registered with the General Medical Council when travelling to or dealing with an emergency.

Blue warning beacons and other special warning lamps may only be used on emergency vehicles (ie ambulance, fire brigade or police service vehicles; Forestry Commission fire-fighting vehicles; military bomb disposal vehicles; RAF Mountain Rescue vehicles; Blood Transfusion Service vehicles; British Coal mines rescue vehicles; HM Coastguard and Coast Life Saving Corps vehicles; RNLI vehicles; and those used primarily for transporting human tissue for transplanting).

In all cases such beacons should be fitted with their centres no less than 1,200 mm from the ground and visible from any point at a reasonable distance from the vehicle. The light itself must show not less than 60 and not more than 240 times per minute.

Swivelling Spotlights (Work Lamps)

White swivelling spotlights may be used only at the scene of an accident, breakdown or roadworks to illuminate the working area or work in the vicinity of the vehicle provided they do not cause undue dazzle or discomfort to the driver of any vehicle.

Rear Retro-Reflectors

Motor vehicles must be fitted with two red reflex retro-reflectors facing squarely to the rear. Reflectors must be fitted not more than 900 mm and not less than 350 mm from the ground. For normal goods vehicles and trailers they must be within 400 mm of the outer edge of the vehicle or trailer and not less than 600 mm apart. Reflectors must be capable of being seen from an angle of 30 degrees on either side.

Triangular Rear Reflectors

Triangular rear reflectors must not be used other than on trailers or broken-down vehicles being towed.

Side Retro-Reflectors

Vehicles more than 6 metres long first used since 1 April 1986 (more than 8 metres long if first used before 1 April 1986) and trailers more than 5 metres long must be fitted with two (or more as necessary) amber side retro-reflectors on each side. One reflector on each side must be fitted not more than 1 metre from the extreme rear end of the vehicle and another no more than 4 metres from the front of the vehicle with further reflectors at minimum 3 metre intervals (or can be 4-metre intervals) along its length. They must be mounted not more than 1,500 mm and not less than 350 mm from the ground. On pre-April 1986 vehicles one reflector must be positioned in the middle third of the vehicle length and the other within 1 metre of the rear. Where such reflectors are mounted within 1 metre of the rear of the vehicle/trailer they may be coloured red instead of amber.

Front Retro-Reflectors

Trailers built since 1 October 1990 must be fitted with two obligatory front retro-reflectors, white in colour and mounted facing forwards, at least 350 mm but not more than 900 mm from the ground and no more than 150 mm in from the outer edges of the trailer and at least 600 mm apart.

Vehicle Markings

Number (Registration) Plates

All vehicles first registered since 1 January 1973 must be fitted with number plates made of reflecting material complying with BS AU 145a. This requirement does not apply to goods vehicles over 7.5 tonnes gross weight, which are required to display rear reflective markers (see pp 366–72) or works trucks, agricultural machines and trailers or pedestrian-controlled vehicles. If a vehicle over 3,050 kg unladen is exempt from the requirement to fit rear reflective markers then it must be fitted with reflective number plates. Regulations specify the precise style of letters and numerals to be used on vehicle registration plates, in particular the spacing between each individual character. It is an offence to alter, rearrange or misrepresent the characters or to alter the spacings to form words or names. It is also an offence to use a number plate with a patterned or textured background. Three possible repercussions may result from the illegal presentation of vehicle registration numbers:

- a fine of up to £1,000 may be imposed on conviction;
- the registration number (mark) may be withdrawn;
- the vehicle may fail its MoT test.

From this it will be seen that the use of so-called 'fun' number plates in which spacings between letters and numbers are rearranged to produce key words is prohibited and will result in police action (usually an order to get the plates changed within five days, but possibly more serious consequences as listed above). Italicized, computer-type and shadow lettering on vehicle number plates will also invite police action. It is useful to note that the firms making and selling these plates commit no offence – only the person who uses them on the road.

A new scheme introduced by the DVLA requires number plate manufacturers to be registered as part of the campaign to curb vehicle crime. Eventually number plates will carry an electronic 'chip' which will be read by roadside microwave beacons and cameras.

Vehicle Registration Numbers

From 1 September 2001 a new system of vehicle registration numbers was introduced in the UK requiring that number plates conform to a new British Standard (BS AU 145d) which replaces the previous standard referred to above. Since that date all new number (ie registration) plates must comply with the following format:

AB51 DVL

The letters 'AB' identify the local area in which the vehicle is registered (see Appendix VII). The number '51' identifies the date of first registration (ie 51 representing September 2001) and will change every six months in September and March each year (eg 10 being March 2010 and 60 being September 2010, etc). The last three letters (in the above example DVL) are chosen at random.

Also from 1 September 2001, all new number plates must display the mandatory fonts (in both style and size – see below) specified in the Road Vehicles (Display of Registration Marks) Regulations 2001. No lettering other than in the specified standard font may be used (ie computer, script-type and other 'fun' lettering are banned). The name and trademark of the maker and the postcode of the supplying outlet may be used.

Mandatory Character Font

From 1 September 2001 all new number plates must display the new mandatory font as shown here and characters must be of the regulation size:

123456789
ABCDEFGH
JKLMNOPQ
RSTUVWXYZ

Height	79mm
Width	50mm
Stroke	14mm
Side margin	11mm
Top & bottom margin	11mm
Space between characters	11mm
Space between groups	33mm

(Applicable to all vehicles except motorcycles and vehicles manufactured before 1973.)

Existing number plates will not have to be changed to conform to the new style provided the font used is 'substantially the same' as the new style. However, number plates must be replaced if they have been customized with either:

- stylized letters and figures such as italics; or
- number plate fixing bolts that alter the appearance of the letters or numbers.

Failure to replace such number plates may result in the vehicle keeper risking prosecution.

Nationality Symbols

It is a legal requirement (under the Vienna Convention on Road Traffic) for vehicles travelling in a country other than that in which they are registered to display at the rear a nationality plate showing the official symbol for the country of registration (eg GB for Great Britain, F for France and D for Germany). These plates, usually in the form of a self-adhesive sticker, should be of an approved pattern, oval in shape (at least 17.5cm by 11.4cm) and contain the relevant national symbol in black letters on a white background.

However, under new provisions contained in EC Regulation 2411/98/EC, vehicles travelling within EU member states are exempted from the above requirement provided they are fitted with so-called 'Euro-plates'. These are the new-style number plates (as described above) which incorporate, in a panel on the left-hand side, the EU symbol comprising a circle of 12 gold stars on a blue background surrounding the nationality letters of the country in which the vehicle is registered (eg GB). Vehicles displaying this symbol on the number plate will no longer need to use the traditional black GB on a white oval background sticker mentioned above

Switzerland (not an EU member state) has been asked by the EU to recognize these plates as being legal.

Vehicle owners/operators who wish to do so may now legally display their national flag on number plates (ie the union flag with 'GB' for Great Britain; the cross of St George with 'ENG' for England; the Saltire – the cross of St Andrew – with 'SCO' for Scotland; or the Red Dragon for Wales or Cymru).

NB: *With these national symbols displayed but no 'GB' or 'Euro stars' on the number plate a separate oval, black-on-white GB plate must be displayed for travel in Europe.*

Weight Markings

Goods vehicles must not display any weight markings other than their plated weights, any weights required to be displayed under the C&U regulations, or weights required under other regulations (eg the Motor Vehicles (Authorisation of Special Types) General Order). This means that maximum weights shown on 'Ministry' plates and maximum laden weights (so long as these do not exceed 'Ministry' plated weights) may be shown on either one or both sides of a vehicle.

Motor tractors and locomotives must have their unladen weight shown in a conspicuous place on the outside of the vehicle where it can easily be seen.

Dimensions Marking

Goods vehicles over 3.5 tonnes and trailers made since 31 May 1998 must be fitted with a plate showing their length and width, unless this information is already shown on either the manufacturer's plate or a 'Ministry' plate.

'Ministry' Plates

Goods vehicles over 3,500 kg maximum gross weight and goods carrying trailers over 1,020 kg unladen weight must display a 'Ministry' plate and/or a manufacturer's plate showing the maximum permissible gross vehicle weight and individual axle weights (see Chapter 14).

Special Types Plates

Vehicles carrying abnormal loads must display a manufacturer's plate showing the maximum weights at which the vehicle can operate and the relevant speeds for travel at those weights. The weights shown must be those approved by the vehicle or trailer manufacturer and the vehicle must not exceed specified Special Types speed limits when travelling loaded to the weight shown on the plate (see details of speeds for different classes of Special Types vehicles, pp 254–55).

Food Vehicles

Vehicles which are used in connection with a food business or from which food is sold must display in a clearly visible place the name and address of the person carrying on the business and the address at which the vehicle is kept or garaged. If the vehicle bears a fleet number and is kept or garaged on that person's premises the garage address is not required but the local authority must be notified.

Height Marking

The travelling height of vehicles and trailers carrying engineering equipment, containers and skips, where the height of the vehicle and load exceeds 3 metres, must be marked in the cab where the driver can see it. Further provisions extend this by requiring the fitment of warning devices where vehicles carry 'high-level equipment' (see pp 298–99 for further details).

Hazard Marking

Vehicles which carry hazardous, radioactive or explosive loads must display appropriate hazard warning symbols on the vehicle, whether a bulk tanker, a tank container or a normal delivery vehicle used for carrying hazardous consignments, and on the individual packages too in the latter case. Further details are given in Chapter 20.

Outline (Contour) Marking of Large Vehicles

Increasing use is being made of reflective outline marker tape on the sides (yellow tape) and rear (red tape) of large goods vehicles (ie contour marking) to make them more visible at night, thus enhancing road safety. Although this is not yet a statutory requirement, it is anticipated that it will become so in due course under EC legislation. A European specification for such markings already exists, namely ECE104.

Rear Reflective Markings

All vehicles with a maximum permissible weight exceeding 7,500 kg and trailers with a maximum permissible weight exceeding 3,500 kg must be fitted with rear reflective markers which make them more conspicuous at night and in poor visibility (Figures 13.1 and 13.2). The markers may also be displayed on loads such as builders' skips (see below).

For new vehicles first used from 1 April 1996 and trailers manufactured on or after 1 October 1995, which under the regulations require the fitment of rear reflective markings as described below, fitment of a new type of rear marking (in accordance with ECE Regulation 70) is necessary.

Types of Markers

For pre-1 April 1996-used vehicles and pre-1 October 1995-built trailers, there are two types of markings, each in two sizes:

- alternating red fluorescent and yellow reflective diagonal strips – diagrams 1, 2, and 3 in Figure 13.1a;
- a central yellow reflective panel overprinted with the words LONG VEHICLE and having a red fluorescent surround – diagrams 4 and 5 in Figure 13.1a.

For post-1 April 1996-used vehicles and post-1 October 1995-built trailers, the markings comprise two types:

- alternating red fluorescent and yellow retro-reflective diagonal strips – diagrams 1, 2, 3 and 4 in Figure 13.1b;
- a central yellow retro-reflective panel surrounded by a red fluorescent border – diagrams 5, 6, 7 and 8 in Figure 13.1c.

Specification for Markers

Markers of the type illustrated in Figure 13.1a must comply with the regulations regarding size and colour and they must be in the form of durable plates stamped with the mark BS AU 152/1970. Those of the type illustrated in Figures 13.1b and 13.1c must also comply with the regulations as above and be stamped with a designated approval mark. They must not be simulated by being painted on the vehicle and the plates must not be defaced, cut or modified to aid fitting to the vehicle.

Which Markers to Be Fitted

Pre-1 April 1996-used Vehicles and Pre-1 October 1995-built Trailers

Vehicles not exceeding 13 metres in length and trailers in combinations not exceeding 11 metres must be fitted with the markers shown in diagrams 1, 2 or 3 in Figure 13.1a. Alternatively, they may be fitted with the markers shown in diagrams 1, 2, 3 or 4 in Figure 13.1b.

FIGURE 13.1a Rear reflective markers required on certain goods vehicles. The plates comprise red fluorescent material background. The lettering is in black on yellow reflex reflecting material

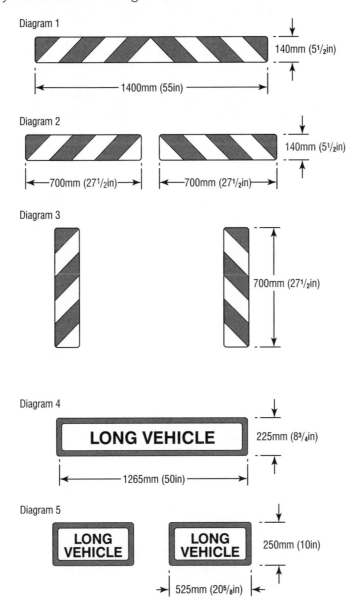

Vehicles more than 13 metres long and trailers in combinations more than 13 metres long must be fitted with the markers shown in diagram 4 or 5 in Figure 13.1a (or alternatively those shown in diagrams 5, 6, 7 or 8 in Figure 13.1c).

FIGURE 13.1b   Rear markings for post-1 April 1996-used vehicles and post-1 October 1995-built trailers

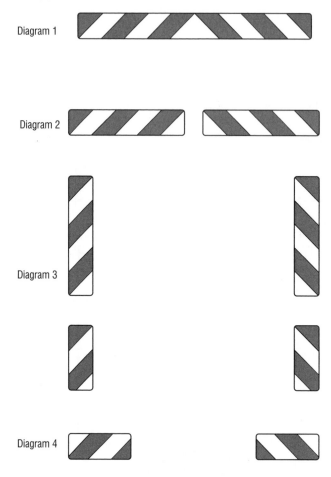

Trailers in combinations of more than 11 metres but not more than 13 metres may be fitted with the markers shown in diagram 1, 2, 3, 4 or 5 in Figure 13.1a or those in diagrams 1 to 8 in Figures 13.1b and 13.1c.

Post-1 April 1996-used Vehicles and Post-1 October 1995-built Trailers

Vehicles not exceeding 13 metres in length and trailers in combinations not exceeding 11 metres must be fitted with a marker or set of markers of the types shown in diagrams 1, 2, 3 or 4 in Figure 13.1b.

Vehicles more than 13 metres long and trailers in combinations more than 13 metres long must be fitted with the markers shown in diagrams 5, 6, 7 or 8 in Figure 13.1c.

Trailers in combinations of more than 11 metres but not more than 13 metres must be fitted with a marker or set of markers of the types shown in diagrams 1 to 8 in Figures 13.1b and 13.1c.

FIGURE 13.1c New-type rear markers for use on long vehicles first used from 1 April 1996 and trailers built since 1 October 1995

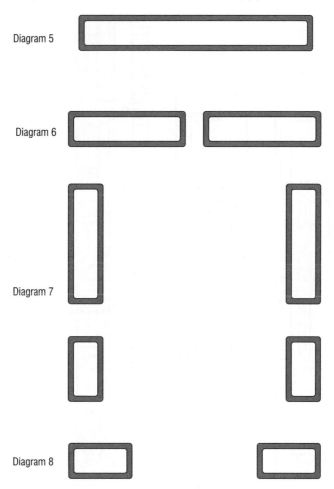

Diagram 5

Diagram 6

Diagram 7

Diagram 8

Fitting Position

The height from the ground to the lower edge of the marker when fitted must not exceed 1,700 mm but must be at least 400 mm. It must be fitted parallel to the ground and be facing square to the rear.

Alternative Fitting Position

When a vehicle which by law requires rear reflective markers to be displayed is carrying a load which obscures partly or wholly the markers so that they are not clearly visible from the rear, the reflective markers may be fitted to the rear of the load.

FIGURE 13.2 Vehicles which must carry reflective rear markers and the alternative fitting arrangements

Rigid vehicles not more than 13 metres (42' 7⁷/₈")
overall length (if more than 3 tonnes unladen)

Trailers in combinations not more than
11 metres (36' 11⅛") overall length (if trailer
weight more than 1 tonnes unladen)

Trailers in combinations more than
11 metres (36' 11⅛") but less than
13 metres (42' 7⁷/₈") overall length

Trailers in combinations more than
13 metres (42' 7⁷/₈") overall length

Exemptions

Certain vehicles as indicated in the following list are exempt from the requirement to fit these markers:

- vehicles with a maximum gross weight not exceeding 7,500 kg;
- passenger vehicles other than articulated buses;
- land tractors, land locomotives, land implements, land implement conveyors, agricultural tractors or industrial tractors;
- works trucks or works trailers;
- vehicles in an unfinished condition proceeding to a works for completion or to a place where they are to be stored or displayed for sale;
- motor vehicles constructed or adapted for the purpose of forming part of articulated vehicles;
- broken-down vehicles while being drawn in consequence of the breakdown;
- engineering plant;
- trailers, not being part of an articulated bus, drawn by public service vehicles;
- vehicles designed for fire fighting or fire salvage purposes;
- vehicles designed and used for the purpose of servicing or controlling aircraft;
- vehicles designed and used for the transportation of two or more motor vehicles carried thereon, or of vehicle bodies or two or more boats;
- vehicles proceeding to a place for export;
- vehicles brought temporarily into Great Britain by persons residing abroad;
- vehicles in the service of a visiting force or of a headquarters;
- motor vehicles first used before 1 January 1940;
- vehicles owned or in the service of the army, navy or air force;
- vehicles designed for heating or dispensing tar or similar material for road construction or maintenance;
- trailers being drying or mixing plant designed for the production of asphalt, bitumen or tarmacadam;
- trailers made before 1 August 1982 with an unladen weight not exceeding 1,020 kg;
- trailers with a gross weight not exceeding 3,500 kg.

Previously it was illegal to fit the markers to these vehicles, but a change in the regulations permits the fitting of such markers to exempt vehicles on a voluntary basis, provided the vehicles exceed the specified weight limit. It is illegal to display these markers on vehicles which do not require them by law except as mentioned above.

Builders' Skips

Rear reflective markings of the type described above (as shown in diagram 3, Figure 13.1a) must be fitted to the ends of builders' skips which are placed on the highway.

They must be fitted as a matched pair as near to the outer edge as possible, mounted vertically and no more than 1.5 metres from the ground to the top edge. They must be kept clean, in good order and be visible from a reasonable distance. Such skips are required to be illuminated when standing on roads at night.

Conspicuity Markings

Conspicuity marking material is required to be fitted to new heavy goods vehicles and trailers from 10 July 2011. This requirement aligns the UK Road Vehicles Lighting Regulations (RVLR) with UNECE Regulation 48.

The legislation covers the following vehicles:

- Goods vehicles with a gross vehicle weight exceeding 7,500kg first used on or after 10 July 2011
- Trailers with a gross vehicle weight exceeding 3,500kg manufactured on or after 10 July 2011

Certain vehicles as follows are exempt from the requirements:

- A vehicle which is not a goods vehicle.
- Goods vehicles not exceeding 7,500kg gvw.
- Trailers not exceeding 3,500kg gvw.
- Chassis cabs.
- Incomplete vehicles proceeding to a works for completion or to a place where they are to be stored or displayed for sale.
- Articulated tractive units.
- Vehicles/trailers with an overall width not exceeding 2.1 metres do not require rear markings.
- Vehicles/trailers with overall length not exceeding 6 metres do not require side markings.

The conspicuity marking legislation requires a full contour marking on the rear of the vehicle (ie horizontal and vertical markings to outline the shape of the vehicle, and partial contour markings on the side). Partial contour markings consist of a horizontal line showing the length of the vehicle and 'tick' marks showing the upper corners of the vehicle. Where the shape, structure, design or operational requirements make it impossible to install the mandatory contour marking, a line marking is acceptable.

Goods Vehicle Plating, Annual Testing and Vehicle Inspections

M ost goods vehicles are required to be tested annually to ensure they are safe to operate on the road and meet the legal requirements relating to mechanical condition. In particular, this annual inspection is intended to determine whether vehicles and trailers meet the standards specified in the Road Vehicles (Construction and Use) Regulations 1986 (as amended). Additionally, it is necessary for certain goods vehicles and trailers to be 'Ministry plated' to show the maximum permissible gross weight and maximum axle weights at which they may be operated on roads in Great Britain. The requirement for annual plating and testing of goods vehicles is contained in the Road Traffic Act 1988 and is detailed in the Goods Vehicles (Plating and Testing) Regulations 1988 as amended.

The Vehicle and Operator Services Agency (VOSA) is responsible for the operation of goods vehicle testing stations – of which there are currently 100 front-line stations plus numerous HGV 'designated premises' (DPs) in the UK. It is also the main enforcement authority involved in roadside checks on goods vehicles.

Since May 2009 VOSA has been undertaking a programme of test centre closures. The stations concerned are to be replaced by privately run but VOSA-manned Authorised Testing Facilities (ATFs). Operators using these private centres will have to pay an additional fee as shown in the table of test fees on page 376.

NB: A full and up-to-date list of the VOSA Goods Vehicle Testing Stations and Authorised Testing Facilities (ATF) together with contact details can be found on the internet at: **http://www.transportoffice.gov.uk**.

Annual Testing

Articulated tractive units, rigid goods vehicles over 3,500 kg gross weight, goods carrying semi-trailers and drawbar trailers over 1,020 kg unladen weight and converter dollies must be tested annually at either a goods vehicle testing station, ATF or at one of the designated operator workshops (ie designated premises – DPs) – for which a test fee surcharge applies, plus any additional charge made by the DP.

Certain specialized vehicles are exempt from the test, as shown on pp 386–88, and the regulations do not apply to vehicles used under a trade licence. Goods vehicle test stations also carry out the Class V test, which is the MoT-type test, on large passenger vehicles which cannot get into normal MoT test garages (see also Chapter 15).

The Class VII test provides for MoT testing of goods vehicles of more than 3,000 kg but not more than 3,500 kg design gross weight which were formerly subject to goods vehicle plating and testing when they had an unladen weight exceeding 1,525 kg.

Types of Test

There are various types of goods vehicle test as follows:

- *First test:* the first annual test of the vehicle or trailer (carried out no later than the end of the anniversary month in which it was first registered) at which the information shown on the vehicle's official (ie 'Ministry') plate (issued from Swansea) is verified.
- *Parts 2 and 3 retests*: re-examination of vehicles which have failed their first test or a retest.
- *Periodical test*: the annual test which applies to all relevant vehicles after the first test.
- *Part 4 test*: a test provided for in the regulations which may be required if a notifiable alteration has been made to the vehicle, or if the operator wants the plating certificate amended to show different weights as a result of changes to the vehicle or, for example, if different tyre equipment has been fitted.
- *Retest following appeal*: retests carried out following an appeal to the test station manager or subsequently the VOSA Regional Manager.

Test Dates

Vehicles may be submitted for test at any one of the full-time or part-time goods vehicle test stations selected by the vehicle operator. Vehicles are due for test each year no later than the end of the anniversary month in which they were first registered (eg a vehicle registered on 1 January 2010 would be due for its first test no later than 31 January 2011 and for subsequent tests by 31 January in each following year).

Trailer Test Dates

The first test for trailers is due by the end of the first anniversary month from when they were sold. When application is made for a first trailer test a serial number is given, and this number must be stamped on or permanently attached to the trailer prior to its test. It is a condition of acceptance for test that this number is on the trailer.

Year of Manufacture/Registration

There is an anomaly with due test dates when a vehicle or trailer is manufactured in one year and is not registered (or sold in the case of a trailer) before 1 July of the following year. In this case it must be tested by the end of December in the year in which it was first registered or sold.

Phased Programmes and Missed Test Dates

VOSA allows vehicle operators the facility of having vehicles tested before their due date to accommodate phased programmes of test preparation, rather than having a large number of vehicles due for preparation and test in any particular month of the year.

Test Applications

Initial application for a first test of vehicles and trailers has to be made direct to the Goods Vehicle Centre, Welcombe House, 91/92 The Strand, Swansea SA1 2DH (not to be confused with the DVLA at Swansea). Application for subsequent tests can be made either to Swansea or direct to any test station. The following forms, which may be obtained from good vehicle test stations or Traffic Area Offices, are used for making the application:

VTG1   First test of a vehicle
VTG2   First test of a trailer
VTG40   For subsequent tests of both vehicles and trailers
VTG15   To be completed and submitted every time a dangerous goods vehicle is presented for test.

Time for Application

Applications for test should be made during the two months prior to the month in which the test is required to take place (ie the last day on which the vehicle may legally operate without a test certificate). Applications should ideally be made at least one month before the date on which the test is preferred by the operator (see note below about the Saturday testing facility).

Saturday and Out-of-Hours Testing

Saturday and out-of-hours testing is available at most test stations at an additional fee. Operators wishing to take advantage of this facility must mark their applications very clearly 'SATURDAY TEST' and show the appropriate date.

Test Fees

The appropriate test fee, as follows, should be sent to the Goods Vehicle Centre with the first test application form (VTG1 or VTG2), while fees for subsequent tests should be sent direct to the test station. (Operators can open a direct debit account with VOSA to enable any fee to be collected for any test station.) The test fees listed here were effective from 1 April 2010.

Test type		At VOSA *DPs or *ATF	Out of hours at VOSA
First tests/Annual tests Prohibition clearances (full inspections) Retests after 14 days	2 Axle	£95.00	£133.00
	3 Axle	£120.00	£158.00
	4 or more Axles	£145.00	£183.00
Retests within 14 days Prohibition clearances (partial inspections)	2 Axle	£38.00	£58.00
	3 Axle	£53.00	£73.00
	4 or more Axles	£70.00	£90.00
Part-paid Retests	Any Number of Axles	£13.00	£13.00
Notifiable Alteration		£29.00	£40.00
Replacement Documents	£13.00		

*DPs = Designated premises   *ATF = Approved Testing Facility

NOTE A: These fees now include £38.52 contribution to the cost of enforcement and compliance functions previously charged via Operator Licence vehicle related fees which have been reduced.
RETEST FEES: Part-paid retests will only be available for the failure items marked on the Inspection Document (PG14) with L or _. Part-paid retests must be carried out on either the same day as the test or the next working day.

Heavy Goods Vehicle Testing – Trailers (From 1 April 2010)			
Test type		At VOSA	Out of hours
First tests/Annual tests Prohibition clearances (full inspections) Retests after 14 days	1 Axle	£43.00	£67.00
	2 Axle	£57.00	£81.00
	3 or more Axles	£68.00	£92.00
Retests within 14 days Prohibition clearances (partial inspections)	1 Axle	£19.00	£32.00
	2 Axle	£27.00	£40.00
	3 or more Axles	£36.00	£49.00
Part-paid Retests	Any Number of Axles	£7.00	£7.00
Notifiable Alteration		£27.00	£40.00
Duplicate Certificates	£13.00		

NOTE B: These fees now include £14.98 contribution to the cost of enforcement and compliance functions previously charged via October Licence vehicle related fees which have been reduced.

Testing for LEZ Compliance

Hauliers can book low-emission certificate (LEC) tests at VOSA goods vehicle testing stations to confirm whether their older vehicles comply with the London low-emission zone (LEZ) requirement that began in February 2008. The cost is £28.

Trailer Testing

Many operators have more semi-trailers and trailers than tractive units or drawing vehicles and in order to have these additional trailers tested it may be necessary for them to be submitted for test with a vehicle which has already been tested and has a current valid test certificate. In these cases only the trailer will be examined and the fee payable will be the trailer fee only.

Test Appointments

Following application to the Goods Vehicle Centre for a first or subsequent test (see note above about Saturday testing facility), the test station selected by the operator will confirm the test booking in due course with an appointment letter, and all further communications regarding the test must be made with the test station, not with Swansea. If, owing to excessive workload or staff shortage, the chosen test station cannot accommodate the test an appointment will be made at the nearest alternative test station and a letter will be sent from that station. The appointment letter and the vehicle registration document must be produced on arrival at the test station.

It is essential that vehicles arrive at the test station at the appointed time. Late or non-arrival of a vehicle can mean cancellation of the test and the fee will be forfeited unless an acceptable reason citing 'exceptional circumstances' is put forward. Exceptional circumstances include accident, fire, epidemic, severe weather, failure in the supply of essential services or other unexpected happenings. Breakdown, mechanical defect or non-availability of the vehicle because of shortages in spare parts supply or for operational reasons for example are not looked upon as exceptional circumstances.

Cancellations

If it is necessary to cancel a test booking after making application, provided seven days' notice is given to the test station, either a new test date will be arranged or the fee will be refunded after deduction of a £1.50 charge. In exceptional circumstances, such as an accident to the vehicle on the way to the test station, if notification is given to the station within three days of the accident the fee will be carried forward or refunded less £1.50. If other exceptional circumstances arise within seven days of the due date for the test, provided satisfactory evidence is given to the test station, the fee will be similarly carried forward or refunded less £2.50.

Refusal to Test

Test station officials have the right to refuse to test a vehicle or trailer for the following reasons, in which circumstances form VTG12 will be issued:

- Arrival after the appointed time.
- Appointment card or vehicle registration document not produced.
- If it is found that the vehicle brought to the test station does not conform to the details given on the application form.
- If the vehicle was booked for the test with a trailer but the trailer is not taken to the test station.
- If the chassis number cannot be found by the examiner or if the serial number given for the trailer by VOSA is not stamped on it.
- If the vehicle is in a dirty or dangerous condition.
- If the vehicle does not have sufficient fuel or oil to enable the test to be carried out.
- If the test appointment card specified that the vehicle should be loaded for the test and it is taken to the test station without a load. Under normal circumstances the decision whether the vehicle is to be tested in a laden or unladen condition is left to the owner to suit his convenience but in some circumstances the test station may request that the vehicle is fully or partially loaded to enable the brakes to be accurately tested on the roller brake tester.
- In the case of a trailer if the vehicle submitted with it is not suitable to draw it.
- If the vehicle breaks down during the test.
- If the vehicle is submitted for its annual test (ie not for the first test) or a retest and the previous test and plating certificates are not produced.

Test Procedure

Goods vehicle test stations vary in size and in the number of examination staff. Testing normally takes approximately 45 minutes during which the driver must be available to assist and move the vehicle as required. Examination of vehicles is carried out by VOSA examiners based at the station in accordance with the *Heavy Goods Vehicle Inspection Manual* published by VOSA and available free online at **www.dft.gov.uk/vosa**. All items which have to be inspected are listed in the *Manual* together with, where necessary, details of how the inspection of each item should be carried out and the reasons for failing the item. Under the 'reasons for rejection' column in the *Manual*, where the item inspected is one that is subject to wear, the maximum tolerance will be indicated. Also shown are the standards at which a prohibition notice may be issued during the Annual Test.

Additional items have been added to the vehicle test list from 2011 in accordance with UK law. These items include, for example, airbags, the functioning of Electronic Braking System (EBS) warning lights and main-beam telltale lights.

The Smoke Test

Free acceleration smoke emission testing of diesel engines by means of a calibrated smoke meter (to measure the density of smoke in a vehicle exhaust) was introduced as part of the goods vehicle annual test from 1 September 1992. Where it is necessary to carry out a purely visual test, the driver is asked to depress the accelerator pedal firmly from the engine idle position (preferably with the engine already warm) to the maximum fuel delivery position and, immediately the governor operates, release the pedal until the engine slows to a steady idling speed. Smoke emission from the first attempt at this procedure is ignored but the procedure has to be repeated for a maximum of 10 times until the smoke emission is considered to be of equal density for two successive accelerations.

Inspection Card

During the test the examiner has an inspection card (form PG14/2) on which all items in the *Inspection Manual* are listed and in the case of failure of any item the card is marked accordingly.

A computerized test card is used which allows the examiner to produce:

- a test 'pass' certificate;
- an advice note (for action required);
- a failure notice;
- a PG9 prohibition notice; or
- a PG14 refusal of test certificate.

Tachograph Testing

Tachograph testing is part of the annual test and comprises an inspection of the:

- tachograph scale marking in kilometres per hour (additional mph marking is allowed);
- presence of the tachograph serial number and appropriate 'e' marking;
- tachograph installation/calibration plaque (its presence, condition and calibration date);
- 'K factor' plaque to ensure its presence, condition and that the 'K factor' is clearly visible;
- condition and presence of seals (checking particularly for evidence of interference).

Note Regarding Tachograph-Exempt Vehicles Using a Tachograph as a Speedometer

A vehicle must have a tachograph fitted unless the person presenting the vehicle for test claims that it is exempt from the tachograph regulations. If a tachograph is fitted on an exempt vehicle and used in place of a speedometer, the tachograph must be calibrated and sealed in accordance with the Community Recording Equipment Regulations. However, provided the seals remain intact there will be no requirement for two-yearly inspections or further calibration. If the above vehicle legally requires a speed limiter and has the speed signal operating the limiter transmitted from the tachograph head, then all the seals including the gearbox sender unit must remain intact to avoid the requirement for re-calibration. If the vehicle does not legally require a speed limiter (or the speed limiter does not receive the speed signal from the tachograph head) then the tachograph head seals (excluding the gearbox sender unit seal) must remain intact to avoid the requirement for re-calibration.

Speed Limiter Checks

An electronic device is used during testing to check the function and setting of the speed limiter under test item 33 above and failure of the item will jeopardize the whole vehicle test.

Dedicated ABS/EBS Cables

Where tractive units and trailers are fitted with ISO 7638 sockets to power ABS and and/or EBS braking systems, these sockets must be connected by a dedicated ABS cable (where one or the other does not have an ISO 7638 socket, the ABS is powered through the stop light circuit). Vehicles presented for test after 1 April 2002 without such a cable will receive notice VTG 12, 'refusal to test a vehicle'. Also from 1 April 2002, vehicles stopped at roadside checks that are found to have an ISO 7638 socket on both tractive unit and trailer, but do not have an ABS cable connecting them, will receive a prohibition notice (PG9 – see p 394).

Where a vehicle and trailer are fitted with an electric braking system (EBS) as well as ABS, a seven-core cable connection must be used instead of the normal ABS five-core cable. Vehicles found during roadside checks to have only a five-core instead of the requisite seven-core cable will receive a Defect Note (PGDN 35). On presentation at the test station such vehicles will receive an advisory notice to replace the cable.

Test Pass

When a goods vehicle is found to be in satisfactory order a test certificate is issued by the test station. For goods vehicles the certificate is form VTG5 and for goods-carrying trailers it is VTG5A, which is issued together with a trailer test disc (VTG5B). The trailer test disc is included with the certificate and this must be removed and fixed on to the trailer in a protective holder in a position where it is conspicuous, readily accessible and clearly visible from the nearside.

The heavy goods vehicle test certificate must be produced when applying for an excise licence for a vehicle which comes within the scope of these regulations and otherwise at the request of a competent authority.

Replacement Documents

Replacement test certificates and trailer test date discs and replacement plates and plating certificates (see later in chapter) may be obtained from local test stations or the Goods Vehicle Centre at Swansea at a cost of £13.00 each. Application in both cases should be made on form VTG59, obtainable from goods vehicle test stations or Traffic Area Offices. Automatic replacement of lost or defaced documents is not guaranteed. The Secretary of State has powers to order a retest before issuing such replacements, in which case full test fees become payable.

Test Failure and Retests

When the vehicle is sent for test, it is recommended that a mechanic with a toolkit and minor spares items (light bulbs, for example) accompanies it so that any minor defects can be rectified on the premises and the test can be completed. The examiner may allow certain minor defects to be repaired during the test if they do not take up too much time (usually no more than 20 minutes) and delay the test schedule. In some instances the vehicle may be allowed to be taken out of the test line for minor repairs to be carried out but this again is at the discretion of the examiner.

If it is necessary to take the vehicle away to get the defects rectified and it is submitted again later that day or during the next working day, no additional charge is made. These free retests are restricted to those cases where the vehicle failed because of certain prescribed defects in items as follows:

- legal plate position;
- legal plate details;
- bumper bars;
- spare wheel carrier;
- cab doors;
- mirrors;
- view to front;
- speedometer;
- audible warning;
- oil leaks;
- fuel tanks, pipes and system;
- obligatory sidelamps;
- obligatory rear lamps;
- reflectors;
- direction indicators;
- head lamps – vertical aim;
- obligatory head lamps;
- obligatory stop lamps.

If the vehicle which fails the test is submitted to the same test station again within 14 days, a reduced retest fee is charged and only the items on which the test was failed are re-examined. See page 376 for retest fees. Arrangements for retests have to be made with the manager of the test station concerned.

Appeals against Test Failure

If a vehicle or trailer undergoing test or retest failed for a reason which the operator believes is not justified, he has a right of appeal to the test station manager or VOSA Regional Manager, by completing form VT17 and paying the relevant fee (ie the same as the test fee for that vehicle). The person who submitted the appeal will receive notification as to where and when he must submit the vehicle for re-examination.

Reduced Pollution Examination of Vehicles

Operators wishing to gain the reduced rate of VED for 'reduced pollution' vehicles (see pp 218–19) may submit their vehicles to a goods vehicle testing station for examination by VOSA.

The reduced pollution requirement may be satisfied by:

- a new vehicle meeting the required standard;
- the fitting of a new engine to a vehicle; or
- the fitting of a type-approved device for which there is a Certificate of Conformity issued by the vehicle manufacturer.

The reduced pollution requirements are satisfied if the rate and content of a vehicle's particulate emissions do not exceed the number of grams per kilowatt-hour specified in the table below:

Item	Instrument setting standard to which vehicle was first used	Rate and content of particulate emissions after adaptation (grams per kilowatt-hour)
1.	Directive 88/77/EEC	0.16
2.	Directive 91/542/EEC (limits A)	0.16
3.	Directive 91/542/EEC (limits B)	0.08
4.	European Commission Proposal (Com [97] 627) for a European and Council Directive amending Council Directive 88/77/EEC	0.04

NB: A vehicle first used before 1 April 1991 shall be taken to be a vehicle falling within item 1 above.

Examinations of goods vehicles for the purposes of determining whether they meet the reduced pollution requirements are carried out by an authorized examiner, following which a 'reduced pollution certificate' is issued, providing conclusive evidence that the statutory requirements have been met. A reduced pollution certificate must be produced on application for a vehicle licence at a reduced rate of duty.

Fees for examinations conducted for this purpose are:

	Normal	Out of hours
With annual test	£19.00	£31.00
Without annual test	£32.00	£44.00

Procedures are established for:

- the re-examination of a certified vehicle;
- issue of a rectification certificate where a vehicle is found no longer to satisfy the requirements;
- the revocation, surrender and cancellation of certificates;
- making appeals against the refusal or revocation of a reduced pollution certificate.

Hauliers whose reduced pollution certificated vehicles are found to be emitting black smoke will lose the certificate and the benefit of reduced duty.

Plating of Goods Vehicles and Trailers

Manufacturer's Plating

All new goods vehicles and new trailers over 1,020 kg unladen weight must be fitted with a plate by the manufacturer which shows specified information as follows:

- the manufacturer's name;
- the date of manufacture;
- vehicle type;
- engine type and power rating;
- chassis or serial number;
- number of axles;
- maximum weight allowed on each axle;
- maximum gross weight for the vehicle (including the weight imposed on the tractive unit by a semi-trailer in the case of articulated vehicles);
- maximum train weight.

The plate containing this information is normally fitted inside the driver's cab on the nearside.

For trailers, the information shown on the plate is:

- the manufacturer's name;
- date of manufacture;
- chassis or serial number;
- number of axles;
- maximum weight allowed on each axle;
- maximum weight imposed on the drawing vehicle in the case of semi-trailers;
- maximum gross weight for the trailer.

The plate for trailers is usually riveted to the chassis frame on the nearside.

Design Weights

The weights stated are those at which the manufacturer has designed the vehicle to operate. Where these weights exceed those permitted by law (ie in the C&U regulations) for the type of vehicle in question then, until such time as the vehicle is plated by VOSA, the lower statutory weight limits apply. Conversely, if the manufacturer's design weight is lower than that permitted by law for the type of vehicle then it is the lower limit which applies.

Vehicle Dimensions

Goods vehicles over 3.5 tonnes gross weight and trailers manufactured since 31 May 1998 must be fitted with a plate showing their length and width, unless this information is already shown on either the manufacturer's plate or a 'Ministry' plate.

'Ministry' Plating

When Type Approved goods vehicles over 3,500 kg gross weight are first registered, an official plate (ie commonly referred to as a 'Ministry' plate) is issued showing the maximum permissible gross vehicle weight and individual axle weights at which the vehicle or trailer is allowed to operate within Great Britain.

A plating certificate (form VTG7 – for all vehicles and trailers) and a plate (form VTG6 blue – for pre-1 April 1983 vehicles; VTG6T red – for post-1 April 1983 vehicles; VTG6A green – for all trailers and, on special request (apply on form VTG101), for goods vehicles used in international operations), giving similar details to those on the manufacturer's plate, are issued by the Goods Vehicle Centre at Swansea after receipt of the necessary documents (including the Type Approval Certificate) when a new vehicle is first registered. The plating certificate must be retained by the vehicle operator but the plate (made of paper and protected in a laminated casing, not metal as is the manufacturer's plate) which is also issued must be fixed to the vehicle in an easily accessible position. Generally it should be fitted inside the cab of vehicles on the nearside (but not affixed to the door) and in a suitable position on the nearside of trailers (it is usually fitted to the chassis frame). In all cases the plates should be protected against the weather, kept clean and legible and secure against accidental loss.

NB: *The red, blue and green plates referred to above are being phased out and replaced by computer-generated plates.*

Tractive units and semi-trailers in articulated outfit combinations are plated separately and the individual plates must be fixed separately to the tractive unit and the trailer.

Down-Plating of Vehicles

Down-plating to obtain the benefit of lower rates of Vehicle Excise Duty (VED), will be carried out on request using form VTG10.

Where no alteration has been made to the vehicle, inspection by VOSA will not be necessary. However, it should be noted that in no circumstances will a vehicle that has an inefficient braking performance, is not maintained to required safety standards or which otherwise does not comply with legal requirements be plated at lower weights to compensate for these defects. In such cases examiners at the Goods Vehicle Testing Station will refuse to issue the vehicle with a test (pass) certificate.

The procedure for down-plating is to complete the form for Notifiable Alterations (VTG10), obtainable from goods vehicle test stations and the Goods Vehicle Centre at Swansea, and then:

- hand it in at the time of presenting the vehicle for its annual goods vehicle test;
- contact the local goods vehicle test station at any time for an appointment to submit the vehicle for down-plating; or
- send the form and the fee (see below) to the Goods Vehicle Centre at Swansea.

On payment of the statutory fee of £27.00 to £40.00 if carried out after hours a new vehicle plate (to be fitted in the vehicle cab) and plating certificate will be issued.

International Plates

International Proof of Compliance plates are available and may be voluntarily fitted to vehicles by international hauliers. These plates show compliance with the weights and dimension requirements of EC Directive 96/53/EC. They have been introduced to speed up clearance times through Customs for vehicles on international journeys, showing that the vehicles to which they are fitted do meet the regulations on weights, widths and lengths. Operators wishing to fit these plates should apply to the Goods Vehicle Centre at Swansea using application forms obtainable from Swansea direct or from heavy goods vehicle testing stations. Eventually the new-style plate will replace the present style of 'Ministry' plates.

Vehicles and trailers manufactured since 31 May 1998 should be fitted with these 'dimensions' plates, unless the information is already shown on the manufacturer's plate or on a 'Ministry' plate issued for the vehicle or trailer.

Notifiable Alterations

Operators who make any alteration to the structure of their vehicles must notify VOSA before the vehicle is used on the road. Details of the alterations which require notification on form VTG10 are as follows:

a *Alterations to the structure or fixed equipment of a vehicle which vary its carrying capacity*
   These include alterations to any of the following items:
   (i)   *Chassis frame or structure*
         Any alteration which increases or decreases the front or rear overhang by more than 1 foot. Any structural alteration (other than normal adjustment of an extensible structure) which reduces or extends the wheelbase (or in the case of a semi-trailer the equivalent distance). Any other extension, deletion or alteration including cutting, welding, riveting, etc, which materially weakens the chassis frame or structure or changes its torsional stiffness.
   (ii) *Steering suspension, wheels and axles (including stub axles and wheel hubs)*
         The fitting of steering gear, axles, hubs or road springs of a different design or load-bearing capacity. The fitting of additional wheels and axles, or the removal of such items. Any addition, deletion or alteration which reduces the inherent strength of the above components.
   (iii) *The fitting of an alternative body of different design, construction or type*
         Any alteration which reduces materially the strength of the body structure or the means by which it is attached to the chassis. Any alteration which causes the body to extend beyond the rear of the chassis frame.

b *Alterations to braking system*
   These comprise alterations which adversely affect either the braking system or the braking performance of the vehicle. They include the addition or deletion of components such as reservoirs, servomotors, brake actuators, exhausters and compressors. They would also include the addition of any equipment

which it is necessary to connect to any part of the braking system, and the fitting of different brake drums or shoes or liners of a smaller contact area.

c *Other alterations to the structure or fixed equipment*
Any other alteration made in the load-bearing structure or fixed equipment of the vehicle, eg the coupling gear, which could make the vehicle unsafe to travel on roads at any weight shown on the plate and plating certificate. In the case of a motor vehicle this could include such alterations as changing the type of engine or repositioning the engine or its mountings (eg petrol to diesel, normal control to forward control, etc).

NB: *Any trailer that is over eight years old submitted for examination under the notifiable alterations procedure must have its braking system brought up to the latest standard applicable at the time of its rebuilding.*

Exemptions from Plating and Testing

Vehicles which are subject to the Goods Vehicle (Plating and Testing) Regulations 1988 (as amended) are exempt from the need to hold current plating and testing certificates while being taken to a test station, when used on a road during the test, returning to base from the test station after a test and being taken (unladen) to a working or repair centre for work to be carried out on them in connection with the test.

Temporary Exemption

Temporary exemption from the need to hold a test certificate for not more than three months can be granted by the test station manager if for some special reason it is not possible for a vehicle or trailer to be submitted for test by the last day of the month in which it was due to be tested.

Temporary exemption may be granted in the event of severe weather, fire, epidemic, a failure in the supply of essential services, an industrial dispute, or other unexpected happenings to either a vehicle or the test station. A normal mechanical breakdown of the vehicle will not be considered a circumstance for temporary exemption. A certificate (form VTG33) confirming the exemption will be issued and this can be produced either to the police or examiners of VOSA if they ask for the test certificate, or when applying for an excise licence for the vehicle.

Exempt Vehicles

Vehicles to which the regulations do not apply are as follows:

- dual-purpose vehicles not constructed or adapted to form part of an articulated vehicle;
- mobile cranes as defined in Schedule 1 of the Vehicle Excise and Registration Act 1994;
- breakdown vehicles;
- engineering plant and movable plant and equipment specially designed and constructed for the special purposes of engineering operations;

- trailers being used for drying or mixing plant designed for the production of asphalt or of bituminous or tarmacadam;
- tower wagons as defined in Schedule 2 of the Vehicle Excise and Registration Act 1994;
- road construction vehicles as defined in Schedule 2 of the Vehicle Excise and Registration Act 1994 and roadrollers;
- vehicles designed for fire fighting or fire salvage purposes;
- works trucks, straddle carriers used solely as works trucks, and works trailers;
- electrically propelled motor vehicles;
- motor vehicles used solely for clearing frost, ice or snow from roads by means of a snow plough or similar contrivance, whether forming part of the vehicle or not;
- vehicles constructed or adapted for, and used solely for, spreading material on roads to deal with frost, ice or snow;
- motor vehicles used for no other purpose than the haulage of lifeboats and the conveyance of the necessary gear of the lifeboats which are being hauled;
- living vans not exceeding 3,500 kg design weight;
- vehicles constructed or adapted for, and used primarily for the purpose of, carrying equipment permanently fixed to the vehicle which equipment is used for medical, dental, veterinary, health, educational, display or clerical purposes, such use not directly involving the sale, hire or loading of goods from the vehicle;
- trailers which have no other brakes than a parking brake and brakes which automatically come into operation on the overrun of the trailer;
- vehicles exempted from duty because they do not travel on public roads for more than six miles in any week and trailers drawn by such vehicles (Vehicle Excise and Registration Act 1994, Schedule 3);
- agricultural motor vehicles;
- agricultural trailers and trailed appliances drawn on roads only by a land tractor;
- passenger-carrying vehicles and hackney carriages;
- vehicles used solely for the purpose of funerals;
- goods vehicles proceeding to a port for export and vehicles in the service of a visiting force;
- vehicles equipped with new or improved equipment or types of equipment and used solely by a manufacturer of vehicles or their equipment or by an importer of vehicles, for or in connection with the test or trial of any such equipment;
- motor vehicles temporarily in Great Britain;
- motor vehicles for the time being licensed in Northern Ireland;
- vehicles having a base or centre in any of the following islands, namely Arran, Bute, Great Cumbrae, Islay, Mull or North Uist, from which the use of the vehicle on a journey is normally commenced;

- trailers temporarily in Great Britain, a period of 12 months not having elapsed since the vehicle in question was last brought into Great Britain;
- track-laying vehicles;
- steam-propelled vehicles;
- motor vehicles manufactured before 1 January 1960 used unladen and not drawing a laden trailer, and trailers manufactured before 1 January 1960 and used unladen;
- three-wheeled vehicles used for street cleansing, the collection or disposal of refuse, and the collection or disposal of the contents of gullies;
- vehicles designed and used for the purpose of servicing or controlling aircraft, while so used on an aerodrome within the meaning of the Civil Aviation Act 1982 or on roads to such extent as is essential for the purpose of proceeding directly from one part of such an aerodrome to another part thereof or, subject as aforesaid, outside such an aerodrome unladen and not drawing a laden trailer;
- vehicles designed for use, and used on, an aerodrome mentioned in the preceding paragraph, solely for the purpose of road cleansing, the collection or disposal of refuse or the collection or disposal of the contents of gullies or cesspools;
- vehicles provided for police purposes and maintained in workshops approved by the Minister as suitable for such maintenance, being vehicles provided in England and Wales by a police authority or the receiver for the Metropolitan Police or, in Scotland, by a police authority or a joint police committee;
- heavy motor cars or motor cars constructed or adapted for the purpose of forming part of an articulated vehicle which are used for drawing only a trailer of a type described above or a trailer being used for, or in connection with, any purpose for which it is authorized to be used on roads under the Special Types General Order;
- play buses.

NB: *The following definitions apply in the above exemptions:*

- 'Breakdown vehicle' means a motor vehicle on which is permanently mounted apparatus designed for raising one disabled vehicle and for drawing that vehicle when so raised, and which is not equipped to carry any load other than articles required for the operation of, or in connection with, that apparatus, or for repairing disabled vehicles.
- 'Engineering plant' means movable plant or equipment being a motor vehicle or trailer (not constructed primarily to carry a load) specially designed and constructed for the purposes of engineering operations.
- 'Works truck' means a motor vehicle designed for use in private premises and used on a road only in delivering goods from or to such premises, to or from a vehicle on a road in the immediate neighbourhood, or in passing from one part of any such premises to another or to other private premises in the immediate neighbourhood, or in connection with roadworks while at or in the immediate neighbourhood of the site of such works.

Taxing Exempt Vehicles

When applying for a vehicle excise licence for a vehicle exempt from plating and testing, it is necessary to complete declaration form V112G (available from VROs) in order to obtain the licence without a valid test certificate.

Tachograph Testing

Inspection of tachographs is now included in the annual test, but only in respect of the following items:

- that a tachograph is fitted (ie where the vehicle requires to have it fitted by law);
- that it can easily be seen from the driving seat;
- the condition of the instrument;
- that the instrument can be illuminated;
- that all seals are present and intact.

Operators submitting vehicles for test, which are exempt from the requirement for tachograph fitment, must declare the exemption on an appropriate form which lists the exempt categories (see pp 120–23 for list of tachograph exemptions).

Production of Documents

The police and examiners of VOSA can request production of both test and plating certificates for goods vehicles when such vehicles have been involved in an accident or if they believe an offence has been committed. If these documents cannot be produced at the time, they may be produced within seven days at a police station convenient to the person to whom the request was made, or as soon as reasonably practicable thereafter.

Enforcement Checks on Vehicles

Euro-Wide Enforcement Link-Up

Enforcement agencies from most EU member countries are teaming up to harmonize spot checks on vehicles and legal documentation. Under the EU's *Karolus* programme, national civil servants are participating in exchange programmes throughout the Community for the purposes of enforcing a range of single market legislation, including road transport matters such as drivers' hours and tachograph use, mechanical condition of vehicles and overloading. In time, harmonized enforcement documentation will be issued by way of standardized prohibition notices and enforced rest notices.

VOSA's Operator Compliance Risk Score (OCRS) scheme

Using its Operator Compliance Risk Score (OCRS) system, a key element of its 'targeted enforcement' policy, VOSA scores each O-licence holder from 0 to 10 to indicate how many times the holder has been caught breaking the rules. Operators are also graded red, amber and green - those with a higher score and a red coding are warned that they can expect much closer attention from VOSA until they mend their ways. The scores are based on results from annual tests, vehicle inspections and prosecution records.

VOSA Examiners have a small mobile compliance device, known as an MCD, which they use when carrying out roadside checks on goods vehicles to identify those vehicles which should be checked. They key in vehicle registration numbers or operator licence information and the device displays information about the operator, including his OCRS scores. This data also enables VOSA to prioritize investigations of those operators most likely to be operating outside the law.

Roadside Checks

In addition to carrying out annual vehicle tests at the goods vehicle testing stations, examiners of VOSA operate roadside checks on commercial vehicles. These roadside checks are carried out at intervals on main roads by examiners who usually take over a lay-by which will accommodate several large vehicles. VOSA has stepped up its normal system of roadside checks in recent times and occasionally carries out checks during the night and during weekends. A police officer, in uniform, standing on the road directs vehicles which are required for examination into the lay-by, where they are inspected mainly for visible wear and defects of the brakes, steering gear, silencers, tyres, lights and reflectors and for the emission of black smoke when the engine is revved up. The examiners only have a limited amount of equipment on these checks so the extent of their examination is likewise limited but nevertheless the inspection is undertaken by skilled and observant people and very little escapes their attention.

NB: VOSA *examiners use a guide called* Categorisation of Defects *when considering the prohibition of vehicles found to be defective during roadside checks or while undergoing their annual test. Copies of this guide (price £25.00) can be obtained from goods vehicle testing stations.*

Vehicle Inspections on Premises

Besides roadside checks, VOSA examiners and police officers in uniform are, at any reasonable time, free to enter any premises on which goods vehicles are kept and examine the vehicles. The owner's consent is not needed in this case but to examine any vehicle (ie other than goods vehicles) the owner's consent has to be obtained to carry out the examination or he must be given at least 48 hours' notice of such a proposal to carry out an examination; *if the notice is sent by recorded delivery post the period is increased to 72 hours.* In the latter case the consent of the owner of the premises, if different from the vehicle owner, must also be obtained. If on these inspections defects are found on the vehicles examined, the same procedure applies regarding the prohibition of their use as explained for roadside checks.

A police officer in uniform or a VOSA examiner, on production of suitable identification, can instruct a driver in charge of a stationary goods vehicle on a road (by the issue of form GV3) to take the vehicle to a suitable place to be examined but this must not be for a distance of more than 5 miles.

Prohibition notices can be issued by examiners at a goods vehicle test station if defects of a serious enough nature are found. Also, the police may be notified if prosecution is warranted, although it is not usual for vehicles in such a precarious state to be submitted for test.

Powers of Police, VOSA Examiners and Certifying Officers

The Road Traffic Act 1988 gives authorized examiners (specifically, examiners of VOSA, London taxi examiners, authorized police officers and persons appointed for the purpose by a chief officer of police and certifying officers appointed under the Road Traffic Act 1991) powers to test and inspect vehicles (and examine vehicle records), on production of their authority, as follows:

- They can test any motor vehicle or trailer on a road to check that legal requirements regarding brakes, silencer, steering, tyres, lights and reflectors, smoke and fumes are complied with, and may drive the vehicle for this purpose.

- They can test a vehicle for the same purposes on premises if the owner of the premises consents or has been given at least 48 hours' notice, except where the vehicle has been involved in a notifiable accident, when there is no requirement to give notice. If the notice given is in writing it must be sent by recorded post and the time limit is extended to 72 hours.

- They may at any time enter and inspect any goods vehicle and goods vehicle records, and may at a reasonable time enter premises on which they believe a goods vehicle or goods vehicle records are kept.

- They can request a driver of a stationary goods vehicle to take the vehicle to a place for inspection up to five miles away.

- They can at any reasonable time enter premises where used vehicles are sold, supplied or offered for sale or supply or exposed or kept for sale or supply, to ensure that such vehicles can be used on a road without contravening the appropriate regulations. They may drive a vehicle on the road for this purpose.

- They may enter at any reasonable time premises where vehicles or vehicle parts are sold, supplied, offered for sale or supply, exposed or kept for sale or supply.

- They may require the person in charge of any vehicle to take it to a weighbridge to be weighed. If the vehicle is more than five miles from the place where the request is made and the vehicle is found not to be overloaded, the operator can claim against the highway authority for any loss sustained.

- When a goods vehicle has been weighed and found to exceed its weight limit and its use on a road would be a risk to public safety, they can prohibit its road use by the issue of form TE160 until the weight is reduced to within the legal limit.

- If they find that a goods vehicle is unfit or likely to become unfit for service they can prohibit the driving of the vehicle on the road either immediately or from a later date and time by the issue of a prohibition notice (form PG9 – see below).
  NB: *Police powers in this respect are restricted under the provisions of the Road Traffic Act 1991 (effective from 1 July 1992) to the issue only of immediate prohibitions in circumstances where they consider that the driving of a defective vehicle would involve a 'danger of injury to any person' as opposed to the VOSA examiner's right to prohibit a vehicle which is 'unfit for service'.*

- Where a prohibition order has been placed on a vehicle for various reasons, they are empowered to remove the prohibition (by the issue of form PG10) when they consider the vehicle is fit for use. *Since 1 July 1992 clearance of prohibitions has required the vehicle to be subjected to a full roadworthiness test by VOSA at a goods vehicle testing station – and payment of the full test fee (currently £145.00 and £68.00 respectively for the largest vehicles and trailers).*

- They can ask the driver of a goods vehicle registered in an EU member state, fitted with a tachograph, to produce the tachograph record of the vehicle when it is used in this country and ask to examine the official calibration plaque in the instrument. They can at any reasonable time enter premises where they believe such a vehicle is to be found or that tachograph records are kept, and may inspect the vehicle and records (ie tachograph charts).

Powers of Police Constables

- A police constable *in uniform* can stop a moving vehicle on a road ('constable' includes any rank of uniformed police officer). They can test any motor vehicle or trailer on a road to check that legal requirements regarding brakes, silencer, steering, tyres, lights and reflectors, smoke and fumes are complied with. They may drive the vehicle for this purpose.

- They can test a vehicle for the same purposes on premises if the owner of the premises consents or has been given at least 48 hours' notice (or 72 hours if given by recorded post), except that consent is not necessary where the vehicle has been involved in a notifiable accident.

NB: *This authority applies to all constables even if not specially authorized under the Road Traffic Act 1988 as mentioned above.*

Enforcement Powers for VOSA and DSA Examiners

Specially selected and trained enforcement officers of VOSA have powers to stop moving vehicles. These officers, known as Enforcement Support Officers (colloquially referred to as 'stopping officers') and accredited by Chief Constables under provisions contained in the Police Reform Act 2002, are uniformed and operate with liveried and fully marked vehicles (silver Ford Galaxy cars with amber beacons and 'Follow Me' lighting).

Further new powers under The Road Vehicles (Powers to Stop) Regulations 2011 (SI 2011 No. 996), which amend the Road Traffic Act 1988 and came into effect from 30 March 2011, allow the Secretary of State for Transport to appoint VOSA 'stopping officers' throughout Great Britain (and in Northern Ireland) who may *stop* and inspect commercial vehicles for specified purposes as listed below. Under the previous legislation such officers in England and Wales had to be individually accredited by Chief Officers of police in the constabulary in which they operated once they had completed the necessary training.

Now the DfT says the new changes will speed up the enforcement process and free up police involvement in the administration of the current road stopping scheme. Once VOSA stopping officers have received the appropriate training they will have the powers to:

- stop commercial vehicles;
- carry out vehicle roadworthiness inspections;
- carry out vehicle weight checks;
- inspect documents, records and tachograph equipment;
- ensure that O-licence discs are correctly exhibited;
- ensure that a valid O-licence is held;
- ensure that drivers carry evidence of their Driver CPC training, or exemptions from such.

Resisting or obstructing a VOSA stopping officer is a criminal offence.

Powers of Trading Standards Officers

Trading Standards Officers (ie employed by local authorities) can request the driver of a vehicle which is carrying goods that need an official conveyance note (ie ballast which includes sand, gravel, shingle, ashes, clinker, chippings, including coated material, hardcore and aggregates) to take that vehicle to a weighbridge to be weighed. Goods may have to be unloaded if necessary.

Inspection Notices and Prohibitions

Vehicle Inspection Notice – Form PGDN35

Following an inspection of a vehicle which is found to have no serious road safety defects, form PGDN35 (commonly known as an inspection notice) is issued to indicate to the user either that one or more minor defects were found which it is in his interest, and the interests of other road users, to have rectified at an early date – it is not actually a prohibition – or that the vehicle has no apparent defects – subject to a disclaimer – to save further inspection later on that journey or that day.

Direction Notice

Form GV3 is authorization for VOSA examiners to direct a vehicle to proceed to a specified place to be inspected (normally not more than five miles away).

Prohibition Notices

The driver of any vehicle found by VOSA examiners to have serious defects is given a form PG9 on which these are listed. Form PG9 is the examiner's authority to stop the use of the vehicle on the road for carrying goods. Depending on how serious the defects are, the prohibition will either take effect immediately, in which case the vehicle, if loaded, has to remain where it is until either it is repaired or has been unloaded and then taken away for repair, for which the examiner will give authority by issuing form PG9B, or it may be delayed for 12 to 24 hours or more depending on the seriousness of the fault (see p 395). In this case the vehicle may continue to operate until the limit of the period of exemption of the prohibition by which time, if it is not repaired and cleared, it must be taken off the road. If defects recorded as requiring immediate attention are repaired quickly on the roadside (either by the driver or by a mechanic or repair garage staff who come out to the vehicle) the examiner may issue a variation to the PG9 notice with form PG9A, which then allows the vehicle to be removed and used until the new time specified on the variation notice (the forms are described further individually below).

C&U Offences

If defects are found at a roadside check which make the vehicle unsafe to be on the road (usually brakes, steering or suspension defects) or if the defects are such that an offence under the Construction and Use Regulations is committed (particularly in respect of lights, reflectors, smoke emission or the horn), VOSA examiners will report these items to the police in attendance for consideration for prosecution.

Prohibition Forms

A number of official forms as described below are used by VOSA examiners in the process of inspecting vehicles, recording defects and prohibiting the use of those which are defective.

Form PG9

When an inspection by a VOSA examiner reveals defects of a serious nature form PG9 will be issued, specifying the defects and stating the precise time at which the prohibition preventing further use of the vehicle comes into force (which could be the time when the notice is written out – ie with immediate effect – or later). A copy of the PG9 is given to the driver and this must be carried on the vehicle until the prohibition is removed. Further copies of the notice are sent to the vehicle operator and, if the vehicle is specified on an 'O' licence, to the relevant Traffic Commissioner (TC).

If the PG9 has immediate effect, this means that the vehicle cannot be driven or towed away (see below).

Form PG9A

This form (Variation in the Terms of a Prohibition…) is issued if the VOSA examiner wishes to vary the terms of a PG9 notice by either suspending the PG9 until a future time (eg midnight on the day of issue), altering the time (which is effectively the same thing as suspending the notice as mentioned above) or altering the list of defects shown on the PG9 notice.

Form PG9B

A VOSA examiner may, after issuing a PG9, exempt the vehicle (Exemption from a Prohibition…) from the terms of the prohibition and permit its movement provided that the vehicle:

- is unladen;
- proceeds at a speed not in excess of a specified figure;
- does not tow a trailer;
- is towed on a rigid tow bar;
- is towed on a suspended tow;
- is not used after lighting-up time (if it has lighting defects);
- proceeds only between two specified points.

Other conditions may be added as appropriate.

Form PG9C

When a vehicle which is subject to a PG9 notice is presented to a VOSA examiner for clearance of the defect and the examiner is not satisfied that it is fit for service, he may issue form PG9C (Refusal to Remove a Prohibition…), which means that the original PG9 notice remains in force until the defects are satisfactorily rectified.

Form PG10

If the defects specified in a PG9 notice have been repaired to the satisfaction of the VOSA examiner to whom the vehicle is presented for clearance and the examiner is satisfied that the whole vehicle is in a satisfactory condition for use on the road, he will issue a PG10 notice (Removal of Prohibition…), which removes the prohibition. The TC must be notified of the clearance if the vehicle is specified on an 'O' licence.

Form TE160

This notice (*which does not have a PG prefix*) relates to prohibition on the use of overweight vehicles. It effectively requires the driver of the vehicle to take the vehicle to a weighbridge and, if it is found to be overloaded, reduce the gross weight to legal limits before proceeding on his journey.

NB: It is a defence to a charge of overloading that the vehicle was on its way to the nearest practicable weighbridge or that at the time of loading the weight was within legal limits and was subsequently not more than 5 per cent heavier despite not having any additions to the load en route.

Effects of Prohibition

A vehicle must not, under any circumstances, be used to carry goods while it is the subject of a PG9 prohibition notice, but despite the prohibition notice a vehicle may be driven unladen to a goods vehicle test station or to a place agreed with a goods vehicle examiner (both by previous appointment only) in order to have the vehicle inspected. The vehicle may also be driven on the road for test purposes, provided it is unladen, within three miles of where it has been repaired.

Forms PG9 and PG9A have a panel of boxes identified by letters of the alphabet from A to M. These boxes are used by enforcement staff to codify certain aspects of the vehicle check as follows:

A Whether the vehicle was laden or unladen.

B Whether examination took place on the roadside, at a test station, during the annual test, following an accident, during a fleet check or on any other occasion.

C If defects appeared to be from a significant failure in maintenance arrangements a letter 'S' is entered; 'X' is used if the examiner can attach no undue significance to the defect (ie it could have happened on the journey); and the box is left blank if the examiner is not able to form an opinion as to the cause of the defect.

D To indicate whether a prosecution will follow (the letter 'P' in this box indicates prosecution by the police and 'V' by VOSA).

E If vehicle is issuing smoke ('S' equals smoking in service; 'S/A' equals smoking under free acceleration when vehicle is stationary).

L Indicates number of pages of prohibition notice served at the time (ie page 1 of 1, page 1 of 2). This indicates to the examiner who is asked to clear the prohibition that there was another sheet(s) to the prohibition notice issued at the time.

F, G, H, K and M Not currently used.

Appeals against the Issue of Prohibition Notices

There is no appeal against the imposition of a PG9 prohibition notice, but there is a right of appeal against refusal to remove a prohibition after repair.

Clearance of Prohibition

An operator having a vehicle placed under an immediate or a delayed prohibition notice has to get the defects repaired and then submit the vehicle to his local goods vehicle testing station either for a full roadworthiness examination in the case of serious defects (with payment of the relevant fees as shown on p 376) or, in the case of minor defects, a 'partial clearance' or 'mini' test. A clearance certificate, PG10, is issued if the examiner is satisfied with the repair. If the examiner is not satisfied with the repair he will issue a form PG9C 'Refusal to Remove a Prohibition', or form PG9A if some of the defects are cleared and others are not. If because of the better inspection facilities at the test station he finds further defects another form PG9 may be issued.

VDRS for Trucks

A vehicle defect rectification scheme for heavy commercial vehicles similar to the one operated by the police for defective cars and light vehicles (see pp 408–409) was introduced nationwide (late in 1996) following the success of pilot schemes in Durham and Essex. Operators of vehicles found with minor defects are given 14 days in which to rectify them, and produce evidence of the repair (ie by means of an invoice).

Light Vehicle Testing

Light goods vehicles up to 3,500 kg gross weight and dual-purpose vehicles (see p 220 for definition) under 2,040 kg unladen weight are required to be tested on the third anniversary of the date of their original registration and annually thereafter (commonly known and referred to as the MoT test). The tests are carried out at private garages approved by VOSA and displaying the blue and white triple-triangle sign. For full details of the testing scheme for these vehicles, see Chapter 15, which deals with light vehicle testing.

Northern Ireland Certification of Vehicles

The United Kingdom system of goods vehicle plating and annual testing does not apply in Northern Ireland. The Province has its own Goods Vehicle Certification scheme (commonly known and referred to in the Province as the PSV test) which requires heavy goods vehicles to be submitted to the Department of the Environment (NI) for an annual mechanical examination. Under the Goods Vehicles (Certification) Regulations (Northern Ireland) 1982, owners of goods vehicles (other than those specifically exempted – see pp 400–401) must obtain a test certificate for each vehicle no later than one year from the date of first registration and annually thereafter (see p 406).

Application for a certificate must be made to the following address at least one month before the date on which the certificate is to take effect: Department of the Environment, Vehicle and Driving Test Centre, Balmoral Road, Belfast BT12 6QL.

Retest fees apply where application is made within 21 days from the date of service of the notice and the vehicle is presented for re-examination within 28 days.

Applications by Non-NI-Based Bodies

Where an application is made by a corporate body with its principal or registered office outside Northern Ireland or by a person residing outside Northern Ireland the following conditions must be observed:

- During the currency of the certificate a place of business must be retained in NI.

- They must be prepared to accept, at such a place of business, any summons or other document relating to any matter or offence arising in NI in connection with the vehicle for which the certificate is applied for.
- They must undertake to appear at any court as required by such a summons or by any other document.
- They must admit and submit to the jurisdiction of the court relative to the subject matter of such summons or other document.

Failure to comply with any of the above-mentioned requirements will involve immediate revocation of the certificate.

Examination of Vehicle

When notified by the Department the applicant must present the vehicle for examination, in a reasonably clean condition, together with the registration book and previous certificate, if any, at the time and at the centre specified in the notice.

Issue of Certificate

If, after examining the vehicle, the Department is satisfied that it complies in all respects with the regulations in respect of the construction, use, lighting and rear marking of vehicles, a certificate will be issued.

Refusal of Certificate

If the vehicle does not meet the requirements of the regulations a certificate will be refused and the applicant will be notified of the reasons why.

Re-examination of Vehicles

When a certificate has been refused and the defects specified in the notice have been put right, an application may be made for a further examination of the vehicle. A reduced retest fee will be payable if the retest is conducted within 21 days of the original test.

Refund of Fees

Prepaid test fees may be refunded in the following circumstances:

- If an appointment for an examination of a vehicle is cancelled by the Department.
- If the applicant cancels the appointment by giving the Department (at the centre where the appointment is made) three clear working days' notice.
- If the vehicle is presented to meet the appointment but the examination does not take place for reasons not attributable to the applicant or the vehicle.
- If the applicant satisfies the Department that the vehicle could not be presented for examination on the day of the appointment because of exceptional circumstances which occurred no more than seven days before the day of the

appointment, and providing notice is given to the centre where the examination was to take place within three days of the occurrence.

Duplicate Certificates

Duplicate certificates may be issued in replacement of those which have been accidentally lost, defaced or destroyed. A fee is payable for replacement certificates. If subsequently the original certificate is found, it must be returned to the nearest examining centre or to any police station.

Display of Certificates

The certificate issued on satisfying the examiners must be attached to the vehicle in a secure, weather-proof holder and must be displayed on the nearside windscreen or on the nearside of the vehicle not less than 610 mm and not more than 1,830 mm above the road surface so that the particulars of the certificate are clearly visible (ie at eye level) to a person standing at the nearside of the vehicle.

Conditions of Certificate

It is a condition of the certificate that the vehicle owner:

- must not permit the vehicle to be used for any illegal purpose;
- must not deface or mutilate the certificate or permit anybody else to do so;
- must, at all reasonable times, for the purpose of inspection, examination or testing of the vehicle to which the certificate relates:
  - produce the vehicle at such a time and place as may be specified by any Inspector of Vehicles;
  - afford to any Inspector of Vehicles full facilities for such inspection, examination or testing including access to his premises for that purpose;
  - must ensure that the vehicle and all its fittings are maintained and kept in good order and repair and must take all practical steps to ensure that all parts of the mechanism, including the brakes, are free from defects and are in efficient working order;
  - must immediately notify the nearest examination centre of any alteration in design or construction of the vehicle since a certificate was issued.

Transfer of Certificates

If a vehicle owner sells or changes the ownership of a vehicle, he must return the certificate for the vehicle to the nearest examination centre and notify the Department of the name and address of the transferee. The Department may then transfer the certificate on request by the new owner.

If a vehicle owner dies or becomes infirm of mind or body, on application of any person the Department may transfer the certificate to such a person.

Change of Address

If a certificate holder changes his address during the currency of a certificate, he must notify details of such changes to the nearest examination centre.

Markings on Vehicles

When certificates have been issued for vehicles, those vehicles must be marked with:

- the name and address of the owner in legible writing and in a conspicuous position on the nearside of the vehicle; and
- where the unladen weight of the vehicle exceeds 1,020 kg, the unladen weight should be painted, or otherwise clearly marked, in a conspicuous position on the offside of the vehicle. In the case of articulated vehicles the unladen weight of the tractive unit and the trailer must be marked on the respective unit and trailer.

Offences

It is an offence to operate when a certificate has expired, or to alter, deface, mutilate or fail to display a certificate. Failure to observe such rules will result in the certificate being declared invalid. It is also an offence to assign or to transfer a certificate to another person with the same resultant penalty. Fines or six months' imprisonment may be imposed on summary conviction for such offences or up to two years' imprisonment upon any further conviction or indictment.

Renewal of Certificates

At least one month before the expiry date of a certificate the holder should apply for a new one using an application form obtainable from any examination centre or Local Vehicle Licensing Office of the Department.

Exemptions from Certification

The following vehicles are exempt from the requirements of NI certification:

- vehicles constructed or adapted for the sole purpose of spreading material on roads or used to deal with frost, ice or snow;
- a land tractor, land locomotive or land implement;
- an agricultural trailer drawn on a road only by a land tractor;
- a vehicle exempted from duty under section 7(i) of the Vehicles (Excise) Act (Northern Ireland) 1972 and any trailer drawn by such a vehicle;
- a motor vehicle for the time being licensed under the Vehicles (Excise) Act 1971, paragraph (a);
- a trailer brought into NI from a base outside NI if a period of 12 months has elapsed since it was last brought into NI;

- a pedestrian-controlled vehicle;
- a track-laying vehicle;
- a steam-propelled vehicle;
- a vehicle used within a period of 12 months prior to the date of it being registered for the first time in NI or the UK; or, where a vehicle has been used on roads in NI or elsewhere before being registered, the exemption applies for the period of 12 months from the date of manufacture rather than from the date of registration. For this purpose any use before the vehicle is sold or supplied retail is disregarded.

Light Vehicle (MoT) Testing

Private cars, motor caravans (irrespective of weight), dual-purpose vehicles (see p 220 for definition) under 2,040 kg unladen weight and light goods vehicles not exceeding 3,500 kg gross weight are subject to annual testing (commonly referred to as the MoT test) at VOSA-approved commercial garages, starting on the third anniversary of the date of their first registration and each year thereafter.

Cars and light goods vehicles may be tested up to one month before the due date of their first test and the test certificate will extend for 13 months to expire on the anniversary of the first registration date.

Testing is carried out at garages displaying the blue and white MoT triple-triangle symbol, and application is made direct with the garage for a suitable appointment. Some centres claim to provide MoT testing 'while you wait'. There is no application form to be completed.

A new computer system has been installed in MoT testing stations which facilitates checks on a vehicle's MoT status and reduces theft and forgery of MoT test certificates. Records of all MoT tests are held on a secure central database, which comprises the definitive proof of a valid test pass. MoT certificates are produced as A4-format receipts which have no value to thieves and there are no blank certificates to steal. With the new-type computerized test certificate a vehicle can be re-taxed online at **www.direct.gov/motoring** as well as at a post office.

Fees for the light vehicle test (as at July 2010) – payable to the garage at the time of the test – are as follows:

Class IV & IVa (Class IVa includes seat belt installation check)

Vehicle type	Age first test certificate required (years)	Fee
Cars (up to 8 passenger seats)	3	£54.85
Motor caravans	3	£54.85
Dual purpose vehicles	3	£54.85
PSVs (up to 8 seats)	3	£54.85
Ambulances and taxis	1	£54.85
Private passenger vehicles and ambulances (9–12 passenger seats)	1	£57.30
Class IVa	–	£64.00

Class V (with more than 13 passenger seats)

Vehicle type	Age first test certificate required (years)	Fee
13–16 passenger seats	1	£59.55
More than 16 passenger seats	1	£80.65

Class Va (includes seat belt installation check)

Vehicle type	Age first test certificate required (years)	Fee
13–16 passenger seats	–	£80.50
More than 16 passenger seats	–	£124.50

Class VII

Vehicle type	Age first test certificate required (years)	Fee
Goods vehicles (over 3,000 kg up to 3,500 kg DGW)	3	£58.60

Duplicate test certificates cost £10 or half of the above amounts.

NB: *The term 'DGW' as used above means 'design gross weight'.*

Vehicle Classes

Vehicles subject to the MoT test are classified as follows:

Class I   Light motor bicycles not exceeding 200 cc cylinder capacity with or without sidecars.

Class II   All motor bicycles (including Class I) with or without sidecars.

Class III   Light motor vehicles with three or more wheels (excluding Classes I and II) not exceeding 450 kg unladen weight.

Class IV   Heavy motor cars and motor cars (excluding Classes III and V); ie any vehicle with an unladen weight of more than 450 kg which is:
(a) a passenger vehicle (ie private car, taxi, vehicle licensed as private, with 12 passenger seats or less, or small public service vehicle with less than 8 passenger seats);
(b) a dual-purpose vehicle not exceeding 2,040 kg unladen weight (see p 219 for definition);
(c) a goods vehicle not exceeding 3,000 kg gross weight;
(d) a motor caravan irrespective of weight.

Class V   Large passenger carrying vehicles; ie motor vehicles which are constructed or adapted to carry more than 12 seated passengers in addition to the driver, and which are not licensed as public service vehicles.

Class VI   Public service vehicles other than those in Class V above.

Class VII   Goods vehicles of 3,001 kg to 3,500 kg gross weight (these vehicles may be tested at MoT garages – where the facility to test such vehicles is available – or at goods vehicle testing stations).

Exemptions

Public service vehicles with seats for eight or more passengers excluding the driver, track-laying vehicles, vehicles constructed or adapted to form part of an articulated vehicle, works trucks and all trailers are excluded from the above classes and the following vehicles are also exempted from the test:

- heavy locomotives;
- light locomotives;
- goods vehicles over 3.5 tonnes gross weight;
- articulated vehicles other than articulated buses;
- vehicles exempt from duty under the Vehicle Excise and Registration Act 1994;
- works trucks;
- pedestrian-controlled vehicles;
- vehicles kept and used by invalids;
- vehicles temporarily in Great Britain;
- vehicles proceeding to a port for export;
- vehicles provided for use by the police force;

- imported vehicles owned or in the service of HM navy, army or air force;
- vehicles which have Northern Ireland test certificates;
- electrically propelled goods vehicles not exceeding 1,525 kg unladen weight;
- certain hackney carriages.

Many of these vehicles are subject to the goods vehicle testing and plating scheme (see Chapter 14 for details).

There is also an exemption which applies to vehicles which come within the MoT test scheme while they are being driven to a place by previous arrangement for a test or bringing it away, if it fails, to a place to have work done on it. This means that such vehicles can be driven on the road without a valid test certificate being in force, but only in the circumstances mentioned and no other.

The Test

Testing is carried out in accordance with *The MoT Tester's Manual* – copies available from The Stationery Office. (*Note: This publication should not be confused with* The Heavy Goods Vehicle Inspection Manual, *which relates solely to the goods vehicle annual test and which is also available from The Stationery Office.*)

When presenting a vehicle for test the following conditions must be observed:

- The vehicle registration document must be produced.
- The vehicle must be sufficiently clean so as not to make the test unreasonably difficult.
- The vehicle must have sufficient petrol and oil to enable the test to be completed.
- If the vehicle is presented for the test in a loaded condition (ie in the case of light goods vehicles) the load must be secured or else removed.

Refusal and Discontinuance of Test

Failure to observe any of the above conditions can lead to a refusal to test the vehicle, and the test fee will be refunded. Furthermore, if the tester finds a defect of a serious nature which, in his opinion, makes it essential to discontinue the inspection on the grounds of risk to his own safety, risk to the test equipment or to the vehicle itself, he may do so and issue form VT30 showing the defects which caused the test to be discontinued.

Items Tested

The following items are tested and must meet the conditions specified in *The MoT Tester's Manual*:

Section I   Function of obligatory front and rear lamps
             Function of obligatory head lamps

Function of stop lamps
Obligatory rear reflectors
Function of direction indicators
Aim of head lamps

Section II   Steering wheel and column
Steering mechanism
Power steering
Front wheel bearings
Suspension
All suspension types
Suspension assemblies (springs, torsion bars, etc)
Shock absorbers

Section III   Parking brake and operating lever
Parking brake mechanism (under vehicle)
Service brake operating pedal
Service brake mechanism under vehicle
Brake performance test

Section IV   Tyres
Road wheels

Section V   Seat belts

Section VI   Function of windscreen washers
Function of windscreen wipers
Exhaust system
Function of audible warning device
Condition of the vehicle structure.

Additional Test Items

Since 1 November 1991 the examination has covered additional items such as exhaust emissions (see below) – particularly in light goods vehicle tests; ABS (ie anti-lock braking system) warning lights; rear seat belts (ie where fitted); rear wheel bearings; more extensive corrosion checks.

Since 1 January 1993 additional items have been included in the MoT test in accordance with EU requirements. These include checks on the following vehicle components and systems:

- mirrors – a motor car must have a mirror on the driver's side and either an exterior mirror on the passenger side, or an interior mirror; they must be in good condition, capable of adjustment and be secure;

- windscreens – damage (ie a crack) to a windscreen, exceeding 10 mm in zone A (an area 290 mm wide centred on a vertical line passing through the centre of the steering wheel and within the area swept by the windscreen wipers), will result in test failure as will obscuring clear vision with stickers or other obstructions;

- fuel tanks and feed pipes – must be in good condition and secure (including the tank filler cap);

- bodywork and body security – must be sound;

- seat fixings – must be secure and backrests lockable;
- security of doors and other openings – all doors must be capable of being opened from the inside and outside and they must latch securely;
- number (ie registration) plates – must be secure and in good condition and the letters and numbers must be correctly spaced (incorrect spacing of letters and numbers to make up names or other words will result in test failure);
- vehicle identification number – must be present and capable of being clearly read;
- number plate lamps (at rear) – must be fitted and working correctly;
- rear fog lamps – vehicles first used after 1 April 1980 must have one and it must work and an interior warning light must be provided and must work;
- hazard warning devices – must work with the ignition on or off and there must be an interior warning light which works.

Exhaust Emission Checks

A check is made on emissions from diesel-engined vehicles subject to the test. These tests were reintroduced in 1994 after being temporarily suspended.

Cars, light goods vehicles and particularly goods vehicles within the weight range 3,001 kg to 3,500 kg gross weight which fall within the *Class VII* MoT test are subjected to additional exhaust emission checks during their annual roadworthiness test, as well as checks for excessively smoking exhausts. This involves measurement of the levels of carbon monoxide (CO) and hydrocarbons (HC) to ensure that engines are properly tuned. The current maximum level of carbon monoxide acceptable for post-1 August 1983 registered vehicles is 4.5 per cent (6 per cent for vehicles first registered prior to this date). The limit for hydrocarbons for post-1 August 1975 registered vehicles is 1,200 parts per million (ppm).

Higher standards (ie lower permissible emissions), originally intended for introduction in 1996, were brought forward to come into effect from 1 September 1995, as follows:

- light goods vehicles in Class II (ie between 1,250 and 1,700 kg gross weight):

carbon monoxide (CO) limit –	5.17 kg/km
hydrocarbon/nitrous oxide –	1.4 g/km
particulates –	0.19 g/km

- light goods vehicles in Class III (ie 1,700 kg to 3,500 kg gross weight):

carbon monoxide (CO) limit –	6.9 kg/km
hydrocarbon/nitrous oxide –	1.7 g/km
particulates –	0.25 g/km

Emission standards tests as described above do not apply to motorcycles, three-wheelers or diesel-engined vehicles.

Regulations permit tests for exhaust emissions to be carried out on the roadside as well as at approved MoT test garages.

Seat Belt Checks

Additional seat belt checks have been included in the MoT scheme since 1 August 1998. From this date the condition of seat belts in all vehicles (whether required to be fitted mandatorily or fitted on a voluntary basis) will be examined to determine whether the belts are likely to fulfil their intended function in the event of an accident. Similar checks on seat belts will be carried out during roadside and other enforcement spot checks.

Certain vehicles are to be subject to a once-only check of the quality of their seat belt installations – during subsequent MoT checks only the condition of the belts, as normal, will be checked. Vehicles affected by these additional checks are those falling into Class IV, Class V and Class VI (see p 403). The checks will be carried out only at Class V MoT testing stations, VOSA testing stations and VOSA PSV designated premises by appropriately trained vehicle examiners.

A one-off additional fee is to be charged for these installation-quality inspections.

Test Failure

If the vehicle fails to reach the required standard of mechanical condition a 'notification of refusal of a test certificate' (form VT30) is issued. This indicates the grounds on which the vehicle failed the test (ie it names the faulty components or component area and the actual fault).

Retests

If a vehicle fails the test, no further test fee is payable if it is left at the garage for the necessary repairs to be carried out before the end of the 10th working day from the day of the initial test. However, if the vehicle is taken away following the test failure, a three-tier system of retests and fees applies as follows:

- Tier 1 Full Test. Where a vehicle is presented for retest more than 10 working days after the day of the initial test or if the original MoT tester is not available for a tier 2 test, a full test must be carried out and the full test fee is payable.

- Tier 2 Partial Retest. Where a retest is necessary that requires the use of a major piece of testing equipment (including hoist or pit, brake performance tester, exhaust gas analyser (EGA), diesel smoke meter (DSM) and head lamp aim equipment), or where a repair has been carried out by welding, or there has been a repair to the steering or braking system (excluding stop lamps), provided that the retest is carried out by the same tester at the same MoT garage before the end of the 10th working day from the day of the initial test a partial retest will be carried out and only two-thirds of the full test fee will be payable.

- Tier 3 Partial Retest. Where a retest does not require the use of a major piece of testing equipment, provided it is carried out at the same MoT garage before the end of the 10th working day from the day of the initial test, only one-third of the full test fee will be payable.

Where any vehicle does not fall into tier 2 or 3 above, a full re-examination in accordance with tier 1 must be carried out. Only one partial re-examination is permissible per full examination.

Issue of Test Certificate

On completion of the test, if the vehicle is found to be in satisfactory condition and in compliance with the law, a test certificate (form VT20) is issued. Additionally, a copy of form VT29 is issued to indicate to the vehicle owner the general state of the vehicle and to point out components which may need attention in the future to keep it in good, safe working order. Comments on form VT29 are made against the following headings:

I   Lighting equipment
II   Steering and suspension
III Braking system
IV   Tyres and wheels
V   Seat belts
VI   General items.

Appeals

A vehicle owner can appeal if he is not satisfied with the result of the test. He must complete form VT17 and send it to the local Traffic Area Office within 14 days of taking the test.

Production of Test Certificates

It is necessary to produce a current, valid test certificate when taxing a vehicle to which the regulations apply, otherwise an excise licence will not be issued. A police officer can ask to see a vehicle test certificate. If the driver does not have it with him he can be asked to produce the certificate at a police station nominated by him within seven days.

As mentioned MOT test certificates are now computerized and these can be used to re-tax a vehicle online.

Vehicle Defect Rectification Scheme

Operators of light vehicles (up to 3,500 kg gross weight) found on the road with non-endorsable minor vehicle defects (ie lights, wipers, speedometer, silencer, etc) in certain areas may be offered the VDRS procedure by the police whereby no prosecution will result if:

1 Immediate arrangements are made for the repair of the defect.
2 The repaired vehicle and VDRS notice are presented to an MoT garage for examination and certification that the defects have been rectified.
3 The certificate is sent to a local Central Ticket Office.

Failure to follow the procedure on receipt of a VDRS notice will result in prosecution.

Vehicle Maintenance and Maintenance Records

The requirements of the Road Traffic Act 1988 for the annual testing of goods vehicles and trailers, the requirements of the current Construction and Use Regulations, and the parts of the Transport Act 1968 setting out the conditions relating to vehicle maintenance under which an 'O' licence will be granted create a situation whereby operators must ensure that their vehicles and trailers are always safe, are in a fit and roadworthy condition and that their maintenance, vehicle inspection and maintenance record systems meet the requirements laid down in the legislation.

In order for operators to meet these requirements they must maintain their vehicles and trailers (no matter how old they are) to a sufficiently high standard to enable them to pass the stringent annual goods vehicle test, which they should be able to do on the test day *and on every other day when they are on the road*. To be able to do this, it is not sufficient merely to take the vehicle off the road for a short period once a year just before test day and work frantically to get it up to scratch, and for the rest of the year allow it to run on the road in a condition which is something below the required standard.

The risk of the vehicle encountering a roadside check, or being on the operator's premises when examiners of the Vehicle and Operator Services Agency (VOSA) or the police decide to make an inspection, as they are empowered to do, is too great to take when the penalties for failure to maintain vehicles are so high. Besides the risk of heavy fines, there is the possibility that the operator may lose his 'O' licence since a satisfactory state of maintenance is one of the factors taken into account by the Traffic Commissioner in considering applications and renewals for such licences.

Maintenance Advice

A VOSA team along with operator associations have produced a Code of Practice on vehicle maintenance for transport operators – *Guide to Maintaining Roadworthiness: Commercial Goods and Passenger Carrying Vehicles* – available from The Stationery Office, Traffic Area Offices and heavy goods vehicle testing stations and it can be freely downloaded from the VOSA website at **www.vosa.gov.uk/publications**. Additionally, there is the DfT's free guide *A Guide to Goods Vehicle Operators' Licensing* (reference GV74), which contains some specific advice on vehicle maintenance arrangements for licence applicants. The following notes are included as an appendix to the *Guide*.

There are two separate vehicle checks and inspections which should be carried out:

- daily running checks;
- vehicle safety inspections and routine maintenance at set intervals on items which affect vehicle safety, followed by repair of any faults.

Daily running checks are normally carried out by drivers before a vehicle starts its daily journey. They are checks on such basic items as engine oil, brakes, tyre pressures, warning instruments, lights, windscreen wipers and washers and trailer coupling.

Vehicle safety inspections and routine maintenance should be carried out at set intervals of either time and/or mileage, whichever occurs first. How often these inspections are done should be decided by the nature of the operator's business. A vehicle used on long-distance work will need inspecting at different intervals from one employed in heavy traffic on local work with frequent stops and starts. The items inspected should include wheels, tyres, brakes, steering, suspension, lighting, and so on. More detailed information can be found in VOSA's publication *The Heavy Goods Vehicle Inspection Manual* (available from The Stationery Office or ordered online, see above). Vehicle checks and inspections are extra to a routine maintenance schedule. It is vital to the vehicle's safety that both types of checks and inspections are done.

Staff doing inspection checks must be able to recognize faults they find, such as excessive wear of components. They should also be aware of the acceptable standard of performance and wear of parts. Trade associations offer regular inspections for their members' vehicles.

Records

Records must be kept of all safety inspections to show the history of each vehicle. These records must be kept for at least 15 months. If vehicles from several operating centres are inspected and repaired at a central depot, the records may be kept at that depot, although VOSA examiners are entitled to request inspection of records at the operating centres where vehicles are based.

If an outside garage does the inspections and repairs, you must still keep maintenance records. You are responsible for the condition of any vehicle or trailer on your licence.

Facilities

These will depend on the number, size and types of vehicles to be inspected. It must be possible to inspect the underside of a vehicle with sufficient light and space to examine individual parts closely. Ramps, hoists or pits will usually be necessary, but may not be needed if the vehicles have enough ground clearance for a proper underside inspection to be made on hard-standing. Creeper boards, jacks, axle stands and small tools should be available.

As well as providing facilities for checking the underside of vehicles, operators should whenever possible use equipment for measuring braking efficiency and setting headlights. If many vehicles have to be inspected, it may be worthwhile providing a roller brake tester.

Drivers' Reports

Drivers must report vehicle faults to whoever is responsible for having them put right. The maintenance system should allow for these reports, which must be recorded in writing either by the driver himself or by the person responsible for maintaining the vehicle. Owner-drivers must note faults as they arise and keep these notes as part of their maintenance record.

Hired Vehicles and Trailers

In the case of hired, rented or borrowed vehicles or those belonging to other operators used in inter-working arrangements, it is the user who is responsible for their mechanical condition on the road. If disciplinary action is taken as a result of a mechanical fault, it is against the user's licence, not the company from whom the vehicle is hired, or the owner.

The Choice: To Repair or Contract Out

The first decision an operator has to make when planning his vehicle maintenance is to determine whether it is to be carried out in his own workshops, by his own staff, or whether it is to be contracted out to a repair garage. The size of the fleet and what existing facilities and premises he already has will usually determine the method to be used. It is unlikely to be an economic proposition for a very small operator with a fleet of less than five or six vehicles to establish his own workshop unless he actually does the work himself. On the other hand it is unlikely to be an economic proposition for a large operator to contract out the work. There are, however, many examples in industry where the opposites apply, and very successfully too; so it remains very much a matter for operators to assess their own requirements, balance out the costs of the alternatives and make arrangements accordingly.

Choice of Repairer

When choosing a repairer to do the work preference should be given to a garage which is a main distributor for the make of vehicle operated or an agent for that make of vehicle. The reason for this is that such a firm, as part of its arrangement with the manufacturer it represents, will have had to send some of its mechanics to the factory for training in the repair and servicing of that particular make of vehicle. This ensures that skilled staff are working on the vehicle. Moreover, the distributors are also usually required by the manufacturer to hold considerable stocks of spare parts, with a predominance of fast-moving items. By using such a garage the risk of a vehicle being kept off the road waiting for spare parts is therefore considerably reduced, and since vehicle downtime is a heavy cost burden these days this is an important consideration. If a garage of this type is not available locally and a second choice has to be made, this should be a firm which is experienced in heavy vehicle repair work and which has suitably trained staff and the necessary equipment. A garage which normally only handles motor car repair work should not be used.

Repair Arrangements

Any arrangements made with a repairer should be in writing. The 'O' licence application form requests that copies of any maintenance contract should be sent with the application but in any event the Traffic Commissioner (TC) will want to know what arrangements have been made with a repairer. Verbal arrangements or the practice of sending vehicles in for repair as necessary on an ad hoc basis are not acceptable to the TCs, some of whom have said that a verbal agreement for these purposes is no agreement at all.

Maintenance Agreements

The agreement should include provisions for the repairer to be responsible for supplying the operator with suitable records of the inspections and repair work carried out. The operator should ensure that he can escape reasonably quickly and easily from any agreement in the event of the standard of work deteriorating and thereby placing his 'O' licence at risk.

Care should be taken when discussing or making an agreement that the repairer is aware of the consequences of any negligent action on his part on the livelihood of the operator, remembering that it is the vehicle 'user' who remains responsible at all times for the safe and satisfactory mechanical condition of the vehicle, and it is he or she who is responsible for keeping and producing records of vehicle inspections and other maintenance work.

There is no standard or recommended form of maintenance agreement in universal use; it is left to the parties concerned to agree on terms.

NB: *A suitable format for agreements is suggested by the DfT in its* Guide to Maintaining Roadworthiness. *A copy of a suitable agreement is also included in the 'O' licence application pack and is available online at* **www.businesslink.gov.uk.**

The agreement should clearly set out in detail the work to be done, the intervals at which it is to be done, the responsibilities of the operator and the garage, the form which records should take and the action to be taken if defects are discovered or repairs over a certain value are found to be necessary.

Maintenance Contracts

In recent years there has been a proliferation of contract maintenance schemes, many of them offered by truck manufacturers who are looking to retain future business. However, the advice given in this chapter remains relevant even with such sophisticated schemes. It is worth pointing out here that no matter how good the contract scheme or how reputable and reliable the repairer, it remains the responsibility of the operator to ensure that vehicles are in a fit, serviceable and safe condition when on the road and that they comply fully with the law. (This is covered in more detail later in the chapter.)

Some of the prominent commercial vehicle repair specialists offer contract maintenance schemes. There are usually a number of options in such schemes which, for instance, give the operator a choice of having his vehicles inspected only at set intervals; inspected and serviced according to the manufacturer's recommendations; or inspected, serviced and all repair work carried out (excluding damage caused by the vehicle having been involved in an accident), including the supply of materials except for such things as tyres and batteries.

The charges (both labour and materials) for the various options are usually incorporated in the contracts and these remain fixed for the period of the contract with a clause which enables the garage to make additional charges if the vehicle exceeds, by a large margin, the mileage estimated by the operator at the time of negotiating the contract. The additional charges are usually based on the excess mileage at an agreed figure per mile.

In offering a fixed charge agreement to include all normal repair work, the garage is dependent to quite an extent on the good faith of the operator in using his vehicles in a manner which is not likely to involve the garage in excessive costs above what may be normally estimated in advance. Again, a clause may be included in the contract stating that additional charges will be raised for the repair of damage or defects because of misuse by the owner.

If a full maintenance contract under one of these schemes is negotiated, the garage usually accepts the responsibility for ensuring that the vehicle is always in a fully roadworthy condition, able to pass through VI roadside checks and pass its annual test without difficulty. In the event of a vehicle getting a PG9 prohibition for defects, the operator has some grounds for a claim against the garage but, unfortunately, he has no defence to present to the TC if he is called to explain why the vehicle was not maintained to the required standard because of the condition of 'O' licensing which makes the vehicle user totally responsible for the condition of his vehicles on the road (see below).

The garage offering a full fixed-price contract maintenance scheme will prefer, wherever possible, to negotiate a contract for a vehicle from the day it is new because it is much easier to plan and cost the amount of work likely to be necessary for an estimated annual mileage and the spare parts required.

The effective working of a contract agreement needs the co-operation of both parties if it is to be successful. Operators may feel that in return for paying the garage a fixed price for full maintenance they are left with little responsibility. But they must make it their business to ensure that whatever other considerations may be pressing, a vehicle is sent to the garage when it is required if the contract is one in which the garage calls the vehicle in at specified intervals for the work to be done.

Although armed with what appears to be a fair agreement with a reputable repairer, operators should not become complacent. It is strongly recommended that wherever possible they should arrange for a physical check of the work that the repairer claims to have carried out. While this is not to suggest that a repairer is likely to claim to have done work that he knows has not been done, it must be remembered what is at stake and an operator should therefore doubly check the quality of the work.

Contract Maintenance Schemes

A number of package contract maintenance schemes are available to operators. Whichever they choose, if indeed they choose any, will depend on a number of considerations: the make of the vehicles they own, the trade association to which they belong, the availability of a suitable repairer, etc.

Freight Transport Association Maintenance Services

Under the FTA quality control maintenance inspection service member operators contract to have their vehicles inspected one or more times a year by Association inspectors (only skilled and highly experienced people are appointed) to see that they meet the requirements of the law. The inspections can be used by operators either as a second check on their own inspection and maintenance system, or as the sole means of inspection of their vehicles to comply with the law in this respect; the actual maintenance work being carried out by their own staff. Alternatively, the scheme can be used as a means of checking the maintenance work carried out by a repair garage or agent.

The FTA vehicle check system is not purely a maintenance scheme as such. It is an inspection and maintenance advisory service available to Association members as a do-it-yourself scheme using the documents, checklists and advice provided. It can include contract inspections of vehicles by a qualified inspector.

After carrying out a vehicle check, the inspector completes a checklist indicating whether items are satisfactory, within reasonable tolerances, or whether attention is needed. When the inspector returns to carry out the next check on the vehicle he will expect to see that his previous recommendations have been followed. If they have not, the operator is told that there is little point in paying for a service which is not being used to its fullest advantage.

Following the experience of many operators who have received PG9s on brand new vehicles, the FTA offers a service whereby it will conduct a full inspection of a brand new vehicle before it goes into service. One of the obvious advantages of this independent check is that it provides the operator with evidence to support claims to the vehicle supplier and manufacturer for new vehicles delivered in faulty condition.

Responsibility for Maintenance

The major point to remember when making any arrangements with a garage is that it is the operator (ie the vehicle 'user' – see pp 14–15 for definition), not the repairer, who remains responsible for the mechanical condition of the vehicle, even where defects are due to negligence by the repairer. In *A Guide to Operators' Licensing*, available from local Traffic Area Offices, the following warning is given:

'Operators who contract out their inspections and maintenance work are still the legal "users" of their vehicles and as such will be held fully responsible by the TC for the arrangements they make and the condition of their vehicles. If either are unsatisfactory it is the operator's licence which will be placed in jeopardy.'

The same responsibility applies in the case of vehicles hired without drivers and trailers even if the hire company, as part of the agreement, carries out the inspection and repair work.

Responsibility for Records

Operators are also responsible for ensuring that proper records of maintenance work are kept. Even if the repairer makes the records and holds them on file it is up to the operator to ensure, first, that they are properly kept with all the necessary information recorded and, second, that they are retained on file, available for inspection, for a minimum period of 15 months. In completing the 'O' licence application 'undertakings' the vehicle operator promises to 'keep records'. This can be interpreted as meaning that the operator keeps the record rather than the repair garage keeping it on his behalf (see also Chapter 16).

Negligence by Repairers

Unfortunately, however satisfactory the arrangements made with a garage may be in other ways, there is very little that operators can do contractually to protect themselves completely from negligence on the part of the repairer or the repairer's employees. It is unlikely that the repairer would agree to be party to a contract in which he has fully to indemnify the operator against failure of his employees to carry out work to a required standard, even though he may agree that morally he should be held responsible (moral responsibility, incidentally, has no standing in law). Moreover, most small operators are not likely to be in a position to have sufficiently persuasive powers to get the repairer to agree to such terms.

Operators have no protection against poor workmanship other than relying on the reputation of the garage. However, if they are members of one of the trade associations (the Freight Transport Association for own-account operators and the Road Haulage Association for haulage contractors) they could try to enlist their help in pressing a claim.

In-House Repairs

The advantages of operators having their own workshop and being able to do their own safety inspections and repairs are many, provided that sufficient vehicles are operated to justify the overheads involved. Principal among them is that by employing the staff they have direct control over the work carried out, the standard of the work, and the record keeping which is so important.

If operators provide their own maintenance facilities they must be of a suitable standard, although once again no specific details are given in the regulations. The main requirement is for a covered area with hard-standing and facilities including adequate lighting for conveniently inspecting the underside of vehicles. Ideally this means that either a pit in the ground or a hydraulic lift should be provided. The former is the most commonly used and it is very much the cheaper of the two alternatives. Suitable lighting, either fixed in the pit shining upwards to the underside of the vehicles or by means of portable inspection lamps, is necessary.

The remainder of the tools and machines with which a workshop should be equipped are left entirely to the operator's choice, but such items as a beam-setter and a portable Tapley brake-efficiency recorder are useful to check that vehicles comply with the test requirements. Servicing equipment such as jacks, high-pressure greasing equipment, high-pressure washing or steam-cleaning equipment make maintenance work much less of a chore. Hand tools are, of course, essential and in general the better the equipment available (including the availability of the special tools often needed to carry out work on today's sophisticated vehicles) the more likelihood there is of the work meeting the required standard.

Vehicle Inspections

Vehicle inspections are an essential part of the maintenance programme, and legislation covers this aspect. Section 74 of the Road Traffic Act 1988 requires operators of goods vehicles to have them regularly inspected by a 'suitably qualified person' to ensure that they comply with Construction and Use Regulations (Chapter 12) and, of course, it is in the operator's best interests to have vehicles regularly inspected to ensure that they are kept in a fully safe and roadworthy mechanical condition.

Frequency of Inspection

Legislation does not specify the intervals at which vehicles should be inspected, what form the inspection should take or what is meant by a 'suitably qualified person'. In the case of the first-mentioned, it is very much a question of the type of operation on which the vehicle is used. A tipping vehicle, for example, which spends much of its time on rough sites, with perhaps a fairly high mileage on the road as well, certainly should be inspected at least weekly. The same applies to a vehicle which, although it remains on normal roads, does perhaps 800 to 1,200 miles a week. On the other hand, a monthly inspection may be quite sufficient for a local delivery vehicle doing low weekly mileages on good roads and spending a great deal of its time standing while deliveries are being made.

Operators' own experience of their type of operation should indicate the intervals between which wear and tear takes place and defects become apparent. It has even been suggested that vehicles standing out of use in depots should be checked at least monthly. Although there is some suggestion that inspection intervals can be based on either a time or miles/kilometres alternative it is becoming clear that some TCs at least will not accept anything other than a time-based frequency from 'O' licence applicants. The VOSA Code of Practice on vehicle maintenance referred to on page 411 recommends that the maximum time interval between safety inspections should be six weeks with no mileage alternative. It also recommends operators to have flow charts covering at least 12-monthly periods to indicate when vehicle safety inspections are due.

Items for Inspection

A full list of the items to be inspected at regular intervals is not laid down in regulations but it is obviously necessary that the inspection at the very least covers all the items set out in *The Heavy Goods Vehicle Inspection Manual* (see pp 403–05), with particular emphasis on those items (eg brakes, steering, wheels, tyres, suspension systems and lights) that have special relevance to the safe operation of the vehicle. Tyres on vehicles used on site work or on local delivery work should receive particularly careful examination for damage.

The Inspector

There are no specified qualifications for a vehicle inspector. Clearly, the most obvious one is wide experience in the repair of heavy commercial vehicles. A person with such experience would know where and how to look for wear and for defects and would recognize the symptoms of hidden faults, such as uneven tyre wear indicating that the steering is out of alignment or that kingpins or wheel bearings are worn.

It is possible, however, to train a person specifically as a vehicle inspector, and this is being done in the industry. The emphasis in training in such cases must be on following a predetermined list, such as *The Heavy Goods Vehicle Inspection Manual*, examining every individual item carefully and methodically, testing the wear in components and measuring the tolerances of moving parts accurately.

It is desirable, although not a legal requirement, that the person carrying out the vehicle inspection should not be expected to carry out repairs, however small, at the time of making the inspection. To have to do this would cause a lack of concentration and could lead to other items being missed if repairs took up too much of the inspector's time. In the case of an owner-driver carrying out his own inspections and repairs this can be a difficult situation and in such instances it is useful to have the work verified and an audit-type check carried out by an outside agency, such as the FTA, to ensure that the vehicle is kept up to a high standard.

Authority to Stop Use of Vehicles

The inspector, besides being suitably qualified and experienced to spot defects, should have the authority to prevent a vehicle being taken on the road in the event of a serious or potentially dangerous defect being found.

Vehicle Servicing

Regular servicing as opposed to specific inspections and repairs is an important part of vehicle maintenance and as such it should be carried out with unfailing regularity at predetermined intervals of time or mileage. The importance of servicing cannot be too highly emphasized for two reasons: first, because the vehicle must meet the requirements of the law and second, because operators will benefit by always having their vehicles ready for work and able to carry out a job without breakdowns and delays. It also increases the life of the working parts and consequently of the whole vehicle as well as reducing downtime costs and disrupted delivery schedules.

The intervals at which servicing should be carried out are left to the owner's discretion depending on the work on which the vehicle is employed, in much the same way as the intervals for inspection are decided. To give owners some guidance, however, vehicle manufacturers usually provide a service schedule which owners can use in their own workshop or which their agent will use when vehicles are sent in for servicing. A useful guide to service intervals is 5,000/6,000-mile services carried out at least monthly with more extensive services at 15,000/20,000- mile/three-monthly intervals and 30,000/40,000-mile/six-monthly intervals. Progressively, service intervals are being extended with the use of longer-life components and particularly improved filters and lubricating oils, which can go for very much longer periods these days without detriment to their lubricating properties.

Cleaning of Vehicles

Particular reference is made in the instructions to operators submitting vehicles for VOSA heavy goods vehicle tests, that those which are not sufficiently clean will be refused the test. Again, it is difficult to specify a standard of cleanliness for the underside of a vehicle, but the main point is that all the components listed for the examination must be easily visible so that inspectors can see without difficulty if wear or damage exists. To achieve and keep a suitable standard of cleanliness it is desirable for vehicles to be washed with either a steam cleaner or a high-pressure water washer at regular intervals and certainly immediately before they are taken to the test station.

If the maintenance of the vehicles is contracted out to a garage on a maintenance scheme, the operator should arrange either for the garage to clean the vehicle before inspection or for one of the many specialist vehicle cleaners to do it.

Enforcement of Maintenance Standards

There has been increasing concern in recent times about the standards of vehicle maintenance. As a result of this concern, VOSA has stepped up the levels of checking on vehicles by enforcement staff, particularly at night and at weekends. The purpose of these additional checks is to catch vehicles operating outside normal working hours – many legitimately but some possibly deliberately running the gauntlet.

Maintenance Records

There is a legal requirement under the Road Traffic Act 1988 for goods vehicle operators to keep records of maintenance work carried out on their vehicles. When completing form GV79, 'O' licence application, operators have to make the statutory 'declaration of intent' in which they promise to fulfil undertakings made at that time throughout the duration of the 'O' licence. A number of items in the declaration of intent relate to maintenance records. From this can be determined what records are needed by law.

In the declaration of intent the operator promises to ensure that the following records will be kept:

- safety inspections;
- routine maintenance;
- repairs to vehicles.

A promise is also made that drivers will report 'safety faults' in their vehicles and the Traffic Commissioners insist that these reports should be in writing and therefore they become part of the vehicle record-keeping system. The operator promises to keep all these records for a minimum period of 15 months and to make them available on request by Vehicle and Operator Services Agency (VOSA) examiners or the Traffic Commissioner (TC).

Additionally, operators are frequently asked by vehicle examiners and the TCs to keep a wall chart showing vehicles in the fleet and when they are due for inspection, service and annual test. The VOSA Code of Practice on vehicle maintenance (see p 412) recommends annual flow charts showing vehicle inspection-due dates.

Driver Reports of Vehicle Faults

It is a specific requirement (and part of the declaration of intent on an 'O' licence application form) that arrangements must be made for drivers to have a proper means of reporting 'safety faults' (ie defects) in the vehicle they are driving as soon as possible. As already mentioned, the TCs expect these defect reports to be made in writing, not verbally. Ideally, the report should be made either on an individual form which is completed and handed in by the driver, or in a defect book reserved for recording defects found on a vehicle which is kept in a convenient place where all drivers have easy access to it, and where whoever is responsible for ensuring that repair work is carried out can also easily reach it. To reiterate, it has been made abundantly clear that verbal reporting of defects is not in itself a system acceptable to the TCs.

Whichever method is used it is important that the repair of the defects is recorded on the form or in the book by a note of the work done and the signature of the person who has done it (see also under repair records). It is also important for operators to ensure that whatever system of defect reporting is used, they make regular checks on drivers and repair staff to see that the procedure is being followed correctly. This requirement has been pointed out by the TCs on a number of occasions. Using separate pads of defect sheets is the best alternative and where these can be made out in duplicate they provide the driver with his own copy of the report for future reference.

Systems of defect reporting which rely on a centrally located defect book or on verbal reports by drivers are open to the risks of drivers forgetting to report defects when they return to base. If a driver's attention is distracted by his manager who wants to talk to him, for example, just as he is about to report a defect, the defect is not reported and another driver may take the vehicle out next day with a defect which could result in a prohibition notice being issued in a roadside check. A driver may also forget to report a defect when he returns late from a journey and is in a rush to get home or if he cannot find the defect book.

It is the operator's responsibility to make sure that the system used is infallible in all these circumstances, first because it is an offence to fail to cause the defect to be reported and second because the vehicle could be found on the road subsequently with a safety fault not reported and not repaired.

Drivers' tachograph records should clearly indicate the time spent on their 'walk round' checks prior to taking a vehicle on the road. Where such records show drivers to have commenced driving immediately on starting their shift it will be interpreted by VOSA that they have not:

- carried out the 'walk round' check as required; or
- if they claim to have carried out the check;
- they have not made an accurate record; or
- that they have falsified their record.

In any event, they will have committed one or more offences.

Inspection Reports

The Road Traffic Act 1988 requires that records of regular safety inspections to vehicles must be made. For this purpose the vehicle inspector (see p 419) should have a sheet on which are listed all the items to be inspected (preferably in accordance with the contents of *The Heavy Goods Vehicle Inspection Manual*).

The inspection sheet should identify the necessary items for inspection with a cross-check reference number to the *Inspection Manual* to enable, if necessary, full details of the method of inspection of that item – and the reason for its rejection as not being within acceptable limits – to be determined. The sheet should have provision for the inspector to mark against each item whether it is 'serviceable' or 'needs attention' and space to comment on defects for immediate rectification and other items for attention at a future date or on which a watch should be kept if attention is not required immediately. The form should contain space for the inspector to sign his name and add the date.

Defect Repair Sheets

Besides ensuring that proper records are kept of vehicle safety fault reports made by drivers and of regular safety inspections, the operator must also keep a record showing that any defects reported or found on inspection are rectified in order to keep the vehicle in a fit, serviceable and safe condition. Records of such repairs may be added to the driver defect report or the inspection report to provide combined records, or a separate repair or job sheet may be used. The important points about repair records are, first, that they should show comprehensive details of the actual repair work carried out, identifying components which were repaired or replaced and new parts added, and, second, that there should be a matching repair sheet for every defect reported or found on inspection so that the vehicle examiners, when they visit to examine records, can see the report of the defect and then subsequently a report of the repair work carried out to rectify it. Reports of defects which do not have a corresponding repair record can arouse suspicion in the examiner's mind that perhaps the necessary repair has not been carried out and that the defect still exists. This is a good reason for him then to consider examining that vehicle, or perhaps the whole fleet.

Service Records

In addition to the records of defects and vehicle inspections which have to be kept, a record should also be kept of all other work carried out on the vehicle, whether it is repair or replacement of working parts or normal servicing (oil changes and greasing, etc).

Retention of Records

It is a legal requirement that records of maintenance must be retained by operators. The original inspection report, or a photocopy of it, with the inspector's comments, the date and the mileage at which the inspection was carried out, must be retained and kept available for inspection if required by the VOSA examiners for 15 months from the date of the inspection. Work sheets showing the repair work carried out following the inspection and all other work done on the vehicle, including repairs following defect reports by drivers, as well as defect reports themselves, must be kept for 15 months, available for inspection by VOSA examiners or the TC, if requested.

Repair Records from Garages

When vehicle safety inspections, servicing and repair work are carried out for the operator by repair garages, the operator should obtain from the garage comprehensive documentation to enable him to meet the legal requirements detailed above. In many cases VOSA examiners are quite happy if the garage retains the records of inspection and repair, so long as they can be made available for examination when required. The operator must be certain, in these instances, that the garage is keeping proper records (for a period of 15 months) which satisfy the legal requirements and that they are being kept available for inspection, not bundled away out of easy reach in a store with thousands of others.

In the event of failure of the garage to keep records as required, the operator's licence would be at risk but there would be no penalty imposed on the garage. On the form GV79 undertaking (see p 421) the operator promised that he would 'make proper arrangements so that records are kept for (15 months) of all driver defect reports, safety inspections, routine maintenance and repairs to vehicles and trailers and these are made available on request'.

It is important to note that in this respect, invoices, or copies of invoices from garages, for repair work are not in themselves sufficient to satisfy the record-keeping requirement. It is the actual inspection sheet and repair sheets, or photocopies of them, which are needed because of the greater and more precise detail which they contain. Similarly, maintenance records in computer printout form are unlikely to satisfy the requirement of enforcement staff to examine actual records – they will still want to see the original inspection sheets. This is an important point to consider with the increasing application of computers to transport operations and vehicle maintenance functions.

Location of Records

Where companies hold operators' licences in a number of separate Traffic Areas the maintenance records for the vehicles under each licence should be kept in the area covered by the individual licence (preferably at the vehicle operating centre). With the sanction of the local TC, records may be kept centrally at a head office or central vehicle workshop, although the vehicle examiners may ask for them to be produced for inspection at the operating centre of the vehicles in the Traffic Area – probably giving three days' to one week's notice to enable the records to be obtained from the central files.

Wall Planning Charts

While it is not strictly a legal requirement, the Traffic Commissioners like to see operators using wall planning charts (see note above about use of flow charts in accordance with the VOSA Code of Practice on vehicle maintenance) to provide a visual reminder of important dates such as:

- vehicle/trailer due for inspection;
- vehicle/trailer due for service;
- vehicle/trailer due for annual test;
- excise duty due.

Such charts usually provide facilities for a whole year's recording of these items for the fleet (either shown by vehicle registration number or by fleet number).

Vehicle History Files

For efficiency in record keeping, a system of vehicle history files – one for each vehicle and trailer in the fleet – is most useful. This provides the facility for keeping all relevant records relating to individual vehicles and trailers together and in one place. Individual files can have all the important details of the vehicle/trailer on the front cover for easy reference.

Safety – Vehicle, Loads and at Work

Transport operators, along with all other sectors of business and industry, are under constant pressure to become ever more conscious of the need for safety in their operations, in the provision of facilities for their employees, and in the way their employees work and conduct themselves on work premises. Predominantly, this is influenced by the demands of the Health and Safety at Work etc Act 1974 and the stringent requirements which it imposes on employers and employees alike. But in transport, the requirements of the Road Vehicles (Construction and Use) Regulations 1986 (as amended), regarding the safety of vehicles and loads, place additional legal burdens on operators and drivers. The problems of safe loading and avoidance of vehicle overloading are not new, but increased enforcement activity has accelerated concern in these areas. There is concern also on the wider front of safety in load handling and in the use of loading aids (forklift trucks for example) and with regard to vehicle manoeuvring in depots and works premises, which alone results in many workplace deaths and injuries annually.

According to the Health and Safety Executive (HSE), 151 workers were killed in 2009 and many others are forced to leave work each year and are unable to work again due to neglect of proper health and safety management procedures. According to the HSE, being struck by a moving vehicle is one of the most common causes of fatal injury among workers: in 2000–01 the figure was 22 per cent of all fatalities.

C&U Requirements

The Road Vehicles (Construction and Use) Regulations 1986 require that all vehicles and trailers, and all their parts and accessories, and the weight, distribution, packing and adjustment of their loads, shall be such that no danger is caused or likely to be caused to any person in or on the vehicle or trailer or on the road. Additionally, no motor vehicle or trailer must be used for any purpose for which it is so unsuited as to cause or be likely to cause danger or nuisance to any person in or on the vehicle or trailer or on the road.

Under the regulations, provisions relating particularly to bulk and loose loads make it an offence if a load causes a nuisance as well as a danger to other road users and such loads must be secured, if necessary by physical restraint, to stop them falling or being blown from a vehicle.

These regulations include two notable terms relating to load safety: one is the use of the term 'nuisance' in addition to the term 'danger' so that to commit an offence the operator does not have to go so far as causing danger; merely causing nuisance is sufficient to land him in trouble. The other term is 'physical restraint', which clearly implies the need for sheeting and roping any load, such as sand or grain, hay and straw and even builders' skips carrying rubble that may be blown from the vehicle.

The Safety of Loads on Vehicles

A Code of Practice – The Safety of Loads on Vehicles (third edition, available from The Stationery Office) sets out general requirements in regard to the legal aspects of safe loading, information on the forces involved in restraining loads, the strength requirements of restraining systems and load securing equipment, and then details specialized requirements for containers, pallets, engineering plant, general freight, timber, metal and loose bulk loads. It provides a list of dos and don'ts for drivers and others concerned with the loading of vehicles as shown below. The 2003 version includes advice on anchor points and restraint methods.

For particular note is the basic principle on which the Code is based, which is that 'the combined strength of the load restraint system must be sufficient to withstand a force not less than the total weight of the load forward and half the weight of the load backwards and sideways'.

Dos	Don'ts
1. Do make sure your vehicle's load space and the condition of its load platform are suitable for the type and size of your load.	1. Don't overload your vehicle or its individual axles.
2. Do make use of load anchorage points.	2. Don't load your vehicle too high.
3. Do make sure you have enough lashings and that they are in good condition and strong enough to secure your load.	3. Don't use rope hooks to restrain heavy loads.
4. Do tighten up the lashings or other restraining devices.	4. Don't forget that the size, nature and position of your load will affect the handling of your vehicle.

Dos	Don'ts
5. Do make sure that the front of the load is abutted against the headboard, or other fixed restraint.	5. Don't forget to check your load: a. before moving off; b. after you have travelled a few miles; c. if you remove or add items to your load during your journey.
6. Do use wedges, scotches etc, so that your load cannot move.	6. Don't take risks.
7. Do make sure that loose bulk loads cannot fall or be blown off your vehicle.	
Safe loading Your own life and the lives of others may depend upon the security of your load	

Taken from the original Code of Practice on the Safety of Loads on Vehicles (DfT)

The Code of Practice is available on the DfT website: **www.dft.gov.uk**.

Distribution of Loads

When loading a vehicle, care must be taken to ensure that the load is evenly distributed to ensure stability of the vehicle and to conform to the vehicle's individual axle weights as well as the overall gross weight, and is secure so it cannot move or transfer its weight during transit. It is important on multi-delivery work to make sure that when part of the load has been removed in the course of a delivery, none of the axles has become overloaded because of the transfer of weight. This can happen even though the gross vehicle weight is still within permissible maximum limits and in such cases it is necessary for the driver to attempt to correct the situation by shifting the load, or part of it.

All loads should be securely and safely fixed, roped and sheeted, and chained or lashed if necessary. It is an offence to have an insecure load or a load which causes danger to other road users. Furthermore, it is a legal requirement of the C&U regulations that loads must not cause or be likely to cause a danger or nuisance to other road users and that they should be physically restrained (ie roped and sheeted) if necessary to avoid parts of the load falling or being blown from the vehicle.

NB: *tipping vehicles (and others), which carry loose loads that could emit dust into the atmosphere, must be sheeted before travelling on the road under the separate provisions of the Environmental Protection Act.*

It is an offence also for the securing ropes or other devices and sheets to flap and cause nuisance or danger to other road users. Heavy penalties, with maximum fines of up to £5,000, can be imposed on conviction for offences relating to these matters.

Axle Load Calculations

Imposed axle loads can be calculated to determine whether a vehicle is operating legally in particular circumstances by using the following formula:

- Determine the vehicle wheelbase.
- Determine the weight of the load (ie payload).

$$\text{Weight on rear axle} = \frac{\text{front load base}}{\text{wheelbase}} \times \text{payload}$$

$$\text{Weight on front axle} = \text{payload} - \text{weight on rear axle}$$

Vehicle specification:
Maximum gross weight – 14,000kg
Maximum front axle weight – 5,000kg
Maximum rear axle weight – 9,000kg

1. Rear axle weight calculation:

$$\frac{\text{front load base}}{\text{wheelbase}} \times \text{payload} \quad = \text{payload weight on rear axle}$$

$$= \quad \frac{2.2\text{m}}{3.5\text{m}} \quad \times 9,000\text{kg} \quad = 5,657\text{kg}$$

2. Front axle weight caculation:

Payload　−　rear axle weight = payload weight on front axle

9,000kg　−　5,657kg　　　= 3,343kg

3. Total vehicle weight distribution:

Rear axle:　payload weight + rear axle unladen weight
　　　　=　　　　5,657kg + 3,000kg　　　　= 8,657kg

Front axle:　payload weight + front axle unladen weight
　　　　=　　　　3,343kg + 1,500kg　　　　= 4,843kg

- Calculate the front load base (ie centre line of front axle to centre of gravity of load).
- Apply the formula as above.

Road Safety

Government statistics show the following road casualties in Great Britain in 2008: 2,538 people killed and 26,034 people seriously injured. In all, there were 230,905 casualties. The figures do not identify the numbers of goods vehicle driver or passenger casualties.

BRAKE Campaign

A vigorous campaign to improve vehicle mechanical standards (especially in regard to heavy vehicle braking) and reduce death on the road is being conducted by road safety lobby group BRAKE. Among its specific activities are to promote the Road Risk Forum (supported by leading truck and component manufacturers and a number of major national transport fleet operators), whose aim is to develop road safety initiatives and promote best practice in road safety. BRAKE also publishes a booklet called *Procedures Following a Death on the Road*, designed to help bereaved relatives and provide information on criminal prosecutions, claiming compensation and the way the police investigate a death on the road.

BRAKE can be contacted at PO Box 548, Huddersfield HD1 2X7; fax: 01484 559983; e-mail: **brake@brake.org.uk**.

Safety Report

A report entitled *Transport Kills* (The Stationery Office) produced by the Health and Safety Executive (HSE) and based on a study of fatal accidents in industry indicates that motor vehicles are one of the biggest causes of industrial deaths. These motor vehicle-related deaths occur during vehicle loading, unloading, maintenance and, of course, movement and are mainly caused by poor management, failure to provide safe working systems and inadequate training.

Included in the report is a checklist which is intended to help transport operators and others to reduce unnecessary risks and dangers. Companies should use it to help examine their current practices and to institute new and safer procedures. The checklist (reproduced below with acknowledgement to the HSE) is only a general guide, and it is emphasized that safety requirements vary with different types of operation. *However, it is important to note that firms could face prosecution if they do not meet the minimum safety standards outlined in the list.*

This checklist is intended as a general guide only. It will not necessarily be comprehensive for every operation and all points will not be relevant for all work.

Organization, Systems and Training

- Have all health and safety aspects of the transport operation been assessed?
- Has an organization (and arrangements) for securing such safety been detailed in the safety policy?
- Has a person been appointed to be responsible for the transport safety?
- Have safe systems of work been set up?
- What monitoring is carried out to ensure that the systems are followed?

- Have all drivers been adequately trained and tested?
- Is there a satisfactory formal licensing or authorization system for drivers?
- Have all personnel been trained, informed and instructed about safe working practices where transport is involved?
- Is there sufficient supervision?

External Roadways and Manoeuvring Areas

- Are they of adequate dimensions?
- Are they of good construction?
- Are they well maintained?
- Are they well drained?
- Are they scarified when smooth?
- Are they gritted, sanded, etc, when slippery?
- Are they kept free of debris and obstructions?
- Are they well illuminated?
- Are there sufficient and suitable road markings?
- Are there sufficient and suitable warning signs?
- Are there speed limits?
- Is there a one-way system (as far as possible)?
- Is there provision for vehicles to reverse where necessary?
- Are there pedestrian walkways and crossings?
- Are there barriers by exit doors leading on to roadways?
- Is there a separate vehicle parking area?
- Is there any storage positioned close to vehicle ways?
- Is the yard suitable for internal works transport, eg smooth surface, hard ground, no slopes?

Internal Transport

- Are internal roadways demarcated and separated where possible from pedestrian routes with crossings and priority signs?
- Are there separate internal doors for trucks and pedestrians? Have these vision panels?
- Are blind corners catered for by mirrors, etc?
- Are trucks kept apart from personnel where possible?
- Do the trucks use a satisfactory warning system?

Vehicles

- Is there a maintenance programme for vehicles and mobile plant?
- Is there a fault reporting system?
- Are there regular checks to ensure that the vehicles are up to an acceptable standard?
- Are keys kept secure when vehicles and mobile plant are not in use?
- Are vehicles and mobile plant adequate and suitable for the work in hand?
- Is suitable access provided to elevated working places or vehicles?
- Are tractors and lift trucks equipped with protection to prevent the driver being hit by falling objects and from being thrown from his cab in the event of overturning?
- Are there any unfenced mechanical parts on vehicles, eg power take-offs?
- Are there fittings for earthing vehicles with highly flammable cargoes?
- Are loads correctly labelled (especially hazardous substances)?
- Are the vehicles suitable for use in all the areas they enter? Do they need to be to Division I or II standards, etc?
- If passengers ride on vehicles, do they have a safe riding position?

Loading and Unloading

- Do loading positions obstruct other traffic? Do pedestrian ways need diverting?
- Are there special hazards, eg flammable liquid discharge? Do pedestrians need to be kept clear?
- Is there a yard manager to supervise the traffic operation, to control vehicular movement and to act as a banksman during reversing?
- Has he received satisfactory training? Does he use recognized signals, and has he cover during his absences?
- Are there loading docks? Will the layout prevent trucks falling off or colliding with objects or each other?
- Are there any mechanical hazards caused by dock levellers, etc?
- Are methods of loading and unloading assessed? Are loads stable and secured?
- Are safe arrangements made for sheeting?
- Is there a pallet inspection scheme?

Motor Vehicle Repair

- Are appropriate arrangements made for tyre repair and inflation?
- Are arrangements made for draining and repair of fuel tanks?
- Is access available to elevated working positions?

- Are arrangements made to ensure brakes are applied and wheels checked?
- Is portable electrical equipment low voltage and properly earthed?
- Are moving vehicles in the workshop carefully controlled?
- Are vehicles supported on both jacks and axle stands where appropriate?
- Are engines only run with the brakes on and in neutral gear?
- Are raised bodies always propped?

Health and Safety at Work

Stringent UK legislation on health and safety at work implements the EU's 'Framework Directive', namely EC Directive 391/1989. The overall objective of this Directive is to impose on employers a duty to encourage improvements in the health and safety of people at work.

The main legislation is contained in the Health and Safety at Work etc Act 1974, plus the regulations listed below – the so-called 'six pack' – which were introduced to implement EC Directive 391/1989 (the 'Framework Directive'). Additionally, there are many other relevant provisions dealing with such matters as fire protection and safety signs. Collectively, this legislation has largely replaced both the Factories Act 1961 and the Offices, Shops and Railway Premises Act 1963 which formerly applied.

- Management of Health and Safety at Work Regulations 1999;
- Workplace (Health, Safety and Welfare) Regulations 1992;
- Manual Handling Operations Regulations 1992;
- Health and Safety (Display Screen Equipment) Regulations 1992;
- Provision and Use of Work Equipment Regulations 1998;
- Personal Protective Equipment at Work Regulations 2002.

Additionally, there are the Lifting Operations and Lifting Equipment Regulations 1998.

The Health and Safety at Work etc Act 1974

Since the original introduction of the Health and Safety at Work etc Act 1974 employers have had to take positive steps to draw up policy statements regarding health and safety at work, appoint safety representatives and establish safety committees in addition to ensuring that workplaces meet all the necessary safety requirements of the law. These responsibilities apply equally to employers in transport, and it should be remembered that here the requirements of the law apply to the transport operator's premises (ie offices, workshops, warehouses and yard) and to the vehicles which constitute the workplace of drivers.

The Act replaced certain parts of the Factories Act and the Offices, Shops and Railway Premises Act, and added other provisions. There are four parts to the Act:

- Part I relates to health, safety and welfare at work;
- Part II relates to the Employment Medical Advisory Service;

- Part III amends the law regarding building regulations;
- Part IV covers a range of general and miscellaneous provisions.

The main effects of the Act are:

- To maintain and improve standards of health and safety for people at work.
- To protect people other than those at work against risks to their health or safety arising from the work activities of others.
- To control the storage and use of explosives, highly flammable or dangerous substances, and to prevent their unlawful acquisition, possession and use.
- To control the emission into the atmosphere of noxious or offensive fumes or substances from work premises.
- To set up the Health and Safety Commission and the Health and Safety Executive.

Duties of Employers

The Act prescribes the general duties of all employers towards their employees by obliging them to ensure their health, safety and welfare while at work. This duty requires that all plant (including vehicles) and methods of work provided are reasonably safe and without risks to health. A similar injunction relates to the use, handling, storage and transport of any articles or substances used in connection with the employer's work. Provisions contained in the Data Protection Act mean that employers are no longer permitted to design health questionnaires for completion by employees or to screen or interpret employees' medical data. Now, only qualified health professionals may carry out these functions.

Provision of Necessary Information

In order that employees are fully conversant with all health and safety matters, it is the duty of the employer to provide all necessary information and instruction by means of proper training and adequate supervision.

Employers must either: 1) display the 'Health and Safety Law' poster; or 2) distribute the 'Health and Safety Law' leaflet to employees. (Copies can be obtained from: HSE Books, PO Box 1999, Sudbury, Suffolk CO10 2WA.)

Condition of Premises

Workplaces generally, if under the employer's control, must be maintained in such a condition that they are safe and without risks to health, have adequate means of entrance and exit (again this applies equally to vehicles as it does to 'premises') and must provide a working environment that has satisfactory facilities and arrangements for the welfare of everybody employed in the premises.

Statements of Safety Policy

It is necessary for an employer of five or more employees to draw up and bring to the notice of all his workforce *a written statement of company policy* regarding their health and safety at work with all current arrangements detailed for the implementation of such a policy. Stress is laid on the necessity of updating the 'statement' as the occasion arises and of communicating all alterations to the personnel employed.

Appointment of Safety Representatives

Involvement of all employees in health and safety activities is envisaged by the appointment (by a recognized trade union) or election of safety representatives from among the workforce. A safety representative should be a person who has been employed in the firm for at least *two years* or who has had two years' similar employment 'so far as is reasonably practicable'. The broad duties of safety representatives are concerned with the inspection of workplaces, investigating possible hazards and examining the cause of accidents, investigating employees' complaints regarding health and safety matters and making representations to their employer on health and safety at work matters.

Safety Committees

At the written request of at least two safety representatives employers must establish a safety committee to review health and safety at work matters. The establishment of a safety committee creates a joint responsibility with the employer for concern with all health and safety measures at the workplace, together with any other duties arising from regulations or codes of practice.

Duty to the Public

Employers and self-employed persons are required also to ensure that their activities do not create any hazard to members of the general public. In certain circumstances, information must be made publicly available regarding the existence of possible hazards to health and safety.

Summary of Duties of Employers to their Employees

- It shall be the duty of every employer to ensure so far as is reasonably practicable the health, safety and welfare at work of all his employees. That duty includes, in particular:
  - the provision and maintenance of plant and systems of work that are so far as is reasonably practicable safe and without risks to health;
  - arrangements for ensuring so far as is reasonably practicable safety and absence of risks to health in connection with the use, handling, storage and transport of articles and substances;
  - the provision of such information, instruction, training and supervision as is necessary to ensure so far as is reasonably practicable the health and safety at work of employees;
  - so far as is reasonably practicable the maintenance of any place of work that is under the employer's control in a condition that is safe and without risks to health, and the provision and maintenance of means of access to and egress from it that are safe and without such risks;

- – the provision and maintenance of a working environment for employees that is so far as is reasonably practicable safe and without risk to health and adequate as regards facilities and arrangements for their welfare at work.
- Except in such cases as may be prescribed it shall be the duty of all employers to prepare and as often as may be appropriate revise a written statement of their general policy with respect to the health and safety at work of their employees and the organization and arrangements for the time being in force for carrying out that policy, and to bring the statement and any revision of it to the notice of all employees.
- It shall be the duty of any person who erects or installs any article for use at work in any premises where the article is to be used by persons at work to ensure, so far as is reasonably practicable, that nothing about the way in which it is erected or installed makes it unsafe or a risk to health when properly used.
- No employer shall levy or permit to be levied on any employee any charge in respect of anything done or provided in pursuance of any specific requirement of the relevant statutory provisions.

As well as these statutory duties, employers have a common law duty of care. Where a breach of that care results in negligence (eg where careless conduct results in injury to a person), they may be liable to pay compensation.

Duties of Employees

The Act states in general terms the duty of employees to take reasonable care for their own safety and that of others and to co-operate with others in order to ensure that there is a compliance with statutory duties relating to health and safety at work. In this connection no person shall interfere with or misuse anything provided in the interests of health, safety or welfare either intentionally or recklessly.

Summary of Duties of Employees at Work

- It shall be the duty of all employees while at work:
  - – to take reasonable care for their own health and safety and of other persons who may be affected by their acts or omissions at work, and
  - – as regards any duty or requirement imposed on their employer or any other person, to co-operate with them so far as is necessary to enable that duty or requirement to be performed or complied with.
- No person shall intentionally or recklessly interfere with or misuse anything provided in the interests of health, safety or welfare.

General Duties of Employers and Self-Employed to Persons Other than Their Employees

- It shall be the duty of all employers and self-employed persons to conduct their undertaking in such a way as to ensure so far as is reasonably practicable that persons not in their employment are not thereby exposed to risks to their health and safety.

- It shall be the duty of all employers and self-employed persons to give to persons not in their employment, who may be affected, the prescribed information about such aspects of the way in which they conduct their undertaking as might affect such persons' health and safety.

Improvement and Prohibition Notices

Improvement Notice

An improvement notice may be served on a person by a health and safety inspector in cases where he believes (ie is of the opinion) that the person is contravening or has contravened, and is likely to continue so doing or will do so again, any of the relevant statutory provisions. Such a notice must give details of the inspector's reason for his belief and requires the person concerned to remedy the contravention within a stated period.

Prohibition Notice

A prohibition notice with immediate effect may be served on a person under whose control activities to which the relevant statutory provisions apply are being carried on, or are about to be carried on, by an inspector if he believes that such activities involve or could involve *a risk of serious personal injury*. A prohibition notice must specify those matters giving rise to such a risk, the reason why the inspector believes the statutory provisions are, or are likely to be, contravened, if indeed he believes that such is the case. The notice must direct that the activities in question shall not be carried on unless those matters giving rise to the risk of serious personal injury, and any contravention of the regulations, are rectified.

Remedial Measures

Both improvement and prohibition notices may include directions as to necessary remedial measures and these may be framed by reference to an approved Code of Practice and may offer a choice of the actions to be taken. Reference must be made by the inspector to the fire authority before serving a notice requiring, or likely to lead to, measures affecting means of escape in case of fire.

Withdrawal of Notices and Appeals

A notice, other than a prohibition notice with immediate effect, may be withdrawn before the end of the period specified in the notice, or an appeal against it made. Alternatively, the period specified for remedial action may be extended at any time provided an appeal against the notice is not pending.

Penalties for Health and Safety Offences

Conviction for an offence under the Health and Safety at Work etc Act 1974 may lead to a fine of £20,000, but where the case is tried in the Crown Court the amount of fine which may be imposed is unlimited. However, it should be stressed that while generally the fine imposed is intended to reflect the gravity of the particular offence and the employer's attitude towards health and safety matters, the Court will also bear in mind the offender's resources and the effects of a heavy penalty on his business and may reduce the penalty accordingly.

Corporate Manslaughter

In a situation where a death is caused through the negligence of an employer, whether health and safety related or as a result of a road accident, the employer risks facing a charge of corporate manslaughter.

It has been ruled by the courts that for an indictment on such a charge to be sustained, three key issues must be established by the jury as follows:

- The defendant owed a duty of care to the person killed.
- The defendant had breached his duty of care and that breach of care led to the death.
- The defendant's negligence was so gross that a jury would consider it justified to bring in a criminal conviction.

From 6 April 2008 the Government's Corporate Manslaughter and Corporate Homicide Act 2007 came into force. The Act applies solely where fatalities after this date are held to have been caused by gross mismanagement.

On conviction for such an offence it is likely that a fine of an unlimited amount would be imposed (possibly as much as 5 per cent of a company's annual turnover for the past three years) plus potential disqualification for the company's directors.

The corporate manslaughter offence (or corporate homicide in Scotland) will apply to both corporate organizations and Crown bodies such as government departments – which will be on the same footing as their private-sector counterparts when carrying out similar activities. The offence is focused on corporate liability and does not apply to individual directors or others. Prosecutions against individuals will continue to be possible for existing offences – including manslaughter/culpable homicide and health and safety offences – where they themselves are personally at fault.

The Management of Health and Safety

The so-called 'management' regulations (p 433) are both wide-ranging and general in nature, overlapping with many existing regulations. They have to be viewed as a 'catch-all' regulation, sitting astride other more specific health and safety provisions (eg the COSHH regulations – see p 448). The Health and Safety Executive, in its Approved Code of Practice, advises that where legal requirements in these management regulations overlap with other provisions, compliance with duties imposed by the specific regulations will be sufficient to comply with the corresponding duty in the management regulations. However, the HSE says, where duties in the Management of Health and Safety at Work Regulations 1999 go beyond those in the more specific regulations, additional measures will be needed to comply fully with the management regulations.

Specifically, these regulations cover:

- Requirements for employers (and self-employed persons) to make assessments of the risks to the health and safety of:
  - employees while they are at work;
  - other persons not in their employ, arising out of or in connection with their conduct or the conduct of their undertaking.
- Employers with five or more employees must record the significant findings of their risk assessment (ie make an effective statement of the hazards and risks which lead management to take relevant actions to protect health and safety).
- Employers and self-employed persons must make and give effect to such arrangements, as are appropriate to the nature of their activities and the size of their undertaking, for the effective planning, organization, control, monitoring and review of preventive and protective measures.
- Health surveillance must be provided for employees as appropriate to the risks to their health and safety as identified by the assessment.
- Employers must appoint one or more (competent) persons to assist them in undertaking the measures necessary to comply with the requirements and prohibitions of this legislation.

The Workplace Regulations

These regulations (see second item in the list of new legislation on p 433) add further to existing legislation on workplaces. They apply to new workplaces as of 1 January 1993 and to any modifications or conversions to existing workplaces started after this date. Existing workplaces (ie which are unaltered) must comply from 1 January 1996.

Specifically the regulations impose requirements on the:

- maintenance of workplaces;
- ventilation of enclosed workplaces and temperatures of indoor workplaces and the provision of thermometers;
- lighting (including emergency lighting);
- cleanliness of the workplace, and of furniture, furnishings and fittings (also the ability to clean floors, walls and ceilings) and the removal of waste materials;
- room dimensions and unoccupied space;
- suitability of workstations (including those outside) and the provision of suitable seating;
- condition of floors, and the arrangement of routes for pedestrians or vehicles;
- protection from falling objects, and from persons falling from a height, or falling into dangerous substances;
- material of and protection of windows and other transparent or translucent walls, doors or gates, and to them being apparent;

- way in which windows, skylights or ventilators are opened and their position when left open and the ability to clean these items;
- construction of doors and gates (including the fitting of necessary safety devices), and escalators and moving walkways;
- provision of suitable sanitary conveniences, washing facilities and drinking water (including cups and drinking vessels);
- provision of suitable accommodation for clothing and for changing clothes, for rest and for eating meals.

Manual Handling

The Manual Handling Regulations 1992 are intended to reduce back and other injuries suffered through the manual handling of loads. Employers must reduce the risk of injury to employees by using more mechanical aids, providing training in load handling, and providing precise information about load weights, centres of gravity and the heaviest side of eccentrically loaded packages.

Employers must avoid having employees undertake manual handling operations which involve risk of injury. Where it is not possible to avoid this, they have a duty to assess potential injury risks and take steps to reduce those risks to the absolute minimum or, better still, find an alternative way of achieving the same objective which does not involve manual handling, for example by mechanization of certain handling tasks or by eliminating some activities altogether.

Where such activities must take place, the employer should ensure that employees:

- are well trained in good handling techniques;
- understand how operations have been designed to ensure their safety; and
- make proper use of systems of work provided.

In particular, employees should understand:

- how potentially hazardous handling operations can be recognized;
- how to deal with unfamiliar operations;
- the proper use of handling aids;
- the proper use of personal protective equipment;
- features of the working environment that contribute to safety;
- the importance of good housekeeping;
- factors affecting individual capability; and
- good handling techniques.

Training in good handling techniques should be tailored to the particular handling operations likely to be undertaken, beginning with relatively simple examples and progressing to more specialized handling operations.

It is especially useful to train employees to:

- recognize loads whose weight as well as their shape and other features, and the circumstances in which they are handled, might cause injury;

- treat unfamiliar loads with caution and not assume that apparently empty drums or other closed containers are in fact empty;
- test loads first by attempting to raise one end; and
- apply force gradually when lifting or moving loads until either undue strain is felt, in which case an alternative method should be considered, or it is clear that the task can be accomplished without injury.

The HSE booklet *Manual Handling* (available from The Stationery Office) provides excellent guidance on the regulations and their application. Additionally, these notes will provide useful information to employers on many aspects of manual handling.

The Use of Display Screen Equipment

For the purposes of these regulations (fourth item in the list on p 433), a display screen is any form of alphanumeric or graphic display screen regardless of the process involved – generally termed Visual Display Units (VDUs). Under the regulations employers are required to protect VDU users (ie those who habitually use VDUs for a significant part of their normal work) from the risks associated with habitual VDU use – mainly visual fatigue, mental stress, backache and upper limb pain. This must be done by controlling the design of workstations and actual working conditions. Employers must make an assessment of the risks to which VDU users are exposed and reduce these to the lowest reasonably practicable level. Work at VDU screens must be periodically interrupted by breaks or a switch to other work and employers must provide eye and eyesight tests for relevant employees and, where necessary, also provide special corrective appliances (ie spectacles) where normal spectacles cannot be used. Both existing and new VDU users must be given health and safety information about, and training in the use of, the workstation.

Provision and Use of Work Equipment

The Provision and Use of Work Equipment Regulations 1998 require employers and the self-employed to ensure that equipment provided for use at work complies with the regulations. The law applies to owned, hired, leased and second-hand equipment and all machinery, appliances (including cranes, lift trucks and vehicle hoists), apparatus, tools or component assemblies so arranged as to function as a whole unit. Work equipment must be:

- suitable for its intended purpose;
- assessed as to any risks associated with the equipment;
- subject to a recorded inspection where such an inspection would assist in identifying health and safety risks; and
- maintained in efficient working order, in an efficient state and in good repair, and a maintenance log kept.

Personal Protective Equipment

Employers are required to provide suitable personal protective equipment (PPE) to employees where there are risks to their health and safety which cannot be adequately controlled by other means – it is a last-resort measure. Self-employed persons must provide their own protective equipment where necessary. PPE is not suitable unless:

- It is appropriate for the identified risks.
- Account has been taken of the environment that it will be used in, ergonomic factors such as the nature of the job, the need for communication and the health of the wearer.
- It fits the wearer correctly and comfortably and is capable of being adjusted.
- It is effective, so far as is practicable, against the risks it is intended to control.

PPE is described as being any equipment designed to be worn or held by persons to protect them from one or more risks, including against extreme temperatures, poor visibility and adverse weather. Work clothing and uniforms, sports equipment and road safety protective wear such as crash helmets are excluded.

A recent fatal accident to a lorry driver on a motorway hard shoulder has highlighted the need for drivers, and others, to wear high-visibility clothing when working in vulnerable situations. In this particular case the driver was criticized for being careless with his own safety in not wearing his reflective jacket.

Lifting Operations

The Lifting Operations and Lifting Equipment Regulations 1998 (LOLER) apply to all lifting equipment which is defined as 'work equipment for lifting and lowering loads and includes its attachments used for anchoring, fixing or supporting it'. These regulations obviously apply to forklift trucks and to automated goods storage and retrieval systems and front-end loaders on tractors.

It is important to note that these regulations also apply to tipping vehicles. In this context it is important that the operator ensures he receives from the manufacturer adequate information about safe operation and correct methods of use and that such information is passed on to the driver, who should also be properly trained as per all health and safety requirements.

The regulations make provisions regarding:

- the strength and stability of lifting equipment;
- the safety of lifting equipment for lifting persons;
- the way lifting equipment is positioned and installed;
- the marking of machinery and accessories for lifting, and lifting equipment which is designed for lifting persons or which might so be used in error;
- the organization of lifting operations;
- thorough examination and inspection of lifting equipment in specified circumstances;

- evidence of examination to accompany it (ie the lifting equipment) outside the firm's premises;
- exceptions for winding apparatus at mines;
- the making of reports of thorough examinations and records of inspections; and
- the keeping of information in the reports and records.

Additionally, according to the Health and Safety Executive's *Simple Guide to the Lifting Operations and Lifting Equipment Regulations 1998,* operators must ensure that:

- Lifting operations are planned, supervised and carried out in a safe manner by people who are competent.
- Where equipment is used for lifting people it is marked accordingly, and it should be safe for such a purpose, eg all necessary precautions have been taken to eliminate or reduce any risk.
- Where appropriate, before lifting equipment (including accessories) is used for the first time, it is *thoroughly examined.* Lifting equipment may need to be thoroughly examined in use at periods specified in the regulations (ie usually at least six-monthly for accessories and equipment used for lifting people and, at a minimum, annually for all other equipment) or at intervals laid down in an examination scheme drawn up by a competent person. All examination work should be performed by a competent person.
- Following a thorough examination or inspection of any lifting equipment, a report is submitted by the competent person to the employer to take the appropriate action.

Work-Related Stress

All employers have a duty in law to ensure that their employees are not made ill by their work. Work-related stress is becoming recognized as a major cause of employee illness and absenteeism. Transport employers, in particular, need to recognize that stress can make their employees ill because the work involved, especially driving, is renowned as a stressful occupation.

Stress is a person's natural reaction to excessive pressure and thus it is not a disease. However, excessive and long-term stress can lead to mental and physical ill health causing, for example, depression, a nervous breakdown and even heart disease. Stress in one person can lead to stress in other people who have to cover their work.

The costs of stress can be high: high staff turnover, increased absence through sickness, reduced work performance, increased lateness and more customer complaints. An employer who ignores signs of stress among employees or who fails to take the necessary action to reduce stress may face claims for compensation from employees who have suffered ill health from work-related stress. Half a million people in Britain are thought to be suffering from work-related stress, according to the HSE, and this is costing industry £3.75 billion in lost time.

Where stress has been caused in a workplace, or made worse by work, it is the employer's duty to assess the risks among employees, in particular:

- looking for pressures at work that could cause high and long-lasting levels of stress;
- judging which employees may be affected or harmed by stress;
- deciding whether sufficient measures are being taken to prevent harm from stress;
- determining what further measures can be taken to reduce the stress-inducing pressures of work.

Employers are not responsible for preventing ill health from stress caused by problems occurring outside work, but they should be able to recognize the effects of such stress, for example, people being unable to cope with their work, or performing below their normal standard. In such cases, adopting an understanding attitude would be helpful to the individual concerned and is in the employer's best interests.

Ban on Smoking

Since 1 July 2007 (2 April 2007 in Wales) virtually all enclosed public places and workplaces in England have been smoke-free under provisions contained in the Health Act 2006. This has health benefits for workers and others by ensuring a healthier environment, so that everyone can work, travel, relax, shop and socialize free from second-hand smoke. The ban also applies to work vehicles that are used by more than one person.

Under the legislation employers must:

- display no-smoking notices (in/on both premises and vehicles);
- develop and implement smoke-free policies;
- remove ashtrays from premises;
- inform anyone smoking that they are committing an offence; and
- request that offenders extinguish their smoking materials immediately or leave the premises/vehicle.

Since the commencement date mentioned above, a number of new criminal offences have been created, as shown in Table 17.1.

Electric Storage Batteries

The Health and Safety Executive has issued guidance on the safe charging and use of electric storage batteries in motor vehicle repair and maintenance. This is to help reduce the number of injuries which occur annually when batteries explode through mishandling and improper use, generally causing acid burns to face, eyes and hands as well as other injuries.

In a freely available leaflet the HSE warns of the dangers of charging batteries, particularly those described as maintenance free but which still give off flammable

TABLE 17.1 Criminal offences created by the Health Act 2006

Offence	Who is liable?	Fixed penalty notice (if paid in 15 days)	Fixed penalty notice (if paid in 29 days)	Court-awarded fine
Smoking in a smoke-free place	Anyone who smokes in a smoke-free place	£30	£50	Up to £200
Failing to display required no-smoking signs	Anyone who manages or occupies the smoke-free premises or vehicle	£150	£200	Up to £1,000
Failing to prevent smoking in a smoke-free place	Anyone who manages or controls the smoke-free premises or vehicle	N/A	N/A	Up to £2,500

SOURCE: Table by courtesy of *Roadway* magazine, June 2007

hydrogen gas, which on contact with a naked flame will burn and cause the battery to explode. The advice it gives is as follows:

General Precautions

- Always wear goggles or a visor when working on batteries.
- Wherever possible, always use a properly designated and well-ventilated area for battery charging.
- Remove any metallic objects from hands, wrists and around the neck (eg rings, chains and watches) before working on a battery.

Disconnecting and Reconnecting Batteries

- Turn off the vehicle ignition switch and all other switches or otherwise isolate the battery from the electrical circuit.
- Always disconnect the earthed terminal first (often the negative terminal, but not always – CHECK) and reconnect it last using insulated tools.
- Do not rest tools or metallic objects on top of a battery.

Battery Charging

- Always observe the manufacturer's instructions for charging batteries.
- Charge in a well-ventilated area. Do not smoke or bring naked flames into the charging area.
- Make sure the battery is topped up to the correct level.
- Make sure the charger is switched off or disconnected from the power supply before connecting the charging leads, which should be connected positive to positive, negative to negative.
- Vent plugs may need to be adjusted before charging. Carefully follow the manufacturer's instructions.
- Do not exceed the recommended rate of charging.
- When charging is complete, switch off the charger before disconnecting the charging leads.

Jump Starting

Preparation:

- Always ensure that both batteries have the same voltage rating.
- If starting by using a battery on another vehicle, check the earth polarity on both vehicles.
- Ensure the vehicles are not touching.
- Turn off the ignition of both vehicles.
- Always use purpose-made, colour-coded jump leads with insulated handles – red for the positive cable and black for the negative cable.

Connection for vehicles with the *same earth* polarity:

- First connect the non-earthed terminal of the good battery to the non-earthed terminal of the flat battery.
- Connect one end of the second lead to the earthed terminal of the good battery.
- Connect the other end of the second lead to a suitable, substantial, unpainted point on the chassis or engine of the other vehicle, away from the battery, carburettor, fuel lines or brake pipes.

Connection for vehicles with *different* earth polarity:

The HSE warns that in view of the potential for confusion this should be attempted only by skilled and experienced personnel.

- First connect the earthed terminal of the good battery to the non-earthed terminal of the flat battery.
- Connect one end of the second lead to the non-earthed terminal of the good battery.
- Connect the other end of the second lead to a suitable, substantial, unpainted point on the chassis or engine of the other vehicle, away from the battery, carburettor, fuel lines or brake pipes.

Starting

- Ensure the leads are well clear of moving parts.
- Start the engine of the 'good' vehicle and allow to run for about one minute.
- Start the engine of the 'dead' vehicle and allow to run for about one minute.

Disconnection

- Stop the engine of the 'good' vehicle.
- Disconnect the leads in the reverse order to which they were connected.
- Take great care in handling jump leads; do not allow the exposed metal parts to touch each other or the vehicle body.

The Batteries Directive

The EU's Batteries Directive (2006/66/EC) came into force in the UK on 5 May 2009. It provides for controls of the environmental impacts of batteries, in particular setting limits for the content of certain heavy metals within batteries. Whereas the former directive on this issue applied to less than 10 per cent of batteries, the new directive applies to all types of battery and it also specifies tighter limits for the heavy metal content of batteries and sets targets for recovery, recycling, labelling and producer responsibility.

Two particular and connected environmental hazards are associated with batteries. First, they often contain heavy metals such as cadmium and mercury, which can pose a threat if released into the environment. Second, the disposal sources for many batteries are either landfill sites or incineration plants, the use of either being likely to lead to polluting releases into the environment.

The Directive includes all types of batteries and accumulators, and divides batteries into three main categories:

- Portable batteries: These include household batteries, such as those used to power portable electronic equipment and torches.
- Industrial batteries: These include lead-acid batteries used in heavy machinery and industrial power tools.
- Automotive batteries: All batteries used to power motor vehicles. These are commonly lead-acid batteries.

The main aims of the Directive include:

- restricting the use of mercury and cadmium in batteries;
- setting out labelling requirements for new batteries (to help consumers in choosing batteries and in deciding how to send them for recycling);
- setting targets for collecting waste portable batteries:
  - 25 per cent by September 2012, rising to
  - 45 per cent by September 2016;

- prohibiting the disposal by landfill or incineration of waste industrial and automotive batteries, which implies a 100 per cent collection and recycling target;
- introducing producer responsibilities.

So far as the UK is concerned, a significant increase in recycling will be needed to meet these proposed new limits, which poses a challenge – current recycling facilities for batteries are inadequate, especially for alkaline-manganese and zinc-carbon batteries, which make up about 80 per cent by weight of all portable batteries.

The Government legislation is contained in the Waste Batteries and Accumulators Regulations 2009.

Control of Substances Hazardous to Health (COSHH)

There are many situations where the use of chemicals or other hazardous substances at work can put people's health at risk; consequently employers are legally required to control exposure to such hazardous substances to prevent ill health under the Control of Substances Hazardous to Health Regulations 2002 (COSHH) (as amended). Eight basic measures are established that employers, and sometimes employees, must take as listed below. If an employer fails to control hazardous substances adequately, employees or other persons may become ill with anything from mild eye irritation to chronic lung disease; occasionally, even death may occur. Employers must undertake an assessment of their work environment to determine the potential hazards and to take steps to minimize any such hazards. They must inform employees of any risks which exist and train them in safety procedures such as the handling of hazardous materials and the monitoring of the work environment. Failure to comply with the regulations will result in prosecution under these regulations and under the Health and Safety at Work etc Act.

The eight essential steps of COSHH as recommended by the HSE are:

Step 1   Assess the risks.

Step 2   Decide what precautions are needed.

Step 3   Prevent or adequately control exposure.

Step 4   Ensure that control measures are used and maintained.

Step 5   Monitor the exposure.

Step 6   Carry out appropriate health surveillance.

Step 7   Prepare plans and procedures to deal with accidents, incidents and emergencies.

Step 8   Ensure employees are properly informed, trained and supervised.

Acknowledgement: The above list is reproduced from the Health and Safety Executive guide to the COSHH regulations and may be freely downloaded from the HSE website at: **www.hse.gov.uk/pubns**.

Notification of Accidents (RIDDOR)

The Reporting of Injuries, Diseases and Dangerous Occurrences Regulations 1995 (commonly referred to as RIDDOR) require employers to notify fatal accidents, major accidents and those causing more than three days' incapacity for work, work-related diseases, gas incidents and any dangerous occurrence whether or not anybody is injured.

The report of any notifiable accident or occurrence must be made to the appropriate authority (see below) by a 'responsible person'. Usually this is the employer in the case of employees, but if the accident or occurrence involves a member of the general public, the responsible person is the person who controls the premises.

In cases where an accident occurs to an employee away from base (as may be the case with lorry drivers and sales representatives, for example), although it remains the responsibility of the employer to report the accident or occurrence, the Health and Safety Executive suggests that it would be helpful if the owner or occupier of the premises where the event occurred were to advise the person's employer as soon as possible (although there is no legal obligation to do so). Where a dangerous occurrence involves the carriage of dangerous goods by road the person responsible is the 'O' licence holder.

Under new proposals being considered by the HSE, employers may be required to report all accidents involving their vehicles as part of the RIDDOR system. This would allow safety inspectors, as well as the police, to investigate on-road accidents and incidents and to determine whether employers have adequate on-road risk assessment systems in force.

Reporting Authorities

Reports of fatal and injury accidents and notifiable dangerous occurrences must be made to the 'enforcing authority' (ie the authority responsible for enforcing the Health and Safety at Work Act). Principally, the authority is the HSE but reports should be made to its individual Inspectorates as listed below, depending on the type of premises activity:

Premises by main activity	To whom to report
Factories and factory offices	HM Factory Inspector
Mines and quarries	HM Mines and Quarries Inspector
Farms (and associated activities), horticultural premises, and forestries	HM Agricultural Inspector
Civil engineering and construction sites	HM Factory Inspector
Statutory and non-statutory railways	Inspecting Officer of Railways
Shops, offices, separate catering services, launderettes	District Council (or equivalent)
Hospitals, research and development services, water supply, postal services and telecommunications, entertainment and recreational services, local government services, educational services and road conveyance	HM Factory Inspector

Reporting an Accident

Reports should be made to the local office of the enforcing authority as soon as possible, preferably by telephone, of:

- any accident causing death or major injury to an employee;
- any accident which occurs on premises which are under a person's control causing death or major injury to a self-employed person or to a member of the public;
- any notifiable dangerous occurrence; incidents of these types affecting the work or equipment either of a firm or of self-employed persons working on premises which are under a member of the firm's control should be reported even if nobody is injured.

'Major injury' is defined as follows:

- fracture of the skull, spine or pelvis;
- fracture of any bone:
  - in the arm other than a bone in the wrist or hand;
  - in the leg other than a bone in the ankle or foot;
- amputation of a hand or foot;
- the loss of sight of an eye; or
- any other injury which results in the person injured being admitted into hospital as an inpatient for more than 24 hours, unless that person was detained only for observation.

If the person responsible does not know whom to report to, he should tell the nearest office of the HSE who will pass on the report.

Details of the accident/dangerous occurrence should be entered in the record book (or other record system). Within seven days a written report must be sent, on form F2508 (available from HSE offices), to the enforcing authority. This form should be used to report on all accidents causing fatal or major injury and notifiable dangerous occurrences. In the case of a reportable disease form F2580A is used.

Other injuries to employees are also notifiable if they result in more than three days' absence from normal work, but all that is needed is to:

- enter details of the accident in the accident record book (or other record system);
- complete form B176 (relating to a claim for Industrial Injury Benefit) when requested to do so by the local DSS office.

Accident Books

Since 31 December 2003 firms should have been using the new-style Accident Book (form BI 510) devised by the HSE. The reason for this change is that the old-type book (also using the same form number, BI 510) does not comply with data protection legislation because anyone entering accident details is able to read personal information contained in previous entries. The new book also contains useful information on first aid and how to manage health and safety in the workplace so as to avoid accidents in the first place.

Dangerous Occurrences

The list of dangerous occurrences in the regulations is selective, the aim being to obtain information about incidents with a high potential for injury but with a low frequency of occurrence.

It is important to note that dangerous occurrences must be reported even though no injury was actually caused to any person.

Examples of incidents which constitute dangerous occurrences are as follows:

- failure, collapse or overturning of lifts, hoists, cranes, excavators, tail-lifts, etc;
- explosion of boiler or boiler tube;
- electrical short circuits followed by fire or explosion;
- explosion or fire which results in stoppage of work for more than 24 hours;
- release of flammable liquid or gas (ie over 1 tonne);
- collapse of scaffolding;
- collapse or partial collapse of any building;
- failure of a freight container while being lifted;
- a road tanker to which the Hazchem regulations apply either overturning or suffering serious damage to the tank while a hazardous substance is being carried.

Note 1: This list is abbreviated. Where appropriate the regulations themselves should be consulted.

Note 2: A useful leaflet on the subject is available free from local offices of the HSE.

Risk Management

Risk management may be defined as the process of measuring or assessing risks (ie in the workplace) and then developing strategies to manage those risks. Generally, the strategies adopted would include either transferring the risk to another party, avoiding the risk, reducing the negative effect of a particular risk, or deciding to accept some or all of its consequences. Traditionally, risk management focuses on risks arising from physical or legal causes (eg natural disasters or fires, accidents, death, and lawsuits) or malpractices in the workplace. Ideally, risk management should follow a prioritization process whereby the greatest risks (ie those likely to cause most harm to people or damage to equipment) are dealt with first, while those with a lower probability of occurrence and less likelihood to cause harm or damage are dealt with later. In practice, careful decisions need to be made about these issues. Most large companies have risk management teams, but even the smallest of firms and even one-man owner-driver businesses need to have focused risk management procedures.

Risk Management for Transport Operators

Running a safe operation is crucial in today's increasingly litigious world. When something goes wrong, particularly a serious accident or incident, it is increasingly the directors of a company that are held accountable, while the true costs of road traffic accidents are often overlooked when considering insured costs such as property damage and injury compensation. In any event, the impact on profitability of the following should not be underestimated:

- loss of revenue through vehicles being unavailable for use;
- the cost of replacement drivers following injury to regular drivers;
- loss of business through damage to customer relationships;
- damage to brand image if a liveried vehicle is involved in a fatal accident.

Risk Assessment

Many accidents could be prevented by simply examining what actually goes on in your business, removing and controlling hazards as far as possible and taking the necessary managerial and supervisory steps to make sure that what is supposed to happen does happen. For example:

STEP 1: Look for the hazards
STEP 2: Decide who might be harmed and how
STEP 3: Evaluate the risks and decide whether the existing precautions are adequate or whether more should be done
STEP 4: Record your findings
STEP 5: Review your assessment and revise it if necessary
SOURCE: *RHA Haulage Manual 2006*

NB: A hazard is simply something that can cause harm. Risk is the chance of anyone suffering harm from such a hazard.

Road Risk

Road risk is the new 'in' term for transport management to contend with. While knowledge of and compliance with the *Highway Code* is essential for both drivers and managers alike, the DfT's free guideline publication *Driving at Work – Managing Work-Related Road Safety* is now also essential reading for transport management and for anybody who drives on company business, ie managers and staff as well as commercial vehicle drivers, those who drive full-time and those who drive only occasionally and, of course, self-employed drivers. In fact, according to road safety guru Dr Will Murray, these two documents go together like 'bacon and eggs'. The guidelines show how legal responsibilities under health and safety at work provisions must be complied with in addition to existing road traffic and vehicle construction and use provisions. They describe how to manage work-related road safety, assessing risks on the road and how to evaluate those risks. Overall, the aim is to cut the number of road accidents involving people at work – estimated by the HSE to account for over 20 fatalities and 250 serious injuries *every week*.

Fire Safety

All employers are required by law to carry out a fire risk assessment and introduce appropriate safety measures within their workplaces. This applies irrespective of whether the employer's premises are covered by a Fire Certificate or not, whereas previously this duty did not apply where a Fire Certificate was in force.

The Regulatory Reform (Fire Safety) Order 2005 which came into effect in England and Wales from 1 October 2006 (separate legislation applies to Scotland) revokes or repeals all previously existing fire legislation including the Fire Precautions Act 1971, the amended 1997 Fire Precautions (Workplace) Regulations, plus 100 other pieces of fire related legislation. Fire certificates are no longer valid.

This regulatory Order is a fire risk assessment-based approach where the person responsible for the premises or area they control must decide how to address the risks identified, while meeting certain requirements. By adopting this fire risk assessment approach, the responsible person will need to consider how to prevent fire from occurring in the first place, by removing or reducing hazards and risks (ie such as ignition sources), then consider the precautions necessary to ensure that people are adequately protected if a fire were still to occur. The fire risk assessment must also take into consideration what effect a fire may have on any person in or around your premises plus in neighbouring property.

While the Order is intended to be less burdensome and clearer than former legal provisions, the main emphasis of the regulations remains in fire prevention so risk assessments will need to be kept under regular review.

The Order applies to all non-domestic properties, including those of voluntary organizations and is subject to monitoring and where appropriate enforcement by the Local Authority Fire Service (LAFS).

Summary of the Order

- All existing fire legislation has now been repealed or revoked, which includes the Fire Precautions Act 1971, the amended 1997 Fire Precautions (Workplace) Regulations plus 100 other pieces of fire related legislation.
- Fire certificates have been abolished and are no longer issued.
- A 'Responsible Person' is to be responsible for fire safety and they must conduct a fire risk assessment regardless of the size of the risk.
- The identified responsible person(s) will carry full corporate liability.
- The Order extends the scope of consideration to include property safety, firefighter safety and the environment around the site. The responsible person has a duty to protect all risks.

- Unlike the previous legislation, this Order places emphasis on business continuity and containing and preventing the spread of small fires.

Protection is explicitly extended to occupants of all premises, including employees, visitors, contractors and passers-by all of whom have to be considered in the fire risk.

First Aid

Regulations require employers to train members of their staff in first aid techniques and to provide first aid equipment and facilities under the Health and Safety (First Aid) Regulations 1981. An approved Code of Practice established by the Health and Safety Commission provides both employers and the self-employed with practical guidance on how they may meet the requirements of the regulations. Further, The Stationery Office has published a booklet in its health and safety series entitled *First Aid at Work* HS(R) 11; price: £2.50.

The regulations state that 'an employer shall provide, or ensure that there are provided, such equipment and facilities as are adequate and appropriate in the circumstances for enabling first aid to be rendered to his employees if they are injured or become ill at work'.

Trained First-Aiders

The employer must provide suitable persons to administer first aid and these persons must have had specific (see Code of Practice) training or hold appropriate qualifications – occupational first-aiders are no longer considered to be 'suitable persons' for this purpose.

First Aid Boxes

First aid boxes must be provided. These should be properly identified as first aid containers, preferably with a white cross on a green background, and contain sufficient quantities of first aid material *and nothing else*. In particular, the boxes should contain only material which a first-aider has been trained to use. The old style of contents list, according to the numbers of persons covered, has been scrapped in favour of a single specification list as follows:

> 1 × guidance card;
> 20 × individually wrapped sterile, adhesive dressings of assorted sizes;
> 2 × sterile eye pads, with attachment;
> 6 × individually wrapped triangular bandages;
> 6 × safety pins;
> 6 × sterile, unmedicated wound dressings (approx 13 cm × 9 cm);
> 2 × sterile, unmedicated wound dressings (approx 28 cm × 17.5 cm);
> one pair of disposable gloves (latex).

Soap and water and disposable drying materials, or suitable equivalents, should also be available. Where tap water is not available, sterile water or sterile 9 per cent saline, in sealed disposable containers (refillable containers are banned) each holding at least 300 millilitres, should be kept easily accessible, and near to the first aid box, for eye irrigation.

The contents of first aid boxes should be replenished as soon as possible after use and items which deteriorate will need to be replaced from time to time. Items should not be used after the indicated expiry date on the packet. For this reason boxes and kits should be examined frequently to make sure they are fully equipped.

It is unwise to store non-listed medical supplies (ie proprietary items such as painkiller tablets, etc) or indeed any other items in first aid boxes. This may contravene the COSHH or other regulations and could result in prosecution – as in one case when a firm was prosecuted because an HSE inspector discovered its staff had placed nail varnish and acetate varnish remover in the box 'for safety'!

Travelling First Aid Kits

An employer does not need to make first aid provisions for employees working away from his establishment. However, where the work involves travelling for long distances in remote areas, from which access to NHS accident and emergency facilities may be difficult, or where employees are using potentially dangerous tools or machinery, small travelling first aid kits should be provided.

The contents of such kits may need to vary according to the circumstances in which they are likely to be used. The regulations suggest that in general the following items should be sufficient:

1 × guidance card;
6 × sterile adhesive dressings;
1 × large sterile, unmedicated dressing;
2 × triangular bandages;
2 × safety pins;
a supply of individually wrapped, moist cleaning wipes.

First Aid on the Road

Over 300,000 people are injured in road traffic accidents annually, with unfortunately some 3,500 of them dying as a result. Any help that a road user can give at the scene of an accident may just save a life, or may give much-needed comfort to a traumatized casualty. The following guidelines have been established for dealing with casualties at the scene of a road accident:

1 Assess the situation:
  – What has happened?
  – Is there any further danger to you or the casualty? (Remember, roadsides are particularly dangerous places to treat a casualty.)
  – How many people are injured?
  – Is anybody else able to help?

2 Assess the casualty:

- What is wrong with the casualty?
- Is it necessary to move the casualty, or can he/she be left safely in his/her current position?
- Remember, further injuries can be caused through unnecessary movement of the casualty.

3 Do you need assistance?

- Do you need assistance from the emergency services?
- Don't forget, other first-aiders/bystanders can help you.
- When you ask for help from the emergency services they will need to know:
  - the precise location of the incident;
  - what happened;
  - the injuries involved;
  - how many people are injured.

4 Make a diagnosis:

- What happened to the casualty? Did he or she fall, faint or have a bump on the head?
- Look for signs such as bleeding, swelling or unaligned limbs.
- If the casualty is conscious, ask him or her where he or she feels pain or if he or she went dizzy before the accident.

5 Priorities:

The priorities of first aid are usually referred to as the ABC of first aid:

- *Airway*: check inside the mouth and remove any visible obstruction. Put your fingertips under the point of the casualty's chin. Lift the chin to open the airway.
- *Breathing*: spend at least 10 seconds looking, listening and feeling for breathing. If the casualty is breathing, put him/her in the recovery position. Continue to monitor the patient's breathing.
- *Circulation*: look, listen and feel for normal breathing, coughing or movement by the victim. Only if you have been trained to do so, check the carotid pulse.

6 Priorities of general treatment (the three Bs):

- *Breathing* (see above).
- *Bleeding*. Stop bleeding by raising the injured limb above the heart. Apply pressure to the wound with pad, bandage, clean handkerchief or towel.
- *Bones*. If necessary immobilize a broken arm in a sling. If a broken leg is suspected, keep the casualty still.

7 While you are waiting for the arrival of the emergency services:

- Look for changes in the casualty's condition, monitoring the vital signs.
- Check your treatment is adequate and successful.
- Co-operate with the emergency services when they arrive.

Safety Signs

A safety sign is defined as one which combines geometrical shape, colour, and a pictorial symbol to provide specific health or safety information or an instruction as to whether or not any text is included on the sign. Regulations concerning the specification of safety signs in work premises have applied to all such signs since 1 January 1986. Specifications for various types of safety sign are given in BS 5378 (Part I). They are briefly described as follows:

- **Prohibition Sign:** round in shape with a white background and a circular band and cross-bar in red. The symbol must be black and placed in the centre of the sign without obliterating the cross-bar. Typical examples of such signs are those prohibiting smoking, pedestrians or the use of water for drinking purposes.

- **Warning Sign:** triangular in shape with a yellow background and black triangular band. The symbol or words must be black and placed in the centre of the sign. Typical examples of such signs are those warning of the danger of fire, explosion, toxic substances, corrosive substances, radiation, overhead loads, industrial trucks, electric shocks, proximity of laser beams, etc.

- **Mandatory Sign:** round in shape with a blue background, with the symbol or words placed centrally and in white. Typical examples of such signs are those advising that certain pieces of protective clothing must be worn (eg goggles, hard hats, breathing masks, gloves, etc).

- **Safety Sign:** square in shape with a green background and white symbol or words centrally placed. Typical examples of such signs are those for fire exits, first aid posts and rescue points.

Vehicle Reversing

Among the statistics of industrial accidents and road accidents, those resulting from vehicles reversing feature significantly. According to the HSE, nearly one-quarter of all deaths involving vehicles at work occur while vehicles are reversing. In a new booklet entitled *Reversing Vehicles* (available from the HSE) the HSE gives the following advice to those concerned:

- Identify all the risks and decide how to remove them.
- Remove the need for reversing.
- Exclude people from the area in which vehicles are permitted to reverse.
- Minimize the distance vehicles have to reverse.
- Make sure all staff are adequately trained.
- Use a properly trained banksman or guide (the booklet illustrates the signals such a person should use to ensure safety when vehicles are reversing).
- Decide how the driver is to make and keep contact with the banksman.

- Make sure all visiting drivers are briefed.
- Make sure all vehicle manoeuvres are properly supervised.

Additionally:

- Increase the area the driver can see.
- Fit a reversing alarm (see below).
- Use other safety devices (ie trip, sensing and scanning devices, and barriers to prevent vehicles overrunning steep edges).

It is in consequence of dangers of reversing that legislation permits the voluntary fitment of reversing bleepers on certain goods and passenger vehicles (see p 344 for full details). With the introduction of these voluntary provisions, there is the risk that any operator deciding not to fit such equipment on a voluntary basis, who then has one of his vehicles involved in a reversing accident, could face proceedings under the Health and Safety at Work etc Act for not taking sufficient care in safeguarding the health of others. A number of successful prosecutions on this account have been reported and in some cases very heavy fines were imposed.

Safe Tipping

Another area where concern has been expressed over safety measures involves the use of tipping vehicles (and vehicles with lorry-mounted cranes and suchlike) whereby elevated bodies (or crane jibs) come into contact with overhead power cables or are sufficiently close for arcing to occur in wet conditions. The specific danger lies in touching the vehicle body or tipping controls while in contact with the power cable. Drivers are safe when a cable is touched provided they remain in the cab, where the vehicle tyres prevent completion of an electrical circuit. A spokesperson for the electricity supply industry advises drivers to remain in their cabs and drive clear. If this is not possible they should jump from the cab and NOT touch any part of the vehicle, remaining well clear until an electricity engineer has been contacted and reports that it is safe to return to the vehicle.

Tipper operators should also be aware of the provisions of the Lifting Operations and Lifting Equipment Regulations 1998 described on pp 442–43.

Sheeting of Loads

A variety of load types need to be sheeted for both legal and operational reasons; particularly loads comprising waste skips, bricks, sand, gravel, ash, grain and various types of agricultural produce. Other loads need to be sheeted for weather protection and security reasons.

Many aspects of health and safety legislation and various Codes of Practice are relevant and should be carefully observed to avoid any breach of health and safety law. Also, specifically, it is an offence under C&U regulations to allow loose loads of any type to cause nuisance or danger to other road users as a result of such material falling or being blown from the vehicle. These loads must be adequately restrained by sheeting or by covering with netting.

Sheeting and un-sheeting of loads is a notoriously high-risk procedure. Those carrying out this activity may slip or fall while walking on top of the load or balancing on vehicle sides or as a result of pulling on ropes that break. Employers have a statutory duty to assess such risks and to put in place safe working practices.

Health and safety guidelines suggest that priority should be given to the use of closed vehicles or, where this is not feasible, to vehicles with mechanically operated sheeting systems or, at the very least, with mechanical systems that can be operated from ground level. Alternatively, consideration should be given to the provision of gantries from which operatives can sheet loads with minimal risk to their personal safety.

Useful guidance on safe sheeting methods is to be found in a number of official publications as follows:

- Health and Safety Executive publications:
  - *Workplace Transport Safety* – HS(G)136;
  - *Sheeting and Un-sheeting of Tipper Lorries* – HS(G)148.
- Department for Transport:
  - *Code of Practice – Safety of Loads on Vehicles* (third edition, 2002).

Safe Parking

Many accidents occur with parked vehicles and trailers. In particular, within transport depots there should be proper procedures for parking, especially in regard to parking areas and level standing for detached semi-trailers. A common failing is not ensuring that semi-trailers are dropped on to hard and level ground, allowing the landing gear on one side to sink and the trailer to topple over to the side. Nose-diving is another common accident, where nose-heavy semi-trailers are not supported with trestles when left detached. Ground sinkage can also be a cause of difficulty when recoupling tractive units.

Recently reported cases (in *Commercial Motor*) of unsafe parking practices resulting in driver deaths concern the braking of parked semi-trailers. When recoupling tractive units, drivers insert the red air-hose which releases the emergency brakes on the semi-trailer without checking that both the semi-trailer ratchet brake and the tractive-unit handbrake are fully applied. In such circumstances the vehicle combination can move while the driver is out of the cab. Other potential sources of accidents are when articulated combinations are coupled near to walls and loading bays, where there is always a danger of an unseen person walking behind the trailer. Again, if brakes are not properly set the semi-trailer is likely to shunt backwards as the tractive unit is driven under the coupling plate.

Work at Height

Another new set of regulations concerning health and safety matters, and very likely to have a significant impact on the road haulage industry, are the Work at Height Regulations 2005 (SI 2005 No 735), which came into effect from 6 April 2005. These regulations are intended to help prevent the many accidents involving falls from height. In 2007–08 these accounted for 58 fatal accidents at work and over 3,600 major injuries; in fact they are the biggest single cause of workplace deaths and major injury. Replacing earlier regulations, they consolidate previous legislation and implement EC Directive 2001/45/EC.

The new rules apply to most 'work at height' situations where there is a risk of a fall likely to occasion person injury – as, for example, climbing into or out of a vehicle cab or the load area. The employer's duty is to ensure that current practices are safe and to take steps to prevent falls and ensure that relevant staff are trained, that work is planned accordingly and that work is suspended when weather conditions endanger health or safety. Provision in these regulations also relates to falling objects, which should be safeguarded against. In the context of this legislation, 'at height' means a place from which a person falling could be injured – and it also includes below ground level. Working means moving around at a place of work.

Noise at Work

According to the HSE, more than 1 million workers are exposed to noise levels that put their hearing at risk. In fact, it is estimated by the HSE that around 170,000 people in Britain actually suffer deafness, tinnitus and other hearing problems caused by noise at work. Hence, from April 2006 all workers in the transport industry are brought within the scope of the Control of Noise at Work Regulations 2005. As well as goods vehicle drivers, the regulations also include workers in garages, warehouses, and in bodybuilding, repair and paint shops, for example.

Where appropriate, employers are required to provide hearing protection (eg ear defenders) – and insist that employees use it – and regular hearing tests as well as training on minimizing the risk of hearing loss where the noise exceeds 80 decibels. Noise control must be implemented where noise levels exceed 85 decibels and there is an absolute maximum limit of 137 decibels above which no employee should be subjected. Fines of up to £5,000 may be imposed for breaches of these regulations.

Further information can be obtained from the HSE website: **www.hse.gov.uk/ noise**.

Forklift Truck Safety

There has been much concern in recent years about the high level of industrial accidents which are caused by or which result from forklift truck misuse. In consequence of this a system of forklift truck driver licensing is to be established in order to ensure a safe standard of operation.

The scheme is voluntary but a Code of Practice* has been established which employers will be bound to follow if they wish to avoid conflict with the Factory Inspectorate, who have powers to order an employer to have drivers trained, to order that the use of forklift trucks must be stopped immediately if they believe that danger is being caused, and to take an employer to court if an untrained driver causes an accident with a forklift truck.

* NB: *This Code of Practice is available from HSE Books, price £5.00, ISBN 0 7176 2455 2.*

Freight Container Safety Regulations

Owners and lessees and others in control of freight containers must ensure that they comply with the International Convention for Safe Containers – Geneva 1972. The Freight Containers (Safety Convention) Regulations 1984 apply to containers designed to facilitate the transport of goods by one or more modes of transport without intermediate reloading, designed to be secured or readily handled or both, having corner fittings for these purposes and which have top corner fittings and a bottom area of at least 7 square metres or, if they do not have top corner fittings, a bottom area of at least 14 square metres.

Containers must have a valid approval issued by the Health and Safety Executive or a body appointed by the HSE (or under the authority of a foreign government which has acceded to the Convention) for the purpose of confirming that they meet specified standards of design and construction and should be fitted with a safety approval plate to this effect. If they are marked with their gross weight such marking must be consistent with the maximum operating gross weight shown on the safety approval plate. Containers must be maintained in an efficient state, in efficient working order and in good repair. Details of the arrangements for the approval of containers in Great Britain are set out in a document *Arrangements in GB for the Approval of Containers*, available from the HSE.

The safety approval plate (issued by the HSE) as described in the regulations must be permanently fitted to the container where it is clearly visible and not capable of being easily damaged and it must show the following information:

CSC SAFETY APPROVAL

- Approval Reference;
- Date Manufactured;
- Identification Number;
- Maximum Gross Weight . . . kg . . . lb;
- Allowable Stacking Weight for 1.8g . . . kg . . . lb;
- Racking Test Load Value;
- Next Examination Date.

Operation of Lorry Loaders

The use of hydraulically operated lorry loaders or lorry-mounted cranes, as they are more commonly called (in fact the name Hiab is becoming a generic term for this equipment), 'has reduced the risk of accident from the arduous and potentially injurious manhandling of loads and they reserve the strength of the driver for safe conduct of the vehicle', according to the Association of Lorry Loader Manufacturers and Importers of Great Britain (ALLMI). But, the Association says, despite the inherent safety of a properly designed and installed lorry loader, accidents still occur through lack of knowledge and understanding. For this reason ALLMI has published an excellent booklet called *Code of Practice for the Safe Application and Operation of Lorry Loaders*. Copies are available from the Association (tel: 0844 8584334).

See also Chapter 7 dealing with driver training for lorry-loader operatives.

Safety in Dock Premises

Under the Docks Regulations 1988 made under the Health and Safety at Work etc Act 1974, when goods vehicle drivers work in or visit docks premises, including roll-on/roll-off ferry ports, they must be provided with high-visibility clothing to be worn when they leave the vehicle cab. The clothing may take the form of fluorescent jackets, waistcoats, belts or sashes and must be worn at all times when out of the cab on such premises, including when on the vehicle decks of the ferry. Protective headgear (hard hats) must be supplied and worn in such areas where there is likely to be danger of falling objects from above (eg where cranes are working).

Drivers must leave the vehicle cab when parked on a straddle-carrier grid or where containers are being lifted on to or off the vehicle.

The HSC has published an approved Code of Practice – *Safety in Docks* – which is available from The Stationery Office.

Loads – General, Livestock, Food, etc

In addition to the regulations referred to in Chapter 12 regarding the way in which vehicles are constructed and used, operators will find many more regulations imposed on them which depend on the types of load they carry. Some of these provisions are included in the Road Vehicles (Construction and Use) Regulations 1986, and its many amendments, but others are to be found elsewhere. This chapter deals with both the length and width of normal loads and also covers some of the special points applicable to carrying food, livestock, sand and ballast, solid fuel and containers.

Length and Width of Loads

Loads on normal goods vehicles (ie which come within the C&U regulations) in excess of the actual vehicle dimensions of length and width may be carried provided that certain special conditions are met, as indicated here. Details of the requirements relating to abnormal and projecting loads are given in Chapter 19.

Length

When moving a vehicle, which complies with C&U regulations, and its load, which is more than 18.65 metres long, the police must be notified two clear days in advance and a statutory attendant must also be carried. If a long load is carried on an articulated vehicle which is specially designed to carry long loads but in all other respects complies with the C&U regulations, the 18.65-metre dimension is measured excluding the length of the tractive unit. Notice must also be given to the police and an attendant carried if the combination of a number of vehicles carrying one load is more than 25.9 metres long.

An overall limit of 27.4 metres is set for the length of a trailer and its load (the length of the towing vehicle is excluded from this dimension), above which movement can only be allowed by special order from the Secretary of State for Transport.

Further details of the requirements for markers, police notification and attendants on long loads are given in Chapter 19.

Width

The overall width of a normal load (ie not an indivisible load) carried on a vehicle complying with the C&U regulations must not be more than 2.9 metres. The load itself must not project more than 305 millimetres on either side of the vehicle. There is an exception to this requirement when loose agricultural produce is carried.

If an indivisible load is carried on a normal vehicle which complies in all respects with the C&U regulations and the load is more than 2.9 metres wide, two days' notice must be given to the police of every district through which it is to pass. If such a load exceeds 3.5 metres width then the police must be notified as stated and an attendant must be carried.

If the load on a vehicle is more than 5 metres wide, two days' notice must be given to the police, a statutory attendant must be carried and a Special Order must be obtained from the Secretary of State for Transport on form VR1.

Carriage of Livestock

A completely new set of rules concerning the welfare of animals during transit came into effect from 5 January 2007, replacing most of the former regulations. Council Regulation 1/2005/EC is a very long and detailed document for which the Department of Environment, Food and Rural Affairs (DEFRA) has provided a summary of the main requirements as follows.

The most important and overriding provision to note is that 'No animal shall be transported unless it is fit for the intended journey, and all animals shall be transported in conditions guaranteed not to cause them injury or unnecessary suffering' *(Source: Council Regulation 1/2005/EC on the protection of animals during transport and related operations and amending Directives).*

All persons who take animals on a journey, whatever the length, should always apply the following good transport practice by ensuring that:

- the journey is properly planned and time is kept to a minimum and the animals are checked and their needs met during the journey;
- the animals are fit to travel;
- the vehicle and loading and unloading facilities are designed, constructed and maintained to avoid injury and suffering;

- those handling animals are trained or competent in the task and do not use violence or any methods likely to cause unnecessary fear, injury or suffering;
- water, feed and rest are given to the animals as needed, and sufficient floor space and height are allowed.

The Regulation applies to all those involved with the transport of live vertebrate animals in connection with an economic activity, for example:

- livestock and equine hauliers;
- farmers; and
- commercial pet breeders.

The Regulation also applies to those working at:

- markets;
- assembly centres; and
- slaughterhouses.

The Regulation does not apply to the transport of animals:

- where the transport is not in connection with an economic activity;
- to or from veterinary practices or clinics under veterinary advice, where the animal is an individual animal accompanied by its owner (or other responsible person) and is fit for the journey; or
- where animals are pet animals accompanied by their owner on a private journey.

Animals that Cannot Be Transported

Animals that fall into the following groups cannot be transported:

- unfit animals;
- very young animals (eg calves of less than 10 days of age, pigs of less than 3 weeks and lambs of less than 1 week) – except if the journey is less than 100 km;
- calves of less than 14 days of age – journeys exceeding 8 hours are not permitted;
- pregnant female animals – not considered fit for transport if they have reached the latest stage of gestation (within 10 per cent of the estimated time of the gestation before birth) and for a period of one week after giving birth;
- cats and dogs under 8 weeks of age – may not be transported commercially unless accompanied by their mother.

Transporter Requirements for Journeys up to 65 Kilometres

Transporters are *not* required to have vehicle authorization or training and certificates of competence. However, they must comply with the technical rules on fitness to travel, means of transport and transport practices as set out in Annex 1 of Council Regulation 1/2005/EC.

Transporter Authorization for Journeys over 65 Kilometres and Under Eight Hours' Duration

Authorization will be granted, and will be valid for five years, if transporters can comply with the following:

- They have an established business or, in the case of businesses established outside the UK, are represented in the UK.
- They can demonstrate that they have appropriate staff, equipment and operational procedures to transport animals in compliance with the new Regulation.
- They have no record of serious infringements of animal welfare legislation in the three years preceding application.

Transporter Authorization for Journeys of Over Eight Hours' Duration

The authorization will be valid for five years. Authorization will be granted if transporters can comply with the following:

- They have an established business or, in the case of businesses established outside the UK, are represented in the UK.
- They can demonstrate that they have appropriate staff, equipment and operational procedures to transport animals in compliance with the new Regulation.
- They have no record of serious infringements of animal welfare legislation in the three years preceding their application.

The transporter must provide:

- valid certificates of approval for vehicles and containers;
- details of procedures enabling transporters to trace and record the movement of road vehicles under their responsibility and to contact the drivers at any time;
- contingency plans in the event of emergencies;
- from 2008, valid certificates of competence for drivers and attendants.

All new vehicles used for the transport of horses (except registered horses) or farmed animals must have a satellite navigation system. This requirement applies to all vehicles (old and new) used for the transport of horses (except registered horses) or farmed animals from 2009.

Training and Competence for Drivers and Attendants and Assembly Centre Personnel

From 5 January 2008, drivers or attendants responsible for the transport of farmed animals, horses and poultry over distances greater than 65 kilometres are required to hold a certificate of competence. Assembly centre staff are *not* required to obtain a certificate of competence but will need to have undergone training.

Training courses will cover the technical and administrative aspects of the rules and regulations that apply to the protection of animals during transport. These include:

- general conditions of transporting animals;
- the documents that are required;
- fitness for transport;
- journey planning;
- animal physiology and feed needs, animal behaviour and the concept of stress;
- practical aspects of handling animals;
- impact of driving behaviour on welfare of animals and on the quality of meat;
- emergency care for animals;
- safety of personnel handling animals.

The certificate of competence will be awarded once an independent assessment of knowledge of the above has been made.

Exporting of Animals

When animals are exported out of Great Britain the transporter must ensure that the journeys are properly planned and that a route plan is submitted to the Divisional Veterinary Manager at DEFRA for approval. Without this approval an export health certificate will not be issued. Operators based outside Great Britain will require an authorization from their own domestic authorities to transport animals.

Journey Logs

From 5 January 2007 anyone exporting farm livestock or unregistered horses is required to complete a journey log. This needs to be approved by the relevant Animal Health Divisional Office for the place of departure. The journey log replaces the existing route plan form (ERA 20).

Animal Transport Certificates

Animal transport certificates (ATCs) are required for journeys of any species of animal over any distance or duration *except* journeys involving farm livestock and unregistered horses on export journeys of over eight hours, which require a journey log instead. The Animal Transport Certificate is required to provide the following information:

- origin and ownership of animals;
- place of departure and destination;
- date and time of departure and expected duration of journey.

NB: *Farmers transporting their own animals in their own means of transport on journeys of up to 50 kilometres from their holding are exempt from this requirement.*

The requirement for an Animal Transport Certificate (ATC) is not new and, as previously, there is no prescribed format in which the information required has to be presented. Any other document containing the required information – such as an Animal Movement Licence – may be used, if preferred.

Vehicle Inspection and Approval

From 5 January 2007 vehicles used for transporting farm livestock and horses on long journeys (those in excess of eight hours) must be inspected and approved by the competent authority of a member state or a body designated by a member state. In the UK this will include such organizations as the Freight Transport Association, EFSIS Agriculture and CMI Certification. In Scotland the approved authority is the Scottish Food Quality Certification Board.

Food

The Food Standards Agency established under provisions contained in the Food Standards Act 1999 controls and regulates food safety and standards in the UK, particularly including such issues as the transport of livestock, fresh meat and other foods. It will have power to intervene if hauliers jeopardize food safety.

Special regulations (the Food Safety (General Food Hygiene) Regulations 1995) apply to vehicles used for the carriage of food, excluding milk and drugs. All mobile shops and food delivery vehicles and the equipment carried by such vehicles must be constructed and maintained so that the food carried can be kept clean and fresh.

The driver of a food vehicle should wear clean overalls and if meat or bacon sides are carried, which the driver has to carry over his shoulder, he should wear a hat to prevent the meat touching his hair. He must not smoke while loading or unloading or serving the food (but he may do so in the cab of the vehicle if this is separate from the part of the vehicle in which the food is carried), and any cuts or abrasions on his hands must be covered with waterproof dressings.

If a driver or any other person concerned in the loading and unloading of food develops any infectious disease, his employer must notify the local authority health department immediately.

Food vehicles must have the name and address of the person carrying on the business shown on the nearside and the address at which the vehicle is garaged if this is a different address. If, however, a vehicle based in England or Wales has a fleet number clearly shown and is garaged at night on company premises, then the garage address is not required.

A wash handbasin and a supply of clean water must be provided on vehicles which carry uncovered food (except bread) unless the driver can wash his hands at both ends of his journey before he has to handle the food. When meat is carried, soap, clean towels and a nail brush must be provided on the vehicle. In Scotland all food-carrying vehicles must be provided with these items.

Mobile shops and food delivery vehicles must not be garaged with food still inside unless it can be kept clean.

An authorized officer of a council may enter and detain (but not stop while it is in motion) any food-carrying vehicle except those owned by a rail company or vehicles operated by haulage contractors.

Perishable Food

A whole range of legislation covers the carriage of food and particularly perishable food both in the UK and in Europe. When perishable foodstuffs are carried on international journeys to and through Austria, Belgium, Bulgaria, the CIS, the Czech Republic, Denmark, Finland, France, Germany, Italy, Luxembourg, Morocco, the Netherlands, Norway, Poland, Slovakia, Spain, Sweden and the former Yugoslavia the conditions of the Agreement on the International Carriage of Perishable Foodstuffs (known as the ATP agreement) must be observed.

The ATP agreement also applies in Britain (viz the International Carriage of Perishable Foodstuffs Act 1976) and under its provisions vehicles used to carry perishable food must be constructed and tested (at six-yearly intervals) to certain specified standards and must display an ATP approval plate to this effect. The principal requirement is that vehicles carrying certain specified perishable foodstuffs must comply with the body and temperature control equipment test standards and must be certified to this effect. The ATP agreement applies broadly to quick-frozen, deep-frozen, frozen and non-frozen foodstuffs but not fresh vegetables and soft fruit.

Information relating to food transport may be obtained from the Department of Health and Social Security, which has published a number of Codes of Practice, and from the Department for Environment, Food and Rural Affairs.

Chilled Food Controls (ie Temperature-Controlled Food)

Following a series of food poisoning (salmonella and listeria) outbreaks in 1989 changes in legislation resulted in the introduction of the Food Hygiene (Amendment) Regulations 1990, which control the maximum temperature at which chilled food can be transported. The Regulations apply to goods vehicles exceeding 7.5 tonnes gross weight carrying 'relevant food' products (which are listed in the schedules to the regulations). Such vehicles must have equipment capable of maintaining the temperature of the food at or below the specified temperature (1 April 1993, –5°C for certain foods as listed in the schedules and –8°C for other 'relevant' foods) or at or above 63°C as appropriate.

Vehicles up to 7.5 tonnes used for local deliveries must be capable of keeping relevant food at or below the specified temperature or at or above 63°C as appropriate.

However, in a case where the regulations specify that food is to be kept at 5°C, provided it is not kept in the vehicle for more than 12 hours, it may be at a higher temperature, not exceeding 8°C.

There are exemptions to these requirements: where food is to be sold within two hours (ie if prepared at 63°C or over) or four hours (ie if prepared below 63°C). Other variations (ie not exceeding 2°C for a maximum of two hours) may be permitted in certain specified circumstances such as variations in processing; while equipment is defrosted; during temporary breakdown of equipment; while moving food from one place or vehicle to another; or any other unavoidable reason.

Regulations (ie the Food Safety (Temperature Control) Regulations 1995 and the Food Safety (General Food Hygiene) Regulations 1995) which came into effect in September 1995 implement various provisions of EU Directive 43/93/EEC on these matters and parts of the so-called 'Water Directive' (EU Directive 778/80/EEC), which relates to the use of water for food production purposes. These regulations only marginally affect transport operations and for that reason they are not detailed here.

Quick-Frozen Foodstuffs

The UK Quick-frozen Foodstuffs (QFF) Regulations 1990 are effective in setting general conditions for the quality and use of equipment for storing and transporting food labelled 'Quick-frozen' (but not ice cream). These regulations require certain temperatures to be maintained within a percentage range of −18°C, or colder, as follows:

- during transport (other than local distribution) a tolerance for brief periods of 3°C (but not warmer than −15°C);
- during local distribution 6°C (but not warmer than −12°C).

The Quick-frozen Foodstuffs (Amendment) Regulations 1994, which took effect from 1 September 1994, require refrigerated transport operators to fit temperature recorders to vehicles carrying frozen foodstuffs (but not chilled foods) and to keep the records for at least 12 months.

Waste Food

Vehicles used to collect unprocessed waste food, intended for feeding to livestock and poultry, must be drip-proof, covered and enclosed with material capable of being cleansed and disinfected.

Vehicles must be thoroughly cleansed and disinfected on the completion of unloading. No livestock or poultry or foodstuff or anything intended for use for any livestock or poultry may be carried in any vehicle which is carrying unprocessed waste food intended for feeding to livestock or poultry. Furthermore, processed and unprocessed waste food may not be carried in the same vehicle at the same time.

Grain Haulage

Grain hauliers are faced with new rules banning them from using grain trailers for the carriage of other loads (such as glass, toxins, waste, bonemeal and manure) which may contaminate the trailer. Auditors from UKASTA (the United Kingdom Agricultural Supply Trade Association) will monitor standards and check hauliers' records and invoices to ensure they have not broken the Association's code, which is based on provisions in the Food Safety Act 1990. A new-style 'grain passport' must be carried on vehicles, otherwise loads may be rejected by consignees if they are not satisfied as to the origin or standard under which loads have been carried.

Sand and Ballast Loads

The movement of sand and ballast came to the attention of the former Department of Trade and Industry and Trading Standards inspectors principally because under the Weights and Measures Act 1985 these materials must be sold in weighed quantities (normally by volume in metric measures – in multiples of 0.2 cubic metre) and carried in calibrated vehicles which display a stamp placed on the body by the Trading Standards department of the local authority.

When sand and ballast (including shingle, ashes, clinker, etc) loads are carried, the driver must have a signed note (ie conveyance note) from the supplier indicating the following facts:

- the name and address of the sellers;
- the name of the buyer and the address for delivery of the load;
- a description of the type of ballast;
- the quantity by net weight or by volume;
- details of the vehicle;
- the date, time and place of loading the vehicle.

The document containing these details must be handed over to the buyer before unloading, or if he is not there it must be left at the delivery premises. Where a delivery is to be made to two or more buyers each must be given a separate document containing the details shown above. Similar requirements apply to the carriage of ready-mixed cement.

Quarry Tax

From April 2002, in an effort to increase the use of alternative recycled materials, a new 'quarry' tax of £1.60 per tonne applies to all primary aggregates such as sand, gravel and crushed rock taken from quarries. Recycled materials include wastes from construction, demolition, clay and coal extraction. Some of the revenue earned from this tax will go into an 'aggregates sustainability fund'.

Solid Fuel Loads

When solid fuel is carried a document giving similar details to those mentioned above for sand and ballast carrying must be held by the driver of the vehicle. When solid fuel is carried for sale in open sacks a notice on the vehicle in letters at least 60 mm high must contain the following words: 'All open sacks on this vehicle contain 25 kg or 50 kg'.

Container Carrying

Container carrying has come to the fore in recent years, and while there are no specific regulations on this subject apart from the general safety provisions of the C&U regulations and the vehicle weight limitations, the authorities are concerned about the dangers arising from inadequate securing of containers. Containers, ideally, should be carried only on vehicles fitted with proper twist locks or, failing this, should be secured by chains of sufficient strength with tensioners for adjustment and taking account of the recommended strength of restraint systems given in the DETR code of practice *Safety of Loads on Vehicles* (see pp 427–28).

The use of ropes for securing containers should be avoided because the corner castings through which they are passed are rough and will cut through the rope. Containers where possible should be loaded against the headboard and directly on the platform of the vehicle, not on timber packing, which is liable to move.

Under the Freight Containers (Safety Convention) Regulations 1984 owners and lessees and others in control of freight containers used or supplied must ensure that they comply with the conditions of use as stated in the International Convention for Safe Containers 1972 (see also Chapter 17).

Fly-Tipping

The Control of Pollution (Amendment) Act 1989, implemented in 1991, tightened up existing measures to prevent the illegal tipping (fly-tipping) of waste, demolition rubble and such materials in unauthorized places. Among the specific measures legislated for under regulations called the Controlled Waste (Registration of Carriers and Seizure of Vehicles) Regulations 1991 are requirements for registration of waste transporters and tipper operators, the licensing of authorized operators, restriction of tipping to authorized sites and further powers to impound (and possibly sell) vehicles belonging to operators who dump loads illegally (such powers also exist under the Criminal Justice Act 1988).

Offences such as fly-tipping can result in fines of up to £20,000 and three months' imprisonment for magistrate's court convictions under the Environment Protection Act 1990. Where a case goes before a Crown court, much higher penalties may be imposed.

NB: See Chapter 20 for more information on the carriage and disposal of waste materials.

Loads – Abnormal and Projecting

After a prolonged period of consultation, a new set of rules on the carriage of abnormal indivisible loads (AILs) on Special Types vehicles was made late in 2003 with the introduction of the Road Vehicles (Authorization of Special Types) (General) Order 2003 under Section 41 of the Road Traffic Act 1988. These provisions are concerned primarily with four different types of vehicle, now referred to as Part 2 vehicles and vehicle combinations, as follows:

- abnormal indivisible load vehicles;
- mobile cranes;
- engineering plant;
- road recovery vehicles.

Abnormal Indivisible Loads

For the purpose of regulations, abnormal indivisible loads (sometimes abbreviated to AILs) are loads which cannot, without undue expense or risk of damage, be divided into two or more loads for the purpose of carriage on the road and which cannot be carried on a vehicle operating within the limitations of the C&U regulations as described in Chapter 12.

Number of Abnormal Loads

While normally the carriage of only one abnormal load is permitted, two such abnormal loads may be carried on one vehicle within Category 1 or Category 2 (see below) provided the loads are from the same place and are destined for the same delivery address.

Engineering Plant

In the case of engineering plant, such plant and parts dismantled from it may be carried on the same vehicle (ie to constitute more than one or two loads) provided that the carriage of the parts does not cause the overall dimensions of the vehicle and the main load to be exceeded and that the parts are loaded and discharged at the same place as the main load.

Special Types Vehicles

Dimensions

Width Special Types vehicles, locomotives and trailers and their loads are normally permitted to be up to 2.9 metres wide but, if necessary to ensure the safe carriage of large loads, they may be up to a maximum of 6.1 metres wide.

Length The overall length of a Special Types vehicle and its load must not exceed 27.4 metres, which applies normally, but where the abnormal load is carried on a combination of vehicles and trailers or on a long articulated vehicle the dimension of 27.4 metres is measured excluding the drawing vehicle.

Weight The permissible maximum weight of a Special Types vehicle must not exceed 150,000 kg. There is a limit on the maximum weight which may be imposed on the road by any one wheel of the vehicle of 8,250 kg and the maximum weight imposed by any one axle must not exceed 16,500 kg. These limits may be exceeded only if authorization by Special Order is obtained from the Secretary of State for Transport (DfT).

Vehicle Categories

The Special Types Order specifies three separate weight categories for abnormal load vehicles as follows:

> Category 1 – up to 50 tonnes gcw
> Category 2 – up to 80 tonnes gcw
> Category 3 – up to 150 tonnes gcw

Category 1 Vehicles

Vehicles within this category will normally fall within the C&U regulations in regard to permissible maximum weight, axle spacings and axle weights but where it is a five-axle articulated vehicle the weight may exceed 38 tonnes up to a maximum of 50,000 kg (ie 50 tonnes) provided the following minimum relevant axle spacings are observed:

Relevant axle spacing	Maximum weight
At least 6.5 metres	40,000 kg
At least 7.0 metres	42,000 kg
At least 7.5 metres	44,000 kg
At least 8.0 metres	50,000 kg

Category 2 Vehicles

Vehicles within this category may operate up to a maximum weight of 80,000 kg (ie 80 tonnes) but they must have a minimum of six axles with a maximum weight of 50,000 kg on any group of axles and they must meet the minimum axle spacing requirements specified below.

Individual wheel and axle weight limits are as follows:

Distance between adjacent axles	Maximum axle weight	Maximum wheel weight
At least 1.1 metres	12,000 kg	6,000 kg
At least 1.35 metres	12,500 kg	6,250 kg

Minimum axle spacings and applicable maximum weights are as follows:

Distance between foremost and rearmost axles	Maximum weight
5.07 metres	38,000 kg
5.33 metres	40,000 kg
6.00 metres	45,000 kg
6.67 metres	50,000 kg
7.33 metres	55,000 kg
8.00 metres	60,000 kg
8.67 metres	65,000 kg
9.33 metres	70,000 kg
10.00 metres	75,000 kg
10.67 metres	80,000 kg

Category 3 Vehicles

A minimum of six axles is needed on Category 3 vehicles operating up to a permissible maximum weight of 150,000 kg (ie 150 tonnes) with a limit of 100,000 kg on any group of axles or 90,000 kg on any group of axles where the distance between adjacent axles is less than 1.35 metres. Vehicles in this category must meet the minimum axle spacing requirements specified below.

Individual wheel and axle weight limits are as follows:

Distance between adjacent axles	Maximum axle weight	Maximum wheel weight
At least 1.1 metres	15,000 kg	7,500 kg
At least 1.35 metres	16,500 kg	8,250 kg

Minimum axle spacings and applicable maximum weights are as follows:

Distance between foremost and rearmost axles	Maximum weight
5.77 metres	80,000 kg
6.23 metres	85,000 kg
6.68 metres	90,000 kg
7.14 metres	95,000 kg
7.59 metres	100,000 kg
8.05 metres	105,000 kg
8.50 metres	110,000 kg
8.95 metres	115,000 kg
9.41 metres	120,000 kg
9.86 metres	125,000 kg
10.32 metres	130,000 kg
10.77 metres	135,000 kg
11.23 metres	140,000 kg
11.68 metres	145,000 kg
12.14 metres	150,000 kg

VED for Special Types Vehicles

A separate VED taxation class applies to Special Types vehicles – see Chapter 8 for details.

Braking Standards

Vehicles operating within Category 1 must meet the C&U regulation braking standard requirements and those operating within Categories 2 and 3 from 1 October 1989 must meet the EU braking standards (ie EC 230/71, 132/74, 524/75, 489/79).

Identification Sign

Vehicles operating under the Special Types Order must display an identification sign at the front. This sign, on a plate at least 250 mm × 400 mm, must have white letters on a black background as follows:

letters 105 mm high

letters and figures 70 mm high

NB: A figure 1, 2 or 3 must follow the word 'CAT' as appropriate depending on the category of vehicle.

Special Types Plates

Vehicles falling within Category 2 and 3 which have been manufactured since 1 October 1988 must display Special Types plates (in a conspicuous and easily accessible position) showing the maximum operational weights recommended by the manufacturer when travelling on a road at varying speeds as follows: 12, 20, 25, 30, 35, 40 mph. The weights to be shown are the permissible maximum gross and train weights and the maximum weights for each individual axle. Plates on trailers (including semi-trailers) must show the permissible maximum weight for the trailer and the maximum weights for each individual axle. The plates must be marked with the words 'Special Types Use'.

Speed Limits

Maximum permitted speeds* are specified for Special Types vehicles as follows:

Vehicle category	Motorways	Dual-carriageways	Other roads
1. Up to 50 tonnes	60 mph	50 mph	40 mph
2. Up to 80 tonnes	40 mph	35 mph	30 mph
3. Up to 150 tonnes	30 mph	25 mph	20 mph

Speeds for Wide Loads

Vehicles carrying loads over 4.3 metres but not over 6.1 metres wide are restricted to 30 mph on motorways, 25 mph on dual-carriageways and 20 mph on other roads.

NB: It is important to note that tyre equipment on vehicles and trailers must be compatible with both the gross weight of the vehicle and the authorized maximum speed of operation.

Attendants

An attendant must be carried on Special Types vehicles:

- when the vehicle or its load is more than 3.5 metres wide;
- if the overall length of the vehicle is more than 18.3 metres (not including the length of the tractive unit in the case of articulated vehicles);
- if the length of a vehicle and trailer exceeds 25.9 metres;
- if the load projects more than 1.83 metres beyond the front of the vehicle;
- if the load projects more than 3.05 metres beyond the rear of the vehicle.

If three or more vehicles carrying abnormal loads or other loads of dimensions that require statutory attendants to be carried travel in convoy, attendants need only be carried on the first and last vehicles in the convoy.

Police Notification

The police of every district through which a Special Types combination is to be moved must be given two clear days' notice (excluding Saturdays, Sundays and bank holidays) in the case of notification under the Special Types General Order (STGO) and excluding Sundays and bank holidays for notification under the C&U regulations) if:

- the vehicle and its load is more than 2.9 metres wide;
- the vehicle and its load (or trailer and load) is more than 18.3 metres long;
- a combination of vehicles and trailers carrying the load is more than 25.9 metres long;
- the load projects more than 3.05 metres to the front or rear of the vehicle;
- the gross weight of the vehicle and the load is more than 80,000 kg.

The notice given must include details of the vehicle and the weight and dimensions of the load, the dates and times of the movement through the police district and the proposed route to be followed through that district.

In the case where notice has been given to the police of the movement of an abnormal load, they have the power to delay the vehicle during its journey if it is holding up other traffic or in the interests of road safety.

Under the provisions of the new STGO, which came into effect from 1 January 2004, responsibility for escorting abnormal loads has transferred to private escort companies. These companies, a list of which is available from the RHA must meet laid down criteria of standards and comply with a newly devised Code of Practice established jointly by the Highways Agency, the Association of Chief Police Officers (ACPO), ACPOS (Scotland) and the transport trade associations.

It should be noted that despite these new arrangements, notification about the movement of abnormal loads must still be made to the police, and that Chief Constables retain the right to escort vehicles 'where appropriate'.

Notification of Highway and Bridge Authorities

If a Special Types vehicle and its load weighs more than 80,000 kg, or the weight imposed on the road by the wheels of such a vehicle exceeds the maximum limit laid down in the C&U regulations (see pp 290–91), five clear days' notice must be given to the highway and bridge authorities for the areas through which the vehicle is to pass. Two days' notice is required when only the C&U axle weight limit is exceeded. The operator of such a vehicle is also required to indemnify the authorities against damage to any road or bridge over which it passes. These requirements also apply to vehicles which exceed the C&U gross weight limits and those which exceed their plated axle weight limits, plus mobile cranes and engineering plant which exceed the limits specified.

Stopping on Bridges

The driver of a vehicle carrying an abnormal load must ensure that no other such vehicle and load are on a bridge before he drives on to the bridge and once on the bridge he must not stop unless forced to do so.

Where a vehicle weighing more than 38,000 kg gross has to stop on a bridge for any reason it must be moved off the bridge as soon as possible. If it has broken down, the advice of the bridge authority (usually the Highways Department of the local authority) must be sought before the vehicle is jacked up on the bridge. In the event of damage being caused to a road or bridge by the movement of a heavy or large load over it the highway authority can take steps to recover from the vehicle operator the costs of repairing the damage.

Notification to Railtrack

All movements of abnormal loads over rail bridges must be notified to the BR Property Board National Helpline 08457 114141.

Special Orders

Written approval has to be obtained from the Secretary of State (DfT) in cases where a Special Types vehicle and its load exceeds 5 metres in width. Application is made on form VR1 (ie the movement order) and a copy of this completed form must be carried on the vehicle. The route specified, and the date and timings for the journey notified in the application, must be adhered to, otherwise further approval will have to be sought.

Dump Trucks

When dump trucks (ie vehicles designed for moving excavated material) are used on the road the maximum permissible gross weight is limited to 50,800 kg and the maximum axle weight allowed for such vehicles is 22,860 kg. They must not exceed a speed of 12 mph on normal roads and an attendant must be carried if the width exceeds 3.5 metres. If a dump truck is more than 4.3 metres wide, permission in the form of a Special Order from the Secretary of State is required before it is moved. Where three or more such vehicles over 3.5 metres wide travel in convoy only the first and last vehicles need carry attendants.

Other Plant

The Special Types General Order also makes special provision for other items of plant such as grass-cutting machines and hedge trimmers, track-laying vehicles, pedestrian-controlled road maintenance vehicles, vehicles used for experimental trials, straddle carriers, land tractors used for harvesting, mechanically propelled hay and straw balers, vehicles fitted with movable platforms and engineering plant. Any person proposing to move such items on public roads is advised to check that the appropriate legal requirements are met.

Internet Notifications for Abnormal Loads (ESDAL)

The Highways Agency, together with its agents SERCO, has launched a free website called ESDAL (Electronic Service Delivery for Abnormal Loads) which is designed to ease the complex statutory notifications which operators must make when planning to move abnormal loads. The scheme is said to 'cut bureaucracy' by making it easier for operators to find out who they must contact in both the police and the highway authorities in order to make these notifications.

The web address on which operators can register their details and obtain more information on this topic is: **www.highways.gov.uk/esdal**.

High Loads

While there are no general legal height restrictions on vehicles or loads (except those specific instances mentioned on pp 298–99), clearly vehicles must be loaded so that they can pass under bridges on the routes to be used.

In particular it should be noted that motorway bridges are built to give a clearance of 16 ft to 16 ft 6 ins and overhead power cables crossing roads are set at a minimum height of 19 ft (5.8 metres) where the voltage carried does not exceed 33,000 volts and at 6.0 metres where this voltage is exceeded (see also the note on p 483 about tipping vehicle dangers in regard to contact with overhead power cables). When planning to move loads above 19 ft it is a legal requirement to make contact with the National Grid Company or the appropriate regional electricity distribution company (ie previously the regional electricity boards) beforehand. It is also recommended that contact should be made with British Telecom regarding the presence of its overhead lines on the routes to be used. Some police forces now report that they will not action notification of abnormal load movements until both National Power and British Telecom have been notified.

Projecting Loads

Projecting loads may be carried on normal C&U regulation vehicles as well as on Special Types vehicles as described above. A projecting load is one that projects beyond the foremost or rearmost points or the side of the vehicle and, depending on the length or width of the projection, certain conditions apply when such loads are carried on normal vehicles, including requirements for lighting and marking.

Side Projections

Loads more than 4.3 metres wide cannot be moved legally under the C&U regulations although they can be carried on vehicles which comply with those regulations. In such cases the provisions of the Special Types General Order apply (see above).

The normal width limit for loads is 2.9 metres overall or 305 mm on either side of the vehicle except in the case of loose agricultural produce and indivisible loads. Where an indivisible wide load extends 305 mm or more on one or both sides of the vehicle or exceeds 2.9 metres overall, the police must be given two clear days' notice in advance and end marker boards must be displayed front and rear (fitted within 50 mm of the edge of the load), and if it exceeds 3.5 metres, police notification, end marker boards and an attendant are required.

Forward Projections

A load projecting more than 2.0 metres beyond the foremost part of the vehicle (on C&U vehicles) must be indicated by an approved side and end marker board (Figure 19.1) and an attendant must be carried. On Special Types vehicles only, where the load projects more than 1.83 metres to the front, an end marker must be displayed and an attendant carried.

If a load projects more than 3.05 metres beyond the front (on both C&U and Special Types vehicles), the police must be given two days' notice of its movement, both side and end approved marker boards must be displayed and an attendant must be carried.

If a load projects more than 4.5 metres beyond the front of the vehicle the provisions mentioned above must be observed and additional side marker boards must be carried within 2.5 metres of the first set of side markers.

Rearward Projections

Where a load projects more than 1.0 metre beyond the rear of a C&U vehicle (1.07 metres on Special Types vehicles) it must clearly be marked (the form which this must take is not specified, but a piece of rag tied to the end is usually sufficient). If the rear projection is more than 2.0 metres on C&U vehicles (1.83 metres on Special Types vehicles) an end marker board must be displayed.

Where the rearward projection is more than 3.05 metres the police must be notified, an attendant carried and approved side and end marker boards displayed. An end marker is not required if the projecting load is fitted with a rear reflective marker. If the rearward projection exceeds 5.0 metres additional side marker boards must be carried within 3.5 metres of the first set of side markers.

Marker Boards

Marker boards carried in accordance with the requirements described above must conform to the dimensions and colours shown in Figure 19.1 and they must be indirectly illuminated at night.

FIGURE 19.1 The approved-type marker boards which must be displayed when projecting loads are carried

Front or rear marker

Side marker

Lighting on Projecting and Long Loads

Rearward Projections

When carrying a load projecting more than 1.0 metre beyond the rear end of the vehicle an additional red rear position light must be carried within 1.0 metre of the end of the load or if the projecting load covers the rear lights and reflectors of the vehicle, additional lights and reflectors must be fixed to the load. This is usually best accomplished by having a complete lighting set and reflectors fitted to a board which can be fixed to the load.

Side Projections

When a load projects sideways more than 400 mm beyond the front and rear position lights of a vehicle, front position lights must be carried within 400 mm of the outer edges of the load and additional rear lights must also be carried within 400 mm of the outer edges of the load. White front and red rear reflectors must also be carried within 400 mm of the outer edges of the load.

Long Vehicles

A vehicle or combination of vehicles which, together with their load, are more than 18.3 metres long must, when on the road during the hours of darkness, carry side marker lights on each side positioned within 9.15 metres of the front of the vehicle or load and within 3.05 metres of the rear of the vehicle or load and other lights positioned between these at not more than 3.05-metre intervals. These requirements do not apply if approved illuminated marker boards are carried or if the combination is formed of a towing vehicle and a broken-down vehicle.

In the case of a combination of vehicles carrying a supported load (a load not resting on a vehicle except at each end) when the total length of the combination exceeds 12.2 metres but not 18.3 metres, side marker lights must be carried when on the road during the hours of darkness, positioned not more than 1.53 metres behind the rear of the drawing vehicle, and if the load extends more than 9.15 metres beyond the drawing vehicle an additional side marker light must be carried not more than 1.53 metres behind the centre line of the load.

Loads –
Dangerous,
Explosive
and Waste

According to the Health and Safety Executive (HSE), approximately 100 million tonnes of a wide range of dangerous goods are transported annually on British roads and railways. Legislation on the carriage of dangerous goods is both extensive and complex, and should be studied in detail by those responsible for such operations. Failure to comply with the strict provisions of the law can lead to harsh penalties. It could also result in risk to health and human life and cause serious environmental pollution.

Legislation Summary

The latest item of dangerous goods legislation is known by the name of REACH. This is a new European Community regulation (EC 1907/2006) on chemicals and their safe use. It deals with the registration, evaluation, authorization and restriction of chemical substances. The regulation came into force on 1 June 2007 and its aim is to improve the protection of human health and the environment through the better and earlier identification of the intrinsic properties of chemical substances.

The REACH Regulation gives greater responsibility to industry to manage the risks from chemicals and to provide safety information on the substances. Manufacturers and importers will be required to gather information on the properties of their chemical substances that will allow their safe handling, and to register the information in a central database run by the European Chemicals Agency (ECHA) in Helsinki.

UK national legislation on the carriage of dangerous goods by road is now aligned with the European Agreement Concerning the International Carriage of Dangerous Goods by Road (ADR) under Council Directive 94/55/EC, which harmonizes the law throughout the European Union. A so-called consolidated 'restructured' edition of ADR was published for 2005, taking effect from 1 January 2005. The main changes are listed in the following text in summary form on a part-by-part basis. The current edition of ADR is that for 2011, effective from 1 July 2011 – described further below.

UK Carriage by Road Regulations

The current dangerous goods regulations, namely the Carriage of Dangerous Goods and Use of Transportable Pressure Equipment Regulations 2009 (SI 2009 No 1348), generally referred to as the Carriage Regulations, deal with the carriage by road and rail of dangerous goods (other than explosives and radioactive material) in packages or in bulk in any container, tank or vehicle. An updated version of these regulations for 2011 is awaited as this *Handbook* goes to press. However, unlike former UK domestic dangerous goods legislation, these regulations implement ADR in the UK and cross-reference to the provisions set out in the Agreement.

These regulations, in Part 2(5) state that no person may carry dangerous goods, or cause or permit dangerous goods to be carried, where that carriage is prohibited by ADR or where that carriage does not comply with any applicable requirement of ADR. In other words, all carriage of dangerous goods by road must be in accordance with the ADR Agreement as described in this chapter.

The ADR Convention

The international carriage of dangerous goods by road within Europe is governed by the 'European Agreement concerning the International Carriage of Dangerous Goods by Road' (known conveniently as 'the ADR Convention' or 'the ADR Agreement') and most European countries are contracting parties to it. All EU Member States are signatories to it and their respective domestic legislation on dangerous goods carriage is based on this Convention, which is regularly updated. It is an agreement between Member States with no overall enforcing authority – the relevant authorities in contracting countries prosecute contravention of the ADR requirements under their own domestic legislation. The Agreement is a substantial document, the current edition of which has been updated for 2011.

ADR is published in two-volume book form or is available on CD, both from The Stationery Office (TSO) and is consistent with the United Nations' Model Regulations on the Transport of Dangerous Goods (13th revised edition – 2003), the International Maritime Dangerous Goods Code and the International Civil Aviation's Technical Instructions for the Safe Carriage of Dangerous Goods by Air, and is fully harmonized with the Regulations concerning the International Carriage of Dangerous Goods by Rail (RID).

Volume 1 of this edition contains the text of the actual ADR Agreement and the Protocol of Signature and Parts 1 to 3 of Annex A, which cover the general provisions and provisions concerning dangerous substances and articles as follows:

- Part 1 deals with the scope of the Agreement, definitions and units of measure, training of persons involved in the carriage of dangerous goods, safety obligations of the participants in the carriage of such goods, various derogations and transitional measures, the general requirements for the carriage of Class 7 goods (ie radioactive material), checks and other measures to ensure compliance with safety requirements, the rights of Contracting Parties to the Agreement to restrict or prohibit the carriage of certain dangerous goods for reasons other than safety, and it lists in an Appendix to Part 1 the competent authorities in each of the signatory states. In the UK this is the Department for Transport (DfT).
- Part 2 deals with the general provisions concerning the classification of dangerous goods and lists the nine main Classes and Sub-classes. It also describes the test methods to be used for the classification of dangerous goods and cross-references the procedures to the United Nations' *Manual of Tests and Criteria*.
- Part 3 is taken up with the actual Dangerous Goods List in which all relevant substances are classified across 20 column headings under their UN Number and also by their names in alphabetical order.

Volume 2 contains:

- Continuations of Annex A and Part 3 from volume 1;
- Part 4 dealing with packing and tank provisions;
- Part 5 dealing with consignment procedures;
- Part 6 dealing with the construction and testing of packagings and IBCs;
- Part 7 dealing with carriage by road, loading and handling of dangerous goods;
- Part 8 dealing with vehicle crews and equipment;
- Part 9 dealing with the construction and approval of dangerous goods carrying vehicles.

Definition and Classification of Dangerous Goods

Definition

Dangerous goods are defined as being those substances and articles the carriage of which is prohibited by ADR (or RID in the case of carriage by rail), or authorized only under the conditions prescribed in these Agreements.

In general terms the following types of article and substance would be defined as dangerous goods:

- goods named in the ADR classification list as set out in ADR Part 2 (see also SI 2004/568, regulation 15);
- other goods which have one or more hazardous properties;
- explosives; or
- radioactive material.

Dangerous articles or substances falling within the scope of the legal requirements may range from:

- quite small quantities of individually packaged goods such as domestic cleaning products;
- tanker loads of acids and corrosive substances;
- explosives (both substances and explosive articles – eg detonators, etc);
- radioactive substances.

Identification

The purpose of, and legal necessity for, identifying dangerous goods is to determine their classification and identify their most hazardous properties and the dangers which may arise or be created when they are loaded, transported and unloaded. In many cases such goods have a number of hazards, not all of which may be immediately apparent.

It is for the manufacturer or consignor initially to determine the classification for dangerous goods intended to be consigned for carriage by deciding whether they are:

- explosives;
- radioactive material;
- named individually in the ADR Chapter 2;
- not named individually in the ADR Chapter 2.

Dangerous Goods Named Individually in the ADR Dangerous Goods List

Most of the commonly transported dangerous goods are named individually in ADR under their proper name, in alphabetical order and with their UN number. If the goods comprise a mixture or preparation of substances these too may be listed, as may dangerous goods that have a generic name. This 'dangerous goods list' is to be found in ADR Chapter 3.2.

Dangerous Goods Not Named Individually in the ADR Dangerous Goods List

Where the dangerous goods are not 'named individually' the most appropriate generic entry (where the goods are of one chemical family) must be established or, alternatively, the relevant 'Not Otherwise Specified' (NOS) entry for those goods. This is done by first establishing the hazardous properties of the goods and then checking to see whether any alternative name can be found in the List that could be used to classify the goods.

Classification

It is important to note that the carriage of dangerous goods is prohibited unless their classification, packing group and any subsidiary hazards have been determined. An established classification system applies to the carriage of dangerous goods as set out in the United Nations so-called *Orange Book** and in ADR Part 2 as follows:

The internationally recognized recommendations for the classification, package testing and marking requirements for the transport of dangerous goods. It is in two volumes comprising a set of model regulations (volume I) and tests and criteria (volume II) – currently in their 10th revised edition.

The UN system classifies dangerous goods into:

- classes (of which there are nine);
- divisions;
- packing groups.

The nine classes cover the main types of dangerous goods (eg explosives, gases, flammable and oxidizing substances, etc) – see full list below. Each of these classes is further subdivided into a number of divisions which more specifically identify dangerous goods falling within each of the classes. A further degree of classification is achieved by assigning goods to a packing group according to the degree of danger they present.

Classes and Divisions

The following list shows the classes and divisions for dangerous goods:

- Class 1: Explosive substances and articles.
  - Division 1.1: Substances and articles which have a mass explosion hazard.
  - Division 1.2: Substances and articles which have a projection hazard, but not a mass explosion hazard.
  - Division 1.3: Substances and articles which have a fire hazard and either a minor blast hazard or a minor projection hazard or both, but not a mass explosion hazard.
  - Division 1.4: Substances and articles which present no significant hazard.
  - Division 1.5: Very insensitive substances that have a mass explosion hazard.
  - Division 1.6: Extremely insensitive articles that do not have a mass explosion hazard.
- Class 2: Gases.
  - Division 2.1: Flammable gases.
  - Division 2.2: Non-flammable, non-toxic gases.
  - Division 2.3: Toxic gases.

- Class 3: Flammable liquids.
- Class 4: Flammable solids, substances liable to spontaneous combustion and substances which, on contact with water, emit flammable gases.
  - Division 4.1: Flammable solids, self-reactive and related substances and desensitized explosives.
  - Division 4.2: Substances liable to spontaneous combustion.
  - Division 4.3: Substances which, in contact with water, emit flammable gases.
- Class 5: Oxidizing substances and organic peroxides.
  - Division 5.l: Oxidizing substance.
  - Division 5.2: Organic peroxides.
- Class 6: Toxic and infectious substances.
  - Division 6.1: Toxic substances.
  - Division 6.2: Infectious substances.
- Class 7: Radioactive material.
- Class 8: Corrosive substances.
- Class 9: Miscellaneous dangerous substances and articles.

UN Numbers and Proper Names

Besides the system of classification described above, dangerous goods are assigned a UN number comprising four digits which are used in conjunction with the letters 'UN' (eg UN 2426, which identifies ammonium nitrate liquid in a hot concentrated solution); and a proper shipping name according to their hazard classification and depending on their composition (eg as above).

UN Packing Groups

Dangerous substances are allocated UN packing groups as follows:

- Packing group I   for goods presenting high danger;
- Packing group II   for goods presenting medium danger;
- Packing group III   for goods presenting low danger.

UN Table of Precedence

The UN *Orange Book* sets out a table of precedence to take account of situations where dangerous goods not specifically identified in the Dangerous Goods List (in ADR Chapter 3.2) have more than one risk, or where dangerous goods have multiple risks. In such cases the most stringent packing group (ie Packing group I) takes precedence over other packing groups.

The following tables indicate the relevant classifications for dangerous goods, along with their packing group number (ie I, II or III), their class number and any optional lettering to be shown on packages (Table 1) and the relevant danger signs for dangerous goods indicating the symbol to be used and the colouring of the lettering and background (Table 2).

TABLE 1

Classification	Packing group	Class no	Optional lettering
Non-flammable, non-toxic gas	–	2.2	Compressed gas
Toxic gas	–	2.3	Toxic gas
Flammable gas	–	2.1	Flammable gas
Flammable liquid	I, II or III*	3	Flammable liquid
Flammable solid	I, II or III*	4.1	Flammable solid
Spontaneously combustible substance	I, II or III*	4.2	Spontaneously combustible
Substance which in contact with water emits flammable gas	I, II or III*	4.3	Dangerous when wet
Oxidizing substance	I, II or III*	5.1	Oxidizing agent
Organic peroxide	II	5.2	Organic peroxide
Toxic substance	I, II or III*	6.1	Toxic
Infectious substance	–	6.2	Infectious substance
Corrosive substance	I, II or III*	8	Corrosive
Miscellaneous dangerous goods	–	9	–

* NB: Depending on its relevant properties

TABLE 2

Description of sign	Symbol	Lettering	Background
Non-flammable, non-toxic gas	Black gas cylinder	Black or white	Green
Toxic gas	Black skull & crossbones	Black	White
Flammable gas	Black flame	Black or white	Red
Flammable liquid	Black flame	Black or white	Red
Flammable solid	Black flame	Black	Vertical white/ red stripes
Spontaneously combustible substance	Black flame	Black or white	White top/red bottom
Substance which in contact with water emits flammable gas	Black flame	Black or white	Blue

Description of sign	Symbol	Lettering	Background
Oxidizing substance	Black 'O' & flame	Black (5.1)	Yellow
Organic peroxide	Black 'O' & flame	Black (5.2)	Yellow
Toxic substance	Black skull & crossbones	Black	White
Infectious substance	Black symbol	Black	White
Corrosive substance	Black symbol	White	White top/ black bottom
Miscellaneous			Vertical white/ black stripes at top

Responsibilities

Responsibility for Classification of Dangerous Goods

Responsibility for the classification of dangerous goods rests with:

- the appropriate competent authority (eg the United Nations) in publishing the classification system; and
- the manufacturer of the goods and the consignor (ie the sender) – these may be one and the same or separate entities who must:
  - identify their hazards;
  - determine the most appropriate description for them; and
  - establish their correct UN identification number (ie a four-digit number) by reference to the ADR Dangerous Goods List and their packing group.

Responsibility for Applying ADR

The competent authorities applying ADR requirements in the UK rests with the Department for Transport (DfT) – (Dangerous Goods Branch), the police and the Health and Safety Executive.

Responsibility for Ensuring that Legal Requirements Are Met

Responsibility for ensuring that relevant legal requirements are met (including the task of correctly identifying and classifying dangerous goods) rests with:

- the competent national authority, which in the UK is the DfT;
- consignors of dangerous goods; and

- those who load, unload and transport such goods, namely:
    - employers/carriers;
    - dangerous goods safety advisers (DGSAs);
    - drivers of dangerous goods carrying vehicles;
    - employees and other people.

Employer Responsibilities

Firms (described in the legislation as undertakings) or individuals involved in the loading, unloading or transport (ie carriage) of dangerous goods by road must comply with statutory requirements on the prevention of risks to the health and safety of persons, or to damage of property or the environment. They also need to appoint a qualified safety adviser (DGSA) (SI 2004 No 568, regulation [12]) and ADR 1.8.3). An 'undertaking' is any legal body (eg limited liability company), association or group (eg voluntary and charitable organizations), or any official body that transports, loads or unloads dangerous goods.

Employers are responsible for ensuring that:

- a qualified DGSA is appointed, where relevant; and
- dangerous goods vehicle drivers:
    - hold vocational training certificates; and
    - are trained in emergency action procedures.

Rules for Drivers

Drivers must not:

- carry unauthorized passengers on vehicles transporting dangerous goods (ADR 8.3.1);
- open any package containing dangerous goods unless authorized to do so (ADR 8.3.3);
- carry matches or lighters (or anything else capable of producing a flame or sparks) on vehicles carrying dangerous goods (except where the only goods on the vehicle are infectious substances), nor must the vehicle crew smoke during handling operations inside or in the vicinity of the vehicle (ADR 8.3.4 and 8.3.5).

Responsibility for Safety

Responsibility for compliance with the dangerous goods regulations, in particular in relation to safety issues, rests with the participants, who are defined in ADR 1.4 as the consignor, the carrier and the consignee together with other personnel such as loaders, fillers, packers, etc (ADR 7.5.1 and SI 2004 No 568, regulation 23[5]). In particular, these participants must take appropriate measures according to the nature and extent of foreseeable dangers, so as to avoid damage or injury and, if necessary, to minimize their effects. Where there is an immediate risk that public safety may be jeopardized, the participants must immediately notify the emergency services and make available to them the information they need to take appropriate action. Chapter 1.4 of ADR specifies the individual responsibilities of the three main participants as outlined below.

The Consignor

The consignor must ensure, when handing over dangerous goods for carriage, that consignments conform to the requirements of ADR, in particular by:

- ensuring that the goods are classified and authorized for carriage in accordance with ADR;
- giving the carrier relevant information, data and the required transport documents;
- using only packaging, intermediate bulk containers (IBCs) and tanks (ie tank vehicles, demountable tanks, battery vehicles, MEM, portable tanks and tank containers) approved for and suited to the carriage of the substances concerned and displaying the markings prescribed by ADR;
- complying with the requirements on the means of dispatch and on forwarding restrictions; and where he uses the services of other participants (packers, loaders, fillers, etc), he must still ensure that the consignment meets the requirements of ADR.

The Carrier

The carrier must ascertain that:

- the dangerous goods to be carried are authorized for carriage in accordance with ADR;
- the next due test date for tank vehicles, portable tanks and tank containers has not passed;
- vehicles are not overloaded;
- visually, vehicles and loads have no obvious defects such as leakages, cracks or missing equipment, etc;
- appropriate danger labels and prescribed markings have been affixed to the vehicle;
- prescribed documentation is being carried on board the vehicle; and
- the equipment prescribed in the driver's written instructions is on board the vehicle.

If, in carrying out the above checks, the carrier observes any infringement of the ADR requirements, he must not allow the consignment to be shipped until the matter has been rectified. Similarly, if during the journey, an infringement is detected which could jeopardize the safety of the operation, the consignment must be stopped as soon as possible bearing in mind the requirements of traffic safety, the safe immobilization of the consignment, and of public safety.

The Consignee

Consignees may not defer acceptance of a consignment of dangerous goods without compelling reasons. They must also, after unloading, verify that the requirements of ADR have been complied with.

Other Participants

Other participants may be involved with the carriage of dangerous goods consignments, such as employees described as tanker operators, loaders, packers, fillers, etc. Broadly, such employees have a duty to ensure that their actions and the loads they deal with comply in all relevant respects with the requirements of ADR.

Duty of Care

Employers have a general duty of care towards their employees under the Health and Safety at Work Act etc 1974, to ensure their health, safety and welfare. They also have a duty to ensure that their premises are safe and without risk to the health of those who are not employees but who use the premises as a place of work. Employees must take reasonable care for their own health while at work. Employers and self-employed persons must ensure that their work activities do not expose other persons (ie not in their employ) to risks to their health and safety through their work activities.

The relevant Northern Ireland legislation is the Health and Safety at Work (Northern Ireland) Order 1978.

Exemptions

A number of exemptions to ADR are specified in Chapter 1.1 (ie 1.1.3) and in SI 2004 No 568, regulation 7 and are set out in simplified form in *Working with ADR* (pp 5–7) as follows:

- the carriage of dangerous goods by private individuals where the goods are packaged for retail sale and are intended for their personal or domestic use or for their leisure or sporting activities;
- the carriage of machinery or equipment not specifically listed in the Dangerous Goods List and which contain dangerous goods in their internal or operational equipment;
- carriage undertaken by enterprises which is ancillary to their main activity;
- carriage by, or under the supervision of, the emergency services, in particular by breakdown vehicles carrying vehicles which have been involved in accidents or have broken down and contain dangerous goods;
- emergency transport intended to save human lives or protect the environment.

Special Provisions Exemptions

Certain special provisions of the ADR (ie Chapter 3.3) exempt, either partially or totally, the carriage of specific dangerous goods from the requirements of ADR, as identified in column 6 of the Dangerous Goods List (Chapter 3.2, Table A), against the appropriate entry for that article or substance.

Limited Quantities Exemptions

Exemptions also relate to dangerous goods packed in limited quantities where a 'limited quantity' code Q1–Q29 (see table at ADR 3.4.6) appears in column 7 of the appropriate entry of the Dangerous Goods List, in which case that article or substance is exempted from the requirements of ADR, but only if it meets packaging and marking requirements; and the prescribed maximum quantities per inner packaging, and per package, are not exceeded.

When the code LQ0 appears in column 7 of the Dangerous Goods List (ADR 3.2), the substance or article is not exempted from any of the requirements of ADR (unless otherwise specified).

Transport Unit Exemptions

This class of exemptions is sometimes also referred to as being a 'limited quantities exemption', but it should not be confused with the limited quantities exemption described above. In this case, the exemption applies where:

- a specified maximum total quantity per transport unit, depending on its transport category (ADR 1.1.3.6) is not exceeded; or
- where the dangerous goods carried in the transport unit are in more than one transport category and the total quantity carried does not exceed the value calculated in accordance with ADR 1.1.3.6.4.

Transport categories and maximum quantities per transport unit

Transport category	Max total quantity per transport unit*
0	0
1	20
1A	50
2	333
2A	500
3	1,000
4	unlimited

*NB: For articles, gross mass in kilograms (for articles of Class 1, net mass in kilograms of the explosive substance); for solids, liquefied gases, refrigerated liquefied gases and dissolved gases, net mass in kilograms; for liquids and compressed gases, nominal capacity of receptacles (see definition in ADR 1.2.1) in litres.

If either of the two bullet point conditions (above) applies, the dangerous goods may be carried in packages in a single transport unit and the following requirements of ADR will not apply.

Other Exemptions

ADR	Covering
5.3	Placarding and marking of containers, etc
5.4.3	Documentation – instructions in writing
7.2 except for V5, V7 and V8 of 7.2.4	Carriage in packages
CV1 of 7.5.11	Prohibitions on loading and unloading in public places
Part 8, except for 8.1.4.2–8.1.4.5, 8.2.3, 8.3.4, 8.4 and S1(3), S1(6), S2(1), S4, S14–S21 of 8.5	Vehicle crews, equipment operation and documentation
Part 9	Construction and approval of vehicles

ADR also includes exemptions relating to:

- the carriage of gases;
- the carriage of liquid fuels;
- empty uncleaned packaging;
- carriage in a transport chain including maritime or air carriage;
- the use of portable tanks approved for maritime transport; and
- carriage other than by road.

Transport Information and Documentation

Information to Be Provided

Consignors of dangerous goods must provide the transport operator (ie carrier) with a transport document showing:

- the designation, classification code and UN number for the goods;
- any additional information needed to determine their transport category and their control and emergency temperatures;
- for packaged goods, the number and weight or volume of individual packages, or the total mass or volume in each transport category;
- for bulk loads, the weight or volume in each tank or container and the number of tanks or containers;
- the name and address of both consignor and consignee;
- any other information which the operator must give to the driver;

- a 'consignor's declaration' that the goods may be carried as presented, that they, their packaging and any container or tank in which they are contained is fit for carriage and is properly labelled.

It is an offence to provide false or misleading information and where one transport operator sub-contracts a dangerous goods consignment to another operator he must, by law, pass on the information provided by the consignor.

Documentation to Be Carried during Carriage

Drivers of vehicles carrying dangerous goods must be provided with the following 'transport documentation', in writing:

- the information provided by the consignor (see above);
- details of the weight or volume of the load;
- the relevant hazard identification number or the emergency action code (where appropriate);
- emergency information comprising:
  - the dangers inherent in the goods and safety measures;
  - what to do and the treatment to be given should any person come into contact with the goods;
  - what to do in the event of fire and what fire-fighting appliances or equipment must not be used;
  - what to do in case of breakage or deterioration of packaging or of the goods, particularly where this results in a spillage on to the road;
  - what to do to avoid or minimize damage in the event of spillage of goods likely to pollute water supplies;
- any relevant additional information about the particular type of dangerous goods being carried.

It is an offence to provide false or misleading information to drivers about the particular type of dangerous goods being carried.

Drivers must keep the transport documentation readily available during dangerous goods journeys and produce it on request by the police or a VOSA goods vehicle examiner. Where a dangerous goods carrying trailer is detached from the towing vehicle the transport documentation (or an authenticated copy) must be given to the owner or manager of the premises where it is parked, or attached to the trailer in a readily visible position.

Documentation relating to dangerous goods no longer carried on a vehicle must be either removed completely, or placed in a securely closed container clearly marked to show that it does not relate to dangerous goods still on the vehicle.

Operators must keep a record of journey transport documentation for at least three months (SI 2004 No 568, regulation 54).

Instructions in Writing

Since 2009 operators have had a responsibility to give drivers 'instructions in writing' to help them with any emergency that may arise. The key features are:

- they are to be issued by the carrier not the consignor;
- they must be in a language that the driver and/or crew members can read and understand before starting their journey not in languages of the country of origin, transit and destination;
- vehicle crews are required to familiarize themselves with the emergency arrangements for the dangerous goods loaded *before* commencing a journey;
- A new four-page model of the revised instructions in writing consists of:
  - action to be taken in the event of an emergency;
  - guidance on the hazards and actions to be taken for each class of dangerous goods.

Information to be Displayed on Containers, Tanks and Vehicles

Containers, tanks and vehicles used for carrying dangerous goods must display information as described below. All panels and danger signs must be kept clean and free from obstruction.

It is an offence to display information when the container, tank or vehicle is not carrying dangerous goods, and to cause or permit the display of any information likely to confuse the emergency services.

Signs and panels relating to dangerous goods no longer being carried must be covered or removed. Where an orange-coloured panel is covered, the covering material must remain effective after 15 minutes' engulfment in fire. Danger signs, hazard warning panels, orange-coloured panels or subsidiary hazard signs need not be covered or removed if the mass or volume of dangerous goods in packages falls below the following limits:

Transport category	Total mass/volume (kg/litres)
0	0
1	20
2	200
3	500
4	unlimited

It is an offence to remove panels or signs from a container, tank or vehicle carrying dangerous goods (except for updating the information) and to falsify information on any panel or sign.

Danger Signs and Panels

A reflectorized orange-coloured, black-bordered panel (plain with no letters or figures) must be displayed at the front of vehicles carrying dangerous goods. A similar panel must be attached to the rear of vehicles carrying dangerous goods in packages.

Single Load Labelling

Where a *single load* of dangerous goods is carried in a container, tank or vehicle an orange-coloured panel showing the appropriate UN number and emergency action code (see Figure 20.1) must be displayed:

- one at the rear of the vehicle;
- one on each side of the vehicle, the container or the tank;
- and, in the case of a tank, one on each side of the frame of the tank, or on the vehicle positioned immediately below the tank.

Multi-load Labelling

Where a vehicle is carrying a *multi-load* in tanks, or in bulk in separate compartments of the vehicle, or in separate containers, an orange-coloured panel showing the appropriate emergency action code only (see below) must be displayed at the rear of the vehicle.

Additionally, orange-coloured panels as follows are required on both sides of each tank (or, if it has multiple compartments, on each compartment), on each compartment of the vehicle or on each container on the vehicle:

- at least one on each side showing the appropriate UN number and emergency action code (Figure 20.1); and
- the remainder showing only the appropriate UN number.

Alternatively, for dangerous goods carried in a tank, the panels may be displayed on both sides of the frame of each tank, or on the vehicle positioned immediately below the tank or tank compartment concerned.

Where diesel fuel or gas oil or heating oil (UN 1202), petrol, motor spirit or gasoline (UN 1203), or kerosene (UN 1223) is carried in a multi-compartment road tanker it may be labelled as a single load only, showing the UN number and emergency action code for the most hazardous of the products carried.

FIGURE 20.1 Orange panel showing the emergency action code and the UN number identifying the dangerous substance being carried

All black borders 15mm or less

Horizontal black line at mid height of 15mm stroke width

Height not less than 300mm

Base 400mm

Detail of Panels

The orange-coloured panels must be either:

- a rigid plate fitted as near vertical as possible; or
- in the case of a vehicle carrying dangerous goods in a tank container or in bulk in a container,
  - orange-coloured self-adhesive sheets; or
  - orange-coloured paint (or equivalent), provided the material is weather-resistant and ensures durable marking.

UN numbers and emergency action codes must be shown in black, at least 100 mm high and 15 mm wide – but where the emergency action code is white on a black background, it must appear as orange on a black rectangle at least 10 mm greater than the height and width of the letter. Except where panels comprise self-adhesive sheets or are applied by paint, UN numbers and emergency action codes must be indelible and remain legible after 15 minutes' engulfment in fire (not applicable to tanks constructed before 1 January 1999).

Where there is insufficient space for full-sized panels, these may be reduced to 300 mm wide by 120 mm high with a 10 mm black border.

Emergency Action Codes

The emergency action codes are as follows:

1 By numbers 1 to 4 indicating the equipment suitable for firefighting and for dispersing spillages (ie 1 = water jets, 2 = water fog, 3 = foam, 4 = dry agent).

2 By letters indicating the appropriate precautions to take as follows:

Letter	Danger of violent reaction	Protective clothing and breathing apparatus	Measures to be taken
P	Yes	Full protective clothing	Dilute
R	No	Full protective clothing	Dilute
S	Yes	Breathing apparatus	Dilute
S*	Yes	Breathing apparatus for fire	Dilute
T	No	Breathing apparatus	Dilute
T*	No	Breathing apparatus for fire	Dilute
W	Yes	Full protective clothing	Contain
X	No	Full protective clothing	Contain
Y	Yes	Breathing apparatus	Contain
Y*	Yes	Breathing apparatus for fire	Contain
Z	No	Breathing apparatus	Contain
Z*	No	Breathing apparatus for fire	Contain

* These symbols, shown as orange (or can be white) letters reversed out of a black background, remain valid but are not included in the latest versions of the EAC.

Where a letter 'E' is shown at the end of an emergency action code this means that consideration should be given to evacuating people from the neighbourhood of an incident.

Display of Telephone Number

A contact telephone number, comprising black digits at least 30 mm high on an orange background, must be shown on vehicles carrying single or multi-loads of dangerous goods in tanks, positioned:

- at the rear of the vehicle;
- on both sides of the tank (or each tank if more than one), the frame of each tank, or the vehicle; and
- located in the immediate vicinity of the orange-coloured panels.

Instead of a telephone number, the words 'consult local depot' or 'contact local depot' may be substituted, but only if:

- the name of the operator is clearly marked on the tank or the vehicle; and
- the fire chief for every area in which the vehicle will operate has been notified in writing of the address and telephone number of that local depot, and has confirmed in writing that he is satisfied with the arrangements.

Display of Danger Signs and Subsidiary Hazard Signs

Where a vehicle is carrying:

- packaged dangerous goods in a container:
  - any danger sign or subsidiary hazard sign required on the packages must also be displayed on at least one side of the container;
- dangerous goods in a tank container or in bulk in a container:
  - any danger sign or subsidiary hazard sign required on the packages containing such goods must be displayed on each side of the tank container or container, and where such signs are not visible from outside the carrying vehicle, the same signs must also be shown on each side of and at the rear of the vehicle;
- dangerous goods in a tank, other than a tank container, or in bulk in a vehicle, but not in bulk in a container on a vehicle:
  - any danger sign or subsidiary hazard sign required on the packages containing such goods must be displayed on each side of and at the rear of the vehicle.

Danger signs for a particular classification, or subsidiary hazard signs, need not be shown more than once on the sides or rear of any container, tank or vehicle.

Danger signs and subsidiary hazard signs must have sides at least 250 mm long; have a line the same colour as the symbol 12.5 mm inside the edge and running parallel to it; and be displayed adjacent to one another and in the same horizontal plane.

Display of Hazard Warning Panels

Despite the requirements described above for the display of orange-coloured panels the regulations permit, wherever such a panel is required on the sides or rear of a container, tank or vehicle, the alternative use of existing-type combined hazard warning panels (see Figure 20.2) on vehicles operating within the UK.

These are mainly orange with black borders and lettering – except for the white background where a reduced-size (ie 200 mm sides) danger sign is located and any subsidiary hazard sign must be the same size and displayed adjacent to it and in the same horizontal plane.

All danger panels and signs required on the front or rear of a vehicle must be positioned at right angles across its width, and those on the sides of a container, tank or vehicle at right angles along its length. All signs must be clearly visible.

Vehicles operating internationally under ADR may display a similar orange board with a three-digit ADR Kemler Code instead of an Emergency Action Code – as with most European dangerous goods vehicles. The UN number is shown in the lower half of the panel, as with UK transport. Foreign vehicles running under ADR tend not tohave integrated Hazchem boards (as shown in Figure 20.2), with the class diamonds (referred to as 'placards' in the ADR regulations) being displayed separately.

FIGURE 20.2 Existing UK-type combined hazard warning panel which may be used on the sides and rear of a bulk chemical tanker vehicle or container

Emergency Procedures

Vehicles carrying dangerous goods must be equipped so that the driver can take emergency measures, as follows:

- At least one portable fire extinguisher with a minimum capacity of 2 kg of dry powder (or other extinguishant with an equivalent test fire rating of at least 5A and 34B – defined in British Standard BSEN 3–1: 1996), suitable for fighting a fire in the engine (unless the vehicle has an automatic extinguisher system) or cab, and not likely to aggravate a fire in the load.

  NB: Such an extinguisher is not required on a detached trailer.

- At least one portable fire extinguisher with a minimum capacity of 6 kg of dry powder (or other extinguishant with an equivalent test fire rating of at least 21A and 183B – defined as above)*, suitable for fighting a tyre or brake fire, or a fire in the load, and not likely to aggravate a fire in the engine or cab. Fire extinguishers with a minimum total capacity of 12 kg are required.

  *NB: Where the vehicle has a gross weight under 3.5 tonnes, a 4 kg dry powder extinguisher (or another suitable extinguishant with a test fire rating of at least 5A and 34B) will suffice.

Portable fire extinguishers must not be liable to release toxic gases into the driver's cab, or under the heat of a fire. They must be marked in compliance with a recognized standard; fitted with a seal verifying they have not been used; and be inscribed with the date for their next inspection – it is an offence to carry an extinguisher with an overdue inspection date.

A fire extinguisher is not needed where only infectious substances are carried.

Where toxic gases are carried, vehicles must carry respiratory equipment to enable the crew to escape safely.

Other equipment to be carried includes:

- a shovel and a plastic collecting container (eg a 9-litre bucket with lid);
- non-sparking torch;
- protective gloves;
- eye protection and eye-rinsing liquid.

Accidents and Emergencies

In accident or emergency situations drivers must comply with the emergency information given to them and apply the emergency procedures for which they are trained and which are stated on the emergency action information given to them (eg on the Tremcard), including:

- notifying the relevant emergency services by the quickest practical means;
- taking steps to prevent chemical contamination of the environment (eg watercourses);
- taking steps to prevent the risk of fire;
- keeping the public away from the scene;
- applying first aid where necessary.

Accident Investigation and Reports

All accidents and dangerous goods incidents must be reported and investigated to determine how and why they were caused and how any such event may be prevented in the future – possibly by changing procedures and the issue of fresh safety instructions.

Dangerous Goods Safety Advisors (DGSAs) have a statutory duty to prepare reports on serious accidents, incidents or legal infringements occurring during the loading, unloading and transport of dangerous goods and to implement appropriate measures to avoid recurrence of such events.

Reporting to the Health and Safety Executive

Accidents and serious incidents involving dangerous goods must be reported to the HSE as required under the Reporting of Injuries, Diseases and Dangerous Occurrences Regulations 1995 (SI 1995/3163 – commonly known as RIDDOR). The report must be made to the HSE both immediately by telephone and in writing within 10 days (using HSE Form 2508) concerning any such occurrence causing:

- death or major injury to an employee;

- any injury occasioning an employee to be away from work for more than three days;
- any work-related disease.

Any dangerous occurrence (even if it does not result in personal injury to any person) must also be reported, including:

- splitting or collapse of a tank or tank container;
- failure of pipework or valves resulting in spillage;
- overturning of a dangerous goods carrying vehicle;
- a dangerous goods carrying vehicle catching fire; or
- a fire in the loading or unloading premises.

In Northern Ireland the relevant legislation is the Reporting of Injuries Diseases and Dangerous Occurrences Regulations (Northern Ireland) 1997 (SR No. 455).

Road Traffic Accidents

The procedures to be followed in the event of a road traffic accident, apart from the special considerations relating to the carriage of dangerous goods as set out above, are those described on pp 277–78 of this *Handbook*.

Security Provisions

From 22 July 2005, in response to new measures included in the revised ADR 2005, the Government has introduced new security provisions relating to the carriage of all dangerous goods except nuclear materials. The requirements fall into four groups as shown below; namely, general provisions, provisions relating to High Consequence Dangerous Goods, training requirements and the need to implement security plans.

General Provisions

These require that:

- All persons engaged in the carriage of dangerous goods must consider the security requirements for the carriage of dangerous goods commensurate with their responsibilities.
- Dangerous goods may only be offered to carriers that have been appropriately identified.
- Areas within temporary storage terminals, temporary storage sites, vehicle depots, berthing areas and marshalling yards used for temporary storage during carriage of dangerous goods must be properly secured, well lit and, where possible and appropriate, not accessible to the general public.
- Each crew member of a vehicle carrying dangerous goods must carry with them means of photographic identification.
- Safety inspections must cover appropriate security measures.

High Consequence Dangerous Goods

Dangerous goods that have the potential for misuse in a terrorist incident and which may, as a result, produce serious consequences such as mass casualties or mass destruction are now defined as High Consequence Dangerous Goods (see list below).

Training Requirements

Additional provisions relating to training require that up-to-date registers of all valid training certificates must be maintained by the competent authorities and that relevant training, and refresher training, must include elements of security awareness, in particular addressing the following issues:

- the nature of security risks;
- how to recognize security risks;
- how to address and reduce such risks;
- what actions to take in the event of a breach of security.

Security Planning

Another key new provision is that all carriers (eg road hauliers), consignors and other participants engaged in the carriage of High Consequence Dangerous Goods (as listed below) must formulate, implement and comply with a security plan that covers at least all the requirements specified below:

- The plan must specifically allocate responsibility for security to competent and qualified persons with appropriate authority to carry out their responsibilities.
- Records must be kept of the dangerous goods or types of dangerous goods involved in the carriage.
- A review must be undertaken of current operations and assessment of security risks, including at any stops necessary to the transport operation, the keeping of dangerous goods in the vehicle, tank or container before, during and after the journey and the temporary storage of dangerous goods during the course of intermodal transfer or transhipment between units.
- A clear statement must be made of the measures that are to be taken to reduce security risks, commensurate with the responsibilities and duties of the participant, including:
  - training matters;
  - security policies;
  - operating practices;
  - equipment and resource use to reduce security risks.
- Effective and up-to-date procedures must be established for reporting and dealing with security threats, breaches of security or security incidents.
- Procedures must be put in place for the evaluation and testing of security plans and actions.

- Measures must be taken to ensure the physical security of transport information contained in the security plan.

- Measures must be taken to ensure that the distribution of information relating to the transport operation contained in the security plan is limited to those who need to have it.

- A process needs to be established to cooperate in the exchange of security threat information, to apply appropriate security measures and to respond to security incidents.

- Steps must be taken to prevent the theft of vehicles carrying High Consequence Dangerous Goods or their cargo by means of suitable security devices, equipment or arrangements. These must be kept operational and effective at all times, but must not jeopardize any emergency response.

- Transport telemetry or other tracking methods or devices should be used to monitor the movement of High Consequence Dangerous Goods, when it is appropriate to do so and when such systems are already fitted.

High Consequence Dangerous Goods are those listed in the table opposite and carried in quantities greater than shown.

Enforcement

In the interests of public safety, the police and authorized examiners of the Vehicle and Operator Services Agency (VOSA) are given wide-ranging powers to ensure compliance with the law on dangerous goods carriage. For example, they can demand production of the statutory information which drivers must carry when on a dangerous goods journey as well as production of the driver's own Vocational Training or ADR Certificate, which he must carry at all times during such journeys.

VOSA is empowered to enforce certain aspects of dangerous goods law relating solely to vehicles (the HSE retains its responsibility for premises-based inspections). VOSA inspectors are authorized to serve Prohibition Notices and prosecute offenders for breaches of the law, but they *will not* serve Improvement Notices as these are not normally appropriate for on-the-road work.

Class	Division	Substance or article	Quantity Tank (ltrs)	Bulk (kg)	Packages (kg)
1	1.1	Explosives	a	a	0
	1.2	Explosives	a	a	0
	1.3	Compatibility group C explosives	a	a	0
	1.5	Explosives	0	a	0
2		Flammable gases (classification codes including only the letter F)	3,000	a	b
		Toxic gases (classification codes containing the letters T, TF, TC, TO, TFC or TOC) excluding aerosols	0	a	0
3		Flammable liquids of packing groups I and II	3,000	a	b
		Desensitized explosives	a	a	0
4	4.1	Desensitized explosives	a	a	0
	4.2	Packing group I substances	3,000	a	b
	4.3	Packing group II substances	3,000	a	b
5	5.1	Oxidizing liquids of packing group I	3,000	a	b
		Perchlorates, ammonium nitrate and ammonium nitrate fertilizers	3,000	3,000	b
6	6.1	Toxic substances of packing group I	0	a	0
	6.2	Infectious substances of Category A	a	a	0
7		Radioactive material	3,000 A1 (special form) or 3,000 A2, as applicable, in Type B or Type C packages		
8		Corrosive substances of packing group I	3,000	a	b

Offences and Penalties

Dangerous goods legislation is complex and extensive with a large number of potential offences which may be committed, either singly or in conjunction with other offences. Offenders can expect to be prosecuted and dealt with severely by the courts on conviction.

On summary conviction in the magistrate's court (sheriff's court in Scotland) for an offence under the HSWA 1974, currently a fine of up to £5,000 may be imposed, while in more serious cases indictment by the Crown Court for an offence may lead to an unlimited fine and/or a two-year prison sentence.

Obstruction of an inspector who is fulfilling his statutory duties is a serious offence carrying a fine of up to £5,000 on conviction while breach of any notice served by an inspector can result in a fine up to £20,000 on conviction or in either case an unlimited fine on indictment.

Defence

A person charged under these regulations can, in his own defence, prove that the offence was due to the act or default of another person (other than his own employees), and that he had tried to avoid committing the offence, but he must give the prosecutor, in writing, at least seven days before the court hearing and to the best of his knowledge, information identifying or assisting in the identification of that other person.

Carriage of Explosives

This topic will be updated in the next edition of *Lowe's Transport Manager's and Operator's Handbook*. For further information on the carriage of explosives refer to the ADR regulations at http://www.unece.org/trans/danger/publi/adr2011/11 contentsE.html

Radioactive Substances

Complex legislation controls the carriage of radioactive substances. In particular, the Radioactive Material (Road Transport) Regulations 2002 made under the provisions of the Radioactive Material (Road Transport) Act 1991 apply to the carriage of such materials, while the Ionising Radiations Regulations 1985 and the Ionising Radiations (Outside Workers) Regulations 1993 cover controls on radiation doses received by persons working with such materials. Further, *A Code of Practice for the Carriage of Radioactive Materials by Road* is available (from TSO) which sets out the law and gives advice on all aspects of transporting these materials.

Driver Training

Drivers of vehicles carrying dangerous goods must be instructed and trained so they understand the dangers of the particular goods being carried and the emergency action to be taken, as well as their duties under the Health and Safety at Work etc Act 1974, and current dangerous goods legislation. Operators must keep training records and give copies to the drivers concerned.

The driver training specified in ADR 8.2 applies (from the time of loading until the goods have been unloaded and, where appropriate, the compartment has been cleaned or purged) to drivers of the following dangerous goods vehicles:

- road tankers exceeding 1 m^3 capacity;
- those carrying tank containers exceeding 3 m^3 capacity;
- those carrying dangerous goods:
  - in bulk;
  - as a road tanker with a capacity not exceeding 1,000 litres;
  - in a tank container with a capacity not exceeding 3,000 litres;
  - where any of the goods are in transport category 0;
  - comprising more than 20 kg/litres* of category 1 goods in packages;
  - comprising more than 200 kg/litres* of category 2 goods in packages;
  - comprising more than 500 kg/litres* of category 3 goods in packages;
- those carrying explosives;
- those carrying radioactive materials.

* NB: This refers to 'total mass or volume' (ie as measured in kilograms or litres).

Vocational Training Certificates

Transport operators must ensure their drivers hold valid 'vocational training certificates' appropriate to the dangerous goods work they are employed in. This includes drivers of all vans as well as larger vehicles and is necessary irrespective of how short the journey.

These certificates, issued under the auspices of The Scottish Qualifications Authority (formerly the City & Guilds Institute dealt with these matters), are granted to drivers on successful completion of an approved course of theoretical study and practical exercises and passing an approved examination. Certificates are valid for five years and may be extended for further five-yearly periods if in the 12 months preceding their expiry the holder has successfully completed a refresher course and passed the examination.

Current driver ADR certificates (if valid for the type of operation engaged in) are accepted as vocational training certificates for these purposes.

Certificates to Be Carried and Produced to the Police

Drivers must carry their vocational training certificates on all dangerous goods journeys and produce them on request by the police or a goods vehicle examiner.

Minimum Training Requirements for Issue of Vocational Training Certificates

Approved training for drivers must cover at least:

- general requirements on dangerous goods carriage;
- main types of hazard;
- environmental protection in the control of the transfer of wastes;
- preventive and safety measures appropriate to various types of hazard;
- what to do after an accident (first aid, road safety, the use of protective equipment, etc);
- labelling and marking to indicate danger;
- what to do and not do when carrying dangerous goods;
- the purpose and operation of technical equipment on vehicles used for carrying dangerous goods;
- prohibitions on mixed loading in the same vehicle or container;
- precautions during loading and unloading of dangerous goods;
- civil liability;
- multi-modal transport operations.

For drivers of vehicles carrying packaged dangerous goods, training must also cover the handling and stowage of packages, and for road tanker or tank container drivers training must cover the behaviour of such vehicles on the road, including load movement during transit.

Dangerous Goods Safety Advisers (DGSAs)

From 31 December 1999, firms which load, unload or carry dangerous goods by road (and by rail and inland waterway) must appoint a qualified Dangerous Goods Safety Adviser (DGSA) under provisions contained in EU Directive 96/35/EC. This also applies to self-employed persons, who must become qualified and appoint themselves. The person appointed must hold a valid Vocational Training Certificate confirming they have passed the official DGSA examination conducted by the Scottish Qualifications Agency (SQA – appointed by the DfT to conduct all UK DGSA examinations). *Details of the examination system and a copy of the syllabus may be obtained from the SQA, Customer Contact Centre, tel: 0845 279 1000; fax: 0845 213 5000, or it may be downloaded from the SQA's website:* **www.sqa.org.uk/dgsa/**.

To qualify as a DGSA it is necessary to study the subject material contained in the official syllabus, sit the relevant examinations and pass in at least three of the following subjects:

- the core examination, which is compulsory for all candidates;
- one modal paper covering either Road, Rail or Inland Waterways;
- at least one dangerous goods Class paper covering either:
  - Class 1;
  - Class 2;
  - Class 3 (specifically UN 1202, 1203 and 1223 – ie mineral oils);
  - Class 7;
  - General Chemical Classes (3, 4.1, 4.2, 4.3, 5.1, 5.2, 6.1, 6.2, 8 and 9);
  - all classes.

It has been illegal to carry on a business in which dangerous goods are loaded, unloaded or transported since 31 December 1999 unless a qualified DGSA has been appointed and taken up his duties as outlined below.

Tasks and Functions of DGSAs

Appointed DGSAs must effectively carry out the legal duties and bear the responsibilities set out in law as follows:

- monitor compliance with the law on the transport of dangerous goods;
- advise their employer on the transport of dangerous goods;
- prepare an annual report to their employer on the firm's activities in transporting dangerous goods (to be kept for five years and made available to the authorities on request).

The DGSA must also monitor:

- procedures for identifying dangerous goods being transported;
- practices for taking account of any special requirements in connection with dangerous goods being transported;
- procedures for checking equipment used in the transport, loading or unloading of dangerous goods;
- employee training and maintenance of training records;
- emergency procedures to be taken in the event of accidents that may affect safety during the transport, loading or unloading of dangerous goods;
- investigation and preparation of reports on serious accidents or legal infringements during the transport, loading or unloading of dangerous goods;
- implementation of steps to avoid the recurrence of accidents, incidents or serious legal infringements;
- account taken of the legal requirements in the choice and use of sub-contractors;
- operational procedures and instructions that employees must follow;
- introduction of measures to increase awareness of the risks inherent in the transport, loading and unloading of dangerous goods;

- verification procedures to ensure that vehicles carry the documents and safety equipment required and that they comply with the law;
- verification procedures to ensure that the law on loading and unloading is complied with.

Controlled and Hazardous Waste

Many transport operators (and skip-hire firms) are concerned with the disposal of 'waste' and, as such, they are affected by newly imposed and strictly enforced legislation. For these purposes waste may be considered in two forms:

- controlled waste which comprises 'household, industrial and commercial waste or any such waste' (ie including waste paper, scrap metal and recyclable scrap);
- hazardous waste which is material defined as 'special waste' in the controlled waste legislation, or material which falls within the classification of dangerous substances for the purposes of the road tanker or packaged dangerous goods legislation described earlier in this chapter.

A range of legislation applies in this area of activity including the Disposal of Poisonous Waste Act 1972 (which makes it an offence to dispose of poisonous waste in an irresponsible way), the Criminal Justice Act 1988 (which provides powers for the authorities to impound vehicles engaged in illegal fly-tipping) and the Control of Pollution (Amendment) Act 1989, the Controlled Waste (Registration of Carriers and Seizure of Vehicles) Regulations 1991 and the Controlled Waste Regulations 1992. Two other sets of regulations are important, the Waste Management Licensing Regulations 1994 and the Hazardous Waste (England and Wales) Regulations 2005 (SI 2005 No 894).

Controlled Waste

Controlled waste should not be disposed of, or transported away by, a person or firm not legally authorized for this purpose.

Registration of Operators

The law (see above) requires operators who transport controlled waste within Great Britain to register with the appropriate waste regulation authority (ie in the area in which they have their business). It is an offence to fail to register or to carry controlled waste when not registered. Besides fines following prosecution and conviction for such offences, legislation provides powers for the seizure and disposal of vehicles used for such illegal purposes.

Exemptions are provided for charities, voluntary organizations, domestic householders disposing of their own waste, waste collection authorities and producers of controlled waste. Builders and demolition companies are not exempt and must register and otherwise comply with the legislation.

A new, and quite complex, charging scheme has been instituted by the Environment Agency from 2008. Full details can be viewed on the agency's website at: **http://publications.environment-agency.gov.uk**.

Duty of Care

Under the Environmental Protection Act 1990 firms and individuals that produce, import, store, treat, process, recycle, dispose of or transport controlled waste (see above for definition) have a statutory 'duty of care'. This places responsibility for the completion of paperwork (ie 'Waste Transfer Notes') and to take all reasonable steps to stop waste escaping and ensuring its safety and security.

Waste Transfer Notes

Waste transfer notes comprise written descriptions of waste handed over to other persons to transport and/or dispose of, and a transfer note signed by both parties (allowable as a single document) containing the following details:

- what the waste is and the quantity;
- the type of container in which it is carried;
- the time and date of transfer;
- the place where the transfer took place;
- the names and addresses of both parties (ie consignor and recipient);
- detail as to which category each falls into (eg producer and registered waste carrier);
- a certificate number if either or both parties hold waste licences and the name of the authority from whom it/they was/were issued;
- reasons for any exemption from registration or waste licensing.

Copies of documents (ie descriptions of waste and/or transfer notes) given and received must be retained for at least two years. Both or either party may be required to produce these and prove in court where particular consignments of controlled waste originated.

Seizure of Vehicles

The seizure of vehicles aspects of the legislation are a new method of penalty in the UK – and incidentally, are also being sought in regard to 'O' licence offenders. The law gives powers to waste regulation authorities to seize the vehicles of offenders, remove and separately store or dispose of loads as necessary, and dispose of (or destroy) vehicles following set procedures to publicize details of the seizure in local newspapers. Attempts will be made to seek out legitimate owners, who may reclaim their vehicles on satisfactory proof of entitlement and identification.

Hazardous Waste Disposal

Broadly, the law on hazardous waste requires that waste which is poisonous, noxious or polluting is not deposited on land where its presence is liable to give rise to an environmental hazard. And it is necessary for anyone removing or depositing poisonous material to notify both the local authority and the river authority before doing so.

An environmental hazard is defined as waste that is deposited in a manner or in such quantity that it would subject persons or animals to material risk of death, injury or impairment of health or threaten the pollution or contamination of any water supply. A booklet, *Guidelines on the Responsible Disposal of Wastes,* is available from the Confederation of British Industry. The European Commission has also produced a booklet on this subject for local authorities in EU member states.

There are additional controls over the carriage and disposal of particularly hazardous waste. The Control of Pollution (Special Waste) Regulations 1980 were introduced in order to comply with EU Directives:

The main requirements of these regulations are outlined below:

- Certain types of waste are to be regarded as special waste and subject to the additional controls. These are wastes that are regarded as dangerous to life as set out in the regulations.

- Waste producers have to give not less than three days' and not more than one month's prior notice to waste disposal authorities of their intention to dispose of a consignment of special waste.

- A set of consignment notes must be completed when special wastes are transported. This means that a consignment of special waste can be transported from the producer to the disposal site only if each person has signed for it and taken on responsibility for it. This is to ensure that waste disposal authorities know who is carrying the waste and they have to be informed within 24 hours of when it reaches the disposal site. Waste producers should take particular note of the requirement that all notices must be made on the statutory forms. Each form contains a unique reference number to assist an authority in making sure that waste is safely disposed of.

- A record of the location of the point of disposal on site of all special wastes must be kept in perpetuity. This is to ensure that proper arrangements can be made to bring the site back into use after the waste disposal operation has ceased.

- Proper registers of consignments must be kept by the producers, carriers and disposers.

- There will be a 'season ticket' arrangement for regular consignments of special wastes of similar composition disposed of at the same site. The waste disposal authorities will decide which producers and disposers in their areas qualify.

- The Secretary of State will have emergency powers to direct receipt of special wastes at a particular site. This is likely to be rarely used.

- Radioactive waste which also has the characteristics of special waste will be subject to the new controls.

Failure to comply with any of the requirements of the regulations is an offence.

Advice on particular problems can be obtained from waste regulation authorities (usually the district or county council).

Waste Site Licensing

The site licensing provisions of the Control of Pollution Act 1974 require all commercial, industrial or domestic wastes to be disposed of at a site licensed for that purpose and nowhere else. The licences are issued by the waste disposal authorities (these are the county councils in England and the district councils in Wales and Scotland). These licences, which are a matter of public record, set conditions for the operation of each site including the types of waste which can be disposed of at that site, the manner of disposal, site supervision, boundary fences, noticeboards, etc. Waste disposal authorities must inspect sites regularly and make sure the operators are following the conditions of the licence. Failure to comply with licence conditions is a criminal offence. In addition to prosecution, an authority can amend or even revoke the licence. See also the section dealing with unauthorized tipping of waste (ie fly-tipping) on p 472.

Packaging Waste

The Producer Responsibility Obligations (Packaging Waste) Regulations 1997, made under the Environment Act 1995, are designed to encourage businesses to recover value from products at the end of their life with the aims of:

- achieving a more sustainable approach to dealing with packaging waste;
- reducing the amount of packaging waste going to landfill;
- implementing the recovery and recycling targets in the EC Directive 94/621/EC on packaging and packaging waste.

Businesses affected by the regulations are those with an annual turnover in excess of £5 million (reducing to a threshold of £1 million annually since 1 January 2000) and which handle more than 50 tonnes of packaging or packaging material annually. If one or other of the thresholds are not met the business is excluded from the regulations.

The regulations impose three main obligations on relevant businesses, namely:

- registration;
- recovery and recycling;
- certifying.

Registration

Registration requires producers to register with the Environment Agency in England or Wales, or with the Scottish Environment Protection Agency (SEPA) if their principal place of business or registered office is in Scotland. A registration fee must be paid and packaging data must be provided on a data form (set out in Schedule 4 to the regulations) which will be provided by the Agency.

The deadline for businesses continuing their registration or registering for the first time is 1 April each year.

Recovery and Recycling

Recovery and recycling obligations started in 1998 and require producers to take reasonable steps to recover and recycle specific tonnages of packaging waste calculated on the basis of three factors:

- the tonnage of packaging handled by the producer in the previous year;
- the 'activities' that the producer performs and the percentage obligation attached to each activity; ie
    - manufacturing packaging raw materials;
    - converting materials into packaging;
    - packing and filling packaging;
    - selling packaging to the final user;
- the national recovery and recycling targets (as set out in the regulations).

Certifying

Producers must write to the Environment Agency* by 31 January following the end of the calendar year in which they fall within the scope of the regulations (ie by virtue of turnover and the tonnage of packaging waste handled), certifying that they have recovered and recycled the necessary tonnages of packaging waste. The person writing must be an 'approved person' (ie a director of a company, a partner in a partnership business or a sole trader).

*National Customer Contact Centre
PO Box 544
Rotherham
S60 1BY
www.environment-agency.gov.uk

Fleet Car and Light Vehicle Operations

T ransport managers and other staff responsible for the operation of large goods vehicles within companies frequently have additional responsibilities for the operation of company-owned motor cars used by management, sales and service personnel, and light commercial vehicles, which are outside the general scope of much of the legislation explained in this book. It is equally important that such vehicles should be operated strictly within the law. Most of the offences and penalties described in earlier chapters apply when operating such vehicles and the consequences of operating illegally can be serious. As already mentioned, for example, Traffic Commissioners will take account of failure to operate light vehicles safely and within the law when deciding whether an applicant is fit or is of sufficient good repute to hold an 'O' licence for larger vehicles.

For the purposes of this chapter, light goods vehicles are vehicles with a gross plated weight not exceeding 3.5 tonnes (ie below the 'O' licensing, LGV plating and testing and the EU drivers' hours and tachograph requirement thresholds).

Much of the legislation applicable to the use of private motor cars and light goods vehicles has already been dealt with under such headings as excise duty, insurance and traffic regulations. The same system as described previously in Chapter 8 applies to the registration and excise licensing of such vehicles and the legal requirements for insurance cover have been outlined in Chapter 9.

Most of the traffic restrictions, particularly with regard to parking and waiting, road signs, motorway lights, breath tests and zebra crossings, which apply equally to the private car and light vehicle driver and to the large goods vehicle driver, have been dealt with in Chapter 10. Nevertheless, some of these items of legislation are worth emphasizing here for the benefit of the light vehicle fleet manager along with other matters applicable to such operations within firms.

Excise Duty

Private-type motor cars owned by firms and used for business purposes can be licensed at the private/light goods (PLG) rate of duty. See Chapter 8 for details of VED rates. If a private car is adapted for carrying goods, or an estate car is used for carrying goods, tools or samples, the appropriate goods rate of duty must be paid if the permissible maximum weight exceeds 3,500 kilograms.

In determining whether an estate car or dual-purpose vehicle (see p 220 for definition) is subject to the goods vehicle rate of duty, if its permissible maximum weight exceeds 3,500 kilograms then consideration has to be given to the nature of the goods or burden carried. No specific guidelines are laid down but local Vehicle Registration Offices take the view that if any goods or samples, service equipment or spare parts are carried in connection with a business from which profit may result, then the vehicle should be taxed as a goods vehicle. Samples which can be accommodated in a normal briefcase would not generally constitute goods for this purpose.

The tax (ie VED) disc must be displayed on the windscreen of the vehicle on the nearside where it can be easily seen. See Chapter 8 for details of vehicle excise duty requirements.

Registration and Licensing of Foreign Vehicles

Foreign-registered cars and light vehicles brought into Great Britain temporarily by overseas residents are exempt from UK registration and licensing.

A vehicle which is properly registered and taxed in its home country may be used by a visitor for up to 6 months in 12 without being subject to domestic registration and licensing. To qualify for this, a visitor must have his normal residence outside the country he is visiting. Any vehicle used in the UK for more than six months has to be registered and licensed in the normal way.

If a vehicle displaying foreign registration plates is stopped by the police, the keeper must demonstrate that he is eligible to use it in Britain without registering and licensing it here.

Insurance

Private-type motor cars and light goods vehicles, like all other vehicles, are required by law to be covered for third-party insurance risks as a minimum, but clearly in the case of fleet cars additional cover would be taken out, and in most instances comprehensive cover is advisable. Most insurance policies contain a variety of option clauses, some of which are included in the basic premium and others are available at extra cost.

Correct Cover

Of importance to the fleet manager is the need to ensure that company cars are fully insured for business use by employees of the company. The difference in insurance classification for business cars used for commercial travelling and for those which are not used for this purpose is an important point for the fleet manager to consider. Most policies differentiate between such use, and in a car fleet where vehicles are used by both salesmen and other staff and management, it is essential to ensure that either the policy covers the whole of the car fleet for commercial travelling or, if it does not do so, the sales force should be restricted to driving only those cars which have this cover. If a salesman, or indeed any other staff member, uses a car for a purpose which can in any way be described as soliciting an order, then in insurance terms this use is classed as commercial travelling and the cover on the car must include this clause.

Dual-purpose vehicles registered and licensed as goods vehicles must be insured with cover permitting goods to be carried for business purposes.

Cover for Special Cars

There can be problems in a fleet with certain individual cars on insurance cover which may not be driven by certain employees. For example, if the managing director has a high-powered sports-type car it is likely that the insurers would impose severe restrictions on the driving of that car, for whatever purpose (chauffeuring, ferrying back and forth for service or repairs, for example), by relatively inexperienced drivers or by, say, young drivers under 25 years of age. Alternatively, such cars may be restricted to named drivers only.

Private Use of Company Cars

A further point which needs consideration is cover for the employee's use of a company car for private purposes. It is general practice for firms to allow their employees this concession both for commuting to work and for family motoring at the weekends and for holidays. The cover taken out for fleet cars should specifically include this provision if such use is permitted, otherwise the vehicle owner (the firm) may be guilty of permitting the use of an uninsured car. In these circumstances, if an accident and claim were to result, the consequences for the employee could be very serious in terms of meeting damage claims and in prosecution for using an uninsured car. The same provisions should be applied if the firm permits the employee's wife (or husband) or even his children (if they are qualified drivers) to drive the car at any time.

Employees' Use of Own Cars

If employees are ever required, or likely to be required, to use their own private car for business purposes, even for only the occasional errand, the fleet manager should ensure that they have adequate insurance cover on their own vehicle for such purpose. This usually means that employees' own policies must include provision for their car to be used in connection with the business of their employer.

The fleet manager, confronted with this type of situation, should ask to see evidence of the cover (ie a valid Certificate of Insurance or a temporary cover note showing the conditions for use covered by the policy) and not just rely on the word of the employee. Similarly, the fleet manager would be wise to inform all other persons in the firm, management and staff alike, that employees should not use, or be requested to use, their own car on company business without first having the insurance cover verified.

To avoid the dangers which could arise from an employee using his own private car for business purposes when it was not covered for such use, when the policy was not in force at all because the premium had not been paid, or because the policy was invalid as a result of the employee giving incorrect information at the time of completing the policy application, the company can take out a motor contingency policy which will indemnify it against any claims arising from an accident involving an employee undertaking company business in his own uninsured car. This type of policy is very cheap to obtain and well worth the cost when considered against the risks. For example, if the employee had an accident causing serious injury to one or more third parties and his own insurance proved to be void, the third parties would look to the employer on whose business the employee was engaged at the time of the accident to meet their claims.

Dual Car Use

When an employee who is provided with a company car also owns a car which his wife uses, an anomalous situation on insurance cover can arise if his own car is insured in his, and not his wife's, name. This problem occurs because the cover provided on his own car automatically provides him with third-party cover while driving any other car not belonging to him. Consequently, when driving the firm's car for pleasure purposes he has the double cover provided by both the firm's policy and his own policy. If he should then be involved in an accident resulting in a third-party claim, his own insurers could be held partially liable for the damages arising out of the claim.

In order to overcome this particular problem the major insurance companies have made an undertaking indicating that it is not their intention to take advantage of the cover provided by the driver's own personal insurance policy in such circumstances. However, not all insurance companies are party to this undertaking.

Payment by Passengers

Payment by passengers towards the cost of petrol consumed on a journey no longer infringes the 'hiring' exclusion clause on insurance cover. However, payment towards other motoring expenses such as parking fees or depreciation could still fall within the 'prohibition of hiring' clause in most insurance policies. In cases where this situation arises a check should be made with insurers to ascertain the current position.

When an employer makes a company car available for the private use of an employee a 'benefit in kind' value has to be calculated in relation to the car, and the fuel if that is also provided for private use. The calculator, which is available on the Inland Revenue website at **http://www.hmrc.gov.uk/calcs/cars.htm**:

- allows the 'benefit in kind' value of a company car to be calculated and, if appropriate the car fuel benefit;
- provides an indication of the Income Tax liability for the provision of the company car and car fuel benefit.

The calculator was updated in January 2010 to allow calculations for the tax years 2004–05 to 2010–11 inclusive.

Changes to the Car Benefit Rules

The car benefit charge for a full year is obtained by multiplying the price of the car for tax purposes (in most cases, its list price plus accessories less capital contributions) by the 'appropriate percentage'. More detailed guidance is available for employees and for employers in free HMRC booklets available via the website.

From 2010–11 onwards the lower threshold (ie the CO_2 emissions figure which sets the 15 per cent rate) will be reduced from 135 to 130 g/km. The appropriate percentage for cars which cannot in any circumstances emit CO_2 by being driven (eg 'zero emission cars', including those powered solely by electricity) is reduced to 0 per cent for five years with effect from 6 April 2010.

The appropriate percentage for cars with CO_2 emissions figures not exceeding 75g/km is reduced to 5 per cent for five years with effect from 6 April 2010, subject to the diesel surcharge where appropriate.

According to HMRC, from 2011–12 the car benefit rules will be significantly simplified. For example, from 6 April 2011:

- There will no longer be any reductions for alternative fuels (hybrids, bi-fuels and cars manufactured to run on E85 – types H, B and G).
- The diesel surcharge will apply to all diesels (including type L diesels approved to Euro IV emissions limits and first registered before 1 January 2006).
- The £80,000 limit for the price of a car for car benefit purposes will no longer apply.
- The lower threshold (the CO_2 emissions figure which sets the 15 per cent rate) will be reduced from 130 to 125 g/km.
- The number of letters used to describe cars will therefore be reduced to three: E for electric-only cars (as at present), D for all diesels (current types D and L) and A for all other types (current types H, B, C, G, P).

Fuel Benefit Charge

HMRC holds that free fuel 'incentivizes unnecessary motoring, which is contrary to the Government's environmental objectives. Taxing the benefit-in-kind represented by free fuel therefore serves to discourage unnecessary driving'.

(Source: Explanatory memorandum to the car and van fuel benefit order 2010, No. 406, 7.1. Website: **http://www.opsi.gov.uk/si/si2010/em/uksiem_20100406_en.pdf**).

Currently, the system for valuing the benefit for cars from free fuel, based on the multiplier and the appropriate percentage was introduced by the Finance Act 2002, replacing previous fuel scale charges. The multiplier was originally set at £14,000 for the years 2003–04 to 2007–08 and increased to £16,900 for the year 2008–09 onwards. From 6 April 2010 the figure rises to £18,000 per year and for the year 2011–12 the amount is £18,800. The benefit charge is intended to reflect a notional value for the fuel received.

Private Use of Vans

Legislation introducing a flat-rate fuel charge for the use of vans was introduced by the Finance Act 2004. This was originally set at nil for the years 2005–06 to 2006–07 and £500 for the years 2007–08 and onwards. From 6 April 2010 the tax figure is £550. Vehicles over 3.5 tonnes will be exempt from this arrangement, as will any pooled van which is not normally kept at or near an employee's home.

In a case where an employee who is provided with a van is allowed to use it for private purposes he is treated as having a taxable benefit of £3,000. If the employer pays for fuel used for private purposes this will count as an additional benefit worth £550 as already mentioned above. This means that a 22 per cent taxpayer would face a tax bill of around £781 for these 'benefits in kind' regardless of the age or size of the van.

Where a van is used solely for business travel to and from work, with only occasional private use, the benefit in kind rules do not apply.

National Insurance on Private Fuel Usage

Where employees are provided with free fuel for private use there is a liability to pay National Insurance contributions on the value of the benefit to the employee. Where such value has not been taken into account by the employer there is a risk of claims by the DSS for retrospective payment of contributions going back one year.

Construction and Use Regulations

Apart from the sections of the C&U regulations which apply to private cars concerning their construction, lighting, noise, silencing and all the provisions which require the motor car to be maintained in accordance with the regulations, they are not involved in the special requirements relating to goods vehicles, unless the car has in any way been adapted to carry goods, for example, by removing seats or fitting racks on which goods can be carried. In this case the goods vehicle rate of excise duty applies and the vehicles become subject to certain aspects of the C&U regulations regarding goods vehicles (see Chapter 12).

It should be remembered that the overriding requirement of the C&U regulations for all vehicles to be maintained at all times in such a condition that they shall not cause danger to people carried on the vehicle and other road users applies equally to private cars and to goods vehicles irrespective of their size or weight.

New cars manufactured for sale in Britain must meet the braking system requirements of EC Directive 71/320 unless the system is of the dual-line type. This directive specifies maximum stopping distances equivalent to a braking efficiency of 27 per cent.

Also as a result of EU Directives, reversing lamps and four-way hazard warning flashers are compulsory on all cars made in Britain. Regulations require rear fog lights to be fitted to new vehicles manufactured since 1 October 1979 and first used since 1 April 1980 (see p 355-56 for more details).

Towing

From 1 August 1998, all tow bars fitted to new cars must be EC Type Approved and marked accordingly. It is an offence to fit – or have fitted – a tow bar which does not comply with Euro-legislation contained in Directive 94/20/EC.

Local Authority Emissions Testing

Several local authorities, including Birmingham, Bristol, Canterbury, Glasgow, Middlesbrough, Swansea and the City of Westminster, are operating pilot schemes of roadside emissions testing. Drivers of vehicles which fail the test will be issued with a fixed penalty notice requiring payment of £60, rising to £90 if unpaid within 28 days. The test levels are the same as those that vehicles would be expected to meet at the annual test. Commercial vehicles that fail an emission test invariably have poorly maintained engines. The scheme covers all types of vehicles, including commercial vehicles, and if the tests prove successful they will be extended nationally.

Safe Use of Mobile Phones, etc

Mobile telephones emit electrical energy when transmitting and should be switched off before entering a filling station. Receiving incoming calls presents the same hazards as when making outgoing calls. A number of serious fires have resulted from mobile phone use in filling stations.

The Highway Code prohibits the use of hand-held mobile phones or microphones while driving. It also says that using hands-free equipment may distract a driver's attention from the road. It is an offence to fail to exercise proper control of a vehicle at all times. If a driver is caught using a hand-held mobile phone whilst driving there is a £60 fixed penalty and three points added to the drivers' licence. Larger fines can be imposed if the offender goes to court (up to £2,500 for drivers of goods vehicles).

A similar injunction applies in regard to in-vehicle (or on-board) systems such as those used for route guidance, navigation and congestion warning, and the use of laptop or hand-held PCs and multi-media, etc.

In all instances, when it is necessary to use such equipment the driver should stop the vehicle in a safe place (ie not on the hard shoulder of a motorway except in an emergency).

Carrying Dangerous Goods in Cars

According to the National Chemical Emergency Centre (NCEC), the carrying of small quantities of dangerous goods, such as samples, in company cars can present both legal problems and safety risks.

The legal situation is determined by the type of goods carried, the size of the receptacles in which they are carried, and the total size of the load. The quantity thresholds for UK carriage are shown in the CDG Road regulations (schedule 1, Table 2) – see pp 486–91 for further details.

For the most part, it is unlikely that sufficient quantities of such goods in Class 3 (Flammable), Packing Group III (Transport Category 3) would be carried in a private car to require the full legal gamut of vehicle placarding, the provision of Tremcards and the need for driver training. Provided these goods are in receptacles with a volume of 25 litres or less it would be difficult to exceed the quantity threshold of 500 litres above which these legal requirements apply.

However, should the samples fall within the requirements for Packing Group I substances (Transport Category 1), goods must then be in a receptacle with a capacity of 1 litre or less, with a total volume of 20 litres or less, to avoid these requirements.

So far as the risk element is concerned, it is necessary to consider what would happen in the event of a road accident. With no Tremcards on the vehicle, there is no emergency information available for either the driver or the emergency services, nor, invariably, is there likely to be any emergency equipment such as the appropriate fire extinguishers, first aid kit, respirator, gloves, spill kit or emergency warning triangle to place on the road.

Besides all the dangers implicit in the carrying of dangerous samples, there is the question of the vehicle insurance to consider. Generally, it may be expected that an insurance company would repudiate any claim if they were not advised beforehand of the carriage of such goods, especially if legal requirements were not being met at the time.

Drivers' Hours and Records

Light goods vehicle drivers (ie of vehicles not exceeding 3.5 tonnes gross weight) coming within the scope of this chapter and employees driving company-owned private-type motor cars are exempt from the EU driving hours regulations – consequently, only the relevant British provisions apply in certain cases.

The applicable limits for drivers of goods vehicles not exceeding 3.5 tonnes gvw are as follows:

- maximum daily driving time 10 hours;
- maximum daily duty time 11 hours.

There are no specified break or daily or weekly rest period requirements; no limits on continuous duty or weekly limits on duty or driving.

Drivers of light goods vehicles of not more than 3.5 tonnes gross plated weight and dual-purpose vehicles (see p 220 for definition) of any weight used for certain specialized duties are required to observe only a daily maximum driving time of 10 hours. This applies to light goods vehicles used:

- by doctors, dentists, nurses, midwives or vets;
- for any service of inspection, cleaning, maintenance, repair, installation or fitting;
- by a commercial traveller and carrying only goods used for soliciting orders;
- by an employee of the AA, the RAC or the RSAC;
- for business of cinematography or of radio or television broadcasting.

Record Keeping

Light goods vehicle drivers (ie vehicles under 3.5 tonnes gross weight) and drivers of dual-purpose vehicles are exempt from the requirements to keep records of their driving, duty and rest periods.

Employees driving vehicles in this category remain exempt from the requirements of the goods vehicle drivers' hours and record requirements, but only so long as they do not drive vehicles to which these requirements do apply. If at any time an employee who normally drives only light goods vehicles or motor cars also as part of his work needs to drive a goods vehicle to which the drivers' hours regulations do apply then any time spent driving a van or a private car (his own or the company's) for his firm's business must be counted within his total daily working time (ie duty time). If the goods vehicle exceeds 3.5 tonnes gross weight the driving of the car should be shown on his record sheet (ie tachograph chart) for the day on which he drives a goods vehicle as 'other work'.

Full details of the goods vehicle drivers' hours and records are given in Chapters 3 and 4.

Tachographs

Light goods vehicles of not more than 3.5 tonnes gross plated weight are exempt from the EU tachograph regulations requiring tachograph fitment and use, but if such a vehicle is coupled to a goods-carrying trailer so that the total of the combined gross weights exceeds 3.5 tonnes then the vehicle will come within the scope of the EU tachograph regulations, unless it is otherwise exempt due to special use. This means that a fully calibrated tachograph must be fitted and must be used by the driver when the trailer is drawn (see Chapter 5 for full details of the tachograph regulations) and the EU drivers' hours rules must be followed (see Chapter 3 for details).

Speed Limits

Private cars and dual-purpose vehicles not drawing trailers are restricted to maximum permitted speeds on certain roads in accordance with the restriction signposted on the section of road and to overall maximum speeds of 60 mph on single-carriageway roads and 70 mph on dual-carriageways and motorways.

Speed limits for cars and light goods vehicles are as follows:

	Motorways	Dual-carriageways	Other roads
Cars and car-derived vans	70	70	60
Cars and car-derived vans towing trailer	60	60	50
Rigid goods vehicles not exceeding 7.5 tonnes	70	60	50
Articulated vehicles and rigid goods vehicles not exceeding 7.5 tonnes drawing trailer	60	60*	50

* In Northern Ireland the limit for this category of vehicle is 50 mph.

NB: *In all cases of speed restrictions mentioned above, if specific lower limits are in force on any section of road, then it is the lower limit which must be observed.*

Speed Limiters for Large Vans

Since 1 January 2007 all goods vehicles over 3,500 kg gvw fitted with Euro-III engines and first registered from 1 October 2001 to 31 December 2004 should have been fitted with a speed limiter calibrated to a maximum speed not exceeding 56 mph (90 kph).

Euro-III vehicles have the facility to have a top speed limiter already built into the engine electronic control unit, thus ensuring that the calibration procedure does not involve the fitment of brackets, air cylinders or piping.

From the same date, 1 January 2007, vans over 3.5 tonnes gross weight have been prohibited from using the outside lane of a three-, or more, lane motorway.

Seat Belts

Compulsory fitment of seat belts applies in the case of the following light vehicles (see also pp 279–81):

- Goods vehicles not exceeding 1,525 kg unladen (first registered since April 1967).
- Goods vehicles not exceeding 3,500 kg maximum gross weight (first registered since 1 April 1980).

- Dual-purpose vehicles first registered since 1 January 1965.
- Private cars first registered since 1 January 1965.

Vehicles to which the regulations apply first used since 1 April 1973 must be fitted with belts which can be secured and released with one hand only and must also be fitted with a device to enable the belts to be stowed in a position where they do not touch the floor. The belts must be maintained in a fit and serviceable condition and kept free from permanent or temporary obstruction which would prevent their being used by a person sitting in the seat for which the belt is provided. Failure to comply with these requirements is an offence and can lead to failure of the MoT test.

In cases where the regulations apply, as above, belts must be provided for the driver and one front seat passenger.

Wearing of Seat Belts

The wearing of front seat belts in vehicles fitted with them by law has been compulsory since 1 January 1983.

Since 1 September 1989 children up to 14 years of age riding in the back seats of motor cars fitted with rear seat belts or child restraints must wear those belts or restraints.

Since 1 July 1991 adult rear seat passengers travelling in cars or taxis fitted with rear seat belts must wear the belts provided, irrespective of the age of the vehicle.

Certain exemptions to the wearing of belts have been included in the regulations (see pp 280–81 for list of exemptions).

Heavy fines may be imposed on conviction for failing to wear a seat belt as required by law. The responsibility for seat belt wearing rests with the person sitting in the seat for which the belt is provided except that responsibility for ensuring that children wear seat belts as required by law either in the front or rear seats rests with the driver of the vehicle (ie not the parent or guardian who may be accompanying the child).

Fuel Consumption Tests

Concern about energy conservation led to the Energy Act 1976 and the Passenger Car Fuel Consumption Order 1977 being enacted. Because of interest among readers of the *Handbook* in this subject, details of the legal requirements and the scheme are outlined here.

Since 1 April 1978 new cars on display in showrooms and on forecourts must carry a label showing official fuel consumption figures for that model of car. Every dealer must have details of officially approved fuel consumption tests for all cars listed in a booklet available in his showroom for buyers to consult on request. In addition, where reference is made in promotional literature, such as advertisements, technical specifications and sales brochures, to the petrol consumption of a new car the test results must be included. In all such cases the results of all tests carried out must be quoted (urban cycle, 90 kph – and 120 kph where appropriate) in both miles per gallon and litres per 100 kilometres. These requirements do not apply in the Channel Islands or the Isle of Man.

Official Tests

The official tests are carried out in approved laboratories or on test tracks. They have been designed to be representative of real-life driving situations and the results achieved provide a guide to the models which are likely to be more economical in their fuel use.

The test results do not guarantee the fuel consumption of any particular car. Each new car has not itself been tested and there will inevitably be differences between cars of the same model. The driver's style, the loading of the car, road, weather and traffic conditions, the overall mileage of the car and its standard of maintenance will all affect its fuel consumption. For all these reasons the fuel consumption achieved on the road will not necessarily accord with the tests results.

The Standard Test

The tests follow an internationally agreed procedure and consist of two compulsory parts:

Part 1. A cycle simulating urban driving.
Part 2. A constant speed test at 56 mph (90 kph).

Models Included in the Tests

Almost all types of new passenger cars are covered by the tests. However, certain types are excluded as follows:

- Cars manufactured before 1 January 1978.
- Second-hand cars.
- Cars adapted to carry more than eight passengers (excluding the driver).
- Three-wheelers.
- Invalid carriages.
- Van-derived passenger cars.
- Cars built specially for export.
- Cars operating on four-wheel drive only.
- Cars whose engines run on diesel, liquefied petroleum gas or other such fuels.

These vehicles will not, therefore, be labelled in the showrooms. Heavy goods vehicles, vans and motorcycles are also excluded from these tests. Also, a small number of manufacturers and importers have been granted exemption from testing because of the low volume of production involved. Consequently, these particular makes and models are not likely to be of significant interest or concern to the fleet user.

Urban Test Cycle

The urban test cycle is carried out in a laboratory where equipment simulates the loads experienced under normal driving conditions and the standard patterns of urban driving. The car is driven from a fully warmed-up start and is taken through a cycle of acceleration, deceleration and idling with a maximum speed not exceeding 31 mph (50 kph).

Constant Speed Test

The constant speed test at 56 mph (90 kph) is intended to be representative of open-road driving. It may be carried out in the laboratory or on a test track (under strictly controlled road and weather conditions).

Optional Constant Speed Test

This test is carried out at 75 mph (120 km/h) in a laboratory or on a test track. Although it is recognized that this test exceeds the UK maximum speed limit, it is included to illustrate to car drivers the worsening fuel consumption at higher speeds. It may also be useful to manufacturers exporting to some parts of Europe where speed limits are higher.

Only one production car is tested as a representative of each model. It must have been run in and have been driven for at least 1,800 miles (3,000 km) before testing. In some cases several models which do not differ significantly in certain technical characteristics thought to be important in determining fuel consumption may be grouped together into a 'class'. Only one car in the class needs to be tested.

Testing

The responsibility for testing lies with the manufacturers and importers themselves. They must either carry out the tests themselves or arrange for them to be carried out on their behalf. Department of Transport officials have the right to inspect the test laboratories and to witness tests in progress to ensure that they are being carried out correctly.

Manufacturers must submit their fuel consumption test results to the Department of Transport, who record the results in an official fuel economy certificate.

SAFED Training for Van Drivers

A new Department for Transport scheme launched in mid-2006 offers free driver training under its SAFED (Safe and Fuel Efficient Driving Standard) initiative for van drivers (ie drivers who fall below the 7.5-tonne threshold for LGV licensing).

SAFED for vans is a one-day course and the acclaimed benefits for drivers are as follows:

- reduced risk of accidents while driving;
- reduced stress levels and enhanced satisfaction of driving;
- increased confidence in vehicle control and driving technique;

- enhanced job efficiency and professionalism;
- potential financial incentives.

There are also many benefits for employers (ie owner-drivers and fleet operators), such as:

- reduced accidents;
- less vehicle downtime due to a reduction in accidents;
- reduced fuel bills;
- increased productivity and vehicle utilization;
- improved resale value of vehicles;
- reduced running costs (particularly relating to maintenance and tyres);
- potential reductions in insurance premiums;
- reduced environmental impact.

Further details of the scheme can be obtained by telephoning the free hotline on 0300 123 1133 or by e-mailing **info@vanbestpractice.org.uk**.

Vehicle Fuel Efficiency

N ext to wage costs, fuel is the most expensive goods vehicle operating cost item, accounting for up to one-third of road transport operating costs. It is a high-cost commodity which is a major budget feature of all vehicle fleet operations. It is also subject to occasional and dramatic shortages as a result of political unrest in some of the major oil-producing countries, as we have seen with the Middle East. Scientists predict total extinction as world supplies of crude oil are consumed ever more rapidly by developed nations, which have become increasingly dependent on transportation systems powered by oil-based fuels. Even the once much-heralded finds of oil in offshore waters of the British Isles are now known to have limited life expectancy.

While the search for and research into acceptable alternative fuels and power units goes on, it is important to take steps to minimize consumption of our present fuel supplies. As well as being a problem for nations, this is a problem which concerns all fleet operators, whatever their size. Besides any conscience they may have about energy conservation they will readily appreciate that fuel consumption must be reduced in the campaign to keep vehicle operating costs down.

Fuel and Vehicle

Fuel consumption is substantially related to the type of vehicle, its power unit and drive line, its mechanical condition, the use to which it is put and how it is driven. In recent times manufacturers have offered fuel economy models within their ranges so the cost-conscious operator can choose between economy or outright performance.

The fuel-conscious operator who is in a position to buy new vehicles will undoubtedly choose fuel economy models where these are suited to his particular needs. However, for the most part, fleet operators have to stick with the vehicles they already have in their fleets and are faced with the need to consider how improved fuel economy can be achieved with existing vehicles. Three principal areas exist for improvement in the vehicle itself. These are as follows:

- mechanical condition;
- efficient use;
- addition of fuel economy aids.

Mechanical Condition

A vehicle which is poorly maintained will inevitably consume more fuel. Particular attention should be paid to efficient maintenance of the following items:

- **Fuel system** (fuel tank, pipe lines, filters, pump and injectors). There should be no leaks and the vehicle should not emit black smoke. Both of these are causes or consequences of excessive consumption as well as matters which could result in test failure and prosecution. Fuel pumps and injectors should be properly serviced as recommended by the manufacturers.
- **Wheels and brakes.** Wheels should turn freely and without any brake binding. Front wheels should be correctly aligned. Brake binding and misalignment cause unnecessary friction which is only overcome by the use of more fuel. Axles on bogies should be correctly aligned because tyres running at slip angles have a high rolling resistance and therefore are a source of increased fuel consumption.
- **Driving controls.** Throttle cables and clutch and brake pedals should be correctly adjusted so the driver has efficient control over the vehicle. In particular, engine tick over should be accurately adjusted to save throttle 'blipping' to keep it running when the vehicle is stationary.

Efficient Use

Inefficient use of vehicles constitutes the greatest waste of fuel. The following activities should be avoided by careful route planning, scheduling and prior thought about the cost consequences:

- vehicles running long distances when only partially loaded;
- vehicles covering excessive distances to reach their destination;
- large vehicles being used for running errands or making small-item deliveries which could be accomplished more efficiently, and certainly more economically, by other means;
- vehicles running empty.

It is frequently argued that traffic office staff have little control over these matters, since customer demands for orders and the need to give drivers freedom to choose routes are dictates which overrule efficient planning. Nevertheless, attempts should be made to persuade those concerned of the need for restraint, in the quest for saving fuel and thereby reducing costs.

Fuel Economy Aids

The quest for fuel saving has led to a market for economy aids which can be added to existing vehicles. These aids fall into three general categories:

- streamlining devices such as cab-top air deflectors, under-bumper air dams, front corner deflectors for high trailers and box vans, in-fill pieces for lorry and trailer combinations and shaped cones for addition to the front of van bodies – radiusing or chamfering the front edges of the body is perhaps the simplest means of reducing air drag;
- road speed governors which restrict maximum speed – one of the greatest causes of excessive fuel consumption (speed limiters are now a mandatory requirement on certain heavy vehicles – see Chapter 12);
- engine fans and radiator shutters which are designed to ensure that diesel engines are always operating at the correct temperature to give the most efficient performance and fuel economy.

All these types of device can be economically justified to a varying degree, but it is important to note that fitting streamlining devices in isolation only reduces fuel consumption if vehicle speeds are kept down. If the driver is able to use the few extra miles per hour which these devices provide – which he will do unless otherwise restricted – then there will be little fuel saving and the cost of fitting would not be wholly justified.

Fuel and Tyres

The type and condition of tyres on a vehicle play a significant part in its fuel consumption. It is a proven fact that the lower rolling resistance inherent in radial-ply tyres adds considerably to the fuel economy of the vehicle compared to the greater resistance of cross-ply tyres.

Improvements in fuel consumption of 5 to 10 per cent can be expected from the use of radial-ply tyres. Low-profile tyres which offer a number of operational benefits over conventional radial tyres – such as reduced platform height and reduced overall height – also offer further possibilities for fuel saving.

The savings mentioned will only be achieved if the tyres are in good condition, are correctly inflated to the manufacturer's recommended pressures and are properly matched, especially when used in twin-wheel combinations. Neglect of tyre pressures is common in fleets and under-inflation is one of the major causes of tyre failure. It is also a major contributor to excessive fuel consumption.

Fuel and the Driver

Driving techniques, above all else, influence the overall fuel consumption of vehicles. A driver with a heavy right foot will negate all fuel-saving measures and devices and destroy any expectations of acceptable fuel consumption. Poor driving which has these consequences falls into two categories:

- high-speed driving;
- erratic, stop-go driving.

Fast driving consumes excessive fuel: this fact is beyond question but the extent of the extra consumption is difficult to assess accurately. Tests carried out some time ago (but still making a valid point) on an articulated vehicle on motorway operation indicated that fuel consumption increased quite dramatically when the vehicle was travelling at over 40 mph. In the tests, at 40 mph the fuel consumption was 10.5 mpg, at 50 mph this reduced by 2.6 mpg to 7.9 mpg and at 60 mph a further reduction of 1.5 mpg was experienced, making a 3.75 mpg difference between 40 mph and 60 mph travelling speeds. This represents a 35.7 per cent increase in fuel consumption. The real significance of these figures will be fully appreciated when annual motorway travel is calculated and this is multiplied by the increase in consumption, by the number of vehicles in the fleet and by the cost per gallon of diesel fuel.

The effects of erratic driving are more difficult to determine in quantitative terms, but it is sufficient to say that it results in abnormally high fuel consumption as well as causing excessive wear and tear on vehicle components. Impatience behind the wheel and an inability to assess in time what is happening on the road ahead leads the driver to see-saw between fierce acceleration to keep up with the traffic and violent braking to avoid running into the vehicle in front – hence the excessive use of fuel.

More economical driving is achieved by concentration on the road and traffic conditions ahead, anticipating well in advance how the traffic flow will move and what is happening in front, so that acceleration and braking can be more progressive and a smooth passage assured.

One other fuel-saving practice which the driver can adopt is to stop the engine while the vehicle is stationary rather than letting it tick over for unnecessarily long periods. If he feels this is necessary because his battery is in poor condition, then it is much cheaper to deal with the battery and charging problems than pay for the extra fuel to compensate.

Fuel and Fleet Management

Fleet operators can take a number of basic steps to reduce fuel consumption besides ensuring that the measures already mentioned are implemented.

Bulk Supplies/Buying

Control over the buying of bulk supplies and issues and over the buying of supplies outside from filling stations at the higher pump prices are important aspects for management attention. So too is accurate record keeping, without which it is impossible to compare the fuel consumption of vehicles or to see which vehicles are consuming excessive amounts of fuel. Without records to identify these problems, there is no hope of remedying high fuel costs.

Recording Issues

Overfilling of vehicle tanks, causing spillage, is a common occurrence which wastes fuel and prevents accurate consumption records being obtained, as well as causing a mess and a health hazard. Accurate recording of issues against individual vehicles is another area which demands close attention. Modern electronic and computerized fuel-dispensing systems are available which ensure security of bulk supplies by preventing access except with a known key or card. This stops unauthorized drawing of fuel and it monitors issues to identified vehicles or keyholders. The cost of such systems can be quickly recouped through savings in missing or unaccounted fuel and through better record keeping, which enables high vehicle consumption to be quickly identified and investigated.

Buying Away from Base

Where bulk supplies are available at base, drivers should be discouraged from buying supplies from outside sources at higher prices except when absolutely necessary and even then they should buy only sufficient to get them home. Commonly, drivers fill tanks to the top, which is enough to cover the trip home and to do further journeys as well on fuel which cost much more than that which they could have drawn once they got back to base. It is important to keep watch on the purchase of outside fuel supplies, especially for cash, because of the incentives which are offered to drivers to fill to the top. If outside fuel drawings are necessary then recognized bunkering card systems should be established.

Long-Range Tanks

In the case of vehicles which operate regularly on long distances – on international work, for example – the fitting of long-range tanks is an economic proposition because of the savings achieved by using bulk-purchased supplies. A word of caution though: the extra fuel carried should not be at the expense of payload unless this can be justified, and on international work there is the cost of fuel levies or taxes to be borne in mind. These are chargeable when entering some countries and are based on the amount of fuel in the tank. British hauliers returning to the UK may also find they have to pay an excess fuel tax on supplies bought outside the UK.

Following a number of cases where road hauliers have been stopped for using overlarge diesel fuel tanks on vehicles, the RHA has reminded its members of the official definition for 'standard' fuel tanks.

Under Article 8a of Council Directive 92/81/EEC, the diesel tanks fitted to new vehicles are defined as follows:

> The tanks permanently fixed by the manufacturer to all motor vehicles of the same type as the vehicle in question and whose permanent fitting enables fuel to be used directly, both for the purpose of propulsion and, where appropriate, for the operation, during transport, of refrigeration and other systems.

In the case of used vehicles, the RHA advice is that:

any tank already fitted to such a vehicle when purchased by its current owner, would satisfy the 'standard tank' criteria. This means that should the original tank have been replaced by a new, larger tank prior to purchase by a subsequent owner, then that larger tank would be regarded as having been fitted by the manufacturer for the purpose of the legal definition.

HM Revenue & Customs has warned that the focus of attention on fuel import issues is on the misuse of duty relief and has emphasized that fuel brought into the UK may only be used by the particular vehicle carrying it and should not be offloaded from that vehicle for use by other vehicles or for transfer to a bulk fuel installation.

Route Planning/Scheduling

Better planning of vehicle schedules and routes offers the prospect of quite considerable fuel savings, besides other savings which may also result. A reduction in the miles travelled to fulfil particular delivery schedules will inevitably result in fuel savings. If the schedules can be planned so that fewer vehicles are needed to carry out the operation then, besides the broader savings in vehicle costs, the fleet as a whole will use less fuel. Therefore, the elimination of unnecessary trips or trips where vehicles are only partly loaded is a major priority in the search for fuel cost savings.

Tachographs in Fuel Saving

The use of tachographs in vehicles and detailed analysis of tachograph charts are steps which have provided many fleet operators with fuel savings if nothing else. The value of chart recordings in this connection should not be overlooked.

Agency Cards

There are a number of agency and fuel cards available to fleet operators. Generally they can be categorized between those from the major oil companies (eg Shell, Esso, BP) and those from other commercial organizations.

Principally these systems offer the opportunity to buy fuel at pump prices, paying only when fuel is actually purchased. The differences in the various schemes is in the levels of service which they offer.

Fuel Economy Checklist

Check

- Fuel systems free from leaks.
- Fuel pump and injectors serviced and correctly adjusted.
- Exhaust not emitting black smoke.
- Air cleaners not blocked.
- Engine operating at correct temperature.

- Wheels turning freely.
- Controls properly adjusted and lubricated.

Tyres

- Condition and inflation pressures.
- Possibility of changing to radials on all vehicles.

Drivers

- Speed limits not being exceeded.
- Driving methods smooth and gentle.
- Engines stopped when vehicle standing.

Management

- Control over supplies and issues.
- Avoidance of spillage, loss and unauthorized use.
- Purchases from outside suppliers kept to a minimum.
- Record systems accurate and up to date.
- Possibility of installing fuel issue and monitoring systems.
- Possibility of fitting fuel economy aids (deflectors, engine fans, etc).
- Possibility of using long-range fuel tanks on vehicles.
- Routeing and scheduling practices to reduce wasted journeys and unnecessary mileage.
- Fuel economy programme to ensure all possible steps being implemented efficiently and recorded accurately.

Energy Efficiency Best Practice Programme

The Government has produced a comprehensive *Fuel Management Guide* for the road haulage industry, providing advice on fuel economy, under its Energy Efficiency Best Practice Programme (EEBPP). The guide covers many aspects of best practice in fuel efficiency, including easy methods of capturing and monitoring of data, vehicle specification and maintenance as well as driver training.

NB: The Energy Efficiency Best Practice Programme promotes energy efficiency through free, impartial, authoritative information and advice for industry, buildings and transport. The website can be found on: **www.energy-efficiency.gov.uk/transport.**

Freight Best Practice

This scheme is funded by the Department for Transport (D*f*T) and managed by AECOM to promote operational efficiency within UK road freight transport operations. It offers essential information, free of charge, for the freight transport industry covering topics such as fuel saving, skills development, the use of efficient equipment and systems, operational efficiency and performance management.

A quarterly newsletter, *Freight Future,* often highlighting successful efficiency case studies, is published. This, together with a list of free guides on many aspects of road transport efficiency, can be downloaded from the Freight Best Practice website, **www.freightbestpractice.org.uk**, or can be ordered via a Hotline telephone number: 0300 123 1250.

Reducing Fuel Bills

The University of Huddersfield has published a 20-point plan to help transport and distribution companies reduce their fuel bills following recent increases in fuel duty. It says the following aspects are key to improving fuel efficiency:

- Ensure that you have accurate fuel consumption figures.

- Get the best from your present fleet.

- Make fuel-efficient purchasing decisions when buying new or second-hand equipment.

It also suggests following the points listed below:

- Check that weekly or monthly averages are produced by total distance divided by total fuel used rather than average of the daily averages. Quarterly summaries (using average of the daily averages) have been found to be inaccurate by as much as half a mile per gallon (mpg).

- In most cases there is a seasonal pattern to mpg, which peaks in July and August and bottoms out in December and February. It is very important to know this if you are going to test products that claim to improve mpg.

- When you find a large discrepancy in daily mpg, investigate it. Don't just average it or ignore it. Take measures to prevent it from happening again.

- If you want to accurately determine the effect of different equipment under controlled conditions, then enter the Institute of Road Transport Engineers (IRTE) fuel trials, which are run every year in June. It is a lot cheaper than hiring a facility on your own and you get the benefit of mixing with like-minded fleet managers and engineers.

- Driver training consistently achieves better miles per gallon (mpg), but it needs a reinforcement mechanism otherwise it will fail.

- Reinforcement mechanisms for fuel efficient driving can be:
  - simple feedback on a noticeboard;

- individual letters to drivers; or
- a fuel bonus; however, while an annual bonus can be based on the annual average mpg, shorter-term bonus systems (eg weekly or monthly) should not use the annual average mpg. (Remember too that bonuses must not endanger road safety.)

- The most senior person with an LGV licence should be trained first.
- Identify the most fuel-efficient vehicles and, if possible, bearing in mind other operational factors, place them on the operations or routes that use the most fuel.
- Think of aerodynamics. For example, ensure that the gap between the back of the cab and the front of the trailer is minimized to reduce aerodynamic resistance. Tippers with easy sheets should have them closed when empty to prevent the airflow hitting the inside of the tailboard.
- If adjustable air deflectors are fitted, get the drivers to adjust them for maximum effect. If the deflector is too low, you will see a tidemark on the front of the trailer.
- Specify the correct bodywork – it should be no higher or wider than the job requires.
- Monitor maintenance records – poor mpg and short brake-lining life are good indicators of a driving style that wastes fuel.
- When buying new vehicles, calculate which is best over the life of the vehicle. Is there a better residual at the end of the vehicle's life from a larger engine, or are there reduced fuel costs from a smaller engine that is just as capable of doing the job? Remember to include the effect of the 'fuel escalator' in the fuel costs.
- Specify trailers or bodywork with rounded leading edges (minimum 200 mm radius).
- Aerodynamic aids may not be cost-effective on vehicles that do not undertake long, high-speed journeys as part of their regular work.
- Beware of claims made for aerodynamic equipment tested at 56 mph and translating the saving to your vehicle(s). Aerodynamics is highly sensitive to speed. As a rough guide, calculate the average speed of your vehicle(s) and ask for test results conducted at that speed.
- When buying a new vehicle, consider specifying a tachograph with the fourth needle activated to record engine speed. While you can get more information from electronic systems, activating the fourth needle will be far cheaper. However, you must be prepared to use the information, otherwise you are wasting your money.
- Specify and activate an engine speed limiter. (In some vehicles these are a legal requirement.)
- When buying a second-hand vehicle, take it for a test drive and note the engine speed at 56 mph. If the vehicle is being purchased for medium- or long-distance work, you do not want to purchase a vehicle that is geared for local

work. If you get this wrong, you will end up cruising at too high an engine speed and subsequently wasting a lot of fuel.

- When purchasing a new vehicle, get the manufacturer to provide free driver training. Most do, now, so take advantage of it.

Gas-Powered Heavy Trucks

Increasingly, environment-conscious transport operators are looking to natural gas for powering heavy vehicles. Among the key players is the Somerfield supermarket group, which has put 300 compressed natural gas-powered, Detroit-engined ERF vehicles into service. Besides the savings in fuel costs, these vehicles are much quieter than conventional diesel-powered vehicles – quieter than a saloon car, it is said, thus allowing night-time deliveries to stores without upsetting local residents.

There are three main types of gaseous fuels in use in the UK:

1 liquefied petroleum gas (LPG);
2 compressed natural gas (CNG);
3 liquefied natural gas (LNG).

All these three types of gas are used by both van and truck operators due to their environmental benefits, particularly:

- clean exhaust emissions;
- reduced engine noise;
- favourable duty treatment (ie 29 per cent reduction in road fuel gas duty in the 1999 Budget).

The Government's National Air Quality Strategy requires the monitoring of airborne pollutants such as NO_x (oxides of nitrogen) and particulates while the Air Quality Regulations 1997 oblige local authorities to assess air quality. As a result of this, a number of councils are now running gas-fuelled vehicles.

Further details on saving energy can be obtained from the Energy Saving Trust (tel: 020 7222 0101). See also the website: **www.energysavingtrust.org.uk**.

Low-Sulphur Diesel

The International Road Transport Union (IRU) called for supplies of low-sulphur diesel fuel to be made readily available throughout Europe long before the EU's current proposal for universal supplies from 2009. With legislation requiring all new heavy vehicles from October 2006 to meet Euro-IV exhaust emission standards, this fuel is essential since these engines need fuel that does not exceed a sulphur content of 10 parts per million (ppm) whereas current diesel supplies have a sulphur content of up to 50 ppm. The IRU is concerned that without adequate supplies of the low-sulphur diesel operators will not be inclined to invest in new Euro-IV vehicles until they are absolutely forced to do so by compulsory legislation.

Biodiesel

Biodiesel is a diesel-equivalent, clean-burning processed fuel derived from biological sources (such as vegetable oils), which can be used in unmodified diesel-engined vehicles. It differs from straight vegetable oils (SVO) or waste vegetable oils (WVO), used as fuels in some diesel vehicles. It is biodegradable and non-toxic – in fact, it is said to biodegrade as fast as sugar and be less toxic than table salt. It typically produces about 60 per cent less net carbon dioxide emissions than petroleum-based diesel, as it is itself produced from atmospheric carbon dioxide via photosynthesis in plants.

Biodiesel is claimed to be better for the environment because it is made from renewable sources which can be grown in the UK and elsewhere, which consequently decreases Britain's dependence on foreign oil supplies and contributes to our own national economy.

Some vehicle manufacturers are positive about the use of biodiesel, citing lower engine wear as one of its benefits. However, as biodiesel is a better solvent than standard diesel, it 'cleans' the engine, removing deposits in the fuel lines, and this may cause blockages in the fuel injectors. For this reason, manufacturers recommend that the fuel filter be changed a few months after switching to biodiesel (this part is often replaced anyway in regular servicing). Other vehicle manufacturers remain cautious over its use. For example, in the UK many only maintain engine warranties for use with maximum 5 per cent biodiesel, blended in with 95 per cent conventional diesel – which is generally considered to be overly cautious. Peugeot and Citroën are exceptions in that they have both announced that their HDI diesel engines can run on 30 per cent biodiesel. Scania and Volkswagen are other exceptions, allowing most of their engines to operate on 100 per cent biodiesel.

Mobile Communications and Information Technology in Transport

Technology developments in mobile communications have moved on apace and it is now commonplace for vehicle drivers to be in almost constant touch with their home base by mobile phone and being directed to their exact destination by a satellite navigation (sat-nav) system.

It used to be a common experience in transport operations for considerable cost to be wasted through late, changed, redirected and cancelled orders and instructions. Try as they might, transport or fleet managers could rarely avoid their share of these annoying frustrations and there was nothing that they could do, usually because they could not contact the driver while he was travelling. Vehicle-based mobile communications at today's level of sophistication have changed all this and the wasted costs of the past can be turned into savings and even into profit quite simply by being able to contact the driver, relay details of the changed plans and generally divert vehicles to meet the current needs of the business. The savings in wasted time and miles, the avoidance of heavy vehicles returning home empty, because they can be directed to pick up return loads, and the response to last-minute customer demands are significant benefits which in themselves, or with other benefits, add up to offset the capital costs of buying and installing communications equipment and the ongoing costs of rentals and call charges.

Mobile Phones

The advent of the mobile phone system has revolutionized mobile communications. Today it is possible to have a telephone interconnected to the national and international telephone networks from a vehicle-based (ie mobile) installation or from a unit carried in a jacket pocket. Such systems provide the user with the facility to dial direct to almost any telephone number in the UK or to reach such numbers via the British Telecom operator, and to make international calls and calls to any other cellular telephone. Similarly, any telephone user can dial direct to a mobile cell-phone number.

Safety

The *Highway Code* includes a special section on the use of microphones and car telephones. It prohibits using a hand-held microphone or telephone handset while driving, except in an emergency. It says the driver should only speak into a fixed, neck-slung or clipped-on microphone when it would not distract attention from the road. Drivers should not stop on the hard shoulder of a motorway to answer or make a call, no matter how urgent.

Satellite-Based Communications Systems

The Global Positioning System

The Global Positioning System (GPS), originally devised by the US military to assist navigation of both ground and air crew, incorporates 24–32 satellites orbiting the earth in outer space. As the system developed, it has been utilized for civilian purposes, in particular the marine, leisure and commercial markets.

The nature of the satellite signal enables the GPS receiver, ranging in size from a standard mobile phone to a small television set, to track it accurately and efficiently. At least three satellites are in view of the receiver at any one time, and this decodes the information to display global position in longitude and latitude, and a number of different coordinate formats. Because it does not rely on radio signals GPS can be used anywhere in the world.

'In-vehicle GPS systems' are capable of incorporating CD, radio and GPS in a single unit. For navigation purposes, it is just a case of entering a destination (such as a postcode or the name of a road) and within seconds the distance, route and travel time is calculated and displayed. A voice gives commands for turning at the correct junctions, while a map on the screen is a useful navigation aid.

Siemens VDO System

Siemens VDO Automotive was the first company in the UK to incorporate the recently introduced Traffic Message Channel service (TMC) into its aftermarket satellite navigation systems, enabling it to combine satellite navigation with real-time traffic information. TMC provides up-to-the-minute information on current traffic conditions which is relayed to vehicles equipped with any VDO Dayton or Philips CARiN navigation system (the two brands are owned by Siemens VDO) using RDS TMC, a digital data stream carried by radio broadcaster Classic FM. Data is gathered from a wide variety of sources, including real-time information from vehicles actually out on the road. The system is also 'intelligent', being capable of differentiating between different types of delays, for example slow-moving traffic, accidents, fog or roadworks. TMC data can also be used by the navigation system to automatically plan alternative routes around incidents or congested areas and to predict arrival times. This form of real-time traffic information significantly adds to the usefulness of on-board navigation, turning it into a driving aid that can assist in reducing journey times, even for drivers travelling on routes they use regularly.

Information Technology in Transport

Information technology (IT) is quite simply the means by which information is collected accurately, fully analysed, transmitted to all relevant functions within and without an organization, and disseminated by those charged with decision making. Many efficient transport and distribution operations these days are totally dependent on reliable IT systems (for example, 'just-in-time' stocking principles hinge on rapid and efficient communications) for communication with customers, suppliers and contractors.

Within IT systems, one of the fastest-growing areas is that of Electronic Data Interchange (EDI), whereby transport and distributor firms receive orders, delivery documentation and invoices direct from their customers' computers into their own (compatible) systems via direct communications links, completely eliminating the delays, errors and other difficulties associated with the creating and movement of paper documents via postal and courier systems. EDI systems provide the benefits of rapid and accurate order passing and processing (at less direct cost) and with the potential for reducing stock levels.

Electronic Data Interchange (EDI)

Widescale computerization in the road freight, shipping and export/import industries and by Revenue & Customs departments has led to the introduction of modern systems for passing shipping and export/import data between traders, shippers and Revenue & Customs. This is now done via direct or indirect computer links without the need for paper documents to pass or confirm information. This whole concept is known as EDI (Electronic Data Interchange), sometimes called paperless systems of trading, and its use results in automatic handling and actioning of data. To ensure uniformity in this method of trading the United Nations has set a standard for EDI known as EDIFACT (an acronym for Electronic Data Interchange for Administration,

Commerce and Transport), under which there are standard procedures and messages for passing such matter as shipping instructions.

Computerization in Transport

Computerization provides many facilities of value to the transport industry, especially vehicle routeing and load scheduling systems which determine the most cost-effective and load-efficient delivery routes and schedules.

Bar coding systems allow packages to be scanned for data both in the warehouse and on the vehicle, allowing data to be transferred back to base as soon as a consignment has been delivered to its destination. In the office, all manner of data can be held on file, readily accessible by staff, to give information about employees, vehicles, customers, loads, etc.

Computerized tachograph chart analysis systems can be installed for compliance with the legal requirement to check drivers' tachograph charts on a regular basis.

The current trend is towards the development of on-board systems to allow vehicle drivers to remain in constant communication via computer with their base for transmitting data and instructions. Precise vehicle location (ie to within a few metres irrespective of where the vehicle is) can be determined via the GPS (global positioning satellite) and other tracking systems, which is particularly useful for tracking high-value cargo vehicles and stolen vehicles.

Additionally, a full range of data recording, information and analysis operations, including accounting, staff records and vehicle maintenance records, can be accessed by all relevant staff and management, both in the office and away from base on laptop or hand-held computers via an internet connection.

The use of e-mail and internet connection to the world wide web has led to enormous improvements in business efficiency and information, providing rapid person-to-person communication and access to unlimited data on just about every subject under the sun.

Intelligent Transport Systems

Intelligent Transport Systems (ITS) that use telematics (ie the combination of information technology and telecommunications) provide online (electronic) information and control systems for all modes of transport, including vehicle-based systems. Typical of these systems used in road transport are those that operate:

- variable message signs (VMS) for use on, for example, motorways;
- on-board route and traffic information, such as Trafficmaster;
- traffic control and enforcement signs, such as the new-type digital speed cameras;
- electronic road charging;
- traffic monitoring;

- vehicle-to-base communications;
- electronic ticketing.

Teleroute

Teleroute is a leading European online matching service for freight and vehicle space, providing freight forwarders and road hauliers with opportunities to maximize efficiency and increase profits. Established in 1985, the system has over 200,000 freight offers posted and consulted online daily by more than 70,000 subscribers in 16 European countries. Each year more than 120 million tonnes of freight are efficiently transacted in 40 different countries.

Teleroute claims to provide:

- more efficient and strategic transport planning and reduced empty running;
- flexible reaction to customers' needs;
- better load combinations;
- new UK and international contacts;
- improved time management;
- immediate results with only data that really matter;
- increased profitability through optimized efficiency;
- lower communication costs.

Contact: **www.teleroute.co.uk**.

The Data Protection Act 1998

The Data Protection Act 1998 is designed to protect living and identifiable persons from the misuse or unauthorized disclosure of any information about them, including the expression of any personal opinion. Thus firms or individuals such as self-employed road hauliers who hold personal data on file, especially in electronic – ie computerized – format, about employees, job applicants and customers, fall within the scope of the Act. Exemptions apply when information is held:

- by persons for their own family or domestic purposes;
- for historical or statistical research;
- in certain instances relating to journalism, art and literature;
- for the purposes of national security.

In road haulage, for example, if customer names and addresses held on file include the name of an individual person (such as the managing director, transport manager, etc) then such data falls within scope of the Act. The Act defines data as information that is:

- being processed by means of automatic equipment;

- recorded to be processed by such equipment;
- kept as part of a filing system, or with that intention;
- relating to certain health and associated records.

Processing of personal data means obtaining, recording or holding information or data or carrying out any operation on it, including its:

- organization, adaptation or alteration;
- retrieval, consultation or use;
- disclosure by transmission, dissemination or otherwise making it available;
- alignment, combination, blocking, erasure or destruction.

Special rules apply to the processing of 'sensitive' data such as an individual's racial origin.

Any firm or individual holding personal data must: 1) register with the Data Protection Commissioner; 2) conform to the data protection principles set out in the Act.

It is a criminal offence (punishable by a fine of up to £5,000) for an unregistered person to hold or disclose personal data about any person, and no processing of data should take place until after registration under the Act and an entry has been made in the Data Protection Register.

It is the responsibility of data controllers (ie those who process and determine the use of personal data) to operate within the terms of their Register entries. They can be held liable to pay compensation for any damage or associated distress suffered as a result of holding or disclosing inaccurate personal data.

On registration, a data controller must notify the Data Protection Commissioner of:

- the name and address of their principal place of business; in the case of limited companies, the address of the registered office;
- the name and address of any nominated representative for the purposes of the Act, where this differs from that of the company's registered office;
- a description of the personal data to be or being processed, and the category or categories of data subject to which they relate;
- a description of the purpose or purposes for which the data are to be or are being processed;
- a description of the recipients to whom the data will be disclosed;
- the names of countries outside the European Economic Area (EEA) to which the data controller will directly or indirectly transfer the data.

It is illegal for a registered data user to:

- hold personal data of any description other than that specified in their entry in the Data Protection Register;
- hold or use any such data for purposes other than those described in their entry;
- obtain or hold data, or the information to be contained in such data, from any source that is not described in the register entry;

- disclose the data they hold to any person who is not described in the register entry, or directly or indirectly transfer data they hold to any country or territory outside the EEA which does not have similar data protection laws.

The Act sets out eight so-called 'data protection principles' under which registered data users must ensure that data are:

1 processed fairly and lawfully;

2 used only for specified and lawful purposes;

3 adequate, relevant and not excessive;

4 accurate and up to date;

5 not kept longer than necessary;

6 processed in accordance with the rights of data subjects under the Act;

7 protected against unauthorized or unlawful processing and against accidental loss, destruction and damage;

8 not transferred outside the European Economic Area (EEA), unless an adequate level of protection exists for the rights and freedoms of data subjects.

Individuals who know or believe that a firm or organization holds information about them have a statutory right to request details of the information held. Thus, for example, an employee may ask his employer about the information held about himself. This is a right under the Data Protection Act and under other employment legislation. In the case of health records, some information must be statutorily provided on request. However, there are certain areas where information about data held will not be given, for example, by the police about their records while 'enquiries' are in progress.

Warnings

Two disturbing factors have come to light regarding application of the Data Protection Act, as follows.

First, road hauliers could face fines of up to £5,000 for operating unregistered CCTV systems in their premises for security purposes. Such systems must be registered under the Act and a £35 registration fee paid to the Information Commissioner (formerly the Data Protection Registrar).

Second, demands (including official-looking red 'Final Demands') for a £95 payment plus VAT by an organization called the Data Protection Act Registration Agency, and a number of similar names, have been shown to be a scam. The registration fee, legally due under the Act, is payable direct to the Information Commissioner and is only £35 except for very large companies (ie more than 250 staff and a turnover exceeding £25.9 million).

Transport and the Environment

24

O ne of the most important and widely discussed issues in transport continues to be the impact which the industry as a whole, and heavy lorries in particular, has on the environment. So-called 'green' issues feature in every aspect of transport operation, from the siting of vehicle depots to the routeing of heavy goods traffic and the disposal of certain loads, especially waste.

This *Handbook* charts in earlier chapters the legal requirements regarding choice of vehicle operating centres to satisfy 'O' licensing requirements, and the need for licence applicants to advertise their proposals in this regard and defend their premises against potential environmental representations from local residents. In the technical section, legal requirements concerning the emission of noise, smoke, fumes and exhaust pollutants are detailed (together with new information on qualifying for lower rates of VED with 'Reduced Pollution' vehicles), and in Chapter 20 the subject of waste carriage is covered with descriptions of the legal requirements regarding hazardous waste and the more recent legislation on 'controlled' waste – which is basically everyday waste emanating from commercial and industrial premises and is now subject to stringent control as to its carriage and disposal.

Many of the UK's major transport groups have developed clear environmental policies. These initiatives are concentrated mainly on fuel conservation at this stage, which has a direct payback benefit by way of cost savings and an indirect benefit in the shape of an improved company 'image', as well as achieving actual reductions in the amount of carbon dioxide which their respective company vehicles discharge into the atmosphere. This in turn helps to reduce global warming, which scientists have identified as being a problem of catastrophic proportions. However, there are many other ways in which these and other firms are contributing to the environmental effort, even down to the use of recycled paper for routine stationery needs, for example.

Major steps towards tackling the environment 'problem' have been taken with reports by the Royal Commission and more recently the Government's consultation documents on roads and on developing an integrated transport policy – both aiming to find ways of reducing traffic congestion and the adverse effects of air pollution from road traffic. These consultation exercises came to fruition in 1998 with a White Paper in which positive and sustainable solutions were put forward.

In the meantime, one step towards improving the environmental impact of transport and distribution operations has been taken by the Institute of Logistics with the publication of a three-part practical handbook covering three distinct aspects of the subject – namely, Volume 1, which deals with transport, Volume 2, which covers non-transport and specialized logistics operations, and Volume 3, which concerns environmental management.

Impact of Transport

Transport impacts on the environment in a variety of ways; some are more distinctly controllable by fleet operators than others; some produce more tangible benefits both to the vehicle operator and to the community than others; but it has to be remembered that, inevitably, any form of transport, serving any and every need imaginable, has an adverse impact on the environment. There is no such thing as a totally environmentally acceptable form or means of transport. What there can be, however, are means and systems of transport which are more 'friendly' towards the environment, and which can be controlled and managed in such a way that the environmental impact is minimized.

So far as transport operations are concerned the following list identifies some of the main areas of environmental impact which can be, and should be, challenged by management:

Vehicle Depots

- siting;
- noise, fumes, vibration and light emitted;
- disposal of waste.

Vehicle Operations

- engine, exhaust, tyre, body and load noise;
- smoke, fumes, gases, spray emitted;
- fuel/oil consumption;
- visual impact;
- routes and schedules;
- load utilization.

Oil Storage

Regulations, which came into effect from 1 September 2005 to protect against water pollution, will apply to road hauliers who store more than 200 litres of oil on any site that is located near to a river, waterway, borehole or even close to the water table. These regulations, the Control of Pollution (Oil Storage) Regulations 2001, require the person with custody of the oil to carry out such works or to take such precautions or actions as are necessary to minimize the risk of oil-related water pollution. The regulations specify technical details relating to the storage facility, particularly its bund base and wall, which must be checked regularly, and the pipework, valves and gauges. It is essential that the tank or its pipework is not positioned where there is a risk from vehicle impact, especially when reversing.

To prevent oil-contaminated water entering the public surface water sewer, an 'interceptor' should be incorporated into the operating centre's internal drainage system. This interceptor will separate the oil from the remainder of the surface water run-off. The unpolluted surface water will be allowed to leave the site and enter the public sewer, and the collected oil will be retained for safe collection and disposal by a waste-processing company.

Other products, such as fuel or chemicals that might be spilled, should also be prevented from entering the drainage system. Spill kits containing items such as retaining booms, absorbent granules and waste bags should be used to retain and mop up any spillages. The resultant polluted waste would have to be removed by a specialist waste-processing organization.

In addition to these more environmentally controllable aspects of transport, there are other aspects which have a powerful impact, but over which the transport manager has virtually no control, namely vehicle design and manufacture, road planning and building, legislative controls which are not necessarily environmentally oriented and customer demand, which is influenced more by commercial pressure and financial consideration than by the vehicle operator's quest to, among other things, reduce fuel consumption, deliver during non-congested times, or combine loads to improve vehicle efficiency.

Possible Solutions

Transport managers and small fleet operators are undoubtedly limited in the steps they can individually take towards improving the environment, but this does not mean they should take no steps at all. Simple measures are available to them which will make a valuable contribution. The following list provides just a few examples:

In the Depot

- Examine the way that waste material is stored and disposed of.
- Ensure that controlled waste (see Chapter 20) is correctly and safely stored on site and then handed over to licensed disposal contractors.
- Avoid burning of waste, which can cause pollution and lead to complaints.
- Ensure that recyclable material is identified and saved for proper disposal – including waste paper and packing materials from office and stores.

- Take steps to ensure that vehicle washing does not result in dirty (ie grease-laden) water draining on to neighbouring properties as well as into sewage systems.
- Ensure that oil and fuel spillages do not pollute drains.
- Consider the use of recycled products such as paper for administrative uses and packing.
- Undertake regular depot clean-up campaigns (in particular, ensuring that the outside appearance of the depot is 'environmentally friendly' to local residents, business visitors and others).

On the Vehicle

- Ensure that legal requirements regarding noise, smoke, exhaust emissions and spray suppression are fully complied with.
- Take steps to economize on fuel consumption.*
- Provide driver training to ensure courtesy and consideration on the road and the use of defensive driving methods* (which saves on wear costs).
- Fit speed limiters (now a legal requirement on certain vehicles – see Chapter 12).
- Ensure that drivers obey rules about parking and causing obstruction with their vehicles, and are aware of the problem of visual intrusion, noise and vibration on domestic properties (contravention of these matters can jeopardize 'O' licences – see Chapter 1).
- Route vehicles and plan journeys to avoid congestion – ensure full utilization of vehicles to avoid extra or unnecessary journeys (which add to congestion, air pollution, and the operator's own costs).
- Consider the visual impact of vehicles in terms of their general appearance and livery (change aggressive liveries to present a 'softer' image).

NB: These matters are discussed in more detail in Chapter 22.

In the Community

- Consider the sponsorship of local community efforts to improve the environment and encourage staff to undertake environmental protection projects.

The International Organization for Standardization (ISO) has developed a set of internationally recognized standards so that businesses can monitor and control the environmental effects of their activities. The key stages in developing an Environmental Management System in compliance with the ISO 14001 standard are as follows:

- Draw up an environmental policy.
- Set targets and make plans to achieve those targets.
- Implement the plans and ensure that information is communicated to all relevant staff.

- Measure results and compare these to the set targets, take corrective action where necessary and implement a system for regular reviews of the policy.

Natural Gas Vehicles

In an effort to make towns and cities cleaner and quieter places in which to live and work, the Government is making progress in cutting vehicle emissions and noise by encouraging greater use of cleaner vehicles.

A Government Minister speaking at the Commercial Vehicle show at the NEC in Birmingham in May 2002 said that natural gas vehicles are part of the solution, offering transport operators an opportunity to contribute to a cleaner, quieter environment as well as save money on their fuel bills. The Government is encouraging the wider availability of natural gas vehicles by offering demonstration grant funding through the Energy Saving Trust's 'TransportAction' initiative. This supports part of the cost of introducing new natural gas vehicles on to the market (see below).

Vehicles powered by natural gas – essentially the same product as used for domestic cooking and heating – can offer substantial environmental benefits, in particular compared with equivalent diesel vehicles. They are much quieter than diesel vehicles and emit lower levels of the two air pollutants of most concern in the UK, particulates and oxides of nitrogen.

Business Management in Transport

Quality Management

Increasingly, road hauliers are facing demands from customers, and from principal contractors, to meet recognized standards of quality assurance in the form of certification to the ISO 9000 series standard in the United Kingdom. This chapter outlines the basic requirements for meeting quality assurance standards to achieve recognized certification to these standards.

A great deal has been written about the subject of 'quality', and many myths have been spread, but it is quite simply the concept of doing things right first time, and right every time. This saves having to repeat operations at extra cost, and annoyance to the customer, whether in production of goods or the provision of a service – road haulage for example. It means supplying customers with the service they need, not what suppliers think they can best provide. In haulage, it means, particularly, providing cost-effective deliveries – on time, to the right address, with the load intact and undamaged and delivered by a courteous driver in a presentable vehicle. It does not mean a service which causes customer complaint.

The concept of 'quality' is not new. It has been applied to production for many years, especially by the Japanese, who have captured world markets for cars, motorcycles, electronics and cameras due to the inherent quality, reliability, durability and desirability of their products. Only more recently has the quality concept been applied to service industries, and particularly to road haulage. Achieving quality assurance (QA) certification involves complex steps, changed ideas, new thinking and acceptance that 'old ways' must be replaced by new methods, despite extra paperwork, form filling, writing of manuals, checking and rechecking of standards, and visits from inspectors. What are quality systems and quality management? A quality system is one where problems, queries, faults, and anything which could give rise to customer dissatisfaction or complaint, are identified and eliminated. Every aspect of operating procedure is critically examined to ensure that nothing unexpected (short of pure accident, and contingencies can even be established for these) can arise to jeopardize service to the customer. Quality management is the management of quality systems – a totally new way of doing business, hence the expression 'total quality management' (TQM).

Quality Assessment and Accreditation

Quality assessment and accreditation is the process by which a firm demonstrates to an accredited certification body that its services meet pre-established quality standards, followed by certification of this fact.

Accreditation

The British Standards Institution (BSI) standard for quality management systems is designated ISO 9000. This incorporates the provisions of both the International and European standards and is fully accepted in the member states of the European Community and the four European Free Trade Association (EFTA) members – Norway, Iceland, Switzerland and Liechtenstein.

Firms whose quality systems meet specified standards may register with an approved body and, on satisfactory completion of the formalities, receive accreditation 'Registered Firm' status when they may use the accreditation body's symbol of approval on its company literature (ie letterheads, brochures) and on vehicles. A road haulier quality accredited in the UK is additionally accepted as meeting both European and international quality standards, an essential ingredient for trading in the single European market.

Standards

The essence of a quality haulage service is that every step in fulfilling customer orders is undertaken in accordance with a documented standard – a set of rules governing the best way to operate and against which day-to-day operations are compared. Thus, performing to standard means performing as set out in the rules. BS 5750 is a standard for quality systems which identifies the basic disciplines and specifies the procedures and criteria to be applied to ensure that services are of a quality that will always meet specified customer requirements.

Assessment by Accreditation Certification Bodies

Assessment for accreditation involves a number of stages. Among these, one is the need to establish, document and maintain a quality system demonstrating a commitment to quality and to meeting customer service needs. Another is the selection of an appropriate accreditation body to which application for registration is made. This involves providing information about the business, its size and scope, the number of employees, how many locations are involved, the particular nature and manner of its operation and the services provided. Applicants must submit their documented quality system for examination and approval. The accreditation body checks this to ensure it covers all aspects of the quality system standard and then follows up with site visits to thoroughly review the operation in practice. These inspections – made by specialists in quality assessment – are a key element in quality assurance. Documented procedures are examined in detail and systems observed in operation to ensure that day-to-day procedures follow the documented quality system in every respect and comply with the laid-down standards of the accreditation body.

Monitoring

A process of continuous monitoring for compliance with standards is maintained through inspectors from the accreditation body making regular visits – up to four times each year. Any drop in performance will require renewed efforts to bring procedures back to standard. Continued failure to meet the standard will result in withdrawal of registration.

Establishing a Quality System

To establish a quality system within a firm, it is necessary to identify key aspects of the business where quality principles are to be applied and record precisely how these should be carried out. This is achieved by translating individual tasks into descriptive text in manual form, and by making step-by-step checklists or by establishing Codes of Practice. The key aspects will include:

- setting company policy and objectives for quality systems;
- determining the structure of the organization and responsibilities;
- preparing instructions and Codes of Practice for quality work standards;
- monitoring sub-contracted supplies and services for quality;
- establishing operational methods and controls to meet specified standards;
- inspection and monitoring of the transport service;
- controlling defective work;
- determining corrective actions before problems arise;
- measuring and recording quality performance;
- determining training requirements;
- establishing quality audit and review procedures.

Determining Customer Needs

Quality starts with the customer; the need to determine exactly what every customer wants. Never *assume* that one customer's service requirements are identical, or even remotely similar, to those of another. Each must be asked individually about his precise expectations when making enquiries and placing orders. They will differ widely: a customer may even have differing service requirements in differing circumstances. These requirements, whether few or many, whether standard in all circumstances or varying widely for individual consignments, must be clearly understood by the haulier, leaving no doubt whatsoever as to what is needed and expected in all circumstances. This information should be carefully recorded (and regularly updated) to form the basis for the quality system. It will become the standard against which all future responses to each customer's demands will be measured to ensure satisfaction.

The next step is to consider internal workings of the haulage operation to determine how these relate to the provision of a quality service. This task should be split into individual components or identifiable activities and for each there should be a documented set of procedures to be followed. The following are some examples of such activities:

- receipt of customer orders;
- planning daily work schedules;
- allocation of work to vehicles and drivers;
- preparation of collection/delivery note sets;
- instruction of drivers;
- preparation of vehicles;
- confirmations to customers;
- driver conduct on arrival;
- driver debriefing on completion of deliveries;
- recording/confirmation of work completed;
- invoicing.

Documenting the System

The individual tasks mentioned above – and many more if appropriate – should be written down in the form of checklists to ensure that no matter who takes the order, who allocates the vehicle or driver, who prepares the delivery notes or who carries out any other of these functions, the established step-by-step procedure is followed and no key element is missed which could lead to customer dissatisfaction. Documenting the system fully, effectively means preparation of a 'Quality Manual'.

Quality Procedures Manual

A quality procedures manual is a statement of the firm's commitment to quality, a constant reminder to management of their obligation to the firm's customers based on these documented procedures. It becomes the bible of operating practice for the staff, which has to be followed from when a customer first rings with an enquiry to when the job papers are finally filed away. It should detail:

- the organizational structure of the company;
- relationships between, and the responsibilities of, individual operating departments and functional managers;
- how the company's quality system is to work in practice:
  - every day;
  - every time an order is received;
  - every time a customer rings up;
  - every time a load is scheduled; and
  - every time a driver/vehicle is allocated to a job.

No matter what process or function is carried out, the manual should define it, who does it, how he does it, when, where and in what sequence, what follow-up action is carried out, by whom, to whom everyone reports in the event of difficulties or potential problems, what records are kept and so on. It is the ultimate guidebook to the firm: every single company operation is described, and cross-referenced to every other related function.

Mistakes may still be made, but the procedures manual should take account of such possibilities by detailing the action to be taken when errors are discovered (or pointed out by customers), and by whom, as well as to whom in the firm such matters should be reported, what reports should be written and to whom they are to be submitted. These 'failure reports' should be acted upon promptly, and details of the corrective action taken should also be recorded for future reference. By documenting failures, they should progressively be eliminated from the system.

Manuals within Manuals

A simple manual would have an opening section containing basic reference material as follows:

- firm's name;
- description of the business in which it is engaged (eg haulage of aggregates and excavated materials, also contract haulier to. . .);
- number of locations (eg one only or head office and vehicle base at. . .);
- general description of resources (eg 'x' number of vehicles/plant);
- names/functions of key departments (eg traffic/administration/workshop);
- names/titles of key managers/personnel;
- job descriptions for key positions (eg operations manager/fleet engineer/ company accountant/marketing manager);
- date(s) and name(s) of person(s) compiling manual;
- names of persons issued with the quality manual and those responsible for keeping it up to date;
- statement of firm's quality policy;
- name(s) of person(s) with ultimate responsibility for compliance with quality policy.

From this point, the manual could divide into sections covering each functional department (eg traffic operations/accounts and administration/workshop). For each there could be a general statement of departmental responsibility; the names, positions and individual responsibilities of key personnel; and the lines of reporting and communication (ie upwards to the company's top management or board of directors, downwards to supervisors, shift leaders, etc, and sideways by liaison with other departmental heads).

To compile the procedures manual, the work of each department must be examined in detail to see what current practices exist, who does what job (routine ones, special ones, urgent ones, etc), what controls are imposed and what safety procedures, if any, are followed to avoid failures (eg loads missed, jobs not invoiced, vehicles missing out on services, etc). Every step should be categorized within a functional heading (eg receipt of customer orders, recording orders on daily work sheets, allocating orders to vehicles, planning vehicle loads and so on) and the correct procedure for carrying out each step needs to be recorded. It is necessary to describe how details relating to the job should be entered, in what form or sequence, and the safety measures necessary to ensure that no essential information (eg a customer's special instructions) are missed.

The manual must be capable of being read – and the procedures understood and followed – by any member of the firm and by the inspector from the quality accreditation organization which checks the procedures. If the wording is tortuous and the manual littered with technical terms and unexplained abbreviations its point will be lost. For this reason manual writing demands the use of clear and simple language. Jargon should be avoided and technical terms kept to a minimum. When they are essential they should be defined or explained. Essential legal obligations (such as goods vehicle drivers' hours, tachographs, safe loading, etc) must be explained or cross-referenced to a source of detailed legal information.

Manuals in a form other than full-size pages in ring binders (eg pocket-size handbooks) may be more appropriate for drivers. These should detail the rules to be followed on drivers' hours, the correct use of tachographs, safe loading, dangerous load procedures, routine daily vehicle inspections, what to do in an emergency or the event of an accident and many other instructions. Workshop staff could have their own handbooks concentrating on safety procedures, what to do in the event of injury or accident, use of tools and equipment, procedures for drawing spare parts and consumable supplies and so on. Fitters who are required to road test vehicles should also be issued with a copy of the driver's handbook.

Other Documentation

Besides the main manual, other documentation systems are needed – a 'day book' in which to record customer orders, collection notes, delivery notes, receipt notes or combined consignment note sets, invoices, statements and suchlike. Many of the forms may relate to ongoing or periodic events such as the annual examination of employee driving licences; annual medical examinations and eyesight tests; inspections of safety equipment and safety signs, workshop equipment, fire-fighting equipment and first aid kits. Other forms would record company meetings with staff, drivers, workshop staff, and training sessions on new procedures or new legislation. Examples of all forms used should be included in the procedures manual to show which form to complete in any particular set of circumstances, where supplies of the form can be found, how it should be completed and what to do with it following completion.

Training to Achieve Quality Standards

All staff within a firm seeking quality accreditation should be properly trained to operate in accordance with specified quality procedures (ie to perform to standard). Management, staff and workers should be updated on the latest techniques and new developments. For example, heavy vehicle drivers may need refresher courses in driving skills to eradicate bad habits and training in efficient and economical driving techniques for new vehicles, or vehicle equipment such as new types of gearbox; they need reminders and updating on essential safety procedures and the use of safety equipment, on legal requirements (such as on drivers' hours rules and tachograph use) and on the use of mechanical loading aids.

At all levels from management to driver/operative, training improves job skills. Additionally, it contributes to the individual's motivation and job interest and provides an incentive to do that job better and take more of an interest in the firm's overall objectives – namely, to provide a quality service. The following list shows examples of training from which various grades of management and staff may benefit:

Top management –
> Management techniques.
> Sales/marketing/public relations.
> Control of people.
> Motivational skills.
> Employment legislation.
> Financial controls.
> Taxation matters.

Middle management –
> Administrative controls.
> Business systems.
> Computer familiarization.
> Management techniques.
> Motivational skills.
> Health and safety law.

Functional management –
> Transport legislation.
> Safety systems.
> Engineering skills.
> Computer techniques.
> Accounting practices.

Goods vehicle drivers –
    Economic driving.
    Safety procedures.
    Legal requirements.
    Dealing with customers.
    Dangerous loads requirements.

Loaders –
    Safety matters.

Forklift truck drivers –
    Driver training.
    Safety procedures.
    Truck maintenance.

Vehicle workshop staff –
    Safety procedures.
    Vehicle manufacturer training.
    Component training.
    First aid.

Administrative and secretarial staff –
    Office procedures.
    Computer.
    Telephone techniques.
    Use of office equipment (photocopiers/fax machines, etc).
    First aid.

While the range of courses and training opportunities is endless, there is a need to identify activities which demand acquired skills; for example, where special competence is legally required such as for goods vehicle vocational driving licences and dangerous goods training. These require priority over other training because failure could result in prosecution, or loss of operating licences.

Training Records

All training should be carefully recorded, whether a 30-minute in-company explanation of new legislation or the desired telephone answering techniques, or a longer external training course for management. This should show dates, who attended, who presented the training session, the duration, the location, the facilities/ aids used, the objectives of the session, the results achieved and any other relevant data, including any follow-up action necessary. Similarly, where staff achieve other qualifying standards as a result of company-sponsored incentives (eg attendance at evening or day-release classes or by home-study learning), or on a voluntary basis, these should be recorded.

Monitoring of Quality Standards

Successful operation of quality management systems involves a continuous monitoring process to ensure quality procedures are maintained and do not slip back into old inferior methods. A variety of monitoring methods may be employed. The establishment of Quality Circles is one, with groups or teams of volunteer employees meeting to discuss the application of quality, particularly in relationship to their own departments or work sections. They identify quality 'problem' areas and put forward suggestions as to possible solutions.

In the small firms, where the cost structure does not warrant full-time monitoring, two methods in particular will ensure that standards are maintained. The first is regular monitoring of customers' perception of the quality of service they are receiving; customers should be asked to point out any deficiencies and their answers noted, analysed and corrective action taken. Second, maintaining full and clear communication in the firm will ensure that everybody, from top to bottom, is on the same quality wavelength and working towards the same goals. In this way the whole firm will feel united in the quest for total quality management.

Further Information

Further information on the establishment of quality systems in road haulage may be obtained from the following:

British Standards Institution (BSI)
Business Development Advice
Tel: 020 8996 9001
Website: **www.bsigroup.co.uk**

Department for Business, Innovation and Skills (BIS)
Tel: 020 7215 5000
Website: **www.bis.gov.uk**

Debt Collection

The Late Payment of Commercial Debts (Interest) Act 1998, which came into force on 1 November 1998, allows small businesses to claim interest on commercial debts that relate to the supply of goods and services that are paid late. It does not apply to consumer debt. In effect, interest becomes chargeable from the day after the agreed date for payment. Where no specific date has been agreed for payment, interest becomes payable after 30 days from either: 1) the date on which the contract was formed; or 2) the date of invoice, or notice of the amount of the debt (whichever is the later).

For these purposes, small businesses are limited liability companies with an annual turnover not exceeding £2.8 million or a balance sheet value not exceeding £1.4

million, or if they are not an incorporated limited company, they should have no more than 50 employees. This obviously includes many road haulage businesses and some own-account vehicle operators.

The rate of interest chargeable is the bank base rate plus 8 per cent.

The Act is being implemented in stages, the first part having been applied since 1 November 1998 to small businesses as mentioned above; the second part having been applied since November 2000, allowing small businesses to claim against all businesses and the public sector. The final part was implemented from 7 August 2002, since when all businesses and the public sector have been able to claim interest from all other businesses.

Insolvency

People often refer to a company being insolvent, but what does that actually mean? It is important at the outset to establish exactly what form of insolvency you are dealing with. Each type of insolvency has its own specific office holder, who has differing obligations, duties and powers. This will undoubtedly affect how you act, and whether or not you have any chance of recovery of a debt from that company.

Administration

The holder of office is called 'the administrator' and is appointed by the court following a petition. His aim is either to achieve the survival of the company and the realization of assets and liquidation, or to enable a Company Voluntary Arrangement. The effect is a moratorium preventing any creditor action. While the administrator owes a duty to creditors in general, he will not agree creditors' claims, nor has he the power to distribute funds to the creditors.

Administrative Receivership

The holder of office is called 'the receiver' and is appointed by someone holding a debenture over (substantially) all the assets and undertaking of the company. The receiver's aim is to continue trade with a view to sale of the business as a going concern. The directors remain in office, albeit the receiver has day-to-day control of the business. There is no moratorium preventing creditor action, but the administrative receiver's duty is solely to get in and realize the assets of the company, sufficient to repay the indebtedness of the debenture holder.

Liquidation

There are different types of liquidation. These are:

- compulsory liquidation;
- creditors' voluntary liquidation;

- members' voluntary liquidation; and
- pre-pack administration.

In the first three cases the office holder is called 'the liquidator', but his appointment is different, depending on what type of liquidation it is.

- In the case of compulsory liquidation the company is placed in liquidation by the court following the making of a winding-up order.
- In the case of creditors' voluntary liquidation, the liquidator is appointed by the directors/shareholders where the company is insolvent and unable to pay its debts.
- In the case of members' voluntary liquidation, the liquidator is appointed by the directors/shareholders where the directors have sworn a statutory declaration of insolvency. The aim of the liquidation is to realize assets, shut down the company and distribute the assets in accordance with a strict order of priority.

With company voluntary arrangement (CVA), the office holder is called 'the supervisor' and his rights and powers are set out in a document entitled *the proposal*, which is put to and voted upon by the company's creditors. The company can, and invariably will, trade under the auspices of a CVA, which is often used to effect a reconstruction or reorganization of the company's trading enterprise. The proposal that leads to the making of the CVA forms a private contract between the company and its creditors. If the proposal is approved, creditors are bound to accept the terms in full and final settlement of their indebtedness.

Insolvency Pre-Pack Administration

An insolvency pre-pack is a deal whereby an insolvent (ie company's assets) are sold, or a deal for their sale, is negotiated before the company actually goes into formal insolvency. The deal to sell the business (eg to the management, the staff or others), usually as a going concern will have invariably been agreed before the Insolvency Practitioner is appointed, but it will be executed by the Insolvency Practitioner shortly after his appointment. If the conditions are appropriate, a pre-pack can be advantageous for all involved, and can be the best way of extracting value from a dire situation.

Pre-packs mean a business can be sold without negative publicity, which could destroy the value of the business and lead to loss of customers and staff. This is often the case with haulage companies which are owner-managed businesses and where most of the value is in key staff who may leave, or assets that may lose considerable value once the administration or liquidation process is announced. Hence, the business is usually sold with little or no open market promotion. Unsecured creditors are normally only informed of the pre-pack after it has been completed. By contrast secured creditors are often aware of the transaction ahead of the formalized deal as it will generally require them to release their security.

The main advantage of pre-pack insolvency is that the debts of the business remain with the old company and therefore the new (often called a 'phoenix' company) can start again with a clean slate. At the point when the sale is agreed the existing company will move into Administration or Liquidation and the new company will start trading immediately. Therefore, the whole process will be seamless to the business, the staff and the customers.

The Competition Act

The Competition Act 1998, which came into force on 1 March 2000, is designed to ensure that UK businesses remain competitive. It applies to all businesses irrespective of the trade in which they are engaged and their size. It even applies to sole traders such as owner-driver road hauliers.

Principally, the Act prohibits anti-competitive agreements and abuse of a dominant position in the market.

Anti-Competitive Agreements

The prohibition on anti-competitive agreements covers agreements and practices that prevent, restrict or distort competition, or are intended to do so. These can be formal or informal, written or not. In particular, they include agreements to:

- fix purchase or selling prices or other trading conditions;
- limit or control production, markets, technical development or investment;
- share markets or sources of supply;
- apply different trading conditions to equivalent transactions, which will put some parties at a competitive disadvantage;
- make contracts subject to unrelated supplementary conditions.

The effect of an agreement must be 'appreciable' to be caught by the Act. There are certain exemptions and exclusions.

Abuse of a Dominant Position

Whether a business is in a dominant position will depend on how much it can act independently of its competitors and customers. As a general rule, a dominant position is unlikely if its market share is less than 40 per cent. This will, however, depend on the structure of the market. Examples of abuse are:

- imposing unfair purchase or selling prices or other unfair trading conditions;
- limiting production, markets or technical development to the prejudice of consumers;
- applying different trading conditions to equivalent transactions, which will put some parties at a competitive disadvantage;
- making contracts subject to unrelated supplementary conditions.

The Director-General of Fair Trading has wide-ranging powers to investigate suspected breaches of the law. His officials can enter premises and demand relevant documents, and may even get a warrant to make a search. They can order offending agreements or conduct to be terminated. Businesses can be fined up to 10 per cent of their UK turnover; prohibited agreements will be made void and unenforceable, and any third party harmed by an unlawful agreement or conduct may be able to sue for damages.

If Your Business Is a Victim of Unfair Competition

A complaint may be made to the Office of Fair Trading (OFT) by anyone who suspects that the competition rules are being broken. This may be in writing or by telephone and the complainant's identity may be protected although evidence will be needed to back up any such complaint. The OFT may launch a formal investigation if there are reasonable grounds for suspecting that an offence is being or has been committed.

Where a business finds that it is part of an illegal cartel and provides information voluntarily to the OFT, it may receive a significant reduction in any financial penalty imposed or, if it is the first to notify the OFT of the situation, it may gain complete immunity from financial penalty.

Further information can be obtained from:

The Office of Fair Trading
Field House Room 107
15–25 Bream's Buildings
London EC4A 1PR
e-mail: **enquiries.competitionact@oft.gov.uk**

International Haulage

S ince the removal of barriers to inter-Community trading from January 1993, UK road hauliers have been largely free to operate, uninhibited, across the whole of the EU, which now comprises 27 countries and a consumer market of some 490 million people.

Transport Implications

The transport implications of the single European market (SEM) are very significant and whole new horizons have been opened up. In the past, road freighting across Europe was impeded by restrictive Customs procedures and road haulage permit requirements resulting in excessive administrative burdens, frustrating delays and inhibiting costs. In the wider arena of distribution, past inhibition has been rather more to do with the inability to trade across frontiers. Now, with all these constraints swept away, road freighting into Europe and the setting up of Euro-wide distribution networks is basically no more complex and no more fraught with bureaucracy than operating in the domestic marketplace. Our concepts of what is 'local' and what is 'regional' in terms of distribution are undergoing considerable change.

NB: In 2009, 2.38 million goods vehicles travelled from the United Kingdom to mainland Europe (14 per cent lower than the 2008 figure).

Entry to the International Road Haulage Market

Access to the European haulage market is governed solely by a system of quality licences much on the lines of the present UK scheme of operators' licensing – which was amended in 1978 to align with the original EU requirement for establishment of a professional competence qualification for those wanting access to the road haulage industry. Entrants to the haulage business must meet standards of good repute, financial standing and professional competence, and the granting of licences is dependent on satisfactory proof that these standards are met. Past convictions, mainly, but not exclusively, for transport and vehicle-related offences will result in licence penalty – even revocation – and inability to sustain adequate finances will have a similar effect. Licence holders have to prove resources or provide financial guarantees (this topic is dealt with in detail in Chapter 1).

Community Authorization

A system of 'Community Authorizations' was implemented from 1 January 1993 enabling EU road hauliers to operate freely (ie to undertake as many journeys as they wish) *between* member states* – not to be confused with the quite separate cabotage authorizations which are needed by hauliers wishing to collect and deliver goods *within* EU member states other than their own (see below). International hauliers operating within the EU (apart from when operating domestically within their own state) must hold a Community Authorization issued by the transport authority in their own member state.

NB: Valid Community Authorizations also permit cross-border operations into three European Economic Area (EEA) states – namely, Liechtenstein, Norway and Iceland.

It is important to note the continuing requirement for bilateral and ECMT permits (see p 578) for road haulage journeys *outside* the EU (and the three EEA states mentioned above) and for international furniture removals, and the particular requirements relating to journeys to and through Austria which are described later in this chapter.

Regulation 881/92/EEC

The system of Community Authorizations for intra-EU road haulage operations is established under Council Regulation (EEC) 881/92 and implemented in the UK by the Goods Vehicles (Community Authorisations) Regulations 1992 (SI 1992 No 3077). Regulation 881/92 amended earlier legislation (ie Council Regulation (EEC) 3164/76 as amended by Council Regulations (EEC) 1841/88 on Access to the Market in the International Carriage of Goods by Road) by effectively introducing qualitative criteria in place of the previous system of quantitative restriction. The qualitative criteria are as specified in Council Regulation (EEC) 561/74 as amended by Council Regulation (EEC) 438/89, namely a requirement that the road haulage operator be of good repute, of adequate financial standing and professionally competent in road haulage operations.

Issue of Community Authorizations

Community Authorizations are issued in the UK by the Traffic Commissioners (TCs) on an automatic basis to all standard international operator ('O') licence holders (ie there is no need for UK operators to make separate application for these authorizations). It should be noted that such 'O' licences are granted only to those applicants who fully satisfy the qualitative standards of the EU, in other words the legal requirements for good repute, adequate financial standing and professional competence in road haulage operations.

The authorization comprises an original document to be retained safely at the licence holder's main place of business, and a number of certified true copies equalling the total number of vehicles authorized on the operator's licence. One of the certified true copies of the authorization must be carried in each vehicle undertaking international journeys within the EU. Community Authorizations and the certified true copies carried on vehicles must be produced for inspection on request. Failure to do so, and to carry the certified true copy on a vehicle while on an international journey within the EU, is an offence.

Penalties for Infringement of the Law

UK-based international hauliers who jeopardize their 'O' licences by failing to meet the requirements of good repute, financial standing or professional competence also jeopardize their Community Authorization. In other words, where circumstances arise which, as a result of infringement of the law or failure to meet the qualitative requirements of good repute, financial standing and professional competence, require the TC to suspend, curtail or revoke an 'O' licence, the Community Authorization will also be automatically suspended, curtailed or withdrawn (ie revoked). The precise action taken by the TC will depend on the seriousness of the offence or offences. Serious or repeated minor infringement of carriage regulations (ie the Community Authorization regulation itself) will result in temporary or partial suspension of the certified true copies of the authorization.

In member states where 'O' licences of the type issued in the UK or its equivalent are not used, failure by international hauliers based in those states to meet (or maintain) the standards of good repute, financial standing and professional competence required under the EU regulation will, nevertheless, result in jeopardy of the Community Authorization.

It is a specific requirement of the regulation that where one member state becomes aware of infringement of Community Authorization legislation by a haulier from another member state, it shall inform the authorities in that member state and may ask that state to impose sanctions on the haulier in accordance with the regulations (ie for temporary or partial suspension of certified copies or withdrawal of the Community Authorization).

Validity and Duration of Authorizations

Community Authorizations are made out in the original licence holder's name and are not transferable to any third party and remain valid while the 'O' licence is in force unless otherwise revoked. Certified copies, as mentioned above, must be carried on the relevant vehicle when on an international journey and must be produced by the driver for examination whenever he is required to do so by an authorized inspecting officer.

On the expiry of a Community Authorization after five years, it is a requirement that the issuing authority (ie in the UK, the TC) must verify whether the operator still satisfies the legal conditions for its issue. Since these conditions are identical to those on which renewal of the haulier's 'O' licence depends, namely good repute, financial standing and professional competence, in the UK at least, operators whose 'O' licences are renewed can rest assured that their Community Authorization will be automatically renewed at the same time.

Community Authorization Documents

Annex I to EU Regulation (EEC) 881/92 specifies a model for the Community Authorization, the front page of which contains details of the haulier (ie name and full address), the date from which it is valid and the name of the authority by whom it is issued and the date of issue; on the rear are printed the general provisions for the use of such authorizations, in particular that while within the territory of any member state the holder (ie both the road haulage operator and the vehicle driver) must comply with the 'laws, regulations and administrative provisions in force in that state', especially in regard to transport and traffic.

Exemptions from Community Authorization Procedure

Certain transport operations are specifically exempt from the requirement for Community Authorizations in accordance with Annex II to the EU regulation as follows:

- Carriage of mail as a public service.
- Carriage of vehicles which have suffered damage or breakdown.
- Carriage of goods in vehicles with a permissible laden weight (including that of any trailer drawn) which does not exceed 6 tonnes or the maximum permitted payload of which does not exceed 3.5 tonnes.
- Carriage of goods* in vehicles owned (including hired) by an own-account firm solely for its own purposes and where the transport is no more than ancillary to its overall activities and where the vehicle is driven only by an employee of the firm.
  * NB: *The goods concerned may be the property of the firm, or have been sold, bought, let out on hire or hired, produced, extracted, processed or repaired by the firm.*
- Carriage of medicinal products, appliances, equipment and other articles required for medicinal care in emergency relief, in particular for natural disasters.

Road Haulage Cabotage

Cabotage operation is provided for under the Treaty of Rome.

Cabotage is quite simply internal haulage by foreign transport operators – the collection and delivery of goods by road within a country by a road haulier whose business is established in another country. The significance of cabotage, of course, is that it protects internal haulage markets against incursion – or in this case the abstraction of domestic traffics – by outsiders (see below). Hence the reason why, hitherto, it has always been an illegal practice, but now, with the liberalization policies of the SEM in force, such restrictive practices have been swept away and road freight cabotage within EU member states is permitted by regulation.

Cabotage by EU own-account road transport operators is permitted, but only on the same basis as defined above (ie the fourth item under exemptions from Community Authorization requirements).

The New Cabotage Regime

New EU rules on road haulage cabotage came into effect from 14 May 2010 in accordance with articles 8 and 9 of Regulation 1072/2009/EC. This follows many years of discussion within the EU and much uncertainty for international road hauliers who have not known what, precisely, the cabotage rules allowed and prohibited.

For the purposes of this regulation, cabotage is defined as 'national carriage for hire or reward carried out on a temporary basis in a host Member State in conformity with this regulation'.

Under these new regulations, international road hauliers holding a Community Licence (issued to UK-based hauliers by the Traffic Commissioners to holders of international 'O' licences), and whose driver, if he is a national of a third country, holds a Driver Attestation document in accordance with the same regulation (ie Article 5 of 1072/2009/EC), is permitted to undertake cabotage operations. This means that they may carry out national road haulage for hire or reward on a temporary basis (ie not regularly) within a Member State other than the one in which they are registered. But in so doing they must comply with the legal requirements on road traffic applicable in the host country.

Within a period of seven days following on from the delivery of an incoming loaded international journey into the Member State, road hauliers may undertake three loaded domestic journeys within that other Member State, using the same vehicle, provided the work is not permanent or continuous. It is emphasized that the last unloading in the course of a cabotage operation before the haulier leaves the host country must take place within seven days from the last unloading of goods comprising the incoming international journey.

It should be noted that cabotage work is not permissible if:

- the activity is permanent and exercised continually and regularly;
- the activity is carried out systematically and not just on an ad hoc basis;
- the activity involves a vehicle belonging to a non-resident haulier, where the vehicle in question never left the territory of the host state.

Hauliers are required to be able to provide suitable clear evidence of their compliance with the rules – ie of the incoming international journey and of the subsequent cabotage journeys carried out. For these purposes the following information is required as evidence:

a the name, address and signature of the sender;

b the name, address and signature of the haulier;

c the name and address of the consignee as well as his signature and the date of delivery once the goods have been delivered;

d the place and the date of taking over of the goods and the place designated for delivery;

e the description in common use of the nature of the goods and the method of packing, and, in the case of dangerous goods, their generally recognized description, as well as the number of packages and their special marks and numbers;

f the gross mass of the goods or their quantity otherwise expressed;

g the number plates of the motor vehicle and trailer.

Additionally, hauliers engaging in cabotage operations must observe the law and administrative provisions in force in host Member States relating to, among other things:

- the conditions governing transport contracts (these should be checked to see if any particular conditions apply);
- the maximum weights and dimensions of road vehicles permitted in host states for national traffic – these limits must not be exceeded even if limits in the haulier's home country are greater;
- the requirements relating to the carriage of certain categories of goods, in particular dangerous goods, perishable foodstuffs and live animals;
- drivers' hours law and tachograph records;
- VAT on transport services (VAT has to be charged at the rate applicable in the country of operation (ie the host country) – this may require the haulier to be VAT registered in each country in which he proposes to carry out cabotage operations or to appoint an agent for VAT purposes in these countries).

VAT on Cabotage Operations

Internal transport operations under cabotage authorization require operators to comply with national VAT regulations. For this purpose, operators may need to register in the member states in which they are operating or appoint a suitable VAT agent or fiscal representative to handle these matters on their behalf.

Road Haulage Permits

Certain road haulage operations from the UK and other EU member states to non-EU member states still require the issue of a bilateral road haulage permit. At the present time road haulage journeys to or through Belarus, Georgia, Kazakhstan, Morocco, Russia, Tunisia, Turkey and Ukraine require such permits for specified transport operations. Third-country permits are required for journeys from either Germany or Romania.

Bilateral road haulage permits are not required for transport operations within the EU. However, hauliers on transit journeys across Community territory to non-EU destinations must be in possession of a Community Authorization.

Permits are available from VOSA in Cambridge. **www.dft.gov.uk/vosa/forms**.

Validity of Permits

Where bilateral road haulage permits are required as described above, such permits are available covering single journeys only, allowing just *one* return journey to be undertaken between the dates shown on the permit. Outside of these dates the permit is invalid and it would be illegal to commence or continue the journey. In the case of Turkey, single journey permits as described above are available as well as multiple journey permits authorizing four journeys.

Third-Country Traffic

Third-country traffic, which is the carriage of goods between two countries other than the country in which the vehicle is registered, is permissible in certain cases (ie between any EU country) but not in others. For UK hauliers, journeys are permissible between any two EU countries.

NB: Permits valid for third-country traffic are available and full details can be obtained from VOSA.

Issue of Permits

Road haulage permits where necessary as described above are issued by the relevant authority in each member state. Normally, this involves completion of application forms, advance payment of the relevant fee and submission by the applicant of a copy of his authority to operate (eg his Community Authorization).

Return of Used Permits

Used and expired permits must be returned to the issuing authority not later than 15 days after the relevant journey has been completed or the permit expiry date, whichever is earlier.

Journey record sheets issued with period permits (eg the four-journey permit for Turkey) must be returned within the same timescale.

Lost or Stolen Permits

Road haulage permits are valuable transit documents and as such should be treated with care and appropriate security. They are not transferable to another operator and such misuse is illegal throughout the Community, with harsh penalties imposed on offenders (see also below). Replacement of lost or stolen permits is not normally automatic, and in any case a full written explanation of the circumstances surrounding the loss or theft is required, together with a copy of the police report.

Journeys to or through Non-Agreement Countries

If vehicles are to travel to or through a country with which an EU member state has no agreement, permission to operate in that country has to be sought direct from its transport authority. Application should be made well before the journey is due and full details of the vehicle, the load and the route should be given.

ECMT/ITF Multilateral Permits

NB: *The former European Conference of Ministers of Transport (ECMT), which had existed since 1953, has been transformed into a new intergovernmental organization called the International Transport Forum (ITF). Its principal aim is to help both policymakers and the general public gain a deeper understanding of the essential role played by transport.*

A number of ECMT/ITF permits are allocated to the UK for haulage journeys between ECMT member countries (ie all EU member states plus (as at 1 January 2009): Albania, Armenia, Azerbaijan, Belarus, Bosnia-Herzegovina, Croatia, FYR Macedonia, Georgia, Malta, Moldova, Montenegro, Norway, Russian Federation, Serbia, Switzerland and Turkey.

These ECMT/ITF permits allow journeys between member countries, including laden or empty transit journeys and third-country journeys to other ECMT countries, which are prohibited by certain bilateral agreements. However, they cannot be used for transit of ECMT countries on journeys to non-ECMT states or for cabotage. They are for hire or reward journeys only and may not be used by unaccompanied trailers or semi-trailers. They are valid for one calendar year and allow an unlimited number of journeys within that period, but they may be used with only one vehicle at a time. The quota for their issue is limited, so these permits are allocated before the beginning of the year in which they are issued. Usually no further supplies are available during the course of the year, but should the quota be increased an announcement is made in the trade press.

ECMT Removals Permits

These permits are quota-free and can be used for international removals between, or crossing, ECMT member countries. They are available only to firms employing the specialized equipment and staff needed to undertake such operations and are valid for one year from the date of issue.

Details available from **www.businesslink.gov.uk**.

Permit Checks

As a result of the exposure of a number of cases of permit frauds, stringent regulations exist to prevent vehicles on international journeys travelling without valid permits (where relevant – see above) and checks are made on vehicles to ensure that these regulations are complied with. A vehicle will be prevented from continuing its journey if it does not carry a valid permit. In the UK it is an offence to forge or alter permits, to make a false statement to obtain a permit or to allow one to be used by another person.

Own-Account Transport Operations

Own-account transport operations within Community territory (including cabotage as defined above) are now free from all bilateral permit requirements (under the provisions of EU Regulation 881/92 Annex II) provided that goods are carried solely in connection with the trade or business of the vehicle user and are not carried for hire or reward, and that the following conditions are also met:

- The goods carried must be the property of the business (of the vehicle user) or must have been sold, bought, let out or hired, produced, extracted, processed or repaired by the business.
- The purpose of the journey must be to carry the goods to or from the business or to move them, either within the business or outside for its own needs.
- Motor vehicles used for the carriage must be driven by employees of the business.
- The vehicles carrying the goods must be owned by the business, bought on deferred terms or hired by it (this does not apply where a replacement vehicle is used during a short breakdown of the vehicle normally used).
- Road haulage must not be the major activity of the business.

Own-account operations between the UK, Austria, Cyprus and Hungary are free from permit requirements but in the case of such journeys, drivers should carry on the vehicle a document containing the following information to confirm that the operation is solely for own-account purposes:

- The name and address of the vehicle operator (ie user).
- The nature of the operator's trade or business.
- The nature of the goods being carried.
- The location of the loading and unloading points.
- The registration number of the vehicle on which the goods are carried.
- Details of the route to be followed.

In all cases, own-account vehicle operators (and their drivers) should be aware that they may be asked to provide satisfactory evidence to help the authorities to determine the ownership of the goods and that they are being carried solely for own-account purposes.

International Carriage of Goods by Road – CMR

Transport operators – whether just a one-man haulage business (ie owner-driver) or a large firm – carrying goods for reward on international road haulage journeys must comply* with the Convention on the Contract for the International Carriage of Goods by Road 1956 (*Convention Relative au Contrat de Transport International de Marchandises par Route* – commonly referred to as the CMR Convention). This Convention is applied in the UK under English law by the provisions of the Carriage of Goods by Road Act 1965. The Convention defines the carriers' liability and the documents to be carried on vehicles engaged in the international movement of goods between different countries, of which at least one is a party to the CMR Convention.

* NB: Since, in effect, CMR applies automatically to an international road haulage journey, the haulier has no choice in the matter – but may be carrying out the operation in ignorance of this fact.

The following countries are party to the CMR convention: Austria, Belgium, Bulgaria, the Czech Republic, Denmark, Finland, France (including its overseas territories), Germany, Gibraltar, Greece, Hungary, Italy, Luxembourg, the Netherlands, Norway, Poland, Portugal, Romania, Slovakia, Spain, Sweden, Switzerland, United Kingdom (including Northern Ireland), and the former Yugoslavia.

Applicable Law

International conventions such as CMR override the relevant provisions of national law but only insofar as they cover the point at issue. However, not all points of issue that may arise by way of dispute or claim out of a contract for international carriage are covered by the CMR Convention, in which case relevant national law would apply (basically this means the law of the country in which the dispute or claim arose and to whose courts the matter is referred). In deciding the outcome of any dispute or claim, the courts may refer to either the French or English language texts of the Convention although the French text is not reproduced in the schedule to the Carriage of Goods by Road Act 1965. When referring to this Act, a court is still free to consider the French language version of the Convention for clarification should difficulty be found in determining the precise meaning of any aspect of the English text.

Non-CMR Operations and Journeys

For the CMR Convention to apply there must be clear evidence of a contract for the international carriage of goods for reward. In other words, the carriage of goods on an international journey at no charge, and therefore outside of a contract for carriage as specified in the Convention, would not be covered by CMR. Furthermore, the carriage must be of *goods* to allow the Convention to apply.

Besides these exclusions arising from defining the precise terms of applicability, the Convention has a number of more specific exemptions. Namely, its terms do not apply to:

- own-account operations which involve international journeys;
- furniture removals;
- funeral consignments which are transported abroad;
- carriage under an International Postal Convention.

The Convention is also *not* applicable in respect of international haulage operations between the United Kingdom (including Northern Ireland) and the Republic of Ireland, or to contracts for the carriage of goods between the UK mainland and the Channel Islands (ie Guernsey, Jersey, Alderney, Sark and Herm) such operations not being legally classed as international journeys. Cabotage journeys (ie internal journeys within a country by a road haulier from another country) are also outside the provisions of the CMR.

Basic Requirements of CMR

The CMR Convention automatically applies to every contract for the international carriage of goods by road in vehicles for reward, even when the vehicle containing the goods is carried over part of its journey by sea, rail or inland waterway, although other conventions may also apply and take precedence over CMR. A CMR-type consignment note must be completed for the journey. There is no escape from the Convention's provisions and road hauliers may not opt out (by agreement with consignors or otherwise) from its legal (ie liability) requirements. Thus, for example, if a road haulier was induced to carry goods for reward on an international journey knowing nothing of the CMR and its provisions and his consequential liability responsibilities, and even without a CMR consignment note in force, the provisions of the Convention would still apply. Should a legal dispute or claim subsequently arise he could be liable to pay substantial compensation not covered by his domestic Goods in Transit insurance policy.

Even in circumstances where a road haulier may not be aware that a load being carried on one of his vehicles is destined to continue on, or has previously been moved on, an international journey, and where he is not aware of the conditions and implications of CMR, the Convention's provisions still apply. This is particularly relevant where loaded articulated semi-trailers are collected or delivered – it is the load and that part of the vehicle which are together at the time of crossing national boundaries which determines that a particular journey is legally an international journey to which CMR applies. The Convention is not relevant where containers are carried domestically after having been transferred from the vehicle or rail wagon which crossed national boundaries; or where loads are trans-shipped between the vehicle which undertook the international part of the journey (to which CMR did apply), and local delivery vehicles (to which CMR does not apply).

CMR Conditions for International Road Haulage Journeys

An outline of the principal conditions of the Convention is given here:

1 The Convention applies to every contract for carriage of goods, whether wholly by road or partly by road and partly by rail, sea or inland waterway, as long as the goods remain in the original vehicle, on a journey from one country

to another, one of which is a contracting party to the Convention (with the exception of UK–Eire and UK mainland–Channel Islands journeys which are ruled not to be international journeys for this purpose). Exemptions to CMR apply to carriage under international postal conventions, funeral consignments and furniture removals.

2 The carrier (ie road haulier) is responsible under the Convention for the actions and omissions of his agents and any other persons whose services are used in carrying out the movement. Even if the original road haulier contracted to undertake the movement sub-contracts the whole of the operation to another road haulier (whose name appears on the CMR consignment note) the first (original) haulier remains fully liable under CMR should a dispute or claim arise. This can present problems in a case where, for example, the first (original) haulier operates only in domestic transport and thus is covered only by, say, Road Haulage Association Conditions of Carriage and is insured accordingly – not being insured to the much higher CMR level of liability.

3 A contract for the international carriage of goods for reward is confirmed by making out a CMR consignment note in three original copies which should be signed by the sender and carrier. Each keeps a copy and the third copy travels on the vehicle with the goods. While a CMR consignment note confirms that a contract exists, the absence of, or failure to raise such a note does not invalidate the contract or dis-apply the terms of the Convention.

4 If the goods are carried under a single contract in different vehicles or are divided owing to their different nature, the carrier or the sender can specify that a separate consignment note should be made out for each vehicle or each load of goods.

5 The consignment note must contain certain specified details (see pp 582–84) and may also contain additional information of use to the parties to the contract. It must state that the carriage is subject to CMR. Although not a 'title' to the goods, the consignment note is evidence of the facts it contains (ie the details shown are presumed to be correct), such as the number of packages, etc, and any claim which disputes such facts would have to be backed by substantial independent evidence to the contrary. Normally a standard note such as that available from the International Road Transport Union (IRU) is used (or in the UK from the Road Haulage Association or the Freight Transport Association – both IRU members).

6 The sender is responsible for all expenses, loss and damage sustained by the carrier as a result of inaccuracies in completion of the consignment note in relation to information supplied by him – even if the road haulier completes the note from information given to him by the sender.

7 On receipt of the goods, the carrier must check the accuracy of the details shown in the consignment note, particularly, for example, as to the number of packages, the apparent condition of the goods, their packaging and how they are marked. Any discrepancies or comments about other relevant matters such as the condition of the goods or packages should be noted by a 'reservation' on the note. Should the sender request the carrier to check the contents of

packages or to have the consignment weighed he must reimburse the carrier any costs incurred in doing so.

8 The sender is liable to the carrier for damage and expenses due to defective packing of the goods unless the defects were known to the carrier when taking over the goods and he indicated this fact by way of a 'reservation' on the note. The absence of such a reservation means that the carrier, if he was aware of the damage, accepted any likely risks of subsequent claims.

9 The sender must attach to the consignment note or make available to the carrier the necessary documents to complete Customs formalities. The sender is liable to the carrier for any damage caused by the absence, inadequacy or irregularity of such documents.

10 The sender has the right of disposal of the goods and may stop transit of the goods or change the delivery address up to the time of delivery to the consignee unless he has stated on the consignment note that the consignee has this right. Once the goods are delivered to the address on the consignment note, the consignee has the right of disposal.

11 A carrier who fails to follow the instructions on the consignment note or who has followed them without requesting the first copy of the consignment note to be produced is liable for loss or damage caused by such failure.

12 The carrier must provide the consignee with a second copy of the consignment note at the time of delivering the goods.

13 If the carrier cannot follow the instructions on the consignment note for any reason, he must ask the sender or the consignee, depending on who has the right of disposal (see item 10 above), for further instructions.

14 The carrier is liable for the total or partial loss of the goods and for any damage to them occurring between the time when he takes over the goods and the time of their delivery unless the loss, damage or delay was caused by a wrongful act or neglect of the claimant. The burden of proof in this case rests with the carrier.

15 Failure to deliver goods within 30 days of a specified time limit, or within 60 days from the time when the first carrier took them over if there is no time limit for delivery, results in the goods being considered to be lost.

16 When goods of a dangerous nature are consigned, the carrier must be informed of the nature of the danger and the precautions to be taken.

17 Calculation of compensation in the event of loss or damage is related to the value of the goods at the place and time they were accepted for carriage but will not exceed a set value (ie related to SDR – see p 582 for explanation).

18 Carriage charges, Customs duties and other charges in respect of the carriage are refunded in the case of total loss of the goods and proportionately in the case of partial loss.

19 Higher levels of compensation may be claimed where the value or a special interest in delivery has been declared or where a surcharge has been paid in respect of a declared value exceeding the limit mentioned in item 17 above.

20 In the case of damage the carrier is liable for the amount by which the value of the goods has diminished.

21 The claimant may demand interest in respect of the amount of any claim at 5 per cent per annum from the date on which the claim was sent to the carrier.

22 A carrier cannot avail himself of exclusions or limiting clauses if damage to goods was caused by his wilful misconduct or default which constitutes wilful misconduct.

23 The consignee is considered to have accepted the goods in a satisfactory condition if he does not indicate his reservations at the time of delivery or within seven days (excluding Sundays and public holidays).

24 In legal proceedings, the plaintiff may bring an action in any court or tribunal of a contracting (ie CMR contracting) country, or of a country in which the defendant is normally resident or has his principal place of business, or of a country where the goods were taken over by the carrier or where they were designated for delivery, and in no other courts or tribunals.

25 The period of limitation for an action under the Convention is one year, or three years in the case of wilful misconduct.

26 Where successive road carriers are involved in a contract under the Convention, each one of them is responsible for the whole operation as a party to the contract. Each successive carrier must give the previous carrier a dated receipt and must enter his name and address on the second copy of the consignment note.

27 A carrier who has paid compensation arising from a claim may recover the compensation plus interest, costs and expenses from other carriers who were parties to the contract subject to:

(a) the carrier responsible for the loss or damage paying the compensation;
(b) each carrier responsible for loss or damage jointly caused shall be liable to pay proportionate compensation, or compensation proportionate to their share of the carriage charges, if responsibility cannot be apportioned.

28 If a carrier who is due to pay compensation is insolvent, his share must be paid by the other carriers who are party to the contract.

In particular, road hauliers should note that the terms of the carriage contract require the carrier taking over the goods to check the accuracy of the statements in the consignment note as to the number of packages, their marks and numbers, the apparent condition of the goods and their packaging – and they should obviously do so for their own protection in the event of later disputes or claims. Under the Convention the carrier is responsible for loss, damage or delay from the time of taking over the goods until the time of their delivery.

Furthermore, where goods are handled by a number of carriers on an international journey (eg by transferring a loaded articulated semi-trailer from one to another), provisions are contained in CMR to apportion the liability for loss or damage between all the carriers (based on the relative proportions of the total carriage cost charged by each one of them). This is because of the difficulties which may arise in pinpointing the exact time and place when the damage occurred (unless specific responsibility can be determined), but should one or more of the carriers in this situation default (ie through insolvency) in meeting their share of any claim for damage to or loss of the goods then the remaining carrier or carriers will have to meet the share of those defaulting.

CMR Liability

As stated above, in international road haulage operations (but not own-account road transport operations) the carriage automatically comes within the terms of the CMR Convention under which the carrier's liability for claims resulting from loss of or damage to the goods carried is determined by comparison with a measure known as 'Special Drawing Rights' (SDRs), whereby compensation must not exceed 8.33 units of account per kilogram of gross weight short (gws). Special Drawing Rights are defined by the International Monetary Fund (IMF) as being a unit for converting currency values based on a 'basket' of the currencies of the key member states of the IMF and are converted to the national currency of the country in which any claim is dealt with in court, and is assessed as to value on the date of the judgement, or on a date agreed to by the parties. A treasury certificate stating the value for that day is taken to be conclusive proof of that fact.

NB: *The value or exchange rate of SDRs on the date of judgement or agreement referred to above must not be confused with the date of calculation of the value of the goods which are subject to the claim as referred to in item 17 on p 580).*

SDR Conversion Rate

The daily conversion rate for SDR to national currencies can be found in the financial newspapers. With changing values it is essential that the current value should be established at any particular point in time, and adequate insurance cover to at least this level of liability should be carried. To give an approximate idea of what this value represents, on 26 July 2010 a conversion of SDR to sterling at a rate of £1.00 = 1.0239500000* SDRs per kilogram represented a value of £8,135.16 per tonne (ie calculated as £1.00 divided by 1.0239500000 = £0.976610186 × 8.33 × 1,000 kg).

* NB: *It is important to note that the SDR rate may change daily.*

CMR Consignment Notes for International Haulage Journeys

Road hauliers carrying goods for hire and reward on international journeys under the provisions of the Convention on the Contract for the International Carriage of Goods by Road (CMR) as described above must complete special CMR consignment notes to be carried on the vehicle. These consignment notes confirm that the carriage is being conducted under a contract subject to the terms of the CMR Convention, but even in the absence of a CMR note, the carriage will still be subject, under international law, to the terms of the Convention although the carrier may not have been aware of this fact.

The consignment note is made out in three original copies all of which should be signed by both the carrier and the consignor of the goods. One copy of the note (with red lines) is retained by the consignor, the second copy (with blue lines) is for the consignee, and the third copy (with green lines) is for the carrier and must travel forward with the vehicle and remain with it while the goods are on board – a fourth copy (with black lines) may be retained on file by the originator of the document.

Where a consignment is divided to travel by different vehicles or by separate means, separate CMR consignment notes can be made out for each individual part of the consignment.

The following details must be entered on CMR consignment notes:

Box 1   Sender (name, address, country)
Box 2   Customs reference/status
Box 3   Sender's/agent's reference
Box 4   Consignee (name, address, country)
Box 5   Carrier (name, address, country)
Box 6   Place and date of taking over the goods
Box 7   Successive carriers
Box 8   Place designated for delivery of goods
Box 9   Marks and numbers; number and kind of packages; description of goods*
Box 10   Gross weight (kg)
Box 11   Volume (m³)
Box 12   Carriage charges
Box 13   Sender's instructions for Customs
Box 14   Reservations
Box 15   Documents attached
Box 16   Special agreements
Box 17   Goods received
Box 18   Signature of carrier
Box 19   Company completing the note
Box 20   Place, date, signature
Box 21   Copies to:
          (i)   Sender
          (ii)   Consignee
          (iii) Carrier

For dangerous goods indicate:
          (i)   Correct technical name (ie proper shipping name);
          (ii)   Hazchem class;
          (iii) UN number;
          (iv)   Flashpoint (°C), if applicable.

Where applicable, the consignment note must also contain the following particulars:

- A statement that trans-shipment to another vehicle is not allowed.
- The charges which the sender undertakes to pay.
- The amount of 'cash on delivery' charges.

- A declaration of the value of the goods and the amount representing special interest in delivery.
- The sender's instructions to the carrier regarding insurance of the goods.
- The agreed time limit within which the carriage is to be carried out.
- A list of documents handed to the carrier.

The consignor or consignee can also add to the consignment note any other particulars which may be useful to the road haulier.

Consignment Notes for Own-Account Carriage by Road

Own-account operators are not required to use the CMR consignment note for international journeys. For most journeys a simple consignment note is all that is necessary to prove that the journey is on own-account (ie not for hire or reward). It should contain details of the following:

- the vehicle operator;
- his trade or business;
- the goods being carried;
- their loading and delivery points;
- the vehicle being used (ie by registration number, etc);
- the route to be followed.

In the case of own-account traffic to Germany a more detailed document is required containing the following particulars:

- the place at which the document was made out and the date it was made out;
- the name and address of the own-account operator and an accurate description of the nature of his business;
- if the goods are to be accepted from, or delivered to, any other person, the name and address of that person and an accurate description of the nature of his business;
- details of the loading point or points;
- details of the place or places at which the vehicle is to deliver;
- details of the nature of the load (ie a description of the goods carried);
- the gross weight or other indication of the quantity of the load;
- the carrying capacity of the vehicle by weight;
- the index mark and registration number of the vehicle or, if these do not exist, the chassis number;
- the distance of the loaded journey in Germany in kilometres;
- the point or points at which the frontier is to be crossed;
- a signature of the operator or his authorized representative.

Customs Procedures and Documentation

Many changes have taken place in Customs procedures in recent years, both Euro-wide and domestically within the UK; not least, in the latter case, a merger and rebranding of the Government departments that deal with the issues of tax and Customs duties. From April 2005 a so-called 'super-agency' was created known as Her Majesty's Revenue & Customs (HMRC).

Authorized Economic Operators (AEOs)

The horrific events in the United States on 11 September 2001 significantly raised the profile of international security issues, not only for counterterrorism purposes, but also in the fight against organized crime and other threats to society. Among a number of subsequent initiatives was the introduction of the concept of Authorized Economic Operator (AEO). EU member states successfully voted on the detailed legal provisions to implement the concept, effective from 1 January 2008. The Security Amendment (Council Regulation 648/2005/EC) and its implementing provisions (Commission Regulation 1875/2006/EC) are available on the Commission's Europa website.

The aim of the AEO concept is to provide business with an internationally recognized quality mark that will demonstrate that they operate within a secure supply chain and that their internal customs controls and procedures are efficient and compliant. Under the new legislation, businesses that satisfy certain EU-wide criteria may apply for, and be granted, the status of AEO by HMRC. When a member state has granted a business AEO status, this status will be recognized across all member states. AEOs will be able to benefit from facilitation of customs controls or simplifications of customs rules or both, depending on the type of AEO certificate.

Community Transit

There have been other changes in Customs procedures, most notably the removal of barriers to intra-Community trade with the opening of the Single European Market (SEM) from 1 January 1993. Many former complicated document systems have been replaced with simplified paperwork systems and the term 'export' no longer applies to shipments within the territories of the EU. The EU's key procedures for dealing with this trade, known as Community Transit and Common Transit in their current manifestation (as described in the *HM Customs and Excise Guide to Exporting and Importing* – version 5 of December 2004), are Customs procedures that allow respectively:

- goods that are not in free circulation, and in certain cases, EC goods to move between two points in the EC, including two points in a single member state, with the duties and other charges suspended. The procedure is also used to control the movement of goods to and from Andorra, San Marino and the 'special territories' of the Community (such as the Channel Islands) – Community Transit; and

- the movement of both Community and 'non free circulation' goods to, from and through European Free Trade Association (EFTA) countries such as Iceland, Norway, Liechtenstein – Common Transit.

For Community Transit (CT) purposes goods are said to have a particular customs 'status' which is based on their liability to customs duty and other charges (eg excise duty and VAT) or claims to Common Agricultural Policy (CAP) refunds. Goods are divided into two distinct categories as follows, either:

1 Goods which have Community status (ie Community goods). These are goods which:

- originate in the Community;

- have been imported from a non-EC country and have been put into free circulation (see below) in the Community; or

- have been manufactured in the Community from materials or parts imported from a non-Community country provided the imported materials or parts are in free circulation.

The term 'free circulation' is used to describe imported goods on which all import formalities have been complied with and any customs duties or equivalent charges which are payable have been paid and not repaid in whole or in part. Goods originating in the Community are also in free circulation unless a CAP export refund or other refund has been claimed on them. Consequently, as a general rule, Community goods can move within the EC without any customs controls.

or

2 Goods without Community status (ie 'non-Community goods').

The Tariff

All the information and advice needed to help with importing and exporting procedures is to be found in 'The Tariff' (ie *The Integrated Tariff of the United Kingdom*). This document, published in three volumes and to the same format in all EU member states, contains all the relevant commodity codes (more than 65,000 of them); duty rates; procedures, including a box-by-box completion guide for C88 documents (see below); as well as references to the legal provisions.

Customs Documentation

An eight-part Customs document (C88), known as the 'Single Administrative Document' (SAD), is used throughout the Community and EFTA countries for the purposes of import, export and transit controls. A Community Transit declaration comprises completed copies of pages 1, 4 and 5 of the SAD. In certain circumstances a Community status document (T2L) may be used where required to provide evidence to Customs of Community status. A T2L can be either a copy 4 of the SAD, or a commercial document such as an invoice or a transport document or a manifest.

The SAD (form C88) comprises an eight-part document set, but not all of it is used since the opening of the SEM. Only the following copies are now required:

Copy 1   Copy for the Customs office of departure.
Copy 3   Consignor/exporter's copy.
Copy 4   For Customs office of destination, or Community status (T2L) declaration.
Copy 5   Return copy from Customs office of destination to prove that the goods arrived intact.
Copy 7   Statistical copy for Customs in the country of destination.

Copies 1 and 3 remain in the country of origination (ie export) and copies 4, 5 and 7 travel forward with the goods, copy 5 eventually being returned to the office of departure.

Community Transit Movements

There are two types of CT procedure:

1   The external CT procedure. This is mainly used to control the movement of non-Community goods and to control the movement of Community goods which are subject to a Community measure involving their export to a third country, eg CAP (Common Agricultural Policy) goods which are liable to an export refund. This procedure is also known as the 'T1' procedure.

2   The internal CT procedure. This procedure controls the movement of free circulation goods to or from the special territories, to or via the EFTA countries and between the EFTA countries. This procedure is also known as the 'T2' procedure (or the 'T2F' procedure for goods moving to or from the special territories).

Control Procedures

All transit movements are the responsibility of a 'Principal', who is the person or company who undertakes to ensure that the goods are delivered to the office of destination within the prescribed time limit. The Principal must put up a guarantee to secure the relevant duties and other charges in case the goods do not arrive intact at the office of destination. The guarantee can be cash (lodged at the office of departure), vouchers (purchased from a guaranteeing association) or a guarantee undertaking (provided by a guarantor).

To start a CT movement the completed declaration must be presented to Customs at an 'office of departure' where it will be authenticated and a time limit for completing the movement will be set. The goods may also be sealed and an itinerary set. Copies 4 and 5 of the CT declaration (ie the SAD) must travel together with the goods until they reach the EU member state or EFTA country where the movement is to end. Here the declaration and goods must be presented to the appropriate Customs at the 'office of destination'. This office will then stamp copy 5 of the SAD and return it to the office of departure so that the movement can be discharged. If copy 5 is not received within two months the Principal is contacted and asked to provide proof that the procedure has ended correctly. If proof is not provided within four months, the enquiry procedure is initiated to recover the potential debt.

There is a range of transit simplifications available for use by compliant and reliable traders. These include the use of comprehensive and reduced guarantees or waivers, becoming Authorized Consignors and Consignees, using trader seals on vehicles, special loading lists, having an exemption from prescribed itineraries, goods moved by pipeline, use of other simplified procedures and being able to use commercial documentation instead of the SAD in the case of air, rail and sea environments. All of these simplifications are subject to authorization by the Customs authorities.

NCTS

The New Computerized Transit System (NCTS) is a European-wide system, based on the concept of electronic declaration and processing, and is designed to replace, in due course, the existing, paper-based Community Transit system and to provide better management and control of CT. It involves all EU member states and the EFTA countries, 31 countries in all. Each country develops its own NCTS processing system, according to centrally defined architecture, and these systems are connected, through a central domain in Brussels, to all of the other countries – some 3,000 European Customs offices.

The UK, in common with many other participating countries, is using the Minimal Common Core (MCC) software developed by the European Commission, which provides all of the basic data capture and messaging functionality for effective connection to the European network. It is important to note that UK NCTS is a completely separate system from CHIEF (see below) and is not interconnected to it in any way, and separate declarations for transit will continue to be required.

Customs Handling of Import and Export Freight

CHIEF is one of the largest and most advanced Customs declaration processing systems in the world, providing a sound technological platform for Customs & Excise and international trade. Its sophisticated computer software controls and records the UK's international trade movements, whether by land, sea or air, and links with several thousand businesses. It uses the latest technology and is designed to cope with continuous growth in international trade. While it enhances Customs & Excise control of imports and exports, it is also claimed to improve the service provided to the international trade community and reduce overall administrative costs.

Further details of the extensive CT procedures can be found in *The Transit Manual* on the European Commission website at **http://europa.eu.int/comm/taxation_ customs/resources/documents/customs/procedural_aspects/transit/common_ community/transit_manual_en.pdf**.

Information on UK Customs procedures can be found at **www.hmrc.gov.uk**.

The TIR Convention

The TIR Convention system applies to road journeys to all countries (except member states of the EU) which are party to the Convention but only where the haulier elects to conform to the Convention's requirements.

Under the Customs Convention on the International Transport of Goods by Road (TIR Carnets) 1959, to which the UK is party, goods in Customs-sealed vehicles or containers may travel through intermediate countries *en route* to their final destination with the minimum of Customs formalities provided a TIR Carnet has been issued in respect of the journey (UK vehicles may operate on international haulage journeys outside the EU without the protection of TIR but in this case they will be subject to the full weight of Customs formality and bureaucracy (and delay) at each border crossing and on arrival at destination – see also below).

The Carnet is a recognized international Customs document intended purely to simplify Customs procedures; it is not a substitute for other documents, nor is it mandatory for any operator to use it; it does not give any operator the right to run vehicles in any European country. Use of a Carnet frees the operator from the need to place a deposit of duty in respect of the load he is carrying in each country through which the vehicle is to pass.

The issuing authorities for the Carnets (in this country the FTA and the RHA – see Appendix I for addresses) act as guarantors on behalf of the IRU (International Road Transport Union – the international guarantor), and for this reason Carnets are issued only to bona fide members of these two associations.

Goods may only be carried under a TIR Carnet provided the vehicle in which they are carried has been specifically approved by the Vehicle and Operator Services Agency (VOSA). This means complying with constructional requirements so that the load-carrying space can be sealed by Customs, after which it must not be possible for any goods to be removed from or added to the load without the seals being broken, and there must be no concealed spaces where goods may be hidden.

Detailed requirements are laid down concerning the structure of the body, particularly regarding the manner in which it is assembled, so that there is no possibility of panels being removed by releasing nuts and bolts and so on. The manner in which doors and roller shutters are secured must also meet stringent specifications. Sheeted vehicles or containers may be used provided conditions relating to the construction of the sheet are observed and as long as when the closing device has been secured it becomes impossible to gain access to the load without leaving obvious traces.

VOSA examines vehicles (by appointment at Goods Vehicle Test Stations) to ensure that they meet the technical requirements for operation under the TIR Convention and issues a certificate of approval, which must be renewed every two years and must be carried on the vehicle when it is operating under a TIR Carnet. This point is particularly important as Customs authorities carry out checks on vehicles leaving the UK to ensure that this certificate is being carried where necessary.

Application for TIR Certification

Application for the examination of vehicles or containers must be made to the Clerk to the Traffic Commissioner for the traffic area in which they are available for inspection. These offices provide the application form GV 62, and a leaflet setting out the technical conditions which have to be met. If a TIR-approved vehicle is sold to another operator, the TIR certificate (form GV 60) is not transferable and the new owner must have the vehicle re-certified if he wishes to use it for TIR operations

The fee for examination of a vehicle for TIR purposes is £106.00, unless it is not of a previously approved TIR design type, in which case the fee is £644.00. The fee for a TIR certificate is £14.00. For a re-inspection of a failed vehicle, the fee is £70.00.

TIR Plates

When a vehicle has been approved it must display at the front and the rear a plate showing the letters 'TIR' in white on a blue background. Such plates are obtainable from the FTA and RHA. They should be removed or covered when the vehicle is no longer operating under TIR.

TIR Carnets

TIR Carnets are internationally recognized Customs documents. Carnets are in pairs and have counterfoils in a bound cover. They are in four parts and contain 6, 14 or 20 pages (ie *volets* in French). A 6-page Carnet is valid only for a journey between the UK and one other country. Journeys to more than one other country require 14- or 20-page Carnets, which are valid for two months and three months respectively. A Carnet covers only one load and if a return load is to be collected, a separate Carnet is needed (each individual voucher covers one frontier crossing) and the driver should take this with him on the outward journey. At each Customs point *en route* a voucher is detached and the counterfoil is stamped. Careful attention must be paid to the completion of the Carnet if delays and difficulties are to be avoided during the journey.

Carnets are valid for limited periods only (see above), and if not used they must be returned to the issuing authority for cancellation. Those which are used and which bear all the official stampings acquired *en route* must also be returned within 10 days of the vehicle's return.

Strict instructions regarding the use of Carnets are supplied by the issuing authorities for both the operator and the driver. For example, the driver should never leave the Carnet with any Customs authority without first obtaining a signed, stamped and dated declaration quoting the Carnet number and certifying that the goods on the vehicle conform with the details contained in the Carnet. Drivers should also ensure that the Customs officials at each departure office, transit office and arrival office take out a voucher from the Carnet and stamp and sign the counterfoil accordingly.

The four parts of the Carnet comprise the following:

1 Details of the issuing authority, the Carnet holder, the country of departure, the country of destination, the vehicle, the weight and the value of the goods as shown in the manifest (see 3 below).

2 A declaration that the goods specified have been loaded for the country stated, that they will be carried to their destination with the Customs seals intact and that the Customs regulations of the countries through which the goods are to be carried will be observed.

3 A goods manifest giving precise details of the goods, the way in which they are packed (the number of parcels or cartons) and their value.

4 Vouchers which Customs officials at frontier posts will remove, stamping the counterfoil section which remains in the Carnet.

Before obtaining a Carnet the applicant must sign a form of contract with the issuing authority, agreeing to abide by all the necessary legal and administrative requirements. A financial guarantee is required to ensure that any claims which may be made against the applicant will be met.

Seal Breakage

If a Customs seal on a TIR vehicle is broken during transit as a result of an accident or for any other reason, Customs or the police must be contacted immediately to endorse the Carnet to this effect.

Non-TIR Journeys

Goods may be sent abroad in vehicles without TIR cover and no Carnet is required. In this case, however, it is necessary to comply with the individual Customs requirements of each country through which the vehicle passes. A guarantee in lieu of import duty, or a deposit against such duty, will have to be paid before the vehicle is allowed to enter the country to which it is travelling, or any country through which it needs to pass, and the vehicle will be subject to stringent Customs scrutiny not only at the port of exit from the UK and the port of entry to the Continent, but at all further frontier crossings during the journey.

Further information is available on the TIR website at: **www.unece.org/tir/ convention/bases.htm**.

The ADR Agreement

When dangerous goods are transported on international road journeys the provisions apply of the European Agreement concerning the International Carriage of Dangerous Goods (the ADR Convention). The current edition is that for 2009, applicable from 1 January 2009. This is a long and complex document contained in two large volumes. However, for most general purposes, if the reader refers to the provisions of our dangerous goods legislation in Chapter 20 of this *Handbook* he will find all the information he needs, since UK rules are based on the international ADR requirements.

Carnets de Passage

Most countries to which vehicles are likely to travel permit the temporary importation of foreign vehicles and containers (not to be confused with the loads they carry) free of duty or deposit and without guaranteed Customs documents.

However, a Customs document known as a *Carnet de Passage en Douane* is required for the following:

- vehicles and trailers entering Iran, Iraq, Jordan, Kuwait, Saudi Arabia, Syria, Turkey and other Middle Eastern countries;
- vehicles remaining in Italy for more than three months;
- vehicles remaining in Greece for more than 10 days;
- vehicles remaining in Pakistan for up to three months.

A triptyque is required for vehicles carrying spare parts into Portugal.

Where *Carnets de Passage* are needed for travel they can be obtained from the Royal Automobile Club (RAC) and the Royal Scottish Automobile Club (RSAC).

ATA Carnets

Goods that are being imported only temporarily into certain countries,* such as samples, professional equipment and items for display at exhibitions and fairs, and which, eventually, will be returned to the UK can be moved under an international Customs clearance document known as an ATA Carnet. These documents, valid for 12 months from the date of issue, are issued by chambers of commerce to members without the need for payments of, or deposits against, duty. It should be noted, however, that holding an ATA Carnet does not relieve the operator from observing Customs requirements in each individual country.

* NB: *The countries to which this is applicable include all EU member states plus Gibraltar, Israel, Switzerland and Turkey.*

Further information is available at the following website: **www.londonchamber.co.uk**.

'De Suivi' Document

Drivers of UK haulage and own-account vehicles entering France must be able to produce a 'de suivi' document in addition to the normal CMR or own-account consignment note.

There is no official or formal layout for this additional document, it being left to operators to determine how they present the relevant information which can be added to the existing CMR document if space permits. The relevant information required is as follows:

- date the consignment was drawn up;
- transport operator's name and address;
- transport operator's VAT number;
- date when goods were taken into charge;
- nature, weight and volume of goods;
- name of the consignor;
- address of loading point;
- name of consignee;
- address of unloading point.

Space must be provided on the note for entering of the following information:

- time of vehicle arrival at loading point;
- time of departure of loaded vehicle;
- required time of arrival at destination.

A separate document must also be made out to show:

- date and time of arrival at destination;
- date and time of departure of unloaded vehicle.

On international journeys the driver must also carry a further document showing the relationship between the transport operator and the driver (ie whether he is a direct employee, an owner-driver or an employee of a sub-contractor).

Road Tolls

The Austrian 'Maut' System

The former Austrian Eco-points system described in previous editions of this *Handbook* has been completely abolished and replaced by a new 'Maut' (toll) 'per mile' system for trucks over 3.5 tonnes gross weight similar in concept to the German LKW-Maut system mentioned below. The previous Austrian 'Vignette' sticker system has also been replaced. The system requires relevant vehicles to be fitted with an easy-to-install DSRC-TAG electronic (microwave) transponder, colloquially called a 'GO-Box', and payment is via the internet or at point-of-sale terminals, located mainly at roadside fuel filling stations.

All 2,000 kilometres of Austria's motorways are wired for DSRC (short-range electronic tolling) to operate the nationwide toll system, which is achieved with the aid of an electronic transponder or by off-road payment, normally by internet or at one of 200-odd point-of-sale terminals, mostly located at fuel filling stations. When paying the toll the truck driver enters his registration number, which is recorded on a list of payers. When the vehicle is seen on the road by cameras mounted on some 400 overhead gantries, it is matched against the so-called 'white' payment list.

	Category 2 2 axles	Category 3 3 axles	Category 4+ 4 and more axles
A EURO emission category EURO EEV & VI	0,1440	0,2016	0,3024
B EURO emission category EURO IV & V	0,1540	0,2156	0,3234
C EURO emission category EURO 0 to III	0,1760	0,2464	0,3696

A higher toll rate is charged for use of a number of special road sections on the A9, A10, A11, A13 (the Brenner Pass) and A16 motorways. VAT at 20 per cent is added to the tolls.

The German LKW-Maut System

Germany's distance-based LKW-Maut road toll system, operated by Toll Collect, applies to all trucks, domestic and foreign, of 12 tonnes gross weight and above.

Toll payments can be made in several alternative ways as follows:

- LogPay plan (direct debit);
- Road Account;
- fuel card payment;
- credit account payment;
- EC card payment;
- credit card payment;
- cash payment.

LogPay Plan (Direct Debit) and Toll Charges

Under the LogPay scheme fees are listed on a monthly toll log statement and debited directly to the bank account provided by the registered user with Toll Collect. The amount of toll is also based on vehicle exhaust emission rating and on the number of axles on the truck. Category A applies to Euro-V and EEV trucks; Category B to Euro-III and -IV trucks; and Category C to Euro-I, -II and -III trucks plus those that do not belong to any emissions category.

For vehicles or vehicle combinations with up to three axles, the toll (in EUR, €) per kilometre from 1 January 2010 is:

- EUR (€) 0.140 in Category A;

- EUR (€) 0.168 in Category B;
- EUR (€) 0.224 in Category C; and
- EUR (€) 0.287 in Category D.

and for vehicles or vehicle combinations with four or more axles the toll is:

- EUR (€) 0.154 in Category A;
- EUR (€) 0.182 in Category B;
- EUR (€) 0.224 in Category C; and
- EUR (€) 0.287 in Category D.

The toll is a public-sector levy and is therefore not subject to VAT.

Eurovignettes

Motorway charges (ie tax) must be paid (in accordance with EC Directive 1999/62 EC – the so-called Eurovignette Directive) for goods vehicles of 12 tonnes maximum weight and over, including those towing trailers where the combined maximum weight is 12 tonnes or more, when travelling in or through the Netherlands, Belgium, Luxembourg, Denmark and Sweden. The tax is charged in euros (€), payable in advance, and is based on a sliding scale according to the pollution emission rating of the vehicle engine (ie Euro-0, Euro-I or Euro-II/III – see Chapter 11), the number of axles and the amount of time during which the motorways will be used (eg day, week, month, etc), as per the following table. Payment covers journeys in all five countries.

A new range of Eurovignette charges apply for 2010 as follows:

Daily charge for all vehicle categories: €8.
All other charges are based on emissions ratings as follows:

Annual tariff		
Emission group	1-3 Axles	4 or more axles
EURO 0	96,000	155,000
EURO I	85,000	140,000
EURO II	75,000	125,000
EURO III	75,000	125,000
EURO IV	75,000	125,000
EURO V	75,000	125,000
EURO VI	75,000	125,000

Monthly tariff Emission group	1-3 axles	4 or more axles
EURO 0	9,600	15,500
EURO I	8,500	14,000
EURO II	7,500	12,500
EURO III	7,500	12,500
EURO IV	7,500	12,500
EURO V	7,500	12,500
EURO VI	7,500	12,500
Weekly tariff Emission group	1-3 axles	4 or more axles
EURO 0	2,600	4,100
EURO I	2,300	3,700
EURO II	2,000	3,300
EURO III	2,000	3,300
EURO IV	2,000	3,300
EURO V	2,000	3,300
EURO VI	2,000	3,300

When the tax is paid, a certificate/receipt called a Eurovignette is issued, showing the vehicle registration number, the date and period of validity, and the amount paid. The vignette must be carried on the vehicle at all times as proof of payment. Failure to obtain a vignette or to be able to produce it on request can result in a fine of up to £5,000.

Eurovignettes can be purchased at petrol stations, motorway service areas and near motorway access points. In England they are obtainable from P&O at Dover, the Ferry Terminal at Ramsgate, the Port Services Office at Harwich and from Eurotunnel at Folkstone.

Other Motorway Tolls in Europe

The Czech Republic introduced a one-day Eurovignette on 1 January 2001. Belgium planned to introduce a new motorway tax disc for all LGVs from January 2008. Hungary introduced in 2008 an electronic payment toll system for trucks weighing more than 7.5 tonnes on all its main roads (mostly trans-border routes). France, too, has a new e-Toll system ('TIS PL') for trucks over 3.5 tonnes using its motorways, with automatic billing via an electronic box system. However, use of the system is not compulsory, although frequent users who sign up to the system will be eligible for rebates.

European Lorry Bans

Many European countries impose restrictions on the movement of goods vehicles on certain routes and at certain times. Usually these apply at weekends, during public and annual holiday times, at religious or traditional festival times and when and where severe weather conditions may be expected. Severe penalties may be imposed on drivers who flout these restrictions. Operators are advised to check the current position via the internet or with the Road Haulage Association before scheduling vehicles for weekend and holiday working.

Environmental Plaques on Heavy Lorries

The International Transport Forum European Conference of Ministers of Transport (ITF/ECMT) scheme (see above), for the issue of multilateral quota road haulage permits, allows for an additional quota of permits for those countries participating in the so-called 'green lorry' scheme. In order to gain the additional quota the vehicles used on ECMT multilateral permit journeys must comply with specified minimum standards for noise emissions and chemical exhaust emissions for diesel engines as well as certain other safety requirements. Compliance with these standards is confirmed by the issue of an environmental certificate of conformity, which must be carried on the vehicles during relevant journeys, and by the display of an environmental plaque – usually stuck in a prominent place on the vehicle front bumper or cab front. These plaques and certificates indicate to the relevant authorities, while in cross-border and internal transit, that the vehicle in question meets ECMT standards for either 'green' or 'greener and safe' lorries; the former with Euro-I specification engines and the latter with Euro-II spec engines. Vehicles with Euro-III engines are required to display a plaque showing the number '3'.

These requirements are set out in the ECMT's document *Guide for Government Officials and Carriers on the Use of the ECMT Multilateral Quota*. This document can be viewed and/or downloaded from the ECMT's website at: **http://www. internationaltransportforum.org/publications/roadtransport**.

Also accompanying the *Guide* is a document called *Documents to be on Board a Tractor Vehicle*.

The plaques (referred to in the *Guide* as stickers) fall into the following categories:

- *For 'green' lorries*: a green circular plaque of 200 mm diameter with a 20mm-wide white border and displaying:
  - a white letter 'E' (Environment) or white letter 'U' (Umwelt), denoting vehicle with a Euro-I engine.
- *For 'greener and safe' lorries*: a green circular plaque of 200 mm diameter with a 20mm-wide white border and displaying either:
  - a white letter 'S' (Sicher/safe), denoting a vehicle with a Euro-II engine and safety features;* or
  - a white figure '3' denoting a vehicle with a Euro-III engine and safety features.*

NB: These safety features include rear under-run protective devices, lateral protection, rear-view mirrors, lighting and light signalling devices, tachograph, speed limiters, rear marking plates, anti-lock braking systems and steering, all of which must comply with relevant EC/EEC/ECE/UN Directives and Regulations.

Austria and Germany have their own plaques to indicate vehicles that meet low noise standards as follows:

- 'L' – denoting *Lärmarm Fahrzeug* (ie low-noise vehicle): Austrian version of the symbol for 'quiet' diesel vehicles, which are:
  - small and medium-sized lorries of no more than 150 kW producing noise levels no greater than 78 dB; and
  - heavy lorries exceeding 150 kW with noise levels no greater than 80 dB.
- 'G' – denoting *Geräuscharm Fahrzeug* (ie noiseless/quiet vehicle): German version of the Austrian 'L' plate for use only on diesel vehicles meeting German low-noise requirements – similar to those for Austria as above.

Emissions Standards

ECMT-specified noise emission and chemical exhaust emission requirement standards for so-called 'green' vehicles are as follows.

Noise Emissions Standards for 'Green', 'Greener and Safe' and 'Euro-III Safe' Lorries

- For vehicles with maximum power output up to 150 kW = 78 dB.
- For vehicles with maximum power output over 150 kW = 80 dB.

Chemical Exhaust Emissions for Diesel Engines

	'Green lorries'	'Greener and safe lorries'	'Euro-III safe lorries'
CO	4.9 g/kWh	4.0 g/kWh	2.1 g/kWh
HC	1.23 g/kWh	1.1 g/kWh	0.66 g/kWh
NO_x	9.0 g/kWh	7.0 g/kWh	5.0 g/kWh
Part.	0.4 g/kWh^2	0.15 g/kWh^2	0.10 g/kWh^2

Other Vehicle Markers

In some European countries, particularly Germany and Austria for example, vehicles may also be seen displaying other plaques such as the following:

- 'A' – required in Germany on all vehicles carrying waste;
- 'K' – required in Germany for vehicles making use of exceptions to the Motor Tax Law.

In Italy the following plaques (displayed on the rear and on both sides of the vehicle) are used to indicate vehicles carrying special products and which are therefore exempt from weekend driving bans as follows:

- 'a' – for vehicles carrying easily perishable foodstuffs;
- 'd' – for vehicles carrying milk.

In Austria, three plaques are used to indicate vehicles that have had their maximum weight modified under certain conditions:

- 'R' – for vehicles authorized for use only on special routes;
- 'H' – for vehicles that have had their maximum permissible weight increased;
- 'E' – for vehicles that have had their maximum permissible weight reduced.

Miscellaneous Requirements

Trailer Certification

UK international road hauliers travelling in Germany and Italy are required by these countries to carry legal documentation relating to the trailer/semi-trailer. Principally, this means a Certificate of Ownership (available from VOSA at a cost of £20) and from the second year of service, a copy of the plating certificate which shows the trailer's roadworthiness.

Driver Contracts for France

Drivers travelling to or through France must carry either:

- a copy of their contract of employment with their current employer; or
- a letter of engagement from their employer; or
- a valid recent (ie their last) payslip.

Impounding in Italy

The Italian authorities are strict on law compliance and increasingly use vehicle impounding as a means of penalty for infringements – sometimes holding vehicles for as long as three months even for relatively minor infringements, according to FTA reports.

Speed Limits in France

Speed-limit offenders in France face instant loss of their driving licence if they exceed statutory limits by more than 40 kph (ie approximately 25 mph). Heavy vehicles in France are restricted to 90 kph (ie approx 56 mph) on motorways, 80 kph (ie approx 50 mph) on dual carriageways, 80 kph on country roads (only 60 kph (ie approx 37 mph) for vehicles drawing trailers) and 50 kph (ie approx 31 mph) in built-up areas.

Euro Currency

The euro officially came into use from 1 January 2002. The exchange rate for the euro against the pound sterling is published daily in newspapers and on the internet.

Attestation of Activities

UK LGV drivers, particularly on international journeys, may be asked to provide evidence of their activities that are not covered by a valid tachograph record. For this purpose the EU has devised an official form of attestation. A version of this form should be completed by the employer and issued to drivers on such journeys. The form is illustrated below and copies can be downloaded from the EU's website at: **http://www.ecos.ba/doc_upload/POTVRDA%20DIREKTIVA%20561_2006.pdf.**

ATTESTATION OF ACTIVITIES UNDER REGULATION (EC) NO 561/2006
OR
THE EUROPEAN AGREEMENT CONCERNING THE WORK OF CREWS
OF VEHICLES ENGAGED IN INTERNATIONAL ROAD TRANSPORT
(AETR) (*)

To be filled in by typing and signed before a journey
To be kept with the original tachograph records wherever they are required
to be kept
False attestations constitute an infringement

1 Name of the undertaking: _____

2 Street address, Postal code, City, Country: _____, _____, _____, _____

3 Telephone number (including international prefix): _____

4 Fax number (including international prefix): _____

5 E-mail address: _____

I, the undersigned

6 Name: _____

7 Position in the undertaking: _____

declare that the driver

8 Name: _____

9 Date of birth: _____

10 Driving licence number or Identity card number or Passport number:
_____

for the period

11 from (time-day-month-year) _____-_____-_____-_____

12 to (time-day-month-year) _____-_____-_____-_____

13 ☐ was on sick leave (**)

14 ☐ was on annual leave (**)

15 ☐ drove a vehicle exempted from the scope of Regulation (EC) No 561/2006 or AETR (**)

16 For the undertaking, place _____date _____signature _____

17 I, the driver, confirm that I have not been driving a vehicle falling under the scope of Regulation (EC) No. 561/2006 or AETR during the period mentioned above.

18 Place _____date _____Signature of the driver _____

(*) This form is available in an electronic and printable version on the internet at ec.europa.eu.

(**) Only one of the boxes 13, 14 or 15 may be chosen.

Drink Driving Limits

Drivers are warned that while the UK drink-driving (ie blood-alcohol level) limit at 80 mg per 100 ml of blood may appear to be strict, the limits in many other European countries are as strict or even stricter, as the following list indicates:

- 0 mg - Estonia, Lithuania, Malta, Romania, Slovakia, Czech Republic, Hungary (this means *zero* tolerance);
- 20 mg – Norway, Poland, Sweden;
- 50 mg – Belgium, Bulgaria, Denmark, Germany (Germany is 30mg if you're in an accident), Finland, France, Greece, Italy, Serbia/Montenegro, Croatia, Latvia, Macedonia, Netherlands, Austria, Portugal, Slovenia, Spain, Turkey, Cyprus (North);
- 80 mg – UK, Ireland, Luxembourg, Malta, Switzerland;
- 90 mg – Cyprus (South).

NB: *Lower limits apply in some countries to new drivers and those found well above the limits can expect to be dealt with very severely.*

More information on safe driving in Europe can be found on the Safe Travel website at: **http://www.safetravel.co.uk.**

Driver Health Cover Abroad

Drivers engaged on international journeys should carry their own personal EHIC (European Health Insurance Card) to provide cover for any medical treatment required as a result of accident or illness while in any European Economic Area (EEA) country. The card (which has replaced the former E111 document) is obtainable free of charge and can be applied for on the internet – just enter EHIC in the Google search facility. The card enables holders to obtain free medical attention from state-run hospitals and medical centres on the same basis as the local populace; however it does not cover:

- treatment in private medical facilities abroad;
- repatriation when the patient is well enough to travel;
- the cost of recovering the vehicle;
- the cost of hospital visits by relatives;
- the costs of funeral transport from abroad.

All these additional items, if required, should be covered by private medical insurance taken out by the driver or his employer.

Intermodal Freight Transport

Intermodal freighting is a form of transport operation in which two or more individual transport modes are used in combination (such as road and rail, or road and inland waterway) to form an integrated transport chain. Principally, the concept is intended to achieve more operationally efficient and cost-effective delivery of goods in an environmentally sustainable manner from their point of origin to their final destination.

In recent years, the concept of intermodal freight transport and indeed, the wider concept of multi-modalism, have become of increasing interest to the UK road haulage industry and freight shippers in general. This interest is being driven forward by a number of key incentives as follows:

- Government pressure to remove heavy freight traffic from the roads and onto rail and inland waterways.
- To effect a reduction in road traffic congestion and road accidents.
- To reduce the consumption of scarce fossil fuels.
- To reduce adverse environmental pollution caused by vehicle exhaust emissions and noise.

Intermodalism is far from a new idea; in fact, freight containers of wooden construction were being transferred to and from horse-drawn wagons onto rail as long ago as the late 1800s. However, the 1994 Report of the Royal Commission on Environmental Pollution, *Transport and the Environment*, determined that an important objective for a sustainable transport policy must be founded on the concept of increasing 'the proportions of… freight transport [carried] by environmentally less damaging modes and to make the best use of existing infrastructure'.

The Report effectively warned that the likely consequences of taking more and more land to provide new infrastructure to cope with the forecast massive growth in road use could not be sustainable, so alternatives had to be devised and developed. It highlighted the fact that the projected growth of heavy goods vehicle traffic between 1989 (when the National Road Traffic Forecasts were made) and 2025 was no less than 140 per cent and it concluded that even with a large-scale shift to rail, road transport would remain the dominant mode for freight transport and therefore it was important to explore all possible ways of limiting its adverse environmental impact.

In 1998 a 'new approach' was adopted with publication by the Department for Transport (DfT) of its White Paper *A New Deal for Transport: Better for Everyone*, signalling that the Government was looking for a radical change in transport – in particular, seeking to achieve a more integrated transport system to tackle the growing problems of congestion and pollution. Prior to publication of this White Paper, a number of other key documents set out the Government's strategies for overcoming the adverse effects of the motor vehicle – especially the heavy lorry – on our lives.

While some freight movements may use, and justify the use of, a number of different transport modes such as road and rail, or road and inland waterway or either short-sea or deep-sea shipping, thus making them multi-modal operations, in the majority of instances efficient movements are invariably achieved by the use of just two modes: most commonly road haulage collection and final delivery journeys combined with a rail freight trunk-haul journey in what is commonly known as a 'combined road–rail' operation. However, where operational circumstances dictate or a feasible alternative option is available, road haulage or rail freighting may be combined instead with an inland waterway journey via river or canal or with a short-sea shipping operation – typically a coastal or a cross-Channel sailing.

Combined transport operations involving either road haulage or rail freight in conjunction with deep-sea container services or with an airfreight operation also feature in intermodal and multi-modal scenarios, albeit the latter occurring in only a relatively small number of instances and small scale in terms of the freight volumes shipped.

Determining the choice of mode or modes to be used depends on circumstances; sometimes cost alone will be the deciding factor, but frequently other considerations are decisive. For instance, operational practicalities like frequency of service, speed of delivery, the availability of special handling facilities, the ability to meet particular packaging requirements, security considerations or the sheer volumes of freight to be moved may be a factor, or indeed it may be that a number of these various service 'pluses', in combination, produce the ideal solution. But other less tangible issues may also enter the equation such as the need to follow corporate environmental policies or to assuage a shipper's social conscience.

Freighting by intermodal or multi-modal combinations is the alternative to consigning loads for the whole of their journey by a single mode – as is the case with some 68 per cent of domestic freight moved in Great Britain (according to the DfT's *Transport Statistics for Great Britain – 2007* publication) being transported by road. It is a fact that the haulage of goods by road from their source direct to their final destination remains the preferred method in the majority of cases, and it is this preference that individuals, corporate bodies and Government departments alike who champion the cause of intermodal transport are trying to break down.

Since by far the largest proportion of freight traffic commences and ends its journey on the back of a lorry, intermodalism is principally understood to mean the use of an alternative mode to undertake the middle, long-haul or trunk leg of the journey. Typically this involves transhipping the unitized load from a lorry at a railhead or inland waterway terminal or at a seaport, for onward shipment by rail, inland waterway barge or sea-going ship, and then transhipping it back again onto a lorry for the final delivery leg to the customer – the consignee. In some instances it is not just the unitized load that is transhipped, but the whole road vehicle, or at least its semi-trailer, which is loaded aboard a rail freight wagon, an inland waterway barge, a short-sea vessel – invariably a roll-on/roll-off ferry ship, or an ocean-going ship for onward transportation.

No matter what the particular freighting arrangement, the essence of the whole operation is to utilize the key characteristics of each individual transport mode to its best advantage. The lorry has the benefits of immediacy and flexibility in its favour plus the ability to effect collections and deliveries of goods from locations that have no rail sidings or waterway quays for loading. Rail freighting offers a lower-cost alternative for multiple loads carried over longer transits and a much less polluting effect on the environment, as does barge traffic shipped on the navigable rivers and canals of inland waterway networks. Thus road haulage in any combination with rail freighting, inland waterway, short-sea and coastal shipping may prove to be the most viable option, both economically and operationally. But in certain cases, particularly where no roll-on/roll-off vehicle ferry service or road or rail tunnel facility exists, shipping by container vessel may be necessary, and especially for trans-global freight movements.

It is useful to explain here the various constituent parts of a freight movement.

Unit Loads and Loading Units

A unit load is a consignment of freight – usually, but not always, comprising a combination of small consignments, as in a groupage load, which is unitized to save transhipment and repacking time and cost at each individual stage of the journey, and also for ease of handling. Such loads are usually consolidated into an ISO shipping container or a swap body built to internationally recognized and accepted standards, or into an articulated lorry semi-trailer. Unitization of freight into standard loading units in this manner is a vital element of the intermodal transport concept, providing speed and efficiency in handling, security for the load in transit and reduced risk of damage.

Bimodal Systems

'RoadRailer' is a brand name for an interchangeable, bimodal road–rail trailer system conceived in the United States of America by Wabash National Inc. of Indiana. It is based on the use of a road-going semi-trailer with a six-wheel undercarriage that is pneumatically raised, allowing the front and rear ends of the trailer to be mounted on rail bogies and formed into a train for rail transit.

Rolling Motorway Systems

A rolling motorway system is one where complete road vehicles are driven onto specially built rail wagons for the rail transit. The system gets its name because, in effect, vehicles are driven straight off the motorway onto the rail wagon at one end of the journey, then off again and onto the motorway at the other end of the trunk leg, the driver travelling on the train accompanying his vehicle. Hence the rail link is seen as a continuation of the motorway journey.

Eurotunnel's freight shuttle service through the Channel Tunnel between the UK and France is a rolling motorway system, having special transfer wagons enabling vehicles to be driven onto the train from the platform, and off again at the other end of the through-Tunnel journey. By this means loading and unloading is both easily and rapidly accomplished, reducing journey delays to an absolute minimum – one of its main advantages over roll-on/roll-off ferry ship operation where there are often delays in loading and unloading.

Piggyback Transport

Unaccompanied articulated semi-trailers are carried on certain UK and European rail services by a method known as 'piggyback' transport. The semi-trailers are either:

- lifted onto special low-height rail wagons by container crane or by straddle carriers fitted with grapple arms which locate into strengthened pockets in the trailer under frame; or are
- shunted, by a terminal tractor, onto special rail wagons with a swivelling, tilting load-bed, which rotates and lowers to form a ramp.

Neither the tractive unit nor the driver travels on the train, the unaccompanied semi-trailer being picked up from a rail terminal at the other end of the journey by another tractive unit and driver for final delivery to its destination.

Piggyback was at one time seen to be one of the most promising methods of switching long-haul freight from road to rail, and a number of major studies have been carried out in connection with its potential development. For example, the European Conference of Ministers of Transport (ECMT) issued a report in 1992 on improvements in so-called piggyback links across Europe, while in the UK a consortium of consultants and operators, among others, studied and for a while vigorously promoted this particular concept of road–rail transport. However, for its development to progress in the UK, substantial and very costly infrastructure works are needed to increase the rail loading gauge to provide both top corner and platform clearance for the passage of normal height semi-trailers and 9 ft 6 in high ISO containers.

Rail Freight

The rail freight element – now mainly operated by DB Schenker (formerly EWS) and Freightliner in the UK – relies on the use of a variety of intermodal wagons specifically designed to carry ISO shipping containers, standard swap bodies or whole vehicle combinations (eg piggyback style). The former are usually skeletal-framed flat wagons, built to provide a low loading height to accommodate 9 ft 6in tall 'high-cube' ISO containers and are fitted with twist locks at 20 ft and 40 ft centres.

Vehicular traffic (ie semi-trailers and whole-vehicle combinations) are carried on special pocket wagons or on spine wagons which provide safe and secure accommodation for vehicles in transit, their road wheels sitting low on the wagon to provide adequate overhead clearance for bridges and tunnels (known as 'loading gauge' clearance). Depending on the system being used, the vehicles are either lifted on or off the rail wagon or are driven on or off via special loading ramps built into the wagon. The Channel Tunnel freight shuttle also uses a direct drive-on system.

Inland Waterways

Intermodal freight traffic on the inland waterways is carried on barges equipped to accommodate either complete road vehicles, but more usually ISO containers stacked both in the cargo hold and on deck. Rarely are such vessels seen on UK inland waterways, but they are a common sight on major European rivers such as the Rhine, the Elbe and the Danube which, along with other inland navigations, carry a great deal of freight traffic, a fair proportion of which is intermodal traffic.

Short-Sea Shipping

Increasingly, short-sea shipping (SSS) is being seen as a key alternative to road freighting and a solution to the burdens caused by traffic congestion and air pollution across the whole of Europe (this not just a UK problem). The ships used in these types of operation are familiar enough to anybody making a port visit. They are generally small freighters (or coasters in common terminology to differentiate them from ocean-going vessels), typically of some 1,000–5,000 deadweight tonnes (dwt).

Containers

Freight, or shipping containers as they are usually termed, are generally constructed of steel for strength and to meet the requirements of legislation and to standard dimensions established by the International Organization for Standardization (ISO) – hence the term ISO container. They are capable of being lifted from the top corner twist-lock castings by purpose-built container cranes, straddle carriers or stackers, or from the bottom by heavy-duty forklift trucks, for which purpose many containers also have strengthened fork pockets in the underside. These containers are sufficiently rigid and strong to be stacked 8, or even in some cases 9 or 10 units high in container terminals or within specially built cellular container ships where they are subjected to considerable stress. Standard ISO containers are 20 ft, 30 ft, 40 ft and 45 ft long by 8 ft wide (2.44 metres); and 8 ft 6 in and, increasingly, 9 ft 6 in high (now said to comprise 45–50 per cent of all containers coming into the country – and likely to amount to 80 per cent by 2015).

Container ship capacity is measured and container industry statistics are compiled in relation to a single 20 ft ISO container defined as 1 teu (ie a 20 ft equivalent unit). Thus a 40 ft container is counted as 2 teu. The largest of the current generation of sea-going container ships carry 10,000 or more 20 ft equivalent containers (ie 10,000 teu) – a first arrival of a 14,000 teu container ship into the Port of Felixstowe was reported early in 2009.

Twenty-foot and 40 ft ISO units are those most commonly used since they provide greater flexibility in loading and more effectively match the legal dimensions for road vehicles – 30-footers being an odd size and square-ended 45-footers being too long for legal carriage on European road vehicles. However, 45 ft containers with the Geest patented type of twist-lock corner casting are now becoming increasingly common and these overcome the difficulties of meeting the legally specified 'swept circle' dimension for maximum length semi-trailers thus allowing the 45-footer to be carried legally.

A variety of different container designs are used for special purposes including half-height types for carrying particularly heavy, low capacity freight such as machinery or sheet steel, refrigerated units with built-in 'reefer' units, and bulk liquid or powder tanks mounted within standard-dimension steel container frames.

All these containers are fitted with standard design corner castings that enable them to be quickly and safely secured and released from matching twist lock equipment mounted on road vehicle trailers, rail wagons and lifting and loading equipment. Twist locks on vehicles and rail wagons may be recessed within load platforms to allow a clear deck for general freight carrying, or mounted on special purpose-built skeletal frames – hence the term skeletal trailer.

These can be used for no other purpose than container or swap body carrying, but by their nature they weigh less than a standard platform body and therefore provide a lower unladen vehicle weight which in turn allows a greater load-carrying capacity within legal gross weight limits. Other non-standard, non-stackable containers and demountable bodies used in domestic transport and builders' skips are not included in this definition, and are not found in intermodal transport operations.

A new generation of ISO pallet-wide containers is now in use, patented by GESeaCo and brand-named 'SeaCell'. These units have a revolutionary sidewall construction permitting sideways stowage of two, 1,200 millimetre, standard Euro-pallets within the standard ISO exterior dimensions (45 ft by 8 ft). This configuration increases load capacity from 27 Euro pallets (ie 1,200 mm by 800 mm) to 33 pallets.

Swap Bodies

Swap bodies (in French, *caisses mobiles* – a term frequently encountered) are loading units sufficiently strong for lifting, when loaded, to or from road vehicles and rail wagons with ease. Many of the shorter (ie 7.15 m and 7.45 m) units have fold-down legs so they can be free-standing. All swap bodies are equipped with specially strengthened lifting pockets, located at standard dimensions, in the underside of the base frame for lifting by stacker or by overhead crane with grapple arms. They are built to a lighter construction than an ISO container thus saving on tare weight and increasing payload potential, but in consequence they are not sufficiently strong for top lifting or stacking like a container, although some more recent versions allow for stacking when empty.

A variety of bodywork types are encountered: the solid closed type, or those with curtain sides, or open with drop-down sideboards and tailboard for ease of loading and unloading. When used exclusively in intermodal operations, they are built to standard dimensions of 7.15 m, 7.45 m, 7.82 m and 13.6 m lengths; 2.5 m, 2.55 m or 2.6 m wide; and up to 2.77 m high, allowing them to be carried within legal limits on European road vehicles and providing sufficient gauge (ie bridge and tunnel) clearance for rail freighting.

In Europe, intermodalism has grown significantly; typically with such operations as the French and German road–rail systems of Novatrans and Kombiverkehr respectively which carry containers, swap bodies and road vehicles on long-haul, trans-European rail journeys.

Among the many catalysts which prompted such developments, was the fact that (pre-Single European Market, 1 January 1993) international road hauliers wishing to cross France or Germany needed road haulage permits authorizing transit through these countries. These were available only on a very limited allocation basis, but hauliers willing to load their vehicles on to rail, piggyback-style (ie on the 'Kangourou' system in France and the 'Kombi-Trans' system in Germany), from one side of the country to the other, were granted transit rights without the need for one of these scarce permits. Such permits are no longer required in the free market.

Appendices

Appendix I

The Traffic Area Network (TAN)

National number for all queries: The telephone contact number for all Traffic Area Offices is 0870 60 60 440. This is the VOSA national telephone number, which is manned by staff trained to deal with all general enquiries between the hours of 07.30–17.30 Monday to Friday, and 08.00–14.30 Saturdays.

Note: Under new arrangements effective from the beginning of 2007 'O' licence application administration is centralized at the following address:

VOSA Licensing Application Services
Hillcrest House
386 Harehills Lane
Leeds LS9 6NF

Post for the public inquiry and regional intelligence units, and personal post for the Traffic Commissioners, should continue to be sent to local offices.

Traffic Area	Areas Covered
North-Eastern Hillcrest House, 386 Harehills Lane, Leeds LS9 6NF Tel: 0870 606 0440 Fax: 0113 248 9607 *Traffic Commissioner:* *Tom Macartney*	The Metropolitan Boroughs within South Yorkshire, Tyne and Wear and West Yorkshire; the Counties of Durham, Northumberland, Nottinghamshire and North Yorkshire; the Districts of Darlington, East Riding of Yorkshire, Hartlepool, Kingston upon Hull, Middlesbrough, North Lincolnshire, North East Lincolnshire, Nottingham, Redcar and Cleveland, Stockton on Tees and York.

North-Western
Hillcrest House,
386 Harehills Lane,
Leeds LS9 6NF
Tel: 0870 606 0440
Fax: 0113 248 9607
Traffic Commissioner:
Beverley Bell

The Metropolitan Boroughs within Greater Manchester and Merseyside; the Counties of Cheshire, Cumbria, Derbyshire and Lancashire; the Districts of Blackburn with Darwen, Blackpool, Derby City, Halton and Warrington.

West Midland
38 George Road,
Edgbaston,
Birmingham B15 1PL
Tel: 0870 606 0440
Fax: 0121 608 1001
Traffic Commissioner:
Nick Jones

The Metropolitan Boroughs within the West Midlands; the Counties of Shropshire, Staffordshire, Warwickshire and Worcestershire; the Districts of Herefordshire, Stoke on Trent and Telford and Wrekin.

Eastern
City House,
126–130 Hills Road,
Cambridge CB2 1NP
Tel: 0870 606 0440
Fax: 01223 309684
Traffic Commissioner:
Richard Turfitt

The Counties of Bedfordshire, Buckinghamshire, Cambridgeshire, Hertfordshire, Essex, Leicestershire, Lincolnshire (except the Districts of North Lincolnshire and North East Lincolnshire), Norfolk, Northamptonshire and Suffolk; the Districts of Leicester, Luton, Milton Keynes, Peterborough, Rutland, Southend on Sea and Thurrock.

Wales
38 George Road,
Edgbaston,
Birmingham B15 1PL
Tel: 0870 606 0440
Fax: 0121 608 1001
Traffic Commissioner:
Nick Jones

Counties of Clwyd, Dyfed, Gwent, Gwynedd, Mid Glamorgan, Powys, South Glamorgan and West Glamorgan.

Western
2 Rivergate,
Temple Quay,
Bristol BS1 6EH
Tel: 0870 606 0440
Fax: 0117 929 8352
Traffic Commissioner:
Sarah Bell

The Counties of Cornwall, Devon, Dorset, Gloucestershire, Hampshire, Oxfordshire, Somerset and Wiltshire; the Districts of Bath and North East Somerset, Bournemouth, Bracknell Forest, Bristol, Isle of Wight, North Somerset, Plymouth, Poole, Portsmouth, Reading, Slough, Southampton, South Gloucestershire, Swindon, Torbay, West Berkshire, Windsor and Maidenhead and Wokingham.

South-Eastern and Metropolitan
Ivy House,
3 Ivy Terrace,
Eastbourne BN21 4QT
Tel: 0870 606 0440
Fax: 01323 721057
Traffic Commissioner:
Philip Brown

Greater London; the Counties of Kent, Surrey, East Sussex and West Sussex; the Districts of Brighton and Hove, the Medway Towns.

Scottish
'J' Floor, Argyle House,
3 Lady Lawson Street,
Edinburgh EH3 9SE
Tel: 0870 606 0440
Fax: 0131 529 8501
Traffic Commissioner:
Joan Aitken

Scotland.

International Road Freight Office

The issue of authorizations and permits for international road freight transport is dealt with by VOSA in Cambridge at:

City House,
126–130 Hills Road
Cambridge CB2 1NP
Tel: 01223 531030
Fax: 01223 309684

Appendix II

Transport Trade Associations and Professional Bodies

Freight Transport Association
Regional Offices
Head Office:
Hermes House
157 St John's Road
Tunbridge Wells
Kent TN4 9UZ
Tel: 01892 526171
Fax: 01892 534989

Midlands, West and Wales:
Hermes House
20 Coventry Road
Cubbington
Leamington Spa
Warwickshire CU32 7JN
Tel: 01926 450020
Fax: 01926 452765

Northern:
Springwood House
Low Lane
Horsforth
Leeds LS18 5NU
Tel: 0113 258 9861
Fax: 0113 258 6501

Scottish (including Northern Ireland):
Hermes House
Melville Terrace
Stirling FK8 2ND
Tel: 01786 457500
Fax: 07186 450412
(Belfast: Tel: 028 9046 6699
Fax: 028 9046 6690)

London and South-eastern:
Hermes House
157 St John's Road
Tunbridge Wells
Kent TN4 9UZ
Tel: 01892 526171
Fax: 01892 552352

Cardiff:
Regus House
Falcon Drive
Cardiff Bay CF10 4RU
Tel: 029 20 504070

Enquiries regarding management
training should be made to Training and
Personnel Services
Hermes House
Tunbridge Wells (see Head Office).

Road Haulage Association
District Offices
Head Office:
Bretton Way
Bretton
Peterborough
PE3 8DD
www.rha.uk.net

Scotland and Northern Ireland:
Roadway House
The Rural Centre
Ingliston
Newbridge EH28 8NZ
Tel: 0131 472 4180
Fax: 0131 472 4179

Northern:
Roadway House
Little Wood Drive
West 26 Industrial Estate
Cleckheaton
West Yorks BD19 4TQ
Tel: 01274 863100
Fax: 01274 865855

Southern and Eastern:
Roadway House
Bretton Way
Bretton
Peterborough PE3 8DD
Tel: 01733 261131
Fax: 01733 332349

Midlands and Western:
Roadway House
Cribbs Causeway
Bristol BS10 7TU
Tel: 01179 503600
Fax: 01179 505647

Other Trade Associations
Local Government Association
Local Government House
Smith Square
London SW1P 3HZ
Tel: 020 7664 3000

Association of Lorry Loader
Manufacturers and Importers (ALLMI)
Unit 76
Prince Maurice House
Cavalier Court
Bumpers Farm
Chippenham, Wilts
SN14 6LH
Tel: 0844 858 4334
www.allmitraining.co.uk

Association of Load Restraint
Equipment Manufacturers (ALREM)
Tel: 01538 382312

Association of Vehicle Recovery
Operators (AVRO)
1 Bath Street
Rugby CV21 3JP
Tel: & Fax: 01788 567320

British Association of Removers (BAR)
Tangent House
62 Exchange Road
Watford, Herts
WD18 0TG
Tel: 01923 699480
www.bar.co.uk

British Industrial Truck Association
Scammell House
High Street
Ascot
Berkshire SL5 7JF
Tel: 01344 623800
Fax: 01344 291197

British International Freight Association
(BIFA)
Redfern House
Browells Lane
Feltham
Middlesex TW13 7EP
Tel: 020 8844 2266
Fax: 020 8890 5546

British Vehicle Rental and Leasing
Association (BVRLA)
River Lodge
Badminton Court
Amersham
Bucks HP7 0DD
Tel: 01494 434747
Fax: 01494 434499

Chemical Industries Association
Kings Buildings
Smith Square
London SW1P 3JJ
Tel: 020 7834 3399
Fax: 020 7834 4469

Joint Approvals Unit for Periodic
Training (JAUPT)
14 Warren Yard Office Village
Milton Keynes MK12 5NW
Tel: 0844 8004184

National Association of Waste Disposal
Contractors (NAWDC)
154 Buckingham Palace Road
London SW1W 9TR
Tel: 020 7824 8882
Fax: 020 7824 8753

National Tyre Distributors Association
(NTDA)
8 Temple Square
Aylesbury, Bucks
HP20 2QH
Tel: 0844 967 0707

Retail Motor Industry Federation (RMI)
201 Great Portland Street
London W1N 6AB
Tel: 020 7580 9122
Fax: 020 7580 6376

Road Operators Safety Council
395 Cowley Road
Oxford O4 2DJ
Tel: 01865 775552
Fax: 01865 711745

Skills for Logistics
12 Warren Yard
Warren Farm Office Village
Stratford Road
Milton Keynes MK12 5NW
Tel: 01908 313360
Fax: 01908 313006

Society of Motor Manufacturers and
Traders (SMMT)
Forbes House
Halkin Street
London SW1X 7DS
Tel: 020 7235 7000
Fax: 020 7235 7112

Transfrigoroute (UK) Ltd
Sanderum House
Oakley Road
Chinnor
Oxford OX39 4TW
Tel: 01844 355560
www.transfrigoroute.co.uk

Transport Association
PO Box 374
Leatherhead
Surrey KT22 2EY
Tel: 07507 785845

UK Warehousing Association
Walter House
418–422 Strand
London WC2R 0PT
Tel: 020 7836 5522

Vehicle Builders and Repairers
Association (VBRA)
Belmont House
Finkle Lane
Gildersome
Leeds LS27 7TW
Tel: 0113 253 8333
Fax: 0113 238 0496

Professional Bodies in Transport

Institute of Advanced Motorists
IAM House
510 Chiswick High Road
London W4 5RG
Tel: 020 8996 9600
Fax: 020 8996 9601

Institute of Grocery Distribution
Grange Lane
Letchmore Heath
Watford
Hertfordshire WD25 8GD
Tel: 01932 857141
Fax: 01923 852531

Chartered Institute of Logistics and Transport (UK)
Earlstrees Court
Earlstrees Road
PO Box 5787
Corby
Northamptonshire NN17 4AX
Tel: 01536 740100
Fax: 01536 740101

Institute of the Motor Industry (IMI)
'Fanshaws'
Brickendon
Hertford SG13 8PQ
Tel: 01992 511521
Fax: 01992 511548

Institution of Mechanical Engineers (IME)
1 Birdcage Walk
London SW1H 9JJ
Tel: 020 7222 7899
Fax: 020 7222 4557

Institute of Transport Administration (IoTA)
The Old Studio
25 Greenfield Road
Westoning
Beds MK45 5DJ
Tel: 01525 634940

Society of Operations Engineers
22 Greencoat Place
London SW1P 1PR
Tel: 020 7630 1111
Fax: 020 7630 6677

Appendix III

Other Organizations Connected with Transport and Transport Journals

Automobile Association (AA)
www.theaa.com

BRAKE (for safe road transport)
PO Box 548
Huddersfield HD1 2XZ
Tel: 01484 559983
Fax: 01484 559983
e-mail: **brake@brake.org.uk**

British Standards Institution (BSI)
389 Chiswick High Road
London W4 4AL
Tel: 0845 367 0242

British Transport Advisory Consortium
6 Byland
Glascote
Tamworth
Staffs B77 2QA
Tel: 07968 406673

CENEX (Centre for Low Carbon and Fuel Technologies)
Holywell Park
Loughborough University
Ashby Road
Leicester LE11 3TU
Tel: 01509 635750

Department for Transport
Enquiry Helpline
Tel: 0300 330 3000
www.dft.gov.uk

Driving Standards Agency
Tel: 0300 200 1122
www.dsa.gov.uk

Freight Best Practice (DfT)
www.businesslink.gov.uk

International Road Freight Office
See page 614

International Road Transport Union (IRU)
Centre International
3 rue de Varembe
PB 44
1211-CH Genève 20
Switzerland
Tel (from UK): 00 + 41 22 734 13 30
Fax: 00 + 41 22 733 06 60

Green Flag National Breakdown
Tel: 0845 246 1557
www.greenflag.com

Royal Automobile Club (RAC)
RAC House
M1 Cross
Brent Terrace
London NW2 1LT
Tel: 020 8452 8000
Fax: 020 8208 0679

OCR
Westwood Way
Westwood Business Park
Coventry CV4 8JQ
For vocational examination enquiries
Tel: 02476 851509

Recruitment and Employment Federation
36–38 Mortimer Street
London W1W 7RG
Tel: 020 7462 3260
Fax: 020 7255 2878

Royal Society for the Prevention of Accidents (RoSPA)
Cannon House
Priory Queensway
Birmingham B4 6BS
Tel: 0121 248 2000

Skills for Logistics
12 Warren Yard
Warren Farm Office Village
Stratford Road
Milton Keynes MK12 5NM
Tel: 01908 313360
Fax: 1908 313806
e-mail: **rhdtc@dial.pipex.com**

Vehicle & Operator Services Agency (VOSA)
Berkeley House
Croydon Street
Bristol BS5 0DA
Tel: 0870 6060 440
Fax: 0117 954 3212

Transport Journals
Commercial Motor
Quadrant House
The Quadrant
Sutton
Surrey SM2 5AS
Tel: 020 8652 3673/3302

Export and Freight
The Old Coach House
12 Main Street
Hillsborough
Co. Down BT26 6AE
Northern Ireland
Tel: 01762 334272
Fax: 01762 351046

Logistics and Transport Focus (Journal of Institute of Logistics and Transport)
Supply-Chain Centre
PO Box 5787
Corby
Northants NN17 4XQ
Tel: 01536 740100
Fax: 01536 740103

Freight (Journal of FTA)
Hermes House
St John's Road
Tunbridge Wells TN4 9UZ
Tel: 01892 26171

International Freighting Weekly (IFW)
Informa Freight Publishing
69-77 Paul Street
London EC2A 4LQ
Tel: 020 7505 3551

Motor Transport
Quadrant House
The Quadrant
Sutton
Surrey SM2 5AS
Tel: 020 8661 3500

Removals and Storage (Journal of
British Association of Removers)
3 Churchill Court
58 Station Road
North Harrow HA2 7SA
Tel: 020 8861 3331

Roadway (Journal of RHA)
Roadway House
Bretton Way
Bretton
Peterborough
PE3 8DD
www.rha.uk.net

Transport Engineer
22 Greencote Place
London SW1P 1PR
Tel: 020 7630 1111
Fax: 020 7630 6677

Transport News Digest (TND)
38 Portobello Road
London W11 3DH
Tel: 020 7727 0253

Trucking
30 Monmouth Street
Bath
BA1 2BW
www.truckingmag.co.uk

Appendix IV

Vehicle and Operator Services Agency (VOSA) Weighbridges

This list shows the geographical location of VOSA dynamic axle weighbridges within Traffic Areas. Locations marked * provide a self-weighing facility.

North-Western

A5, Holyhead, Anglesey, North Wales.

Wallasey Tunnel (East), Liverpool, Merseyside.

Wallasey Tunnel (West), Liverpool, Merseyside.

M62, Junction 20, Thornham, Greater Manchester.

A59, Samlesbury, Preston, Lancashire.

A556, Rostherne, Cheshire.

A5117/M56, Dunkirk, Cheshire.

A74, Harker, Carlisle, Cumbria.

A494, Ewloe, Clwyd, North Wales.

North-Eastern

A1, Scotch Corner, Middleton Tyas, North Yorkshire.

A19, Wellfield, County Durham.

A1/A659, Boston Spa, Wetherby, West Yorkshire.

A63, South Cave, North Humberside.

*Nepshaw Lane, Gildersome, Morley, Leeds, Yorkshire.

A1, Robin Hoods Well, Skellow, Doncaster, South Yorkshire.

Blackley New Road, Ainley Top, Huddersfield, West Yorkshire.

A61, Barnsley Road, Tankersley, Barnsley, South Yorkshire.

*King George V Docks, Kingston upon Hull, Humberside.

*A15, Approach Road, Humber Bridge, Hessle, South Humberside.

A46/52, Saxondale, The Old Nottingham Road, Bingham, Nottinghamshire.

A449, Link Road, Warndon, Nottinghamshire.

West Midlands

A5, Wall Island, Lichfield, Staffordshire.

M6, Doxey, Nr Stafford, Staffordshire.

A45/M45, Thurleston Island, Dunchurch, Rugby, Warwickshire.

M5, Junction 3, Quinton, Nr Birmingham, West Midlands.

*A40, Three Crosses, Ross-on-Wye, Gloucestershire.

Eastern

A43, Towcester, Northamptonshire.

A17/A15, Holdingham, Sleaford, Lincolnshire.

A428/M1, Junction 18, Crick, Northamptonshire.

*Stone Grove Road, The Dock, Felixstowe, Suffolk.

Old A45 Road, Risby, Suffolk.

A1, Southbound, Connington Fen, Sawtry, Cambridgeshire.

A1, Northbound, Lower Caldecote, Sandy, Bedfordshire.

A414/M11, Junction 7, Harlow, Essex.

M1, Junction 14, Newport Pagnell, Buckinghamshire.

Southlands Road, Denham, Buckinghamshire.

South Wales

A40, Penblewin, Narberth, Dyfed.

M4, Coldra, Newport, Gwent.

Western

*Millbay Docks, Plymouth, Devon.

A303, Wylye, Wiltshire.

Off A361, Sampford Peverell, Tiverton, Devon.

*Continental Freight Ferry Terminal, New Harbour Road, Poole, Dorset.

A38, Anchor Inn Lay-by Kennford, Devon.

A35, Lay-by, Puddletown, Dorchester, Dorset.

*Portsmouth Docks, Portsmouth, Hampshire.

A46, Tormarton, Avon.

A34/A415, Marsham Road, Abingdon, Oxfordshire.

South-Eastern and Metropolitan

A30, Staines Bypass, Surrey.

M25, Junction 9, Leatherhead interchange, Surrey.

A13, Barking, Essex.

A3, Burpham, Nr Guildford, Surrey.

A1, Holloway Road, London (North).

*Dover, East Dock, Dover, Kent.

*Dover, West Dock, Dover, Kent.

A23, Handcross, West Sussex.

Stockers Hill, Boughton, Kent.

A27, Beddingham, East Sussex.

A26/A22, Millpond, Maresfield, East Sussex.

*A27, Withy Patch, Lancing, West Sussex.

Sheerness Docks, Sheerness, Kent.

Scottish

A75, Castle Kennedy.

*A90, Cramond.

*A92, Findon, Nr Aberdeen.

A74, Beattock Summit.

M9, Craigforth, Stirling.

*Tayside Truckstop, Smeaton Road, Dundee.

For a fully detailed list of currently available weighbridges consult the *Commercial Motor* list or visit **www.chrishodgetrucks.co.uk** and click on weighbridges.

Appendix V

Police Services in Great Britain (for Notification of Abnormal Load Movements)

In most cases, police forces require fax notifications of abnormal load movements to be clearly identified as such in the heading or prefix to the message. Communications should be addressed to the Chief Constable, unless a specific department is indicated. Up-to-date information on the Police Service can be found by following the links at **www.police.uk**.

England

Constabulary/Force	Address/Tel/Fax Nos for Notification
Avon and Somerset	Abnormal Loads Dept, PO Box 37, Valley Road, Portishead, Bristol BS20 8QJ. Tel: 01275 816885; Fax: 01275 816884
Bedfordshire	Abnormal Loads, 4th Information Room, Woburn Road, Kempston, Bedford MK43 9AX. Tel: 01234 842249; Fax: 01234 842051
Cambridgeshire	Hinchingbrooke Park, Huntingdon PE29 6NP. Tel: 0845 456 4564; Fax: 01480 414448/412848
Cheshire	Clemends Way, Oakmere Road, Winsford CW7 2VA. Tel: 0845 458 0000
City of London Police	Abnormal Loads Dept, 37 Wood Street, London EC2P 2NQ. Tel: 020 7601 2190; Fax: 020 7601 2760 *For City of London movements only – not Metropolitan area.*
Cleveland	Ladgate Lane, Middlesbrough, Cleveland TS8 9EH. Tel: 01642 326326; Fax: 01642 301200

Cumbria	Carleton Hall, Penrith, Cumbria CA10 2AU. Tel: 0845 3300 247
Derbyshire	Butterley Hall, Ripley, Derbyshire DE5 3RS. Tel: 0845 123 3333
Devon and Cornwall	Abnormal Loads Office, Middlemoor, Exeter EX2 7HQ. Tel: 08452 777444
Dorset Police	Winfrith, Dorchester, Dorset DT2 8DZ. Tel: 01305 223731; Fax: 01202 223678
Durham	Operational Support, Aykley Heads, Durham DH1 5TT. Tel: 0191 386 4929; Fax: 0191 375 2160
Essex Police	POBox 2, Springfield, Chelmsford CM2 6DA. Tel: 01245 491491; Fax: 01245 452424
Gloucestershire	No. 1 Waterwells, Waterwells Drive, Quedgeley, Gloucestershire GH2 2AN. Tel: 0845 090 1234
Greater Manchester	Traffic Management Section, PO Box 22, Manchester M16 0RE. Tel: 0161 827 5050; Fax: 0161 856 1676
Hampshire	West Hill, Romsey Road, Hants SO22 5DB. Tel: 0845 045 4545; Fax: 01983 538650 For Isle of Wight movements: Tel: 01983 528000
Hertfordshire	Stanborough Road, Welwyn Garden City, Herts AL8 6XF. Tel: 0845 3300 222; Fax: 01707 354572
Humberside Police	Priory Police Station, Priory Road, Hull, HU5 5SF. Tel: 0845 6060 222; Fax: 01482 597645
Kent County	Police HQ Ops Centre, Sutton Road, Maidstone, Kent ME15 9BZ. Tel: 01622 690690; Fax: 01622 654169
Lancashire	PO Box 77, Hutton, Nr Preston PR4 5SB. Tel: 0845 125 3445; Fax: 01772 410788
Leicestershire	Abnormal Loads Dept, St Johns, Narborough, Leicester LE9 2BX. Tel: 0116 222 2222; Fax: 0116 248 2327
Lincolnshire Police	PO Box 999, Lincoln LN5 7PH. Tel: 01522 532222; Fax: 01522 558098
Merseyside Police	Traffic Dept, Canning, Liverpool P11 8SX. Tel: 0151 709 6010; Fax: 0151 777 5760
Metropolitan Police	Room 154, New Scotland Yard, Broadway, London SW1H 0BG. Tel: 020 7230 1212; Fax: 020 7230 2133 *Covers Greater London but not City of London.*

Norfolk	Jubilee House, Falconers Close, Wymondham, Norfolk, NR38 0WU. Tel: 0845 456 4567; Fax: 0845 345 4567
Northamptonshire Police	Woolton Hall, Mereway, Northampton NN4 0JQ. Tel: 0845 700 700
Northumbria Police	Area Operations Room, Ponteland, Newcastle upon Tyne NG20 0BL. Tel: 03456 6060 247
North Yorkshire Police	Force Communications Centre, Racecourse Lane, Northallerton DL7 9HA. Tel: 01609 783131; Fax: 01609 789213
Nottinghamshire Police	Force Control Room, Sherwood Lodge, Arnold, Nottingham NG5 8PP. Tel: 0115 967 0999; Fax: 0115 967 2145
South Yorkshire Police	Abnormal Loads Officer, Snig Hill, Sheffield S3 8LY. Tel: 0114 220 2020; Fax: 0114 252 3250
Staffordshire Police	Abnormal Loads Section, Cannock Road, Stafford ST18 0YY. Tel: 01785 232674; Fax: 01785 232673
Suffolk	Ipswich IP5 3QS. Tel: 01473 613500; Fax: 01473 613737
Surrey	Mount Browne, Sandy Lane, Guildford, Surrey GU3 1HG. Tel: 0845 125 2222 *NB: Certain parts of the county of Surrey fall within the jurisdiction of the Metropolitan Police.*
Sussex Police	Church Lane, Lewes, East Sussex BN7 2DZ. Tel: 0845 6070 999; Fax: 01273 404274
Thames Valley Police	Headquarters, Kidlington, Oxford OX5 2NX. Tel: 01865 846816; Fax: 01865 846726 *Includes movements in Berkshire, Buckinghamshire and Oxfordshire.*
Warwickshire	PO Box 4, Leek, Woolten, Warwick CV35 7QB. Tel: 01926 415260; Fax: 01926 415388
West Mercia	PO Box 55, Worcester WR3 8SP. Tel: 0845 444 888; Fax: 01905 756161
West Midlands Police	Lloyd House, Colmore Circus, Queensway, Birmingham B4 6NQ. Tel: 0845 113 5000; Fax: 0121 322 6039
West Yorkshire Police	Operations Division PO Box 9, Wakefield WF1 3QP. Tel: 01924 375222; Fax: 01924 292182
Wiltshire	London Road, Devizes SN10 2DN. Tel: 01380 734022; Fax: 01380 734135

Wales

Constabulary/Force   *Address/Tel/Fax: Nos for Notification*

Dyfed-Powys Police   PO Box 99, Llangunnor, Carmarthen, Carmarthenshire
                             SA31 2PF.
                             Tel: 0845 330 2000; Fax: 01267 222 185

Gwent   Headquarters, Croesyceiliog, Cwmbran, Gwent
                             NP44 2XJ.
                             Tel: 01633 838111; Fax: 01633 642312

North Wales Police   Central Control Room, Glan-y-Don, Colwyn Bay
                             LL29 8AW.
                             Tel: 0845 607 1002; Fax: 01492 5110777

South Wales   Communications Dept, Bridgend, Mid Glamorgan
                             CF31 3SU.
                             Tel: 01656 655555

Scotland

Constabulary/Force   *Address/Tel/Fax: Nos for Notification*

Central Scotland Police   Randolphfield, Stirling FK8 2HD.
                             Tel: 01786 456000; Fax: 01786 451177

Dumfries and Galloway   Cornwall Mount, Dumfries DG1 1PZ.
                             Tel: 0845 6005701

Fife   Detroit Road, Glenrothes KY6 2RJ.
                             Tel: 0845 6005702

Grampian Police   Queen Street, Aberdeen AB10 1ZA
                             Tel: 0845 6005700

Lothian and Borders Police   Fettes Avenue, Edinburgh EH4 1RB.
                             Tel: 0131 311 3131; Fax: 0131 440 6889

Northern   Old Perth Road, Inverness IV2 3SY.
                             Tel: 0845 6033388; Fax: 01463 230800
                             For Highland Region, Orkney, Shetland and Western
                             Isles.

Strathclyde Police   173 Pitt Street, Glasgow G2 4JJ.
                             Tel: 0141 532 2000; Fax: 0141 207 5758

Tayside Police   PO Box 59, West Bell Street, Dundee DD1 9JU.
                             Tel: 0845 600 5705; Fax: 01382 200449

Appendix VI

Local and Other Authorities (for Notification of Abnormal Load Movements)

Local Authorities (responsible for highways and bridges, or their agents for abnormal load notifications)

Further information may be obtained by accessing the Local Government website: **www.lga.gov.uk**.

England

Counties

County	Address
Bedfordshire	Engineering Policy and Planning, Bedfordshire County Council, County Hall, Bedford MK42 9AP Tel: 01234 363222
Buckinghamshire	Head of Transportation, Buckinghamshire County Council, County Hall, Walton Street, Aylesbury, Bucks HP20 1UY Tel: 01296 382420; Fax: 01296 383990
Cambridgeshire	Assistant Director (Highways and Engineering) Department of Environment and Transport, Cambridgeshire County Council, Castle Court, Shire Hall, Castle Hill, Cambridge CB3 0AP Tel: 01223 717715

Cheshire	Director of Environment Services, Cheshire County Council, County Hall, Chester CH1 1SF Tel: 01244 603770; Fax: 01244 603608
Cornwall	Director of Planning, Transportation and Estates, Cornwall County Council, County Hall, Truro TR1 3AY Tel: 01872 322000
Cumbria	Director of Community Economy and Environment, Cumbria County Council, Citadel Chambers, Citadel Road, Carlisle CA3 8SG Tel: 01228 606060; Fax: 01228 606755
Derbyshire	Director of Environmental Services, Traffic Section, Derbyshire County Council, County Offices, Matlock DE4 3AG Tel: 01629 580000 extn 7591; Fax: 01629 585255
Devon	County Environment Directorate, Devon County Council, Lucombe House, County Hall, Topsharn Road, Exeter EX2 4QW Tel: 0 1392 383249; Fax: 01392 382135
Dorset	Head of Highways and Transportation, Dorset County Council, Colliton Park, County Hall, Dorchester, Dorset DT1 1XJ Tel: 01305 251000
Durham	Director of Environment and Technical Services, Durham County Council, County Hall, Durham DH1 5UQ Tel: 0191 386 4411
East Sussex	Director of Transport and Environment, East Sussex County Council, County Hall, St Anne's Crescent, Lewes, East Sussex BN7 1UE Tel: 01273 481000
Essex	Head of Transportation and Operational Services, Essex County Council, County Hall, Chelmsford CM1 1QH Tel: 01245 437065
Gloucestershire	Executive Director: Environment, Gloucestershire County Council, Shire Hall, Gloucester GL1 2TH Tel: 01452 425523; Fax: 01452 541305
Hampshire	Director of Environment, Hampshire County Council, The Castle, Winchester S023 8UJ Tel: 01962 841841; Fax: 01962 847055
Hertfordshire	Director of Environment, Hertfordshire County Council, County Hall, Hertford SG13 8DE Tel: 01992 555201; Fax: 01992 588900

Kent	Director of Strategic Planning, Kent County Council, Sessions House, County Hall, Maidstone, Kent ME14 IXQ Tel: 01622 221612
Lancashire	Environment Director, Lancashire County Council, Guild House, Cross Street, Preston PR1 8RD Tel: 01772 264468; Fax: 01772 262154
Leicestershire	Director of Planning and Transportation, Leicestershire County Council, County Hall, Glenfield, Leicester LE3 8RJ Tel: 0116 265 7000; Fax: 0116 265 7962
Lincolnshire	Director of Highways and Planning, Lincolnshire County Council, City Hall (4th Floor), Lincoln LN1 1DN Tel: 01522 553053; Fax: 01522 553149
Norfolk	Director of Planning and Transportation, Norfolk County Council, County Hall, Martineau Lane, Norwich NR1 2SG Tel: 01603 222143; Fax: 01603 223219
Northamptonshire	Highways Service, Northamptonshire County Council, PO Box 221, John Dryden House, 8–10 The Lakes, Northampton NN4 7DE Tel: 01604 237155; Fax: 01604 236393
Northumberland	Director of Environment, Northumberland County Council, County Hall, Morpeth, Northumberland NE61 2EF Tel: 01670 533000; Fax: 01670 533086
North Yorkshire	Director of Environmental Services, North Yorkshire County Council, County Hall, Northallerton, North Yorkshire DL7 8AH Tel: 01609 780780
Nottinghamshire	Director of Environment, Nottinghamshire County Council, Trent Bridge House, Fox Road, West Bridgford, Nottingham NG2 6BJ Tel: 0115 977 4500; Fax: 0115 945 4531
Oxfordshire	Director of Environmental Services, Oxfordshire County Council, Speedwell House, Speedwell Street, Oxford OX1 1NE Tel: 01865 815700
Shropshire	Corporate Director, Community and Environment Directorate, Shropshire County Council, The Shirehall, Abbey Foregate, Shrewsbury SY2 6ND Tel: 01743 253021; Fax: 01743 252505

Somerset	Corporate Director Environment and Property, Somerset County Council, County Hall, Taunton, Somerset TA1 4DY Tel: 01823 355600; Fax: 01823 356107
Staffordshire	Development Services Department, Staffordshire County Council, Riverway, Stafford ST16 3TJ Tel: 01785 276633
Suffolk	Director of Environment and Transport, Suffolk County Council, St Edmund House, County Hall, Ipswich IP4 1LZ Tel: 01473 583305; Fax: 01473 230078
Surrey	Head of Engineering, Surrey County Council, County Hall, Kingston-upon-Thames KT1 2DY Tel: 020 8541 9375; Fax: 020 8541 9447
Warwickshire	Director of Planning, Transport and Economic Strategy, Warwickshire County Council, PO Box 43, Shire Hall, Warwick CV34 4SX Tel: 01926 410410; Fax: 01926 412903
West Sussex	Transport Planning Service, Environment and Development Group, West Sussex County Council, The Grange, Tower Street, Chichester, West Sussex P019 1RH Tel: 01243 777100
Wiltshire	Director of Environmental Services, Wiltshire County Council, County Hall, Trowbridge, Wilts BA14 8JD Tel: 01225 713000

Greater London and Metropolitan County Areas

Greater London

Corporation of London	Director of Technical Services, Corporation of London, PO Box 270, Guildhall, London EC2P 2EJ Tel: 020 7606 3030
Barking and Dagenham	Controller of Development and Technical Services, London Borough of Barking and Dagenham, Town Hall, Barking, Essex IG11 7LU Tel: 020 8592 4500
Barnet	Chief Highways Officer, London Borough of Barnet, Barnet House, 1255 High Road, Whetstone, London N20 0EJ Tel: 020 8359 4481; Fax: 020 8359 4116

Bexley	Chief Engineer Directorate of Environmental Services, Bexley Civic Offices, Broadway, Bexleyheath, Kent DA6 7LB Tel: 020 8303 7777 extn 2929
Brent	Director of Transportation, London Borough of Brent, Brent House, High Road, Wembley HA9 6BZ Tel: 020 8937 5128; Fax: 020 8937 5125
Bromley	Director of Environmental Services, London Borough of Bromley, Bromley Civic Centre, Stockwell Close, Bromley BR1 3UH Tel: 020 8313 4443
Camden	Director of Environment, London Borough of Camden, Argyle Street, London WC1H 8EQ Tel: 020 7974 2605; Fax: 020 7974 5556
Croydon	Planning and Transportation, London Borough of Croydon, Taberner House, Park Lane, Croydon CR9 3JS Tel: 020 8686 4433
Ealing	Executive Director: Environment, London Borough of Ealing, Perceval House, 14–16 Uxbridge Road, Ealing W5 2HL Tel: 020 8825 6859; Fax: 020 8579 5453
Enfield	Director of Environmental Services, London Borough of Enfield, PO Box 52, Civic Centre, Silver Street, Enfield EN1 3XD Tel: 020 8379 3503
Greenwich	Strategic Planning, London Borough of Greenwich, Peggy Middleton House, 50 Woolwich New Road, Woolwich SE18 6HQ Tel: 020 8854 8888 extn 5488
Hackney	Borough Services, London Borough of Hackney, Maurice Bishop House, Reading Lane, Hackney, London E8 1HH Tel: 020 8356 3000; Fax: 020 8356 8142
Hammersmith and Fulham	Environment Department, London Borough of Hammersmith and Fulham, Town Hall, King Street, London W6 9JU Tel: 020 8748 3020 extn 3004
Haringey	Director of Environmental Services, Haringey Council, Tottenham Town Hall, Town Hall Approach Road, London N15 4RY Tel: 020 8489 4537; Fax: 020 8489 4596

Harrow	Head of Environment and Transportation, London Borough of Harrow, PO Box 37, Civic Centre, Harrow, Middlesex HA1 2UY Tel: 020 8863 5611; Fax: 020 8424 1541
Havering	Transportation Planning Manager, Building and Technical Services, London Borough of Havering, The Whitworth Centre, Noak Hill Road, Harold Hill, Romford RM3 7YA Tel: 01708 432804; Fax: 01708 433719
Hillingdon	Head of Transportation, London Borough of Hillingdon, Civic Centre, High Street, Uxbridge, London UB8 IUW Tel: 01895 250111
Hounslow	Head of Traffic and Parking, Environmental Services Department, Borough of Hounslow, Civic Centre, Lampton Road, Hounslow, Middlesex TW3 4DN Tel: 020 8583 4961; Fax: 020 8583 5350
Islington	Head of Planning Transport, London Borough of Islington, PO Box 3333, 222 Upper Street, London N1 1YA Tel: 020 7527 2000
Kensington and Chelsea	Mr Michael Stroud, Executive Director of Environmental Services, Royal Borough of Kensington and Chelsea, Council Offices, Pembroke Road, London W8 6PW Tel: 020 7341 5101; Fax: 020 7341 5155
Kingston upon Thames	Director of Environmental Services, Royal Borough of Kingston upon Thames, Guildhall, Kingston upon Thames KT1 1EU Tel: 020 8546 2121
Lambeth	Head of Transportation and Highways, London Borough of Lambeth, 3rd Floor, Blue Star House, 234–244 Stockwell Road, London SW9 9SP Tel: 020 7926 1236; Fax: 020 7926 2486
Lewisham	Directorate of Regeneration, London Borough of Lewisham, Laurence House, Catford Road, Catford, London SE6 4RU Tel: 020 8314 7167
Merton	Director of Environmental Services, London Borough of Merton, Civic Centre, London Road, Morden, Surrey SM4 5DX Tel: 020 8543 2222; Fax: 020 8545 4105
Newham	Director of Environment, London Borough of Newham, 25 Nelson Street, East Ham, London E6 6EH Tel: 020 8430 2000 extn 22301; Fax: 020 8430 3051

Redbridge	Highways Services, London Borough of Redbridge, Lynton House, 255/259 High Road, Ilford, Essex IG1 1NY Tel: 020 8478 3020; Fax: 020 8708 3970
Richmond upon Thames	Transport Planning Manager, London Borough of Richmond upon Thames, 44 York Street, Twickenham TW1 3BZ Tel: 020 8891 7310
Southwark	Director of Regeneration, London Borough of Southwark, Chiltern House, Portland Street, London SE17 2ES Tel: 020 7525 5000; Fax: 020 7525 5484
Sutton	Head of Transportation, London Borough of Sutton, 24 Denmark Road, Carshalton SM5 2JG Tel: 020 8770 5000
Tower Hamlets	Highways Department, London Borough of Tower Hamlets, 60 Southern Grove, London E3 4PN Tel: 020 7364 5000
Waltham Forest	Head of Street Services, Low Hall Depot, Argyll Avenue, Leyton E10 7AS Tel: 020 8496 2510; Fax: 020 8496 2512
Wandsworth	Director of Technical Services, Wandsworth Borough Council, Town Hall, Wandsworth High Street, London SW18 2PU Tel: 020 8871 6547; Fax: 020 8871 0218
Westminster	Director of Planning and Transportation, Westminster City Council, PO Box 240, Westminster City Hall, 64 Victoria Street, London SW1E 6QP Tel: 020 7641 6000

Metropolitan Borough Councils

Greater Manchester Area

Bolton	Director of Environment, Bolton Metropolitan Borough Council, The Wellsprings, Civic Centre, Bolton BL1 1US Tel: 01204 336470
Bury	Borough Engineer, Development and Environmental Services Department, Bury Metropolitan Borough Council, Lester House, Broad Street, Bury BL9 0AW Tel: 0161 253 5804; Fax: 0161 253 5329

Manchester	Engineering Services Division, Chief Executives Department, Manchester City Council, Town Hall, Manchester M60 2JT Tel: 0161 455 2258; Fax: 0161 455 2151
Oldham	Executive Director, Environment and Transportation, Oldham Metropolitan Borough Council, Henshaw House, Cheapside, Oldham OL1 1NY Tel: 0161 911 4300; Fax: 0161 911 3411
Rochdale	Director of Technical Services, Rochdale Metropolitan Borough Council, PO Box 20, Electric House, Smith Street, Rochdale OL16 1YP Tel: 01706 647474
City of Salford	Director of Development Services, City of Salford, Civic Centre, Chorley Road, Swinton, Salford M27 5BW Tel: 0161 793 3800; Fax: 0161 793 3848
Stockport	Director of Environment and Economic Development, Stockport Metropolitan Borough Council, Stopford House, Piccadilly, Stockport SK1 3XE Tel: 0161 474 4934
Tameside	Head of Engineering Services, Tameside Metropolitan Borough Council, Council Offices, Wellington Road, Ashton-under-Lyne, Tameside OL6 6BL Tel: 0161 342 8355; Fax: 0161 342 3911
Trafford	Executive Director of Economic and Community Regeneration, Trafford Metropolitan Borough Council, Trafford Town Hall, Talbot Road, Stretford, Trafford, Greater Manchester M32 0YX Tel: 0161 912 4453; Fax: 0161 912 4407
Wigan	Director of Engineering Services, Wigan Metropolitan Borough Council, Civic Buildings, New Market Street, Wigan WN1 1RP Tel: 01942 244991; Fax: 01942 404210

Merseyside Area

Knowsley	Head of Transportation and Engineering Services, Department of Planning and Development, Knowsley Metropolitan Borough, PO Box 26, Yorkon Building, Archway Road, Huyton, Knowsley, Merseyside L36 9FB Tel: 0151 443 2235
Liverpool	Executive Director of Regeneration, Liverpool City Council, 2nd Floor, Kingsway House, Hatton Garden, Liverpool L69 2RA Tel: 0151 233 3000; Fax: 0151 225 2924

St Helens
Transport Department,
St Helens Metropolitan Borough Council,
Hardshaw Brook Depot, Warrington New Road,
St Helens, Merseyside WA9 1JR
Tel: 01744 456000

Sefton
Technical Services Director,
Sefton Metropolitan Borough Council, Balliol House,
Balliol Road, Bootle, Liverpool L20 3NJ
Tel: 0151 922 4040

Wirral
Borough Engineer, Metropolitan Borough of Wirral,
Town Hall, Civic Way, Bebington CH63 7PT
Tel: 0151 643 9000

South Yorkshire Area

Barnsley
Transportation Manager, Planning and Transportation,
Barnsley Metropolitan Borough Council, Central Offices,
Kendry Street, Barnsley S70 2TN
Tel: 01226 772629; Fax: 01226 772199

Doncaster
Infrastructure Services,
Directorate of Development and Transport Engineering,
Scarborough House, Chequer Road, Doncaster DN1 2DB
Tel 01302 735113; Fax: 01302 735028

Rotherham
Transportation Unit Manager,
Regeneration and Planning Service, Bailey House,
Rawmarsh Road, Rotherham S60 1QT
Tel: 01709 822953; Fax: 01709 822139

Sheffield
Head of Service, Planning, Transport and Highways,
Sheffield City Council, Howden House, 1 Union Street,
Sheffield S1 2SH
Tel: 0114 273 5499; Fax: 0114 273 5002

Tyne and Wear Area

Gateshead
Head of Transport Strategy, Gateshead Council, Civic Centre,
Regent Street, Gateshead NE8 1HH
Tel: 0191 433 3000; Fax: 0191 477 8422

Newcastle upon Tyne
Planning and Transportation, Newcastle City Council,
Civic Centre, Newcastle upon Tyne NE1 8PD
Tel: 0191 232 8520; Fax: 0191 211 4984

North Tyneside
Environmental Services, North Tyneside Council,
PO Box 113, Station Road, Killingworth,
Newcastle upon Tyne NE12 6WJ
Tel: 0191 219 2198; Fax: 0191 219 2534

South Tyneside	Director of Development Services, South Tyneside Metropolitan Borough Council, Town Hall and Civic Offices, Westoe Road, South Shields NE33 2RL Tel: 0 191427 1717; Fax: 0191 427 717 1
Sunderland	Director of Environment, City of Sunderland, Civic Centre, Sunderland SR2 7DN Tel: 0191 553 1000; Fax: 0191 553 1460

West Midlands Area

Birmingham	Director of Transportation, Birmingham City Council, 1 Lancaster Circus, Queensway, Birmingham B4 7BQ Tel: 0121 303 7400; Fax: 0121 303 1352
Coventry	Director of City Development, Coventry City Council, Tower Block, Much Park Street, Coventry CV1 2PY Tel: 024 7683 2037; Fax: 024 7683 1324
Dudley	Environment, Engineering and Transportation Department, Council House, Mary Stevens Park, Stourbridge, West Midlands DY8 2AA Tel: 01384 814005
Sandwell	Highways Direct, Sandwell Metropolitan Borough Council, PO Box 42, Lombard Street, West Bromwich, West Midlands B70 8RU Tel: 0121 569 4141; Fax: 0121 569 4072
Solihull	Director of Environment Services, PO Box 19, Council House, Solihull B91 3QT Tel: 0121 704 6000; Fax: 0121 704 6404
Walsall	Engineering and Transportation Services, Walsall Metropolitan Borough Council, Civic Centre, Walsall WS1 1DG Tel: 01922 652558; Fax: 01922 649036
Wolverhampton	Head of Transportation, Wolverhampton City Council, Salop Street, Wolverhampton WV3 0SQ Tel: 01902 555700; Fax: 01902 555656

West Yorkshire Area

Bradford	Head of Transportation and Planning, City of Bradford Council, 3rd Floor, Jacobs Well, Bradford BD1 5RW Tel: 01274 754605; Fax: 01274 754583
Calderdale	Calderdale Metropolitan Borough Council, Northgate House, Northgate, Halifax HX1 1UN Tel: 01422 357257; Fax: 01422 392195

Kirklees	Head of Highways Services, Flint Street, Fartown, Huddersfield HD1 6LG Freephone: 0800 731 8765
Leeds	Director of Highways and Transportation, Selectapost 6, 2 Rossington Street, Leeds LS2 8HB Tel: 0113 247 7500
Wakefield	Head of Engineering, Engineering Division Development Department, PO Box 92, Newton Bar, Wakefield, West Yorkshire WF1 1XS Tel: 01924 306009; Fax: 01924 306052

Unitary Authorities

Bath and North East Somerset	Head of Transportation, Access and Waste Management, Bath and North East Somerset Council, Riverside, Temple Street, Keynsham, Bristol BS31 1LA Tel: 01225 394128; Fax: 01225 394335
Blackburn with Darwen	Director of Technical Services, Blackburn with Darwen Borough Council, Town Hall, Blackburn, Lancs BB1 7DY Tel: 01254 841240
Blackpool	Head of Technical Services, Business Services Dept, Blackpool Borough Council, PO Box 117, Westgate House, Squires Gate Lane, Blackpool FY4 2TS Tel: 01253 476111; Fax: 01253 476112
Bournemouth	Director of Development Services, Bournemouth Borough Council, Town Hall Annexe, St Stephens Road, Bournemouth BH2 6EA Tel: 01202 451451; Fax: 01202 451006
Bracknell Forest	Planning and Transportation Department, Bracknell Forest Borough Council, Time Square, Market Street, Bracknell, Berkshire RG12 1JD Tel: 01344 424642; Fax: 01344 3 51260
Brighton and Hove	Chief Executive, Brighton and Hove City Council, King's House, Grand Avenue, Hove BN3 2LS Tel: 01273 290000; Fax: 01273 291003
Bristol City	Director of Environment, Transport and Leisure, Bristol City Council, Colston House, Colston Street, Bristol BS1 5AQ Tel: 0117 922 2000
Darlington	Chief Executive, Darlington Borough Council, Town Hall, Darlington DL1 5QT Tel: 01325 380651; Fax: 01325 382032

Derby City	Transport Policy Officer, Development and Cultural Services, Derby City Council, Roman House, Friar Gate, Derby DE1 1XB Tel: 01332 715034; Fax: 01332 715040
East Riding of Yorkshire	Director of Operational Services, East Riding Council of Yorkshire, County Hall, Beverley HU17 9BA Tel: 01482 887700; Fax: 01482 884944
Halton	Executive Director, Environment and Development, Halton Borough Council, Grosvenor House, Halton Lea, Runcorn WA7 2GW Tel: 0151 424 2061; Fax: 0151 471 7304
Hartlepool	Head of Highways and Transportation, Hartlepool Council, Bryan Hanson House, Hanson Square, Hartlepool TS24 7BT Tel: 01429 523241; Fax: 01429 523541
Herefordshire	County Offices, Herefordshire Council, Engineering Services, PO Box 234, Hereford HR1 2HQ Tel: 01432 260779; Fax: 01432 261983
Isle of Wight	Directorate of Environment Services, Isle of Wight Council, County Hall, Newport, Isle of Wight PO30 1UD Tel: 01983 821000
Kingston upon Hull City	Director of Technical Services, Kingston upon Hull City Council, Kingston House, Bond Street, Kingston upon Hull HU1 3ER Tel: 01482 300300
Leicester City	Director of Environment and Development, Leicester City Council, New Walk Centre, Welford Place, Leicester LE1 6ZG Tel: 0116 254 9922; Fax: 0116 254 5531
Luton	Luton Borough Council, Department of Environment, Regeneration, Engineering and Transportation Division, Town Hall, Luton LU1 2BQ Tel: 01582 546000
Medway	Planning and Development, Front Line Task Force Division, Compass Centre, Chatham Maritime, Chatham, Kent ME4 4YH Tel: 01634 331145; Fax: 01634 331613
Middlesbrough	Head of Transport and Design Services, Middlesbrough Council, PO Box 99A, Town Hall, Middlesbrough TS1 2QQ Tel: 01642 264002

Milton Keynes	Strategic Director Environment, Milton Keynes Council, PO Box 108, Civic Offices, 1 Saxon Gate East, Milton Keynes MK9 3ZL Tel: 01908 691691
North East	Head of Engineering, North East Lincolnshire Council, Lincolnshire Civic Offices, Knoll Street, Cleethorpes DN35 8LN Tel: 01472 313131; Fax: 01472 324302
North	Assistant Director Highways and Transportation, Lincolnshire North Lincolnshire Council, PO Box 42, Church Square House, Scunthorpe DN15 6XQ Tel: 01724 297440
North Somerset	Highway Services, North Somerset Council, Kings Court, 87/89 High Street, Nailsea, Somerset BS48 1AW Tel: 01934 882001; Fax: 01934 882002
Nottingham City	Director of Development and Environmental Services, Nottingham City Council, Lawrence House, Talbot Street, Nottingham NG1 5NT Tel: 0115 915 6225; Fax: 0115 915 6150
Peterborough City	Head of Transport and Engineering Services, Peterborough City Council, Bridge House, Town Bridge, Peterborough PE1 1XG Tel: 01733 453500; Fax: 01733 453444
Plymouth City	Head of Transport, Plymouth City Council, Civic Centre, Plymouth PL1 2EW Tel: 01752 66800
Poole	Chief Executive, Borough of Poole, The Civic Centre, Poole, Dorset BH15 2RU Tel: 01202 633633; Fax: 01202 633706
Portsmouth City	Chief Executive, Portsmouth City Council, Civic Offices, Guildhall Square, Portsmouth PO1 2AL Tel: 0239 282 2251; Fax: 0239 282 8441
Reading	Transport Strategy Manager, Reading Borough Council, Civic Centre, Reading RG1 7TD Tel: 0118 939 0813; Fax: 0118 939 0633
Redcar and Cleveland	Director of Technical Services, Redcar and Cleveland Council, Cargo Fleet Offices, Middlesbrough Road, PO Box South Bank 20, Cleveland TS6 6EL Tel: 01642 444000; Fax: 01642 444600
Rutland	Head of Highways and Transportation, Rutland County Council, Council Offices, Catmose, Oakham LE15 6HP Tel: 01572 722577; Fax: 01572 771616

Slough	Head of Engineering, Slough Borough Council, Wellington House, PO Box 570, Slough SL1 1FA Tel: 01753 552288; Fax: 01753 875296
South Gloucestershire	Director of Planning, Transportation and Strategic Environment, South Gloucestershire Council, The Council Offices, Castle Street, Thornbury BS35 lHF Tel: 01454 863400; Fax: 01454 863642
Southampton City	Chief Executive, Southampton City Council, Civic Centre, Southampton SO14 7LY Tel: 023 8022 3855; Fax: 023 8083 3232
Southend-on-Sea	Technical Services Department, Southend-on-Sea Borough Council, Civic Centre, Southend-on-Sea SS2 6ER Tel: 01702 215731
Stockton-on-Tees	Director of Environment and Technical Services, Stockton-on-Tees Borough Council, Municipal Buildings, Church Road, Stockton-on-Tees TS18 1LD Tel: 01642 391230; Fax: 01642 391316
Stoke-on-Trent City	City Services, Stoke-on-Trent City Council, Cromer Road, Northwood, Stoke-on-Trent ST1 6XB Tel: 01782 234567; Fax: 01782 236257
Swindon	Director of Environmental Services, Swindon Borough Council, Premier House, Station Road, Swindon SH1 1TZ Tel: 01793 466360; Fax: 01793 466165
Telford and Wrekin	Corporate Director, Environment and Economy, Telford and Wrekin Council, Dowby House, Telford TF3 4LB Tel: 01952 202367; Fax: 01952 200764
Thurrock	Head of Strategic Planning, Thurrock Borough Council, Civic Offices, New Road, Grays RM17 6SL Tel: 01375 652207; Fax: 01375 652780
Torbay	Director of Environment Services, Torbay Council, Roebuck House, Abbey Road, Torquay TQ2 5TF Tel: 01803 207701; Fax: 01803 208856
Warrington	Director of Environment and Regeneration, Warrington Borough Council, New Town House, Buttermarket Street, Warrington WA1 2NH Tel: 01925 442700; Fax: 01925 442704
West Berkshire	Highways and Engineering, West Berkshire District Council, Council Offices, Faraday Road, Newbury RG14 2AF Tel: 01635 42400; Fax: 01635 519865

Windsor and Maidenhead	Director of Planning and Environment, Royal Borough of Windsor and Maidenhead, Town Hall, St Ives Road, Maidenhead, Berkshire SL6 1RF Tel: 01628 798888; Fax: 01628 796408
Wokingham	Chief Executive, Wokingham District Council, Council Offices, Shute End, Wokingham RG40 1WQ Tel: 0118 974 6000; Fax: 0118 978 9078
Worcestershire	Director of Environmental Services, PO Box 373, County Hall, Spetchley Road, Worcester WR5 2XG Tel: 01905 763763; Fax: 01905 766899
York	Director of Environment and Development Services, City of York Council, 9 St Leonards Place, York YO1 7ET Tel: 01904 613161; Fax: 01904 551340

Wales

Counties

Cardiff	Head of Highways and Parks Services, Cardiff County Council, County Hall, Atlantic Wharf, Cardiff CF1 5UW Tel: 029 2087 2000; Fax: 029 2087 3653
Carmarthenshire	Director of Environment and Economic Development, Carmarthenshire County Council, Llanstephan Road, Johnstown, Carmarthen SA31 3LZ Tel: 01267 234567
Ceredigion	Director of Highways, Property and Works, Ceredigion County Council, County Hall, Market Street, Aberaeron SA46 0HT Tel: 01545 570881; Fax: 01545 571089
Swansea	Director of Technical Services, City and County of Swansea, County Hall, Swansea SA1 3SN Tel: 01792 636149; Fax: 01792 652712
Denbighshire	Head of Highways and Transportation, Denbighshire County Council, Caledfryn, Smithfield Road, Denbigh LL16 3RJ Tel: 01824 706801; Fax: 01824 706970
Flintshire	Director of Highways, Transportation and Engineering, Flintshire County Council, County Hall, Mold CH7 6NB Tel: 01352 704500; Fax: 01352 703222

Gwynedd	The Surveyor, Highways and Engineering, Gwynedd Council, Council Offices, Caernarfon, Gwynedd LL55 1SH Tel: 01286 679444; Fax: 01286 675961
Isle of Anglesey	Corporate Director of Highways, Transportation and Property, Isle of Anglesey County Council, Council Offices, Swyddfa'r Sir, Llangefni, Anglesey LL77 7TW Tel: 01248 752301; Fax: 01248 724839
Monmouthshire	Head of Highways & Waste Management, Monmouthshire County Council, County Hall, Cwmbran NP44 2XH Tel: 01633 644707; Fax: 01633 644701
Pembrokeshire	Director of Transport, Pembrokeshire County Council, County Hall, Haverfordwest SA61 1TP Tel: 01437 775828; Fax: 01437 775008
Powys	Director of Highways, Transportation and Property, Powys County Council, County Hall, Llandrindod Wells LD1 5LG Tel: 01597 826630; Fax: 01597 826269

County Boroughs

Blaenau Gwent	Director of Community Services, Central Depot, Barleyfield Industrial Estate, Brynmawr NP23 4YF Tel: 01495 355600; Fax: 01495 312357
Bridgend	Director of Environmental and Planning Services, Bridgend County Borough Council, Transportation and Engineering Department, Morien House, Bennett Street, Bridgend Industrial Estate, Bridgend CF31 3SH Tel: 01656 642501; Fax: 01656 642581
Caerphilly	Chief Engineer, Caerphilly County Borough Council, Council Offices, Pontllanfraith, Blackwood NP12 2YW Tel: 01495 235319; Fax: 01495 235012
Conwy	Chief Highways Officer, Conwy County Borough Council, The Heath, Penmaenmawr Road, Llanfairfechan LL33 OPF Tel: 01492 574001; Fax: 01248 681881
Merthyr Tydfil	Head of Engineering, Merthyr Tydfil County Borough Council, Ty Keir Hardie, Riverside Court, Avenue de Clichy, Merthyr Tydfil CF47 8XF Tel: 01685 725000; Fax: 01685 722146

Neath Port Talbot	Director of Technical Services, Neath Port Talbot County Borough Council, Civic Centre, Penllergaer SA4 1GH Tel: 01792 512703; Fax: 01792 512666
Newport	Director of Development and Transportation, Newport County Borough Council, Civic Centre, Newport, South Wales NP20 4UR Tel: 01633 232707; Fax: 01633 244721
Rhondda Cynon Taff	Divisional Director of Transportation, Rhondda Cynon Taff County Borough Council, Sardis House, Sardis Road, Pontypridd CF37 1DU Tel: 01443 494700; Fax: 01443 494888
Torfaen	Director for the Environment, Torfaen County Borough Council, 4th Floor, County Hall, Cwmbran NP44 2WN Tel: 01633 648601
Vale of Glamorgan	Director of Environmental and Economic Regeneration, Vale of Glamorgan Council, Dock Office, Barry Docks, Barry CF63 4RT Tel: 029 206 73000
Wrexham	Chief Transport and Engineering Officer, Wrexham County Borough Council, Crown Buildings, PO Box 1293, Wrexham LL11 1WQ Tel: 01978 292000; Fax: 01978 297103

Scotland

Unitary Councils

Aberdeen	Director of Environment and Property, Aberdeen City Council, St Nicholas House, Aberdeen AB10 1EZ Tel: 01224 523037; Fax: 01224 626301
Aberdeenshire	Director of Transportation and Infrastructure, Aberdeenshire Council, Woodhill House, Westburn Road, Aberdeen AB16 5GB Tel: 01224 665520; Fax: 01224 662005
Angus	Director of Planning and Transport, Angus Council, St James House, St James Road, Forfar DD8 2ZP Tel: 01307 461460; Fax: 01307 461895
Argyll and Bute	Director of Transportation and Property, Argyll and Bute Council, Manse Brae, Lochgilphead PA31 8RD Tel: 01546 602233; Fax: 01546 606618

City of Edinburgh	Director of City Development, City of Edinburgh Council, 1 Cockburn Street, Edinburgh EH1 1ZJ Tel: 0131 529 3595; Fax: 0131 529 3498
City of Glasgow	Director of Land Services, Glasgow City Council, Richmond Exchange, 20 Cadogan Street, Glasgow G2 7AD Tel: 0141 287 9000; Fax: 0141 287 9013
Clackmannanshire	Roads and Transport Manager, Development and Environmental Services, Clackmannanshire Council, Lime Tree House, Alloa FK10 1EX Tel: 01259 452532; Fax: 01259 452530
Dumfries and Galloway	Head of Strategy and Transportation, Dumfries and Galloway Council, Council Offices, English Street, Dumfries DG1 2HR Tel: 01387 260115; Fax: 01387 260111
Dundee City	Director of Planning and Transportation, Dundee City Council, Tayside House, 28 Crichton Street, Dundee DD1 3R13 Tel: 01382 434000; Fax: 01382 433013
East Ayrshire	Head of Roads and Transport, East Ayrshire Council, Greenholm Street, Kilmarnock KA1 4DJ Tel: 01563 576310; Fax: 01563 576312
East Dunbartonshire	Strategic Director, Development and Environment, East Dunbartonshire Council, Tom Johnston House, Civic Way, Kirkintilloch, Glasgow G66 4TJ Tel: 0141 578 8000; Fax: 0141 578 8333
East Lothian	Head of Transportation, East Lothian Council, John Muir House, Haddington, East Lothian EH41 3HA Tel: 01620 827658; Fax: 01620 827923
East Renfrewshire	Head of Roads and Transportation, East Renfrewshire Council, Refuge House, 17/19 Gaule Street, Paisley PA1 1ES Tel: 0141 577 3417
Falkirk	Head of Planning and Transportation, Falkirk Council, Abbotsford House, David's Loan, Falkirk FK2 7YZ Tel: 01324 504820; Fax: 01324 504914
Fife	Head of Transportation, Fife Council, Fife House, North Street, Glenrothes KY7 5LT Tel: 01592 414141; Fax: 01592 416100
Highland	Director of Roads and Transport, The Highland Council, Glenurquhart Road, Inverness IV3 5NX Tel: 01463 702601; Fax: 01463 702606

Inverclyde	Head of Transportation and Roads Service, Inverclyde Council, 71 East Hamilton Street, Greenock PA15 2UA Tel: 01475 714800; Fax: 01475 714825
Midlothian	Head of Transportation, Midlothian Council, Fairfield House, 8 Lothian Road, Dalkeith EH22 3ZN Tel: 0131 270 7500; Fax: 0131 271 3537
Moray	Head of Direct Services, Moray Council, Roads Service, Academy Street, Elgin IV30 1LL Tel: 01343 562500; Fax: 01343 545628
North Ayrshire	Head of Roads, North Ayrshire Council, Perceton House, Irvine KA11 2AL Tel: 01294 225200; Fax: 01294 225244
North Lanarkshire	Director of Planning and Environment, North Lanarkshire Council, Fleming House, Cumbernauld G67 1JW Tel: 01236 616201; Fax: 01236 616206
Perth and Kinross	Director of Roads, Transport and Architectural Services, Perth and Kinross Council, Puller House, 35 Kinnoull Street, Perth PH1 5GD Tel: 01738 475650; Fax: 01738 476510
Renfrewshire	Head of Roads, Department of Planning and Transport, Renfrewshire Council, South Buildings, Cotton Street, Paisley PA1 1LL Tel: 0141 842 5741; Fax: 0141 842 5040
Scottish Borders	Director of Transport and Environmental Standards, Scottish Borders Council, Council Headquarters, Newtown St Boswells, Melrose TD6 0SA Tel: 01835 825075; Fax: 01835 825071
South Ayrshire	Head of Strategy and Design, South Ayrshire Council, Macadam House, 34 Charlotte Street, Ayr KA7 1EA Tel: 01292 612301; Fax: 01292 612342
South Lanarkshire	Head of Roads and Transportation, South Lanarkshire Council, Montrose House, 154 Montrose Crescent, Hamilton ML3 6LL Tel: 01698 454484
Stirling	Director of Technical Services, Stirling Council, Viewforth, Stirling FK8 2ET Tel: 01786 442692; Fax: 01786 443053
West Dunbartonshire	Head of Roads, Transport and Environmental Services, West Dunbartonshire Council, Council Offices, Garshake Road, Dumbarton G82 3PU Tel: 01389 737598; Fax: 01389 737637

| West Lothian | Strategic Services, West Lothian Council, West Lothian House, Almondvale Boulevard, Livingston EH54 6QG
Tel: 01506 777000; Fax: 01506 777102 |

Island Councils

Orkney Islands	Director of Technical Services, Orkney Islands Council, Council Offices, Kirkwall, Orkney KW15 1NY Tel: 01856 873535; Fax: 01856 876094
Shetland Islands	Executive Director Infrastructure Services, Shetland Islands Council, Grantfield, Lerwick, Shetland ZE1 0NT Tel: 01595 744800; Fax: 01595 695887
Western Isles	Director of Technical Services, Comhairle nan Eilean Siar (Western Isles Council), Council Offices, Sandwick Road, Stornoway, Isle of Lewis HS1 2BW Tel: 01851 703773; Fax: 01851 709482

Northern Ireland

Headquarters	Clarence Court, 10–18 Adelaide Street, Belfast BT2 8GB Tel: 028 9054 0540
Belfast	Roads Service, Eastern Division, Hydebank, 4 Hospital Road, Belfast BT8 8X Tel: 028 9025 3000
Coleraine	Roads Service, Northern Division, County Hall, Castlerock Road, Coleraine, Co Londonderry BT51 3HS Tel: 028 7034 1300
Craigavon	Roads Service, Southern Division, Marlborough House, Central Way, Craigavon, Co Armagh BT64 IAD Tel: 028 3834 1144
Omagh	Roads Service, Western Division, County Hall, Drumragh Avenue, Omagh, Co Tyrone BT79 7AF Tel: 028 8225 4111

Tunnel and Bridge Authorities

| Blackwall and Rotherhithe | Tunnels Manager, Greenwich Borough Council, Blackwall Tunnel Office, Naval Row, London E14 9PS
Tel 020 7987 4208/3601; Fax 020 7987 6571 |

Dartford Tunnel	Dartford River Crossing Ltd., Tunnel Operating Division, South Orbital Way, Dartford, Kent DA1 5PR Tel 01322 221603; Fax 01322 294224
Mersey Tunnels	General Manager, The Mersey Tunnels, Georges Dock Building, Georges Dock Way, Pier Head, Liverpool, Merseyside L3 1DD Tel 0151 236 8602 extn 200; Fax 0151 255 0610
Tyne Tunnel	Tyne and Wear PTA, Howdon, Wallsend, Tyne and Wear NE28 0PD Tel 0191 262 4451; Fax 0191 262 1031
Erskine Bridge	The Bridge Manager, Erskine Bridge, Bishopston, Renfrewshire, Strathclyde PA7 5QD Tel 0141 812 7022; Fax 0141 812 6625
Forth Road Bridge	The General Manager, Forth Road Bridge Joint Board, South Queensferry, West Lothian EH30 9SF Tel 0131 319 1699; Fax 0131 319 1903
Humber Bridge	The Bridgemaster, Humber Bridge Board, PO Box 6, Ferriby Road, Hessle, Humberside HU13 0JG Tel 01482 647161; Fax 01482 640838
Severn Bridges	Severn River Crossing, Aust Services, Pilning, Bristol BS12 3BE Tel 01454 633522 (Toll office 01454 632436)
Skye Road Bridge	Skye Bridge Limited, Kyle of Lochalsh Tel 01599 534880
Tamar Road Bridge	Tamar Bridge Authority, Plymouth, Devon Tel 01752 361577
Tay Bridge	The Bridge Manager, Tay Road Bridge Joint Board, Marine Parade, Dundee, Tayside DD1 3JB Tel 01382 21881/2; Fax 01382 201529

Electricity Authorities/Companies

(for notification of high loads – ie above 5.8 metres)

Area	*Board/Company Address*
Eastern	Engineering Director, Eastern Electricity, Wherstead Park, PO Box 40, Wherstead, Ipswich, Suffolk IP9 2AQ Tel 01449 772378; Fax 01449 772396
East Midlands	Power Systems Manager, East Midlands Electricity, PO Box 4, North PDO, 398 Coppice Road, Arnold, Nottingham NG5 7HX Tel 0115 926 9711; Fax 0115 935 8585
London	Transport Manager, London Electricity, 54 Bengeworth Road, London SE5 9AJ Tel 020 7733 5611; Fax 020 7326 6278

Merseyside and North Wales	Chief Engineer, Merseyside and North Wales Electricity Board Plc, Head Office, Sealand Road, Chester CH1 4LR Tel 01244 652234; Fax 01244 652353
Midlands	Chief Engineer, Midlands Electricity, PO Box 8, Mucklow Hill, Halesowen, West Midlands B62 8BP Tel 0121 423 2345; Fax 0121 422 7977
North-Western	Chief Engineer, Norweb Plc, Talbot Road, Manchester M16 0HQ. Tel 0161 875 7111; Fax 0161 875 7456
Northern	Director of Engineering, Northern Electric Plc, Carliol House, Market Street, Newcastle upon Tyne NE1 6NE Tel 0191 221 2000; Fax 0191 235 2211
Scotland	Distribution Operations Manager, Scottish Hydro-Electric Plc, South Inch Business Centre, Shore Road, Perth PH2 8BW Tel 01738 455050; Fax 01738 455055
South-Eastern	Network Operations, Seeboard Plc, Wealdon House, Lewes Road, East Grinstead RH19 3TB Tel 01342 413252; Fax 01342 315620
South of Scotland	General Manager (Operations), Scottish Power Plc, Catheart House, Spean Street, Glasgow G44 4BE Tel 0141 637 7177; Fax 0141 568 2016
South Wales	Chief Engineer, South Wales Electricity Plc, St Mellons, Cardiff CF3 9XW Tel 029 2079 2111; Fax 029 2077 7759
South-Western	Operations Manager, Engineering, South-Western Electricity Plc, Sowton Industrial Estate, Osprey Road, Exeter EX2 7HZ Tel 01392 444111; Fax 01392 444827
Southern	Operations Administration, Southern Electricity Plc, Westacott Way, Littlewick Green, Maidenhead, Berkshire SL6 3QB Tel 01628 822166; Fax 01628 584403
Yorkshire	Systems Operations Manager, Yorkshire Electricity, 161 Gelderd Road, Leeds LS1 1QZ Tel 0113 241 5000; Fax 0113 241 5057

Rail and Water Authorities

(for notification of matters concerning rail crossings, bridges, eg abnormal load movements and damage to bridges caused by goods vehicles)

British Waterways Board	Technical Services Department, Wellington Park House, Thirsk Row, Leeds LS1 4DD Tel 0113 245 0711; Fax 0113 246 0493
Railtrack	Eastern Region – Room B004, Hudson House, York YO1 1HP Tel 01904 522351; Fax 01904 522802
	Western Region – 1 Gloucester Street, Swindon, Wilts SN1 1GW Tel 01793 515898; Fax 01793 515723
	Network SouthEast (South) – Wellesley Grove, Croydon, Surrey CR9 1DY Tel 020 8666 6789; Fax 020 8666 6519
	(North) – Grosvenor House, Room 305, 112 Prince of Wales Road, Norwich NR1 1NZ Tel 01603 285567; Fax 01603 762791
	Regional Railways – 1st Floor West Wing, Stanier House, 10 Holliday Street, Birmingham B1 1TE Tel 0121 654 4251; Fax 0121 654 4528
	ScotRail – ScotRail House, 58 Port Dundas Road, Glasgow G4 0LQ Tel 0141 335 3102; Fax 0141 335 2862
London Underground	4th Floor, 30 The South Colonnade, Canary Wharf, London E14 5EU Tel 020 7308 2571; Fax 020 7308 2700

NB: See note on p 479 about notifications to British Rail Property Board.

Appendix VII

DVLA Local Offices and New Vehicle Registration Marks

Since 1 January 2001 the DVLA's Vehicle Registration Offices have been called Local Offices to reflect the inclusion of driver licensing work and the potential for other Agency business to be undertaken. Telephone numbers are centralized – tel: 0870 850 0007.

Aberdeen
Greyfriars House
Gallowgate
Aberdeen AB10 1WG

Bangor
Penrhos Road
Penrhosgarnedd
Bangor LL57 2JF

Beverley
Crosskill House
Mill Lane
Beverley HU17 9JB

Birmingham
2nd Floor
Edward House
Edward Street
Birmingham B1 2RF

Bournemouth
Bourne Gate
25 Bourne Valley Road
Poole BH12 1DX

Brighton
4th Floor, Mocatta House
Trafalgar Place
Brighton BN1 4UE

Bristol
Northleigh House
Lime Kiln Close
Stoke Gifford
Bristol BS34 8SR

Cardiff
Archway House
77 Ty Glas Avenue
Llanishen
Cardiff CF14 5DX

Carlisle
Ground Floor
3 Merchants Drive
Parkhouse
Carlisle CA3 0JW

Chelmsford
2nd Floor
Parkway House
49 Baddow Road
Chelmsford CM2 0XJ

Chester
Norroy House
Nuns Road
Chester CH1 2ND

Dundee
Caledonian House
Greenmarket
Dundee DD1 4QP

Edinburgh
Department of Transport
Saughton House
Broomhouse Drive
Edinburgh EH11 3XE

Exeter
Hanover House
Manaton Close
Matford Business Park
Marsh Barton
Exeter EX2 8EF

Glasgow
46 West Campbell Street
Glasgow G2 6TT

Inverness
Longman House
28 Longman Road
Inverness IV1 1SF

Ipswich
Podium Level
St Clare House
Greyfriars
Ipswich IP1 1UT

Leeds
1st Floor, 42 Eastgate
Leeds LS2 7DQ

Lincoln
Firth Court
Firth Road
Lincoln LN5 7WD

Luton
2 Dunstable Road
Luton LU1 1EB

Maidstone
Coronet House
11 Queen Anne Road
Maidstone ME14 1XB

Manchester
Trafford House
Chester Road
Manchester M32 0SL

Newcastle upon Tyne
Eagle Star House
Regent Farm Road
Newcastle upon Tyne NE3 3QF

Northampton
Wootton Hall Park
Northampton NN4 0GA

Norwich
11 Prince of Wales Road
Norwich NR1 1UP

Nottingham
Block 6, Government Buildings
Chalfont Drive
Nottingham NG8 3RA

Oxford
Ground Floor, 3 Cambridge Terrace
Oxford OX1 1RW

Peterborough
88 Lincoln Road
Peterborough PE1 2ST

Portsmouth
5th Floor, Baltic House
Kingston Crescent
Portsmouth PO2 8AH

Preston
Fulwood Park, Caxton Road, Fulwood
PR2 9NZ

Reading
77–81 Basingstoke Road
Reading RG2 0ER

Sidcup
12/18 Station Road
Sidcup DA15 7EQ

Sheffield
Cedar House, Hallamshire Court
63 Napier Street
Sheffield S11 8HA

Shrewsbury
Whitehall, Monkmoor Road
Shrewsbury SY2 5DR

Stanmore
Government Building
Canon Park
Honeypot Lane
Stanmore
Middlesex HA7 1BD

Stockton
St Marks House
St Marks Court
Thornaby
Stockton on Tees TS17 6QR

Swansea
Heol Pentre Felen
Swansea SA6 7HG

Truro
Pydar House
Pydar Street
Truro TR1 2TG

Wimbledon
Ground Floor, Connect House
133–137 Alexandra Road
Wimbledon SW19 7JY

Worcester
Clerkenleap Barn
Broomhall
Worcester WR5 3HR

See table of registration marks overleaf.

NB: *In the event of one office receiving an exceptionally high demand that depletes its stock of registration marks, marks may be transferred between DVLA Local Offices.*

Source: Reproduced from DVLA website **www.dvla.gov.uk**

Local memory tag	DVLA office	Local identifier
A	Peterborough	A B C D E F G H J K L M N
	Norwich	O P R S T U
	Ipswich	V W X Y
B	Birmingham	A Y
C	Cardiff	A B C D E F G H J K L M N O
	Swansea	P R S T U V
	Bangor	W X Y
D	Chester	A B C D E F G H J K
	Shrewsbury	L M N O P R S T U V W X Y
E	Chelmsford	A Y
F	Nottingham	A B C D E F G H J K L M N P
	Lincoln	R S T V W X Y
G	Maidstone	A B C D E F G H J K L M N O
	Brighton	P R S T U V W X Y
H	Bournemouth	A B C D E F G H J
	Portsmouth	K L M N O P R S T U V W X Y
		HW Reserved for the Isle of Wight
K	Luton	A B C D E F G H J K L
	Northampton	M N O P R S T U V W X Y
L	Wimbledon	A B C D E F G H J
	Stanmore	K L M N O P R S T
	Sidcup	U V W X Y
M	Manchester	A Y
N	Newcastle	A B C D E F G H J K M N O
	Stockton	P R S T U V W X Y
O	Oxford	A Y
P	Preston	A B C D E F G H J K M N O P R S T
	Carlisle	U V W X Y
R	Reading	A Y
S	Glasgow	A B C D E F G H J
	Edinburgh	K L M N O
	Dundee	P R S T
	Aberdeen	U V W
	Inverness	X Y
V	Worcester	A Y
W	Exeter	A B C D E F G H J
	Truro	K L
	Bristol	M N O P R S T U V W X Y
Y	Leeds	A B C D E F G H J K
	Sheffield	L M N O P R S T U
	Beverley	V W X Y

Appendix VIII

UK Bridge and Tunnel Tolls

Erskine Bridge

Tolls suspended for legislative reasons.

Dartford River Crossing

The Dartford–Thurrock Crossing is now operated by a French consortium called Le Cross Company Ltd.

Vehicle	Single journey	10 pm–6 am
Motor car, including motor car with three wheels or taxi	£1.50	FREE
Light or medium goods vehicle, motor coach, omnibus or tractor, having no more than two axles	£2.00	FREE
Heavy goods vehicle, motor coach or omnibus having more than two axles	£3.70	FREE

Dart-Tag

Discount charges apply to holder of Dart-Tags as follows:

	Day	Night 10 pm–6 am
Car	£1.00	FREE
2-axle goods vehicles	£1.75	FREE
Multi-axle goods vehicles	£3.20	FREE

Proportionate tolls apply where a trailer is drawn (ie double the normal rate).

Charges for Large Vehicles and/or Loads

Passage through the tunnels		
Passage between 6.00 am and 10.00 pm	Wider than 2.75 m Longer than 18.75 m	£42 + toll
Passage between 10.00 pm and 6.00 am	Wider than 2.75 m Longer than 18.75 m	£21 + toll
Passage at any time of day or night	Wider than 6.10 m Longer than 27.40 m Over 150,000 kg	£190 + toll
Height limit:	West tunnel	15 ft 9 in (4.8768 m)
	East tunnel	16 ft 6 in (5.0292 m)
Passage over the bridge		
Passage between 6.00 am and 10.00 pm	Wider than 3.65 m	£42 + toll
Passage between 10.00 pm and 6.00 am	Wider than 3.65 m	£21 + toll
Passage at any time of day or night	Wider than 6.10 m Longer than 27.40 m Over 150,000 kg	£190 + toll

Breakdown Recovery

Breakdown recovery of vehicles causing an obstruction on the carriageway within the Crossing area will be undertaken free of charge to the nearest place of safety at the Crossing.

Forth Road Bridge

Forth Bridge tolls were scrapped from February 2008.

Humber Bridge

	Single crossing	Discounted price per book of 20 tickets
Cars and goods vehicles having a maximum weight not exceeding 3.5 tonnes Motor caravans	£2.70	£48.60

	Single crossing	Discounted price per book of 20 tickets
Goods vehicles having a maximum gross vehicle weight exceeding 3.5 tonnes but not exceeding 7.5 tonnes Vehicles within Class 2 above, with trailers Small buses (with seating for 9–16 passengers)	£4.90	£88.20
Goods vehicles having a maximum gross vehicle weight exceeding 7.5 tonnes with 2 axles Large buses (with seating for 17 or more passengers)	£10.90	£196.20
Goods vehicles having a maximum gross vehicle weight exceeding 7.5 tonnes with 3 axles	£14.60	£262.80
Goods vehicles having a maximum gross vehicle weight exceeding 7.5 tonnes with 4 or more axles	£18.30	£329.40

Abnormal Loads

An additional scale of charges applies to abnormal load movements across the bridge. See **www.humberbridge.co.uk**.

Mersey Tunnel

	Standard	Fast Tag
Private/light goods vehicle up to 3.5 tonnes (ie under 1.525 tonnes unladen)	£1.40	£1.25
Private/light goods vehicle up to 3.5 tonnes, with trailer	£2.80	£2.50
Heavy goods vehicle over 3.5 tonnes, with two axles	£2.80	£2.50
Heavy goods vehicle over 3.5 tonnes, with three axles	£4.20	£3.75
Heavy goods vehicle over 3.5 tonnes, with four or more axles	£5.60	£5.00

NB: *Additional charges are made for escorts and for breakdowns.*

Severn Bridges

Tolls

Cars and motor caravans	£5.70
Small goods vehicles and small buses	£11.50
Heavy goods vehicles and buses	£17.20

Tag Charges	*Monthly*	*Quarterly*
Cars and motor caravans	£100.32	£300.95
Small goods vehicles and small buses	£202.40	£607.20
Heavy goods vehicles and buses	£340.56	£1021.68

NB: Tolls are charged westbound only.

Breakdown Fees

Small vehicles	£40 for first 30 minutes
	£20 for each subsequent 15 minutes or part thereof
Goods vehicles over 3.5 tonnes gvw	£100 for the first 30 minutes
	£50 for each subsequent 15 minutes or part thereof

Skye Bridge

The Skye Bridge toll was removed from 21 December 2004.

Tamar Bridge

	Cash toll	Discount toll
Vehicles up to 3.5 tonnes mgw and up to 8 seats Cars, vans, motorcycle combinations	£1.50	75p
Vehicles over 3.5 tonnes mgw and vehicles with more than 8 seats according to axle count:		
2 axles:	£3.70	£1.85
3 axles:	£6.00	£3.00
4+ axles:	£8.20	£4.10
Vehicles towing trailers	charge is doubled	

Tolls are payable east-bound only.

Special toll rates apply to abnormal loads. See **www.tamarcrossings.org.uk**

Tyne Tunnel

	Standard	*Permit holder*
Car or light van (up to 3,500 kg gross weight)	£1.20	£1.08
Goods vehicle or passenger-carrying vehicle (over 3,500 kg gross weight)	£1.50	£1.35

Recovery Charges

Motorcycles:	£5
Cars:	£28 per hr/min £14
LGV:	£28 per hr/min £14
Breakdown due to fuel shortage:	£17.29 per hr/min £8.30 + recovery charge
Breakdown parking:	£2 per day after 48 hrs

Appendix IX

Dimensions, Weights and Capacities for ISO Containers (Imperial and Metric Units)

ISO Container Type Designation	HEIGHT		WIDTH		LENGTH		WEIGHT	CAPACITY
	External	Internal	External	Internal	External	Internal	Maximum Gross	Minimum
1A	8' 0"	7' 2½"	8' 0"	7' 7¾"	40' 0"	39' 4³/₈"	30 tons	2167.5 cu ft
	2438 mm	2197	2438	2330	12000	11998	30.48 tonnes	61.4 cu m
1AA	8' 6"	7' 8½"	8' 0"	7' 7¾"	40' 0"	39' 4³/₈"	30	2317.5
	2591	2350	2438	2330	12000	11998	30.48	65.7
1B	8' 0"	7' 2½"	8' 0"	7' 7¾"	30' 0"	29' 5⁵/₈"	25	1613.5
	2438	2197	2438	2330	9000	8931	25.4	45.7
1BB	8' 6"	7' 8½"	8' 0"	7' 7¾"	30' 0"	29' 5⁵/₈"	25	1725.4
	2591	2350	2438	2330	9000	8931	25.4	48.9
1C	8' 0"	7' 2½	8' 0"	7' 7¾"	20' 0"	19' 3"	20	1060.1
	2438	2197	2438	2330	6000	5867	20.32	30.0
1CC	8' 6"	7' 8½"	8' 0"	7' 7¾"	20' 0"	19' 3"	20	1135.1
	2591	2350	2438	2330	6000	5867	20.32	32.1
1D	8' 0"	7' 2½"	8' 0"	7' 7¾"	10' 0"	9' 2⁵/₁₆"	10	506.2
	2438	2197	2438	2330	3000	2802	10.16	14.3
1E	8' 0"	7' 2½"	8' 0"	7' 7¾"	6' 8"	5' 10¹/₁₆"	7	321.6
	2438	2197	2438	2330	2000	1780	7.11	9.1
1F	8' 0"	7' 2½"	8' 0"	7' 7¾"	5' 0"	4' 2¹/₈"	5	230.0
	2438	2197	2438	2330	1500	1273	5.08	6.5

Appendix X

Permissible Maximum Vehicle Dimensions in Europe

COUNTRY	HEIGHT	WIDTH	LENGTH		
			Lorry or Trailer	Road Train	Articulated Vehicle
Albania	4 m	2.50 m	12 m	18.35 m	16.50 m
Austria	4 m	2.55 m (3)	12 m	18.75 m	16.50 m
Azerbaijan	4 m	2.50m	12 m	20 m	
Belarus	4 m	2.55 m	12 m	20 m	20 m
Belgium	4 m	2.55 m (3)	12 m	18.75 m	16.50 m
Bosnia-Herzegovina	4 m	2.50 m	12 m	18 m	17 m
Bulgaria	4 m	2.55 m	12 m	18.75 m	16.50 m
Croatia	4 m	2.55 m (3)	12 m	18.35 m	16.50 m
Czech Republic	4 m	2.55 m (3)	12 m	18.75 m	16.50 m
Denmark	4 m	2.55 m (3)	12 m	18.75 m	16.50 m
Estonia	4 m	2.55 m	12 m	18.75 m	16.50 m
Finland (1)	4.20 m	2.60 m	12 m	25.25 m	16.50 m
France	not defined	2.55 m (3)	12 m	18.75 m	16.50 m
FYR Macedonia	4 m	2.50 m	12 m	18 m	16.50 m
Georgia	4 m	2.50 m	20 m	20 m	
Germany	4 m	2.55 m (3)	12 m	18.75 m	16.50 m

COUNTRY	HEIGHT	WIDTH	LENGTH		
			Lorry or Trailer	Road Train	Articulated Vehicle
Greece	4 m	2.55 m (3)	12 m	18.75 m	16.50 m
Hungary	4 m	2.55 m (3)	12 m	18.75 m	16.50 m
Iceland	4.20 m	2.55 m	12 m	22 m	18 m
Ireland	4.25 m	2.50 m (3)	12 m	18.5 m	16.50 m
Italy (2)	4 m	2.55 m (3)	12 m	18.75 m	16.50 m
Latvia	4 m	2.55 m (3)	12 m	18.75 m	16.50 m
Liechtenstein	4 m	2.55 m	12 m	18.75 m	16.50 m
Lithuania	4 m	2.55 m (3)	12 m	18.75 m	16.50 m
Luxembourg	4 m	2.55 m (3)	12 m	18.75 m	16.50 m
Malta	4 m	2.55 m (3)	12 m	18.75 m	16.50 m
Moldova	4 m	2.50 m	12 m	20 m	16.50 m
Netherlands	4 m	2.55 m (3)	12 m	18.75 m	16.50 m
Norway	not defined	2.55 m (3)	12 m	19.50 m	17.50 m
Poland	4 m	2.55 m (3)	12 m	18.75 m	16.50 m
Portugal (2)	4 m	2.55 m (3)	12 m	18.75 m	16.50 m
Romania	4 m	2.55 m (3)	12 m	18.75 m	16.50 m
Russia	4 m	2.55 m (3)	12 m	20 m	20 m
Serbia	4 m	2.50 m	12 m	18 m	16.50 m
Slovakia	4 m	2.55 m (3)	12 m	18.75 m	16.50 m
Slovenia	4 m	2.55 m (3)	12 m	18.75 m	16.50 m
Spain	4 m	2.55 m (3)	12 m	18.75 m	16.50 m
Sweden	not defined	2.60 m	?	?	25.25 m
Switzerland	4 m	2.55 m (3)	12 m	18.75 m	16.50 m
Turkey	4 m	2.55 m (3)	12 m	18.75 m	16.50 m
Ukraine	4 m	2.65 m	12 m	22 m	22 m
United Kingdom	not defined	2.55 m (3)	12 m	18.75 m	16.50 m

1 For vehicles registered in an EEA member country
2 Increased values are applicable for certain types of transport (ie containers, motorcars, etc)
3 Refrigerated vehicles = 2.60 m

With acknowledgement to ECMT, 2 May 2007

Appendix XI

Permissible Maximum Vehicle Weights in Europe (Tonnes)

Country	Weight per bearing axle	Weight per drive axle	Lorry 2 axles	Lorry 3 axles	Road Train 4 axles	Road Train 5 axles and +	Articulated Vehicle 5 axles and +
Albania	10		18	25	40	44	38
Austria	10	11.5	19	39	44 (2)	44 (2)	38 (2)
Azerbaijan				10	37	37	37
Belarus	10		18	25 (1)	36	38	38
Belgium	10	12	19	26	39	44	44
Bosnia-Herzegovina	10		20	26	40	40	40
Bulgaria	10	11.5	18	26 (1)	36	40	40
Croatia	10	11.5	18	26 (1)	36	40	40
Czech Republic	10	11.5	18	26 (1)	36	44 (1)	42/48
Denmark	10	11.5	18	26 (1)	38	48	48
Estonia	10	11.5	18	26 (1)	36	40	40
Finland (3)	10	11.5	18	26 (1)	38	60	48
France	13	13	19	26	38	40	40
FYR Macedonia	10		16	22	36	40	40
Georgia	10				44	44	44

Country	Weight per bearing axle	Weight per drive axle	Lorry 2 axles	Lorry 3 axles	Road Train 4 axles	Road Train 5 axles and +	Articulated Vehicle 5 axles and +
Germany	10	11.5	18	26 (1)	36	40	40
Greece	10	11.5	18	26 (1)	36	40	40
Hungary	10	11	20	24	36	40	40
Ireland	10	11.5	17	26 (1)	35	40	40
Iceland	10	11.5	18	26	37	40	44
Italy (4)	12	12	18	26 (1)	40	44	44
Latvia	10	11.5	18	26 (1)	40	40	40
Liechtenstein	10	11.5	18	26	36	40	40
Lithuania	10	11.5	18	26 (1)	36	40	40
Luxembourg	10	12	19	26	44	44	44
Malta	10.8	11.5	18	25	36	40	40
Moldova	10		18	24	36	40	40
Netherlands	10	11.5	21.5	33	40	50	50
Norway	10	11.5	19	26	39	46	44
Poland	10	11.5	18	26 (1)	36	40	40
Portugal (4)	10	12	19	26	37	40	40
Romania	10	11.5	18	26 (1)	36	40	40
Russia	10		18	25	36	38	38
Serbia	10		18	24	36	40	40
Slovakia	10	11.5	18	26 (1)	40	40	40
Slovenia	10	11.5	18	25		40	40
Spain (4)	10	11.5	18	26 (1)	36	40	40
Sweden	10	11.5	18	26 (1)	–	60	60
Switzerland	10	11.5	18	26 (1)	40	40	40
Turkey	10	11.5	18	25	36	40	40
Ukraine	10				38	38	38
United Kingdom	10	11.5	18	26 (1)	36	40	40/44

1 With air suspension or similar
2 These values are increased by 5% for vehicles registered in an EU member country
3 For vehicles registered in an EEA member country
4 Increased values are applicable for certain types of transport (ie containers, motorcars, etc)

With acknowledgement to ECMT, 2 May 2007

Further Information

Vehicle and Operator Services Agency (VOSA) Goods Vehicle Testing

Heavy goods vehicle testing is changing. While testing continues to proceed in the public sector via the established network of D*f*T Goods Vehicle Testing Stations, more use is being made of existing and new private sector testing stations to provide services at locations and times more convenient for the majority of customers. For example, HGV testing has already been taking place at non-VOSA sites called Designated Premises (DPs), which will remain in existence until further notice. In the meantime the new style of Authorized Testing Facility (ATF) is being implemented where statutory HGV (and PSV) testing is carried out by VOSA staff using approved equipment. These facilities are authorized but not owned by VOSA.

For further details of the new testing arrangements and links to HGV test booking facilities contact: **www.businesslink.gov.uk**.

Driving Standards Agency (DSA) Area Offices and LGV Driving Test Centres

Information on all driving tests and facilities for booking driving tests can be found by following the links on the DSA website at: **www.dsa.gov.uk**.

Training Facilities for Dangerous Goods Drivers

A list of establishments, approved by the SQA on behalf of the Department for Transport, provide training in the handling of various classes of dangerous goods for tanker vehicle drivers and for those drivers whose vehicles carry goods in packages – see Chapters 7 and 20 for full details of the relevant requirements.

NB: The list can be found on the SQA website at: **www.sqa.org.uk.** *Search for DGDT Approved Centre List.*

INDEX

NB page numbers in *italic* indicate figures or tables

Index of Advertisers